W9-CNQ-878

AMERICAN REVOLUTIONARY WAR

A Student Encyclopedia

5/07

AMERICAN REVOLUTIONARY WAR

A Student Encyclopedia

VOLUME III: M–R

Gregory Fremont-Barnes
Richard Alan Ryerson
Volume Editors

James Arnold and
Roberta Wiener
Editors, Documents Volume

FOREWORD BY
Jack P. Greene

A B C 🌓 C L I O

Santa Barbara, California   Denver, Colorado   Oxford, England

REF
973.3
AME

Copyright © 2007 by ABC-CLIO, Inc.

All rights reserved. No part of this publication may be reproduced, stored in a retrieval system, or transmitted, in any form or by any means, electronic, mechanical, photocopying, recording, or otherwise, except for the inclusion of brief quotations in a review, without prior permission in writing from the publishers.

Cataloging-in-Publication Data is on file with the Library of Congress

   ISBN: 1-85109-839-9   e-book: 1-85109-840-2
   ISBN-13: 978-1-85109-839-2   e-book: 978-1-85109-840-8

10   09   08   07   06   05   10 9 8 7 6 5 4 3 2 1

This book is also available on the World Wide Web as an ebook.
Visit abc-clio.com for details.

ABC-CLIO, Inc.
130 Cremona Drive, P.O. Box 1911
Santa Barbara, California 93116–1911

This book is printed on acid-free paper ∞ .
Manufactured in the United States of America

Contents

Volume V: Documents

List of Entries

List of Maps

General Maps

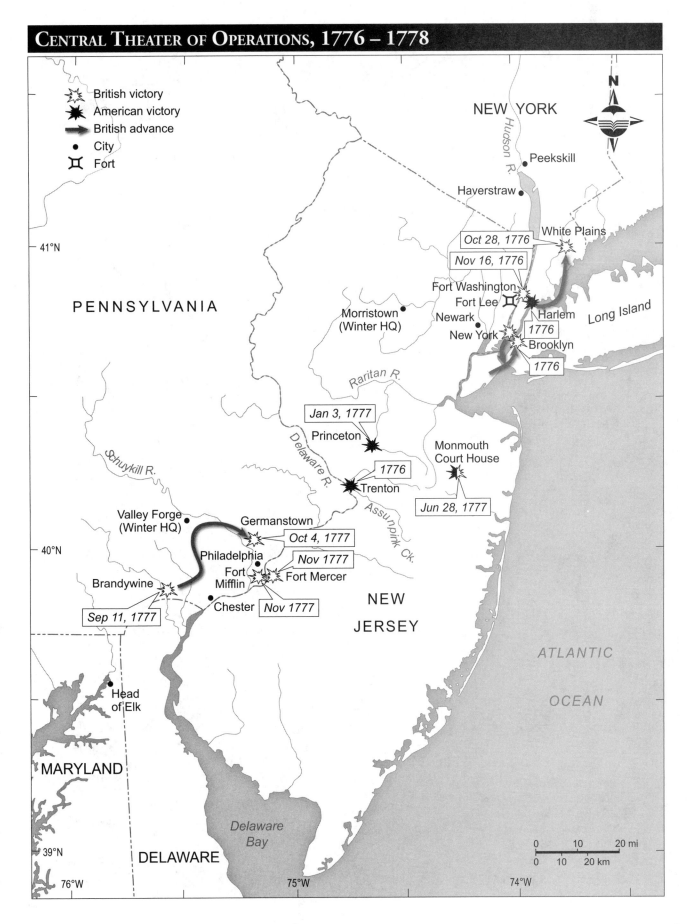

CENTRAL THEATER OF OPERATIONS, 1776 – 1778

British victory
American victory
British advance
City
Fort

NEW YORK

Hudson R.

Peekskill

Haverstraw

White Plains

Oct 28, 1776

Nov 16, 1776

PENNSYLVANIA

Fort Washington
Fort Lee

Morristown
(Winter HQ)

Newark

New York

Harlem

1776

Brooklyn

1776

Long Island

Raritan R.

Jan 3, 1777

Princeton

Monmouth
Court House

Delaware R.

1776

Trenton

Assunpink Ck.

Jun 28, 1777

Schuylkill R.

Valley Forge
(Winter HQ)

Germanstown

Oct 4, 1777

Philadelphia

Nov 1777

Brandywine

Fort
Mifflin

Fort Mercer

NEW

JERSEY

Sep 11, 1777

Chester

Nov 1777

Head
of Elk

ATLANTIC

OCEAN

MARYLAND

Delaware
Bay

DELAWARE

0   10   20 mi
0   10   20 km

NORTH AMERICA, 1783

ARCTIC OCEAN

GREENLAND

Baffin Bay

Baffin Land

ALASKA

50°N

NEW-FOUND-LAND

Hudson Bay

LABRADOR

Area disputed by Spain, Britain and Russia

40°N

RUPERT'S LAND

St. Pierre and Miquelon (FRANCE)

QUEBEC

NOVA SCOTIA

Mississippi R.

Snake R.

30°N

UNITED STATES

ATLANTIC OCEAN

N E W

Area disputed by Spain and U.S.

Rio Grande

PACIFIC OCEAN

FLORIDA

20°N

Bahamas (ENGLAND)

S P A I N

CUBA

JAMAICA

SANTO DOMINGUE

BRITISH HONDURAS

Caribbean Sea

10°N

	United States
	British possessions
	Spanish possessions and claims
	French possessions
	Russian claims
	Unexplored by non-Indians
	Disputed areas

PANAMA

0   250   500 mi

0   250 500 km

120°W   110°W   100°W   90°W

NORTHERN THEATER OF OPERATIONS, 1775–1776

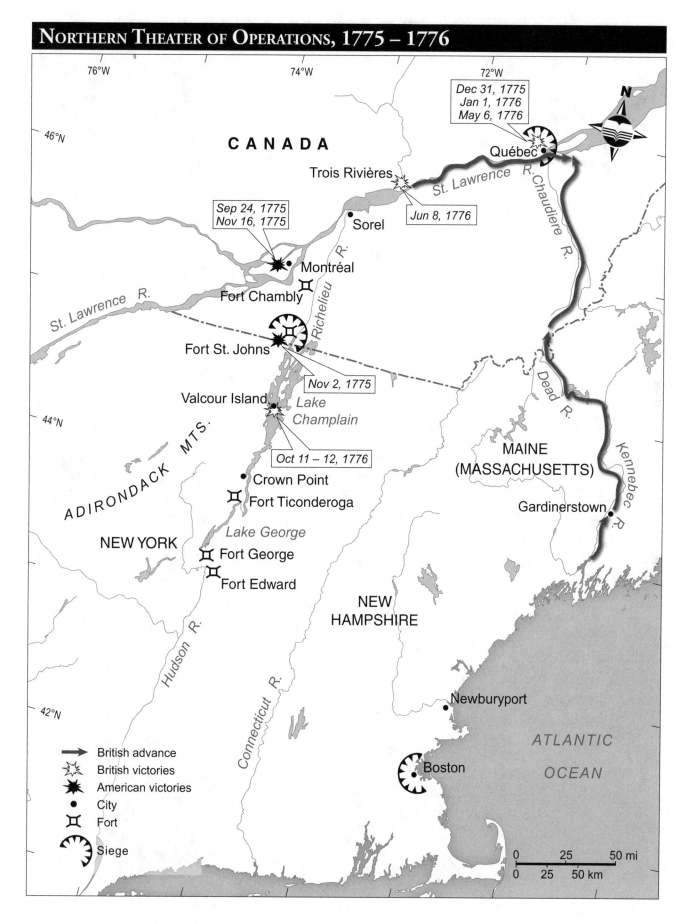

76°W

74°W

72°W

46°N

CANADA

Dec 31, 1775
Jan 1, 1776
May 6, 1776

Québec

Trois Rivières

St. Lawrence R.

Chaudière R.

Sep 24, 1775
Nov 16, 1775

Jun 8, 1776

Sorel

Montréal

Richelieu R.

Fort Chambly

St. Lawrence R.

Fort St. Johns

Nov 2, 1775

Valcour Island

Lake Champlain

44°N

Dead R.

Oct 11 – 12, 1776

ADIRONDACK MTS.

MAINE
(MASSACHUSETTS)

Kennebec R.

Crown Point

Fort Ticonderoga

Lake George

Gardinerstown

NEW YORK

Fort George

Fort Edward

Hudson R.

NEW
HAMPSHIRE

42°N

Connecticut R.

Newburyport

ATLANTIC

OCEAN

Boston

→ British advance

✶ British victories

✸ American victories

● City

Ħ Fort

Siege

0   25   50 mi
0   25   50 km

Legend:
- British victory
- American victory
- Loyalist-Patriot skirmish Jun to Sep 1780
- American-British skirmish
- City

MARYLAND

Chesapeake Bay

Charlottesville

Richmond

Elk Hill

James R.

Williamsburg

Petersburg

Norfolk

Portsmouth

Yorktown
Oct 19, 1781

VIRGINIA

Roanoke R.

Guilford
Court House
Mar 15, 1781

NORTH CAROLINA

Neuse R.

Albemarle Sound

Pamlico Sound

Cape Hatteras

Cape Lookout

Ramsour's Mill
Jun 20, 1780

King's Mountain
Oct 7, 1780

McDowell's Camp
Jul 15, 1780

Pee Dee

Charlotte

Waxhaws
May 29, 1780

Cowpens
Jan 17, 1781

Rocky Mount
Aug 1, 1780

Hanging Rock
Aug 6, 1780

Cheraw

Cape Fear R.

Williams
Plantation
Jul 12, 1780

Hobkirk's Hill
Apr 25, 1781

Ninety Six
May-Jun 1781

Winnsboro

Camden
Aug 16, 1780

Georgetown
Captured by British,
Jul 1, 1780

Cape Fear

34°N

Fort Charlotte

SOUTH CAROLINA

Santee R.

ATLANTIC

OCEAN

Kettle Creek
Feb 14, 1779

Orangeburg

Augusta

Eutaw
Springs
Sep 8, 1781

Savannah R.

GEORGIA

Oconee R.

Briar Creek
Mar 3, 1779

Beaufort

Charleston
1. British attach by sea fails,
Jun 1776
2. City captured by British,
May 12, 1780

Fort Sunbury

Savannah
1. Captured by British, Dec 29, 1778
2. British repel American and French
attack of Oct 9, 1779

Altamaha R.

82°W

80°W

78°W

32°N

0   25   50 mi

0   25   50 km

38°N

New R.

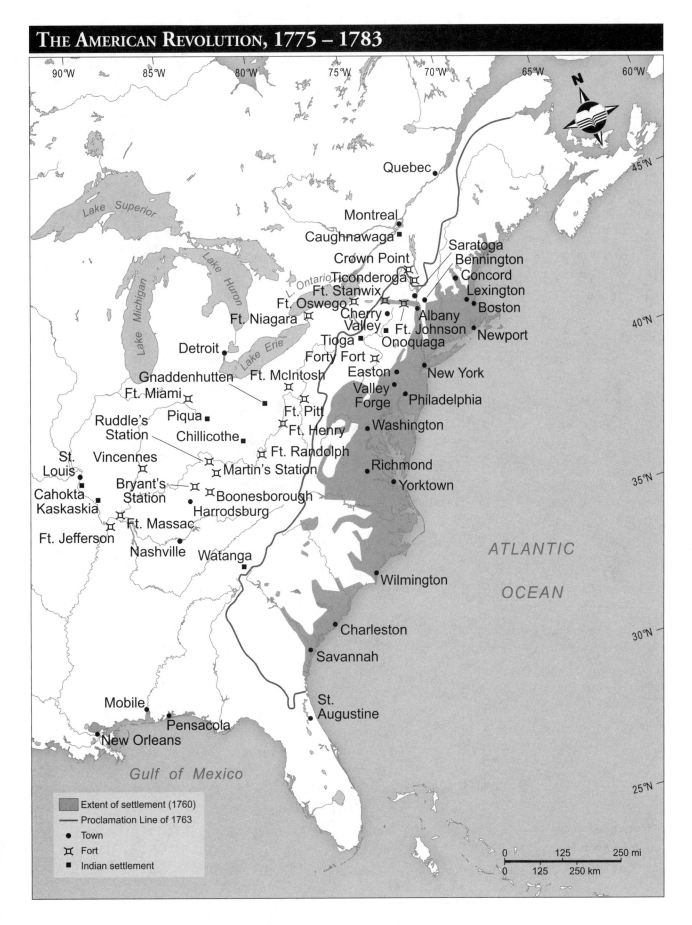

THE AMERICAN REVOLUTION, 1775 – 1783

90°W 85°W 80°W 75°W 70°W 65°W 60°W

N

45°N

Lake Superior

Lake Michigan

Lake Huron

Lake Erie

L. Ontario

Quebec

Montreal

Caughnawaga

Crown Point

Saratoga
Bennington

Ticonderoga
Ft. Stanwix
Ft. Oswego
Ft. Niagara

Cherry
Valley

Concord
Lexington
Boston

Albany
Ft. Johnson

Newport

40°N

Detroit

Tioga

Onoquaga

Forty Fort

Gnaddenhutten
Ft. Miami
Ft. McIntosh

Easton
Valley
Forge

New York

Philadelphia

Ruddle's
Station

Piqua

Chillicothe

Ft. Pitt
Ft. Henry

Washington

St.
Louis

Vincennes

Ft. Randolph

Richmond

35°N

Cahokta
Kaskaskia

Bryant's
Station

Martin's Station

Boonesborough

Yorktown

Ft. Jefferson

Ft. Massac
Harrodsburg

Nashville

Watanga

Wilmington

ATLANTIC

OCEAN

30°N

Charleston

Savannah

Mobile

St.
Augustine

Pensacola
New Orleans

Gulf of Mexico

25°N

Extent of settlement (1760)
Proclamation Line of 1763
• Town
⛫ Fort
■ Indian settlement

0   125   250 mi
0   125   250 km

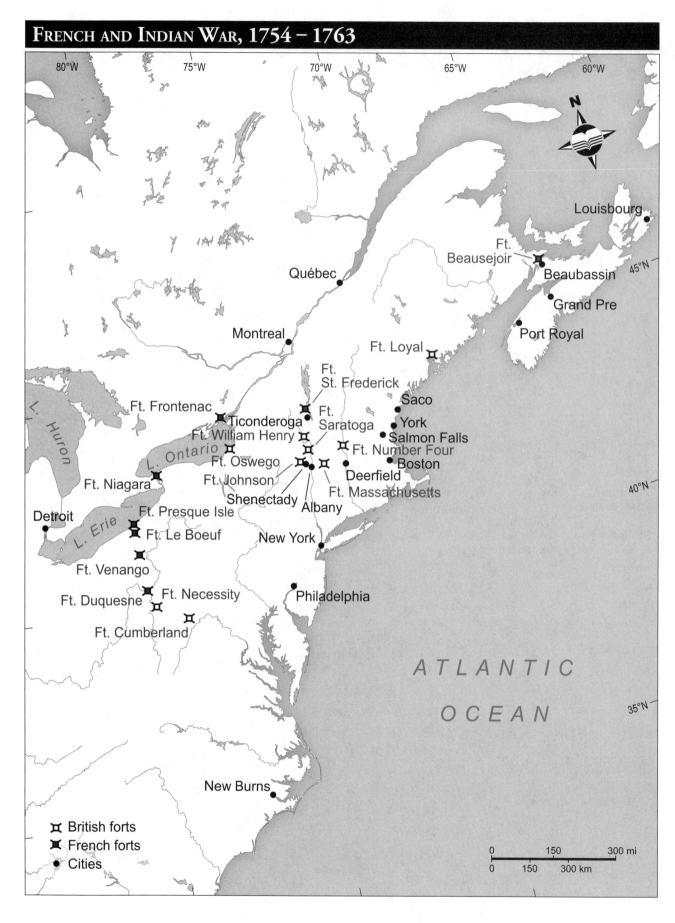

80°W 75°W 70°W 65°W 60°W

N

Louisbourg

Ft. Beausejoir

Beaubassin

45°N

Québec

Grand Pre

Port Royal

Montreal

Ft. Loyal

Ft. St. Frederick

Saco

Ft. Frontenac

Ticonderoga

Ft. Saratoga

York

Ft. William Henry

Salmon Falls

Ft. Oswego

Ft. Number Four

Ft. Johnson

Boston

Ft. Niagara

Shenectady

Deerfield

Albany

Ft. Massachusetts

40°N

Detroit

L. Erie

Ft. Presque Isle

Ft. Le Boeuf

L. Huron

L. Ontario

New York

Ft. Venango

Ft. Duquesne

Ft. Necessity

Philadelphia

Ft. Cumberland

ATLANTIC

OCEAN

35°N

New Burns

British forts
French forts
Cities

0   150   300 mi
0 150 300 km

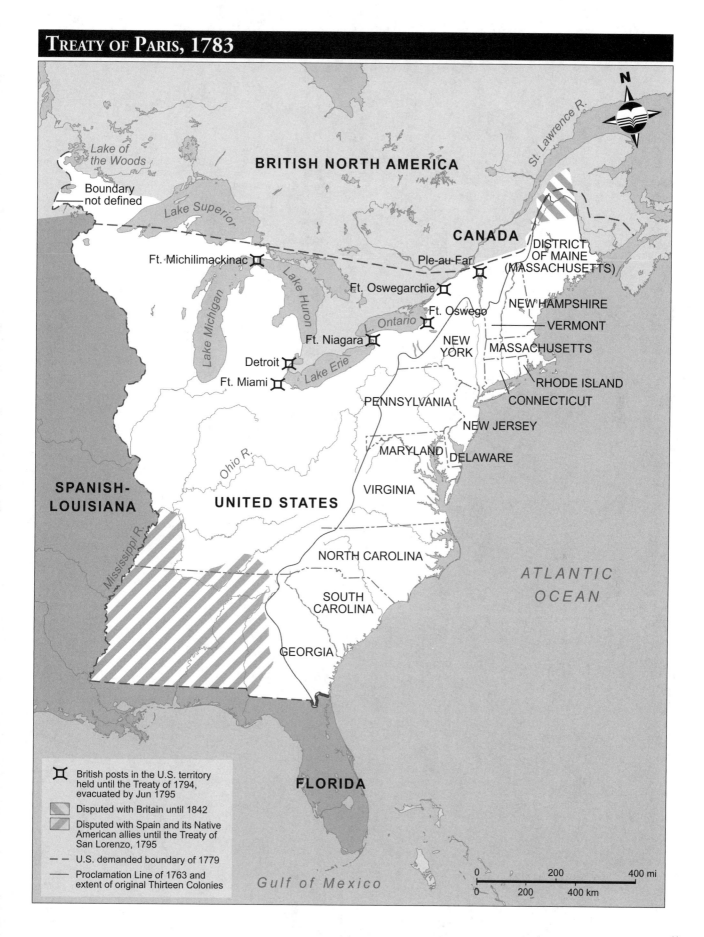

BRITISH NORTH AMERICA

Lake of the Woods

Boundary not defined

Lake Superior

St. Lawrence R.

CANADA

Ft. Michilimackinac

Ple-au-Far

DISTRICT OF MAINE (MASSACHUSETTS)

Ft. Oswegarchie

Lake Huron

Ft. Oswego

NEW HAMPSHIRE

L. Ontario

VERMONT

Ft. Niagara

NEW YORK

MASSACHUSETTS

Detroit

Lake Erie

RHODE ISLAND

Ft. Miami

CONNECTICUT

Lake Michigan

PENNSYLVANIA

NEW JERSEY

MARYLAND

DELAWARE

Ohio R.

VIRGINIA

SPANISH-LOUISIANA

UNITED STATES

Mississippi R.

NORTH CAROLINA

SOUTH CAROLINA

ATLANTIC OCEAN

GEORGIA

FLORIDA

Gulf of Mexico

British posts in the U.S. territory held until the Treaty of 1794, evacuated by Jun 1795

Disputed with Britain until 1842

Disputed with Spain and its Native American allies until the Treaty of San Lorenzo, 1795

U.S. demanded boundary of 1779

Proclamation Line of 1763 and extent of original Thirteen Colonies

0   200   400 mi
0   200   400 km

M

Few, if any, individuals had a more extensive participation in or impact upon the early political development of the United States than James Madison Jr. He served as a state legislator in the Virginia House of Delegates (1776, 1784–1786, and 1799), as a member of the Virginia Council of State (1777–1779), as a Virginia delegate to the Continental and Confederation Congresses (1780–1783 and 1787–1788), as a member of the U.S. House of Representatives for Virginia (1789–1797), as a presidential elector (1800), as U.S. secretary of state (1801–1809), and as U.S. president (1809–1817).

Madison's contributions, however, extended beyond these regular political offices. He was a delegate to two Virginia constitutional conventions in which he aided in the framing and adoption of the state constitutions of 1776 and 1829 and Virginia's 1776 Declaration of Rights. He served as a Virginia delegate to the 1786 Annapolis Convention and was one of the leading promoters and organizers of the 1787 Constitutional Convention, at which he was one of the most active (although occasionally disappointed) participants, and earned the popular, if somewhat exaggerated, reputation as the "father of the Constitution." After the 1787 convention, he was a prominent advocate for ratification of the Constitution, both in the New York press (as the author of several of the most celebrated Federalist Papers essays) and at the Virginia ratifying convention. As a member of the First U.S. Congress, he helped to frame what became the Bill of Rights—the first ten amendments to the U.S. Constitution—as well as the Twenty-seventh Amendment (controlling congressional pay raises), which was ratified more than 200 years later in 1992. Finally, Madison made noteworthy contributions to the era's public discourses on republican government, church-state relations, and the provisions and expected benefits of the U.S. Constitution. His widest and most enduring intellectual legacies are embodied in the Federalist Papers published in New York in 1787–1788, his 1798 *Virginia Resolutions* circulated as a response to the federal Alien and Sedition Acts, and his detailed notes on the deliberations of the 1787 convention posthumously published in 1836.

Madison was born on 16 March 1751, at Port Conway, Virginia, in King George County. Until the age of twelve, he lived on his family's plantation in

Madison, James
(1751–1836)

James Madison represented Virginia in the Second Continental Congress and is often called the "Father of the Constitution" for his critical role in the drafting of the U.S. Constitution. He served as president from 1809 to 1817. (National Archives and Records Administration)

Orange County, Virginia. He was the oldest child of twelve born to his parents, Nelly and James Madison Sr. As a youth, Madison experienced the common privileges associated with his family's local prominence and slavery-created prosperity as well as the expected excitements of living in a large family and, sadly, the sobering infant deaths of four siblings. His childhood education was provided at home until 1762, when he was sent to Donald Robertson's school in King and Queen County, Virginia. He remained a student there until he was about sixteen, mastering a classical and conventional curriculum that included mathematics, literature, and language instruction in Latin, Greek, French, and Spanish.

In 1767 Madison returned to his family plantation, where he received additional private instruction from Reverend Thomas Martin, an Anglican minister who had completed his studies at the College of New Jersey (now Princeton University). Martin's spiritual and educational presence was consequential for Madison, who subsequently decided to attend Martin's alma mater, which at the time was known for its rigorous classical and Christian curriculum.

At the College of New Jersey, Madison joined similarly minded students from dissimilar geographic and cultural backgrounds. The academically inclined Madison thrived under these new intellectual challenges and received liberal exposure to a broad range of philosophical and political thinkers, including Plato, Aristotle, Bacon, Montaigne, Grotius, Hobbes, Newton, Locke, Vattel, Hume, and Montesquieu. Madison received his BA in 1771 but continued his studies for an additional year, learning Hebrew and other subjects under the guidance of John Witherspoon, the college's president. Madison returned to his family plantation in Orange County in 1772, where he continued his bookish habits while periodically considering his future as an adult. The leisure afforded by plantation life coupled with his previous academic studies and the broadly intensifying political conflicts between British authority and American colonial interests in the 1770s primed Madison to become more politically active once the time had come to declare one's ultimate allegiances.

Not surprisingly, Madison's initial engagement in Revolutionary resistance was measured and guided by the decisions of his father and other Orange County leaders. With the aid of his locally prominent father, the twenty-three-year-old Madison was elected to the Orange County Committee of Safety in 1774. In 1776, he was selected to represent Orange County in the Virginia Provincial Constitutional Convention, where he participated in the formation of the new Virginia Constitution and the state's Declaration of Rights—the latter a symbolic reflection of the 1689 English Declaration of Rights and a forerunner to the U.S. Bill of Rights, which Madison subsequently helped to draft in Congress in 1789. At the 1776 state convention, Madison served with George Mason and Patrick Henry on the committee that drafted the new state constitution. Madison also amended the 1776 Declaration of Rights to specify the free exercise of religion as a fundamental individual right, but he failed in his attempt to include a provision disestablishing the Anglican Church in Virginia. As early as 1774, Madison had been deeply affected by the severe religious persecutions he witnessed against non-Anglican religious groups in Virginia, and he expressed an early commitment to the necessity of fundamental reforms in church-state relations.

During the Revolutionary War, Madison refrained from direct military service, apparently for reasons of health, although, again with the aid of his father, he received an appointment as a colonel in the Orange County militia in 1775. In 1776, Madison was elected and served as Orange County's representative in the Virginia House of Delegates. He was not reelected to his seat in 1777, apparently due to his refusal to campaign openly or to treat potential voters with alcoholic incentives. In the same year, however, the General Assembly elected Madison to Virginia's Council of State, a constitutional position charged with providing advice and counsel to the governor. In 1779, the assembly elected Madison one of Virginia's delegates to the Continental Congress, which was then considered a less-prestigious position for those interested in state political careers. Madison's political horizons, however, extended beyond Virginia, and he embraced his return to the role of legislator not only because it required him to move to bustling Philadelphia, where Congress then convened, but also because it offered him opportunities to hone his legislative skills and to have a direct impact upon the Revolutionary War and the young nation's political development.

In Congress, Madison proved to be one of the most diligent and active legislators and one of the most national in his approach to public policy. His voting record more often aligned with New England or the middle-state delegates than with other southern congressmen. Madison's congressional tenure was defined by his commitment to advance policies designed to empower the new national government as well as the interests of Virginia. The national war effort and its economic consequences dominated Congress's agenda throughout his time there. Madison consistently pushed for new taxing powers for Congress, including a 5 percent impost, as a means for solving its ineffectual state requisition system and the young nation's chronic inflation and debt payment problems. He supported close relations with France and negotiations with Spain for the free navigation of the Mississippi River. He also assisted in the resolution of Virginia's extensive western land claims while in Congress, effectively mitigating contentious interstate jealousies and opening the way to the nation's future territorial expansion and economic development.

Madison served in the Continental Congress until 1783, when his term was ended by the three-year limitation in the Articles of Confederation, which the states finally ratified in 1781. He returned to Virginia and in 1784 again was elected to represent Orange County in the Virginia House of Delegates; he was reelected twice and served through 1786. As in Congress, he was an active legislator in the House of Delegates, fulfilling important committee assignments and influencing the ideas of his colleagues and the policies they collectively adopted for the state. In 1784 and 1785, he led a legislative coalition against efforts by Henry to establish a general tax to support organized religious sects. Madison's effort was aided by his "Memorial and Remonstrance against Religious Assessments," a circulated essay in which he argued for individual religious liberty and against governmental support for religion. In 1786, he shepherded a revised version of Thomas Jefferson's Bill for Establishing Religious Freedom through the Virginia General Assembly.

In February 1787, Madison resumed his national legislative career as one of Virginia's delegates to Congress, which then convened in New York City. He remained in Congress through 1788. Following the ratification of the U.S. Constitution, he lost his bid in 1788 for one of Virginia's two U.S. Senate seats; the Virginia General Assembly under the influence of Henry selected Richard Henry Lee and William Grayson. But in February 1789, voters elected Madison over James Monroe for a seat as a Virginia representative in the first U.S. Congress, and he won reelection three subsequent times, serving until 1797.

Madison's public contributions between 1776 and 1789 extended well beyond his legislative achievements and his long list of elected and appointed political offices. Indeed, what separates Madison from others of the era was his lifelong interest in and entrepreneurial pursuit of constitutional change. This interest was evident in his early public career, in which he read widely on ancient and modern federal republics, the laws of nations, and the political history of the New World. With Philip Mazzei, he created the Constitutional Society of Virginia in 1784, one of the nation's first public interest groups committed to the promotion of constitutional reform. The society was chartered to publish information on amending the Virginia Constitution in order to preserve it from corruption by individual ambition and organized factions.

Madison's studied knowledge of the creation and dissolution of constitutional orders was reinforced by his political experiences. He participated in the 1776 Virginia Constitutional Convention and was a member of Congress when the Articles of Confederation were finally ratified. He was also one of only a dozen persons, from just five states, to attend the 1786 Annapolis Convention that sought to advance the reform of the Articles of Confederation. And, of course, he attended and often dominated the 1787 Philadelphia Constitutional Convention. For the Annapolis meeting, Madison completed a lengthy set of notes on the rise and fall of confederacies. For Philadelphia, he clarified his thinking on the necessity of replacing the Articles of Confederation by completing a private memorandum on the vices of the American constitutional order.

Madison's interests and experiences also included the creation of several new state constitutions. In addition to Virginia's first state constitution, in the mid-1780s he advised leaders of the Kentucky statehood movement concerning their new state constitution. He cautiously advised them to leave open the possibility for subsequent constitutional revisions because it was imprudent for initial settlers to believe that they could bind future generations. He insightfully recommended a rule of apportionment for the state legislature that assigned the number of representatives for each county according to the number of the county's electors, and he proposed a periodic reallocation of representation based on population growth—two novel constitutional devices of representation that would be included in the new U.S. Constitution in 1787.

Ironically, given Madison's common monikers as a "nationalist" and the "father of the Constitution," he rejected every proposal to convene a national constitutional convention during his first service in Congress in the early 1780s. In 1782, he refused to endorse a convention proposal advanced by New York delegate Alexander Hamilton. A year later, Madison also opposed a formal proposal advocated by the Massachusetts legislature, opting instead to rely upon the unwieldy and unlikely constitutional amendment process defined in the Articles of Confederation.

Interestingly, after his retirement from Congress in 1783, Madison returned to Virginia to lead the effort to call a convention to rewrite the Virginia Constitution. He visited and actively courted support from leading Virginians such as Mason, Henry, and Lee. After Madison's election to the Virginia General Assembly, he pressed his case for constitutional reform on the floor of the House of Delegates, denouncing the 1776 state constitution for its undemocratic qualities and unequal apportionment of representation among the state's counties and cities. Despite his advance work, however, he clearly had misjudged the level of support for constitutional reform within the General Assembly. Yet Madison's failure to garner support among his legislative colleagues gave him valuable experience in the difficulties of proposing wholesale constitutional change within a legislative body directly affected by the proposed reforms.

Madison's failed state reform kindled his interest in pursuing national constitutional reform. By December 1784, he privately declared that the question no longer was whether the Articles of Confederation needed radical reform but at what moment the attempt should be made to reform it. Under his direction, the Virginia General Assembly proposed a national convention that was to meet in Annapolis to consider the adoption of national commercial regulations. Although initially disappointed that the Virginia legislature did not grant wider latitude to its convention delegates, Madison calculated that the Annapolis Convention created the needed forum for discussion of other constitutional reforms.

Although the Annapolis Convention failed miserably because most states refused to send delegates, Madison and Hamilton used the meeting to call for a second convention to meet the following May in Philadelphia. Madison again gained the endorsement of the Virginia General Assembly and was appointed a delegate to the Philadelphia convention. He also worked to secure the attendance of several states, convinced the widely respected George Washington to attend, and had a heavy hand in drafting and submitting the so-called Virginia Plan, which dominated the early deliberations of the 1787 convention.

Madison arrived in Philadelphia several weeks before the scheduled opening of the 1787 convention and met with other Virginia and Pennsylvania delegates to prepare for the convention and to work on the details of the Virginia Plan. Central to his convention strategy and proposed constitutional reforms was the adoption of a proportional rule of legislative representation to replace the Articles' rule, which gave each state an equal vote in Congress regardless of its population, relative size, or economic significance. His proposed reforms also included the establishment of a national executive and judiciary, a bicameral Congress, popular ratification of the new Constitution, and, most important of all, a more fully empowered and energetic national government that would possess authority to overturn state legislative acts.

Despite Madison's best efforts, however, the convention's deliberations veered away from his expectations and rejected several elements of the Virginia Plan, deadlocking by midsummer over the terms of the new national rule of apportionment. He was greatly disappointed, almost despondent, over the convention's so-called Great Compromise, by which representation would be divided proportionally among the states in the U.S. House of Representatives based on state population but would be equal among all the states, large and small, in the U.S. Senate. He quickly recovered his spirits, however, and participated in the remaining convention deliberations, and he was one of the thirty-nine delegates who signed the original U.S. Constitution.

After the convention, Madison was one of the strongest advocates for ratification of the Constitution. Upon his return to Congress, he and other convention delegates secured the body's unanimous resolution that the states assemble popularly elected ratifying conventions to consider the new document. He monitored and marshaled support for ratification across the states, corresponding with fellow federalists throughout the nation. In Virginia, he openly contested those who opposed ratification, including prominent state leaders such as Mason, Henry, and Lee, and he privately and publicly persuaded others with doubts, such as Governor Edmund Randolph. As a member of the June 1788 state ratifying convention, Madison finally succeeded, along with other Federalists, in winning Virginia's ratification of the Constitution.

Before traveling to Virginia, however, Madison worked to persuade New York to ratify the Constitution by joining the proratification publication campaign of Hamilton and Jay as the third author of the Federalist Papers, a series of commentaries on the provisions and expected benefits of the U.S. Constitution. The three authors wrote under the collective pen name "Publius," a reference to Publius Valerius Publicola, the half-legendary founder and lawgiver of republican Rome. The essays began appearing in New York newspapers in October 1787 and continued through March 1788. Almost immediately thereafter, they were bound and reissued as a two-volume book. While the original essays were read principally by New Yorkers, both the two-volume work and several individual essays were circulated throughout the thirteen states. Madison wrote twenty-nine of the eighty-five Federalist Papers essays, including several coauthored with Hamilton, who wrote fifty-five on his own.

Five of Madison's essays are especially important: Federalist Nos. 10, 39, 47, 48, and 51. In Federalist No. 10, perhaps his most famous, Madison

Madison wrote
twenty-nine
of the eighty-five
Federalist
Papers essays.

focuses on the problem of faction within a republic. Previous republics had fallen prey to the dangers of faction because they permitted a single majority faction, opposed to the common good, to gain power. According to Madison, the cure for the mischief of faction lay in the special character of the United States as an extended and expanding republic. This new type of republic could be expected to include a diversity of factions, which would counteract each other and thereby prevent any one faction from dominating the whole. In Federalist No. 39, Madison explains that the new American republic is neither wholly federal nor wholly national but rather a blend of the best features of both. In Federalist Nos. 47 and 48, he explains the necessity of separation of powers as a check against tyrannical consolidations of power in the same hands. In Federalist No. 51, he argues that as it is beneficial for faction to counteract faction, so also political ambition can be used to counter political ambition. By creating three distinct branches of the national government, by separating the legislature into two houses, and by extending the sphere of the republic, Madison points out that the new Constitution encouraged distinct ambitions, passions, and interests. This diversity made it unlikely for any majority to act on any principles others than justice and the general good.

Madison strongly opposed the addition of amendments to the U.S. Constitution as a condition for ratification. Like others, he believed that the discussion of amendments would extend efforts to weaken the national government or would stop ratification altogether. The states, however, sent more than 200 constitutional amendments to the first U.S. Congress, which convened in 1789. As one of the most prominent members of the first U.S. House of Representatives, Madison led the process of reviewing these amendment proposals, ultimately fashioning a list of nineteen constitutional amendments, of which Congress endorsed and sent twelve amendments to the states for ratification. The states subsequently ratified ten of these amendments, commonly known today as the Bill of Rights because the first nine establish formal protections of individual rights and the Tenth Amendment reserves all powers that are not expressly delegated to the federal government to the states or the people.

Following his service in Congress, as secretary of state to his close friend and political ally Jefferson, and as the fourth president of the United States, Madison retired to his estate at Montpelier, in Orange County, Virginia, where he died in 1836.

CHARLES A. KROMKOWSKI

See also
Articles of Confederation; Congress, Second Continental and Confederation; Constitution, United States; Federalist Papers; Hamilton, Alexander; Henry, Patrick; Jefferson, Thomas; Witherspoon, John

References
Banning, Lance. *The Sacred Fire of Liberty: James Madison and the Founding of the Federal Republic.* Ithaca, NY: Cornell University Press, 1995.

Brant, Irving. *James Madison*, Vols. 1–3. Indianapolis: Bobbs-Merrill, 1941.

Hobson, Charles F. "The Negative on State Laws: James Madison, the Constitution, and the Crisis of Republican Government." *William and Mary Quarterly* 36(2) (1979): 215–235.

Hutchinson, William T., et al., eds. *The Papers of James Madison*, Vols. 1–17. Chicago: University of Chicago Press, 1962–1983.

Ketchum, Ralph. *James Madison: A Biography*. Charlottesville: University of Virginia Press, 1971.

Kromkowski, Charles A. *Recreating the American Republic: Rules of Apportionment, Constitutional Change, and American Political Development, 1700–1870*. Cambridge: Cambridge University Press, 2002.

McCoy, Drew. "James Madison and Visions of American Nationality in the Confederation Period." Pp. 226–258 in *Beyond Confederation: Origins of the Constitution and American National Identity*. Edited by Richard Beeman et al. Chapel Hill: University of North Carolina Press, 1987.

Rakove, Jack N. *James Madison and the Creation of the American Republic*. New York: Longman, 2002.

Wilson, Rick K. "Madison at the First Congress: Institutional Design and Lessons from the Continental Congress, 1780–1783." Pp. 243–263 in *James Madison: The Theory and Practice of Republic Government*. Edited by Samuel Kernell. Stanford, CA: Stanford University Press, 2003.

Madjeckewiss
(1735?–1805?)

This influential Chippewa chief was known by several names spelled in a bewildering variety of ways: Matchiquawish, Matchekewis, Mudjekewiss (translated as "West Wind"), Wachicouess, Kaigwiaidosa, and Mash-i-pi-nash-i-wish (variously translated as "Bad Bird," "Bald Bird," or "Bold Bird"). Before the American Revolutionary War he vacillated between French and British alliances as both warrior and peacemaker, but during and after the war he consistently supported the British against the Americans. One of his most memorable appearances, however, was as a fictionalized character in Henry Wadsworth Longfellow's "The Song of Hiawatha" (1850) as the seducer of Wenonah, mother of Hiawatha.

Madjeckewiss was born in Michigan not far from Saginaw and Thunder Bays. He was a tall and imposing figure, weighing more than 200 pounds even as a youth. During the French and Indian (Seven Years') War, he aligned with the British against France. But in Pontiac's Rebellion (1763–1766), Madjeckewiss turned against the British and helped seize Fort Michilimackinac (now Mackinaw City, Michigan) before joining Pontiac at the unsuccessful siege of Fort Detroit.

Madjeckewiss again allied with the British during the American Revolution and joined General John Burgoyne's invasion of New York in 1777. In 1779, Madjeckewiss attended the great council at L'Arbre Croche (now Cross Village, Michigan), which recruited Indians to fight as British allies. In 1780, he joined Lieutenant Governor Patrick Sinclair at Fort Michilimackinac, and Chief Wapasha of the Santee and Madjeckewiss were commissioned as British generals. They gathered Indian troops to attack Fort San Carlos, a Spanish outpost at St. Louis, Missouri, but the attack was thwarted, preventing Britain from winning control of the Mississippi River. Soon thereafter the war ended, and the Treaty of Paris (1783) gave Americans all upper Mississippi Valley lands once owned by Britain.

Rejecting defeat, Madjeckewiss and other Indians continued to fight the Americans for control of the Northwest. They were initially quite successful but were defeated at the Battle of Fallen Timbers (1794) by American General Anthony Wayne. After their defeat, several Great Lakes tribes, including the Chippewas, negotiated the Treaty of Greenville (1795) with the American government, which established the boundaries between the United States and Indian lands. Madjeckewiss, like other Indian leaders, signed the treaty with his "X" mark, using the name of Mash-i-pi-nash-i-wish.

Madjeckewiss remained concerned with American settler encroachment on Indian lands, and he remained loyal to the British, traveling each summer to British headquarters to request supplies for his people. Some records indicate that Madjeckewiss died in 1806, but his son, also named Madjeckewiss, remembered his father's death as 1805, near the site of Toledo, Ohio. Little is known of Madjeckewiss's family except that he had a son named after himself and a daughter named Sangemanqua (also known as Jeanette Piquette) who married Jean-Baptiste Cadot Jr.

WILLIAM FORD

See also
Native Americans; Northwest Territory; Pontiac's Rebellion; Wayne, Anthony

References
Armour, David A. "Madjeckewiss." In *Dictionary of Canadian Biography Online.* http://www.biographi.ca/EN/ShowBioPrintable.asp?BioId=36645.

Curnoe, Greg. *Deeds/Nations: Directory of First Nations Individuals in South-Western Ontario 1750–1850.* http://www.adamsheritage.com/deedsnations/default.htm.

Danziger, Edmund Jefferson, Jr. *The Chippewas of Lake Superior.* Civilization of the American Indies Series. Norman: University of Oklahoma Press, 1990.

Hindraker, Eric. *Elusive Empires: Constructing Colonialism in the Ohio Valley, 1673–1800.* New York: Cambridge University Press, 1997.

Nolan, Jenny. "Chief Pontiac's Siege of Detroit." *The Detroit News Rearview Mirror.* http://info.detnews.com/history/story/index.cfm?id=180&category=events.

Prucha, Francis Paul. *American Indian Treaties: The History of a Political Anomaly.* 1994. Reprint, Berkeley: University of California Press, 1997.

Snapp, Russell J. *John Stuart and the Struggle for Empire on the Southern Frontier.* Baton Rouge: Louisiana State University Press, 1996.

White, Richard. *The Middle Ground: Indians, Empires, and Republics in the Great Lakes Region, 1650–1815.* 1991. Reprint. New York: Cambridge University Press, 1999.

See Massachusetts

Maine

Manley, John
(1733–1793)

The English-born John Manley was one of America's most successful naval commanders, both as a captain in the Continental Navy and as a privateer, but his largely triumphant career also included two stints as a prisoner of war and one major controversy over his effectiveness as a commander.

Born in Torquay, England, Manley entered the British merchant service as a young man, eventually settling in Marblehead, Massachusetts, where he was master of a merchant ship when the Revolution began. When he offered his services to the American forces surrounding the British in Boston, George Washington gave him the command of the 74-ton schooner *Lee* in October 1775. Manley soon captured several British ships that were supporting their besieged army. The most important of these vessels was the brig *Nancy*, whose cargo of 2,000 muskets, 30 tons of ammunition, and a massive siege mortar proved of great value to the poorly equipped rebels.

As a reward for his service, Congress granted Manley a commission as captain in the Continental Navy on 21 August 1776 and placed him in command of the frigate *Hancock* (32 guns). Manley's career on the *Hancock* was brief, however. Leaving Boston in company with Captain Hector McNeil, commanding the frigate *Boston* (30 guns), on 21 May 1777, Manley captured a small merchantman on 29 May. The following day, however, the *Hancock* had to withdraw from a rash encounter with HMS *Somerset* (64 guns) and was saved only when the *Boston* attacked a British convoy and the *Somerset* had to break off the pursuit to protect the convoy. Two days later, Manley and McNeil combined to capture HMS *Fox*. Instead of celebrating, however, Manley and McNeil began to squabble, first over who could claim the *Fox* as a prize and later over a near collision of the two ships. After pausing to repair their battle damage, the two captains continued their cruise with the *Fox* as a prize.

On 6 July, however, their luck changed. On their way back to Boston, the prize crew of the *Fox* reported British ships on the horizon. The vessels were HMS *Rainbow* (44 guns), *Flora* (32 guns), and *Victor* (10 guns). The ensuing battle ended badly for the Americans, with Manley and McNeil blaming each other for the debacle. The *Flora* engaged the *Boston*, and the two evenly matched ships mauled each other. The *Boston* disengaged downwind to effect emergency repairs. At the same time, Manley opted not to engage the *Rainbow*, believing the British ship to be a 64-gunner, and instead fled to the south while sending the *Fox* eastward to spread the British out. The *Boston* managed to elude capture, eventually reaching safety on the Maine coast. Manley, however, still believing that the *Hancock* was outgunned, struck his flag when the *Rainbow* came into range. And the *Flora* ran down and recaptured the sparsely manned *Fox*.

The British held Manley prisoner in Halifax, Nova Scotia, for two years, until his exchange in 1779. Upon his return, he demanded a board of inquiry to clear his reputation regarding the loss of the *Hancock*. In the subsequent investigation, Manley and McNeil each blamed the other for the disaster. Manley charged that McNeil failed to support him and fled the battle while reiterating his belief that the *Rainbow* outgunned him and claiming that he would have fought the British vessel had he known that the odds were more or less equal. McNeil accused Manley of being the one to flee, charging that the latter had been cowed by his earlier encounter with the *Somerset*. In the end, the board of inquiry cleared Manley of wrongdoing. Public opinion placed most of the blame on McNeil, and he was dismissed from naval service.

With no major warships available for Manley to command, he now turned to privateering. In 1779 and 1780, he successively led three privateers, the *Marlborough*, the *Cumberland*, and the *Jason*, on several successful raids against British shipping in the Caribbean, but in 1780 the British captured him again. After another two years as a prisoner of war, this time in England, another prisoner exchange set him free. In 1782, he was back in Boston in command of the American frigate *Hague* (32 guns). In the last months of the war, he led the *Hague* on a sweep through the Caribbean, taking five prizes before returning to Boston in early 1783. The war ended before Manley could take his ship to sea again. After the war, he returned to the merchant service when the national government all but disbanded the navy. He died in Boston in 1793.

STEVEN J. RAMOLD

See also

Boston, Massachusetts; Continental Navy; Privateering

References

Coggins, Jack. *Ships and Seamen of the American Revolution*. 1969. Reprint, Mineola, NY: Dover, 2002.

Greenwood, Isaac J. *Captain John Manley: Second in Rank in the United States Navy*. Boston: C. E. Goodspeed, 1915.

Peabody, Robert E. *The Naval Career of Captain John Manley of Marblehead*. Salem, MA: Essex Institute, 1909.

Marines, British

British Marines served in two composite battalions during the first years of the American Revolutionary War in the important battles at Lexington, Concord, Bunker Hill, and Long Island. Over the course of the war, the British Marines were deployed with the Royal Navy in their traditional role as sea soldiers, carrying out various raids in North America and, as the war expanded, in the West Indies, India, and Europe. By 1781, more than 20,000 men were serving within the ranks of the British Marines.

While the origins of British sea soldiers can be traced to 1664, the official beginning of the British Marines (Royal Marines after 1802) came only in 1755. Before that date various British Army regiments were raised and served as marines, and there were attempts by senior navy officers, such as Admiral Lord George Anson in the 1740s, to create a formal corps of marines under the command of the Admiralty. With the outbreak of the Seven Years' War, Britain created a formal Marine unit of 5,000 men that served with the

Engraving depicting the shooting of Major John Pitcairn by the African American soldier Peter Salem at the Battle of Lexington during the Revolutionary War. (Bettman/Corbis)

Royal Navy and under its command. The men were divided into three divisions that were further divided into raiding parties, ship parties, composite battalions, and other units.

Unlike the case in previous conflicts, at the close of the Seven Years' War the Marines were kept on the military establishment. They served with Captain James Cook in the Pacific and in garrisons protecting the sea-lanes from Britain to various colonial ports. The period leading up to the American Revolution saw the British Marines organizing themselves along British Army lines, including their creation of light and grenadier companies. The main focus of all military training of the period was linear-style warfare, by which infantry were deployed in extended lines, usually two ranks deep. Marines also engaged in this training, but in smaller units, and recruits trained in companies rather than at the battalion or regimental level utilized by their army counterparts.

There was one critical difference between the officers of the British Army and those of the British Marines. British Army officers bought their commissions and rose steadily through the purchase and patronage system. The British Marine officer did not buy his commission; he rose through the officer ranks on merit alone.

Every Royal Navy ship of seventy-four guns carried an average of eighty to one hundred Marines on board, in part to offer security for the captain against his crew. They also served as raiding and protection forces for the Royal Navy. As tension rose in North America in early 1775, a provisional Marine battalion was sent to Boston, under the command of Lieutenant-Colonel Henry Smith, along with an advance guard under the command of Major John Pitcairn. The troops assembled themselves into a formal battalion organization, with grenadier and light artillery companies, and were noted for their constant drilling. They carried out further tactical training with British Army regulars on Boston Common.

The light infantry of the provisional Marine battalion saw action during the fighting at Concord and Lexington, when they formed part of a composite unit of light infantry made up of several British Army units. The troops fought well but were forced to withdraw toward Boston. In May 1775, a second battalion of Marines arrived to reinforce the British positions. The two battalions stationed in Boston were formally listed as the 1st and 2nd Marine battalions. The 2nd Marines carried out higher-level training during late May and early June.

On 17 June, the British launched an attack against the American positions at Breed's (Bunker) Hill. As at Lexington and Concord, the grenadier and light infantry companies of the Marines were assembled into composite formations with flank companies of British Army units. After two bloody attacks, the British sent in their third and final successful assault. The Marine flank companies participated in both the second and third attacks. The 1st Marine battalion marched with the 47th Regiment of Foot and was able to storm the American positions after the defenders began to run low on ammunition. British forces lost more than 1,000 men dead and wounded, and the Marines in particular lost more than 100 killed and wounded, including 13 officers. The 2nd Marines relieved the 1st Marines on 18 June. British operations in Boston came to a close with the withdrawal of all troops on 17 March 1776.

British Marines were also involved in operations throughout North America. They reinforced Quebec City on the eve of the American attack in December 1775. Marines served in several operations in New York in 1776, at Long Island, Kips Bay, and Manhattan. After 1776, however, the Marines served in most engagements in small numbers. The two Marine battalions were amalgamated into one battalion in 1777 and returned to Britain as tensions with France increased.

Smaller units of Marines, however, continued to serve as raiders and reinforcements from Royal Navy ships in other areas of the conflict. In June 1776, they were involved in the unsuccessful attack on Fort Sullivan (later Fort Moultrie), while in 1777 they successfully raided Norfolk, Virginia. Two grenadier companies served with the British forces in the Philadelphia Campaign of 1777. And Marines served as reinforcements at Castine, Maine, and at Savannah, Georgia, both in 1779. The Marines of the fleet also played an instrumental role in the taking of Fort Moultrie and other batteries outside Charleston, South Carolina, in the 1780 campaign. With the entry of France, Spain, and the Netherlands into the war, the demands made on the Royal

Navy and the Marines increased, and the Marines served in many corners of the globe as the war expanded.

Overall, the British Marines served very well during the American Revolution. They served in composite battalion formations during the early stages of the war, especially in Boston. The demands of the war eventually dictated that the Marines serve in smaller formations, but they continued to contribute as excellent sea soldiers and raiders and created havoc up and down the American coast. As the war became global, the Marines fought throughout the world. Their experience and ability demonstrated during the war helped to cement the British government's decision to retain them during peacetime. The performance of the British Marines in the Seven Years' War and in the early days of the Revolution also influenced the Americans to create their own corps of Marines.

DANIEL PATRICK MARSTON

See also
British Army; Bunker Hill, Battle of; India, Operations in; Lexington and Concord; Long Island, Battle of; Marines, Continental; New York, Operations in; Philadelphia Campaign; Pitcairn, John; Quebec, Siege of; Royal Navy; West Indies

References
Boaz, T. *For the Glory of the Marines: The Organization, Training, Uniforms, and Combat Role of the British Marines during the American Revolution.* Devon, PA: Dockyard, 1993.
Smith, P., and Derek Oakley. *The Royal Marines.* Tunbridge Wells, UK: Spellmount, 1988.

Marines, Continental

The Continental Marines (later the U.S. Marine Corps) had their origin in the American Revolutionary War, although British North Americans had served as Marines, that is, as sea soldiers, in earlier conflicts under the overall command of British forces or of colonial governors. The Continental Marines were initially raised in battalion formation on 10 November 1775 but generally served in smaller units on board ship with the small Continental Navy as a protection force as well as a small raiding force for most of the war. The Continental Marines were a small but welcome addition to the war effort; the corps probably did not exceed 2,000 men. In addition, over the course of the war several state assemblies created small Marine units to serve in local naval expeditions as coastal protection forces.

Marines had been created in other navies, notably the Royal Navy and the Netherlands Navy. The primary role of Marines during the seventeenth and eighteenth centuries was to protect a naval ship's captain from his crew. As this problem decreased over time, the role of the Marines evolved. They began to serve as boarding parties for navy ships as well as amphibious infantry for landings or raids.

The Continental Marines began their career as both seaborne and land-based infantry. While the Continental Congress initially authorized the raising of two Marine battalions specifically to participate in a projected raid on Nova Scotia in 1775, the plans for this operation never came to fruition. The Continental Congress next agreed to raise five companies of Marines. The first captain of the Marines was Samuel Nicholas, who was to serve as the senior Marine officer throughout the war. By December 1775, the companies were filling up with men. As with the Continental Army, the term of enlistment was a year in the first instance. Because the Continental Army had more immediate priorities, however, the new units were not equipped with the required number of weapons.

During this first year of the war, the Continental Congress also authorized the creation of a Continental Navy of thirteen frigates, but because the official Continental Navy was not ready for action until 1777, other ships were pressed into service. The first combined Continental Navy and Marine action occurred in March 1776, when 200 Marines took part in a raid on the British-controlled Bahamas. Over the course of two weeks, the Marines captured Fort Montague and seized more than one hundred cannon and mortars.

The Marines' operations for the rest of 1776 were mainly aboard small frigates that engaged in skirmishes with small frigates of the Royal Navy. The Marines did participate in larger operations in New Jersey at the end of the year. By this time, Congress had raised another four companies. As General George Washington and the Continental Army engaged with British and Hessian forces at Trenton and Princeton, the Marines were ordered to support the attacks. Some one hundred marines served in support of Washington. Some saw service at Trenton, while others served on the west bank of the Delaware River as a defensive force. The major engagement for the Marines was the Battle of Princeton, which took place on 3 January 1777.

The Continental Marines had been raised as an independent corps in 1775, but Congress restructured its armed forces in the spring of 1777 and incorporated the Marines into the Continental Army. More than 600 men had been raised in the ten companies of Marines in 1776. With restructuring, the Marines were to serve in two specific functions: as artillerymen and as ship-based infantry. They would no longer serve as independent infantry forces in the land campaigns. With the introduction of the thirteen formal frigates to the Continental Navy, the role of Marines as protection and as amphibious infantry became critically important.

The Marines deployed to various ships that would sail to Europe and raid the British coast and shipping. The Marines raided the Bahamas in 1778, served along the Ohio River in sloops, and carried out raids into Loyalist territories. They carried out raids in Loyalist villages and towns along the Ohio and Mississippi Rivers as well as in West Florida. The number of Marines began to decline in 1778, however, with the loss of various Continental frigates in engagements with the Royal Navy. In June 1779, Marines participated in the attack on Castine, Maine. The attack involved seven Continental Navy ships as well as state ships. More than 2,500 infantry participated in the attack as well as numbers of Continental Marines and state Marines.

> The first captain of the Marines was Samuel Nicholas.

The 1st Continental Marines recruited by Captain Samuel Nicholas in 1775 for duty in the Revolutionary War. (Bettman/Corbis)

But the Castine operation was a failure. This was not due to any lack of fighting ability among the men but rather to the absence of proper strategic planning for the whole operation. The attack ended with the arrival of a British naval force that destroyed much of the American force, resulting in the Americans' withdrawal to Boston over land. The conduct of the Marines was considered exemplary, but the defeat was such a setback that the Castine operation was the last major amphibious attack carried out by the Marines during the American Revolutionary War.

The Marines' fortunes suffered further damage during the final years of the war. A large number of Marines participated in the defense of Charleston in May 1780, and most of them were captured when the forces surrendered. The defeats suffered by the Continental Navy caused further problems for the Marines. By the end of 1781, there were only two Marine detachments left, both serving on the two remaining Continental frigates.

The Marines served well throughout the conflict. They had been created as an independent corps but were absorbed in 1777 due to the larger strategic needs of the American war effort. They performed well in their capacity as sea soldiers and raiders, carrying out successful raids in the Bahamas as well as in smaller actions in the Delaware and Ohio River areas. With the entry of the French into the war in 1778 and the advent of large-scale sea battles between the French and British navies, the Continental Navy's role diminished further and with it the role of the Marines as sea infantry.

Daniel Patrick Marston

See also

Charleston, South Carolina, Expedition against (1780); Congress, Second Continental and Confederation; Continental Army; Continental Navy; Marines, British; Nicholas, Samuel; Princeton, Battle of; Royal Navy; Trenton, Battle of

References

Aldrich, M. Almy. *History of the United States Marine Corps.* Boston: Henry L. Shepard, 1875.

Heinl, R. *Soldiers of the Sea: The US Marine Corps, 1775–1962.* Annapolis, MD: Naval Institute Press, 1962.

Millett, Alan. *Semper Fidelis: The History of the United States Marine Corps.* New York: Free Press, 1991.

Parker, W. *A Concise History of the US Marine Corps, 1775–1969.* Washington, DC: Historical Division, U.S. Marine Corps, 1971.

Smith, Charles R. *Marines in the Revolution: A History of the Continental Marines in the American Revolution, 1775–1783.* Washington, DC: History and Marines Division, U.S. Marine Corps, 1975.

Marion, Francis
(1732–1795)

A leader of Continental and South Carolina state troops during the American Revolution, Francis Marion achieved fame as a partisan leader, later becoming known as the Swamp Fox because of his resourcefulness in warfare.

Of French Huguenot extraction, Marion was frail in his childhood but during his teen years grew strong. He sailed as a crewman on a schooner to the West Indies at age sixteen and had to abandon ship when the vessel rammed a whale. He was rescued after a week in a jolly boat after two of his companions had died. Settling into life on his father's small plantation, he took over management of the estate in 1750 when his father died. He purchased his own plantation, Pond Bluff, near Eutaw Springs, South Carolina, in 1773, which became his home for life. In 1756, during the French and Indian War, he joined the militia company of Captain John Postell. When Lieutenant-Colonel James Grant organized an expedition against the Cherokee Nation of upper South Carolina in 1761, Marion enlisted as lieutenant in Captain William Moultrie's company. In the Battle of Etchoe, he distinguished himself by leading a group of thirty men in opening the way for Grant's attack on the main Cherokee position.

At the outbreak of the Revolutionary War in 1775, Marion attended the Provincial Congress of South Carolina and voted to organize two state regiments and a cavalry unit to defend the province against Britain. Appointed captain of the 2nd Regiment on 21 June 1775, he assisted in the capture of

Francis Marion, known as the "Swamp Fox," formed a guerrilla band in 1780 and operated independently against British and Loyalist forces in the South. The following year, he began supporting Nathanael Greene's Continental Army, harrassing the enemy in the South Carolina backcountry. (John Clark Ridpath, *Ridpath's History of the World*, 1901)

Fort Johnson on 14 September and was quickly promoted to major. On 28 June 1776, he served gallantly in the repulse of the British assault on Sullivan's Island, off Charleston, and was shortly thereafter promoted to lieutenant colonel in the Continental Army. He served as commander of Fort Moultrie on Sullivan's Island until 1779, and in September of that year he took part in the unsuccessful American assault on Savannah, Georgia. On 9 October, he bravely led his men in an attack on the Spring Hill redoubt but was repulsed with heavy losses. Disgruntled at what he saw as the ineptitude of Patriot commanders, he railed at them for allowing the enemy to entrench before attacking. He was left in temporary command of the army at Sheldon, South Carolina, after Major General Benjamin Lincoln retreated from there to Charleston in late 1779.

In February 1780, Marion was given command of a training camp at Bacon's Bridge on the Ashley River. One evening he jumped out a window to escape a drinking party of his colleagues and broke his ankle. Furloughed home to recuperate, he thus avoided being captured when Charleston surrendered to Sir Henry Clinton's British army on 12 May. In July, as soon as Marion could mount a horse, he set out to join the small Continental Army of 1,400 men under General Baron Johann de Kalb at Coxe's Mill, North Carolina, which had been sent southward by Washington to counter British power. Dispatched on a reconnaissance expedition, Marion rejoined an army that had been taken over by Major General Horatio Gates. In mid-August, Marion was again detached, with orders to sever British communications with Charleston, and thus avoided the Battle of Camden, South Carolina, on 16 August in which Gates's army was routed and subsequently fell back into North Carolina. After the British defeated General Thomas Sumter's army of 700 men two days later at Fishing Creek, Marion's tiny irregular force of 60 men, dubbed Marion's Brigade, was for a time practically the only Patriot military presence in South Carolina.

At the head of this strange command, Marion, recently promoted to brigadier general, began harassing British communications and detachments from a strongly pro-Patriot base around Williamsburg, South Carolina. Scrounging whatever food, military supplies, and soldiers he could manage, he attacked the enemy and quickly retreated into his swampy strongholds. Although his annoying raids seemed almost superhuman achievements to the British, he disliked this mode of warfare and practiced it only because he had no choice. He particularly disliked the way his soldiers kept coming and going at their own discretion. Still, he always managed to keep a few men under his command. On 20 August, at Great Savannah, South Carolina, he captured a British escort of about 25 soldiers under Captain Jonathan Roberts and released 150 American prisoners, while losing just a single man killed and a single man wounded. Striking again on 4 September on the Little Pee Dee River with only 52 soldiers, Marion attacked a Loyalist force of 245 men under Major Micajah Ganey. At a loss of 4 wounded, Marion inflicted 30 casualties and put the rest of the enemy to flight.

On 25 October, with 150 men, Marion routed a Loyalist force under Colonel Samuel Tynes at Tearcoat Swamp, killing 3, wounding 4, and capturing 25. Marion was attacked by Loyalists on 15 November at Alston's Plantation but drove them off with light losses. On 12–13 December, with 700 soldiers, he attacked a force of 200 men under Major Robert McLeroth, pursued the enemy into a swamp, and inflicted 6 casualties. When Major General Nathanael Greene took command in the South in late 1780, he dispatched Lieutenant Colonel Henry Lee and his legion to assist Marion. On 24 January 1781, Marion and Lee led an unsuccessful assault on the British garrison at Georgetown, South Carolina. On 6 March, Marion's militiamen clashed with Lieutenant-Colonel John Watson's force of Loyalists and regulars at Wiboo Swamp but had to withdraw after suffering 6 dead and 12 wounded. Enemy losses were less than half that, but these odds were too great for Marion's strapped command. He battled Watson for two days, 14–15 March, at Lower Bridge, Black River, before forcing Watson to withdraw.

On 23 April 1781, Marion and Lee in joint operations forced Lieutenant James McKay and a garrison of 120 British soldiers to surrender Fort Watson. The same two officers laid siege to Fort Motte on 12 May, compelling the surrender of 150 British troops under Lieutenant Charles McPherson. Serving with Sumter at Quinby Creek Bridge on 17 July, Marion and Lee were dismayed when Sumter imprudently attacked Lieutenant-Colonel John Coates's retreating 19th Regiment and ran out of ammunition. Although the Americans killed 7 of the enemy and wounded 39 more, they suffered 30 killed and 30 wounded. Soon thereafter, Marion and Lee left Sumter in disgust. On 13 August, at Parker's Ferry, Marion and Colonel William Harden with 400 men ambushed 200 Loyalist cavalrymen under Major Thomas Fraser and inflicted 100 casualties. In the major Battle of Eutaw Springs on 8 September, Marion was given command of militia forces in Greene's army. Under Marion's leadership, the militia fought well, composing the front line and firing seventeen rounds before Greene was compelled to surrender the ground to the enemy. At Tydiman's Plantation on 25 February 1782, Marion rallied his men to oppose Colonel Benjamin Thompson, but they broke and ran before a charge. Marion's troopers did better at Fair Lawn on 29 August, stopping a charge by Major Charles Fraser's Loyalists and inflicting 20 casualties. When the British evacuated Charleston on 14 December 1782, Marion's war, and America's war for independence in the South, ended in triumph.

From 1781 to 1791, Marion served his district in the South Carolina Senate, directing much of his energy toward softening laws against the Loyalists. He also devoted much time to restoring his modest estate, which had suffered great damage from enemy depredations during the war. To help relieve his financial misfortunes, he accepted an appointment by the state legislature as commandant of Fort Johnson in 1784, with an annual salary of £500.

Francis Marion became an epic hero, the Swamp Fox, only after his death.

He retained this position until 1790. In 1786, Marion married Mary Esther Videau, a rich and elderly cousin, and his salary was reduced to 5 shillings a day. When a state constitutional convention was called in 1790, he served as a delegate. A quiet, unassuming man, Marion became an epic hero, the Swamp Fox, only after his death, when his friend, Colonel Peter Horry, wrote a biography of him and when Parson Mason L. Weems later developed the theme for a wider audience.

PAUL DAVID NELSON

See also

Camden Campaign; Charleston, South Carolina, Expedition against (1776); Charleston, South Carolina, Expedition against (1780); Eutaw Springs, Battle of; Fair Lawn Plantation, South Carolina, Action at; Fishing Creek, Battle of; Fort Motte, South Carolina; Fort Watson, South Carolina, Actions at; Gates, Horatio; Grant, James; Great Savannah, South Carolina, Action at; Greene, Nathanael; Kalb, Johann, Baron de; Lee, Henry; Lincoln, Benjamin; Moultrie, William; Parker's Ferry, South Carolina, Action at; Quinby Bridge, South Carolina, Action at; Southern Campaigns; Sumter, Thomas; Tearcoat Swamp, South Carolina, Action at

References

Bass, Robert. *Swamp Fox: The Life and Campaigns of General Francis Marion.* 1959. Reprint, Orangeburg, SC: Sandlapper, 1989.

Conrad, Dennis, et al., eds. *The Papers of General Nathanael Greene.* 13 vols. Chapel Hill: University of North Carolina Press, 1976–2005.

James, William Dobein. *A Sketch of the Life of Brig. Gen. Francis Marion and a History of His Brigade.* Charleston, SC: Gould and Riley, 1821.

Lee, Henry. *Memoirs of the War in the Southern Department of the United States.* 1812. Reprint, New York: New York Times, 1969.

Pancake, John S. *This Destructive War: The British Campaign for the Carolinas, 1780–1782.* University: University of Alabama Press, 1985.

Rankin, Hugh F. *Francis Marion: The Swamp Fox.* New York: Crowell, 1973.

Simms, William Gilmore. *The Life of Francis Marion.* New York: G. F. Cooledge, 1844.

Tarleton, Banastre. *History of the Campaigns of 1780 and 1781, in the Southern Provinces of North America.* 1787. Reprint, New York: New York Times, 1968.

Weems, Mason L. *The Life of Gen. Francis Marion: A Celebrated Partisan Officer in the Revolutionary War, against the British and Tories in South Carolina and Georgia.* Philadelphia: Mathew Carey, 1809.

Martin, Josiah
(1737–1786)

Josiah Martin was a British soldier who served as the last royal governor of North Carolina. He briefly studied law at the Inner Temple but chose a military career instead, enlisting in the Antigua militia in 1754. Three years later he was commissioned ensign in the 4th Regiment. After promotion to lieutenant in 1758, he fought the French during the Seven Years' War at Martinique and Guadeloupe as well as in Canada. In 1761 he married his cousin

Elizabeth Martin at Rockhall, the estate of his uncle (also named Josiah Martin) on Long Island, New York. On 24 December 1762, he was promoted to lieutenant-colonel in the 22nd Regiment. He transferred to the 68th Regiment in Antigua in 1764 and a year later was appointed to the island's council. Because of ill health, he sold his commission in 1769 and, with the assistance of his half brother Samuel Martin, a member of Parliament, secured appointment as governor of North Carolina on 14 December 1770, succeeding Governor William Tryon.

When Martin sailed into New Bern on 12 August 1771, he was welcomed by a citizenry who had heard reports of his good character. As governor, he was honest, energetic, and patient, and he labored to promote the public welfare. But he maintained royal prerogatives and was unappreciative of the colonial point of view. The times were not conducive to his success, as Americans everywhere were becoming assertive about their rights. In 1771, he crossed swords with the North Carolina Assembly when he disallowed a discontinuance of the sinking-fund tax. His greatest difficulty came in 1773, when the Assembly refused to enact a court law without a foreign attachment clause, and Martin, under explicit instructions from the Crown, refused assent to any such law. In 1773, too, the judicial system collapsed, and when the governor tried to create courts by decree, the Assembly refused to vote funds for them.

At New Bern in August 1774, Revolutionary leaders defied Martin by holding a provincial congress, electing delegates to the First Continental Congress, and superseding the colony's royal administration. In late May 1775, he fled to the protection of Fort Johnson and British warships on the Cape Fear River, and in July he was driven to take refuge aboard the warship *Cruizer*. There he planned a counterblow against the rebels. With his assistance, Scots Highlanders assembled at Cross Creek in January 1776 under Donald MacDonald but were defeated at Moore's Creek Bridge on 27 February, before British reinforcements arrived. Consequently, Martin sailed for New York and went into semiretirement with his family at Rockhall.

Martin's wife died in 1778, and a year later he joined Sir Henry Clinton's expedition against South Carolina. Martin served as a volunteer in the battle at Camden on 16 August 1780 and at Guilford Courthouse on 15 March 1781. His health now failing, he resigned the governorship of North Carolina in 1781 and sailed with his family for England. There he served as a spokesman for Loyalists until his death in 1786.

PAUL DAVID NELSON

See also
Clinton, Henry; Moore's Creek Bridge, North Carolina, Action at; North Carolina; Tryon, William

Reference
Stumpf, Vernon O. *Josiah Martin: The Last Royal Governor of North Carolina*. Durham, NC: Carolina Academic Press, 1986.

Martinique, Battle of
(29 April 1781)

On 22 March 1781 Rear Admiral François-Joseph de Grasse sailed from Brest with twenty-six ships and a large convoy of troops, bound for Martinique. Six of his warships separated after a week; five went with Pierre-André de Suffren to the East Indies, and one sailed for North America. The remaining twenty ships came within sight of Martinique on 28 April. Leeward of that island, off Pointe des Salines, lay a squadron under Rear-Admiral Sir Samuel Hood, sent by Admiral Sir George Rodney to patrol the waters. That evening, de Grasse and the French commander on shore exchanged intelligence and arranged to cooperate in the fighting that was to follow the next day.

De Grasse's force comprised one ship of the line of 110 guns, fifteen of 74 guns, and one of 64 guns. In addition, there were four other capital ships at Fort Royal: one of 74 guns and three of 64 guns. Hood, who intended to keep these two forces apart, himself had seventeen ships: one of 90 guns, one of 80 guns, twelve of 74 guns, one of 70 guns, and two of 64 guns. Thus, Hood possessed not only fewer ships but also vessels of lower ratings. On the other hand, his whole force had coppered bottoms as a consequence of Rodney's pressure on the Admiralty for this particular innovation. Unlike the French, Hood was not encumbered by a convoy, though he had the disadvantage of being to leeward.

In the early hours of 29 April, de Grasse rounded the southern end of the island, a maneuver that Hood, being too far to leeward, could not prevent. Hood had spent the night attempting to get to windward, but to no avail. Had he been able to do so, he might have fought de Grasse with greater advantage or forced him to abandon his transports to capture. In any event, de Grasse met no opposition in rounding Pointe des Salines. The transports sailed close to the coast, protected to leeward by the warships. Proceeding north, they made for Fort Royal. Shortly after 10:30 A.M. Hood, who had been joined by a 64-gun ship from St. Lucia, tacked to the north, bringing both fleets proceeding in the same direction and with de Grasse's van parallel to Hood's center.

The French began to fire at 11:00 A.M., to which the British, for the moment, offered no reply. Around 11:20, with his van nearing the shore north of the bay, Hood tacked for the south. De Grasse, having safely sailed his convoy into the bay, did the same, bringing both fleets on parallel courses and closer together. Hood's eighteen ships were soon opposed by twenty-four, since the four French vessels in the bay, having the weather gauge, had no difficulty joining the rear of de Grasse's fleet. The British now began to return fire, and at around noon Hood, prevented by the wind from closing the gap with de Grasse, shortened sail, hoping that the French would be brought closer. This had the desired effect. At 12:30 the rival flagships stood abreast of each other, and the fighting intensified down the line, though at extreme range, such that both ships needlessly expended large quantities of powder and shot. The French proceeded on their course, passing the British van.

Once Hood's van passed the southern tip of the island, fresh winds blowing between St. Lucia and Martinique separated it from the center. Hood tried to remedy this at 1:30 by signaling for close order, and at about the same time he ordered his ships to cease firing, for the French were now well beyond effective range. Other vessels, however, continued the action, and four of Hood's ships found themselves assailed by twice their number. One of these, the *Russell*, had been holed in several places and was in danger of sinking. Hood detached it to St. Eustatius, where on 4 May Rodney received news of the battle.

On 30 May, Hood maintained his course and continued to try to put himself to windward of de Grasse. In this he failed. As evening approached and with two of his ships practically crippled, he decided to alter course and proceed north. He could not hope to return to St. Lucia, for so strong were the westerly currents farther south that his damaged ships would not bear the journey. He met Rodney on 11 May in the channel between St. Kitts and Antigua. Rodney had left St. Eustatius on 5 May and, having repaired the *Russell*, brought it, together with the *Sandwich* and the *Triumph*, with him. The fighting had cost Hood 39 killed and 162 wounded. French sources disagree about losses, but they were likely to have been more than 100 killed and perhaps 150 wounded.

Hood had demonstrated boldness at Martinique, eager to fight de Grasse though he led a numerically inferior force. When de Grasse declined the chance for a general engagement, Hood had sought another method: goading his opponent into attack. De Grasse appears to have concentrated his attention on the safety of his convoy. On the following day, Hood, with copper-bottomed ships, easily followed, watching for an opportunity to strike if the numerically superior French should become separated. On the other hand, his superior speed could enable him to disengage if de Grasse chose to fight and the situation deteriorated. It may therefore be said that Hood showed a degree of daring, tempered with caution.

GREGORY FREMONT-BARNES

See also

British West Indies; French West Indies; Grasse, François-Joseph-Paul, Comte de; Hood, Samuel; Rodney, George; Suffren, Pierre André de; West Indies

References

Clowes, William Laird. *The Royal Navy: A History from the Earliest Times to 1900.* Vol. 3 of 7. London: Chatham, 1996.

Gardiner, Robert, ed. *Navies and the American Revolution, 1775–1783.* London: Chatham, 1996.

Ireland, Bernard. *Naval Warfare in the Age of Sail.* London: Collins, 2000.

James, William. *The British Navy in Adversity: A Study of the War of American Independence.* 1926. Reprint, New York: Russell and Russell, 1970.

———. *The Naval History of Great Britain: During the French Revolutionary and Napoleonic Wars.* 4 vols. Mechanicsburg, PA: Stackpole, 2003.

Tilley, J. A. *The Royal Navy in the American Revolution.* Columbia: University of South Carolina Press, 1987.

Maryland

Maryland had little land above tidewater and virtually no frontier.

As a proprietary colony that was partly insulated from direct contact with British officials up to 1776, and then as one of only two states (along with New Hampshire) that saw no engagements within its borders during the entire armed conflict, Maryland played a decidedly secondary role both in the controversies leading up to the American Revolution and in the events of the War for Independence. Throughout the struggle with Britain, however, Maryland produced important civil and military leaders and supplied thousands of effective soldiers for the Continental Army. And in the 1780s, Maryland began to play a more important role in the new nation's political and constitutional development.

Like its proprietary neighbors Delaware and Pennsylvania to the north and east, Maryland had a relatively conservative government through much of the eighteenth century. As executives, Lord Baltimore's appointees, like the deputies of the Penn family, paid attention to the British ministry when they had to, but they worked for the proprietors, not for the Crown. The legislatures in all three colonies were thus insulated from the bitter battles between royal governors and popular assemblies that characterized Massachusetts, New York, South Carolina, and even Virginia for several years before the final imperial crisis.

Yet Maryland began the decade of extensive colonial protest against British imperial policies with at least one claim to leadership. The pamphlet *Considerations on the Propriety of Imposing Taxes on the British Colonies* (1765) by the prominent Annapolis lawyer Daniel Dulany Jr. powerfully stated the Americans' objections to Parliament's argument that its Stamp Act was justified because the colonies were "virtually" represented in the House of Commons. But Dulany soon became an agent for Lord Baltimore, and until the Tea Act of 1773, much of Maryland's energy was devoted to debating proprietor issues, especially the setting of fees for official services. A 1773 newspaper exchange over these fees, however, soon raised issues of home rule for the colony and spelled the end of one colonial career, that of Dulany, and the birth of another, that of Charles Carroll of Carrollton, who as "First Citizen" challenged the proprietor's authority. And Maryland joined several other colonies in firmly rejecting the shipments of East India Company tea.

Maryland's governor, Robert Eden, however, acted as if nothing extraordinary were happening. As Maryland joined other colonies in opposing the Coercive Acts by forming Revolutionary committees of correspondence in the summer of 1774, selecting delegates to the First Continental Congress, and then enforcing the Continental Association of October 1774, Eden performed his duties as Lord Baltimore's representative and paid as little attention to both the British ministry and the radical committees and conventions as possible. This stance worked remarkably well for him for almost two years. While Virginia's royal governor, Lord Dunmore, was fighting an all-out war with his own province, and Carroll, Samuel Chase, and other Patriot leaders were bringing Maryland into the Revolution through provincial congresses and the development of its militia, Eden maintained his composure.

In the spring of 1776, however, as Chase and Carroll urged Marylanders to support independence, Eden's correspondence with Britain's colonial secretary, Lord George Germain, prompted the Second Continental Congress to ask Maryland to arrest its governor. Maryland's Patriot leaders initially refused, but eventually both the governor and the new leadership agreed that royal authority was at an end. On 26 June 1776, just six days before Congress voted for independence, Eden sailed for England, the last British governor to leave his colonial post. In Philadelphia, Maryland's delegates approved independence in July. And in the fall, Maryland's constitutional convention wrote a new republican document with a strong bill of rights for an independent Maryland. Although the colony had been founded by Roman Catholic refugees from England in the 1630s, it had prohibited Catholics from holding public office for much of the eighteenth century. Maryland's constitution of 1776 finally abolished this prohibition, and Carroll immediately took advantage of this new right by becoming a leading member of the new state's senate throughout the Revolutionary War.

The war itself first raged to the north of Maryland and then to the south, but only once, in August–September 1777, did British troops land at the head of Chesapeake Bay and march quickly and without incident across a few miles of the state's northeast corner on their way to defeat George Washington at the Battle of Brandywine. In the War for Independence, however, thousands of Marylanders fought in battles from New York to Georgia. Notable military engagements were those of General William Smallwood's forces at the Battle of Long Island in August 1776 and the brilliant performance of General John Eager Howard's forces at the Battle of Cowpens, South Carolina, in 1780, which was a decisive factor in that one-sided Patriot victory.

In Congress, Marylanders fought a different battle. Virtually alone among states with fairly extensive coastal lands, Maryland had little land above tidewater and virtually no frontier. Massachusetts, Pennsylvania, Virginia, the Carolinas, and even Connecticut all asserted conflicting claims of varying validity to western lands, while Maryland, like tiny Delaware and Rhode Island, had nothing. For several years during the war, Maryland refused to ratify the Articles of Confederation unless its neighbors trimmed back their western claims and ceded some of their frontier to the nation as a whole. In 1781, finally agreeing that its neighbors were taking the issue seriously, Maryland made the ratification of the Confederation unanimous.

The last years of the Revolutionary era in Maryland were devoted to constitutional issues. In 1782 the state revised its constitution and gave a greater role to the upper house of its legislature. In doing so, it developed the novel idea that a senate did not need to be strictly the guardian of privilege but could be an effective second voice for the whole population of any state. This concept soon gained broad currency in other states and played a role in the willingness of the Framers of the U.S. Constitution to create a Senate based on a distinct plan of representation. Maryland was not at the forefront of states in ratifying the new Constitution, and some of its leaders, notably Chase, opposed the document. But in the spring of 1788, by a large margin,

Maryland became the eighth state to ratify the new government. Beginning as an old, fairly prosperous, but rather backward member of the thirteen rebelling colonies in the 1760s and 1770s, Maryland ended the Revolutionary era in a stronger position among its neighbors and with guaranteed access to the West for its citizens.

ARTHUR STEINBERG AND RICHARD ALAN RYERSON

See also

Articles of Confederation; Carroll, Charles; Chase, Samuel; Constitution, United States; Constitution, United States, Ratification of; Dulany, Daniel, Jr.; Eden, Robert; Howard, John Eager; Paca, William; Religion; Smallwood, William; Stamp Act

References

Hoffman, Ronald. *A Spirit of Dissention: Economics, Politics, and the Revolution in Maryland.* Baltimore, MD: Johns Hopkins University Press, 1973.

Land, Aubrey C. *Colonial Maryland: A History.* Millwood, NY: KTO, 1981.

———. *The Dulanys of Maryland: A Biographical Study of Daniel Dulany, the Elder (1685–1773) and Daniel Dulany, the Younger (1722–1797).* Baltimore, MD: Johns Hopkins University Press, 1955.

Onuf, Peter S., ed. *Maryland and the Empire, 1773: The Antilon—First Citizen Letters.* Baltimore, MD: Johns Hopkins University Press, 1974.

Wood, Gordon S. *The Creation of the American Republic, 1776–1787.* Chapel Hill: University of North Carolina Press, 1969.

Mason, George
(1725–1792)

The eminent political theorist, statesman, and planter George Mason is considered the principal author of the Virginia Declaration of Rights and of the first Virginia Constitution. He was also, as a delegate to the Philadelphia Convention of 1787, a leading opponent of the new federal government.

By the time of his birth, Mason's family controlled more than 5,000 acres of agricultural land in Maryland and Virginia, most of it located south of Alexandria in the latter colony. Mason's education came from local schools and private tutors, but following his father's death in 1735, he immersed himself in the law library of his uncle, John Mercer of Marlborough. Mason assumed the role of planter at a relatively young age and entered public life as a justice of the Fairfax County Court in 1749. That same year, his business career prospered after he became a partner in the Ohio Company. In 1750 his marriage to Ann Elibeck extended his political and financial influence, and three years later, he was elected to the Virginia House of Burgesses and commenced work on his relatively small but elegant residence, Gunston Hall. During the French and Indian War, he served as a quartermaster and earned the rank of colonel.

During the 1760s, Mason focused on his business endeavors and cultivated a strong friendship with his close neighbor, George Washington. But

Mason's life was not completely divorced from politics. He sharply criticized the Stamp Act and deplored the sacrifice of British colonists' traditional rights, especially the right to trial by a jury. He greeted the Townshend duties with equal enmity, participated in the Virginia Association's nonimportation agreement, and authored or supported bills in the House of Burgesses that were designed to undermine the enforcement of the new taxes. Mason also wrote numerous essays for local newspapers that called on his fellow Virginians to defend the constitutional rights of Englishmen.

Mason was, nevertheless, basically conservative and was generally cool to the possibility of independence. Following the passage of the Coercive Acts against Massachusetts, however, he drew nearer to the oppositional policy of his close friend, Patrick Henry. Seeing war with Britain as inevitable and the colonists in a state of desperation, Mason attended a meeting of freeholders in Fairfax County in the summer of 1774 where he submitted twenty-four resolutions that were adopted as the Fairfax Resolves. In the resolves, he lamented the breakdown of imperial rule but insisted that once their traditional rights were violated, a people had no recourse but violent resistance. The resolves also hinted at the need to prepare for military confrontation and suggested that Virginians work with other colonists to secure their mutual interests. The most important resolves urged Virginians to cease exporting tobacco and other important goods to Britain.

George Mason, author of the Virginia Resolves and known as "The Father of the Bill of Rights," was a prominent delegate from Virginia to the Constitutional Convention, but ended up opposing the U.S. Constitution. (Library of Congress)

Mason begrudgingly accepted election to the Virginia Convention in 1775 and served on its Committee of Safety, the chief executive arm of the provisional government. He spent most of his first year in the convention preparing plans for defending Virginia, reorganizing the militia system, and prescribing ways to reduce Virginia's exports to Britain. He began 1776, the most important year of his political life, as an elected member of the special convention that produced the first Virginia Constitution. The convention appointed Mason to the committee charged with preparing a draft constitution. Members of the committee agreed that two documents were needed: a constitution and a bill of rights. Several delegates made proposals to both documents, but it was largely Mason's proposals that the committee and, later, the full convention adopted as the Virginia Declaration of Rights.

Mason's explanation of the basis of political power and the rights and responsibilities he proposed for the declaration secured his place as one of the foremost political theorists of eighteenth-century America. His original proposal stipulated that all men were born free and possessed the inalienable rights of "Life and Liberty, with Means of acquiring and possessing Property, and pursueing and obtaining Happiness and Safety." The parallels to John Locke's philosophy were striking: governments existed solely for the benefit of society, and when they ceased benefiting society, the people had an inherent right to rise up and change or abolish their governments. Property rights could not be sacrificed without the consent of property holders. Other rights delineated in the document included trial by jury in civil as well as criminal cases, due process of law, religious toleration, freedom of the press, freedom from ex post facto laws whenever feasible, and freedom from excessive bail and punishments. Mason also insisted that well-regulated militias were the best way of defending a free society. These principles soon found their way into the declarations of rights in the constitutions of Pennsylvania and Massachusetts and ultimately the national Bill of Rights, ratified in 1791.

Virginia's Declaration of Rights was adopted in May 1776, and during the following month Mason proposed a draft constitution. His design merely republicanized the colonial government, sharply limited the new government's power, and retained high property qualifications for officeholders. The convention omitted the steep property qualification for officeholders but kept the qualification for voters. Other than this alteration and a preamble written by Thomas Jefferson, the first Virginia Constitution followed Mason's draft. In writing the constitution, Mason followed a conservative path and kept to it when he was placed on a committee to revise Virginia's laws. Rather than creating a new legal system fashioned after Enlightenment rationalism, he preferred to revise only those laws that were unclear and refused to make any changes to the common law beyond sheer necessity. But in the area of religious toleration, Mason was more innovative. A devout Anglican, he began expressing sympathy for religious dissenters in the early 1770s when he sat on the Fairfax County Court. While serving in Virginia's new Assembly in 1776, he supported the efforts to reform the vestry system and to free dissenters from paying taxes that funded the established Anglican churches. He thus helped lay the groundwork for the eventual granting of complete religious freedom in Virginia, which occurred in 1785.

The final chapter in Mason's political career came in 1787, when he served as one of Virginia's delegates to the Philadelphia Convention. There he opposed the consolidating policies of the nationalists, a move that poisoned his lifelong friendship with Washington. Mason believed that political centralization would jeopardize the rights of Virginians and greatly feared what a federal tariff might do to Virginia agriculture. He was one of only three delegates—along with Virginia's Edmund Randolph and Massachusetts's Elbridge Gerry—who refused to sign the completed Constitution. Mason died on 7 October 1792 and was buried on the grounds of Gunston Hall.

Cary Roberts

See also

Boycotts; Henry, Patrick; Jefferson, Thomas; Militia, Patriot and Loyalist; Virginia; Washington, George

References

Copeland, Pamela C., and Richard K. Macmaster. *The Five George Masons: Patriots and Planters of Virginia and Maryland.* Charlottesville: University of Virginia Press, 1975.

Miller, Helen Hill. *George Mason: Gentleman Revolutionary*. Chapel Hill: University of North Carolina Press, 1975.

Massachusetts

Whether an American Revolution would have occurred without Massachusetts is debatable. Had no British customs officials begun seizing vessels for illegal trade in the 1760s, had the feud between the Otis-Adams and Hutchinson-Oliver factions not been so virulent, had Governor Francis Bernard and the customs officials not insisted on military protection, had the Stamp Act riots and the Boston Massacre not attracted such attention, and, especially, had the British Parliament not passed the Boston Port Act and Massachusetts Government Act in 1774 in response to the Boston Tea Party, it is doubtful that a revolution of the sort that occurred when it did would have happened. Yet while Massachusetts made an important contribution of troops and leaders to the War for Independence and to the new national government that emerged after 1776, the province's exceptional leadership in the Revolution declined after independence.

Massachusetts was especially angry that the burden of post-1760 British imperial policy fell disproportionately on its shoulders, because the province had disproportionately contributed to the common cause during the French and Indian (Seven Years') War (1754–1763). All through the colonial crisis, Massachusetts's leaders, including future staunch Loyalists, protested that the province had repeatedly proven its loyalty by raising expeditions—costly both in lives and money—in every British war since 1689. Massachusetts recruited several thousand soldiers per year from 1756 until 1763; went hundreds of thousands of pounds into debt, which it eliminated through heavy taxation by the early 1770s; and received more than a third of the more than £1 million provided by the British Parliament for the colonies to reimburse them for war expenditures. During this same war, Massachusetts's court or prerogative faction, devoted to zealous prosecution of the war and a hard-money fiscal policy, and headed by Lieutenant Governor Thomas Hutchinson, came to dominate the province politically as well.

Hence, it was a bitter pill that even while the war was still going on, customs officials Charles Paxton and Thomas Lechmere, themselves natives of Massachusetts, began cracking down on the illegal trade with the French and Spanish enemies conducted by the province's merchants. In 1761, James Otis Jr., son of the sometime Speaker of the Massachusetts House of Representatives and leader of the country or popular faction that carefully monitored and criticized the governor's behavior, defended the accused traders on the grounds that General Writs of Assistance, which permitted the customs service to search anywhere, were an unconstitutional violation of the natural right of man to the sanctity of his abode. Hutchinson, whom newly arrived Bernard had appointed chief justice of the superior court the year before (James Otis Sr. was the other, bitterly disappointed candidate), ruled that

BOSTON, December 2, 1773.

WHEREAS it has been reported that a Permit will be given by the Custom-House for Landing the Tea now on Board a Vessel laying in this Harbour, commanded by Capt. HALL : THIS is to Remind the Publick, That it was solemnly voted by the Body of the People of this and the neighbouring Towns assembled at the Old-South Meeting-House on Tuesday the 30th Day of *November*, that the said Tea never should be landed in this Province, or pay one Farthing of Duty : And as the aiding or assisting in procuring or granting any such Permit for landing the said Tea or any other Tea so circumstanced, or in offering any Permit when obtained to the Master or Commander of the said Ship, or any other Ship in the same Situation, must betray an inhuman Thirst for Blood, and will also in a great Measure accelerate Confusion and Civil War : This is to assure such public Enemies of this Country, that they will be considered and treated as Wretches unworthy to live, and will be made the first Victims of our just Resentment.

The PEOPLE.

N. B. Captain *Bruce* is arrived laden with the same detestable Commodity ; and 'tis peremptorily demanded of him, and all concerned, that they comply with the same Requisitions.

Boston Tea Party broadside, 2 December 1773, objecting to the landing of inexpensive British tea. Samuel Adams and other prominent opponents of the Tea Act maintained that tea available at such low prices threatened the livelihoods of Boston merchants, many of whom profited handsomely by smuggling that commodity into Massachusetts. (Library of Congress)

since such writs were issued by British courts, American tribunals could do likewise. (In 1766, Britain's attorney general ruled that the act of Parliament authorizing the writs did not apply to the colonies, but by then the damage was done.) John Adams, who heard Otis's argument, maintained in old age that "then and there the child Independence was born," an exaggerated claim since few people heard the speech, it was not printed, and Massachusetts had already insisted that British activity—such as naval impressments—that violated their natural rights were unconstitutional.

Like the other colonies, Massachusetts's legislature sent written protests to Parliament arguing against the Sugar Act of 1764, which taxed all imported molasses and set up vice-admiralty courts in the colonies. But only when news of the Stamp Act, which taxed printed matter and legal documents, arrived in August 1765 did Massachusetts emerge at the head of colonial resistance. While crowds throughout British North America compelled the officers who had been appointed to distribute the stamps to resign, in Massachusetts a series of riots on 14 August damaged the houses of several royal officials. On 26 August a crowd, led by Hutchinson's enemies to believe that the obnoxious tax was his idea, destroyed his Boston mansion and forced him to flee for his life. He had refused to speak to them to deny the charge, which he did the following day in the superior court. While his plight earned him some sympathy, his refusal to open the province courts without the required stamps—which had been destroyed—lent credibility to his opponents' charges that he had become an enemy to his native land.

In 1765, too, the court party permanently lost control of the legislature as Samuel Adams and John Hancock joined Otis at the head of the popular party. Adams's behind-the-scenes role as the link between the elite merchants, lawyers, and clergymen and the lower and middle classes who provided the muscle for crowd activity remains shadowy because he destroyed most of his papers, but observers both friendly and hostile attested to his skill and power. Hancock, the nephew and sole heir of Massachusetts's richest, recently deceased merchant, provided funds for celebrations and jobs as well as for loans (whose collection he rarely pressed) in Boston's depressed postwar economy. It was no accident that it was the seizure of his ship *Liberty* in 1768 by four newly arrived customs commissioners that provoked the riot that caused the commissioners to flee for protection to Castle William in Boston Harbor.

Joined by Bernard, the commissioners wrote to Britain that Boston had descended to mob rule and that British troops were needed to enforce law and order. In response, Parliament sent 1,200 soldiers to the port in 1768. They were able to protect customs commissioners and other royal officials but were unable to quell protest meetings or riots. No justice of the peace would authorize using the soldiers, and even future Loyalists who were glad to see the redcoats felt intimidated by the crowd. In consequence, soldiers and inhabitants quarreled and fought in the streets, the predictable result being the Boston Massacre of 5 March 1770. Five inhabitants were killed and two mortally wounded when fired upon by a small detachment of British soldiers guarding the customhouse. The soldiers had been taunted both verbally and with rocks and snowballs. The town bells rang out, which usually indicated a fire, and both challenges to "fire" and cries of the assembling inhabitants asking about the "fire" provoked the soldiers to shoot. Only Patriot lawyers John Adams, an emerging leader of the resistance, and Josiah Quincy would dare defend them in the hostile atmosphere. The soldiers escaped with a manslaughter verdict, but Adams was careful not to argue on his clients' behalf that the inhabitants had deliberately plotted to confront the soldiers and drive them out of town. Hutchinson, who had just succeeded Bernard as governor, responded to the Boston Massacre by evacuating the soldiers to Castle William, where they remained until 1774 when substantial reinforcements arrived.

Hutchinson achieved modest gains in support between 1770 and 1773, as Parliament had repealed all the colonial taxes except long-standing customs duties and a small tax on tea. But in 1773, in an effort to save the East India Company, Parliament arranged for the larger tea tax collected in Britain to be refunded on tea that was reshipped to America. British leaders hoped that the colonies would pay the modest tax on tea levied in America, since even with that duty the tea would be cheaper than illegally imported foreign tea. The East India tea, however, was consigned to merchants conspicuous for their loyalty to the Crown over the previous decade. In Massachusetts, the choice fell on Hutchinson's sons and close friends, to the exclusion of Hancock and numerous other merchants. Most colonies persuaded the ship captains who delivered the East India tea that it would be imprudent to land their cargo, but Hutchinson, taking advantage of the presence of naval vessels in Boston Harbor, ordered the tea ships anchored and planned to use the available armed forces to land the tea. When he remained adamant despite protests, a crowd thinly disguised as Indians dumped the tea into Boston Harbor on 16 December.

It was the British response to the Boston Tea Party that provoked Massachusetts and its fellow colonies to raise troops to defend their liberties. In May 1774, Boston learned of the Boston Port Act; in August the province received word of the Massachusetts Government Act. The former act closed Boston Harbor until Massachusetts paid for the tea. The latter banned town meetings—which had met frequently to voice opposition to British policy— except for the annual election of public officeholders and replaced the legislature's elected upper house with an appointed one. A third Coercive (or Intolerable) Act, the Administration of Justice Act, for the first time permitted the transfer (to another colony or to Great Britain) for trial any civil official who was charged with a capital crime in Massachusetts while enforcing

> This statute was specifically referred to in rebellious Massachusetts as the "Murderers' Act" or the "Murder Act."

British retreat from Concord, 19 April 1775. Having clashed with colonial militia earlier in the day at Lexington and destroyed a cache of arms at Concord, a British column marched back to Boston under a continuous harassing fire that would cost them 250 casualties and a good deal of their pride. (National Archives and Records Administration)

British authority. The Quebec Act, which attached the newly conquered Ohio Valley to French Catholic Canada, was a special insult to the still very religious province that had fought the northern papists for the better part of a century. Some 4,000 soldiers were sent to Boston to enforce these laws. Their commander, General Thomas Gage, would be Massachusetts's new governor.

Except for the Boston Port Act, the other measures punished all of Massachusetts for the actions of the Boston crowd and its supporters. Other Massachusetts towns had previously protested British policy, but few had organized alternative sources of authority such as the Boston Sons of Liberty, and none had so thoroughly mobilized the crowd. The Coercive Acts galvanized people throughout the province. The newly appointed mandamus councilors who could not escape to British lines were compelled to resign their commissions, frequently in a humiliating manner by walking between lines of assembled militiamen with their hats in their hands. Crowds prevented the courts, whose judges included many of the councilors and Loyalist sympathizers, from sitting, since they refused to recognize the new laws or the governing officials appointed to enforce them as valid.

But Massachusetts was not content to resist on its own. In early June, Boston drew up the Solemn League and Covenant that declared its refusal to open its port by paying for the tea and instead turned to other colonies, seeking their material aid to support the distressed population. On 17 June, the provincial Massachusetts House of Representatives, in its last official act before Gage dissolved it, appointed four prominent resistance leaders—John Adams, Samuel Adams, Thomas Cushing, and Hancock—to attend the newly proposed Congress in Philadelphia in September. And in early September, Suffolk County (centered on Boston) approved and sent to Congress its Resolves, which called for an immediate and total embargo of trade with Great Britain. Congress, in its Continental Association of late October, did not go quite so far, but it did endorse Massachusetts's essential strategy: a massive commercial boycott until the British ministry changed its colonial policy.

While Massachusetts's orators and writers were busy in Boston and Philadelphia, its militiamen drilled and collected powder and ammunition throughout the province. The British made a few small raids on colonial arms depots in 1774, but when Gage, acting on orders from London, sent British regulars to Concord on 19 April 1775 to seize a major supply of arms and powder—and to arrest Hancock and Samuel Adams, who had fled Boston—the Lexington militia turned out to oppose their march with a symbolic show of force. When a shot of unknown origin rang out at Lexington Green, the American Revolutionary War began. Although the British easily routed Lexington's small contingent, they encountered the rapidly assembling militia of many towns at Concord, began their return march, and were harassed with deadly fire all the way back to Boston.

Troops from other colonies soon joined those of Massachusetts and proceeded to occupy the numerous hills surrounding the British garrison in Boston. On 17 June, the British attacked the besieging force on Breed's Hill in Charlestown (the engagement is known as the Battle of Bunker Hill because that eminence was more imposing). The British finally drove the Americans from the field when the defenders ran out of ammunition, but the redcoats in four assaults suffered more than 1,000 casualties (versus half that number for the rebels). In no condition to pursue this costly victory, the British remained quietly in Boston until 17 March 1776, when the placement of cannon from Fort Ticonderoga on Dorchester Heights overlooking Boston Harbor compelled the new British commander, Sir William Howe, to negotiate a withdrawal with his American counterpart, George Washington, the commander in chief of the new Continental Army, who had replaced Massachusetts's General Artemas Ward the previous July.

Massachusetts saw little military action on its soil for the rest of the war except in Maine, then part of the province. British raiders from Nova Scotia took control of several coastal towns, notably Penobscot. A 1779 flotilla of forty ships manned by some 3,000 men, launched by Massachusetts with little outside assistance to retake that fortified port, was an utter disaster. The expedition failed to dislodge the British, all of the ships were lost, and the cost bankrupted the state and plunged it deep into debt. Thousands of the state's inhabitants, however, served lengthy terms in the Continental Army, and many others served in the militia. Massachusetts supplied more men under arms than any other state during the Revolutionary War. The province also led the new nation in privateering, and that activity greatly increased the prosperity of Salem, the state's second port, and established the fortunes of some of its leading families, notably the Derbys. Prominent soldiers in the Revolution from Massachusetts were Generals Henry Knox, Washington's chief of artillery, and Benjamin Lincoln, the unfortunate commander of the garrison at Charleston, South Carolina, who surrendered the largest body of American troops, some 5,000 men, during the war. The Patriot rider Paul Revere switched from crafting fine silver to making cannon. Samuel Adams became a hard-working but not especially prominent member of Congress, but his cousin John played a crucial role in that body, serving on the committee that wrote the Declaration of Independence (signed so prominently by Hancock, Congress's president), leading the floor fight for independence, and presiding over Congress's Board of War. He concluded his service to Congress with a decade of diplomatic effort, including negotiating the peace with Britain.

John Adams also wrote the Massachusetts Constitution. When news of the Massachusetts Government Act arrived in August 1774, Massachusetts looked beyond its Charter of 1692, which that act had altered, and resumed its Charter of 1629, which stipulated that the freemen—in the eighteenth century, white adult males possessing about £40 worth of property—would elect all officials, including judges, the legislature, and the governor. Alarmed that this extremely democratic system would give too much power to a potentially rambunctious lower class, the legislature in 1778 offered a new frame of government, which was voted down overwhelmingly. Yet a similar constitution, written mostly by Adams and approved by a convention chosen by the voters for that specific purposed, passed in 1780. It provided for a two-house legislature: the Senate was apportioned according to the wealth of the several counties, the House according to population. Increasingly higher levels of property were required for assemblymen and senators as well as for the governor who, unlike those in many of the new states, possessed both a veto power and the right to appoint most public officials and judges. Religion continued to be officially established (Connecticut was the only other state to do this), although people's tithes could support any church they chose to attend.

Although many towns sent representatives to the 1780 constitutional convention, most of them drifted away during a bitter winter, and many of the crucial provisions were passed by small majorities of a small body. Although the constitution was popularly ratified in the spring of 1780, the ratification procedure also raised questions, and the elitist character of the convention came back to haunt the Commonwealth. During the 1780s, Massachusetts attempted to pay off its large, accumulated war debt in hard currency. Added to a postwar depression, which affected subsistence farmers in the western part of the province more than the commercial farmers, merchants, and sailors in the eastern part, this financial policy caused numerous farmers to go bankrupt and suffer the sale of all or part of their property. Local conventions began forming in 1782, and by mid-1786 Westerners marching in military formation were closing county courts and declaring that they would not recognize either the courts, the senate, or the gubernatorial veto as legitimate. They also demanded the sort of paper currency that both the federal government and other states used. Eastern Massachusetts raised some 7,000 men to put down the 3,000 Westerners who participated in what became known as Shays's Rebellion, led by the Revolutionary War veteran Captain Daniel Shays. Although they did not consider themselves rebels but rather citizens marching to protest and redress their grievances, the Shaysites did seek to alter the structure of Massachusetts's government. In any event, the Westerners were easily routed in two engagements with little bloodshed. And a merciful legislature—with the accommodating Hancock replacing the hard-line James Bowdoin as governor—punished most rebels only with disfranchisement for a year and increased the money supply, thereby restoring order.

Massachusetts was fairly evenly divided over ratifying the U.S. Constitution in 1788. The more commercial, cosmopolitan eastern part of the state favored a stronger union; the western part, as the Shaysites' demands suggest, was mistrustful of any authority removed from the immediate locality. But even in Boston and other seaport towns, many artisans opposed the document. Federalists, however, organized political demonstrations to persuade the important Antifederalist Samuel Adams to change his mind, and the vain Hancock was flattered with the possibility that he would become vice president of the new nation or even president if Virginia failed to ratify and Washington could not assume the post. The Massachusetts Convention finally ratified the Constitution by a vote of 187–168, and Hancock was given the honor of introducing the first draft of the Bill of Rights that many wanted to ensure that the new government would not trample on personal or states' rights.

Massachusetts suffered considerable economic damage during the Revolution. Much of Boston burned as the British evacuated, the Maine coast was continually harassed, and trade suffered as many men enlisted in the army. Yet the war was not all suffering for Massachusetts. Compared with several states, the commonwealth had relatively few Loyalists outside members of the elite Hutchinson faction, and most of these left with the British Army in 1776. Privateers did well, Boston helped provision the French fleet, and once the war ended, the Derby family of Salem pioneered new lucrative trades with Asia and the South Seas. By the late 1780s, the economy was recovering.

Although Massachusetts retained its establishment of religion until 1833, the Revolution lessened support for the traditional Congregational Church. Among the elite and in the seaports, especially, many people became Unitarians in the early nineteenth century, and nearly all of Boston's churches embraced this new liberal faith. Inland and among the lower and middle classes, Methodists and Baptists (who had protested discrimination by being forced to support the Congregational Church before the war) increased in numbers. Boston opened its first Catholic church in 1788 and, instead of being criticized as part of a papist conspiracy, became regarded as a bulwark of order during the era of the French Revolution.

Massachusetts supplied more men under arms than any other state.

Socially, one important change that was directly attributable to the Revolution was the formal abolition of slavery in the 1780s. The crucial decision was made by the state's Supreme Judicial Court, based on a straightforward reading of John Adams's bill of rights that introduced the new Massachusetts Constitution. The decision met with almost universal popular approval, and Massachusetts was the first of the thirteen original states to end slavery. With the Revolution completed, however, Massachusetts became, along with Connecticut, politically one of the most conservative and Federalist of the states. Its prominence in bringing the Revolution about suggests that here, in this homogeneous colony with its strong religious roots, the Revolution involved little social turmoil and was largely a conservative defense of a long tradition of self-government. At the same time, certain developments—notably the adoption of a powerful state bill of rights, the abolition of slavery, and the rise of Unitarianism—gave Massachusetts some foundation for a more radical future in the mid-nineteenth century.

WILLIAM PENCAK

See also

Adams, Abigail; Adams, John; Adams, Samuel; Administration of Justice Act; Bernard, Sir Francis; Boston, Massachusetts; Boston, Siege of; Boston Massacre; Boston Port Act; Boston Tea Party; Bunker Hill, Battle of; Coercive Acts; Customs Commissioners, Board of; Dorchester Heights, Massachusetts; Gage, Thomas; Hancock, John; Hutchinson, Thomas; Lexington and Concord; *Liberty* Incident; Massachusetts Government Act; Otis, James, Jr.; Penobscot Expedition; Quincy, Josiah, Jr.; Revere, Paul; Salem, Massachusetts, Incident at; Shays's Rebellion; Stamp Act; Suffolk Resolves; Tea Act; Townshend Acts; Ward, Artemas; Warren, James; Warren, Joseph; Warren, Mercy Otis

References

Alexander, John. *Samuel Adams: America's Revolutionary Politician*. Lanham, MD: Rowman and Littlefield, 2002.

Bailyn, Bernard. *The Ordeal of Thomas Hutchinson*. Cambridge, MA: Harvard University Press, 1974.

Fowler, William M., Jr. *The Baron of Beacon Hill: A Biography of John Hancock*. Boston: Houghton Mifflin, 1980.

Gross, Robert, ed. *In Debt to Shays: The History of an Agrarian Rebellion*. Charlottesville: University of Virginia Press, 1993.

Labaree, Benjamin W. *The Boston Tea Party*. New York: Oxford University Press, 1964.

Pencak, William. *War, Politics, and Revolution in Provincial Massachusetts*. Boston: Northeastern University Press, 1981.

Peters, Ronald M., Jr. *The Massachusetts Constitution of 1780: A Social Compact*. Amherst: University of Massachusetts Press, 1978.

Raphael, Ray. *The First American Revolution: Before Lexington and Concord*. New York: New Press, 2002.

Tyler, John. *Smugglers and Patriots: Boston Merchants and the Advent of the American Revolution*. Boston: Northeastern University Press, 1986.

Zobel, Hiller. *The Boston Massacre*. New York: Norton, 1970.

The Massachusetts Government Act, introduced in Parliament on 15 April 1774, was the second of the so-called Coercive (or Intolerable) Acts. Along with the Boston Port Act, the Administration of Justice Act, and the Quartering Act, the measure was meant to humble and punish the unruly Bostonians and, at the same time, stand as a warning to other potentially disorderly colonies.

The immediate impetus for the Coercive Acts was the Boston Tea Party. Parliament had passed the Tea Act in 1773 in an effort to bolster the floundering East India Company by allowing it to ship tea directly to the colonies without paying any duties in England. In the colonies, however, the East India tea was still subject to the Townshend duty on tea. Even so, the company would be able to undersell its foreign competitors. Two aspects of the Tea Act greatly angered many colonists. First, it seemed that the British ministry was trying to force Americans to accept parliamentary taxation by bribing them to accept the Townshend duty for the sake of cheap tea. Second, only select merchants would be allowed to sell the East India tea. In Massachusetts, these merchants were all friends and relatives of the heartily disliked royal governor, Thomas Hutchinson.

Protests against the Tea Act reached their most fevered pitch in Boston. There, the radical Sons of Liberty went far beyond mere protests to stop the East India ships from landing their cargoes. Instead, on the night of 16 December 1773, they masqueraded as Indians and dumped some 340 chests of East India tea into Boston Harbor. When word reached London of this the next month, Parliament, the ministry, and Britons in general reacted with outrage. Colonials had protested and resisted policy before, but this was wanton destruction of private property and open hostility toward both ministerial policy and royal officials. Lord North and the ministry resolved to crack down and finally put the colonies in their proper place.

They began by closing Boston Harbor until the tea was paid for (the Boston Port Act). This would essentially cripple Massachusetts's economy. Next, the ministry attacked the heart of the province's government—its royal charter of 1691. From its founding, Massachusetts had been very protective of its autonomy. When the Massachusetts Bay Company was chartered, John Winthrop and his partners ensured that no company would be left in London to direct the colony's affairs by taking their charter with them and setting up the colony's sole government in Boston. This gave Massachusetts a government in which all officials, members of the assembly, and even the governor were elected. The first charter came to an end in 1684 when Charles II, in an effort to rein in his autonomous colonies, revoked it. After the turmoil of England's Glorious Revolution in 1688–1689 and the fall of the Dominion of New England in 1689, Massachusetts sought a new charter from William III. To obtain it, Massachusetts had to become a royal colony with an appointed governor, but it was able to maintain its elected council and independent town meetings.

Thus, when the ministry introduced the Massachusetts Government Act in Parliament in April 1774, it was attacking the colony's traditional independence as well as its pride. The act called for a royally appointed council, which was the norm in all other royal colonies. All judges, sheriffs, and most other local officials would be appointed solely by the royal governor. Jury panels would no longer be popularly chosen but would be appointed by the sheriffs. Perhaps worst of all, the towns would be limited to but one meeting a year, which was to be for the purpose of holding elections to the provincial legislature. Any additional meetings would require the permission of the governor. The act was openly designed to end the colony's independence. Moreover, by seizing the right to appoint all judges, sheriffs, and juries, the British hoped to bring to justice the riotous sort of men who would perpetrate such outrages as the Boston Tea Party. Agents for the colony residing in London were not even allowed a hearing to protest the bill. In addition, before the act was even passed, General Thomas Gage, the commander in chief of Britain's North American forces, was appointed Massachusetts's new governor and instructed to use troops to maintain order. Together, the Coercive Acts and Gage's appointment confirmed the colony's worst fears. It looked like the beginning of military dictatorship.

Lord North knew that the Massachusetts Government Act was harsh and violated the old charter, but he declared that the power of Parliament superseded any colonial charter. He explained the need for such harsh measures in Parliament on 22 April, saying that Britain had been too forbearing with Massachusetts for too long in the face of the province's outrageously rebellious subjects. With the Massachusetts Government Act, he hoped to pacify the colony and scare other colonies away from similar acts of disobedience. His plan did not have the intended effect.

Collectively, the Coercive Acts created a spirit of solidarity in British North America. Other colonies quickly rose to Massachusetts's defense. On 24 May, the Virginia House of Burgesses resolved that 1 June, the day the Boston Port Act was to go into effect, was to be a day of prayer and fasting. Virginia's governor, Lord Dunmore, was outraged and dissolved the burgesses, who proceeded to meet illegally at the Raleigh Tavern in Williamsburg. There they called for intercolonial nonimportation and a continental congress to meet in Philadelphia. Finally, the burgesses sent their resolves to the other colonial assemblies, all of which, except Georgia, eventually elected delegates to the First Continental Congress, which would vote to impose nonimportation as the burgesses recommended. Massachusetts would not be isolated, and the other colonies would not be cowed into submission. Lord North and the ministry, rather than pacifying the colonies, had created a firestorm.

AARON J. PALMER

See also

Boston Port Act; Boston Tea Party; Coercive Acts; Massachusetts; North, Lord Frederick

References

Ammerman, David. *In the Common Cause: American Response to the Coercive Acts of 1774.* New York: Norton, 1975.

Brown, Richard D. *Revolutionary Politics in Massachusetts: The Boston Committee of Correspondence, 1772–1774.* Cambridge: Harvard University Press, 1970.

Cobbett, William. *Cobbett's Parliamentary History of England from the Norman Conquest in 1066 to the Year 1803.* London: R. Bagshaw, 1806.

Gipson, Lawrence Henry. *The Coming of the Revolution, 1763–1775.* New York: Harper and Row, 1954.

Labaree, Benjamin Woods. *The Boston Tea Party.* New York: Oxford University Press, 1964.

Maier, Pauline. *From Resistance to Revolution: Colonial Radicals and the Development of American Opposition to Britain, 1765–1776.* New York: Knopf, 1972.

Thomas, Peter D. G. *Lord North.* New York: St. Martin's, 1976.

The soldier and statesman George Mathews served in the Continental Army, commanding Virginia troops at Brandywine and at Germantown, where he was injured and captured. Released before the end of the war, he again served in the army in Georgia. He later sat in the first federal Congress and was elected governor of Georgia.

Mathews was born in Virginia in an area that was prone to Indian raids. At the age of twenty-two he was involved in fighting a group of raiders who had killed an entire neighboring family. In 1774, during Lord Dunmore's War, he led a company at the Battle of Point Pleasant, where he helped to lead the decisive attack. With the outbreak of the Revolutionary War, he was appointed lieutenant colonel of the 9th Virginia Regiment, which was soon placed on the Continental Army establishment. The regiment was first ordered to Chesapeake Bay, where Mathews was to remain for almost two years. During that time the unit suffered several deaths from malaria.

By the middle of 1777, Mathews and his regiment had been placed in the 1st Virginia Division, led by General Nathanael Greene. At the Battle of Brandywine on 11 September 1777, Mathews's unit took position near Chadds Ford. It was here that the battle began when General Wilhelm Knyphausen tried to hold the center of the Continental Army, while the British made a sweeping move on the flank that ultimately forced the Americans to retreat. Mathews was engaged throughout the day, and it was the stout resistance of his regiment, together with other Virginian troops, that allowed the army to withdraw intact.

Mathews's next engagement, on 4 October 1777, was the Battle of Germantown. His troops were delayed in entering the battle, and when they did arrive there was much confusion. But Greene ordered an attack and directed Mathews's regiment to lead it into the right flank of the British force. The 9th Virginia managed to break into Market Square, and the men were convinced of success and began cheering. This alerted the British to the full danger to their flank, and they quickly surrounded Mathews's command. In the firefight that followed, the Virginians suffered heavy casualties, and all the officers were wounded. Mathews received bayonet wounds to the leg and was taken prisoner.

Mathews, George
(1739–1812)

Incarcerated on a prison ship at New York, Mathews wrote to Congress to try to secure his release. He did receive letters from Thomas Jefferson but was not exchanged until the war had almost ended. Mathews then rejoined the Continental Army in the South, once more under the command of Greene, and was given command of the 3rd Virginia Regiment. While serving in Georgia, Mathews bought land there on which he settled after the war ended. As a result of his distinguished service during the Revolution, he was elected governor of Georgia and also served as a member of the first U.S. Congress. He died at Augusta, Georgia, on 30 August 1812.

RALPH BAKER

See also

Brandywine, Battle of; Continental Army; Germantown, Battle of; Greene, Nathanael

Reference

McGuire, Thomas J. *The Surprise of Germantown: Or the Battle of Clivedon, October 4th 1777*. Gettysburg, PA: Thomas, 1996.

Maxwell, William
(1733–1793)

William Maxwell, commander of the New Jersey brigade during the Revolutionary War, was a superb tactician and a resourceful and reliable officer. Immigrating to America from Northern Ireland in 1747, Maxwell and his family settled on a farm along the Delaware River just below present-day Phillipsburg. He received a rudimentary education, and, although he had never lived in Scotland, he spoke with the Scottish brogue of his ancestors and was dubbed "Scotch Willie" by his soldiers.

Maxwell began his military career as an ensign in the New Jersey militia in 1758. During his early service, which lasted until 1760, he was in battle only once, in the rear of the British American army that attacked Fort Ticonderoga in July 1758. He mustered out of service as a lieutenant. After a few years on the farm, he became a commissary agent for the British Army at frontier posts and eventually attached to a contingent of the Royal American (60th) Regiment at Michilimackinac in 1766. He left British service in 1772 and returned to northwestern New Jersey, where he would become a leader of the Revolutionary movement.

In 1775, Maxwell served in the New Jersey Provincial Congress and was appointed by that body as colonel and commander of the western militia district. The Continental Congress accepted him as a colonel and his 2nd New Jersey Regiment into the Continental line on 7 November 1775. He and his New Jersey troops joined the American forces in Canada in March 1776. With the enemy being substantially reinforced and American soldiers devastated by smallpox, however, the American northern army soon had to withdraw from Canada. Maxwell's troops covered the retreat. He fought in the ill-conceived attack on the British at Trois-Rivières, between Quebec and

Montreal, and the American soldiers, suffering heavy casualties, retreated southward down Lake Champlain to Fort Ticonderoga, where they sat out the rest of the campaign.

Maxwell and his regiment, however, continued south and connected with Washington's retreating army just before it crossed the Delaware into Pennsylvania on 7–8 December 1776. Maxwell's first responsibility under Washington was to secure or destroy all watercraft along a 75-mile stretch of the lower Delaware River to give the Americans control of the river for their winter counterattack. At the time of the Battle of Trenton, Maxwell was again in New Jersey, in charge of collecting new troops at Morristown. Congress appointed him a brigadier general on 19 February 1777. From January to May 1777, his troops were continuously involved in skirmishes with British detachments as they provided a protective screen for Washington's army at Morristown and challenged enemy foraging parties. One major engagement occurred at Short Hills (near Metuchen), New Jersey, on 6 June 1777.

In the summer of 1777, Washington created a light infantry corps of 700 soldiers, comprising 100 of the best marksmen from each of seven brigades, and on 30 August appointed Maxwell as the army's first light infantry commander. The mission of the new unit, which was to have a temporary existence, was to perform reconnaissance, function as an advance guard, and harass the enemy on their march. On 3 September 1777, at the battle at Cooch's Bridge and nearby Iron Hill in Delaware, Maxwell and his light infantry fought a running engagement against advancing British and Hessian troops, but the corps eventually ran out of ammunition and, having few bayonets, was forced to retreat.

Maxwell played a similar significant role in the preliminary action of the battle at Brandywine Creek on 11 September. Crossing the creek to contest the advance of the van of the British Army, he positioned his men at four posts, with the men falling back successively to the one post closest to the creek, and then crossing over it to American lines. Maxwell succeeded in slowing down the enemy in this retrograde action, but Lieutenant Colonel William Heath, a Virginia officer under his command, claimed that Maxwell missed opportunities, which "any body but an old-woman would have availd themselves of them—He is to be sure—a Damnd bitch of a General."

In General William Alexander's division, Maxwell and his brigade from a reserve position entered the Battle of Germantown on 4 October 1777 and became involved in trying to dislodge a British regiment in the Benjamin Chew house. Successive assaults failed, as did American artillery trying to breach the structure's thick walls. After the battle, Maxwell was court-martialed, thanks to charges brought by the disgruntled Heath. Maxwell was acquitted, although it was admitted that he was rather too fond of strong drink.

During most of 1778 and early 1779, Maxwell and his brigade had responsibility for guarding the New Jersey shore and the communications route between Washington's army in the Hudson Highlands and Congress in Philadelphia. Maxwell and his troops participated in General John Sullivan's expedition against the Iroquois Indians of central and western New York from June to October 1779, although the expedition did little except destroy

Indian towns and crops. Maxwell's troops helped to stall the advance of British and Hessian troops commanded by General Wilhelm Knyphausen at Connecticut Farms, New Jersey, on 7 June 1780 and again at Springfield, New Jersey, on 23 June 1780.

In the summer of 1780, the relationship between Maxwell and his field-grade officers became unbearable. The cause of the friction is unknown but probably had to do with Maxwell's brusque personality, his renewed heavy drinking, and anxiety about the coming reorganization of the army. With expected troop reduction, one of several colonels would be phased out of the army. Threatening blackmail—to reveal some injurious information about Maxwell—the New Jersey officers forced him from the service. Congress accepted his resignation (which he subsequently unsuccessfully attempted to recall) on 25 July 1780.

Maxwell returned to his parents' farm, which he had inherited. He served one term in the New Jersey Assembly, where he voted for the resumption of confiscating Tory estates and for New Jersey's withholding payment of its share of the national debt. Because he left the army early, Maxwell never received any federal pension or bounty lands. He was, however, a member of the Society of the Cincinnati. In retirement, he spent much time visiting Colonel Charles Stewart, formerly an army commissary of issues, at Union Farm in nearby Hunterdon County. Maxwell generally stayed out of politics but occasionally gave advice when sought. His most noteworthy proposal involved taking a chain of western posts (mostly those to be turned over to Americans by the British) and making them centers of government-sponsored fur trading endeavors. Maxwell died on 3 November 1793 while visiting Stewart at Union Farm.

Maxwell was a hardworking army officer. He was somewhat at a disadvantage with respect to other generals, however, in being relatively poor and hence unable to keep up the pretensions of a gentleman's style of living. Despite his friction with other officers and his early retirement, he retained the full confidence of Washington.

HARRY M. WARD

See also

Brandywine, Battle of; Cooch's Bridge, Delaware, Action at; Germantown, Battle of; Sullivan Expedition

References

Cook, Frederick, ed. *Journals of the Military Expedition of Major General John Sullivan against the Six Nations of Indians in 1779*. Auburn, NY: Knapp, Peck, and Thomson, 1877.

Fleming, Thomas J. *The Forgotten Victory: The Battle for New Jersey, 1780*. New York: Reader's Digest Press, 1973.

Griffith, John H. "William Maxwell of New Jersey: Brigadier General in the Revolution." *Proceedings of the New Jersey Historical Society*, 2nd ser., 13 (1894–1895): 109–123.

May, George S., ed. *The Doctor's Secret Journal, by Daniel Morison, Surgeon's Mate*. Mackinac Island, MI: Mackinac Island State Park, 1960.

Salsig, Doyen, ed. *Parole: Quebec; Countersign Ticonderoga.* Rutherford, NJ: Fairleigh
    Dickinson University Press, 1980.
Ward, Harry M. *General William Maxwell and the New Jersey Continentals.* Westport, CT:
    Greenwood, 1997.

McCrea, Jane
(1753?–1777)

The 27 July killing and scalping of Jane McCrea under controversial circumstances during a critical point in General John Burgoyne's invasion of New York in July 1777 immediately generated one of the more colorful myths of the Revolutionary War and probably played a role in mobilizing local militia units against Burgoyne at Saratoga.

Perhaps no event in the entire Revolutionary War better epitomizes the effect of propaganda (and the racial stereotyping of Native Americans) than the alleged massacre of McCrea and its supposed impact on the Saratoga Campaign. The traditional version has McCrea being escorted to the British camp by Wyandot warriors in order to marry her fiancé, a Loyalist officer. Two of the warriors (drunk or not, according to the various narrators' tastes) argued over who would claim the reward for escorting her, during which one of them killed her with a tomahawk and scalped her. Variations on the story have McCrea's fiancé being responsible for sending out the Indian warriors who killed her (or sending a second war party, whose arrival sparked the argument); McCrea being stripped naked and/or wearing a wedding dress; and the victim being beautiful or homely, raven-haired or blonde. Her murder conveniently fulfilled the need for a "Yankee Joan of Arc," a need identified at the time by Thomas Paine, and was said to have motivated thousands of militiamen to join General Horatio Gates's army, enabling him to entrap Burgoyne at Saratoga. Over time, the story became enshrined in prose and pictures, including the famous 1804 painting by John Vanderlyn and a 1784 novelette, *Miss McCrea*, written in French by Michel René Hilliard-d'Auberteuil, that takes enormous liberties with the facts but is said to be the first work of fiction set entirely in America and dealing solely with an important event in American history.

This traditional version was challenged as early as the 1880s by William L. Stone, who used the papers of Judge John Hay of Saratoga Springs, a highly respected writer on local history who had interviewed eyewitnesses, to tell a different story. McCrea appears to have been the second daughter of the Reverend James McCrea and his first wife, Mary Graham, and probably the last of their seven children. Her mother died in 1753 (possibly around the time Jane was born), and her father then remarried and had five more children. All twelve children were born and raised in Lamington, New Jersey, but the oldest brothers moved north and settled in the Hudson Valley. After the reverend's death in 1769, McCrea left New Jersey to live with her eldest brother John, then an Albany lawyer. In 1773, she accompanied him when he took up farming and acquired land across the Hudson from Fort Edward. Early in the Revolutionary War, McCrea's five full brothers joined the forces of Congress,

The murder of Jane McCrea, a New York Loyalist scalped by Indians during John Burgoyne's campaign of 1777. Patriots exploited the incident for its obvious propaganda value, hoping to demonstrate the ruthlessness of Britain's allies and to encourage men to join their local militia. (Library of Congress)

as did at least one half brother (the only other member of the family to die in the war, shot accidentally by a comrade). Two other half brothers became active Loyalists, as did a childhood friend, David Jones, whose widowed mother had joined the exodus from Somerset County, New Jersey, to Northumberland County, New York.

On the morning of Sunday, 27 July 1777, McCrea went to a house near Fort Edward owned by Sarah McNeill (also spelled McNeal and McNeil). McNeill is usually described as a cousin of Simon Fraser, one of Burgoyne's generals; this may well be true, but it appears unlikely that her father, also named Simon, and General Simon's father, Alexander, were brothers, as some traditions state. McNeill was moving her possessions by boat to Fort Miller, and an escort of twenty men, under a Lieutenant Palmer, had arrived from America's Northern Army, then commanded by General Philip Schuyler (this party is sometimes wrongly identified as British). Before the loading was completed, Palmer and his men left to conduct a brief reconnaissance but were gone longer than expected, so the two women decided to ride down to the boat. Before they could leave, however, McNeill heard gunfire and saw one of Palmer's men being pursued by several Indians, who abandoned the chase and made toward the house. McNeill ordered McCrea, a female servant, and her infant son into the cellar, but the Indians caught McNeill on the stairs and then discovered McCrea but not the servant and her baby.

On Palmer's return, his group was ambushed and all but eight of his men were killed or wounded, Palmer being among the dead (some accounts refer to another officer, named Van Vechten). The Indians decided to withdraw and lifted the two women captives onto the horses, with a Wyandot Indian named Panther—who also had the French name Le Loup, or "Wolf"—leading McCrea's horse. Unfortunately, the somewhat portly McNeill was given a horse with no saddle and kept slipping off, and she was eventually carried by one of the Indians. At this point, another group of American soldiers appeared from Fort Edward and began firing on the Indians. At each volley, the Indians and McNeill threw themselves to the ground, but apparently one volley struck McCrea. Since there would be no reward for rescuing a corpse, Panther scalped McCrea and left her body behind. As McNeill's group had fallen some way behind by this time, she did not directly observe McCrea's death or the scalping. When she was taken to a nearby house, she tried to persuade her guards to return and find McCrea, but they refused. McNeill's party hid until the next day, when she was taken to Burgoyne's camp—though it is not clear if she was stripped naked as is often suggested.

Once there, McNeill was shown a scalp that she identified as that of McCrea. Burgoyne immediately ordered an investigation and interrogated

Panther, who admitted to scalping McCrea but was adamant that she had been killed by enemy fire. Burgoyne appears to have been convinced that Panther had killed McCrea and was prepared to have him executed but was dissuaded by the French officer in charge of the Wyandots, Luc de La Corne, who argued that the Indians would leave the invading army en masse, possibly massacring indiscriminately on their way back to Canada.

The same day that McNeill met Burgoyne, American forces retrieved the corpses of McCrea and Palmer (or Van Vechten). They were rowed down the Hudson and buried by a bridge over a small creek 3 miles south of Fort Edward and 2 miles south of John McCrea's farm. According to different accounts, the operation was directed by either Colonel Morgan Lewis, a deputy quartermaster general to Schuyler, or by John McCrea, who was a militia colonel in Schuyler's army at the time.

According to Stone, Judge Hay interviewed Lewis (by then governor of New York) in a New York City bookstore, some years after the war. Lewis clearly recalled three bullet wounds on McCrea's corpse and stated that he had supervised the removal of the body. Stone remarked that it seemed unlikely that Panther would have used a musket to kill an unarmed woman already under his control, a statement supported by the notoriously conservative attitude shown toward expending scarce ammunition by Indian forces throughout the war. When McCrea's remains were exhumed in the early 1820s and moved to a cemetery at Fort Edward, a local physician, Dr. William Norton, examined the skull and found no signs of a blow. The remains were moved again in 1852 to the Union cemetery between Fort Edward and Sandy Hill to lie beside those of McNeill, and a white marble headstone was erected by McCrea's niece, Sarah Payne, that incorrectly listed her age as seventeen. A tall iron fence was placed around the grave in the 1890s.

Only two witnesses support the traditional version. One was Dr. John Bartlett, a surgeon in the Northern Army, who recorded that McCrea was shot but appears to have automatically attributed the killing to the Indians, which could easily have been based either on confused rumors or on simple hatred of the enemy. He also described a body of British troops standing and watching as the Indians killed this young female Loyalist. The other witness was Samuel Standish, a direct descendant of Miles Standish of the *Mayflower*, who claimed to have been captured by the warriors escorting McCrea and McNeill and to have witnessed an altercation between two chiefs that ended with one of them shooting McCrea. Apart from the fact that no other eyewitnesses, including McNeill and Panther, mention any other prisoners, Standish made no mention of either woman being on horseback, and it seems unlikely that the Indians would have killed McCrea but spared him.

The other McCrea myth—that she became a posthumous recruiting sergeant for the Northern Army—appears in part to belong to the post hoc school of history. While it is possible that her name was a rallying cry three weeks later at the Battle of Bennington (16 August 1777), many of the militia at that battle were from Massachusetts and would only have heard of McCrea—if at all—after joining the local forces. (Interestingly, these same militiamen, having joined the Northern Army, decided to go home just as Burgoyne approached their encampment on Bemis Heights more than a month later.) The respected soldier-historian Colonel John Elting could find no mention of her death in local newspapers, and it did not become an issue for Burgoyne until Gates took over the American army from Schuyler.

Early in September, Gates—in reply to a letter from Burgoyne complaining about the treatment of Loyalist prisoners at Bennington—accused Burgoyne of buying scalps and specifically mentioned McCrea. The letter also had McCrea in her wedding dress, so clearly the rumor mill had already begun to "improve" on the facts. Two of Gates's subordinates, Generals Benjamin Lincoln and James Wilkinson, both felt that the letter went too far, and Burgoyne was clearly offended by its implications. After the Battle of Freeman's Farm on 19 September, more than 3,000 militia joined Gates's army, and another 3,000 arrived in time for the second battle on 7 October. Gates's letter to Burgoyne had been widely published in the first half of September, and if any single version of McCrea's death was responsible for the arrival of the militia, it was likely to have been this.

The stories surrounding Jones, allegedly McCrea's fiancé, can also be dismissed. He did not dispatch the party that collected McCrea from McNeill's house, nor did he offer a barrel of rum to anyone who brought McCrea in, although it seems that he did hire a group of more reliable warriors to try to dissuade the Wyandots from crossing the Hudson River or, failing that, to protect the homes of his mother and of Colonel McCrea from them. There were also no plans for Jones and McCrea to marry immediately upon her arrival. The message sent to her by Jones was an invitation to accompany Burgoyne, along with several other women, on a trip to Lake George. This message was carried by Robert Ayers, one of whose descendants was interviewed by Stone.

BRENDAN D. MORRISSEY

See also

Bennington, Battle of; Burgoyne, John; Loyalists; Native Americans; Propaganda; Saratoga Campaign

References

Elting, John. *The Battles of Saratoga*. Monmouth Beach, NJ: Philip Freneau, 1977.

Lossing, Benson J. *The Pictorial Field Book of the Revolution*. 1951. Reprint, Rutland, VT: Tuttle, 1972.

Stone, William. *Ballads and Poems Relating to the Burgoyne Campaign*. Albany, NY: Joel Munson's Sons, 1893.

Wilson, David. *The Life of Jane McCrea*. Albany, NY: n.p., 1853.

McDougall, Alexander
(1732–1786)

A Continental Army officer, merchant, and politician, Alexander McDougall rose during his lifetime from being a radical New York street politician to a nationally prestigious military commander and capitalist. As a soldier, his major contribution during the War for American Independence was to command Continental troops protecting the strategically important Hudson River Highlands.

McDougall was born on the island of Islay, one of the Inner Hebrides Islands off the west coast of Scotland, and immigrated with his parents to New York City in 1738. Maturing into a rugged, heavyset man, he was plagued with a speech impediment that made it difficult for him to address crowds. He went to sea in his late teens, sailing aboard vessels owned by the Walton family. During the French and Indian War (1756–1763), he sailed on privateers, commanding at different times the *Tyger* and the *Barrington*. After the war, he established himself as an independent merchant in New York City, owning his own vessel, the *Schuyler*, and acting as a moneylender to various friends and associates.

McDougall began his involvement in public life by aligning himself with the Livingston faction of New York politics. As the purpose of this group was to bolster the province's landed interests, the Livingstons and McDougall encouraged moderation in America's resistance to British colonial policies, especially during the Stamp Act crisis of 1765–1766. In 1769, however, McDougall emerged in popular leadership as a Son of Liberty by cultivating his contacts among seamen along the waterfront. He also wrote a broadside, "To the Betrayed Inhabitants of the City and Colony of New-York," that appeared on 16 December. The

Portrait of the New York City Revolutionary leader and Continental Army officer Alexander McDougall. (Geoffrey Clements/Corbis)

broadside, vehemently attacking the General Assembly, was declared libelous by that body, and on 8 February 1770, McDougall was arrested. He refused bail, which was set at £2,000, and languished in jail until after his indictment in April. He immediately became famous, being compared to John Wilkes, a dissident English parliamentarian who had been imprisoned in 1763 for criticizing Parliament. Tensions ran high, as the Sons of Liberty and British soldiers came close to clashing. Although never convicted of any crime, McDougall continued to have difficulty with the General Assembly until March 1771.

From that point forward, McDougall was extremely active in the politics of protest against British attempts to control the American colonies. During the tea crisis of 1773, he took a leading role in organizing New Yorkers to resist the landing of tea in the port of New York City. He was a member of a committee that convinced the captain of the tea ship *Nancy* to take his cargo back to England. When the captain of another tea ship, the *London*, attempted to land his cargo in April 1774, McDougall helped organize a party to dump the tea in the East River. At about this time, he became a member of the New York Committee of Correspondence, and on 6 July 1774, he presided over the famous mass meeting in The Fields (the site of City Hall and the post office). At that time, a nonimportation agreement, drafted by McDougall, was adopted, as were other measures of resistance. He was prominent as a radical leader of the Committee of Fifty-One, a group organized in 1774 to protest Britain's Coercive Acts, and attended the First Continental Congress as an observer in the fall. Returning to New York, he served in the provincial congress and on 5 May 1775 was chosen a member of the Committee of One Hundred to organize a government for New York.

On 30 April 1775, the province of New York organized its army, to consist of four regiments, and on 30 June, McDougall was commissioned colonel of the 1st New York Regiment. He remained in New York City in the summer of 1775 when his regiment was ordered northward to participate in an invasion of Canada. Working actively the following winter to oppose Loyalist sentiment in New York City, he served in several provincial congresses but was criticized for not leading his regiment in the field. He also suffered the death of his son, John, at Laprairie in Canada. Thereafter, McDougall shifted his attention to military affairs. Because of his political prominence, Congress commissioned him colonel of the 1st New York Continental Regiment on 8 March 1776. He worked closely with Major General Charles Lee to plan defenses for New York and during the following summer served under General George Washington in constructing fortifications around the city.

On 9 August, at Washington's behest, Congress promoted McDougall to brigadier general, and the commander in chief immediately put him in charge of a Continental brigade. During the Battle of Long Island on 27 August, McDougall's brigade was in reserve on Manhattan and only crossed over to Long Island the following day. On the night of 29–30 August, he assisted Colonel John Glover in evacuating Washington's army across the East River to Manhattan. After a period of relative inactivity, McDougall's brigade, now augmented by General William Smallwood's Marylanders, was involved in Washington's retreat from Manhattan in October. At the Battle of White Plains on 28 October, McDougall's men were on Chatterton's Hill and were assaulted by Hessian and British troops. Compelled to retreat after their flank became exposed during the fighting, McDougall's brigade, under Lee's command, crossed the Hudson River to New Jersey in early December. At Haverstraw, McDougall was struck down by rheumatism and was compelled to rest in bed for a week. Although still ailing, he joined Washington's army at Morristown on 14 December and learned that Lee had been captured by the British the day before.

In early January 1777, McDougall had recovered enough to accept Washington's offer to take command of the Hudson Highlands. His primary task was to guard against British raids from New York City and protect vital military stores at Peekskill, where his headquarters were located. On 27 March, the enemy sortied with twenty armed ships and 600 troops to test McDougall's defenses. Although McDougall could muster only 300 men to counter this thrust, the British forces retreated the following day in the face of American resistance. Shortly thereafter, McDougall got into an unbecoming shouting match with Colonel Henry Beekman Livingston, which led to no untoward consequences. In May 1777, McDougall asked to be relieved of command and was replaced by General Israel Putnam. McDougall remained in the Highlands during the following summer, helping Putnam complete the construction of Forts Montgomery and Clinton.

On 14 September 1777, Washington ordered McDougall to join the main army in Pennsylvania with his brigade. Arriving at Pennypacker's Mill on 27 September, McDougall took part in the Battle of Germantown on 4 October. Under the command of General Nathanael Greene, McDougall's brigade led the American attack on the British right. Marching down Limekiln Pike to drive into the enemy's rear, McDougall and General John Peter Muhlenberg assaulted the brigades of Generals James Grant and Edward Mathew but were forced to retreat. When Washington's attacks failed all along the line, McDougall's men covered Greene's withdrawal from the battlefield. On 10 October, McDougall was appointed to a court of inquiry, chaired by General William Alexander, Lord Stirling, to investigate the battlefield performance of Anthony Wayne at Paoli, John Sullivan at Staten Island, and Adam Stephen at Germantown. Wayne and Sullivan were found blameless, but Stephen was blamed for the American defeat at Germantown and dismissed from the service.

On 11 October 1777, Washington gave McDougall command of a Continental Army division consisting of two brigades, and nine days later Congress promoted him to major general. He joined Greene in attacking Fort Mercer in late November and once again was debilitated by rheumatism. Retiring to Morristown, he spent seven weeks in bed. In the spring of 1778, he was ordered to the Hudson Highlands to investigate charges against Putnam for losing the Highlands forts to the enemy in the previous campaign. After Putnam was removed from command, McDougall took charge at Fishkill, then rejoined Washington for a time. On 24 November, McDougall reassumed the Highlands command, and in the following months he concentrated on strengthening the defenses at West Point. After Benedict Arnold's treason, McDougall was appointed commander at West Point. He served for a short time in Congress in early 1781 but returned to the army in March. In January 1782, he was court-martialed by General William Heath, with whom he had quarreled. Acquitted of all charges except one, he was reprimanded in general orders and restored to duty.

For some time, McDougall had been sympathetically concerned about discontent among Continental Army officers over pay and other matters. As early as 1780, he had represented the officers as head of a delegation to Congress in Philadelphia, and he spoke for them a year later as a congressman during his short tenure. By 1782, his own finances were in shambles, and many of his fellow officers were no better off. Hence, in August 1782, at Newburgh, New York, he was again chosen by his fellow officers to represent

By the HONOURABLE
Cadwallader Colden, Esq;
His Majesty's Lieutenant Governor, and Commander in Chief of the Province of *New-York*, and the Territories depending thereon in *America*:

A Proclamation.

WHEREAS a certain seditious and libelous Paper, was lately printed, published, and dispersed within the City of New-York, dated *New-York, December* 16th, 1769; directed in these Words,---" To the betrayed Inhabitants of the City and Colony of *New-York*," and containing many insolent, daring, and infamous Reflections on the Honour, Dignity, and Authority of the three Branches of the Legislature of the said Province; which having been taken into Consideration by the General Assembly, the House did, on the Nineteenth Day of *December* Instant, come to the following Resolutions thereupon.

Resolved,
That the said Paper is a false, seditious, and infamous Libel.

Resolved, Nemine Contradicente,
That the said Paper highly reflects on the Honour and Dignity of the House; is calculated to inflame the Minds of the good People of this Colony, against their Representatives in General Assembly; and contains scandalous Reflections on the three Branches of the Legislature.

Resolved, Nemine Contradicente,
That the Proposal therein contained, to come down in a Body to the House, is an audacious Attempt to destroy the Freedom and Independence of this House, and consequently the Rights and Privileges of the Inhabitants of this Colony; introductive of Anarchy and Confusion, and subversive of the Fundamental Principles of our happy Constitution.

Resolved, Nemine Contradicente,
That the Author or Authors, Aiders and Abettors of the said Paper, is, or are guilty of a high Misdemeanour; and a daring Insult on the Honour, Justice, and Authority of this House.

Resolved, Nemine Contradicente,
That an humble Address be presented to his Honour the Lieut. Governor, requesting he will be pleased to issue a Proclamation, offering a Reward of *One Hundred Pounds*, to any Person or Persons, who shall discover the Author or Authors, Aiders and Abettors of the above recited Paper, so that they may be brought to condign Punishment.

I have therefore thought fit, by and with the Advice of his Majesty's Council, to issue this Proclamation, hereby in his Majesty's Name, offering a Reward of *One Hundred Pounds*, to any Person or Persons, who shall discover the Author or Authors, Aiders and Abettors, of the above mentioned seditious Paper, so printed, published, and dispersed as aforesaid; so that he or they be thereof convicted: And over and above the said Reward, I do hereby promise his Majesty's most gracious Pardon to any Accomplice or Accomplices, who shall discover the Author or Authors, Aiders or Abettors, of the seditious Paper aforesaid.

Given under my Hand and Seal, at Arms, at Fort-George, in the City of New-York, *the Twentieth Day of* December, *One Thousand Seven Hundred and Sixty-nine, in the Tenth Year of the Reign of our Sovereign Lord* GEORGE *the Third, by the Grace of* GOD, *of Great-Britain, France, and* Ireland, *King, Defender of the Faith, and so forth.*

CADWALLADER COLDEN.
By his Honour's Command,
Gw. BANYAR, D. Secry.

GOD save the *KING*.

Proclamation to punish Alexander McDougall, the author of a "libelous" paper, begins "To the betrayed inhabitants of New York" and was issued by the lieutenant governor of New York, Cadwallader Colden, in 1769. (Library of Congress)

Alexander
McDougall
joined Henry
Knox in organizing
the Society of the
Cincinnati.

their views before Congress. In early 1783 he presented the officers' arguments, and in March Congress voted to grant them a commutation of half pay for life into five years of full salary. At the end of the War of Independence, McDougall joined Henry Knox in organizing the Society of Cincinnati and became the first president of the New York chapter. On 25 November 1783, McDougall accompanied Washington and other American officers as they formally retook possession of New York City while the British Army under General Sir Guy Carleton withdrew.

For the remainder of his life, despite failing health, McDougall worked to improve his own and New York City's financial positions. He was elected to the New York State Senate on 5 January 1784, serving there until his death and actively promoting a number of legislative initiatives. He also served a short term in the Continental Congress in 1784–1785. Through his son-in-law, John Laurance, McDougall became associated with Alexander Hamilton and became a follower of Hamilton in both national politics and local business matters. Because of this association, McDougall was elected the first president of the Bank of New York, but his health and the tedium of the job caused him to resign after only a one-year term. In the course of his life, he had thus risen from waterfront political organizer to high military rank and capitalist moneyman. He died after suffering through ten weeks of fevers similar to those that had debilitated him so often during the war.

PAUL DAVID NELSON

See also

Alexander, William; Arnold, Benedict; Canada, Operations in; Carleton, Guy; Coercive Acts; Congress, First Continental; Fort Clinton, New York; Fort Mercer, New Jersey, Assault on and Capture of; Germantown, Battle of; Glover, John; Grant, James; Greene, Nathanael; Hamilton, Alexander; Heath, William; Hudson River and the Hudson Highlands; Knox, Henry; Laurance, John; Lee, Charles; Long Island, Battle of; Muhlenberg, John Peter Gabriel; New York, Operations in; Newburgh Addresses; Paoli, Battle of; Peekskill, New York, Raid on; Putnam, Israel; Smallwood, William; Society of the Cincinnati; Staten Island, New York, Actions at; Stephen, Adam; Sullivan, John; Wayne, Anthony; West Point, New York; White Plains, Battle of

References

Becker, Carl Lotus. *The History of Political Parties in the Province of New York, 1760–1776.* Madison: University of Wisconsin Press, 1909.

Champagne, Roger J. *Alexander McDougall and the American Revolution in New York.* Schenectady: New York State American Revolution Bicentennial Commission and Union College Press, 1975.

Countryman, Edward. *A People in Revolution: The American Revolution and Political Society in New York, 1760–1790.* Baltimore, MD: Johns Hopkins University Press, 1981.

MacDougall, William L. *American Revolutionary: A Biography of General Alexander McDougall.* Westport, CT: Greenwood, 1977.

Nash, Gary B. *The Urban Crucible: Social Change, Political Consciousness and the Origins of the American Revolution.* Cambridge: Harvard University Press, 1979.

Shannon, Sister Anna Madeleine. "General Alexander McDougall: Citizen and Soldier, 1732–1786." PhD diss., Fordham University, 1957.

McIntosh, Lachlan
(1725–1806)

Lachlan McIntosh led the Georgia militia during the first battle on Georgia soil, spent the winter of 1777–1778 at Valley Forge with General George Washington, commanded Continental forces in the West in 1778, and was taken prisoner by the British at Charleston in 1780. Yet McIntosh is often most remembered for killing Button Gwinnett, a signer of the Declaration of Independence, in a duel, and for spending the latter part of the war trying to defend himself against criticism of his military leadership.

McIntosh was born in Scotland, where his father was chief of the McIntosh clan, but his family, long impoverished due to their support of the Stuart Pretender during the Jacobite rebellion in 1715, finally immigrated to America in 1736 and settled in Darien, Georgia, where they became planters. McIntosh had received only two years of formal education when he was called on by Governor James Oglethorpe to enter his regiment as a cadet to fight the Spanish, who were threatening the young colony from Florida in the 1740s. Following peace in 1748, McIntosh traveled to Charleston, South Carolina, to work in a countinghouse. There he became friends with Henry Laurens, who would later become president of the Continental Congress. On the eve of the Revolution, however, McIntosh was back in Georgia, living in Savannah and serving as a member of the colony's Revolutionary provincial congress from the Parish of St. Andrew.

Appointed colonel of the 1st Georgia Battalion on 7 January 1776, McIntosh led this unit against the British during the first engagement of the war on Georgia soil. His battalion was soon incorporated into the Continental Army, and he was promoted to brigadier general in that army on 16 September 1776. Problems between him and his political enemies in Georgia, however, now began to affect his career.

Gwinnett, a radical Whig, had become president of the Georgia Committee of Safety following the sudden death of Archibald Bulloch in 1777. After friction with McIntosh, Gwinnett ordered George McIntosh, Lachlan's brother, placed under arrest for trading with the enemy, a charge that was never proven. His brother's arrest permanently strained McIntosh's relationship with Gwinnett. Following the surrender of a small Georgia force to the British and Indians based in St. Augustine, Gwinnett planned an invasion of Florida but would not allow McIntosh to lead the Georgia troops. McIntosh turned his command over to Colonel Samuel Elbert, and the operation was a complete failure. Civil authorities blamed Georgia's military leadership for the defeat. Continued friction and serious political differences between McIntosh and Gwinnett finally led to a duel near Savannah on 16 May 1777, in which both men were wounded. Gwinnett's wound was mortal, and he died three days later.

The Continental Army officer Lachlan McIntosh became an important and controversial figure in Georgia politics. (Library of Congress)

The duel prompted Georgia's radical Whigs to demand McIntosh's removal as brigadier general, but with the aid of George Walton (another signer of the Declaration of Independence) and Laurens, McIntosh received an appointment to command North Carolina troops in Washington's Continental Army. McIntosh's leadership during the terrible Valley Forge winter of 1777–1778 impressed Washington, who granted him command of the Western Department in May 1778. But McIntosh's disappointing performance in suppressing raids by parties of Loyalists and Indians led to criticism by junior officers that he was incompetent and unable to deal effectively with subordinates.

Washington, under pressure from the Continental Congress, replaced McIntosh in western Pennsylvania with Daniel Brodhead. Brodhead had been McIntosh's second in command and primary detractor during the recent campaign against the British and their Loyalist and Native American allies. Ironically, soon after replacing McIntosh, Brodhead decided to end the planned campaign against Fort Detroit altogether, and Detroit remained a main staging area for Loyalist-Indian raids against Americans throughout the war. Washington, however, now used his influence to place McIntosh in command of the 1st and 5th South Carolina Regiments and sent him to Charleston on 18 May 1779. He participated in the failed siege of Savannah in October 1779 and was captured, along with the Southern Continental Army, on 12 May 1780 when Charleston fell to the British.

During his imprisonment, McIntosh discovered that the Continental Congress had rescinded his brigadier general's commission. Papers from Georgia had been delivered to Congress in which the state legislature expressed its dissatisfaction with McIntosh's performance and requested that he be sent to another theater of operations. It is believed that Walton, McIntosh's former friend and ally, carried this document to Philadelphia. It was soon discovered, however, that the letter allegedly by William Glascock, Speaker of the Georgia House, had been forged. Following an investigation, it was determined that Walton had signed the document.

On 16 July 1781, McIntosh's suspension was repealed, restoring his brigadier general's commission, and on 30 September 1783 he was breveted a major general. More importantly, on 24 February 1784, a congressional committee chaired by James Monroe officially thanked McIntosh for his service during the Revolution. Congress also officially charged Walton with forgery, but no records of the case are now extant.

McIntosh was exchanged as a prisoner of war in 1782 for General Charles O'Hara and settled with his family in Virginia until the British Army finally withdrew from Savannah at the end of the war. Returning to the city, McIntosh found himself financially bankrupt. He administered his brother's estate and was elected to Congress in 1784 but never served. He did hold various appointed positions in Georgia and participated in the adjusting of the South Carolina–Georgia boundary. A founding member of the Society of the Cincinnati of Georgia in 1784, he would also serve on the committee that welcomed President Washington to Savannah on his southern tour in 1791. McIntosh died impoverished in 1806 and is buried in Colonial Cemetery in Savannah.

CHRISTOPHER A. MEKOW

See also

Brodhead, Daniel; Charleston, South Carolina, Expedition against (1780); Fort McIntosh, Pennsylvania; Laurens, Henry; Valley Forge, Pennsylvania

References

Berg, Frederick Anderson. *Encyclopedia of Continental Army Units: Battalions, Regiments, and Independent Corps.* Harrisburg, PA: Stackpole, 1972.

Boatner, Mark. *Encyclopedia of the American Revolution.* Mechanicsburg, PA: Stackpole, 1994.

Coleman, Kenneth. *The American Revolution in Georgia, 1763–1789.* Athens: University of Georgia Press, 1958.

Garraty, John A., and Mark C. Carnes, eds. "Gwinnett, Button." Pp. 757–758 in *American National Biography,* Vol. 9. New York: Oxford University Press, 1999.

Malone, Dumas ed. *Dictionary of American Biography,* Vol. 12. New York: Scribner, 1933.

Thomas McKean's career exemplified the upward political mobility achieved by a set of young men of nonelite origins in the proprietary middle colonies of British North America during the Revolutionary era. The complex political cultures nurtured by the region's defining cultural pluralism and the skills and habits that its founding Quakers (also known as the Society of Friends) developed to maintain their political preeminence in Pennsylvania and their viability in Delaware and West New Jersey after the sect became a minority of the population early in the eighteenth century made the mid-Atlantic region a conservative territorial bloc resistant to the emerging ideas of political radicalism and especially independence. But the presence in the region of a second tier of articulate, educated, and politically sophisticated non-Quaker leaders weakened the Friends' political hegemony. When the conservative political system buckled under the strain of the outbreak of war in New England in April 1775, many members of this second cohort rose to power. Some of them stepped immediately into the breach created by the popular loss of confidence in both the Quaker and the proprietary establishments of Pennsylvania and Delaware. Few of them made more of their opportunities than did McKean.

McKean was born in 1734 to an innkeeper and farmer in Chester County, Pennsylvania. After studying at a private academy, he read law with

McKean, Thomas
(1734–1817)

Thomas McKean was one of the most prominent figures in early American politics, serving as a representative from Delaware in the First and Second Continental Congresses and in a number of political and judicial offices. He was president of the Second Continental Congress in 1781 and was also one of the last surviving signers of the Declaration of Independence. (Hayward Circer, ed., *Dictionary of American Portraits*, 1967)

a cousin in New Castle County, Delaware. The presence of a quasi-separate government and political system in the so-called Three Lower Counties on the Delaware River—which would emerge as a fully separate state only with the American Revolution—offered cultural and political apprenticeship opportunities to men such as McKean. These counties shared a proprietary governor, nominated by the Penn family, with Pennsylvania. Since 1702, however, they had been allowed to elect a separate legislative assembly and had their own court system.

A largely invisible phenomenon during the generation before 1776 was the migration of men of talent from Delaware and the northern part of the eastern shore of Maryland into Pennsylvania. As the upper Chesapeake political economy shifted from tobacco to grain cultivation, it increasingly became part of Philadelphia's trading hinterland, and legal, financial, and political decisions for the region were made in the metropolis. From his late twenties, McKean had held a host of offices in Delaware, and he sat in the provincial and then state legislature almost continuously from 1762 to 1779. Yet when he moved to Philadelphia to pursue his legal career in 1773, he was far less prominent than many other men of roughly the same age who had taken this path much earlier, such as Joseph Galloway and John Dickinson. Galloway, the leader of the Pennsylvania Assembly from 1766 to 1774, became an important Loyalist as the Revolution began, while Dickinson exemplified the middle colonies' moderate Whiggism in the Revolution.

McKean, however, sustained a long career in Pennsylvania's radical political community, beginning with his involvement with Philadelphia's Revolutionary committee movement in the 1770s. He chaired Philadelphia's last two Committees of Observation and Inspection in 1775 and 1776 and Pennsylvania's Provincial Conference of June 1776, which prepared the way for independence and a new constitution for the state. While still holding important positions in Delaware, he had become the leading spokesman of Pennsylvania's most radical forces on the eve of independence.

Yet McKean was no newcomer to resisting British policies. He had represented Delaware in the Stamp Act Congress in 1765 and had led the resistance to the Townshend Acts in that colony in the late 1760s. Elected to the First Continental Congress for Delaware in 1774 despite his predominantly Philadelphia residence, he remained a member of Congress for almost a decade. He would eventually become its president, serving in 1781 when the British surrender at Yorktown all but assured American independence. He had supported independence from early in 1776 and helped to assure Delaware's vote for that measure by urgently summoning the colony's third delegate, Caesar Rodney, to Philadelphia in early July to break a tie vote in the delegation. Sometime later (it is not known when), McKean signed the Declaration of Independence.

After 1776, while still playing an important role in Delaware, McKean focused most of his attention on Pennsylvania's turbulent politics. In October 1776, he joined Dickinson in publicly opposing the state's new radical constitution, which had created a strong unicameral legislature, a weak plural executive, an energized electorate, and a provision for "Test Acts" to exclude opponents of the state regime from political participation. But unlike other enemies of the constitution, McKean actively took part in the business of the government while pressing for constitutional revision. In July 1777 he became chief justice of Pennsylvania's Supreme Court, a position that he held for more than two decades. And, just as he had not let holding office in Delaware dissuade him from simultaneously holding office in Pennsylvania (and vice versa), he did not let being a jurist in Pennsylvania dissuade him from continued service in the Delaware legislature or in the Continental Congress or from playing an active role in reforming the Pennsylvania Constitution. But he was first and foremost a jurist, and his persuasive decisions and judicial activism established that court as a fully independent and constitutionally creative branch of the state government.

McKean became gradually more conservative during the 1780s, and he was harshly criticized by Pennsylvania's radicals, especially for judicial decisions that moderated or frustrated their determination to punish Loyalists and other persons accused of treasonous acts during the Revolution. In the mid-1780s he joined James Wilson in advocating the replacement of the Articles of Confederation with a federal constitution. When the U.S. Constitution was presented to the public in September 1787, McKean immediately began working aggressively for its ratification in Pennsylvania. This step energized the state's conservative political community to make its final, and successful, assault on the 1776 Pennsylvania Constitution, an effort in which McKean was deeply involved. That document was replaced in 1790 by one that made the state government much more conventional and thus much more like those of its peers in terms of the structure and function of its public institutions.

Despite McKean's recent moderate conservatism, however, he became a Jeffersonian Republican in national politics after 1790. He disagreed with many of the fundamental premises of Alexander Hamilton's fiscal policy, upon which the Federalist Party was based. Like Jefferson, McKean refused to denounce the French Revolution, even after it took an increasingly radical turn in 1792. And although he supported President George Washington's Neutrality Proclamation in 1793, McKean strongly condemned the Jay Treaty. In 1798, he opposed the patriotic fever that almost drove the United States into a war with France. In 1799, his judicial career ended when he was elected governor of Pennsylvania as a Democratic-Republican.

McKean's gubernatorial career, however, was considerably less distinguished than either his participation in Revolutionary politics or his judicial tenure. He quickly became bogged down in patronage and factional disputes in Pennsylvania's already byzantine partisan political system. He was barely elected to a third term, began nominating avowed Federalists to state offices under his control late in his tenure, and barely avoided impeachment in 1807.

McKean died in 1817, still in considerably more obscurity than many members of the Revolutionary generation who had achieved less than he did in the public arena. Yet the fact that he had achieved as prominent a place as he did early in the Revolution is a testimony to how fundamentally transformative that event was in his native region. His vigorous and varied participation in the debates of his era and especially his role in the development of a culture of judicial independence were important and defining contributions to American politics.

WAYNE BODLE

See also

Congress, First Continental; Congress, Second Continental and Confederation; Declaration of Independence Signers; Delaware; Dickinson, John; Galloway, Joseph; Pennsylvania; Wilson, James

References

Buchanan, Roberdeau. *The Life of the Honorable Thomas McKean*. Lancaster, PA: Inquirer Printing Company, 1890.

Coleman, John M. *Thomas McKean: Forgotten Leader of the Revolution*. Rockaway, NJ: American Faculty Press, 1975.

Rowe, G. S. *Thomas McKean: The Shaping of an American Radicalism*. Boulder, CO: Associated University Press, 1978.

Ryerson, Richard Alan. *The Revolution Is Now Begun: The Radical Committees of Philadelphia, 1765–1776*. Philadelphia: University of Pennsylvania Press, 1978.

McLane, Allan

(1746–1829)

Revolutionary military leader Allan McLane received little recognition for his contributions to winning the War for Independence. His harassing of small parties of British and Loyalists and his foraging and intelligence gathering were tactically important, but they usually redounded to the long-term reputations of his superiors, George Washington, Anthony Wayne, and Henry "Light-Horse Harry" Lee, instead of to himself.

Born the son of a Philadelphia merchant, McLane's original name was McLean, but during the Revolution he changed it to McLane to prevent any confusion with the Scots-Canadian Brigadier-General Allan MacLean, who commanded the British 84th Regiment (Royal Highland Emigrants). McLane had a privileged upbringing, with a proper education and the obligatory grand tour of Europe from 1767 to 1769. Three years after his 1771 marriage to Rebecca Wells of Dover, Delaware, McLane settled near Smyrna, Delaware, as a merchant.

When the War for Independence began, McLane joined the American forces as a volunteer. He was commissioned a lieutenant in September 1775 and served as adjutant to Caesar Rodney's militia regiment. McLane's first engagement was the American rebuff of Virginia Governor Lord Dunmore's force at Great Bridge, Virginia, on 9 December 1775, and he probably accompanied the American force that burned the Loyalist stronghold of Norfolk in January 1776.

McLane soon became noted for his derring-do. He captured a British patrol at the Battle of Long Island in August 1776 and another at White Plains in October. He saw heavy fighting at Trenton and was promoted to captain for his gallantry at Princeton. During the Philadelphia Campaign, he joined Colonel John Patton's Additional Continental Regiment and in September 1777 saw action at Cooch's Bridge, Delaware, and at the Battle of Brandywine.

After Brandywine, McLane depleted his entire fortune raising and equipping a Delaware regiment of about one hundred light horsemen. His was the first American unit to make contact with the British in the Battle of Germantown (4 October 1777). Following that flawed engagement, his dragoons screened Washington's army as it moved to winter quarters at Valley Forge.

The eight-month-long British occupation of Philadelphia gave ample opportunity for McLane and his men to demonstrate their worth by harassing the enemy and gathering essential intelligence for the Continental Army. On 3 December 1777, he warned Washington of an imminent British attack from Philadelphia, which allowed the Americans to be prepared for them at Whitemarsh, Pennsylvania, two days later. On 18 May 1778 when Washington ordered the Marquis de Lafayette to lead a large body of troops

Portrait of Allan McLane, an officer in numerous actions, including Long Island, White Plains, Trenton, Princeton, Brandywine, and Paulus Hook. McLane spent a considerable amount of his personal fortune to arm and equip his company of Delaware troops. (Library of Congress)

across the Schuylkill River to protect Bucks County from British raids, he again wisely consulted with McLane, who had been gathering intelligence on the British and their civilian friends in the area. A British attempt on 19 May to surprise and surround Lafayette's force at Barren Hill was foiled partly by this good intelligence work.

McLane's patrols were so successful in harassing British foraging parties and in intercepting farmers intent on trading their produce for British gold that they were given the nickname "market stoppers." His force also played a significant part during January and February 1778 in gathering livestock from Delaware and Maryland for Washington's troops at Valley Forge and Smallwood's force at Wilmington. And on occasion, McLane's horsemen attacked British outposts on the perimeter around occupied Philadelphia. By creating the illusion of an attack on the outposts on 19 May 1778, McLane's men were able to disrupt the elaborate farewell tournament and joust that were to conclude the Meschianza in honor of retiring General Sir William Howe.

The British and their Loyalist supporters would have liked nothing better than to capture McLane. He narrowly escaped a British ambush on

8 June 1778. This incident is commemorated in James Peale's 1803 painting, *The Ambush of Captain Allan McLane* (now in the Utah Museum of Fine Arts, University of Utah, Salt Lake City; preliminary sketches are in the American Philosophical Society, Philadelphia).

Reported to have been the first American to enter Philadelphia following the British evacuation on 18 June 1778, McLane did not get on well with the newly appointed military governor of the city, General Benedict Arnold. When McLane complained to Washington of Arnold's profiteering, however, he received a stinging rebuke from the commander in chief.

During the British retreat across New Jersey, McLane's horsemen operated with General Philemon Dickinson's militia in impeding British movements by obstructing roads and destroying bridges. McLane also provided Washington's pursuing army with critical intelligence that led to the American attack at Monmouth on 28 June 1778. In this campaign McLane claimed to have captured 300 British stragglers at the expense of only 4 men lost.

The capture of Stony Point by the British on 1 June 1779 threatened both Washington's east-west communications across the Hudson River and the American position at West Point. Washington decided to reconnoiter the British positions and dispatched McLane, disguised as a local farmer, to get inside and examine the British works. McLane spent a whole two weeks collecting intelligence in the fort. Based on his report that the fortifications were only partially complete, Washington decided to let Wayne assault the position in a surprise night attack. In the attack on 15–16 July, McLane and his men were part of Lee's Partisan Corps, which acted as a noisy diversion against the center of the British line while Wayne assaulted and seized the fort from the right. And on 19 August, McLane's dismounted dragoons again were part of Lee's corps in the predawn assault on Paulus Hook, New Jersey.

Since McLane did not get along with Lee, Washington transferred him to General Benjamin Lincoln's army holding Charleston, South Carolina. By failing to reach that besieged city before its surrender in May 1780, McLane avoided spending the rest of the war in a prison camp. With nothing left to do in the Carolinas, he was promoted to major, placed under General Friedrich von Steuben, and returned to the North.

In June 1781, McLane was dispatched to the West Indies to exhort François de Grasse to abandon his attack on Jamaica and instead sail north to support Washington and Jean-Baptiste Vimeur, the comte de Rochambeau, at Yorktown. On his return voyage, McLane obtained the command of the marines on the 24-gun privateer *Congress*, which captured the 16-gun British sloop *Savage*. During the Yorktown Campaign, McLane was busy keeping an eye on General Sir Henry Clinton in New York to ensure that he did not secretly send relief to General Lord Charles Cornwallis in Virginia.

At the end of the war, McLane retired from the army with the rank of brevet major. Having lost his fortune in support of the Revolution, he entered into business with Robert Morris and in the 1790s held the post of marshal of Delaware. McLane also served as collector of the Port of Delaware, a post he held until his death in 1829. During the War of 1812, the elderly McLane commanded the defenses of Wilmington and was sharply critical of the younger officers and soldiers who allowed the British to capture Washington, D.C., in 1814. McLane died bemoaning the lack of recognition he had received for his services during his lifetime.

JOSEPH J. CASINO

See also
Barren Hill, Pennsylvania, Action at; Brandywine, Battle of; Cooch's Bridge, Delaware, Action at; Germantown, Battle of; Great Bridge, Virginia, Action at; Paulus Hook, New Jersey, Action at; Philadelphia Campaign; Stony Point, New York, Capture of; Whitemarsh, Pennsylvania, Action at

References
Allan McLane Papers and Journals, New York Historical Society.
Cook, Fred J. "Allen McLane, Unknown Hero of the Revolution." *American Heritage* 7 (1956): 74–77, 118–119.
Garden, Alexander. *Anecdotes of the American Revolution*. 3 vols. Charleston, SC: A. E. Miller, 1822–1825.
Heitman, Francis B. *Historical Register of Officers of the Continental Army*. 1914. Reprint, Baltimore, MD: Genealogical Publishing Company, 1982.

Mecklenburg Declaration
(20 May 1775)

The Mecklenburg Declaration was said to be a remarkably early statement of independence agreed to at Charlotte, North Carolina, by a meeting of delegates from Mecklenburg County. Passed more than a year before the Declaration of Independence, and even before the creation of the Continental Army and the beginning of formal intercolonial armed resistance to Britain, the document dissolved the political connection between the citizens of Mecklenburg County and the British Crown. Many historians, however, consider the declaration to be spurious because of its publication many years after the fact and because of the similarity of its language to that of the national Declaration of Independence.

On 19 May 1775, a convention did meet in Charlotte to decide what action should be taken against the British for violating the citizens' rights. Supporters of the Mecklenburg Declaration's validity argue that news of Lexington and Concord reached Mecklenburg that morning and inflamed the already anti-English Presbyterian Ulster Scots who dominated the region's population. Said to be ratified at 2:00 A.M. on 20 May and signed by twenty-seven delegates, the declaration consisted of six resolves that identified Parliament as an enemy of the country, absolved the citizens of Mecklenburg County of allegiance to the Crown, and declared that they were a free, independent, and self-governing people. It also adopted former British laws to govern the county, rejected the rights and privileges of the Crown, and affirmed the authority and power of colonial civil and military officials to keep the peace. Finally, it resolved that a copy of the declaration be transmitted to the Continental Congress convened in Philadelphia.

On 30 April 1819, during a national outbreak of nostalgic patriotic zeal, the *Raleigh Register* published the first copy of the Mecklenburg Declaration to appear in public. In 1818 several of the states, particularly Virginia and Massachusetts, began to argue over their place in the American Revolution. Each state claimed that it possessed a unique and decisive position in the struggle for independence. With the publication of the Mecklenburg Declaration, North Carolina made its claim. Senator Nathaniel Macon sent a copy of the declaration to the newspaper. He had obtained the copy from Dr. Joseph McKnitt Alexander, whose father attended the 1775 meeting. The declaration was believed to be genuine until 1829, when a posthumously published letter by Thomas Jefferson to John Adams, written in June 1819, refuted its authenticity and began the controversy that still continues today.

Detractors cite the similarity in the declaration's language to language used by Richard Henry Lee in his resolution for independence to Congress and by Jefferson in the Declaration of Independence. They claim that Alexander used these sources to embellish his father's notes and falsified the Mecklenburg Declaration. Others argue that the similarity in language was due to the universal rhetoric used by politicians during the Revolutionary crisis. Although a fire in 1800 destroyed the records that could have proved the veracity of the declaration, over the years proponents have found interesting sources that do refer either to the document itself or to the fact that the actions of the Mecklenburg delegates were considered revolutionary at the time. It is known that in May 1775 the citizens of Mecklenburg County did meet to defy British authority. However, it is still open to debate whether the document identified as the Mecklenburg Declaration was passed at that meeting.

PETER S. GENOVESE JR.

See also
Declaration of Independence; North Carolina

References
Hoyt, William Henry. *The Mecklenburg Declaration of Independence*. New York: Putnam, 1907.
Maier, Pauline. *American Scripture: Making the Declaration of Independence*. New York: Knopf, 1997.
McNitt, Virgil V. *Chain of Error and the Mecklenburg Declarations of Independence: A New Study of Manuscripts*. Palmer, MA: Hampden Hills, 1960.

Meigs, Return Jonathan
(1740–1823)

Return Jonathan Meigs owed his unusual name to an incident in the courtship of his grandparents. After Hannah Willard turned down the marriage proposal of young Janna Meigs, he rode away from her farm in Wethersfield, Connecticut, vowing never to come back. She called after him, "Return, Janna!" He returned and married Hannah, promising to name one of their children "Return." His fifth child, a hatter and colonial assemblyman, bore the name and passed it on to his own son, who was born in Middleton, Connecticut, in 1740.

Meigs was commissioned a lieutenant of the 6th Connecticut Regiment in 1772 and became a captain in 1774. Shortly after the Battle of Lexington, he marched his men to Massachusetts, where they joined the Continental Army. He was soon raised to the rank of major and participated in Colonel Benedict Arnold's invasion of Canada in 1775. Meigs marched with Arnold through the Maine wilderness and kept a diary of the ill-fated campaign. Meigs was captured during the failed attempt to take Quebec on New Year's Eve 1775.

After a prisoner exchange, Meigs rejoined the Continental Army in New York. He was promoted to the rank of lieutenant colonel and won permission from General George Washington to lead a surprise attack on the British garrison at Sag Harbor on Long Island. On 23 May 1777, Meigs and 170 men rowed across Long Island Sound without being detected by British warships, captured Sag Harbor, and burned all the wharves, transports, and hay. They returned to Guilford, Connecticut, having completed the mission in less than twenty-four hours and with no loss of American lives. Congress awarded Meigs a sword in honor of his bravery.

Return Jonathan Meigs, a Continental Army officer from Connecticut, is best known for his raid on Sag Harbor, New York, in May 1777. He later fought at Stony Point and helped suppress the mutiny of the Connecticut line in 1780. (Library of Congress)

After the surprise attack on Sag Harbor, Meigs and the 6th Connecticut Regiment were sent to Peekskill, New York, and then to West Point, where they built fortifications. In the summer of 1779 they were ordered to join General Anthony Wayne. Meigs and the 6th Connecticut Regiment helped Wayne rout the British from Stony Point on 15 July 1779. During the following year, they again built fortifications around West Point and wintered in Morristown, New Jersey, where Meigs was able to quell a mutiny among his men. The last assignment of the 6th Connecticut Regiment came in September 1780, when Meigs and his men were ordered to West Point to defend the outpost following the defection of Arnold.

After the war ended, Meigs was hired as one of the first surveyors of the Ohio Company. He traveled west with General Rufus Putnam and helped found Ohio's first town at Marietta in 1788. Meigs left Ohio in 1801 when he was appointed agent to the Cherokee Nation, a position he held until his death. His son, Return Jonathan Meigs Jr., became governor of Ohio and led the state during the War of 1812.

MARY STOCKWELL

See also

Arnold, Benedict; Mutiny, Continental Army; Quebec, Siege of; Sag Harbor, Battle of; Stony Point, New York, Capture of; West Point, New York

References

Montross, Lynn. *The Story of the Continental Army, 1775–1783.* New York: Barnes and Noble, 1967.

Meigs, Rick. "Return Jonathan Meigs 1st." *Meigs Family History and Genealogy.* http:/meigs.org/rjm90.htm.

Mercenaries, German

See German Mercenaries

Mercer, Hugh
(1725–1777)

A Scottish immigrant, Virginia doctor, and friend of George Washington before the Revolution, Hugh Mercer became a general in the Continental Army and died of bayonet wounds inflicted by British soldiers at the Battle of Princeton.

Born in Scotland, Mercer trained as a doctor at Aberdeen. At age nineteen, while in the midst of his medical training, he served with Bonnie Prince Charlie's forces in the 1745–1746 Jacobite uprising, taking the post of assistant surgeon. After the bitter defeat at Culloden Moor, Mercer went into hiding in the countryside to escape the brutal retribution being meted out by the British forces of the Duke of Cumberland. Soon thereafter, Mercer fled to the relative safety of the American colonies.

When Mercer arrived in Philadelphia he rapidly pressed on into the Pennsylvania backwoods, where he set about creating a new life for himself. At the outbreak of the French and Indian (Seven Years') War, he got his first glimpse of fighting on the American frontier. While serving in the Pennsylvania militia, he took part in the Kittanning expedition to destroy an important Indian base of operations. In 1758, promoted to lieutenant colonel, he participated in the successful expedition against Fort Duquesne, during which he first met Washington. After the British and Americans had captured Fort Duquesne and renamed it Fort Pitt, Mercer received command of the garrison. This command gave him the kind of military experience that would serve him well during the Revolutionary War. He faced the difficulty of maintaining militia troops through a frontier winter and keeping them in some kind of order. And he successfully supplied his small garrison, no minor feat in the Pennsylvania backwoods, while collecting intelligence on the movements of Indians and French troops.

In January 1761, Mercer was discharged from the Pennsylvania militia, at which time he headed south to Virginia to trade frontier warfare and the rough life of the frontier for the relative comfort and civilization of Fredericksburg, where he would return to the practice of medicine. The following spring, however, he returned to military service part-time by acting as surgeon for a regiment of Virginia militia. In the 1760s, Mercer built a thriving practice, married, and started a family. By 1771 he had prospered enough to open his own apothecary shop and to begin engaging in that favorite activity of the colonial businessman, land speculation. In 1774, Washington sold his mother's home, Ferry Farm, to Mercer.

When the American Revolutionary War began, Mercer needed little encouragement to side against the British. His experiences from thirty years earlier no doubt influenced his decision to embrace the Patriot cause. Mercer's Revolutionary War service began in the Virginia militia, where he was elected colonel of the minutemen of four counties in September 1775. The following January he received an appointment to command the 3rd Virginia Regiment. When he traveled to Williamsburg to meet his troops, he confronted the same problems that plagued so many commanders of the day: forging a fighting unit out of a mass of soldiers eager but untrained in military drill and other important problems such as basic sanitation. But Mercer had little time to train his men; just two months later the 3rd Virginia received orders to head north to defend the Northern Neck of Virginia from Loyalists who supported the royal governor, Lord Dunmore. For the next few months the regiment shuffled back and forth across northern Virginia, still understrength and ill-equipped. While operating so close to several rivers and to Chesapeake Bay, Mercer took a special interest in boats and boatmen as a way to gather intelligence on his enemy's operations and as a means of communication.

Hugh Mercer, physician and brigadier general in the Continental Army, fought at Trenton and at Princeton, where he was killed in action. (National Library of Medicine)

In June 1776, Mercer received an appointment as brigadier general in the Continental Army. He also received the task of creating a defense of the New Jersey coast, based on a concept called the flying camp. In that defensive scheme, Mercer would command a mobile force that could, in theory, rapidly support any coastal garrisons pressed by British attack. In this role, Mercer continually sought ways to strike a blow against the British but was often hampered by the indifferent quality of his troops. In October he raided Staten Island but without success, for the British troops there withdrew into earthworks supported by fire from Royal Navy ships. He then shifted his troops northward to aid Washington's army north of New York City as it tried to hold on to Forts Washington and Lee. When British troops captured Fort Washington, they also captured some of Mercer's best troops.

Shortly thereafter Washington reorganized his army, severely damaged after the failed 1776 campaign to defend New York City, and gave Mercer a small brigade, composed of the remnants of five regiments. That small force continued to dwindle as enlistments expired and desertions rose. Against this background of despair and approaching defeat, Washington launched his brilliant 26 December attack on Trenton, New Jersey, in which Mercer served in the left wing under General Nathanael Greene.

Mercer's 350 remaining troops were in the vanguard several days later when Washington turned north to attack Princeton. Mercer was tasked with capturing the Stony Brook bridge to block the arrival of British reinforcements. His men encountered a determined British force early in the engagement and broke under its fire. British musketry also wounded Mercer's horse, forcing him to dismount. Once on foot, Mercer was surrounded by redcoats who ordered him to surrender, then mortally wounded him with bayonets when he defiantly struck at them with his sword. He lingered for nine days before succumbing to his wounds.

MITCHELL McNAYLOR

See also
Continental Army; Fort Lee, New Jersey; Fort Washington, New York, Fall of; Murray, John, Lord Dunmore; New Jersey; New Jersey, Operations in; Princeton, Battle of; Trenton, Battle of; Virginia; Washington, George

References
Fleming, Thomas. *1776: Year of Illusions.* New York: Norton, 1975.
Ketchum, Richard M. *The Winter Soldiers.* Garden City, NY: Doubleday, 1973.
Waterman, Joseph M. *With Sword and Lancet: The Life of General Hugh Mercer.* Richmond: Garrett and Massie, 1941.

Middleton, Arthur

See Declaration of Independence Signers

Mifflin, Thomas
(1744–1800)

Thomas Mifflin—merchant, member of Congress, Continental officer, and governor of Pennsylvania—began the Revolution as a popular leader but later became embroiled in much unpopular controversy. Nevertheless, after the Revolution he went on to become one of Pennsylvania's most admired public figures. Reared a Quaker, he visited England and France in 1764–1765, then went into business with his brother, George. Mifflin was elected to the American Philosophical Society in 1768. A persuasive public speaker, he opposed the Stamp Act and the Townshend duties and supported nonimportation movements in the 1760s. In 1772, he was elected to the Pennsylvania Assembly, serving four years and sitting on many important legislative committees. He was also a member of various extralegal committees, including the Philadelphia Committee of Correspondence. An early proponent of a congress to deal with British infringements of American rights, he was chosen

Philadelphia's representative to the First Continental Congress in 1774, where he helped write the Association agreement. In all these matters, he allied himself with moderate Whigs, who were in favor of colonial liberties but not democratic leveling.

Mifflin was elected to the Second Continental Congress in 1775, but after the Revolutionary War commenced on 19 April 1775, he turned his attention to military matters. He recruited troops and was appointed major of a volunteer company before becoming, on 23 June, aide-de-camp to General George Washington. As a result, the Quakers read Mifflin out of meeting. On 14 August he was appointed quartermaster general and on 9 November bravely led an attack on a British foraging expedition near Boston. On 22 December he was promoted to colonel, serving ably as quartermaster but wishing to secure a field command. He was promoted to brigadier general on 16 May 1776, and on 5 June, at his own request, was succeeded as quartermaster by Stephen Moylan. Mifflin commanded the covering party during the American retreat from Long Island in August and on 1 October reluctantly resumed the office of quartermaster general when Moylan proved incompetent.

The Continental Army officer Thomas Mifflin was an important figure in Pennsylvania politics both before and after the Revolutionary War. (National Archives and Records Administration)

During the dark period of late 1776, Mifflin was sent by Washington to Philadelphia, where he roused the authorities and people to support the American cause. Mifflin was present at the battles of Trenton (26 December 1776) and Princeton (3 January 1777), and during the following months he used his oratorical skills to keep soldiers in the army when their enlistments expired. On 19 February 1777, he was promoted to major general, but his work as quartermaster began to deteriorate, he was criticized by Congress, and his influence and standing with Washington waned. In the summer of 1777 Mifflin went home, pleading ill health, and on 8 October resigned both as quartermaster general and major general. Congress accepted his resignations but asked him to continue temporarily as quartermaster and major general while also appointing him to the Board of War. Thereafter, discontented and disillusioned, he neglected his duties as quartermaster. Terrible confusion characterized the Department of War, with Washington for some reason refusing to intervene. Mifflin was replaced on 8 March 1778.

In the winter of 1777–1778, Mifflin was associated with the so-called Conway Cabal, a supposed plot by army officers and congressmen to have Washington replaced as commander in chief by Major General Horatio Gates. Both Gates and Mifflin were members of the Board of War in early 1778, and they were good friends. They were also to some degree critics of Washington, and they came in for scathing criticism by Washington's admirers as plotters against the commander in chief. Both men adamantly denied these charges, and there is no evidence that any conspiracy against Washington ever existed. Later, Mifflin declared that Washington was the greatest friend he had ever had in his life. However, Mifflin's usefulness on the Board of War was crippled by the accusations, and on 18 April 1778 he resigned and rejoined the army. Washington accepted him with ill-concealed disgust, appointing him to command a division on 21 May.

Mifflin's tenure in the army was short-lived. On 15 June, Congress decided to investigate his activities as quartermaster general, for his enemies were accusing him of embezzlement. Taking a leave of absence, he began preparing his defense, insisting that he should not be held responsible for his subordinates' mistakes. Washington was also instructed to hold a court of inquiry if he believed that Mifflin was guilty of any improprieties. Although Mifflin welcomed both investigations, he waited in vain for them to commence. Finally, on 17 August 1778, he resigned his commission in order to take his case to the public, although Congress did not accept his resignation. Meanwhile, Congress voted to provide him with $1 million to settle all his public accounts, at the same time deciding that he should be court-martialed by Washington. When Washington refused to comply, Congress accepted Mifflin's resignation on 25 February.

Mifflin was in the Pennsylvania Assembly during 1778–1780, where he opposed the radical Pennsylvania Constitution of 1776. In 1780, Congress appointed him a commissioner to recommend the reorganization of military departments. He was again in Congress from 1782 to 1784 and was elected president of Congress in 1783. He was Speaker of the Pennsylvania Assembly from 1785 to 1788 and president of the Supreme Executive Council from 1788 to 1790. He attended the Constitutional Convention in 1787 and supported the Constitution's adoption in Pennsylvania. He was chairman of the state constitutional convention during 1789–1790 and served for three terms as governor of Pennsylvania during 1790–1799. He personally led state troops during the Whiskey Rebellion of 1794, even though he feared that he might lose favor among Jeffersonian Republicans. After leaving the governorship, he served in the legislature until his death in 1800.

PAUL DAVID NELSON

See also
Congress, First Continental; Congress, Second Continental and Confederation; Conway Cabal; Gates, Horatio; Moylan, Stephen; Princeton, Battle of; Stamp Act; Townshend Acts; Trenton, Battle of; War, Board of

References
Heathcote, Charles W. "General Thomas Mifflin—Colleague of Washington and Pennsylvania Leader." *Picket Post* 62 (1958): 7–12.

Rawle, William. "Sketch of the Life of Thomas Mifflin." Pp. 105–126 in *Memoirs of the Historical Society of Pennsylvania*, Vol. 2. Philadelphia: M'Carty and Davis, 1830.

Rossman, Kenneth R. *Thomas Mifflin and the Politics of the American Revolution*. Chapel Hill: University of North Carolina Press, 1952.

Militia units, both Patriot and Loyalist, played a vital yet controversial role in the American Revolutionary War. Patriot militia forces, which were far more numerous and widespread than their Loyalist counterparts, were especially important in New England at the outset of the war, and many units were tapped by Congress to form the foundation of the Continental Army. They fought both alongside Continental Army regiments and independently in many regions throughout the war and were especially important in such battleground states as New Jersey, Virginia, Georgia, and the Carolinas. They were also severely criticized by George Washington and other Continental officers for their lack of discipline, and on several occasions they retreated in panic, notably at Camden, South Carolina. Yet in many small and midsized engagements in New Jersey, Georgia, and the Carolinas, they performed well and were a vital component to Patriot victories.

After 1776, Loyalist militia units were numerous only in New York and New Jersey and, from 1779 to 1781, in the Carolinas. Most of these forces were organized as Associated Loyalist regiments and, like most Patriot militia units, usually fought only in their own state or in a neighboring state. Both Patriot and Loyalist units from the North, however, fought in the southern campaign of 1779–1781. Loyalist militia often worked closely with British regulars, whose commanders criticized them just as Washington did the Patriot militia. Yet in their own regions they often augmented British power effectively and were able, especially in the Carolinas, to postpone Britain's ultimate defeat.

Modeled on a form of part-time military organization throughout England that had its origin in medieval trainbands, militia units were established from the earliest settlement in several British colonies of North America. By the 1700s in Great Britain, with the growth of the middle class, militia organizations spread throughout the kingdom and were generally officered by the local gentry and nobility. During the American Revolution, so much of the regular British Army was fighting to regain control of the thirteen colonies that the territorial defense of the British Isles fell mostly to the militia.

In most British American colonies, as in Britain, the militia legally included all able-bodied free men between the ages of sixteen and sixty. Every man was expected to possess his own firearm and other equipment. New Jersey law, which was quite typical for the American colonies, required each man eligible for militia duty to keep on hand a musket (with equipment for loading ammunition and firing), a bayonet, a sword or tomahawk, a pound of powder, and three pounds of ball. Transients, slaves, indentured servants, paupers, and Indians generally were excluded from the militia. And men in certain respected occupations were not required to participate, including clergymen, school teachers, doctors, members of the legislature, college professors, fishermen, and captains of sailing ships. In theory, the militia assembled in each community several times a year for drill and could be called out when a threat required their service anywhere in the colony. In practice, by the eighteenth century militia muster days were sloppy social affairs or were skipped altogether.

The membership, use, and discipline of the militia varied considerably from one colony to another. In Virginia, freemen of African descent as well as Indians were excluded from armed service after 1723 but could be required to report unarmed for noncombatant duty as drummers, trumpeters, or any servile labor assigned to them. In Massachusetts and some other New England colonies, no such distinctions were made among freemen.

Many African slaves traded in Massachusetts were sold for a fixed term, like European indentured servants; therefore, many were free and in militia service by 1775. It is known that more than one hundred freemen of African or Indian descent fought in the battles at Lexington, Concord, and Bunker Hill, and many served in the initial core of the Continental Army when Washington took command. It may never be possible to determine their number, but perhaps between 5 and 10 percent of New England Patriot soldiers were black or Indian. Recruiting clerks did not consistently register the color or race of volunteers, nor were there, except in Rhode Island, any distinct black regiments in the militia or the Continental Army like those that appeared so prominently eighty-seven years later during the Civil War.

Pennsylvania had no required militia service prior to the outbreak of the struggle for independence, although many of its citizens formed voluntary armed associations during the French and Indian (Seven Years') War in the 1750s. The Philadelphia militia was organized in May 1775, and its earliest enlistees fought a nine-month debate to define its articles of association. One of the most radical militias in the colonies, most of their members were relatively poor men whose public spirit was not matched by an ability to pay for rifles, muskets, uniforms, and other equipment. Compensation for artisans and wage earners who had to take time off from work was an issue, as was the demand of many militiamen that heavy fines be imposed on wealthier citizens who declined to serve in regular militia units or in the city's Home Guard.

Virginia's militia reflected a social order very different from that of Massachusetts or Pennsylvania. While many New England militia companies elected their officers, Virginia officers came universally from the ranks of the gentry, usually defined by ownership of both a substantial quantity of land and slaves. Millers, miners, and iron founders were exempt from service so that the enterprises of their wealthy employers would not be disrupted, and anyone employed as an overseer of four or more servants or slaves was exempt as a security measure. In fact, any millers or overseers who felt drawn to the excitement, camaraderie, and heavy drinking of the militia muster could be fined twenty shillings for attending in spite of their exemption.

In Virginia and South Carolina, patrols to control and regulate the movement of slaves became a key role for the militia. A 1726 Virginia statute established militia patrols to guard against the danger that might occur from the unlawful gathering of slaves on holidays when they were usually exempted from labor. The 1757 militia statute established monthly patrols by an officer and four men of the militia to visit all slave quarters and any other places where slaves, servants, or any disorderly persons might congregate.

In Virginia, as the conflict with British authority sharpened, new militia bodies were formed, outside the authority of the governor, that claimed to be

> In theory, the militia assembled in each community several times a year.

the authentic military embodiment of the people. When the royal governor, Lord Dunmore, seized the colony's gunpowder supply in April 1775, several of these independent companies demanded its return. A Fredericksburg company declared that any submission to such an arbitrary government act would harm the common cause and encourage further despotic measures.

It has been a traditional element of American national identity to believe that a patriotic citizen militia won the Revolution, overcoming a regular British Army composed of conscripts and mercenaries. In the past century, however, historians have offered many different conclusions about the actual role of the militia in the War for Independence. Much historical analysis has emphasized the more professional military organization of the Continental Army, under the command of General George Washington aided by such generals as Nathanael Greene, Horatio Gates, Daniel Morgan, Philip Schuyler, and Benedict Arnold. It is also important to remember that America's citizen militia was not of a more humble background than its Continental Army. Like the British regular army, America's Continental rank and file—but not its officers—probably contained more landless men, and perhaps more social minorities, than its militia. Although militiamen were criticized by generals of the Continental Army for being apt to simply go home when a battle was not in their favor, militia forces assisted the Continental Army on several important occasions. For instance, militiamen led by William Maxwell slowed down the British retreat from Philadelphia across New Jersey in 1778, allowing Washington's army to catch up with them at Monmouth Court House and give the British a battle they had tried to avoid.

General John Stark leads his New Hampshire militia at the Battle of Bennington in 1777. (North Wind Picture Archives)

And of course, militiamen played the central role in the events in Massachusetts that sparked the open break with the British Crown. John Hancock served as captain of the Boston Cadets, traditionally the royal governor's militia guard of honor. Hancock used the Cadets to take over East India Company tea ships in Boston Harbor in 1773, thereby setting up the Boston Tea Party. In 1774, Massachusetts's Revolutionary Provincial Congress reorganized the militia by raising funds, organizing magazines and supplies, and formulating emergency plans. They placed one quarter of the militia force, known as minutemen, on standby to mobilize within hours. The province soon had 7,500 minutemen, carefully handpicked from the whole militia and properly armed, according to a report made by an agent to the British governor, General Thomas Gage. That report may have been exaggerated, but it was that reorganized provincial militia that fought at Lexington, Concord, and Breed's (Bunker) Hill.

The American militia was usually not able to win major battles against British armies, but various state and local militias played critical roles in maintaining political control in every colony. They effectively prevented any chance of a Loyalist counterrevolution. The measures adopted by provincial congresses and the Continental Congress were enforced by Patriot militiamen, with varying degrees of intimidation and violence. This created and preserved a stable region behind the lines that provided support for the Continental armies. British forces, however, never held enough territory to create supportive behind-the-lines areas anywhere in the thirteen colonies.

There were also several substantial engagements between Patriot and Loyalist militia units. These included Moore's Creek Bridge in North Carolina in February 1776 (where about 1,400 fought on each side), Kettle Creek in Georgia in February 1779, Ramseur's Mill in North Carolina in June 1780, and Kings Mountain in South Carolina in October 1780 (with more than 1,000 men in each of the opposing forces). All four battles were decisive Patriot victories. Across New Jersey and in neighboring parts of New York and Pennsylvania, militiamen fought a "war between neighbors," as a local historian described it, that lasted for five years. Lacking active local support, British commanders had to send out foraging expeditions to supply their armies. Due to constant harassment by local militiamen, these expeditions had to have protection from several hundred or even several thousand British regular soldiers, using up time and supplies, taking casualties, and limiting the results.

There were notable points in the course of the Revolutionary War when the defeat of a British offensive relied primarily on the response of local militia units that were called to aid a small regular army force because significant numbers from the main Continental Army could not be spared. In addition to the initial battles in Massachusetts in 1775, these included important engagements that contributed to the defeat of General John Burgoyne's 1777 invasion from Canada, especially the Battle of Bennington; the struggle to control eastern New Jersey in 1780, when the Continental Army was extremely weak due to desertion and starvation; and the ultimate failure of General Charles Cornwallis's march through the Carolinas in 1780–1781.

At the opening of Burgoyne's campaign in 1777, Washington's main forces were tied down by General William Howe's advance on Philadelphia. Burgoyne's invasion from Canada would have to be met by a relatively small Continental force and whatever militia would respond to the call of the Continental Army officer dispatched to the upper Hudson Valley, General Philip Schuyler (who was replaced before the final battle with General Horatio Gates). Howe doubted that many of the militia would even show up, but by September the Americans had amassed 11,000 men in northern New York, greatly outnumbering the British under Burgoyne. An important victory came in August 1777 when Hessian forces were annihilated by New Hampshire militia under Colonal John Stark and Vermont's Green Mountain Boys under Colonel Seth Warner at Bennington. Inspired by this success, volunteers poured into the upper Hudson Valley to help trap Burgoyne at Saratoga.

Relying on the militia, however, presented difficulties at Saratoga as well as elsewhere. Stark was reprimanded by the Continental Congress for refusing to place his troops under Continental command. Immediately after the 7

Notice sent to John Newton of the Massachusetts militia that he was being drafted into the Continental Army, 1777. Periods of service in the militia were always shorter than those in the regular army, and a conscript could confidently expect to remain under arms for the duration of the war. (National Archives and Records Administration)

October 1777 American victory at Bemis Heights, which would soon lead to Burgoyne's surrender at Saratoga, Stark took his militia home because their enlistment period had expired. And earlier in the Saratoga Campaign, Warner's militia were wary of the New York patrician Schuyler, since New York claimed sovereignty over Vermont.

When more than 5,800 British and Loyalist troops under the Hessian General Wilhelm von Knyphausen invaded New Jersey from Staten Island in 1780, the main Continental Army had been reduced by desertion and starvation to 3,760 men, many of them in a state of near mutiny. The continued existence of Washington's army and the security of its entire arsenal at Morristown depended on the response of the New Jersey militia and a small force of state regular soldiers, led by Maxwell and Colonel Elias Dayton. In theory, New Jersey could turn out 16,000 militiamen. Enough did turn out, although still outnumbered by the British force, so that in two days of fighting they stopped the invasion east of the Watchung Mountains (Short Hills), between Elizabeth Town and Springfield. Subsequent British moves, even with an

Number and Percentage of Males Eligible for Military Service

State	Total Population	White Males over Age 16	Percentage
Connecticut	237,655	60,739	25.56%
Delaware	59,096	11,783	19.94%
Georgia	82,548	13,103	15.87%
Maryland	319,728	55,915	17.49%
Massachusetts	378,556	95,433	25.21%
New Hampshire	141,899	36,074	25.42%
New Jersey	184,139	45,251	24.57%
New York	340,241	83,815	24.63%
North Carolina	395,005	70,172	17.76%
Pennsylvania	433,611	110,559	25.50%
Rhode Island	69,112	16,056	23.23%
South Carolina	249,073	35,576	14.28%
Virginia	747,550	110,936	14.84%
Territories	255,661	61,900	24.21%
Total	3,893,874	807,312	20.73%

additional 4,000 reinforcements brought by General Sir Henry Clinton from the successful siege of Charleston, South Carolina, also ended fruitlessly.

Loyalist militia, generally serving in green uniforms, played important roles in supporting British forces. British officers were dubious about the fighting abilities of the Loyalists, but as the British were often short of troops themselves after 1778, they began to make more use of these bitter American Tories. New York alone provided 15,000 men for Clinton's forces. Lieutenant-Colonel John Simcoe commanded the Loyalist Queen's Rangers, also in green uniforms, who accompanied Clinton's retreat from Philadelphia to New York in 1778 and initiated mounted attacks against rebel snipers who were firing from the cover of trees and houses. The New Jersey Volunteers, more than 1,500 men known as Skinner's Greens, was led by Brigadier-General Cortlandt Skinner, a close friend of New Jersey's Loyalist governor, William Franklin. The Royal Greens, a Loyalist militia commanded by Colonel John Butler, fought under Colonel Barry St. Leger in the Mohawk Valley Campaign in 1777, which was coordinated with Burgoyne's invasion from Canada. But the failure of St. Leger's siege of rebel militia forces at Fort Stanwix relieved Patriot forces of a threat to their western flank and denied Burgoyne the support of nearly 2,000 men.

In the South, Loyalist regiments grouped around the Queen's Rangers were reorganized as the British Legion, commanded by Lieutenant-Colonel Banastre Tarleton. Unlike the Hessian mercenary soldiers employed by the British, Loyalist militia truly hated their rebel enemies. For this reason, they were involved in some of the bloodiest and most ruthless encounters of the war. After the capture of Charleston and the surrender of 5,500 soldiers of the Continental Army in 1780, Cornwallis and Tarleton continued to win victories across South Carolina, dispersing Patriot militia unused to fighting from fixed positions and putting Gates to flight outside of Camden in August 1780, in perhaps the worst showing of the war by Patriot militiamen.

The British could never consolidate these victories, however, because other Patriot militia terrorized Loyalists into inaction, while Greene and

Morgan were able to keep enough militia fighting alongside their Continentals to wear down British forces. At the Battle of Cowpens in January 1781, Morgan inflicted 600 casualties on Tarleton, and at Guilford Courthouse in March the British won only a technical victory at the cost of 500 casualties (one-third of their army). Southern militiamen, properly led, ultimately helped a moderate-sized Continental force drive Cornwallis to Yorktown, where a larger portion of the Continental Army, with vital French assistance, secured his surrender after a classic professional siege operation from fixed positions.

Theoretically, the militia continued to be a resource of both states and the federal government for at least a century after the Revolutionary War, a century in which federal forces were usually quite small. "The right of the people to keep and bear arms," protected by the Second Amendment to the U.S. Constitution, was premised on the need for "a well regulated militia." The militia remained the primary force that state governors could call upon in the event of civil disorder. At the outbreak of the Civil War, both the United States and the Confederate States called for volunteers, assembled by each state under the authority of each governor, to fill the ranks of their respective armies. These recruits to some degree retained the form of a state militia, although state regiments served under the authority and discipline of a regular army command. In the late nineteenth century the militia fell into decline, to be replaced by the National Guard, a more limited body of part-time citizen soldiers trained in military discipline similar to that of the regular army, and early in the twentieth century the militia as such ceased to exist in the United States.

CHARLES ROSENBERG

See also
Arnold, Benedict; Associators; Bennington, Battle of; Boston Tea Party; Burgoyne, John; Camden Campaign; Charleston, South Carolina, Expedition against (1780); Cornwallis, Charles; Cowpens, Battle of; Elizabeth Town, New Jersey, Raids on; English Militia Act; Fort Stanwix, New York; Franklin, William; Gates, Horatio; Green Mountain Boys; Greene, Nathanael; Guilford Courthouse, Battle of; Loyalist Units; McCrea, Jane; Minutemen; Morgan, Daniel; Saratoga Campaign; Schuyler, Philip; Southern Campaigns; Springfield and Connecticut Farms, New Jersey, Raids on; Stark, John; Warner, Seth

References
Breen, T. H., and Stephen Innes. *Myne Owne Ground: Race and Freedom on Virginia's Eastern Shore*. New York: Oxford University Press, 1980.

Fleming, Thomas. *The Forgotten Victory: The Battle for New Jersey, 1780*. New York: Dutton, 1973.

Higginbotham, Don. *War and Society in Revolutionary America: The Wider Dimensions of Conflict*. Columbia: University of South Carolina Press, 1988.

Hoffman, Ronald, and Peter J. Albert, eds. *Arms and Independence: The Military Character of the American Revolution*. Charlottesville: University of Virginia Press, 1984.

Isaac, Rhys. *The Transformation of Virginia, 1740–1790*. Chapel Hill: University of North Carolina Press, 1982.

Pearson, Michael. *Those Damned Rebels: The American Revolution as Seen through British Eyes.* New York: Putnam, 1972.

Quintal, George. *Patriots of Color, "A Peculiar Beauty and Merit": African Americans and Native Americans at Battle Road & Bunker Hill.* Washington, DC: U.S. Department of the Interior, National Park Service, 2002.

Rosswurm, Steven. *Arms, Country, and Class: The Philadelphia Militia and the "Lower Sort" during the American Revolution.* New Brunswick, NJ: Rutgers University Press, 1987.

Trevelyan, George Otto. *The American Revolution.* New York: David McKay, 1965.

Washington and Jackson, on Negro Soldiers. Item 1 in From Slavery to Freedom: The African-American Pamphlet Collection, 1824–1909, Library of Congress, American Memory. http://memory.loc.gov/ammem/aapchtml/aapchome.html.

Minutemen
(1774–1775)

Established by the nascent Revolutionary government of Massachusetts in the fall of 1774, minutemen were elite units drawn from the militia that received extra training, the best equipment, and leaders with military experience. Above all else, they were expected to respond rapidly to any armed threat. Massachusetts created them in order to provide the colony with a means of confronting and repelling British expeditions into the countryside. Though the minutemen are indelibly associated with the Revolution, and particularly with Lexington and Concord, the minuteman concept had a long and distinguished place in Massachusetts' military history.

The first colonists of Massachusetts Bay based their military organizations on the English militia system but modified it to suit local needs. One of these changes occurred in 1645 during the Pequot War when the Massachusetts Council ordered each militia company to keep thirty soldiers well armed, well drilled, and ready to assemble within thirty minutes. The idea was to form an alert force that could quickly gather and march to defend any point in the colony. During King Philip's War in 1675, the system was tested for the first time and proved to be an effective means of defending settlements.

In the first half of the eighteenth century, Massachusetts adapted the concept to the needs of Britain's North American wars with France. To protect its northwest border from attacks by the French and Indians, Massachusetts created the Snow Shoe Men, loosely organized light infantry companies designed to patrol the forests. Their task was not just to respond to attacks but to intercept enemy forces before an assault occurred. Thus, they had an offensive component to their missions. The companies worked in shifts: as some units patrolled, the rest returned home and served as reinforcements ready to provide aid when necessary. By 1745, the system worked so effectively that Massachusetts sent most of its militia on an expedition against the French fortress of Louisbourg on Cape Breton Island, leaving only thirteen companies of Snow Shoe Men to defend the frontier.

Toward the end of the French and Indian (Seven Years') War (1756–1763), the colony again turned to the minuteman concept, and the

Minutemen firing on the British in Lexington, Massachusetts, 19 April 1775. Minutemen were so called because of their ability to stand to arms at a minute's notice. Although companies of minutemen were first formed in Massachusetts, other colonies, including Maryland, New Hampshire, North Carolina, and Connecticut, also formed minutemen companies. (Library of Congress)

first companies calling themselves minutemen appeared. In this conflict, Massachusetts also attempted to refine the system with the Picket Guards, special companies drawn from the militia, composed of volunteers with the best equipment, and designed to serve as strictly defensive units. As planned, the Picket Guards closely resembled the minutemen as eventually established in 1774, but the colony's House of Representatives refused to create them.

By 1774, as tensions mounted between Great Britain and the American colonies, the need to prepare for a possible conflict became apparent to Massachusetts's leaders. Two actions led them to form the minutemen. The first was the passage of the Coercive Acts by Parliament in May, to be enforced by the province's new governor, General Thomas Gage, commander in chief of the British Army in North America, and some 3,000 troops stationed in Boston. The second action transpired in September when units from that army successfully confiscated powder and cannon held at Charlestown and Cambridge. These events convinced the province's leaders of the need to reorganize the militia and create an army capable of defending their entire territory. Seizing the initiative, Worcester County, in its attempt to disarm its Loyalists, ordered its current militia officers to resign, held elections for new officers, and formed seven reorganized regiments. The new officers then enlisted one-third of the men in each town between the ages of sixteen and sixty into units ready to act at a minute's notice. This was the birth of the minutemen of the American Revolution.

On 26 October 1774, to create a more potent military force for the colony, the First Provincial Congress passed resolutions reorganizing the militia along the lines adopted by Worcester County. The resolutions created a provincial Committee of Safety, essentially an army command staff empowered to call out the militia when necessary, and a Committee of Supplies, responsible for provisioning the militia. The Provincial Congress then established the minutemen, decreeing that every militia regiment was to form 25 percent of its men into separate companies of fifty privates. These units would hold themselves in readiness to respond at a moment's notice to orders issued by the Committee of Safety.

Most of the new minutemen units were established on guidelines issued by the Provincial Congress. The minutemen formed into regiments of nine companies. Each company chose a captain and two lieutenants, who then elected the regimental commanders from among themselves. Many minutemen already owned muskets, but the towns provided firearms to those who could not afford their own and gave each man thirty rounds of ammunition and a bayonet, pouch, and knapsack. Some minutemen also received hatchets. The standard musket was the Brown Bess or a similar firearm. The Provincial Congress expected the towns to pay the men unless the troops were called into service, in which case the colony would compensate the troops. Finally, the minutemen were to drill at least three times a week. Not every town followed these guidelines, and a few delayed setting up units. Woburn, for instance, which was immediately adjacent to Lexington, did not create its minutemen unit until 17 April 1775.

The social composition of the minutemen is difficult to determine. In Concord, for which the only historical analysis exists, the town's two companies of enlistees included individuals from every class and town neighborhood. The company captains came from the traditional elite: men in their forties who had previous political or military experience and owned at least one hundred acres of land. The lieutenants were also members of the middle or upper class, though they were younger and less experienced. The rank and file, however, were socially varied but tended to be young (more than half of them were under twenty-five), leading one historian to describe the minutemen of Concord as "the 'embattled farmers' sons." The one class underrepresented was the laboring poor. As a result, the town had to provide only fifteen men with a musket.

In some respects, other minutemen companies seemed to conform to this description of Concord's units. The Massachusetts militia was composed of three bodies. The regular militia included all males between the ages of sixteen and sixty. The minutemen, drawn from the regular militia, contained

> Minutemen were to drill at least three times a week.

both younger men and men with the most military experience. Finally, the alarm companies, comprising boys and old men, were used as a last resort to protect the town. The only groups excluded were Harvard College students, who received a deferment, and the colony's few black slaves. The province's free blacks were not excluded and served in the militia in some numbers, fighting both at Lexington-Concord and at Bunker Hill. In short, most minutemen tended to be both young and experienced, but whether they mirrored the social inclusiveness of Concord's units is not known.

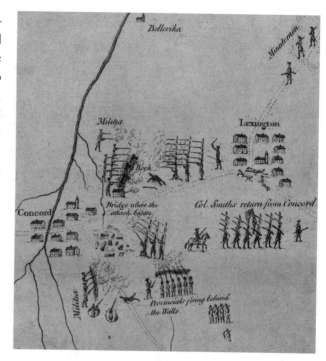

British map showing the engagement at Lexington involving the British troops and the Continental minutemen and militia, 1775. (Library of Congress, Geography and Map Division)

Throughout the winter of 1775, the new companies trained in earnest, compelled by the realization that they might take the field at any time. Due to an unusually mild winter, they were able to drill in the evenings and on weekends, practicing almost as much as the British regulars in Boston. In fact, their drills resembled those used by the British. Virtually all of this training was done at the company level, as few regimental exercises were held primarily because the province could not afford to pay the men. This deficiency was offset by the large number of experienced military personnel in their ranks; perhaps as many as one-third of the men had served in King George's War in the 1740s, the French and Indian War in the 1750s, or both. In this regard, the minutemen compared favorably to the British regiments in Boston, many of which had not seen action for years and contained large numbers of enlisted men and even officers who had never experienced combat.

Massachusetts's efforts to create an army were remarkably effective. By the spring of 1775, the colony had a force of 14,000 well-equipped and well-trained men organized into approximately forty-seven regiments. Of these, seventeen were regular militia, twenty-one were minutemen, and nine were a mixture of both, a mixture that occurred because some militia regiments had not released their minutemen companies to form new regiments. These units had been armed with 20,000 muskets, 10,000 bayonets, powder and ammunition, and some cannon. Amazingly, the British Army in Boston never grasped the extent of Massachusetts's preparations.

The Provincial Congress had established the minutemen to serve as the colony's first line of defense, and events in early 1775 demonstrated the effectiveness of this military organization. Throughout this period, Gage sent small columns of British soldiers into the countryside on practice marches, with orders to confiscate arms and supplies. In January, an attempt to mobilize the minutemen when the British marched on Marshfield, a coastal, heavily Loyalist town, ended in failure when only twelve of the town's men responded to the alarm. Within a month, however, the minutemen's ability to mobilize had improved. At Salem in February and Jamaica Plain in March, the local units quickly assembled and confronted large British columns, although no fighting occurred, as each side sought to avoid bloodshed. Both sides claimed victory, but these incidents convinced Massachusetts's officials that the minuteman system provided them with the means to repel British aggression.

Their confidence was not misplaced, as the events at Lexington and Concord on 19 April confirmed. When Lieutenant-Colonel Francis Smith led his force of 700 regulars into the Massachusetts countryside, the minutemen, adequately warned by the colony's alarm system of riders and signals, assembled in large numbers to confront the British incursion. This time fighting occurred. At Lexington, Captain John Parker's lone company attempted to back away in good order and let the regulars pass, but an unknown individual, whether American or British, fired a shot, and the British opened fire and easily repulsed the heavily outnumbered minutemen. As the British marched on to Concord, however, they entered a region where as many as seventy-five Minutemen and militia companies were at that moment mobilizing to resist them. Concord itself was the geographic center of several county regiments that numbered perhaps 6,000 men.

As the day wore on, many of these regiments arrived at the scene of the fighting, engaging the British in a 15-mile running battle from Concord to Charlestown, just north of Boston. In the end, some 4,000 minutemen and militia participated in the day's engagement. The minutemen proved to be more than a match for the outnumbered regulars. Their training, organization, leadership, and numbers caught the British completely by surprise. Gage, Smith, and other British officers never seemed to have understood that they were not facing ragtag militia units but rather an army of highly motivated, well-trained, and well-armed citizen soldiers defending their farms, homes, and towns.

The minutemen continued in existence for the rest of the Revolutionary War, and the concept was quickly adopted by several other colonies, but they never again achieved the military prominence they enjoyed in the spring of 1775. Following the engagement at Concord, most of the minutemen participated in the siege of Boston, and Massachusetts invited them to enlist in the new Continental Army then being formed, encouraging enlistment by giving their officers preference for commissions. Those who did not volunteer returned home and rejoined the militia units to which they belonged. Massachusetts continued to maintain minutemen companies, and on 18 July 1775 the Continental Congress in Philadelphia recommended that other colonies establish minutemen units for the defense of their own and neighboring colonies. Such units were organized in Connecticut, Maryland, North Carolina, and New Hampshire to defend regions that the Continental Army was unable to protect.

DAVID WORK

See also
Boston, Siege of; Coercive Acts; Gage, Thomas; Lexington and Concord; Massachusetts; Militia, Patriot and Loyalist; Parker, John; Smith, Francis

References
Birnbaum, Louis. *Red Dawn at Lexington.* Boston: Houghton, Mifflin, 1986.

Castle, Norman. *The Minutemen, 1775–1975*. Southborough, MA: Council of the Minute Men, 1977.

Fischer, David Hackett. *Paul Revere's Ride*. New York: Oxford University Press, 1994.

French, Allen. *The Day of Concord and Lexington: The Nineteenth of April, 1775*. Boston: Little, Brown, 1925.

Galvin, John R. *The Minutemen: The First Fight; Myths and Realities of the American Revolution*. 2nd ed. New York: Pergamon-Brassey's, 1989.

Gross, Robert A. *The Minutemen and Their World*. New York: Hill and Wang, 1976.

Quintal, George. *Patriots of Color, "A Peculiar Beauty and Merit": African Americans and Native Americans at Battle Road & Bunker Hill*. Washington, DC: U.S. Department of the Interior, National Park Service, 2002.

Tourtellot, Arthur Bernon. *Lexington and Concord: The Beginnings of the War of the American Revolution*. New York: Norton, 1963.

Ward, Christopher. *War of the Revolution*. 2 vols. New York: Macmillan, 1952.

Mobile Village, Alabama, Action at
(7 January 1781)

The battle at Mobile Village, Alabama, was a military engagement between British and Spanish forces on 7 January 1781. The goal of the British plan to defeat the small Spanish garrison at Mobile Village was to disrupt food and water supplies required by the main Spanish forces across the bay in Mobile. The battle inflicted heavy casualties on the Spanish but ultimately resulted in a British defeat, forcing the latter to withdraw back to Pensacola.

Spain's declaration of war against Britain in 1779 introduced a new theater in the conflict: the former Spanish territory of West Florida. American forces had already engaged British and Loyalist troops in East Florida. However, while Americans had little interest in West Florida as this time, the Spanish eyed it with keen interest. Spanish Governor Bernardo de Gálvez initiated a campaign to capture weakly held British West Florida. Moving from New Orleans, Gálvez seized the towns along the east bank of the Mississippi River and continued his march. Mobile and Pensacola remained as the last, yet strongest, British strongholds in West Florida. Gálvez sailed to Mobile and captured the town and its garrison after a brief siege.

The British forces in Pensacola could wait for an expected attack by Gálvez or launch their own offensive. Their forces were too small in number to both hold Pensacola and conduct an offensive to the west. As an alternative, British General John Campbell sent raiding parties of Native Americans against the settlement of Mobile Village located across the bay from Spanish-held Mobile. Most of Mobile's food and fresh drinking water were being transported to the town from Mobile Village. Successful raids against Mobile Village and its small garrison could cause major disruptions of food and water shipments.

In late 1780, Native Americans raided Mobile Village on two occasions. However, they would not attempt to seize the Spanish garrison after it retreated into a wooden blockhouse. Convinced that British troops could capture the blockhouse, Campbell dispatched 100 soldiers and Loyalists under Colonel Johann von Hanxleden along with 500 Native Americans on 3 January 1781. The British force arrived outside Mobile Village and launched its surprise attack on the early morning of 7 January. The British regulars and Loyalist troops stormed across open ground toward the blockhouse. The startled Spanish soldiers, numbering approximately 200 men, broke in fear and headed for the perceived safety of Mobile Bay, where boats waited. However, the Native Americans were waiting to ambush them in case they attempted a hasty retreat. Many Spanish soldiers fell to the Native Americans before the others decided that it would be safer to take refuge within the blockhouse. The Spanish troops turned back toward the outnumbered British soldiers and fought their way into the blockhouse. Hanxleden fell in the melee. British forces and their Native American allies fired at the blockhouse for the remainder of the day but with little effect. Without artillery, the Spanish were safe within the strong walls of the blockhouse.

The British and Native Americans withdrew from the area in defeat by the end of the day. Native American casualties are not known, but at least twenty British regulars and Loyalists were killed or wounded in the attack. The Spanish soldiers suffered approximately forty total casualties. Britain's defeat at Mobile Village signaled the end of any attempts at a counteroffensive or large-scale raid against Spanish positions to the west of Pensacola. Campbell strengthened his fortifications for the expected attack against his garrison in Pensacola. Gálvez captured the town and its garrison after a siege in May 1781.

TERRY M. MAYS

See also
Campbell, John; Florida; Gálvez, Bernardo de; Mobile, Alabama, Capture of; Pensacola, West Florida, Operation against

Reference
Wright, J. Leitch. *Florida in the American Revolution.* Gainesville: University Press of Florida, 1975.

Molly Pitcher, Legend of

Molly Pitcher, legendary Patriot cannoneer, is both the composite of two female military heroes of the Revolutionary War and a symbolic representative of countless other women who participated in that conflict. Variations on the Molly Pitcher myth range widely but all center on a woman who takes her husband's place at his gun or cannon at either the Battle of Monmouth or the Battle of Fort Washington.

Several historians have pointed to the military career of Margaret Corbin as the inspiration for the myth of Molly Pitcher. Corbin served in an artillery unit, the 1st Company of Pennsylvania, alongside her husband John. Dressed as a male solider but making little attempt to hide her sex, Corbin is sometimes referred to in surviving military records as "Captain Molly." When her husband was killed at the Battle of Fort Washington on 16

Mary Ludwig Hays, known as "Molly Pitcher," at the Battle of Monmouth. According to legend, Hays, a washerwoman with the Continental Army, brought water to the soldiers during the battle. After her husband was injured, she replaced him at an artillery piece. The troops affectionately nicknamed her "Molly Pitcher," and her fame quickly spread throughout the colonies, making her a heroine of the American Revolution. (National Archives and Records Administration)

November 1776, Corbin took his place on the firing line and was wounded in the line of duty. Captured and released by the British, she then served as an invalided guard at West Point before her discharge in April 1783. She died, partly as a result of her combat injuries, in low circumstances around 1800.

The more commonly referenced inspiration for the Molly Pitcher myth is Mary Ludwig Hays McCauley (1754–1832). Mary, also nicknamed Molly, was born in Trenton, New Jersey, but grew up as a family servant in Carlisle, Pennsylvania. In 1769 she married John Caspar Hays, a barber. When he joined the Continental Army in 1775, Molly moved back to her parents' house in Trenton to be near her husband, a common practice among married women during the Revolutionary War. On one terrifically hot day, 28 June 1778, John was serving as an artillery gunner in the 1st Company of Pennsylvania at the Battle of Monmouth, while Molly brought pitchers of water from a nearby well to cool the exhausted and wounded troops. When John fainted, Molly took his place, filling the cannon for the rest of the day. After the war they lived in Carlisle, Pennsylvania, and when John died in 1789, Molly married George McCauley. In 1822 the Pennsylvania legislature awarded "Molly M'Kolly" a yearly annuity of forty dollars for her wartime services. When she died a decade later in Carlisle, however, her obituary failed to mention her wartime service.

Like Hays, there were many women who, while rarely seeing combat or firing a cannon, lived and traveled with the British and American armies during the Revolutionary War. These camp followers blurred the distinction between military and civilian life, some serving as paid nurses, water carriers, cooks, and laundry workers. Others were soldiers' wives or widows, and a small minority were prostitutes. All told, around 20,000 women served in some paid position with the Continental Army, while the unofficial service of many others went unrecorded.

It was in 1876, during the centennial celebration of the Revolution, that the lives of Corbin and Hays, who were both associated with the same Pennsylvania artillery company, first became confused and entangled. The spotty historical record led a generation of poets, memorialists, and local historians to create a composite portrait of a female fighter compelled to heroism after her husband's incapacitation. Such stories played well in the late nineteenth century as Americans romanticized their founding moment. Legend soon had it that General George Washington himself had not only known Molly Pitcher, "the heroine of Monmouth," but had promoted her for her gallantry. Since the centennial, the iconic image of a woman wielding a cannon ramrod in the midst of battle has been repeated and further embellished, creating an enduring if composite symbol of the wartime contributions of a generation of Patriot women.

RICHARD J. BELL

See also
Corbin, Margaret Cochran; Hays, Mary Ludwig; Women

References
Klaver, Carol. "An Introduction to the Legend of Molly Pitcher." *Minerva: Quarterly Report on Woman and the Military* 12(2) (1994): 35–61.

Martin, David G., ed. *A Molly Pitcher Sourcebook*. Hightstown, NJ: Longstreet House, 2003.

Teipe, Emily J. "Will the Real Molly Pitcher Please Stand Up?" *Prologue: Quarterly of the National Archives Records Administration* 31(2) (1999): 118–126.

Monmouth, Battle of
(28 June 1778)

At the Battle of Monmouth, American forces under the command of General George Washington were unsuccessful in destroying the British Army, commanded by Lieutenant-General Sir Henry Clinton. The British were also unable to defeat decisively the American forces arrayed against them, and the battle ended in a draw.

During the winter of 1777–1778, forces from both main armies rested in the area around Philadelphia. General Sir William Howe and his forces were stationed in Philadelphia. American forces under the command of Washing-

General George Washington at the Battle of Monmouth, 28 June 1777. The New Jersey battle, an attempt to intercept British troops withdrawing from Philadelphia to New York, was a hard-won victory for Washington. The action was fought in extreme heat, with losses of approximately 350 men on each side. (National Archives and Records Administration)

ton were stationed to the northwest of Philadelphia, at Valley Forge. Washington had chosen this position to offset any British movement from Philadelphia and to deny the British access to supplies from the countryside.

The American main army passed a difficult winter at Valley Forge. Many militia troops returned to their farms and homesteads, while the Continentals who remained were put through a rigorous training regimen, under the command of a former Prussian officer, Baron Friedrich von Steuben. Steuben recognized that the Continentals needed to be trained in linear tactics but adapted his program with the understanding that Americans were not Prussian and did not have years of discipline to build upon.

The British spent their winter in a hiatus period. Howe, their commander, had offered to resign from his command on 22 October 1777 after the Hessian assault on Fort Mercer. The British government accepted his resignation in February 1778. Clinton was sent to replace Howe but was not due to arrive in Philadelphia until early May.

In addition to a major change in the British high command, the strategy for 1778 was also in a state of flux. Following the British defeat during the Saratoga Campaign and the Americans' improved performance during the Philadelphia Campaign the previous summer, Britain's traditional enemy,

Henry Clinton, the commander in chief of British forces in America, 1778–1782. His decision to abandon Philadelphia and march to New York gave George Washington the opportunity to confront him at Monmouth Court House, in New Jersey. (Library of Congress)

France, had begun open alliance negotiations with the rebellious thirteen colonies. France had been offering covert aid in the form of weapons and officers for some time but had now decided to back the insurrection fully. France and America signed a treaty on 6 February 1778.

France's decision placed the British in a difficult position, as was intended. British officials had to decide what to do about the French threat. Most of the British Army and Royal Navy were stationed in North America, attempting to put down the insurrection. This left the rest of the empire, as well as Britain itself, in a vulnerable position. After a series of plans had been rejected, a strategy was finally formalized in March for the spring and summer campaigns. Clinton was to attempt to bring Washington to a decisive battle at the beginning of the campaign season. If this was not accomplished, Clinton and his army would withdraw to New York City, and in the autumn the British would open a campaign in the South.

The Royal Navy would launch raids against the New England colonies in an attempt to strangle commerce with a naval blockade. The vast majority of British forces would be stationed in the South in the hope that they could be withdrawn periodically to fight in the commercially lucrative regions of the Caribbean.

Later in the month, one significant change was made to this strategy. Since France was seen as the greater threat, Clinton was ordered not to seek a decisive battle with Washington after all. Instead, he was to withdraw to New York as soon as possible and then dispatch troops to the Caribbean to fight the French. Clinton remained in command of all the troops in North America, but he now also had to oversee deployments to Florida, Central America, and the Caribbean as various campaigns were opened.

Clinton took formal command of British forces in early May when he arrived in Philadelphia. He had already received his orders to withdraw to New York by sea and dispatch more than 8,000 of his 12,000-man army to the Caribbean. He countermanded these orders almost immediately as word traveled to the outlying towns that the British were on the verge of withdrawing from Philadelphia. Thousands of Loyalists entered Philadelphia and requested to be withdrawn with the British forces. Rather than following the orders he had received, Clinton decided instead to place a large percentage of the Loyalists with his sick and wounded troops aboard the Royal Navy ships that had originally been sent to convey his army. He requested that his army should instead march to New York; upon arrival, he would divide his army and send the expedition to the Caribbean as originally planned. This change of plans not only benefited the Loyalists but also avoided placing the army in a vulnerable position. The embarkation of the army could have been dangerous, as American forces had received news of the planned withdrawal.

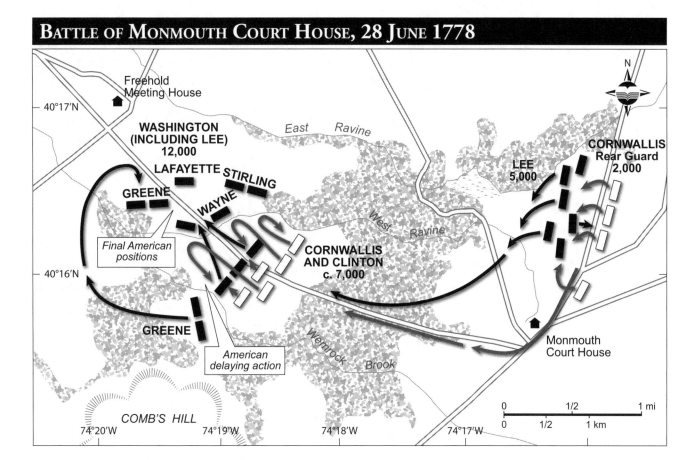

The flotilla of ships carrying Loyalists, sick soldiers, and Howe sailed in early June. The flotilla made it safely to sea. A French fleet had sailed to intercept shipping in the Delaware River area but had failed to catch the British ships. Clinton decided to withdraw his army, refugees, and supplies and march for New York on 18 June.

Washington and his staff discussed possible plans against Clinton. The Americans were aware that Clinton was going to march, but they were unsure where he might go. Some American officers pushed for an attack on the British in Philadelphia, but Washington was against this plan. He decided instead to shadow the British withdrawal and wait for an opportunity to attack the force. At 3:00 A.M. on 18 June, the British began to march to the northeast from Philadelphia.

Washington, realizing that Clinton was marching over land, sent troops to Chadds Ford in case Clinton wanted to move west. Also dispatched was a brigade under William Maxwell, sent to Mount Holly in New Jersey to report on any British movements in that area. At 10:00 A.M. on 18 June, Washington received news that the British had left Philadelphia, marched toward the Delaware River, and were beginning to cross into New Jersey. Washington, still at Valley Forge, ordered six brigades, under the command of the Marquis de Lafayette and Major General Anthony Wayne, to follow the British column closely and harass the rear guard when possible. Washington and the rest of the main army would follow behind the six brigades. A small force of men was sent into Philadelphia to occupy the city.

Clinton divided his forces into two columns marching in a parallel formation in case they were threatened. The British march was extremely slow since, with all the wagons and men, the columns stretched for 12 miles. The weather also played a role in the army's slow progress; the temperature was in the high nineties with humidity to match.

After six days of marching, Clinton and his army arrived at Allentown, New Jersey, 35 miles from Philadelphia. On 23 June, the Americans were closing in on the British columns. Washington was 20 miles to the northwest, and the six brigades sent on ahead were only 10 miles away. Small units of American skirmishers were present on the left and right flanks of the British columns. Clinton decided to move northeast from Allentown toward Monmouth Court House and the road to Sandy Hook. The British planned to rendezvous with the Royal Navy at Sandy Hook and from there evacuate by sea to New York. Clinton was aware that Washington and other American troops were moving to his north and that they could pose a significant obstacle if he attempted to move due north through New Brunswick and on toward Staten Island.

Clinton finalized his preparations and moved out toward Monmouth. Washington and his staff had been carrying out discussions to decide whether to attack and at what point. Washington realized that a British move toward Monmouth might provide an ideal opportunity for attack. There was only one road from Monmouth to Sandy Hook, which would force the British to march in single-column formation, disrupting their defensive cover. Washington decided to strengthen his advance formation. He deployed an additional six brigades to march with Lafayette's units. The advance column was under the command of Major General Charles Lee, and Washington planned to follow behind with the remainder of the army.

Clinton and his forces arrived in the Monmouth Court House area on 27 June. After the long march in extremely hot weather, Clinton decided to rest his troops. Washington decided to attack the British as they moved out from Monmouth. Intelligence reports indicated that the British would move out the next morning, and Washington issued orders to Lee's advance guard of 6,000 men to attack the British rear guard as it moved out. If successful, this plan would destroy the rear guard, as it was deployed as a single column. Washington and the remainder of his army, 8,000 men, would follow as quickly as possible to support Lee and his troops.

At 4:00 A.M. on 28 June, the British formed up and began to march toward Sandy Hook. British forces were divided between Lieutenant-General Baron Wilhelm Knyphausen and Lieutenant-General Charles Cornwallis. Knyphausen led the first column, carrying all the army's baggage and a strong infantry force that included Loyalist troops. Cornwallis was in command of the second column, which consisted of most of the regular troops. Clinton was to accompany Cornwallis and the second column.

Washington received word of his opponent's mobilization and ordered Lee to attack the British rear at 5:00 A.M. Lee, however, was of dubious quality as an officer. He had received orders the previous day to move forward, but he had not carried these out. He began to move his troops forward as ordered on the morning of 28 June but failed to send out orders to his subordinate commanders. Lafayette and Wayne began to move their brigades forward to close in on the British rear, without having received orders from Lee, and other American commanders followed suit. Since no orders had been issued, the troops moved forward in a haphazard manner.

Clinton recognized the impending danger, and so did Cornwallis. They altered direction and proceeded west to meet the Americans, deploying as they did so from column into line before the Americans attacked in strength. The British line extended for 1.5 miles from north to south, just north of the courthouse. Forward American units began to engage the British lines at about 10:00 A.M., but the attack was not coordinated. Lee was still not issuing orders for the attack, and the British took advantage of the confusion and began to repel the initial American attacks.

The American lines began to falter as their right flank began to withdraw, due, according to some sources, to orders from Lee. Wayne, realizing that his right flank was exposed, also began to withdraw. Clinton, recognizing the opportunity now facing his troops, ordered Cornwallis to follow up the American withdrawal as closely as possible. He also ordered Knyphausen to send 3,000 troops back to the area around the courthouse in order to reinforce Cornwallis.

The British pushed home their attack against the American advance guard, and by the time Washington arrived in the area at midday with the remainder of his army, he found the Americans in full retreat. He had expected to push into the line behind Lee, not to encounter retreating soldiers. At this point, Lee, in a heated exchange, was relieved of command by Washington, who then organized various remnants of the advance corps into a last-ditch line under Wayne's command. By that time, the British advance was only 200 yards away following the American advance corps, which had withdrawn about a mile. Wayne was to hold the line as well as he could, while Washington would deploy the remainder of his army into line to the rear of Wayne's line. Major General Nathanael Greene was placed in command of the right wing of the main line, and Major General William Alexander, Lord Stirling, was to command the left wing. Washington and Lafayette attempted to form a reserve line of men from the advance corps that had retreated past Wayne's lines. Wayne was to withdraw from his delaying action when the British attack became too difficult to resist.

The British attack pressed against Wayne's line with considerable force, obliging him to withdraw. Washington, realizing that his main force was still not deployed properly, reinforced Wayne with two regiments. The British moved forward to deal with the second position. According to Clinton, "The second line of the enemy stood the attack with great obstinancy, but was likewise completely routed."

As the British approached Wayne's line once again, a serious exchange of fire ensued. A ravine separated the British from where Wayne was holding his line. Clinton recognized that the American left flank was still not in position in the rear and ordered an additional attack against the American left flank.

Cornwallis deployed more troops to the center to destroy Wayne's position, but Wayne successfully repulsed two major assaults in his final delaying position. At this point, the British received reinforcements from Knyphausen that Clinton shifted to his left wing to attack Greene's line.

The Americans had been able to hold up the British advance long enough to deploy in line. Wayne realized that his delaying action had been successful and ordered his men to withdraw fifty yards to form the center between Greene and Stirling. Officers in the British center mistook this for a full retreat and followed up the withdrawal. Wayne counterattacked, halting the British attack in its tracks and forcing the soldiers back across the marsh.

After his troops had failed to penetrate the American lines, Clinton decided to halt all attacks at around 5:00 P.M. Clinton stated in his official report that "I could press the affair no further; especially as I was confident the end was gained for which the attack had been made." Artillery exchanges became common; both sides were exhausted from long marches in hot weather as well as from the fighting. Exchanges of fire continued all evening, but no further attacks were made.

At 12:00 A.M. Clinton ordered his army to move out toward Sandy Hook. Washington had made plans to attack the next morning. He awoke to discover, much to his amazement, that the British had withdrawn. They had a six-hour head start, and Washington decided not to follow them. Clinton did not flee; he had his rear fully protected and anticipated that Washington would march in pursuit. No additional action occurred on the march, however, and the British arrived at Sandy Hook on 1 July without further incident. They were moved to New York City by 6 July.

The casualties were about the same for both sides, with most estimates suggesting that each lost 400 killed and wounded. Evidence of the intense heat of the day may be gleaned from the fact that both sides lost around 40 men to heat stroke.

In the end, the battle was a stalemate. The British were able to repel the first American attacks. While the British pursued the American advance corps, the main American army was able to hold them off long enough to deploy properly into line formation. A potential rout was turned into a solid defense. The Americans, on the other hand, were not able to destroy the British forces either. The British managed to withdraw to Sandy Hook, thus denying Washington the opportunity for a decisive victory.

DANIEL PATRICK MARSTON

See also
Alexander, William; Clinton, Henry; Cornwallis, Charles; Greene, Nathanael; Howe, William; Knyphausen, Wilhelm, Baron von; Lafayette, Marquis de; Lee, Charles; Loyalist Units; Loyalists; Maxwell, William; Philadelphia Campaign; Saratoga Campaign; Steuben, Friedrich von; Valley Forge, Pennsylvania; Washington, George; Wayne, Anthony

References
André, John. *Major André's Journal: Operations of the British Army under Lieut. Generals Sir William Howe and Sir Henry Clinton.* Tarrytown, NY: New York Times, 1968.
Black, Jeremy. *War for America: The Fight for Independence.* Stroud, UK: Alan Sutton, 1991.

Carrington, Henry B. *Battles of the American Revolution, 1775–1781*. 1876. Reprint, New York: Promontory, 1974.

Clinton, Henry. *The American Rebellion: Sir Henry Clinton's Narrative of His Campaigns, 1775–1782, with an Appendix of Original Documents*. Edited by William B. Willcox. New Haven, CT: Yale University Press, 1954.

Conway, Stephen. *The War of American Independence, 1775–1783*. London: Arnold, 1995.

Ewald, Johann. *Diary of the American War: A Hessian Journal*. New Haven, CT: Yale University Press, 1979.

Higginbotham, Don. *The War of American Independence: Military Attitudes, Policies, and Practice, 1763–1789*. New York: Macmillan, 1971.

Lundin, Leonard. *Cockpit of the Revolution: The War for Independence in New Jersey*. 1940. Reprint, New York: Octagon, 1972.

Mackesy, Piers. *The War for America, 1775–1783*. 1965. Reprint, Lincoln: University of Nebraska Press, 1993.

Smith, Samuel S. *The Battle of Monmouth*. Monmouth Beach, NJ: Philip Freneau, 1964.

Stryker, William S. *The Battle of Monmouth*. 1927. Reprint, Port Washington, NY: Kennikat, 1970.

Ward, Christopher. *War of the Revolution*. 2 vols. New York: Macmillan, 1952.

Wood, W. J. *Battles of the Revolutionary War, 1775–1781*. Chapel Hill, NC: Algonquin, 1990.

Monte Cristi, Actions off
(20 March and 20 June 1780)

In 1780, William Cornwallis, a captain in the Royal Navy, fought two Anglo-French naval actions off the coast of Santo Domingo, in the West Indies. In March 1780, a detached force from the squadron of Vice-Admiral Sir Peter Parker consisting of the *Lion* (64 guns) under Cornwallis and the *Bristol* (50 guns) and the *Janus* (44 guns) was patrolling off the northern coast of Haiti. On 20 March, while this force lay off Monte Cristi, it sighted to the east what was later found to be a French convoy that had sailed from Martinique bound for Cap François. Protecting it was a squadron under Commodore La Motte-Picquet, with two 74-gun ships, one 64-gun ship, one 50-gun ship, and a frigate. The merchant vessels gathered on the port side of the warships, which then pursued Cornwallis.

By 5:00 P.M. the French flagship, the *Annabel* (74 guns), was close enough to exchange fire, albeit distantly, and a general engagement commenced at long range that continued on until after midnight and recommenced at daylight on the next morning. The *Janus* suffered most, having lost its mizzen topmast and foretopgallant mast. Under becalmed conditions the *Janus* could not move and was towed to safety by boats launched from the *Bristol* and *Lion*. Later that morning, two more French line of battle ships joined their number, and intermittent fighting was resumed in the afternoon. In his report to French naval authorities, La Motte-Picquet stated that he had been hesitant to sacrifice his ships and complained of the damage inflicted by the *Janus*.

At dawn on 22 March the two opposing squadrons were again close, and La Motte-Picquet hoped to overtake Cornwallis in an hour-long chase, but he sighted four British ships pursuing him. At 6:30 A.M. he identified three of these vessels as line of battle ships. As the British were now superior in numbers, La Motte-Picquet broke off his own pursuit and made for Cap François. The British ships in question were the *Ruby* (64 guns), the *Pomona* (28 guns), and the *Niger* (32 guns). The opposing forces were, for the French, two 74-gun ships, one 64-gun ship, one 50-gun ship, and one frigate. The British had two 64-gun ships, one 50-gun ship, and three frigates. La Motte-Picquet did not remain long enough to identify the strength of these reinforcements, but even if he had done so and had recognized that, in fact, he was not outgunned and hardly outnumbered, the prevailing French naval doctrine that ships should be preserved would have dictated that he break off the engagement.

Exactly three months later Cornwallis was near Bermuda, having escorted some merchant vessels bound for Britain. His squadron consisted of his own ship, the *Lion*, together with the *Sultan* (74 guns), the *Hector* (74 guns), the *Ruby*, the *Bristol*, and the *Niger*. Early on 20 June, he sighted vessels to the northeast, moving east. This was a group of French transports bound for Rhode Island, protected by seven ships of the line: one 80-gun ship, two 74-gun ships, and four 64-gun ships, all under Commodore Charles Louis, Chevalier de Ternay, who had the important task of escorting 6,000 troops to Rhode Island. While two of the French warships remained with the convoy, the others proceeded on a southwesterly course, in column, intent on confronting Cornwallis.

Cornwallis, meanwhile, was maintaining an easterly course, watching his opponent and assessing his strength. The *Ruby*, however, was a considerable distance to leeward, leaving more than sufficient opportunity for the French to sail between it and the main body, by which they could later take the ship. The *Ruby* sought to reach safety and therefore steered southwest on the port tack, thus putting it on the same course as the French, still approaching Cornwallis's squadron. Cornwallis, in turn, wore his ships, formed into line of battle, and made for the *Ruby*. Here the French made a serious error, for had they kept their wind they would have separated the *Ruby* from the others. If, moreover, Cornwallis chose to come to the *Ruby*'s rescue, he would have no choice but to confront a greatly superior force. Foolishly, Ternay did not keep his wind, and the *Ruby* managed to rejoin its squadron.

When by 5:30 P.M. it became clear to Cornwallis that the French were far enough to leeward to permit the *Ruby* to rejoin the squadron, Cornwallis ordered his ships to tack, bringing them on an easterly course once again. At the same time, the French, moving west-southwest, opened fire as the two lines passed one another. The *Ruby* meanwhile continued until it reached the wake of Cornwallis's column and then tacked as well. The French ships tacked in turn, all in succession, and for a short time the opposing columns fought at long range on a parallel course, with Cornwallis to windward. This commander accepted the folly of continuing an engagement with a force so superior to his own. He consequently broke away, bringing to a close an action in which he might easily have lost the *Ruby*.

Ternay's overcautiousness cost him a possible victory, but it must be borne in mind that he may have hoped to reach Narragansett Bay entirely intact in case he should encounter an equal or superior force on the way. Engaging Cornwallis closely might have caused him damage that he could ill-afford to incur. He did, after all, have 6,000 troops with him. As far as Cornwallis is concerned, he had done well in preserving his force against superior numbers and, as it happened, would do so again in the next war, much to his credit.

GREGORY FREMONT-BARNES

See also
British West Indies; French West Indies; Royal Navy; Ternay, Charles Henri Louis; Toussaint, Jean-Guillaume, Comte de La Motte-Picquet de La Vinoyère; West Indies

References
Clowes, William Laird. *The Royal Navy: A History from the Earliest Times to 1900*. Vol. 3 of 7. London: Chatham, 1996.
Gardiner, Robert, ed. *Navies and the American Revolution, 1775–1783*. London: Chatham, 1996.
Ireland, Bernard. *Naval Warfare in the Age of Sail*. London: Collins, 2000.
James, William. *The British Navy in Adversity: A Study of the War of American Independence*. 1926. Reprint, New York: Russell and Russell, 1970.
———. *The Naval History of Great Britain: During the French Revolutionary and Napoleonic Wars*. 4 vols. Mechanicsburg, PA: Stackpole, 2003.
Tilley, J. A. *The Royal Navy in the American Revolution*. Columbia: University of South Carolina Press, 1987.

Montesquieu, Baron de

See Secondat, Charles-Louis de, Baron de Montesquieu

Montgomery, Richard (1738–1775)

Richard Montgomery, a Continental soldier, was killed early in the Revolutionary War while heroically leading American troops in an assault on Quebec on 31 December 1775.

Born to privilege, Montgomery was the son of Thomas Montgomery, an Anglo-Irish soldier, baronet, and member of the Irish Parliament. During the Seven Years' War, Montgomery's father and elder brother Alexander encouraged him to join the British Army, and on 21 September 1756 he was commissioned an ensign in the 17th Regiment. In 1757, his regiment was sent to Halifax, Nova Scotia, and a year later was in the British expedition to capture Louisbourg, on Cape Breton Island. During this operation he was promoted to lieutenant. In 1759 he served under Sir Jeffrey Amherst in successful

Richard Montgomery was one of the first generals in the Continental Army to be killed in battle, at the attack on Quebec City in 1775. (National Archives and Records Administration)

operations against Forts Ticonderoga and Crown Point. Montgomery was appointed regimental adjutant by Colonel William Haviland in 1760 and took part in the capture of Montreal during the summer.

In 1761, Montgomery went with his regiment to the West Indies and the following year served under Major-General Robert Monckton in a successful expedition to capture the French island of Martinique. On 6 May 1762, Montgomery was promoted to captain of the 17th Regiment, and in the summer he took part in the operations of General George Keppel, Earl of Albemarle, during the siege and capture of Havana, Cuba. Returning to New York, Montgomery was stationed there with his regiment until 1765 and then ordered to England. There, over the next seven years, he became more and more discouraged with Britain's policies toward the American colonies and his own lack of promotion in the British Army. He became friends with several pro-American members of Parliament, such as Isaac Barré, Edmund Burke, and Charles James Fox, and openly opposed ministerial measures directed at taxing Americans without their representation in the House of Commons. In 1771, Montgomery avidly sought an opportunity to purchase an available commission as major, but it finally went to a political favorite of Prime Minister Lord North.

Lacking the political patronage to advance in the military profession, Montgomery sold his captain's commission on 6 April 1772 and began to cultivate a passion for farming. At that time, he wrote that he could cut no figure among British peers and therefore was casting his eye toward America, where his pride and poverty would be more at ease. Fairly well off despite his complaints about money, he removed to New York in late 1772 or early 1773 and purchased a farm of sixty-seven acres at Kingsbridge, 13 miles north of New York City. There he settled happily into the life of an American farmer and began to pay attention to Janet Livingston, whom he had met eight years earlier. She was the daughter of Robert Livingston, judge of the King's Bench, influential landowner, and head of one of New York's most prominent families. After a quick courtship, they were married on 24 July 1773. Montgomery leased his farm, and the couple settled at her home near Rhinebeck, New York, where he constructed a mill and began work on a house to be named Grassmere.

Montgomery's sylvan idyll was rudely interrupted in 1774 by the growing political tensions between America and Britain. He quickly joined his new neighbors in resisting Britain's Coercive Acts and was accepted because of honest and long-standing Whiggish political views. On 16 May 1775, he was elected a representative of Dutchess County to the New York Provincial Congress, even though he had not sought the position. Recognized for his military abilities because of his prior service in the British Army, he was commissioned by Congress a brigadier general in the Continental Army on 22 June. He was ranked second among eight brigadier generals appointed at that time. Although unhappy to be dragged away from his new wife, he reluctantly bowed to the will of an "oppressed people," as he called the Americans. On 26 June, General George Washington appointed him second in command in New York, under Major General Philip Schuyler. After Montgomery and Schuyler were ordered by Congress on 29 June to invade Canada, they established their headquarters at Fort Ticonderoga and began organizing an army for that purpose. Montgomery was dismayed at the general disarray of the troops with which he had to work, calling the New Yorkers "the sweepings of the city streets" and the New Englanders "almost hopeless as soldiers." He swore that he would never again hazard his reputation at the head of such ragamuffins.

Nevertheless, Montgomery and Schuyler managed during July and August 1775 to organize these diverse American citizens, about 500 men, into a semblance of an army. In late August, they advanced from Fort Ticonderoga down Lake Champlain, occupied Île-aux-Noix, and commenced siege operations against St. John's and Chambly. On 16 September, Schuyler's health failed him, and he gave over command of the invasion army to his young subordinate. Suddenly, Montgomery's spirits improved. Writing to his wife, he declared that he had courted fortune and found her kind, and he admonished her not to send him any negative letters that might erode his morale. Despite the seemingly parlous condition of his army, he led by personal example, admonishing his soldiers to accept sacrifice in the American cause. Finally, on 19 October, he captured St. John's and Chambly, and on 11 November the greater prize of Montreal fell into his hands. He then advanced down the St. Lawrence River to Quebec, and on 2 December he joined forces with General Benedict Arnold, who had led an army through Maine to reach the same destination.

Montgomery assumed overall command of American forces in Canada, 900 soldiers in all, and besieged Quebec while working out a plan to capture it. For three weeks, he and Arnold meditated on a scheme of assault, while 2,000 British troops under General Guy Carleton waited within the walls of Quebec for their attempt. With American enlistments about to expire at year's end, Montgomery and Arnold decided that they would attempt a daring direct assault on the well-defended city on 31 December. Discounting Carleton's military abilities, they hoped that the very audacity of the enterprise would mobilize citizens of Quebec to compel Carleton to capitulate. In a two-pronged assault begun at 4:00 A.M. on 31 December, Montgomery and Arnold drove toward the city's walls in a blinding snowstorm. Montgomery led a charge against the lower town, while Arnold attacked the upper town.

As Montgomery pushed forward, urging his men to follow him, he suddenly confronted an enemy gun emplacement that blasted the charging Americans with canister and grapeshot. Montgomery was killed instantly, and the attackers, thrown into confusion, retreated without recovering their commander's body. Arnold's attack also failed after he was wounded in the leg and Captain Daniel Morgan was captured. In the spring of 1776, the American army retreated from Canada. Montgomery died without knowing that Congress had promoted him to major general on 9 December. The day after the battle, the British recovered his frozen corpse and buried it within the walls of Quebec with full military honors. Carleton and other British officers who had served with Montgomery in the British Army remembered his fine personal and martial qualities. On 25 January 1776, Congress honored the memory of the first American general killed in the Revolutionary War by ordering the erection of a marble memorial in the yard of St. Paul's Episcopal Church, New York. In 1818, Montgomery's remains were reinterred under the monument. An inscription on a rock at Cape Diamond, Quebec, marks the place where Montgomery fell.

PAUL DAVID NELSON

See also

Arnold, Benedict; Burke, Edmund; Canada, Operations in; Carleton, Guy; Chambly, Quebec, Action at; Coercive Acts; Fort Ticonderoga, New York; Fox, Charles James; Morgan, Daniel; North, Lord Frederick; Quebec, Siege of; Schuyler, Philip; St. John's, Actions against

References

Allen, Charles W. *Memoir of General Montgomery*. Philadelphia: n.p., 1912.

Armstrong, John. *Life of Richard Montgomery*, Vol. 1, *Library of American Biography*. Edited by Jared Sparks. Boston: Hilliard, Gray, 1834.

Cullum, George W. "Major-General Richard Montgomery." *Magazine of American History* 11 (1884): 273–299.

Hunt, Louise L. "General Richard Montgomery." *Harper's New Monthly Magazine* 70 (1885): 350–359.

O'Reilly, Vincent F. "Major-General Richard Montgomery." *American-Irish Historical Society Journal* 25 (1926): 179–194.

Robinson, Thomas P. "Some Notes on Major-General Richard Montgomery." *New York History* 37 (1956): 388–398.

Shelton, Hal T. *General Richard Montgomery and the American Revolution: From Redcoat to Rebel*. New York: New York University Press, 1994.

Smith, Justin H. *Our Struggle for the Fourteenth Colony: Canada and the American Revolution*. 2 vols. 1907. Reprint, New York: Da Capo, 1974.

Montreal, Operations against

Montreal, in the province of Quebec, was attacked by American forces on 24–25 September 1775 and then finally captured by them on 13 November. It was occupied until 14 June 1776.   (September–November 1775)

Montreal was founded in 1642, on the site of a native village named Hochelaga, and took its name from the 900-foot extinct volcano that provided views of the surrounding countryside as far as the hills at Chambly and the Green Mountains east of Lake Champlain. The main island measured about 30 by 12 miles, with two inlets of the St. Lawrence forming a smaller island 3 miles long and 2.5 miles wide (the Isle de Jesus). Almost 200 miles from Quebec—three weeks' march in winter, given the poor roads, extreme weather,

View of Montreal, Canada, circa 1774. A column under Ethan Allen, holding a defensive position outside the city, was scattered by an Anglo-Canadian force in September 1775, but when British General Guy Carleton withdrew in November and proceeded toward Quebec, the city surrendered to Richard Montgomery without resistance. (Library of Congress)

and limited daylight—Montreal became the second city of New France (Canada) as the fur trade expanded westward, and by 1775 it was about the same size as Quebec, with around 5,000 inhabitants. A series of fires had led to a major redesign of the city, with wide streets and stone buildings. Wooden structures were confined to the outskirts, apart from the grandiosely named Citadel—in reality a log house whose poor condition reflected the state of the other defenses. These comprised a stone wall and dry ditch, dating from 1736 and designed to repel Indian attacks, not European-style sieges. In addition, several nearby hills offered commanding views of the city to enemy artillery.

In September 1775, the Separate Army under Richard Montgomery entered Canada and attacked St. John's. Patrols were dispatched to warn of any relief attempts from Montreal, with John Brown occupying Laprairie and Ethan Allen going to Longueuil. Allen was accompanied by two Americans who had immigrated to Canada, James Livingston and Jeremiah Duggan, who were to recruit Canadians to the American cause. Initially, few habitants joined the Patriots, while local seigneurs and Catholic clergy opposed them. However, the British commander in Canada, Guy Carleton, chose to remain in Montreal, which although correct militarily, discouraged many Canadians from openly supporting the Crown.

American forces near Montreal, November 1775. General Richard Montgomery's troops occupied the city after General Guy Carleton evacuated the place in favor of a more defensible position at Quebec. (Charles McBarron, Army Art Collection, NMUSA)

On 24 September, Allen and Brown met at Laprairie and hatched a plan to capture Montreal. Brown, with 200 troops, would land south of the city; Allen, with 30 of Brown's men and 80 newly recruited Canadians, would attack from the north. Allen ferried his men over during the night of 25 September and by dawn was awaiting Brown's signal. When no signal came (Brown was actually still at Laprairie), Allen sent men into Montreal to contact Thomas Walker, another American who had settled in Canada. Walker tried to persuade other citizens to help him unlock the gates, but a local man had spotted Allen outside the city and informed Carleton, who suddenly found the inertia of the populace dispelled by this more immediate threat. A few families fled to the docks, but 120 French and 80 English volunteers armed themselves and reported for duty, along with 34 men of the 26th Foot, 6 Indians, and 20 Indian Department officers. One Indian Department officer, Major John Campbell, took command and led the contingent out of the city. As the force emerged, Allen's men sought cover in nearby buildings and orchards. Campbell placed the 26th Foot in the center of his line and ordered the volunteers to attack Allen's flanks. At this, Duggan's recruits, guarding the right flank, fled in panic, as did Allen's left wing, leaving him on his own. Allen and 36 of his men were captured; 5 others were killed, and 10 others were wounded. Campbell lost 3 dead and 2 wounded.

The victory saw militia flood into Montreal, until Carleton had 2,000 men. Unfortunately, with no firm intelligence, Carleton could not risk being ambushed and was restricted to improving internal security (issuing a warrant for Walker's arrest) and raids on Longueuil and Boucherville. After four weeks, the militia began drifting away for the harvest and to protect their homes from marauding collaborators, but the arrival of Allan MacLean and 400 reinforcements at Sorel allowed him to be more aggressive. Unfortunately, an attempt to relieve St. John's on 30 and 31 October was thwarted, despite some successes, and Carleton withdrew to Montreal. There, he learned of the fall of St. John's on 4 November, along with news that more Americans were heading for Canada through Maine and that the Royal Navy had refused to transport reinforcements from Boston. Knowing that Montgomery would head for Montreal before winter set in, Carleton embarked the garrison and what stores he could save, destroying the remainder (though he refused to burn the barracks because of the risk to private property).

After sending a detachment to Sorel to prevent Carleton from escaping by water, Montgomery arrived opposite Montreal on 11 November. Aware that the defenses were weak and morale low, he guaranteed every citizen "the peaceable enjoyment of their property of every kind." His magnanim-

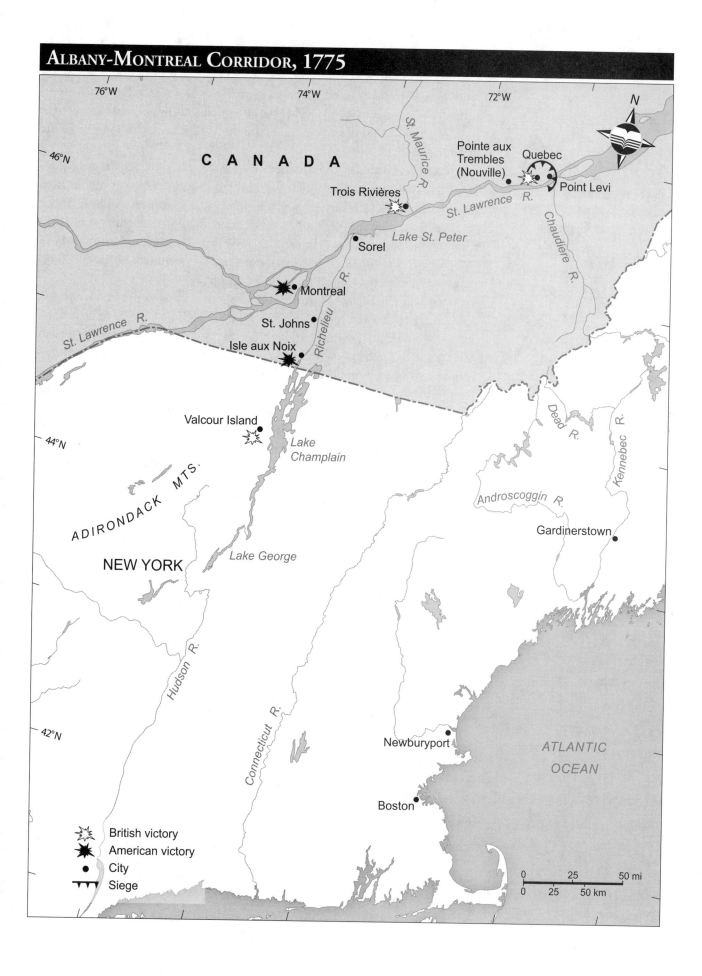

ALBANY-MONTREAL CORRIDOR, 1775

76°W   74°W   72°W

N

46°N

C A N A D A

St. Maurice R.

Pointe aux
Trembles
(Nouville)   Quebec

Point Levi

Trois Rivières

St. Lawrence R.

Chaudiere R.

Lake St. Peter

Sorel

Montreal

Richelieu R.

St. Johns

St. Lawrence R.

Isle aux Noix

Dead R.

Kennebec R.

Valcour Island

44°N

Lake
Champlain

ADIRONDACK MTS.

Androscoggin R.

NEW YORK

Lake George

Gardinerstown

Hudson R.

Connecticut R.

42°N

Newburyport

ATLANTIC
OCEAN

Boston

British victory
American victory
City
Siege

0   25   50 mi
0   25   50 km

ity worked, and on 13 November his troops entered Montreal, occupying the barracks and public storehouses. Unfortunately, the pro-American lobby was less gracious and wanted revenge against the Loyalists. This and Montgomery's decision to leave David Wooster and his ill-disciplined Connecticut contingent to guard the city destroyed all hope of winning the support of the citizens.

Carleton had sailed for Quebec on 11 November but was becalmed for four days, and on 15 November he received a summons to surrender from the American detachment at Sorel. Employing an outrageous bluff, Brown managed to convince the flotilla to surrender, along with 30 guns, more than 300 combatants, and, most valuable of all, 200 pairs of shoes. Also aboard was Walker, who returned to help Wooster "pacify" Montreal. Carleton, however, had escaped to Quebec, disguised as a peasant.

Wooster closed the churches on Christmas Eve, took Loyalists hostage, published lists of "suspects" to be deported to Philadelphia, forbade merchants from dealing with the Indians to deny intelligence to the British posts on the Great Lakes, made the militia swear allegiance to Congress, and introduced new taxes (ironically, given the origins of the war itself, without the consent of the people). Shortage of cash was a particular strain on relations, the invaders rapidly running up more than $35,000 of debts that, in turn, forced the military to confiscate military materials and forcibly enlist local citizens to perform necessary work. When Wooster left for Quebec in January 1776, the city was on the verge of revolt, and while his successors—Moses Hazen and then Benedict Arnold—were more tolerant, matters improved little under them. On 29 April, the three-man commission (Benjamin Franklin, Samuel Chase, and Charles Carroll) appointed by Congress to rebuild relations with the Canadians arrived at Montreal. Despite releasing all political prisoners, it proved impossible to redress Wooster's blunders, and the commission left, blaming Wooster for the disaster and demanding his recall. The defeats at The Cedars and Trois-Rivières made the city vulnerable, and the Americans finally abandoned Montreal in June 1776.

BRENDAN D. MORRISSEY

See also

Allen, Ethan; Arnold, Benedict; Brown, John; Campbell, John; Canada, Operations in; Carleton, Guy; Chambly, Quebec, Action at; Hazen, Moses; MacLean, Allan; Montgomery, Richard; St. John's, Actions against; Trois-Rivières, Action at

References

Hatch, Robert. *Thrust for Canada: The American Attempt on Quebec, 1775–1776*. Boston: Houghton Mifflin, 1979.

Lanctot, Gustave. *Canada and the American Revolution, 1774–1783*. London: Harrap, 1967.

Morrissey, Brendan. *Quebec 1775: The American Invasion of Canada*. Oxford, UK: Osprey, 2004.

Stanley, George. *Canada Invaded, 1775–1776*. Toronto: Canadian War Museum, 1973.

At Moore's Creek Bridge, 20 miles northwest of Wilmington, North Carolina, American Patriots clashed with a larger force of Loyalists that was marching to rendezvous with an anticipated British expeditionary force on the Carolina coast. The small, brief, violent battle, which resulted in a rout of the Loyalist force, was far-reaching in its importance. It marked the end of royal authority in North Carolina and helped thwart a British invasion of the South. It also encouraged the colony's Revolutionary government, on 12 April 1776, to instruct its delegates to the Continental Congress to vote for independence. North Carolina was the first colony to take this momentous step.

As America drifted toward open rebellion against Britain in the mid-1770s, North Carolina's people were divided in their loyalties. The legislature, representing the Patriots, about half the population, was in open conflict with the royal governor, Josiah Martin. In April 1775, Martin informed Lord Dartmouth, secretary of state for the colonies, that his government was powerless to control events. Yet the Loyalists, those who abhorred the idea of taking up arms against the mother country, represented a substantial part of the population. The Loyalists included many Highland Scots, who had immigrated to North Carolina in substantial numbers, and a number of Regulators, who had been defeated in the Battle of Alamance in 1771.

In late May 1775, Carolinians received news of the fighting at Lexington and Concord the month before, and Martin's authority eroded even more. On 31 May, he abandoned the governor's palace in New Bern, fled to Fort Johnson on the lower Cape Fear River, and sent his family to New York. Learning on 15 July that Patriot militiamen were approaching the fort, he sought sanctuary on the British warship *Cruizer*. Three days later he watched in anger and frustration as the rebels burned the fort. Despite these setbacks, he remained convinced that North Carolina was essentially a loyal colony. In a letter to Dartmouth, he proposed to raise an army of 10,000 men, consisting mostly of Highlanders and Regulators, that would march to Brunswick and rendezvous with a British expeditionary force sent to aid them. Dartmouth approved the plan, as did his successor, Lord George Germain. As they envisioned the operation, seven regiments, under the command of General Lord Charles Cornwallis, would depart Ireland for Cape Fear on 1 December 1775 in a powerful fleet commanded by Admiral Sir Peter Parker. At Cape Fear, they would be reinforced by troops from New York under General Sir Henry Clinton. Joining the awaiting Loyalists, they would eliminate Patriot opposition in the Carolinas and Georgia and return these provinces to British rule.

Martin received news that his plan had been approved on 3 January 1776. A week later he issued a proclamation calling for the Loyalists to rendezvous, march to Brunswick by 15 February, and meet the incoming British expedition. Six months earlier, General Thomas Gage, commander in chief of British forces in America, had dispatched Donald MacDonald and Donald McLeod to North Carolina to organize a Highlander battalion. Martin appointed MacDonald brigadier-general and McLeod lieutenant-colonel of Loyalist militia

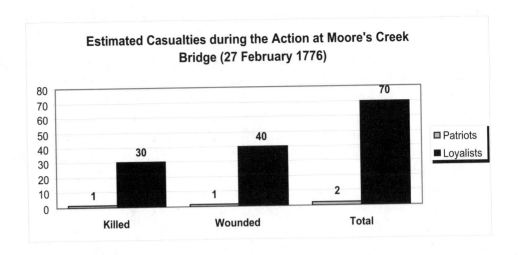

Estimated Casualties during the Action at Moore's Creek Bridge (27 February 1776)

and ordered them and others, such as Alexander and Allan McLean, to raise the royal standard. On 5 February, MacDonald and the other Highlander leaders met at Cross Creek and issued a call for an immediate mobilization. Ten days later, the officers organized about 1,600 Highlanders, Regulators, and Loyalists into an army, and on 20 February they commenced their march down the Cape Fear River to Brunswick.

The Patriot leaders were aware of all this Loyalist activity, but they were hampered by the fact that Colonel Robert Howe's North Carolina Continental regiment was at Norfolk, Virginia. Nevertheless, Colonel James Moore, commander of the 1st North Carolina Continentals, some 650 strong, with five cannon, marched from Wilmington toward Cross Creek. On 15 February, he encamped about 12 miles to the south at Rockfish Creek in a position to block the Loyalists' march toward the coast. There, he was reinforced by 450 militiamen under Colonels Alexander Lillington, James Kenan, and James Ashe. Meanwhile, Patriots at Wilmington constructed defensive breastworks, and militiamen at New Bern mustered under Colonel Richard Caswell then took post at Corbett's Ferry on the Black River. The Loyalist plan was to advance along the south side of Cape Fear, but when MacDonald found his path blocked by Moore's men, he marched eastward toward Caswell's troops, then southward on Negro Head Point Road toward Wilmington.

In response, Moore ordered Caswell to withdraw toward Moore's Creek Bridge, 20 miles northwest of Wilmington, a strategic bottleneck that MacDonald's forces had to cross to reach the coast. Moore also fell back, determined to attack the Loyalists in the rear while Caswell engaged them in front, and detached Lillington's militiamen to join Caswell. Lillington was first to arrive at the bridge, on 25 February, with 150 men. He immediately began constructing a low earthwork on a rise dominating the bridge on the west bank of the stream. Caswell arrived the following day with 850 men, crossed the bridge, and constructed earthworks on the other bank. MacDonald's Loyalists, less than half of them armed, camped only 6 miles away on the night of 26 February. The elderly MacDonald, worn out and ill because of the hard campaigning, had given temporary command to McLeod. The Loyalists now had to decide whether to bypass their enemies once more or fight their way through to Brunswick. The younger officers, wanting to attack, carried the debate, arguing that Caswell's defensive works on their side of the stream would be unsupported by Lillington and thus easily annihilated.

At 1:00 A.M. on 27 February, the Loyalists marched toward Moore's Creek Bridge. Captain John Campbell led the advance guard of 75 handpicked Scots, armed only with broadswords, followed by the main body of troops, with 300 riflemen bringing up the rear. As they approached the American position, they played bagpipes, thus alerting their enemies that they were coming. Unknown to the Loyalists, Caswell had abandoned his position during the night and withdrawn across the creek. His militiamen then had removed half the flooring of the bridge, greased the girders with soap and tallow to make a crossing more treacherous, and placed two artillery pieces to cover the Loyalists' advance. An hour before dawn, McLeod reached Caswell's abandoned lines, organized his men for an attack, and awaited daybreak.

Unable to bear the suspense, McLeod gave the signal to charge, and his advance guard sprinted toward the bridge, shouting "King George and broadswords!" Scrabbling over the exposed and slippery girders, the Loyalists approached the American lines, only to be met with a devastating hail of fire from muskets and cannon. In a matter of minutes, McLeod, Campbell, and several of their men were dead, cut down within a few paces of their objective. Others were killed or wounded while crossing the bridge; a few lost their footing, fell into the deep stream, and drowned. Quickly counter-attacking, the Patriots rushed forward, repaired the bridge, and soon had thrown the Loyalist survivors into headlong retreat. Thirty Loyalists were dead and 40 wounded, while only 1 Patriot was dead and 1 wounded. On 28 February, MacDonald, some other officers, and 850 soldiers were captured, along with £15,000 sterling, 350 muskets, 150 swords and dirks, and 13 wagons. The officers, including MacDonald, were imprisoned or banished from North Carolina, while the soldiers were paroled to their homes.

Martin tried to portray the debacle at Moore's Creek Bridge as only a minor setback of little importance to his grand scheme. But Clinton, commander of the impending British expedition to the American South, knew better. He did not arrive at Cape Fear until 12 March. There, instead of finding Martin's army of 10,000 Loyalists awaiting him, he found the mobilized Patriot militia of the province. MacDonald's movement long before Clinton appeared on the coast to assist him was a most rash and ill-timed maneuver. As for Parker's fleet, which was convoying Cornwallis's troops from Ireland, it was delayed by storms and did not begin to arrive until 18 April. Not until 3 May did the entire fleet, minus a few smaller vessels, finally assemble there. Although Clinton and Parker conducted a reconnaissance in force, burnt some Patriot property, and issued proclamations, they could do nothing more in North Carolina. Instead, they turned their attention to Charleston, South Carolina. Sailing away on 31 May, the British commanders left the province in the firm control of emboldened Patriots, who had already taken the first steps toward American independence. In little more than a month, on 4 July, their dreams would be realized at Philadelphia.

PAUL DAVID NELSON

See also

Cornwallis, Charles; Fort Johnson, South Carolina, Capture of; Gage, Thomas; Germain, Lord George; Howe, Robert; MacLean, Allan; Martin, Josiah; North Carolina; Southern Campaigns

References

DeMond, Robert O. *The Loyalists in North Carolina during the Revolution.* Durham, NC: Duke University Press, 1940.

Hatch, Charles E. *Moore's Creek National Military Park, North Carolina: The Battle of Moore's Creek Bridge.* Washington, DC: Office of History and Historic Architecture, Eastern Service Center, 1969.

Meyer, Duane Gilbert. *The Highland Scots of North Carolina, 1732–1776.* Chapel Hill: University of North Carolina Press, 1961.

Morrill, Dan L. *Southern Campaigns of the American Revolution.* Baltimore, MD: Nautical and Aviation Publishing Company of America, 1993.

Rankin, Hugh F. "The Moore's Creek Bridge Campaign, 1776." *North Carolina Historical Review* 30 (1953): 23–60.

———. *The Moore's Creek Bridge Campaign, 1776.* Conshohocken, PA: Eastern National Park and Monument Association, 1986.

Saunders, William L., ed. *The Colonial Records of North Carolina*, Vol. 10. Raleigh, NC: P. M. Hale, 1890.

Stumpf, Vernon O. *Josiah Martin: The Last Royal Governor of North Carolina.* Durham, NC: Carolina Academic Press, 1986.

Morgan, Daniel
(1735?–1802)

Daniel Morgan, a rough-hewn frontiersman from the valley of Virginia, was a Continental Army officer who saw service in many campaigns during the American Revolution. He achieved renown for his defeat of the famous British cavalryman, Colonel Banastre Tarleton, in the Battle of Cowpens in South Carolina on 9 March 1781.

Estranged from his father at age eighteen, Morgan worked as a farm laborer and became a teamster. He was a stout, active man, once described as perfectly fitted to the toils and pomp of martial life. In 1755, he drove a supply wagon during the campaign of General Edward Braddock against Fort Duquesne but was not involved in the disastrous ambush on 9 July. Morgan knocked down a British soldier who slapped him with a sword and was flogged with 500 lashes on his back. Although he forgave the contrite flogger, his public, painful, and brutal humiliation at the hands of British military authorities was probably remembered twenty years later when he joined the rebellion against Britain. Moreover, when he later commanded troops, he refused to punish soldiers with public whippings. In 1756, he served with a ranger company near Winchester, Virginia, and was seriously wounded when an Indian shot him in the neck and jaw. Two years later Morgan was appointed ensign in the Virginia militia, and in 1763, during Pontiac's War, he was promoted to lieutenant.

In the mid-1760s, Morgan settled into farming near Winchester while continuing to drive wagons for a living. He lived in a common-law relationship with Abigail Curry for ten years, then married her in 1773. They had three children. He served locally as a public surveyor, road supervisor, and deputy sheriff and managed to purchase ten slaves. In 1771, he was appointed captain of the Frederick County militia. Three years later, during Lord Dunmore's War, he and his militia unit accompanied Major Angus McDonald in a campaign against Shawnee Indians near Wheeling, Virginia. At the outbreak of the War for American Independence in 1775, Morgan immediately answered the call of Congress to lead Continental troops. On 22 June, he was commissioned captain of one of two companies of riflemen to be raised in Virginia. Within weeks he and his company joined General George Washington's Continental Army at the siege of Boston. Immediately, the Virginians began using their prodigious skill in sharpshooting to snipe at British sentries and stragglers.

In the fall of 1775, Morgan volunteered to join General Benedict Arnold's expedition against Quebec through the Maine wilderness. Given command of three rifle companies, Morgan led the advance of the Americans up the Kennebec River, finally reaching the St. Lawrence River in November. He was with Arnold's column during the American assault against Quebec on the evening of 31 December, taking command when Arnold was wounded. At first successful in the attack, Morgan was not adequately supported by his fellow soldiers and was compelled to surrender to his British foes. He was held as a prisoner of war in relatively pleasant conditions at Quebec until paroled on 11 August 1776. Taken by ship to New Jersey, he was released in September and returned home to await an exchange. On 12 November, Congress promoted him to colonel of a new regiment, the 11th Virginia Continentals, even though he was not exchanged until January 1777.

Morgan joined Washington's Continental Army at Morristown, New Jersey, in April 1777. He was given command of an elite corps of 500 riflemen that Washington had selected from the army for special duties. This body of sharpshooters, which Washington called the Corps of Rangers, was particularly effective in sniping and dispersed firefights, being capable of harassing enemy troops from concealment at a distance. Morgan effectively employed these troops in early summer 1777 in skirmishes against the British in New Jersey. In August he was ordered northward to assist Major General Horatio Gates in opposing Lieutenant-General John Burgoyne's invasion of upstate New York. Reinforced by the addition of 300 troops under the command of Major Henry Dearborn, Morgan joined Gates's army at Bemis Heights. There Morgan employed his men in reconnoitering British positions, sniping at

Daniel Morgan was the American Revolution's most adept practitioner of tactics involving the use of rifle-armed troops. His leadership and skill played an important part in American success during the Saratoga Campaign of 1777. His subsequent victory at Cowpens, a tactical masterpiece, signaled the decline of British fortunes in the South. (National Archives and Records Administration)

exposed soldiers, and harassing detachments. He won Gates's praise for eliminating Burgoyne's sources of intelligence and thus forcing the enemy to operate blindly.

In the Battle of Freeman's Farm on 19 September, Morgan and his riflemen were in the thick of the fight, picking off British artillerymen and officers. After this battle, Washington, hard-pressed in Pennsylvania by General Sir William Howe's army, requested that Gates return Morgan's corps to him. But when Gates pleaded to retain the riflemen, the commander in chief relented and allowed them to remain with the Northern Army. On 7 October, in the Battle of Bemis Heights, Morgan's corps was again closely engaged with the enemy. During this fight, Morgan instructed one of his riflemen, Timothy Murphy, to shoot Brigadier-General Simon Fraser, a brave and prominent leader of British troops. With the mortally wounded Fraser removed from the battle, the British attack faltered and was soon called off. After Burgoyne surrendered at Saratoga on 17 October, he highly praised Morgan and his forest-wise riflemen for their effectiveness in dispersed woods-fighting. Gates, to whom Burgoyne surrendered, also heaped praise upon Morgan, glowingly recommending him to Congress. Morgan now rejoined Washington's army at Whitemarsh and on 4 December 1777 got into a short but sharp firefight with Major-General Charles Grey's British troops. After wintering at Valley Forge, Morgan and his riflemen arrived too late at Monmouth, on 28 June 1778, to take part in the battle. They did, however, harass and pursue the enemy afterward.

For the remainder of 1778, Morgan's corps was often called upon by Washington to perform various services. Meanwhile, Morgan constantly advocated the importance of coordinating the guerrilla activities of partisans and militia with his own command. In 1779, a year of frustration for him, his rifle regiment was disbanded, and he was appointed colonel of the 7th Regiment. Ill at ease with this less prestigious responsibility, restless and sensitive, suffering from sciatica, and disgruntled with Congress for lack of promotion, he avidly sought command of a new light infantry corps being formed by Washington. When Anthony Wayne was given the position on 21 June, Morgan was deeply chagrined that Washington had not supported his candidacy for the office. Morgan therefore took an honorable furlough from the army on 19 July 1779 and retired to Virginia, where he spent the next few months erecting a new home, Saratoga.

In June 1780, Morgan learned that Congress had appointed Gates commander of the Southern Department and that Gates wanted Morgan to serve under him. Morgan was delighted at this opportunity because Gates recognized his abilities and trusted him. Also, Gates was recommending to Congress Morgan's promotion to brigadier general. However, Morgan suffered a debilitating attack of sciatica and was unable to join Gates at Hillsborough, North Carolina, until mid-September. By that time, Gates had been severely trounced by General Lord Charles Cornwallis in the Battle of Camden. On 2 October, Morgan was given command of an elite light infantry corps that Gates had organized and eleven days later was finally promoted to brigadier general by Congress. Throughout the fall of 1780, Morgan labored without much success to make his light corps the equal of its British counterpart, Tarleton's Tory Legion. Morgan also writhed in enforced inactivity, longing for a chance to test his mettle against the hated "bloody Tarleton," who supposedly had allowed the slaughter of American troops trying to surrender at the Battle of Waxhaws in early December.

Morgan's chance came in December 1780, when Major General Nathanael Greene replaced Gates at Charlotte as commander in the South. Immediately, Greene confirmed Morgan as commander of the elite corps and in mid-December gave him an independent command. Greene ordered Morgan to move southwest into upper South Carolina, collect militia, and oppose Cornwallis's advance northward. On 6 January 1781, Tarleton marched toward Morgan's position at the head of 1,100 men. Morgan, in command of about 1,000 troops, retreated northward until he reached a position called Cowpens, with the Broad River at his back. There he decided to stand and fight. On 17 January, he arranged his troops in three lines on a gently sloping hill, with dragoons and mounted infantry in reserve. He placed his militia forces in the first two lines and his Continental regulars in the third position.

Ordering the militiamen to fire two shots, then retire behind the Continentals, Morgan expected the regulars to bear the brunt of Tarleton's assault. When Tarleton's men charged forward, as Morgan had expected they would, the militia held only a short time, then fell back and regrouped. Morgan then ordered the Continentals to fire point-blank at the advancing redcoats and mount a bayonet charge, while his mounted troops and the regrouped militia lashed Tarleton's flanks in a brilliantly executed double envelopment. The enemy was routed. Although Tarleton escaped, his casualties were about 110 killed, 200 wounded, and another 527 captured. Morgan lost 12 men killed and 60 wounded. For his triumph, one of the decisive victories of the war, he was thanked by Congress and given a gold medal. After the battle, he retreated northward, guarding the rear of Greene's main army as it retired across the Dan River to escape pursuit by Cornwallis. In February, debilitated by sciatica and rheumatism, Morgan went home on leave. Although he assisted the Marquis de Lafayette's army the following summer in defending Virginia, even joining the army for a short time in July, his physical ailments precluded further military activity.

After the war, Morgan applied himself to building his personal fortune, and by 1796 he owned more than 250,000 acres of land. Living comfortably at his new home, Saratoga, he was a well-respected citizen and a devout Presbyterian. He entertained visitors, corresponded with old comrades, and financially assisted former soldiers from time to time. In politics an ardent Federalist and devoted supporter of President Washington, Morgan sincerely believed that the Jeffersonian Republicans were bent on destroying America's constitutional system. In 1793, he was appointed major general of Virginia militia. A year later, during the Whiskey Rebellion, he led light infantry troops in General Henry Lee's federal army that marched against opponents of the excise tax in western Pennsylvania. After the whiskey rebels capitulated without a fight, Morgan was put in charge of the rebellious counties, at the head of 1,500 troops. In May 1795, his little army was disbanded. He ran for the House of Representatives in 1795 but was defeated. Two years later, he won a seat. Serving one term in office, he supported Federalist measures and railed against the Jeffersonians. On one occasion he even threatened to mobilize the militia against his political enemies in Virginia. Living his last years in Winchester, he became incapacitated six months before his death in 1802 as a result of sciatica and rheumatism.

PAUL DAVID NELSON

See also
Arnold, Benedict; Boston, Siege of; Burgoyne, John; Camden Campaign; Canada, Operations in; Cowpens, Battle of; Fraser, Simon; Gates, Horatio; Grey, Charles; Howe, William; Greene, Nathanael; Lafayette, Marquis de; Lee, Henry; Monmouth, Battle of; Morristown, New Jersey, Continental Army Winter Quarters; Quebec, Siege of; Saratoga Campaign; Tarleton, Banastre; Wayne, Anthony; Whitemarsh, Pennsylvania, Action at

References
Callahan, North. *Daniel Morgan: Ranger of the Revolution.* New York: Holt, Rinehart and Winston, 1961.
Conrad, Dennis, et al., eds. *The Papers of General Nathanael Greene.* 13 vols. Chapel Hill: University of North Carolina Press, 1976–2005.
Edwards, William W. "Morgan and His Riflemen." *William and Mary Quarterly* 23 (1914): 73–106.
Graham, James. *The Life of General Daniel Morgan.* 1856. Reprint, Bloomingburg, NY: Zebroski Historical Services, 1993.
Higginbotham, Don. "Daniel Morgan: Guerilla Fighter." Pp. 291–316 in *George Washington's Generals and Opponents: Their Exploits and Leadership.* Edited by George Athan Billias. 1964. Reprint, New York: Da Capo, 1994.
———. *Daniel Morgan: Revolutionary Rifleman.* Chapel Hill: University of North Carolina Press, 1961.
Nelson, Paul David. *General Horatio Gates: A Biography.* Baton Rouge: Louisiana State University Press, 1976.
Nickerson, Hoffman. *The Turning Point of the Revolution, or Burgoyne in America.* Boston: Houghton Mifflin, 1928.
Pancake, John S. *1777: The Year of the Hangman.* University: University of Alabama Press, 1977.

Morgan, John
(1735–1789)

An early leader in American medical education, John Morgan was cofounder of America's first medical school, a surgeon during the French and Indian War, and surgeon general of the Continental Army during the early years of the Revolutionary War.

Morgan was born in Philadelphia in 1735. One of nine children, he was the son of Evan Morgan, a prominent Philadelphia merchant of Welsh descent, and Joanne Biles Morgan. His interest in medicine began when he first served as a hospital pharmacist (1755–1756) in Philadelphia. He is credited with being a pioneer in the development of professional pharmacy in North America. An exacting yet open-minded teacher of medicine, Morgan received his medical training at the University of Edinburgh. He studied under the famous Scottish professor Dr. William Cullen. Morgan received his medical degree in 1763 but was largely prepared for his profession while serving as a colonial army doctor from 1757 to 1760 during the French and Indian (Seven Years') War. After his military service, Morgan completed his medical studies at Edinburgh and pursued further study at Paris and in Italy. His doctoral thesis, which predated the supportive findings of the nineteenth-century German pathologist Julius Cohnheim, pointed out that pus from the human body is secreted by the blood vessels.

In 1765, upon returning permanently to America, Morgan helped establish the College of Medicine in Philadelphia (now part of the University of Pennsylvania) and was appointed the first professor of medicine in North America. One of his best students was Benjamin Rush (who would also become a surgeon general in the Continental Army). As director of the medical school, Morgan advocated the creation of distinct disciplines in the areas of surgery, medicine, and pharmacology. He outlined his views on the significance of

Dr. John Morgan served as surgeon general of the Continental Army. (National Library of Medicine)

distinct disciplines and a liberal medical education in *Discourse upon the Institution of Medical Schools in America* (1765). His views were met with skepticism, as there was considerable opposition by his colleagues trained in the traditional methodologies.

In the pre-Revolutionary years Morgan supported a conciliatory relationship with Britain, but by the late 1760s and early 1770s his views shifted to the point where he became an outspoken Patriot and defender of the cause of liberty. His political convictions and his eminent position within medical circles led the Continental Congress to appoint him as director general to the military hospitals and physician-in-chief to the American army in 1775. Soon afterward, however, Dr. William Shippen, professor of anatomy and surgery, cofounder of the medical school with Morgan, and an army physician, spoke out against him. Shippen was highly critical of Morgan's organizational and leadership skills. During his early tenure in his new position, Morgan was particularly faulted for failing to bring nonmilitary surgeons under general army regulations. He was most successful in dealing with matters of military hygiene during campaigns, a topic he became interested in during the French and Indian War.

Yet in 1777, Congress dismissed Morgan. He vehemently protested his dismissal and bitterly attacked Shippen. Morgan even refused to resume his post as chair at the medical school, despite the popular enthusiasm for his *A Recommendation of Inoculation* (1777) in which he correctly advocated adopting British physician Edward Jenner's method of vaccination against smallpox.

Two years later, in 1779, General George Washington and Congress exonerated Morgan of any malfeasance. Unfortunately, North America's first professor of medicine, member of the French Academy of Surgery, and Fellow of the Royal Society never fully recovered from his dismissal. A recluse the last ten years of his life, Morgan died in poverty in 1789 in the city in which he was born.

CHARLES F. HOWLETT

See also
Continental Army; Diseases; Rush, Benjamin; Shippen, William

References

Bell, Whitefield J. *John Morgan: Colonial Doctor*. Philadelphia: University of Pennsylvania Press, 1965.
Cormer, George W. *Two Centuries of Medicine: A History of the School of Medicine, University of Pennsylvania*. Philadelphia: University of Pennsylvania Press, 1965.
D'Elia, Donald. *Benjamin Rush: Philosopher of the American Revolution*. Philadelphia: American Philosophical Society, 1974.
Flexner, James T. *Doctors on Horseback: Pioneers of American Medicine*. New York: Dover, 1969.

Morris, Gouverneur
(1752–1816)

Gouverneur Morris served as a skillful and principled statesman during the Revolutionary era in several significant roles. As one of the most ardent Federalists among the key Framers, he worked in the Constitutional Convention to shape a strong executive branch, while as chairman of the Committee on Style he crafted much of the Constitution's final wording. Earlier Morris served in the Continental Congress and as deputy to Superintendent of Finance Robert Morris, helping to put the new nation on a sounder financial footing as it struggled to finance the Revolutionary War. Throughout his public career, Morris's energetic and engaging personality served him well, merging intellect and wit with a self-assured speaking presence and the ability to reason patiently and seek conciliation between opposing viewpoints.

Morris was born on 31 January 1752 at Morrisania, his family's estate north of New York City. His aristocratic lineage included a father who served as a judge and a grandfather who had been a colonial governor of New Jersey. As the third son, Morris would receive a limited inheritance and so prepared for a legal career, after graduating from King's College (now Columbia University), under the tutelage of William Smith Jr., a leading lawyer in New York City. At the opening of hostilities between the colonists and Great Britain, Morris feared social upheaval and initially favored compromise. A fundamental commitment to justice soon led him to embrace the ideals of the American Revolution while remaining skeptical of populist democracy and, like many other architects of the republic, determined to maintain a relatively privileged lifestyle. Several Morris family members, however, were

Loyalists throughout the war, including his mother and a half brother who served as an officer in the British Army.

Morris was elected in 1775 to New York's Provincial Congress, a wartime Patriot assembly convened to assume the governance of the colony. There he confronted challenges that he would grapple with later on a national scale, including the writing of a new state constitution in 1776–1777. He successfully advocated a strong executive role for the governor and religious toleration for Catholics while losing a bid to include language encouraging the abolition of slavery in the document. He also served on the state Council of Safety in 1777 and visited the war front to coordinate the state's support of the Continental Army.

In 1777, New York appointed Morris to the Continental Congress. He took his seat in January 1778 and was quickly appointed to the Committee at Camp, which spent early 1778 consulting with General George Washington at Valley Forge. Morris worked vigorously for the Continental Army in Congress, and his support contributed directly to the success of reforms in training and supply. Recognized for the able statesman that he was, he also chaired leading congressional committees and drafted several important state papers. He was not reappointed in 1779, however, as his support in New York waned due in part to differences with the more populist Governor George Clinton.

One of the men credited with writing the final draft of the U.S. Constitution, Gouverneur Morris had a long and varied career as a lawyer, statesman, and diplomat. (Library of Congress)

Morris's right arm was disabled due to a childhood accident. In 1780, his left leg was crushed by a carriage wheel, resulting in its amputation below the knee. Undeterred, Morris was fitted with a wooden prosthesis and continued his active social life, one that he freely acknowledged indulged his natural "taste for pleasure."

In July 1781, Morris began a three-and-a-half-year appointment as assistant to Robert Morris (no relation), the superintendent of the new Finance Office under the Articles of Confederation. The Finance Office worked to stabilize Congress's finances and ensure that American credit would not collapse in the costly struggle against Britain, then the greatest military (and financial) power in the world. Morris authored crucial documents such as the proposal for the Bank of North America and the Report on Public Credit and also introduced the idea of decimal coinage that later was taken up by Thomas Jefferson and became the basis of the nation's currency.

In 1786 the Pennsylvania General Assembly elected Morris to the Constitutional Convention. Records indicate that he was the most frequent speaker at the convention, and the outspoken nationalist debated effectively in support of the formation of an independent executive branch with a strong president to counteract the legislative branch, in contrast to the Articles of Confederation and the weak governorships of most colonies. Key to the legitimacy of the presidency, thought Morris, was its foundation in accountability to the people, and he was influential in assuring the president's indirect popular election rather than his selection by Congress.

Also significant was Morris's chairmanship of the Committee on Style, where as primary draftsman he molded the final version of the Constitution. His federalism favored the recognition of a national identity loyal foremost to the United States rather than to a particular state, and one symbolically significant change in wording that he successfully negotiated was replacing a list of the individual states in the Preamble with its now famous phrasing of "We the people of the United States." Morris also effectively streamlined the document, condensing the original twenty-three articles of the Constitution into the seven known today.

Morris also served as U.S. minister to France from 1792 to 1794. In his sympathy for the dethroned King Louis XVI, whom he attempted to save, and for a more conservative style of government than the revolutionary French could tolerate, Morris became so repugnant to France's rulers that they requested his recall. Yet as the only diplomat who didn't flee Paris during the Reign of Terror, he was able to keep a diary that remains an important record of the turbulent times and richly confirms Morris's fears of the potential for social chaos and abuses under unrestrained radical democracy.

Following his diplomatic service Morris returned to New York, where he tended the 1,400-acre Morrisania estate and rebuilt his finances. He briefly returned to public life to fill a vacated Senate seat from 1800 to 1803. Morris died on 6 November 1816.

SUE BARKER

See also

Congress, Second Continental and Confederation; Constitution, United States; Morris, Robert; New York, Province and State

References

Adams, William Howard. *Gouverneur Morris: An Independent Life*. New Haven, CT: Yale University Press, 2003.

Brookhiser, Richard. *Gentleman Revolutionary*. New York: Free Press, 2003.

Mintz, Max M. *Gouverneur Morris and the American Revolution*. Norman: University of Oklahoma Press, 1970.

Robinson, Donald L. "Gouverneur Morris and the Design of the American Presidency." *Presidential Studies Quarterly* 17(2) (1970): 319–328.

Morris, Robert
(1734–1806)

Robert Morris is often called the "financier of the American Revolution," a reference to his position as superintendent of Finance of the United States from 1781 to 1784 and to his crucial overall role in raising money and supplies for Congress and the Continental Army during the war. As the first of the great American treasury leaders, he helped lay the financial foundations of the United States. He was also a powerful committee chairman in the

Continental Congress; an influential figure in Pennsylvania politics as state legislator, party leader, and first senator from Pennsylvania; and one of the most prominent international businessmen of his day. Morris and Roger Sherman of Connecticut were the only two Founding Fathers to sign all three fundamental testaments of the American Revolution: the Declaration of Independence, the Articles of Confederation, and the U.S. Constitution.

Born in Liverpool, England, in January 1734, Morris was brought to America in 1747 by his father, Robert Morris Sr., who was by then established as a tobacco factor (purchasing agent) in Oxford, Maryland. Sent to Philadelphia for his education, young Morris was apprenticed in 1748 in the merchant house of Charles Willing. In 1750 Morris inherited a moderate estate upon his father's accidental death. After some voyages to the West Indies during 1756 and 1757, during one of which his ship was captured by French privateers, Morris joined Willing's son Thomas in the new firm of Willing & Morris. Due to the younger Willing's growing family and political commitments, Morris gradually became the more active partner, becoming an export-import merchant with connections in Britain, the West Indies, and Continental Europe. By the opening of the Revolutionary War, he had substantial experience not only in all aspects of trade and shipping but also in managing military contracts and privateers. These skills he immediately put to use in the service of the Revolutionary cause.

Robert Morris served as a representative from Pennsylvania to the First and Second Continental Congresses. During the war he played a crucial role in raising money, munitions, ships, and supplies for the Continental Army and Navy. (Library of Congress)

Morris first became involved with the Revolutionary movement in 1765 when he was among the merchants who opposed the Stamp Act and signed a nonimportation agreement. In 1775 the Pennsylvania Assembly appointed him vice president of the Council of Safety and chairman of the subcommittee organizing the state's defense measures. In November 1775, he was elected to the Second Continental Congress, in which he served until 1778. In August 1776, he signed the Declaration of Independence after initially disapproving of the measure as premature. Willing, an opponent of independence, now withdrew from active politics, and Morris moved forward as a political leader of the Patriot wing of Philadelphia's mercantile community.

Almost immediately, Morris became Congress's chief commercial and financial agent. According to Charles Thomson, it was Morris who mobilized the resources that permitted General George Washington's troops to escape from General William Howe's army in New York and regroup in New Jersey and Pennsylvania. In 1775 and 1776, the firm of Willing & Morris secured large contracts for importing war matériel for Congress and for several states. As chairman of Congress's Secret Committee of Trade and as an active member of the Committee of Secret Correspondence and the Marine Committee, Morris was responsible for administering international procurement operations as well as much of Congress's other international and naval affairs.

During these years Morris and his wife, Mary White Morris, also assumed the social and diplomatic functions of introducing foreign officers, merchants, and diplomats into American society, a role they continued to play throughout the war. In December 1776, Morris headed the executive committee that remained in Philadelphia during Congress's flight from the city. Dissolving his firm and leaving Willing behind in Philadelphia during the British occupation of 1777–1778, Morris sojourned at Mannheim, Pennsylvania, where, during a leave of absence from Congress, he unsuccessfully sought to settle the by then controversial and entangled accounts of the Secret Committee. Although he rarely attended Congress during its stay at York, Pennsylvania, he served on the important committee appointed in November 1777 to visit the Continental Army's headquarters at Valley Force and sought to resolve the army's administrative and supply problems. In March 1778, Morris signed the Articles of Confederation.

Unlike some republicans of his day, Morris saw no inherent conflict between public and private interests or between business and government. At least when in public office, and under emergency circumstances, he generally gave higher priority to public than to private good, but he had little faith in the long-term prevalence of disinterested public virtue. Instead, he sought reciprocity of interest by bargaining, by contracts, and by tying private interest to the government through various incentives. His complex mixture of public and private affairs contributed greatly to the success of the war effort. Nevertheless, the potential for corruption and conflict of interest was so great, and so offensive to the ideology of "republican virtue," that he was subject to widespread public criticism and investigation.

This was particularly true during the partisan conflicts known collectively as the Deane-Lee Affair, during which Morris's public and private transactions with Silas Deane in France, and his Secret Committee ventures generally, came under public scrutiny. During this period, Morris also became a leader of Pennsylvania's Republicans, who sought to revise what they considered the excessively democratic or radical Pennsylvania Constitution of 1776. His conspicuous wealth, lavish entertaining, and partisan activities, especially his opposition to depreciating paper money and to price controls, embargoes, and other forms of economic regulation, all led to an investigation of his activities in July 1779 by a local price regulating committee and to the mob action against Morris and his allies known as the Fort Wilson Riot of October 1779. Although no profiteering charges were proven, his reputation was tarnished, and he acquired many inveterate opponents, particularly Arthur Lee and his friends, whose enmity was to follow Morris through the rest of his career.

From 1778 to 1781, ineligible for reelection to Congress under the term limit regulations established by the Pennsylvania Constitution, Morris served in the state assembly and expanded his private business, especially in privateering and in provisioning the French army and navy. By 1781 he had amassed enough wealth and credit to become the preferred candidate for the new post of superintendent of the Office of Finance, one of the executive departments established through the efforts of a strong nationalist movement in the aftermath of the collapse of the Continental currency and of the military defeats in the South in 1780. After Congress agreed that he could retain his prior commercial connections and that he had the power to remove civilian officials responsible for handling public money or property or for examining or settling public accounts, Morris accepted the office of superintendent of finance in May 1781.

Until Morris could institutionalize financial structures that could restore and preserve public credit, he placed his personal credit and reputation as a merchant at the disposal of the Confederation government. To finance the Yorktown Campaign and other urgent public purposes, he issued personally signed "Morris's notes." Initially carrying no indication of public responsibility for their redemption, the notes circulated widely, in part because they were receivable for taxes and because Morris could employ government revenues to redeem them. Nevertheless, he was personally liable for them should government revenues prove inadequate. He had to ensure that arrangements for their redemption were in place before leaving office.

After Yorktown, Morris turned his attention to the reestablishment of confidence in the government and in the public credit. To strengthen the Union, he simultaneously sought to shift the balance of power in the Confederation in favor of the central government. His methods included: (1) keeping government expenditures in check by scrutinizing them for waste and extravagance; (2) establishing a national bank, called the Bank of North America, that would create a stable currency through bank notes, lend money to the government, and provide commercial credit to businessmen; (3) initiating a competitive contracting system for military procurement; (4) erecting a system of federal taxes to provide revenue on a timely, dependable basis; (5) initiating settlement of the states' debts with the Union; and (6) funding the national debt with permanent and increasing domestic revenues vested in Congress through amendment of the Articles of Confederation.

Morris succeeded in cutting expenses and in launching the settlement of public accounts. With the help of French loan funds, he opened the bank and sustained its credit. Military contracts were signed and did improve military provisioning. More foreign loans were secured. However, requisitions on the states, the only access to tax revenues permitted by the Confederation, did not provide anything near the sum that Congress requested. Nor could Morris persuade Congress to pass the funding plan he presented on 29 July 1782. Some states opposed all federal taxation on principle, and others opposed some or all of the particular taxes suggested. Tiny Rhode Island blocked ratification of the most acceptable national tax, the impost, a tax on imports presented to the states for approval in 1781.

By the end of 1782, when most revenue from the requisitions failed to arrive, foreign loan funds were exhausted, and Morris's supply of procrastinating financial expedients ran low, he was unable to pay the army and the military contractors on schedule. Public creditors began to agitate for state assumption of debt payments, a move that would strip the public debt of its role as a potential cement for a unified national government. In December 1782, a delegation of army officers headed by Alexander McDougall arrived

Some states opposed all federal taxation on principle.

in Philadelphia to lobby forcefully for army pay, commutation and payment of half-pay pensions, and settlement and payment of army accounts. Morris tried to persuade them to insist on national rather than state payment. He wanted to unite the army and public creditors as pressure groups for his nationalist approach. On 26 January 1783, declaring that he would not be a "Minster of Injustice," he informed Congress that he would resign effective on 1 May unless Congress adopted a satisfactory funding plan for paying the nation's debts. In March 1783, as peace approached with army issues still unsettled, anonymous inflammatory addresses circulated at the main army encampment at Newburgh, New York, urging the troops either to refuse to fight or to disband unless provisions were made for pay and pensions. During this affair, known as the Newburgh Conspiracy, Morris and his assistant, Gouverneur Morris (no relation), were accused of using the army as a political tool, of fomenting mutiny, and even of encouraging a coup, all of which they denied. Their exact roles in the army protests remain a subject of dispute. Whatever the truth, the effort failed to secure ratification of a funding plan by all the states.

Washington's meeting of 15 March 1783 with the army officers, during which he condemned the anonymous addresses and pledged to appeal to Congress on behalf of army demands, contained the army's discontent in New York. Congress passed legislation for commutation of half-pay pensions and settlement of army accounts and submitted a funding plan to the states for ratification, but one so modified that Morris refused to support it. Nevertheless, under pressure from the army and his political friends, he agreed to remain in office until he provided three months' pay to the army and met his other public commitments (notably the payment of contractors and repayment of bank loans). Finally, on 1 November 1784, after resources from a new Dutch loan enabled him to pay the last of his engagements, Morris turned in his commission as superintendent of finance. When he left office he commented, "It gives me great pleasure to reflect that the Situation of public affairs is more prosperous than when the Commission was issued. The Sovereignty and Independence of America are acknowledged. May they be firmly established, and effectually secured! This can only be done by a just and vigorous Government. That these States therefore may be soon and long united under such a government is my ardent wish and constant prayer."

Although Morris failed to secure all his goals during his administration, his policies contributed to the formation of the coalition of nationalist leaders in various states that ultimately secured adoption of the U.S. Constitution. After participating in the Constitutional Convention, he helped the Washington administration achieve many of the old nationalist goals while serving as a senator from Pennsylvania (1789–1795). In the Senate, Morris backed most of Alexander Hamilton's financial plans, was influential in the enactment of financial and commercial legislation, and played a major role in the compromises that removed the nation's seat of government from New York to its temporary home in Philadelphia and to its ultimate destination on the Potomac.

After playing a major role in the postwar economy through an international network of firms that opened U.S. trade with China and India, managed the tobacco contract signed with the French Farmers General, and secured foreign investment in America, Morris engaged in land speculation on a massive scale, went bankrupt, and landed in debtors' prison from 1798 to 1801. He died in Philadelphia in 1806.

ELIZABETH M. NUXOLL

See also

Continental Army; Congress, Second Continental and Confederation; Hamilton, Alexander; Washington, George; Wilson, James

References

Ferguson, E. James. "The Nationalists of 1781–83 and the Economic Interpretation of the Constitution." *Journal of American History* 56 (1969): 241–61.

———. *The Power of the Purse: A History of American Public Finance, 1776–1790.* Chapel Hill, University of North Carolina Press, 1961.

Ferguson, E. James, John Catanzariti, Elizabeth M. Nuxoll, Mary A. Y. Gallagher, Nelson S. Dearmont, et al., eds. *The Papers of Robert Morris, 1781–1784.* 9 vols. Pittsburgh: University of Pittsburgh Press, 1973–1999.

Nuxoll, Elizabeth Miles. *Congress and the Munitions Merchants: The Secret Committee of Trade during the American Revolution, 1775–1777.* New York: Arno, 1985.

Oberholtzer, Ellis Paxson. *Robert Morris, Patriot and Financier.* New York: Macmillan, 1903.

Sumner, William Graham. *The Financier and Finances of the American Revolution.* 2 vols. New York: Dodd, Mead, 1891.

Ver Steeg, Clarence L. *Robert Morris, Revolutionary Financier, with an Analysis of His Earlier Career.* Philadelphia: University of Pennsylvania Press, 1954.

Wagner, Frederick. *Robert Morris: Audacious Patriot.* New York: Dodd, Mead, 1976.

Young, Eleanor. *Forgotten Patriot: Robert Morris.* New York: Macmillan, 1950.

Morristown, New Jersey, Continental Army Winter Quarters
(1777, 1779–1780, and 1781–1782)

Although its single winter at Valley Forge remains more famous, the Continental Army endured greater hardships during its three winter encampments at Morristown, New Jersey. The site had great strategic value, being close enough to watch British troops in New York City yet far enough away to be out of striking distance from them.

In January 1777, after striking back at Trenton and Princeton, General George Washington moved his army into Morristown for the winter. The British, who had briefly occupied most of northern New Jersey, pulled their troops back closer to New York City in the wake of the two American victories. After months of constant campaigning and many defeats, the Continental Army was a shadow of its former self. Washington had no more than 3,000 men at any given time during midwinter. At Morristown, the small army could rest and refit without fear of surprise attack by the British. Their Morristown base also protected New Jersey farms and supply stores as well as the iron furnaces of the northern counties.

During this encampment, Washington had the army undergo a controversial new procedure, inoculation against smallpox. The effects were

View of George Washington's quarters at Morristown, New Jersey, where the Continental Army spent the winters of 1776–1777, 1779–1780, and 1781–1782. (North Wind Picture Archives)

astonishing: mortality rates fell dramatically. From his headquarters at Arnold's Tavern, Washington saw to the overhauling of his army. Winter was a chance to rest and refit, and new regiments arrived to swell his ranks. By spring, Washington had about 18,000 men, although many were barely trained and lacked reliable weapons.

After leaving their encampment in April 1777, the Continental Army fought several battles in eastern New Jersey and then around Philadelphia, including Brandywine and Germantown. They wintered at Valley Forge, Pennsylvania, during 1777–1778. Here Washington reorganized the army again and improved its drill and logistical support. The Continental Army's only major battle in 1778 was at Monmouth, New Jersey, fought as the British retreated from Philadelphia to New York City.

For the winter of 1779–1780, the army returned again to Morristown. Ten thousand strong, the troops built more than 1,000 log huts. The winter was terrible, but the army had benefited from its experience at Valley Forge. Although the weather was worse in 1779 and 1780 than in 1778, fewer men died here than in Pennsylvania (only 86 deaths compared to 1,859). Morristown was hit by several snow and ice storms that winter, and New York Harbor even froze over. It snowed four times in November, seven times in December, six times in January, four times in February, six times in March, and once in April. One January storm dumped four inches onto the encampment. High winds tore apart tents and damaged huts. And in May 1780, some Connecticut regiments mutinied, demanding better food and pay. Loyal Pennsylvania troops were brought in to surround them, and the situation was defused. Such violence had not happened in the Valley Forge camp, where the supply situation was just as bad.

When spring came the army moved on again, hoping to battle the British near New York City, but again the engagements in that region were fairly minor. During the winter of 1780–1781 a small detachment camped at Morristown, but the main army camped closer to the Hudson River. Lack of pay, improper clothing, and bad food had taken their toll on the men. On New Year's Day 1781, troops from the Pennsylvania line mutinied. They ignored their officers, including the charismatic General Anthony Wayne, and marched on Philadelphia, demanding to be paid and better clothed. At Trenton they met with representatives from Congress and agreed to return to active service in return for back pay and new clothing. To show that they were still loyal to the cause, the Pennsylvanians turned in two British spies. On 20 January, mutiny struck again at Morristown as the New Jersey troops demanded better conditions. They were soon brought under control, but these mutinies illustrate the growing dissatisfaction with the war effort.

Morristown holds special significance as the site of several encampments and as the scene of both smallpox inoculation and three mutinies within the ranks of the Continental Army. Although not as famous as Valley Forge, Morristown was occupied longer and more often by the Continental Army.

ROBERT M. DUNKERLY

See also
Brandywine, Battle of; Germantown, Battle of; Monmouth, Battle of; New Jersey; Princeton, Battle of; Trenton, Battle of; Valley Forge, Pennsylvania; Washington, George; Wayne, Anthony

References
Scheer, George F., and Hugh F. Rankin. *Rebels and Redcoats*. Cleveland and New York: World Publishing Company, 1957.
Weigly, Russell. *Morristown: A History and Guide*. Washington, DC: National Park Service, 1983.

Moultrie, William
(1730–1805)

William Moultrie, Revolutionary soldier and governor of South Carolina, was esteemed in his state as a noble Patriot, even though he was sometimes criticized during the Revolutionary War for not making the best use of his opportunities and troops.

By marriage and hard work, Moultrie came to own a large plantation, Northampton, and 200 slaves in St. John's Parish, Berkeley County. From the 1750s to the outbreak of the Revolution, he was in the South Carolina

William Moultrie commanded the fort on Sullivan's Island during the failed British naval attack on Charleston, South Carolina, in 1776. He was captured during the second British expedition in 1780 but was exchanged two years later. (Library of Congress)

Commons House of Assembly but did not particularly distinguish himself. On 16 September 1760, he was appointed captain in the South Carolina militia, and in 1761 he served in Lieutenant-Colonel James Grant's expedition against the Cherokee Nation of upper South Carolina. Thereafter, Moultrie held a prominent place among the legislators of his colony as a military authority. In 1772 he served on a commission to settle the boundary between North and South Carolina, and in 1774 he was promoted to colonel of militia. He was elected to the First Continental Congress but declined to serve. He attended the First and Second South Carolina Provincial Congresses in 1775–1776 and was elected to the General Assembly in March 1776, after South Carolina adopted a new constitution. On 17 June 1775, he was appointed colonel of the 2nd South Carolina Regiment, and in December he attacked an encampment of escaped slaves on Sullivan's Island, killing 50 and capturing the rest.

In June 1776, Moultrie was appointed commander of Fort Sullivan, a sand and palmetto-log structure on Sullivan's Island at the entrance to Charleston Harbor. He was encouraged by Major General Charles Lee, commander of the Southern Military District, to abandon the position as being untenable, but with the encouragement of South Carolina politicians Moultrie decided to stay put. His garrison consisted of only 435 men, supplied with 31 cannon and 5,000 pounds of powder. He was supported by Colonel William Thompson, commander of 750 soldiers on the east end of the island. On 28 June, General Sir Henry Clinton and Admiral Sir Peter Parker, commanding a large British expedition, assaulted Fort Sullivan with cannon fire from British warships. Although the cannon fired from 11:00 A.M. to 9:00 P.M., the palmetto logs and sand of the fort's walls absorbed the cannonballs with little damage. Meanwhile, Moultrie and Thompson laid down a damaging counterfire that battered the hulls and rigging of Parker's ships and killed 225 seamen. Finally, Clinton and Parker retired and a few days later sailed for New York.

Moultrie was now a national hero, although a few cavilers suggested that he had been too easygoing in his command at Fort Sullivan and had not taken advantage of opportunities. On 20 July 1776 he was voted a resolution of thanks by Congress, and on 16 September he was promoted to brigadier general in the Continental Army. Four days later his troops were taken into the Continental service. During 1777 and 1778, he had no opportunity to conduct significant field operations. He did attempt to organize an invasion of Florida, but the legislature would not provide the necessary funds. In 1778 he was elected to the South Carolina Senate. When Savannah, Georgia, fell to the enemy in December 1778, he was sent to the southern part of the state, ostensibly under the command of Major General Benjamin Lincoln but actually on detached service. Elected again to Congress, Moultrie again declined to serve.

On 3 February 1779, Moultrie defeated a British force at Beaufort, South Carolina, and in April he was left in command of American forces at Charleston when Lincoln marched south to besiege Savannah. On 20 June Moultrie conducted an unsuccessful assault against enemy positions at Stono Ferry. In the spring of 1780, he was rejoined at Charleston by Lincoln, who had abandoned the siege of Savannah. On 12 May, Lincoln's whole army, Moultrie included, surrendered to Clinton, and Moultrie was interned at Haddrell's Point, opposite Charleston. While he was in captivity, Lord Charles Montagu, a former Royal governor of South Carolina, attempted to sway him to the Loyalist side, offering him a colonelcy in the British Army and command of a regiment in Jamaica. Moultrie refused the offer. On 9 February 1782 he was exchanged for Lieutenant-General John Burgoyne and on 15 October was promoted to major general.

In 1783 Moultrie was again elected to the South Carolina House of Representatives and a year later was elected lieutenant governor. He served as president of the South Carolina Society of the Cincinnati from 1783 until his death. He was also a trustee for the College of Charleston. Chosen governor in 1785, he served for two years, advocating sound money, a revival of commerce, and improvements in the militia system. In 1787 he was elected to the Senate, and a year later he served in the state convention to ratify the new U.S. Constitution. He resigned from the Senate in 1791, and in 1792 he was elected as a Federalist to another two-year term as governor. During his final term, he battled against the machinations of Edmond Charles Genêt, the French envoy who was attempting to organize an expedition against Spanish possessions from American territory. Moultrie also continued to advocate improvements in the militia, and he ordered all free black émigrés from Santo Domingo and Haiti to leave the state. He retired to Northampton in 1794 and spent the remainder of his life cultivating rice and cotton in an attempt to recoup heavy financial losses during the Revolution.

PAUL DAVID NELSON

See also
Charleston, South Carolina, Expedition against (1776); Clinton, Henry; Congress, First Continental; Grant, James; Lee, Charles; Lincoln, Benjamin; Savannah, Georgia, Operations against; Savannah, Georgia, British Capture of; Stono Ferry, South Carolina, Action at; Thompson, William

References
Mattern, David B. *Benjamin Lincoln and the American Revolution*. Columbia: University of South Carolina Press, 1995.

McCrady, Edward. *The History of South Carolina in the Revolution, 1775–1780*. 1901. Reprint, New York: Russell and Russell, 1969.

Moultrie, William. *Memoirs of the American Revolution*. 1802. Reprint, New York: New York Times, 1968.

Nadelhaft, Jerome J. *The Disorders of War: The Revolution in South Carolina*. Orono: University of Maine at Orono Press, 1981.

Moylan, Stephen
(1737–1811)

Stephen Moylan served in the Continental Army as muster master, as secretary and aide-de-camp to General George Washington, and as quartermaster general early in the War for American Independence and then as colonel of the 4th Pennsylvania Light Dragoons and finally as a brigadier general.

Moylan was born in 1737 in Cork, Ireland, the son of John Moylan and the Countess of Limerick. After an education in France and mercantile employment in Lisbon, he came to Philadelphia in 1768 at the age of thirty, where he engaged in commerce. In 1770 he became a member of the Gloucester Fox Club, which increased his social status among the city's well-born and well-to-do.

In late July 1775, armed with a letter of introduction from John Dickinson, Moylan presented himself in Massachusetts to the recently appointed commander in chief, George Washington, who named Moylan the muster master general of the Continental Army on 11 August 1775. The army for which he was supposed to secure new recruits was a scene of disorder and confusion, but that was not the full measure of his task. America's tiny, informal navy was designed not to attack British armed vessels but to interrupt unarmed supply vessels without force so as to capture supplies going to British forces in Quebec, and on 4 October 1775 Washington appointed Moylan to fit out sailors for that service as well.

In addition to these duties, Moylan frequently acted as secretary to the commander in chief and on 5 March 1776 became Washington's official secretary. The next day Moylan was also named an aide-de-camp. On 5 June 1776, at New York, he was elected quartermaster general of the army with the rank of colonel, succeeding Thomas Mifflin. But in September, plagued by a lack of funds to perform his duties effectively, Moylan resigned this position.

Soon thereafter, Moylan become colonel of a Continental cavalry regiment, the 4th Pennsylvania Light Dragoons. In this capacity he fought at the Battle of Monmouth in June 1778 and at Bull Ferry in July 1780. He was then assigned to service in the South, but his unit was not properly equipped until June 1781, just in time to join the American campaign against Lord Charles Cornwallis's army in Virginia. There Moylan fought under General Anthony Wayne along the James River and at the siege of Yorktown. In the final order of battle Moylan's horsemen were placed along with Major William Parr's battalion of Pennsylvania riflemen in the first (right) division.

After Cornwallis's surrender at Yorktown, Moylan remained in the army until the formal conclusion of peace. Some scholars have attributed to Moylan an anonymous pamphlet written in the early 1780s in defense of the Society of the Cincinnati against the attack of Aedanus Burke. Moylan was appointed a brigadier general in November 1783, shortly before he retired from the service and returned to Philadelphia to resume his mercantile career.

In 1792 Moylan was appointed register and recorder of Chester County, and in 1793 Mifflin, then serving as governor, appointed him major general of the militia of Chester and Delaware counties. In the same year Moylan was offered the position of federal marshal of Pennsylvania but declined the post. At the end of 1793, however, President Washington appointed Moylan the federal commissioner of loans. In 1796, he was elected president of Philadelphia's Friendly Sons of St. Patrick. He died on 13 April 1811, at the age of seventy-four, after a lingering illness. He left no will and there is no known portrait of him, but as Washington's friend and compatriot, Moylan had served his country with distinction and sacrificed heavily to help his adopted country win its independence.

LINDA MILLER

See also

Bull's Ferry, New Jersey, Action at; Continental Army; Ireland; Monmouth, Battle of; Virginia; Washington, George; Yorktown, Virginia, Siege of

References

Blanco, Richard L. "Moylan, Stephen." P. 1129 in *The American Revolution, 1775–1783: An Encyclopedia*, Vol. 2. Edited by Richard L. Blanco. New York: Garland, 1993.

Griffin, Mark I. J. *Stephen Moylan, Muster Master General, Secretary and Aide de Camp to Washington*. Philadelphia: Griffin, 1909.

Moylan, Stephen. "Selections from the Correspondence of Colonel Stephen Moylan." *Pennsylvania Magazine of History and Biography* 37 (1913): 341–360.

Purcell, L. Edward. *Who Was Who in the American Revolution*. New York: Facts On File, 1993.

Muhlenberg, John Peter Gabriel
(1746–1807)

An ordained minister in Virginia, John Peter Gabriel Muhlenberg left the pulpit to lead a regiment of Virginians in the Continental Army and became known as the "fighting parson."

The son of a Lutheran minister, Muhlenberg was born on 1 October 1746 in Trappe, Pennsylvania. Accompanied by his two brothers, he was sent to Halle, Germany, in 1763 to receive a classical education. Later that year, he contracted to work as an apprentice to a merchant in Lübeck, Germany. The merchant, a grocer, kept him in virtual slavery. After three years, Muhlenberg broke the contract and ran away to enlist in the Royal American Regiment of Foot, a British Army unit comprised of Germans and German colonists in North America. He returned to the colonies as a secretary to one of the unit's officers who was stationed in Philadelphia and was honorably discharged in 1767.

After his brief service in the British Army, Muhlenberg studied to be a pastor in the American Lutheran Church. He was ordained a minister in February 1769 and assisted his father in serving churches in the Philadelphia area. Muhlenberg married in 1770 and shortly thereafter accepted a call from the German Lutheran congregation at Woodstock, Dunmore County, Virginia. Since the Anglican Church was the colony's established church, he traveled to London in 1772 to be ordained a priest by the Anglican bishop of London.

John Muhlenberg, ordained minister and brigadier general, fought in the battles at Brandywine, Germantown, and Monmouth. He was present at the siege of Yorktown and ended the war with the rank of major general. (Library of Congress)

Upon his return to Virginia, Muhlenberg became interested in the political discussions of the day and was soon a follower of Patrick Henry. Entering politics himself, in June 1774 Muhlenberg was elected moderator of a committee of freeholders in Woodstock who organized to protest the Boston Port Act. He then became the chairman of a local committee of correspondence and was elected to the Virginia House of Burgesses that met in Williamsburg in early August 1774. Soon thereafter, however, he briefly followed his father's advice and resigned his political offices to concentrate on the spiritual lives of his congregation. But his neighbors would not leave him to his pastoral duties. In 1775 they reelected him chairman of the Committee of Correspondence and Safety of Dunmore County, and he was present at the Virginia Convention where Henry delivered his famous "give me liberty or give me death" speech. When Muhlenberg's brother Frederick criticized him for mixing religion and politics and called on him to resign his political offices, Muhlenberg replied, "Whether I choose or not, I am to be a politician."

On 12 January 1776, Muhlenberg was appointed a colonel by the Virginia convention meeting in Williamsburg and returned home to raise his regiment. In his farewell sermon to his parish, delivered on 21 January 1776, he is reported to have concluded by saying, "There is a time to pray and a time to fight, and that time has now come!" With that statement, he allegedly threw off his gown at the pulpit, revealing the uniform of a Continental Army colonel. With this exhibition he was able to recruit about 300 members of his parish into the 8th Virginia Regiment, better known as the German Regiment.

The regiment first saw action in the defense of Charleston, South Carolina, in June 1776. Marching through Georgia that summer, the regiment was weakened by disease, and Muhlenberg himself contracted a disease of the liver that would trouble him for the rest of his life and eventually cause his death. He was commissioned a brigadier general on 21 February 1777 and ordered to report to General George Washington's camp at Morristown, New Jersey. Under the command of General Nathanael Greene, Muhlenberg's brigade fought in the battles at Brandywine in September and Germantown in October 1777. During the winter of 1777–1778, he was stationed at Valley Forge. During the Battle of Monmouth, he commanded two Virginia brigades in the Corps de Reserve, the second line. He spent the winter of 1778–1779 at the army's headquarters in Middlebrook, New Jersey. Fighting under the command of General Anthony Wayne, Muhlenberg's brigade contributed to the army's victory at Stony Point in July 1779. He was recognized for his skills as a disciplinarian and for his leadership abilities, and his success as a commander brought him the respect of Washington and Baron von Steuben.

In December 1779, Washington ordered Muhlenberg back to Virginia. The British were threatening the South, and Washington wanted an experienced commander to raise fresh troops to meet the enemy. Because of heavy snows, Muhlenberg did not reach Richmond until March 1780, and his original plan of recruiting troops for the defense of Charleston, South Carolina, was thwarted when that city fell to the British in May. By that time, the British Army was slowly bringing the war to Virginia. Low morale and the impending British threat made Muhlenberg's recruiting efforts more difficult.

In the fall of 1780, Muhlenberg was appointed Steuben's second in command. During the spring of 1781, Muhlenberg distinguished himself while leading his troops in defensive battles against the forces of Banastre Tarleton, Benedict Arnold, and Charles Cornwallis, and under the command of the Marquis de Lafayette, Muhlenberg played a significant role in the siege of the British at Yorktown. His brigade attacked and captured British Redoubt 10, one of the final two British redoubts, on 14 October 1781. Cornwallis surrendered shortly thereafter.

Muhlenberg's actions during that attack, however, became a source of controversy. After the battle, Lieutenant Colonel Alexander Hamilton, the commander of the party that assaulted the redoubt, wrote a report of the action to Lafayette. Lafayette forwarded the report to Washington, who submitted it to Congress. While Hamilton played an important and courageous role in capturing the redoubt, Muhlenberg's name was conspicuously absent from the document when it was published in the newspapers. In fact, Muhlenberg appears to have disappeared from the army for months after the battle. Apparently, the liver disease he contracted early in the war weakened him to the point that he was unable or unwilling to publicize the details of his involvement in the siege of Yorktown.

On 30 September 1783, Muhlenberg was promoted to the rank of brevet major general. He retired from the army on 3 November 1783 and became one of the founders of the Virginia chapter of the Society of the Cincinnati. With his retirement from the military, his parish in Woodstock called on him to return to the pulpit. He declined the invitation, remarking, "It would never do to mount the parson after the soldier."

Immediately after the war, Muhlenberg was appointed by the Virginia Assembly to survey the bounty lands awarded to the soldiers from Virginia. His travels to the West took him to Louisville at the Falls of the Ohio. Returning in June 1784, he reported that the local Indians opposed any further white settlement along the Ohio River. After settling his affairs in Woodstock, Muhlenberg moved back to Pennsylvania, where he was elected to the state's Supreme Executive Council in 1784 as a representative from Montgomery County. From 1785 to 1788, he served as vice president of the state under Benjamin Franklin. In 1789, Muhlenberg was elected to the U.S. House of Representatives as an Antifederalist from Pennsylvania. He joined his brother Frederick, also popular with the German population, in the First Congress, but congressional records show that his contribution to the new legislature was minimal. Only once did he speak on the floor of the House. He also served in the Third and Sixth Congresses.

In 1797, Muhlenberg traveled west again to examine his lands on the Scioto River. After his return, he lived in Trappe, his birthplace. A Democratic-Republican in Pennsylvania and a leader of the German population, he was dubbed "the Moses of the German Israelites" in local newspapers. He was elected to the U.S. Senate on 18 February 1801 but resigned in March, just two days into the opening session, to become the collector of customs for the port of Philadelphia. He died on 1 October 1807 and was buried at the Augustus Church in Trappe.

JOHN DAVID RAUSCH JR.

See also

Brandywine, Battle of; Germantown, Battle of; Greene, Nathanael; Hamilton, Alexander; Henry, Patrick; Lafayette, Marquis de; Monmouth, Battle of; Yorktown, Virginia, Siege of

References

Hocker, Edward W. *The Fighting Parson of the American Revolution: A Biography of General Peter Muhlenberg, Lutheran Clergyman, Military Chieftain, and Political Leader.* Philadelphia: Edward W. Hocker, 1939.

Muhlenberg, Henry A. *The Life of Major-General Peter Muhlenberg, of the Revolutionary Army.* Philadelphia: Carey and Hart, 1849.

Rightmyer, Thomas Nelson. "The Holy Orders of Peter Muhlenberg." *Historical Magazine of the Protestant Episcopal Church* 30 (1961): 183–197.

Wallace, Paul A. W. *The Muhlenbergs of Pennsylvania.* Philadelphia: University of Pennsylvania Press, 1950.

Murphy, Timothy
(1751–1818)

The American soldier, legendary marksman, and frontiersman Timothy Murphy became celebrated for his participation in the Battle of Saratoga, as a member of Daniel Morgan's Rifle Corps, and for his marksmanship on the New York frontier. Murphy's exploits with a rifle and as a scout are legendary although hard to verify, but he is one of the most widely known enlisted soldiers of the American Revolution.

Born in 1751 in Minisink, New Jersey, to Irish immigrant parents, Murphy moved with his family to Easton, Pennsylvania, and then to the region around Sunbury, Pennsylvania. At age twenty-one, he was employed with a surveying crew in Northumberland County, Pennsylvania. In June 1775, he was recruited for a twelve-month enlistment in a rifle company under the command of Captain John Lowdon in the Pennsylvania Rifle Battalion. The unit first participated in actions against the British in the vicinity of Boston. One occasion involving Murphy stands out; he is said to have single-handedly turned back a British boat "a good long mile" off. On a hill overlooking the American shore, he picked off the British in the boat one by one until they were forced to retreat. In this campaign, he began to acquire the reputation as a crack shot in a unit of exceptional marksmen.

In March 1776, Murphy's unit marched to Long Island, where they participated in the major battle there in August. By then his first enlistment had expired, and he joined the 1st Pennsylvania Continental Regiment for three years, serving in Captain John Parr's company. The unit fought in the retreat from Brooklyn to Manhattan and at Trenton and Princeton.

In July 1777, General George Washington, in an effort to block the combined British, Indian, and Hessian army under Lieutenant-General John Burgoyne that was traveling southward to link up with a projected northward-moving British force under General William Howe, sent General Horatio Gates a special force of riflemen under Colonel Daniel Morgan. Morgan's Rifle Corps, in which Murphy was a member of Captain Hawkins Boone's company, was considered an elite force that resembled frontiersmen much more than a line regiment. Their main tasks were to operate independently and attack British outposts and pickets, act as snipers (especially against British officers), and harass and capture foraging parties and supply trains.

Morgan's Rifle Corps took part in the First Battle of Freeman's Farm, near Saratoga, on 19 September 1777. Although this battle was a draw, Gates believed that Morgan's corps was the key force on the American side. In the period between 19 September and the 7 October Second Battle of Freeman's Farm (also called the Battle of Bemis Heights), Murphy demonstrated great audacity and courage. Along with his partner, fellow rifleman David Elerson, Murphy took a British sentry prisoner who revealed the password and countersign, which allowed Murphy and Elerson to enter the British camp. There he took a British officer prisoner after finding him alone in his tent, escaped from the camp with the prisoner, and crossed over into the American lines.

On 7 October 1777, at the Second Battle of Freeman's Farm, Murphy became a legend. British Brigadier-General Simon Fraser commanded the elite advance corps of Burgoyne's army and was considered to be one of the most promising and formidable British officers at Saratoga. While leading a reconnaissance in force against the American position at Bemis Heights, Fraser's men were attacked by Morgan's corps. As Fraser rallied his troops, it became clear that if he was successful he could counterattack into the Americans' overextended line. General Benedict Arnold ordered Morgan to have his riflemen eliminate Fraser. Morgan sent a few men, including Murphy, to the task. Murphy climbed a tree and found a firing position. After two missed shots that have been reported as being anywhere from 200 to 800 or more yards, he hit Fraser, who was carried off the field and died the next day, effectively stopping the British counterattack. While the success of Murphy's marksmanship that day cannot be documented, no person who was present at the event ever disputed that Murphy was the shooter. Murphy was also credited with having shot and killed Sir Francis Clerke, an aide-de-camp to Burgoyne, who, trapped between a large and growing American force and the Hudson River, surrendered his entire army.

After the battle, Morgan's unit returned to Washington's command. By the following July, with the bloody frontier war in New York and Pennsylvania in full swing, Murphy's company was detailed to assist the local militia in New York's Mohawk and Schoharie Valleys. They were in almost constant action against Loyalist troops and their Indian allies. During this period, Murphy earned the reputation as a fierce, effective frontier fighter, often acting independently in gathering information on the enemy. An example of this occurred in August 1778 when Elerson and Murphy eliminated Christian Service (Survass), a Loyalist leader. Murphy and his company also participated in the 1779 campaign of General John Sullivan against the Iroquois and fought in the Battle of Newtown, New York, in August against a combined Loyalist and Indian force. They later marched up the Genesee River, laying waste to all Indian villages and fields in their path and rendering the Indians militarily ineffective for the remainder of the war.

After the Sullivan campaign, Murphy was discharged and returned to the Schoharie Valley of New York to be near the woman he loved, Peggy Fleeck, whose father had forbidden them from courting. She eloped with Murphy in September 1779. He next joined the 15th Regiment of the Albany County Militia, where he spent the majority of his time scouting for Indian and Loyalist raiders. This combined with his previous exploits caused Mohawk chief and Loyalist supporter Joseph Brant to order that Murphy be personally brought to him if he was ever captured. In September–October 1780, some 1,000 British, Hessians, Loyalists, and Indians launched a raid on the Schoharie Valley. Murphy again added luster to his growing legend. Under siege in the valley's middle fort and knowing what would happen to him and his comrades if they were ever taken prisoner, he openly defied the commander of the fort, who wanted to surrender, and three times fired on a Loyalist officer under a flag of truce (close enough to scare him but intentionally missing) in order to deceive the attackers into thinking the fort's occupants were a much stronger force. Sir John Johnson, believing that taking the fort was not worth the effort, retreated back to Canada. It can be argued that Murphy's actions saved the day for the American forces.

While Murphy did fight for the American cause until the war ended, it is not clear if he served out the rest of the war with the 3rd Regiment of the Pennsylvania line and was present at the Battle of Yorktown or if he continued with the Albany County Militia in New York.

Murphy's postwar life was spent in the Schoharie Valley as a farmer and gristmill owner. He and Fleeck had six children before she died on 7 September 1807. He married Mary Robertson in 1812, and they had four children. Though never serving in public office, Murphy was very active in the local political arena. He died of throat cancer on 27 June 1818. He was eventually buried in Middleburgh, New York. Though a simple man, Murphy was able to use his extraordinary talents for the benefits of his comrades in arms and his country. Perhaps what makes him especially remarkable is that he became famous although he was never an officer or a great leader of men, simply a private soldier doing his duty.

SCOTT R. DIMARCO

See also

Arnold, Benedict; Brant, Joseph; Fraser, Simon; Morgan, Daniel; Saratoga Campaign; Sullivan, John

References

Atkinson, C. T., ed. "Some Evidence for the Burgoyne Expedition." *Journal of the Society for Army Historical Research* 26 (1948): 132–142.

Dearing, James. "How an Irishman Turned the Tide at Saratoga." *Journal of the American-Irish Historical Society* 10 (1911): 109–113.

Hubner, Brian E. "Fraser (Frazer, Frazier), Simon." Pg. 594–598 in *The American Revolution, 1775–1783: An Encyclopedia.* Edited by Richard L. Blanco. New York: Garland, 1993.

———. "Murphy, Timothy." Pp. 1130–1132 in *The American Revolution, 1775–1783: An Encyclopedia.* Edited by Richard L. Blanco. New York: Garland, 1993.

Moran, Donald Norman. "The Saratoga Rifleman." *AmericanRevolution.Org.* http://www.americanrevolution.org/murphy.html.

"Tim Murphy: Frontier Rifleman." *New York State Military Museum and Veterans Research Center: New York State Division of Military and Naval Affairs.* http://www.dmna.state.ny.us/historic/articles/murphy.htm.

Trussell, John B. B., Jr. "He Never Missed His Aim." *Parameters, Journal of the US Army War College* 6(1) (1976): 48–59.

Murray, David, Lord Stormont
(1727–1796)

David Murray, 7th Viscount Stormont, 2nd Earl of Mansfield, was a British diplomat and statesman. He served as ambassador to France in the period leading up to France's open financial and military support for the American colonists. In an age of amateur diplomats, he was unusual in that he made a career out of diplomacy. Lord Stormont, the scion of a prominent Scottish family, received a degree from Christ Church, Oxford, in 1748. In that same year, he became the 7th Viscount Stormont upon the death of his father. In 1793, shortly before his death, he became the 2nd Earl of Mansfield as the heir to his uncle, the eminent jurist William Murray, the 1st Earl of Mansfield.

Stormont's career in the diplomatic service began in 1751 when he served as an attaché at the British embassy in Paris. His next posting was to Dresden in 1756, where he was envoy extraordinary to the Court of Saxony. When Frederick the Great invaded Saxony the following year, Stormont attempted to mediate an end to the conflict, though his efforts failed. Beginning in 1763, he served for nine years at the imperial court in Vienna. His services in Vienna were recognized by his government, and he was given the critical diplomatic post of ambassador to France in 1772.

Stormont was a competent diplomat, but he made several errors concerning the intentions of the French during the American Revolution. He arrived in Paris at a time when relations between France and Great Britain were improving, following their nadir during the Seven Years' War. When the American Revolution broke out in 1775, Stormont, who was in Britain on leave, did not bother to return to France immediately because he failed to envision any change in diplomatic relations resulting from the crisis with the colonies. His assessment was not based on an unrealistic view of the extent of the British-French rapprochement but rather was predicated on his belief that economic weakness would force France to pursue a policy of nonintervention.

Stormont's positive assessment of British-French relations remained accurate throughout 1775, but the situation changed the following year. He mistakenly thought that King Louis XVI's chief minister, the comte de Maurepas, was committed to peace between the two nations, but Maurepas supported the comte de Vergennes, France's foreign minister, who saw the situation in the colonies as providing France with an opportunity for winning an advantage over Britain and getting revenge for France's defeat in the Seven Years' War. Vergennes advocated providing the Americans with secret aid and in May 1776 convinced Louis to provide 1 million livres. The British government was caught completely unaware by this change in French policy, with Stormont once again on leave from the French court at this critical juncture. Only when France began to reequip its navy at the end of May did it become clear that they were pursuing a new strategy, and Stormont quickly returned to France even though he remained convinced that war was not inevitable.

Upon his return, Stormont had to deal with the arrival of an American delegation led by the widely popular Benjamin Franklin, who amused his French hosts by punning on the British ambassador's name, coining the word "Stormontir," based on the French word *mentir*, meaning "to lie." Stormont, however, had his own diplomatic resources. While the extent to which the American diplomatic mission was compromised remains open to debate, it is clear that the British ambassador was aided by a network of informants, including Edward Bancroft, secretary to the American commission, who provided him with a steady flow of information, including correspondence intended for the Continental Congress. Stormont used this information to try to hamper French support for the colonists, without letting on how much he knew concerning the ever closer relationship between France and the Americans.

While he was never able to stop the flow of supplies from the French to the Americans, Stormont was able to make things more difficult for the French, who until 1778 did not feel strong enough to openly confront the British. He tried to get the French to agree to at least a partial demobilization of their fleet and, after a meeting with Maurepas in March 1777, thought he had achieved that goal, but a week later Stormont realized that he had been misled and that France would not disarm. He was more successful in persuading the French, in July 1777, to stop their support for American privateers, who were using French harbors as a sanctuary.

Up until the end of 1777, Stormont held to the view that war between Britain and France could be avoided, but when the news reached France in December that General John Burgoyne had surrendered at Saratoga, Stormont realized that war was imminent. When France officially informed Britain of the existence of a Franco-American treaty of alliance in March 1778, he immediately left France without taking leave. Shortly thereafter, Vergennes wrote a brief justification of recent French diplomacy. The historian Edward Gibbon was commissioned by the British government to write a reply, and Stormont turned over his entire correspondence to Gibbon, who incorporated it into his *Justifying Memorial to Serve as Reply to the Exposé*, which was published in serial form in the *General Evening Post*.

In October 1779, Stormont, who sat in the House of Lords as an elected Scottish representative peer, became secretary of state for the Northern Department. With the ineffectual Earl of Hillsborough as secretary of state for the Southern Department, Stormont was in control of British diplomacy. He now had the difficult task of trying to break Britain's diplomatic isolation. At first he assumed that relations with the Dutch were secure, but several months after taking office a crisis emerged after the privateer John Paul Jones sought sanctuary in a Dutch port. Stormont then pursued the idea of Russian mediation in the British-Dutch conflict and offered a full alliance if it was accepted, but he failed to see that Empress Catherine the Great was increasingly interested in neutral rights, which led Russia to issue a Declaration of Neutral Rights in March 1780 and to establish the League of Armed Neutrality with other Baltic powers. Having failed with the Russians, Stormont next turned to the Austrians and in the second half of 1780 and early 1781 tried to conclude an Anglo-Austrian alliance, but this too came to nothing. With the fall of Lord North's ministry in March 1782, Stormont left office. Sitting in opposition, he ended his involvement with the American Revolution by speaking out against the preliminary articles of peace between Britain and the United States when they were debated in February 1783. Stormont died in 1796.

KENNETH PEARL

See also

Diplomacy, American; Diplomacy, British; Diplomacy, French

References

Black, Jeremy. *Natural and Necessary Enemies: Anglo-French Relations in the Eighteenth Century.* Athens: University of Georgia Press, 1986.

Scott, H. M. *British Foreign Policy in the Age of the American Revolution.* New York: Oxford University Press, 1990.

Best remembered as the last royal governor of Virginia, John Murray, 4h Earl Dunmore, launched a war against frontier Indian tribes and then attempted to control, by force, a colony that was moving rapidly toward separation from Great Britain. Of all Britain's royal governors, he mounted the stoutest resistance to the American Revolution.

Dunmore entered Parliament as a representative peer of Scotland in 1761 and held his seat, with only a brief break, until 1790, but while still a member of Parliament he accepted an appointment as governor of New York (1769–1770) and then of Virginia (1770–1776), following the death of the popular Governor Norborne Berkeley Botetourt.

Murray, John, Lord Dunmore
(1730–1809)

John Murray, Lord Dunmore, was royal governor of Virginia from 1771 until he was forced from office in the summer of 1775. Unwilling to return home without a fight, he assembled Loyalist forces, which he commanded at Great Bridge and elsewhere, but in 1776 he finally sought refuge with the British Army and Royal Navy at New York. (Library of Congress)

At first, Dunmore was also quite popular in Virginia. From the Governor's Palace in Williamsburg he aggressively pursued a policy favorable to Virginia's trade and economic interests and strongly defended the province's borders with other colonies. Dunmore himself became a large land speculator with a personal interest in land on Virginia's western frontier. But rising tensions in all the American colonies over their deteriorating relationship with Britain soon affected the mood in the House of Burgesses, Virginia's elected assembly. In 1773, Dunmore dissolved the House of Burgesses following its creation of a Committee of Correspondence to communicate with other colonial assemblies and its expression of support for the Massachusetts Assembly, which Governor Thomas Hutchinson had dissolved.

In early 1774, Dunmore led Virginia's militia to defeat a confederacy of Indian tribes at Point Pleasant on the Ohio River (now in West Virginia). This campaign, often called Lord Dunmore's War, opened more western land to settlers, secured the colony's frontier, and briefly increased the governor's popularity immensely.

Upon returning to Williamsburg, however, Dunmore faced a growing crisis. Virginians were meeting in large gatherings, against his orders, to discuss Britain's new harsh policies in New England. In retaliation for the Boston Tea Party, Parliament had voted to close the port of Boston and alter Massachusetts's charter to get more control of local government. The institution of what they saw as martial law in Massachusetts had many leading Virginia citizens concerned. When the House of Burgesses declared a day of fasting in late May 1774 to show support for Boston's citizens, Dunmore again dissolved the assembly.

Dunmore was able to retain his office and some of his authority for another year, but he quickly lost his influence in Virginia politics. He could keep the House of Burgesses from reconvening, but he could not prevent Virginians from holding an illegal provincial congress that voted to send delegates to the First Continental Congress, where they played a leading role in framing the Continental Association in October 1774. As tensions grew in New England, Dunmore became concerned about the security of royal government in his colony. In April 1775 he ordered the British Marines to remove some of the gunpowder from the magazine in Williamsburg to a nearby warship. Upon the discovery of this deed, the public outcry was tremendous, and Virginia's militia began to organize. Patrick Henry, who in March had anticipated the outbreak of war in Massachusetts, marched his Culpeper County militia to the capital to demand the return of the powder. And by early May, news of the fighting at Lexington and Concord reached Virginia.

In May 1775, Dunmore prohibited the meeting of a provincial convention, and in June he convened a lawful session of the House of Burgesses so

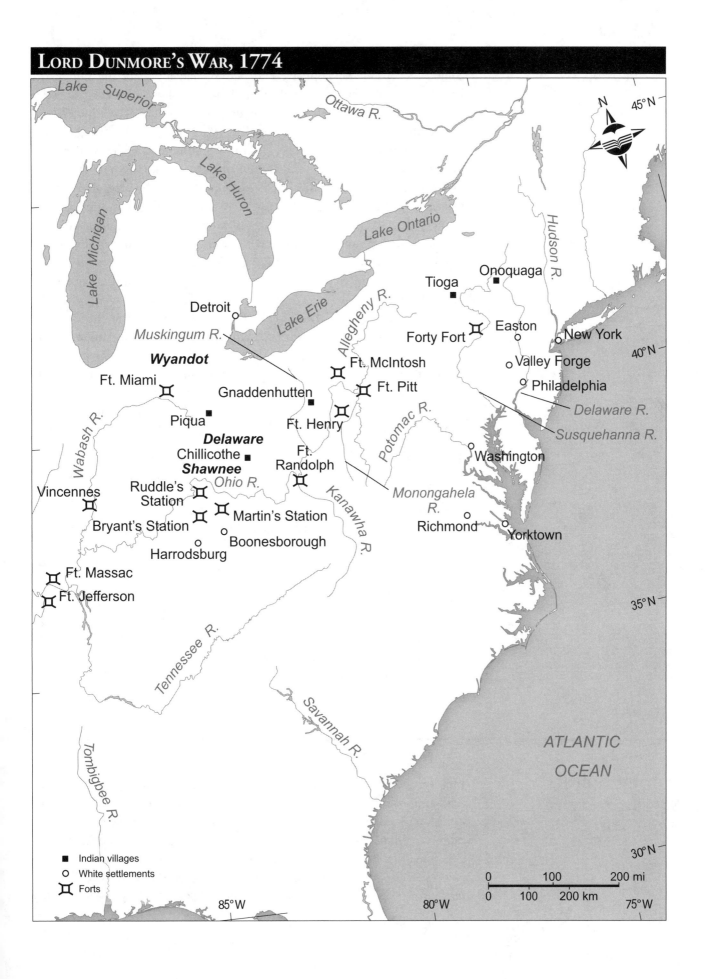

LORD DUNMORE'S WAR, 1774

Lake Superior

Ottawa R.

Lake Huron

Lake Michigan

Lake Ontario

Hudson R.

Lake Erie

Detroit

Muskingum R.

Tioga

Onoquaga

Allegheny R.

Wyandot

Ft. Miami

Gnaddenhutten

Ft. McIntosh

Forty Fort

Easton

New York

Piqua

Ft. Pitt

Valley Forge

Ft. Henry

Philadelphia

Delaware

Chillicothe

Potomac R.

Delaware R.

Shawnee

Ohio R.

Ft.
Randolph

Susquehanna R.

Vincennes

Ruddle's
Station

Washington

Bryant's Station

Martin's Station

Kanawha R.

Monongahela
R.

Harrodsburg

Boonesborough

Richmond

Yorktown

Ft. Massac

Wabash R.

Ft. Jefferson

Tennessee R.

Savannah R.

ATLANTIC

OCEAN

Tombigbee R.

■ Indian villages
○ White settlements
⬡ Forts

0   100   200 mi
0   100   200 km

45° N

40° N

35° N

30° N

85° W

80° W

75° W

that it could consider Lord North's conciliatory proposals. But Dunmore could not control the populace and fled Williamsburg for the safety of a British warship, declared martial law, and called for loyal subjects to organize against the rebels. He also offered freedom to the rebels' slaves and encouraged them to run away and join him. This measure earned him the hatred of many Virginians who had formerly regarded Dunmore as a peer. With a small force of Loyalists, runaway slaves, and British Marines, Dunmore attempted to run Virginia from warships in Chesapeake Bay, and his fleet raided rebel plantations on the James, York, and Potomac Rivers. On land, the House of Burgesses declared that Dunmore, by abandoning the capital, had abdicated his governorship, and they formed themselves into a convention. Using standing committees, the former delegates to the House of Burgesses now ran the colony and called out the militia to keep order and oppose Dunmore's incursions.

In December 1775, Dunmore's troops were defeated at the Battle of Great Bridge, near Norfolk. After the Virginia militia occupied this important seaport, Dunmore's ships shelled it, reducing the town to ruins in January 1776. Unable to control Virginia, Dunmore and his small fleet sailed north to New York City in early summer. There he helped recruit and organize Loyalist soldiers, but he soon returned to England. He promptly entered Parliament again, and after the war he served as governor of the Bahamas. He died in England in May 1809.

ROBERT M. DUNKERLY

See also
Henry, Patrick; Norfolk, Virginia, Raid on; Slaves and Free Blacks; Southern Campaigns; Virginia

References
Boatner, Mark. *Encyclopedia of the American Revolution.* Mechanicsburg, PA: Stackpole, 1994.
Purcell, Edward. *Who Was Who in the American Revolution.* New York: Facts On File, 1993.
White, Bill, and others. *Choosing Revolution Resource Book.* Williamsburg, VA: Colonial Williamsburg Foundation, 1999.

Murray, Judith Sargent Stevens
(1751–1820)

Judith Sargent Stevens Murray was a remarkable woman who gained renown as an author and as one of the earliest American advocates of gender equality.

Murray was born in Gloucester, Massachusetts, and received a typical education for girls of her day: writing, reading, and training in the domestic arts. She later remarked that she wished she had received a better education. Married twice, mother of a daughter, and overseer of the education of several young female relatives and friends, Murray wrote essays, plays, poems, and other works. She began writing poetry at an early age. Often writing anonymously or under the pseudonyms "Constantia" and "Mr. Vigilliusor," she stressed many of the ideals espoused by leaders of the American Revolution, especially liberty and equality.

Murray's letters written during the war years revealed her concern with what was happening around her, and she became interested in expressing the need for female emancipation at this time. Some of her ideas were similar to those of Abigail Adams, with whom she later became acquainted. Murray's letters are particularly effective in revealing the distinctive ways in which women were affected by the war. Because she saved so many of her letters for posterity, one can see in detail how her circle of family, friends, and acquaintances dealt with the war and its aftermath.

After the war, Murray turned from poetry to essays and published several works in the 1780s and 1790s. Her first essay, "Desultory Thoughts upon the Utility of Encouraging a Degree of Self-Complacency, Especially in Female Bosoms," appeared in a 1784 issue of *Gentleman and Lady's Town and Country Magazine.* Her most famous essay, "On the Equality of the Sexes," appeared in *Massachusetts Magazine* in 1790. She also wrote a series of essays called "The Gleaner." Several of these argued that women deserved equal recognition with men, while others were devoted to patriotic political commentary. She used a male pseudonym so that her writings would not be ignored because of her gender. She also wrote plays, the first of which appeared in Boston in 1795.

Strongly influenced by the American Revolution, Murray's works that emerged in the 1780s and 1790s demonstrated her belief in gender independence. The Revolution boosted hopes for freedom among many Americans, and she continually emphasized this. She stressed that women were equal partners in marriage, asserting that in order to achieve true familial harmony and order, women were a necessary part of the domestic sphere, consequently deserving of an equal status in marriage. Arguing that women should be trained in skills other than the domestic arts, she also asserted that women deserved equal access to education, explaining that education not only allowed for personal growth, self-worth, and the development of intellectual skills but also enabled women to achieve a measure of independence not granted to them by the Revolution and certainly not afforded to them in society either before or after that event. She declared that when women received equal access to education, society would benefit. When this happened, she vowed, future generations of women would achieve equality and independence. When Murray died in 1820, she left behind an important body of work that captured life and sentiment from a female perspective during America's formative years.

WENDY A. MAIER

Judith Sargent Murray, a Massachusetts essayist who wrote on many topics including religion, politics, and women's education. (Terra Foundation for American Art, Chicago/Art Resource, New York)

See also

Adams, Abigail; Women

References

Harris, Sharon M., ed. *The Selected Writings of Judith Sargent Murray.* Oxford: Oxford University Press, 1995.

Murray, Judith Sargent. *The Gleaner.* Syracuse, NY: Syracuse University Press, 1993.

Music
(1763–1789)

> Each company had one or two drummers and one fife player.

Most music of the era of the American Revolutionary War was the cultural embodiment of the thoughts and reactions of ordinary citizens. A range of songs communicated the emotions and feelings of Loyalists and Patriots, of British redcoats and American minutemen, and of persons from all walks of life in eighteenth-century America.

Many secular songs that were popular in the 1770s originated during the French and Indian (Seven Years') War (1754–1763). Countless ballads and folk songs were written eulogizing loved ones and military heroes who died doing their duty to God and country, and many of the ballads appeared in widely distributed broadsides. Several ballads also reflected the growing political unrest of the era. In 1765, Peter St. John, a pamphleteer-balladeer and schoolmaster, wrote "American Taxation," a musical protest against the Stamp Act. "Chester," by William Billings, who is now regarded as probably the finest composer in eighteenth-century America, reflected its author's feelings regarding the siege of Boston and became almost as popular as "Yankee Doodle." In times of political upheaval, John Dickinson's "Liberty Song," written before the war began, was sung in local taverns. With the onset of the American Revolution, the colonies already possessed a rich cache of military, secular, and sacred music.

The primary function of both British and American military music was to motivate and inspire soldiers. It was also used as a signaling device for the soldiers in the field, both as part of many marches and in actual combat, and was played in camp as well. This functional music was played by both fife and drum corps and military bands. The fife was derived originally from the Swiss flute and was used by the English from the early sixteenth century. The use of the drum in military music can be traced as far back as ancient Rome, and perhaps earlier. The combination of fife and drum first appeared in the British Army by order of the Duke of Cumberland in 1747, and the Continental Army adopted the fife and drum from British troops stationed in the American colonies. Each company had one or two drummers and one fife player, who were positioned at the right flank of the first unit or platoon. Their repertoire included "To Arms," "The General," and "Rogue's March." Trumpets were added to the Continental Army in 1777 and became associated with cavalry regiments. The military band of this period was a wind band, or *harmoniemusik*, having two each of four common wind instruments of the eighteenth century: bassoons, clarinets, oboes, and French horns. Hired by the officers, these bands played on the battlefield, for military ceremonies, and at unofficial private functions.

One of the most popular British marching songs of the American Revolution was "Yankee Doodle." Although its origin is uncertain, one source attributes it to a British Army surgeon, Richard Shuckburgh, who sought to characterize the unorganized colonial militia he encountered during the French and Indian War. American rebel musicians learned "Yankee Doodle" and "The White Cockade" by hearing them played by British and Loyalist musicians. Indeed, "Yankee Doodle" became one of the most famous tunes in history, and both the British and Patriot forces played it during the Battle of Bunker Hill in June 1775. "The White Cockade" was a lively, immensely popular Jacobite song played on the field at Concord's North Bridge by the Acton Minutemen's fifer Luther Blanchard and drummer Francis Barker. Well after the Revolutionary War, a march composed in honor of President George Washington was first titled "The President's March" but soon became "Hail Columbia," with lyrics written by Joseph Hopkinson, son of Francis Hopkinson, in 1798. It later rivaled "The Star Spangled Banner" in popularity.

Occasionally, both British and Continental Army musicians would use the same tune but sing strikingly different lyrics. One example of this is the redcoats' "God Save the King." The rebels utilized the same tune but sang the lyrics "God save great Washington." (The present version is the British "God Save the Queen," the tune of which is better known to many Americans as "My Country 'Tis of Thee.") Thus, a cross-fertilization of music occurred, extending from the British Army to the Continental Army and throughout the colonies.

On 19 October 1781, General Charles Cornwallis and 8,000 British soldiers surrendered at Yorktown. Two historical records state that "the British stacked arms while their band played *The World Turned Upside Down*. The Continental Army musicians, not to be outdone, played a joyous rendition of *Yankee Doodle*."

Away from the battlefield, and mostly beyond politics, important American composers of this period wrote participatory choral music and songs for private performances in homes. Billings is considered by many to be the most important composer of early American sacred and secular music. Although physically handicapped and trained as a tanner, he taught himself to sing, play, and write music. Billings's friends included Samuel Adams and Paul Revere, and his *New England Psalm-Singer* (1770), engraved by Revere, is the first published collection of music created entirely by an American. Other important Billings compositions include the canon "When Jesus Wept," the Revolutionary hymn "Chester," and the anthem "David's

Archibald McNeal Willard's painting *Spirit of '76* was originally titled *Yankee Doodle* when Willard painted it for the Philadelphia Centennial Exposition of 1876. Art critics dismissed the work as nothing more than a cartoon. However, it quickly came to be admired by the public and toured the country, drawing sell-out crowds wherever it went. (National Archives and Records Administration)

Lamentation." Francis Hopkinson, a congressman from New Jersey and signer of the Declaration of Independence, composed airs for his own secular songs that included "Beneath a Weeping Willow's Shade," "My Days Have Been So Wondrous Free," and "Enraptured I Gaze." James Lyon, a Presbyterian minister and a contemporary of Hopkinson in Philadelphia, published the first English fugue psalm tunes in *Urania* in 1761. Justin Morgan was one of America's most original composers and taught both singing and writing schools. He wrote "Amanda," "Montgomery," and "Weathersfield." This period also saw the creation of some of America's earliest folk music that was originally disseminated by oral tradition. "Johnny's Gone for a Soldier" and "Drink to Me Only with Thine Eyes" are two popular examples.

Several important military and political leaders during the American Revolution were avid amateur musicians in their own right. George Washington was an accomplished flutist. Benjamin Franklin played the guitar, wrote musical criticism, and invented the "glassy-chord," or glass harmonica. Thomas Jefferson played the violin, the cittern, and the harpsichord.

KATHLEEN HITT

See also

References

Brand, Oscar. *Songs of '76*. New York: Evans, 1972.

Chase, Gilbert. *America's Music*. Chicago: University of Illinois Press, 1992.

Commager, Henry S., and Richard B. Morris, eds. *The Spirit of 'Seventy-Six: The Story of the American Revolution as Told by Participants*. 1958. Reprint, New York: Bonanza, 1995.

Fischer, David Hackett. *Paul Revere's Ride*. New York: Oxford University Press, 1994.

Howard, John Tasker, and George Kent Bellows. *A Short History of Music in America*. New York: Crowell, 1954.

Lossing, Benson J. *The Pictorial Field Book of the Revolution*. 1851. Reprint, Rutland, VT: Tuttle, 1972.

Nicholls, David, ed. *Cambridge History of American Music*. Cambridge: Cambridge University Press, 1998.

"U.S. Army Bands in History." *U.S. Army Bands: Serving the Nation through Music*. http://bands.army.mil/history/default.asp.

Winstock, Lewis. *Songs and Music of the Redcoats*. Harrisburg: Stackpole, 1970.

Musket

The standard military weapon of the Revolutionary period was the single-shot, muzzle-loading smoothbore musket. The muskets of the Revolution were well-designed, reasonably efficient weapons that remained in use for most of the eighteenth century. The capabilities and limitations of the musket largely dictated infantry tactics of the day.

The flintlock musket fired by means of a lock mechanism that used flint and steel to create a spark. First, a soldier used his teeth to tear open a prepared cartridge. The cartridge held gunpowder and a round lead ball about an ounce in weight (sometimes buckshot was also used). A little powder was poured into the pan, in front of the cock holding the flint. Closing the pan kept the powder from spilling out. Next, the soldier performed the necessary evolutions so that the ball, paper, and remaining powder were thrust down the barrel. A ramrod drove the charge home. When the soldier put the weapon into full cock position, the weapon was ready to fire. Sparks from the flint scraping the frizzen (a piece of hardened steel located over the pan) set off the main charge, propelling the ball on its way. Thus, with flintlock muskets the soldier experienced an explosion near his face, which ignited the main charge in the barrel.

Such methods, while seemingly straightforward, often went awry. Flintlock weapons were often temperamental. If the powder was wet or even became damp on a humid day, the weapon could misfire and not produce a spark. Moreover, flints often cracked and chipped and had to be replaced frequently. As the musket was fired, black powder residue built up on the lock and in the barrel. This fouling made loading difficult and often prevented ignition of a spark. A soldier could expect his musket to misfire about once in twelve tries.

The most common muskets used in the Revolutionary War were the British Long and Short Land muskets, both commonly called the Brown Bess, and the French Charleville. The Short Land pattern was a smaller, lighter version of the Long Land, but otherwise the muskets were identical. A variety of Spanish, Dutch, and German muskets also found their way into the colonies. For the most part, the Continental Army used captured Brown Besses or imported Charlevilles. In 1777, France shipped 30,000 muskets, ranging in age from new patterns to some from the 1710s, to the Americans.

The Brown Bess fired a .75-caliber ball, while the Charleville accepted a .69-caliber ball. Each weapon weighed about 9.5 pounds. The somewhat longer Charleville is distinct with its retaining barrel bands, whereas small pins held the barrel and stock together on the Brown Bess. The first U.S. Army muskets made after the Revolution were patterned after the Charleville. So reliable were these firearms that they saw service throughout the Napoleonic Wars and up to the start of the American Civil War.

The Brown Bess musket, the standard infantry firearm of the British Army during the American Revolutionary War. Hard-wearing yet inaccurate, like all other smoothbore weapons, it had been in use since the Duke of Marlborough's campaigns at the beginning of the eighteenth century and would continue in British service well into the first half of the nineteenth century. (National Archives and Records Administration)

Throughout the colonies, small armories and local gunsmiths produced Committee of Safety Muskets, which were copies of the Brown Bess. These were used by many militia units at the start of the war. This cottage industry failed to meet the demands for large numbers of weapons, however, and new recruits often arrived at camp unarmed.

The advantage of the musket versus the rifle lay in the relative rates of loading. A musket could be fired by well-trained men about three or four times a minute, whereas the grooves in the barrel of a rifle slowed this process to about one round per minute. In short, the smoothbore and loose-fitting ball allowed the charge to be loaded and rammed home quickly. Muskets were also designed to accept a bayonet, whereas the rifle was not. Military muskets were also mass-produced in factories. They fired a standard-sized ball and had interchangeable parts. These weapons gave armies a huge advantage in the field that American militia, using a variety of weapons, lacked. Rifles could not yet be mass-produced, and while they were more accurate, it was impossible to keep a force of riflemen supplied and stocked with the right ammunition.

Both French and British muskets used a socket bayonet that did not block the muzzle, so the weapon could be loaded and fired with the bayonet fixed. The bayonet was a primary part of the weapon, as bayonet charges often decided a battle. Muskets also had thick wooden stocks reinforced with either brass or steel plates. They could be used effectively as clubs, whereas the stocks of rifles were too thin and delicate for such use.

The main disadvantage to muskets was their inaccuracy. Their effective range was one hundred yards, but they were most effective at fifty yards or closer. Thus, battlefield tactics evolved to accommodate this technology. Combat formations were linear, and troops relied on the volley to break the enemy's formation. Combat consisted of a pattern of loading and firing, followed by a bayonet charge to break the opponent's line.

Men firing shoulder-to-shoulder in ranks could send a steady hail of lead at the enemy. Eighteenth-century armies valued firepower over accuracy, and commanders used many formations such as one, two, and even three ranks to maximize firing. After a series of volleys and after closing in on the enemy, infantry usually employed a bayonet charge as a shock tactic intended to break a wavering enemy line. Strict discipline as well as command and control were vital components of linear warfare. All other things being equal, the side that displayed superiority over its opponents in these regards normally carried the day.

ROBERT M. DUNKERLY

See also
British Army; Continental Army; French Army; Rifle

References
Darling, Anthony. *Red Coat and Brown Bess.* Alexandria Bay, NY: Museum Restoration Service, 1971.
Moore, Warren. *Weapons of the American Revolution.* New York: Funk and Wagnalls, 1967.

Neumann, George. *The History of Weapons of the American Revolution*. New York: Harper and Row, 1967.

Wright, John. *Some Notes on the Continental Army*. New York: Temple Hill Association, 1975.

Mutiny, Continental Army

American officers throughout the War for American Independence were bedeviled by numerous mutinies, some serious, others less so. The cause for most of the unrest was not a lack of honor, loyalty, or patriotism on the part of the mutinying troops, who usually suffered with astounding fortitude an incredible lack of food, clothing, blankets, shelter, and pay. Instead, the blame for the mutinies could be traced to civilian neglect of the soldiers' welfare and pay, mostly for reasons beyond the politicians' control. Sometimes, however, the long-suffering soldiers were forced to endure unfriendly, even contemptuous, dislike from civilians imbued with republican fears of a standing army. Often this dislike took the form of lectures from politicians about the troops being responsible for their own difficulties because of their waste and profligacy.

These soldiers, thoroughly resenting the neglect and haughtiness directed at them by their civilian masters, were forced to find solace among themselves. Ironically, the civilians' attitudes toward soldiers tended to create the very monster they wished away. Also, on occasion some company-level and field-grade officers were too heavy-handed in their treatment of America's soldiers. These insensitive martinets seemed unaware that the troopers were not professionals but citizens in arms, imbued with the idea that military service was a contractual arrangement. The soldiers' most potent weapon of protest against this material and psychological neglect, and also against unpopular officers, was mutiny, which they disliked and tried desperately to avoid. Nevertheless, various state militia units mutinied, and the Continental Army had twenty-eight identifiable mutinies from 1777 to 1783, involving anywhere from a few men to a number of regiments.

Clearly this was not a negligible or ephemeral phenomenon. The problems began during the siege of Boston in September 1775, when a Pennsylvania rifleman was imprisoned for a misdemeanor. On 10 September, a group from Captain James Ross's Pennsylvania company, armed with loaded rifles, set out to free the miscreant, whereupon General George Washington strengthened the guard to 500 men and ordered several regiments under arms. Pursuing the mutineers with Generals Charles Lee and Nathanael Greene, Washington ordered the offending soldiers to ground their arms. They were surrounded by another Pennsylvania company, imprisoned, tried, convicted of mutiny, and fined twenty shillings each. The Continental Army's first mutiny had been handled promptly and effectively, and a great danger appeared to have passed.

Over time, however, the horrible deprivations that the soldiers had to endure overrode their deep-seated patriotic devotion to the cause. Private

> The Continental Army had twenty-eight identifiable mutinies from 1777 to 1783.

Continental troops revolt after their defeat at Brooklyn for want of pay, food, and clothing. Various regiments mutinied during the war, including some from Connecticut, New York, Massachusetts, New Jersey, and Pennsylvania. (National Archives and Records Administration)

Joseph Plumb Martin, among others, explained that he and his comrades loved their country and suffered everything short of death in its service. But eventually, having borne all that human nature could endure, they broke under the strain and mutinied. In February 1776, at Halifax, North Carolina, some newly recruited Continentals mutinied, and at Valley Forge in December 1777, Washington reported to Congress that lack of food had led to an uprising that was suppressed with difficulty. In 1779, Rhode Island and Connecticut troops threatened to mutiny because of civilian neglect.

But the greatest number of serious mutinies came quite close to the end of the war. In early 1780, the Connecticut line again was on the brink of an uprising, complaining about abusive officers and lack of meat and back pay. Two Connecticut regiments prepared to leave camp without authorization in search of food. During an altercation with their officers, a soldier struck Colonel Return Jonathan Meigs on the head, but finally the troops calmed down and returned to their huts. In June 1780, the men of the 1st New York Regiment, stationed at Fort Stanwix in the Mohawk Valley, became disgusted because they had not been paid and their uniforms were in tatters. Thirty-one of them marched away, declaring their intention to desert to the

British at Oswegatchie on the St. Lawrence River. Lieutenant Abraham Handenbergh, a Continental officer, mobilized a band of Oneida Indians to block their escape. Although the Indians managed to shoot thirteen of the deserters, the remainder apparently managed to escape to the enemy.

Toward the end of 1780, some American soldiers were near the end of their tethers. Patriotic or not, they were enduring another harsh winter near Morristown, New Jersey, without uniforms, blankets, provisions, or pay. The Pennsylvania line was particularly disgruntled. Their commander, Brigadier General Anthony Wayne, who was popular among the troops, pleaded with the Pennsylvania Assembly to ameliorate their suffering. On 16 December, the legislators agreed to at least provide the troops with back pay, in specie. But the new legislation would take months to implement, and the soldiers were angry and sullen that they were also devoid of shoes, blankets, rum, and many other necessities. Moreover, they were bitter about their term of service, insisting that they had signed up for only three years and that their obligation was coming to an end. Wayne and the officers insisted that the soldiers had enlisted for the duration of the war. Unfortunately, the national enlistment law, enacted earlier by Congress, was so vaguely worded that it could be interpreted either way.

On 1 January 1781, the Pennsylvania line mutinied, and junior officers attempting to bring the soldiers under control were swept aside. Captain Adam Bettin was killed by the angry men, and two other officers, Captain Samuel Tolbert and Lieutenant Nicholas White, were seriously wounded. Many other officers received injuries from bayonets, stones, and clubbed muskets. A few soldiers were also killed or wounded in the fray. The mutineers seized all four of Wayne's cannon, fired off a few shots across the parade ground, and marched away toward Princeton, New Jersey. Wayne and his senior officers were swept along by this human tide, with the general taking only a moment on 2 January to scrawl a letter to Washington informing him of the mutiny. Wayne also asked the mutineers to appoint a committee of sergeants to represent the soldiers' grievances to him.

After reaching Princeton on 4 January, Wayne wrote to Congress and the Pennsylvania Assembly warning them to be prepared to leave Philadelphia, for he had been informed by the mutineers that they intended to march on both political bodies in that city. He urged Pennsylvania's highest official, President Joseph Reed, to ask the Assembly to send a committee of legislators to negotiate with the rebels, because he believed that the matter should be handled by civilians. Meeting with the committee of sergeants, Wayne learned the soldiers' demands: that men who had enlisted for three years and whose time was up be discharged; that soldiers receive their back pay, in most cases more than a year's worth, immediately and in specie; and that the troops be decently fed and clothed. Although he lacked authority to meet these demands, Wayne did agree to recommend them to Reed. The sergeants, for their part, accepted this procedure and promised that they would quietly await the civilians' response without threatening governments in Philadelphia. As a token of their good faith, they imprisoned two British agents sent by General Sir Henry Clinton to entice them into desertion.

On 7 January, Wayne received a letter from Reed agreeing that he and a committee would negotiate with the sergeants but asking that the mutineers meet the civilians in Trenton rather than Princeton. Reed listed a number of reasons for this request, but the two most important were that the government could more easily supply the army there with the demanded materials and that civil authority could salvage at least a shred of dignity if it could "force" the mutineers to come to it, rather than the other way around. Wayne agreed to this suggestion and prevailed upon the sergeants to go along. On 9 January the troops marched to Trenton, and negotiations began. Meanwhile, Wayne was becoming increasingly more disgusted with and less sympathetic toward the mutineers. Bound by an oath not to molest the soldiers, he nevertheless told Washington and Congress that their demands were so unreasonable that they should be immediately dismissed from the service. Although Washington feared that Reed's committee might be too lenient with the mutineers, he felt that he could not lose that much manpower from his depleted army. All he and Wayne could do was let events play themselves out and hope for the best.

The two sides quickly reached an agreement on 9 January, and the mutiny came to an end. First, Reed promised the sergeants that Pennsylvania's governing authorities would appoint a board to listen to Pennsylvania soldiers who believed that they should be discharged. Only those soldiers enlisted for three years or the duration of the war were eligible for a hearing; the board would accept either written proof or the word of any soldier who claimed the right to the appeal. Second, all Pennsylvania troops would be issued pay warrants, which the state would redeem as soon as it could get the money to do so. Third, all soldiers were guaranteed a shirt, overalls, and shoes, from clothing already collected in Philadelphia by a ladies' committee chaired by Reed's wife, Esther, and Benjamin Franklin's daughter, Sarah Bache. As soon as the agreement was settled, the mutineers turned over to Wayne the two British agents who had attempted to woo Americans into desertion. On 11 January, these two unfortunates were tried before a court-martial, condemned to death, and executed before a firing squad.

Over the next few weeks, Wayne tried everything he could think of to keep his Pennsylvania troops from leaving the army. He cajoled the government of Pennsylvania to provide bonus money for reenlistments, pleaded with the soldiers to remain true to the Revolutionary cause, and urged Philadelphia merchants not to employ any of the discharged soldiers so that they would be compelled to return to the army. He boasted optimistically to Washington on 21 January that the Pennsylvania line soon would be "reclaimed & formidable," but he knew otherwise. Three days later, Congress approved his recommendation of a general amnesty to the mutineers, since in fact there was no other alternative. On 29 January, Wayne wrote to Washington that 1,317 privates and artillerists had been discharged and that he was left with only 1,150 men.

Many officers and politicians feared in early 1781 that the mutiny of the Pennsylvania line would trigger further unrest in the Continental Army. These concerns were justified, for disgruntled veteran soldiers in the New

Jersey Continental line, encamped at Pompton, New Jersey, near Morristown, had been in communication with the Pennsylvania mutineers and sympathized with their demands. These soldiers suffered from the same deprivations and pay problems as the rest of the army. They had recently received five dollars in specie as a token payment of overdue pay, but they were angry that new recruits were receiving better bounties and enlistment terms than they had received. On 20 January, about 200 New Jersey Continentals mutinied, spurred on by their leaders, who made speeches threatening members of Congress. Within a short while, the mutineers had won acceptable concessions and were back under control of their officers.

Washington, however, upon the advice of Wayne and other officers, decided that he must make an example of the New Jersey soldiers. Writing to Congress on 23 January, he declared that unless the rebellious spirit prevailing in the Continental Army was suppressed by force, the army itself would disintegrate. He ordered General Robert Howe to march with 500 New England troops from West Point to Pompton, directed Colonel Israel Shreve to lead reliable New Jersey regulars in support of Howe's troops, and requested that Governor William Livingston call out the state militia. Howe and Shreve were to make sure the mutineers really were subordinate to military authority. More importantly, they were to arrest and summarily execute the most notorious leaders of the mutiny. On 27 January, they surrounded the offending soldiers in their campsite, catching them off guard. Howe then ordered the New Jersey soldiers to assemble without their weapons. Singling out three leaders of the earlier mutiny, he immediately convicted them and sentenced them to summary execution. For their firing squad, he selected nine of the strongest supporters of the condemned men. After two of the soldiers had been executed, Lieutenant Colonel Francis Barber intervened to reprieve the third.

Thus, the mutiny of the New Jersey soldiers ended, only to be followed in May 1781 by another uprising in the Pennsylvania line. Encamped near New York City, the soldiers asserted their newly won personal dignity more than the officers thought was healthy. Wayne began arresting offenders for petty offenses and imposing harsh sentences upon them. On 20 May, he arrested John Fortescue, an artillerist, for mutinous actions and sentenced him to death. The soldiers considered this punishment monstrous and spoke out against it. In response, Wayne arrested five more men for inciting mutiny and also sentenced them to die before a firing squad. Although he pardoned one at the last moment, Fortescue and the other four were executed.

On 25 May, Wayne was confronted with another mutiny when his soldiers, while on parade, suddenly began to demand the pay they had been promised and twelve men stepped forward to exhort their fellows to rebel against their officers' commands. Instantly, Wayne responded by ordering their arrest by other soldiers, who carried out his command. The twelve were court-martialed and ordered shot by a firing squad composed of their closest friends and messmates. After the executions the mutiny died, and Wayne had no more trouble from his Pennsylvania veterans.

The last big mutiny of the war occurred in June 1783 as the conflict was drawing to a close. Several hundred Pennsylvania soldiers were quartered in

Philadelphia at that time, and on 12 June their numbers were increased by 200 Maryland regulars. The following day, a committee of sergeants demanded in a petition that Congress pay the soldiers before they were demobilized and sent home. On 20 June, more soldiers from Lancaster joined the disgruntled troops already in the city. On 21 June, about 300 men marched on the State House where Congress was sitting, surrounded it, posted guards at all the entrances, and demanded their pay. Although the soldiers allowed the congressmen to leave, the legislators informed John Dickinson, president of Pennsylvania, that if the state could not restore order they would adjourn to Trenton or Princeton. They also called on Washington to dispatch troops to the city to suppress the mutiny.

In a meeting on 23 June, Dickinson and the Executive Council refused to ask Washington for assistance or call out the militia, insisting that the rebellious troops could be conciliated. Thereupon, Congress fled to Princeton. The mutiny quickly came to an end, for the soldiers heard rumors that troops were marching toward Philadelphia to quell the uprising. When Dickinson finally did call out 500 militiamen to restore order, the rebellious troops meekly accepted a summons by the governor to gather before the State House. There they heard a lecture on their bad behavior and surrendered, and the soldiers who had come from Lancaster soon departed to march back to that town.

Many observers severely criticized Congress for its hasty departure, but Alexander Hamilton strenuously defended the action, declaring that Dickinson's and the council's refusal to act in a timely manner had forced the legislators to decamp. As for the Continental soldiers who had suffered so much in the Revolutionary cause, they felt hurt and disgusted as the war came to an end. For their loyalty, they had been badly treated by a society that had violated its contractual obligations to the Continental Army. Perhaps their malaise was a result of Washington's calculated ruthlessness in suppressing mutinous New Jersey soldiers in 1781 or because the soldiers' future seemed brighter after 1781 but no better by 1783. Or perhaps it was because the soldiers were too exhausted and dispirited to continue any longer in their struggle against seemingly cold-hearted civilians.

PAUL DAVID NELSON

See also
Congress, Second Continental and Confederation; Continental Army; Dickinson, John; Pennsylvania; Reed, Joseph; Washington, George; Wayne, Anthony

References
Bowman, Allen. *The Morale of the American Revolutionary Army.* Washington, DC: Council on Public Affairs, 1943.

Gragg, Larry. "Mutiny in Washington's Army." *American Heritage Illustrated* 2 (1974): 34–45.

Greene, George Washington. *The Life of Nathanael Greene, Major-General in the Army of the Revolution.* 1871. 3 vols. Reprint, Boston and New York: Houghton, Mifflin, 1897–1900.

Lee, Henry. *Memoirs of the War in the Southern Department of the United States.* 1812. Reprint, New York: New York Times, 1969.

Lender, Mark Edward. "The Enlisted Line: The Continental Soldier of New Jersey." PhD diss., Rutgers University, 1975.

Linn, John Blair, and William H. Egle, eds. *Pennsylvania in the War of the Revolution*, Vol. 1. Harrisburg: L. S. Hart, 1880.

Martin, James Kirby. "A 'Most Undisciplined, Profligate Crew': Protest and Defiance in the Continental Ranks, 1776–1783." Pp. 119–140 in *Arms and Independence: The Military Character of the American Revolution*. Edited by Ronald Hoffman and Peter Albert. Charlottesville: University of Virginia Press, 1984.

Neagles, James C. *Summer Soldiers: A Survey and Index of Revolutionary War Courts-Martial*. Salt Lake City, UT: Ancestry, Inc., 1986.

Nelson, Paul David. "The American Soldier and American Victory." Pp. 35–51 in *The World Turned Upside Down: The American Victory in the War of Independence*. Edited by John Ferling. New York: Greenwood, 1988.

———. *Anthony Wayne: Soldier of the Early Republic*. Bloomington: Indiana University Press, 1985.

Van Doren, Carl. *Mutiny in January: The Story of a Crisis in the Continental Army*. New York: Viking, 1943.

Ward, Christopher. *War of the Revolution*. 2 vols. New York: Macmillan, 1952.

N

Elected governor of North Carolina in 1780, Abner Nash was most noted for his efforts to prepare his state to resist the British attempts to retake the American South.

Nash was born in Prince Edward County, Virginia, to Welsh parents. After legal training, he was qualified to practice law in Prince Edward County in 1757 and was elected to the Virginia House of Burgesses in 1761–1762. In the latter year, he followed his brother, Thomas, and moved to North Carolina with his younger brother, Francis.

Nash again became involved in politics after moving to Halifax, North Carolina, and served in the provincial assembly in 1764, 1765, 1770, and 1771. He also married the widow of Governor Arthur Dobbs and became embroiled in the fight over Dobbs's estate. Upon the death of his wife in 1771, Nash moved to New Bern, North Carolina, where he remarried and established a plantation on the Trent River.

In New Bern, Nash took an even more active role in provincial politics. His relationship with the royal governor, Josiah Martin, became strained during the settlement of Dobbs's estate, and Nash moved into a leadership position in the Patriot movement. With the collapse of royal authority in 1775–1776, Nash played an even stronger role by serving on the Committee of Safety and later on the Provincial Council. He helped prepare North Carolina's resolution on freedom and independence and served as the Speaker of the independent state's newly formed House of Commons. He continued to serve in both the House of Commons and the state Senate throughout the period 1777 to 1780, but he declined a seat in the Continental Congress.

In 1780, Nash was elected the second governor of the State of North Carolina and served until June 1781. His tenure was marked by efforts to defend the state against the invading British Army while also dealing with a growing Loyalist insurgency. He convinced the General Assembly to establish a Board of War to prepare the defense of the state, but the board fought with him over orders to the militia and the purchasing of supplies. The General Assembly also refused to grant Nash additional powers to deal with the wartime crisis.

Nash, Abner
(1740?–1786)

In June 1781, Nash declined a second term as governor. Soon thereafter, his home and papers were burned during the British raid on New Bern in August 1781. He was elected to Congress in 1782 and retained his seat until December 1786, when he died of tuberculosis during a congressional session in New York City.

WILLIAM H. BROWN

See also
North Carolina; Southern Campaigns

References

Crabtree, Beth G. *North Carolina Governors, 1585–1968: Brief Sketches*. Raleigh, NC: State Department of Archives and History, 1968.

Nash, Jacquelin Drane. "Nash, Abner." Pp. 356–357 in *Dictionary of North Carolina Biography*. Edited by William S. Powell. Chapel Hill and London: University of North Carolina Press, 1991.

Russell, Phillips. *Concise Dictionary of American Biography*. New York: Scribners, 1964.

———. *North Carolina in the Revolutionary War*. Charlotte, NC: Heritage Printers, 1965.

National Debt, British

As a result of the Seven Years' War, the national debt of Great Britain increased from £72 million to £132 million. The steps that Great Britain took from 1763 until 1775 to pay off the debt helped bring about the American Revolution. The new imperial taxes levied to manage the debt and control expenses set off a debate between Great Britain and the colonies over the nature of government that in turn led to the creation of the United States of America.

During the early 1760s, taxpayers in Great Britain shouldered most of the debt by paying a variety of new or increased taxes, including a land tax. Parliament also increased revenue for the national treasury through bills such as the Sugar Act of 1764, which placed duties on Madeira wine, sugar, and molasses throughout the empire. The prospect of higher expenditures to garrison 10,000 soldiers along America's western frontier led to the passage of the Stamp Act in 1765. Colonial administrative costs had already jumped from £70,000 in 1754 to more than £350,000 by the mid-1760s. The British hoped that the Stamp Act would allow the colonies to pay for their own defense and not increase the national debt. Parliament believed that the new tax would raise between £60,000 and £100,000 annually in the American colonies.

While the British were convinced that they were managing their national debt in a reasonable way, they had not taken into account how deeply the Americans were tied to their assemblies. The colonists resented the new stamp tax imposed on them by Parliament and saw it as the beginning of a wider attempt to strip them of the self-government they had enjoyed for nearly 150 years. The passage of the Stamp Act set off violent protests throughout the colonies, which only came to an end when Parliament repealed the tax. While the repeal brought temporary peace, the debate over who should tax and ultimately who should rule the American colonies continued and led to open rebellion by 1775.

The attempt to suppress America's rebellion added £114.5 million to the national debt of Great Britain, and the interest on the debt amounted to £9.5 million annually. By 1781, the date of the American victory at Yorktown, Parliament levied just over £25 million in taxes on its citizens each year. When William Pitt the Younger became prime minister, he set out to make the national debt more manageable. First, he funded one-half of it by allowing holders of bonds to exchange them for stock that the government would never fully redeem but on which it would pay interest perpetually. Pitt then established a sinking fund of £1 million allotted annually out of the government's current revenue. A Board of Commissioners drew from the sinking fund to buy back stock from private holders and in turn used the interest on the stock to buy back even more stock. Pitt's reforms held the national debt in check for ten years between the end of the American Revolution and the start of the long war against France, which in turn increased Great Britain's debt to £850 million by 1815.

MARY STOCKWELL

The American Revolution added £114.5 million to Britain's national debt.

See also

Grenville, George; North, Lord Frederick; Pitt, William, the Younger; Stamp Act

Reference

Selley, W. T. *England in the Eighteenth Century*. London. Adam and Charles Black, 1949.

Native Americans

For the overwhelming majority of Native Americans, the American Revolution was a disaster. At least several hundred Indian warriors took part in the conflict on the American side but were too few to have any great impact on the conflict. Many thousands fought on the British side but never in large enough numbers to give the British a significantly improved opportunity to achieve victory in any theater of the war. And most tribes remained neutral through most of the conflict. Yet nearly all suffered when the independent United States, created by hundreds of thousands of aggressive, often land-hungry settlers from Britain and Europe, acquired ultimate sovereignty over the Indians' trade and land.

The term "Native American" refers to all the indigenous peoples of the American continents, but in relation to the American Revolutionary War, a few key groups of indigenous peoples are of special importance. These include the tribes of the Iroquois Confederacy and their allies in New York and Pennsylvania, the Five Civilized Tribes in the southern colonies/states, and the Ohio Valley tribes of the Northwest. While some of the distinctions

Eighteenth-century depiction of an Iroquois warrior. The Iroquois, largely confined to upper New York and Canada though living as far south as North Carolina, in fact consisted of six tribes, whose loyalties were divided between the British and the Patriots. (Library of Congress)

between these three clusters of tribes, like the labels applied to them, are largely the constructions of Europeans, the tribes within each of these groups did have cultural and linguistic similarities as well as common geographic interests that served to delineate their respective memberships. At the same time, they all possessed important commonalities that served to guide European colonial interactions with them. While the ways in which Europeans related to Indians covered a wide spectrum, their most important interactions in the War of Independence revolved around Native American military practices and diplomatic rituals.

Most Native American tribes practiced a method of warfare predicated on stealth and concealment. Raids and ambushes punctuated this form of conflict. Commonly, a small group, or war party, took shape under a leader in order to execute these activities. Usually, the chief action of the group consisted of a brief raid of some sort. Leadership of the war party often fell to the warrior who called it together. The warriors composing the party placed themselves under the direction of the party's leader for the duration of the raid. No set hierarchical command structure existed among most Native American groups, although some leaders, such as Ottawa Chief Pontiac and the Mohawk Joseph Brant, did achieve great visibility among several tribes and considerable fame among Europeans.

Once formed, the war party set out for the location of its chosen foe. The preferred time of attack for the war party was at first light, when their enemy would be least prepared. Most engagements were decided in the initial attack. If they were unsuccessful, the warriors usually retired quickly rather than take part in a set battle and risk heavier losses. If the attack was successful, the raiders would immediately take prisoners and seize plunder. Plunder constituted an important part of warfare among the Native Americans, many of whom lived fairly close to a subsistence level. Goods that could be carried away in brief raids were a mark of the warrior's prowess in battle and were often of considerable value to a tribe's prosperity. Likewise, taking prisoners served an important function in the prosecution of a cultural activity known as the mourning war.

Many members of the Iroquois Confederacy regularly practiced mourning warfare. In mourning war, warriors lost in battle were perceived to leave both a physical and spiritual void in their tribe. In order to fill this void, the tribe had to replace missing members, either physically or symbolically. Consoling the aggrieved tribe was usually accomplished with captives taken in battle. If the prisoners were women of almost any age or children of either sex, they were most often adopted directly into the tribe. Adult male prisoners might be adopted into the tribe, or they could be ritually tortured to death and, in some cases, eaten by their captors. Among the tribes who prac-

Prominent Native American Tribes during the American Revolution

Department	Tribes
Northern	Iroquois Confederacy (Senecas, Mohawks, Oneidas, Onondagas, Cayugas, Tuscaroras)
Southern	Five Civilized Tribes (Cherokees, Chickasaws, Choctaws, Creeks, Seminoles)
Western	Ohio Valley tribes (Shawnees, Delawares, Kickapoos, Miamis, Ottawas, Wyandots)

ticed mourning war, torture was considered a means by which a captured warrior could regain the honor lost when he was captured. If the captive faced his fate stoically, he was deemed to have regained his honor and, in recognition of the fact, was eaten. These practices often led to charges of atrocity from various Europeans. The return of captives taken during conflicts between Native American and Europeans routinely figured in the negotiations at the end of hostilities and could also pose serious challenges during diplomacy.

In the long decade between the end of the French and Indian (Seven Years') War and the outbreak of the American War of Independence, diplomatic negotiations with the various Native American groups were carried out almost exclusively by officials of the British government. There were two royal officials who held primary responsibility for this work. They were the Indian superintendents of the Northern and Southern Departments and reported directly to the colonial secretary in London. From 1756 to 1774, the British Indian superintendent of the Northern Department was Sir William Johnson; following his death, his responsibilities were divided between his relatives John and Guy Johnson. Sir William's death in July 1774 is often cited by historians as one of the reasons for the divisions that wracked the Iroquois Confederacy during the War of Independence. Johnson's responsibilities included all negotiations with the Iroquois Confederacy, the most prominent group in the northern and middle colonies.

The Iroquois Confederacy, whose members referred to themselves as the people of the longhouse, originally included the Onondaga, Oneida, Cayuga, Mohawk, and Seneca tribes. In 1722, the Tuscaroras to the south were admitted, making it the League of the Six Nations. In addition to the Iroquois, to the west there were the tribes of the Ohio Valley, whose territory stretched from western Pennsylvania through present-day Ohio, Indiana, and Illinois to the Mississippi River. While these people were often considered clients of the Iroquois Confederacy in dealing with Europeans, this relationship proved more nominal than real. Because the Ohio Valley Indians were seen as clients of the Iroquois, they had no separate Indian superintendent.

The Ohio Valley tribes were the chief actors in Pontiac's Rebellion (1763–1766). This uprising, which was finally put down by Britain's General Jeffrey Amherst, was a primary reason for the Proclamation of 1763. This royal decree curtailed settlement beyond the line marked by the British government and became a source of great tension between settlers on the frontier and the royal government.

Austenaco, a great warrior, was commander in chief of the Cherokee Nation during the Revolutionary War. (Library of Congress)

For the Southern Department, the Indian superintendent for most of the prewar period was John Stuart. Following his death partway through the Revolutionary War, he was replaced by several officials, including Alexander Cameron and Charles Stuart, both of whom had served as his assistants. Stuart was responsible for overseeing diplomacy with the Five Civilized Tribes: the Creeks, Chickasaws, Choctaws, Cherokees, and Seminoles. The most important of these with respect to the War of Independence were the Cherokees and the Creeks.

Diplomacy between the British Crown and both the Iroquois Confederacy and the Five Civilized Tribes revolved around the ritual practice of gift giving, primarily by the British to the Native American leaders. Gifts were presented at the beginning and end of all conferences. The initial goods were presented in order to wipe away any negative emotion felt by the Native Americans, such as mourning for a fallen member of the tribe. Thus, gifts created a positive climate for the conduct of the business of the conference. At the end of the negotiations, gifts were again presented. These cemented any agreements made at the conference and reaffirmed the bonds of friendship among the participants.

With the outbreak of hostilities between Great Britain and its colonies, both sides in the conflict sent diplomatic missions to the various Native American groups. In these early diplomatic efforts, Crown officials proved more adept, while the rebel diplomats were initially astounded by the expense attached to the gift-giving aspect of diplomacy. The colonies, of course, had to build a diplomatic apparatus from scratch. The Continental Congress set up a plan for the management of Indian affairs that was much the same in its organizational details as that of the British. It did, however, include a Middle Department as well as Southern and Northern Departments. The agendas pursued by both sides had much in common.

Early in the War of Independence, British policy toward the Indians consisted of continuing their friendship while limiting requests for military actions against the rebels. General Guy Carleton, the governor of Canada, was especially reluctant to call upon the Iroquois for military support and thus unleash an Indian war with all of its attendant depredations on the frontier. The American policy, in turn, consisted of expressing friendship and securing pledges of neutrality from the Native Americans, though some Massachusetts Christian Stockbridge Indians were recruited as warriors as early as the siege of Boston. Both British and American emissaries met with considerable failure in their initial efforts.

Among the Iroquois, the first news of conflict between Britain and its American colonies was greeted with confusion and pledges of restraint to both sides. While in theory the Iroquois Confederacy was supposed to act as a single unit, in reality the pull of localism, which placed the interests of the various member tribes ahead of the whole, often prevailed. Only the Mohawk tribe would prove a dependable British ally throughout the war. Much of the tribe's reliability came as the result of the efforts of Brant and his sister Mary, who had been the common-law wife of Sir William Johnson for many years. Mary Brant, in fact, held greater sway among the Mohawks than her brother.

While the first response of the Iroquois had been to wait and see how developments played out between the British and the colonists, the arrival of Chief Brant on the frontier and Guy Johnson in New York City in July 1776 marked the beginnings of a subtle shift in Iroquois policy. The combined efforts of these two men would persuade many of the members of the Iroquois Confederacy to play a much more active role in their support of the British. The Continental Congress's lack of experience in the handling of Indian affairs also allowed most tribes to take a more pro-British stance.

In 1777, many warriors from the various tribes of the Iroquois Confederacy began openly aiding the British and their Loyalist auxiliaries, especially in upstate New York and western Pennsylvania. A number of Indians joined the forces of General John Burgoyne on his march against Albany, New York. A proportionally larger force supplemented Colonel Barry St. Leger's invasion of the upper Mohawk Valley. These warriors took part in a successful ambush of Colonel Nicholas Herkimer and his militia at Oriskany, New York, in August 1777 but could not capture Fort Stanwix, which the rebel forces eventually relieved. Meanwhile, two Native American warriors serving with Burgoyne were accused of perpetrating one of the most highly propagandized "atrocities" of the conflict, the murder of Jane McCrea, an incident that did not help Burgoyne's faltering campaign.

After Burgoyne's surrender at Saratoga in October 1777, the Iroquois and their Loyalist allies worked to make the western and southern reaches of the Mohawk Valley a no-man's-land. This change in tactics led to the outbreak of brutal raids all along the frontier in 1778. The most destructive of these attacks was known as the Cherry Valley Massacre. But the failure of Burgoyne's invasion also initiated conflict within the Iroquois Confederacy as the various tribes and villages took opposing sides in the conflict. The Onondagas, for example, remained divided amongst themselves in their loyalties until 1779. And although most Senecas did join the British, some remained neutral.

By this time, however, General Frederick Haldimand had replaced Carleton as governor in British Canada. Haldimand was far more willing than Carleton to utilize Native American auxiliaries on the frontier against the Americans. This ensured that raids along the frontier in Pennsylvania and New York would increase in 1778. The severity of these attacks, in turn, gave rise to calls for action by Congress to protect the frontier. In 1779, General George Washington launched two major expeditions against the Iroquois. Colonel

Daniel Brodhead commanded the smaller force in western Pennsylvania. A much larger expedition, led by Continental Army General John Sullivan and New York militia commander General James Clinton, marched through the Iroquois territory in northern Pennsylvania and western New York.

The idea of both campaigns was not so much to kill Iroquois warriors as to devastate their crops, thus simultaneously chastising them and making them a greater supply burden on the British. In this respect, the campaigns were a clear success, although they did not end Native American raids on the northern frontier. The importance of these efforts to the Americans, however, is suggested by the fact that the Sullivan expedition was the only major military operation mounted by the Continental Army in 1779.

While there were further attacks by war parties along the northern frontier in both 1780 and 1781, they were greatly reduced in strength, again a signal of the effectiveness of the Brodhead and Sullivan expeditions. Under these reduced conditions, however, frontier warfare continued even after the surrender of Lord Charles Cornwallis at Yorktown in October 1781. But in the later stages of the war, the British were increasingly trying to restrain their Native American auxiliaries. The fate of the Iroquois Confederacy was finally decided by treaty with the United States shortly after the peace with Britain. The Six Nations had to cede much of their land to Pennsylvania and New York, and many Iroquois immigrated to Canada at the invitation of the British and fared better in the future.

In many ways the same story of division and eventual defeat, with its attendant loss of lands, characterizes the experience of Native Americans in the Southern Department. In the South, as in the North, the Native Americans' experience in the American War of Independence was often a struggle for their very survival. Throughout the conflict in the South, there appeared the same types of internal divisions among the Native Americans that were seen in New York and Pennsylvania. The only group to remain steadfast in their support of the British was the Chickasaws.

The chief motivator of the Indians in their support for the British in this region was Stuart. From the start, however, Stuart had his work cut out for him, as the rebel leaders in his base colony, South Carolina, ran such a successful smear campaign against him among both Indians and European settlers that he had to flee to Georgia in 1775. Stuart hoped that Native American warriors would be used in conjunction with the British regulars against the rebels. As he was preparing for this, however, the Patriot leaders of South Carolina attempted to send gunpowder to the Indians on the frontier as a gift in order to secure good relations. Loyalists in the backcountry seized the powder but promptly expended all of it in their unsuccessful siege of a Patriot force at Ninety-Six.

The move to war by Native Americans in the Southern Department came in early 1776, when a delegation of Shawnees, Delawares, and Mohawks from the North came to the Cherokees and urged then to attack the rebel settlers. The Cherokee agreed to attack the colonists, but their plans were leaked, which lost them the element of surprise. In late June 1776, however, the Cherokees of the Lower Towns, those closest to the colonial frontier, raced through the backcountry of South Carolina, burning and plundering as they went. These raids were all the more frightful to the colonists for fear that the Creeks might join the Cherokees on the rampage.

In response, the newly independent southern states launched a concerted counterattack. South Carolina was the first to respond. On 2 August 1776, Colonel Andrew Williamson of South Carolina began a sweep against the Cherokee Lower Towns. On 23 September, he teamed up with General Griffith Rutherford and his North Carolina militia. The final prong of the counteroffensive came with the advance of Colonel William Christian of Virginia into Cherokee territory. By the time of Christian's advance, however, the majority of the Cherokees were ready to negotiate. The quick collapse of the Cherokees was disappointing but not necessarily unexpected by the British. In large part it was due to the fact that the Creeks refused to support the Cherokees. The Cherokees had taken heavy losses in their attacks, and the strong and concerted response of the various states soon quieted them.

The 1776 frontier war broke the power of the Cherokees, and 1777 was a year full of negotiation and little action. Through 1778, most of the attention on the frontier focused on the Creeks, who were threatening settlers in Georgia. But between late 1776 and 1780, relatively little warfare actually took place on the frontier. One important reason for Native American inertia in this region was that Loyalists in the southern backcountry had been effectively muzzled by their own defeats in 1775 and 1776.

Beginning in 1779, the British shifted the focus of their military strategy to the South. The Creeks had more than 300 warriors ready for service with the British in the spring and summer of 1779 but did not support the initial British thrusts into Georgia because they were given no advance notice of British plans. As for the British, their efforts among the Indians in the South changed drastically after Stuart's death in March 1779. His former assistants attempted to take his place and carry out his policies, but their efforts were often subverted by Lord George Germain, Britain's secretary of state for the American colonies, who was now taking a more personal interest in military policy. There was also much competition for Stuart's authority at the local level. Thomas Brown, lieutenant colonel of the East Florida Rangers, a Loyalist unit, was also the superintendent of the Atlantic District of the Southern Indian Department. In this role, he attempted to stretch his powers to take over all of Stuart's old district.

It soon became clear to the British, however, that most Native Americans in the Southern Department were not going to support them. Even the presence of sizable British armies in Georgia in 1779, in South Carolina in 1780, and in North Carolina and Virginia in 1781 did not persuade the Indians to rally to their support. The Creeks did help the British break the first Spanish siege of Pensacola, but the Spanish returned in force, and on 8 May 1781, General John Campbell surrendered Pensacola to them. This event signaled the end of Britain's Southern Indian Department in North America. And the dramatic turn of events in the Southern Department that began with the Battle of Kings Mountain in October 1780, followed by the assumption of the command of the Southern Army by General Nathanael Greene in December, and culminating in the surrender of Cornwallis at Yorktown in October 1781, placed much of the South firmly back under Patriot domination.

By the spring of 1782, the Continental Army and the Patriot militia were in control of the South, making any British communication with Native American tribes quite difficult. The last eighteen months of the conflict in the Southern Department were a time of retrenchment and decline for both the British and the various Native American tribes, and both awaited the final outcome of peace negotiations before launching any new efforts, diplomatic or military. Yet most of the divisive issues between white settlers and Native Americans that were present at the outbreak of the conflict remained at the war's end.

The only region in which there was something resembling even temporary success for Native Americans during the War of Independence was the West, and that success lasted only as long as the war itself. In the Ohio Valley, with the exception of the expedition of George Rogers Clark, Native Americans kept white incursions to a minimum. Clark's expedition into the Illinois Country formed the principal defense north of the Ohio for frontiersmen attempting to set up settlements in the area that would become Kentucky.

The fighting in this region, while it did not approach a definitive possession of territory by either side, did set a precedent exploited by American negotiators in the Treaty of Paris. That agreement ceded all of the area that encompassed the territory of the Ohio Valley tribes to the new United States. This region, organized as the Northwest Territory in 1787, quickly became a site of great tension and eventual conflict between the indigenous inhabitants and the United States.

Most historians of the American Revolution now view the frontier conflict with the Native Americans as an expansionist war waged by the colonists, and then the independent American settlers, in order to gain new territories. They see the Proclamation of 1763, with its attendant restraint on colonial encroachment, as one of the key motivators of people along the frontier. The divided loyalties within the various Native American nations, especially the Iroquois Confederacy, are generally seen as a chief cause of their inability to repel American incursions. And the consensus on such Native American support of American independence as did exist is that it led to a gross injustice on the part of the new nation. Tribes that supported the American bid for independence generally received no consideration of their grievances. In fact, they lost territories with as much regularity as those who fought on the British side. The British, for their part, often turned their backs on allies that had contributed valuable service. The major exception was the Iroquois who immigrated to Canada, where the British gave them the Grand River Valley in Ontario.

JAMES R. MCINTYRE

See also

Atrocities; Border Warfare; Brant, Joseph; Brodhead, Daniel; Brodhead Expedition; Brown, Thomas; Burgoyne, John; Campbell, John; Cherokees, Operations against; Cherry Valley Massacre; Clark, George Rogers; Continental Army; Florida, East and West; Fort Stanwix, New York; Fort Stanwix, Treaty of; Germain, Lord George; Grand Strategy, British; Greene, Nathanael; Herkimer, Nicholas; Johnson, Guy; Johnson, Sir John; Johnson, Joseph; Johnson, Sir William; Kentucky; Loyalists; McCrea, Jane; New York, Operations in; Northwest Territory; Oriskany, Battle of; Pontiac; Pontiac's Rebellion; Proclamation of 1763; Propaganda; Rutherford, Griffith; Saratoga Campaign; Schocharie Valley, New York; St. Leger Expedition; Stuart, John; Sullivan, John; Sullivan Expedition; Williamson, Andrew

References

Calloway, Colin G. *The American Revolution in Indian Country: Crisis and Diversity in Native American Communities*. Cambridge: Cambridge University Press, 1995.

Graymont, Barbara. *The Iroquois and the American Revolution*. Syracuse, NY: Syracuse University Press, 1972.

Horsman, Reginald. *Expansion and American Indian Policy, 1783–1812*. East Lansing: Michigan State University Press, 1967.

Lowell, Harrison H. *George Rogers Clark and the War in the West*. Lexington: University Press of Kentucky, 1976.

Mintz, Max M. *Seeds of Empire: The American Revolutionary Conquest of the Iroquois*. New York: New York University Press, 1999.

Nester, William R. *The Frontier War for American Independence*. Mechanicsburg, PA: Stackpole, 2004.

———. *"Haughty Conquerors": Amherst and the Great Indian Uprising of 1763*. Westport, CT: Praeger, 2000.

O'Donnell, James H. *Southern Indians in the American Revolution*. Knoxville: University of Tennessee Press, 1973.

Richter, Daniel K. *The Ordeal of the Longhouse: The Peoples of the Iroquois League in the Era of European Colonization*. Chapel Hill: University of North Carolina Press, 1992.

Richter, Daniel K., and James H. Merrell, eds. *Beyond the Covenant Chain: The Iroquois and Their Neighbors in Indian North America, 1600–1800*. Syracuse, NY: Syracuse University Press, 1987.

Snow, Dean R. *The Iroquois*. Cambridge, MA: Blackwell, 1999.

Naval Operations, American vs. British

At the outset of the American Revolution, the naval forces of the rebellious colonies and of Great Britain were seriously mismatched, by any account. Britain possessed the most powerful navy in the world, while the Continental Navy, which came into existence only in 1775, much like the Continental Army, was virtually nonexistent. However, as the war progressed from a civil war within the British Empire to a major European conflict, so too would the nature of naval conflicts between the Continental and Royal Navies be transformed, from coastal incursions to major engagements, once France and other European powers intervened, altering the course of the war. For the Americans, the Continental Navy was a symbol of the emerging United States. For the Royal Navy, the American Revolution was a painful defeat,

HMS *Phoenix* and *Rose* under American fire in New York, August 1776. While the Royal Navy enjoyed massive numerical superiority over the Continental Navy and usually outgunned its opponents, it was less effective in ship-to-ship actions. (Library of Congress)

the lessons from which would enable it to emerge victorious in the wars against France shortly thereafter.

On paper, the Royal Navy enjoyed numerous advantages. By the eighteenth century, it had a proud tradition that included the heroics of Sir Francis Drake and others. In addition, the Admiralty had grown to be a complex bureaucracy that oversaw every detail of the Royal Navy all over the world. In 1775, there were 16,000 sailors in service. As the war progressed, the number would increase to an annual average of 82,000. In 1778, the Royal Navy possessed 66 ships of the line (mounting 74 guns or more) alone, with a total of 617 vessels of all types by 1783.

Britain possessed the resources to maintain such a large fleet. Since the Glorious Revolution of 1688, the British government had another revolution in government finances, particularly in the manner of raising revenue. During the war, the government raised £12 million a year through taxation, of which 20 percent came from a land tax, with the rest collected through indirect taxes such as customs and excise and through raising the national debt. Between 1776 and 1783, the British government spent £236 million, of which 40 percent derived from loans. Military spending consumed more of the total budget than any other expense. Spending for the army and navy alone rose to £109 million during the American Revolution, compared to just

£83 million during the Seven Years' War (1756–1763) and £56 million during the War of the Austrian Succession (1740–1748). However, such figures belied the true state of the Royal Navy. After 1763, the quality of the Royal Navy had declined during the years of peace that followed. The Royal Navy had been underfunded, and despite its huge fleet, its vessels, docks, and other facilities were allowed to fall into neglect. Such was the state of the Royal Navy on the eve of the American Revolution.

As the United States came into existence, the Continental Navy had many obstacles to overcome. Even though the American colonists were familiar with the sea, there was no naval tradition to speak of. Before the establishment of the Continental Navy, each individual colony had been responsible for its own coastal defenses. The first to propose provisions for coastal defense was Josiah Quincy of Massachusetts, who wrote to John Adams on 11 July 1775 suggesting row galleys to protect navigation. On 26 August, Rhode Island, which had suffered from attacks by British ships, instructed its delegates to propose to the Continental Congress the creation of a navy to protect all of the colonies. There was much debate over the need to outfit a navy, the cost of which would be prohibitive. However, on 13 October, the Continental Congress authorized the creation of the Continental Navy, under the supervision of the Naval Committee. Four ships had been authorized for construction: the *Alfred*, the *Columbus*, the *Cabot*, and the *Andrew Doria*. The Naval Committee was thus significant in laying the foundations of the Continental Navy not only by providing ships but by establishing the necessary bureaucracy to build, direct, and maintain them; to manage the recruitment of officers; and to draft the first set of rules and regulations by which sailors and officers were to live and work.

Since the Continental Navy only came into existence in 1775, its resources were negligible compared to those of the Royal Navy. In ships of the line alone, the Royal Navy boasted 174, each with sixty to one hundred guns, while in contrast the entire Continental Navy consisted of just 27 ships, averaging only twenty guns each. British ships carried far heavier guns, while American ships had few guns that could load 18-pound round shot. The Royal Navy seriously outmanned the Continental Navy, for the latter at any time never numbered more than 3,000 men. Due to its short existence, the Continental Navy never acquired the naval traditions enjoyed by the Royal Navy. However, despite these disadvantages, it was the Royal Navy that bore the heavier burden in fighting the war.

The North American Squadron, under the command of Vice-Admiral Samuel Graves, formed that portion of the Royal Navy responsible for conducting operations along the eastern seaboard during the American Revolutionary War. Graves had assumed his post before the war when he sailed into Boston Harbor on his flagship, the *Preston*, on 16 April 1774. His command consisted of seven sloops, four schooners, and ten smaller vessels. Four of the sloops, the *Mercury*, the *Lively*, the *Savage*, and the *Tartar*, were stationed in Boston, while the *Active*, the *Fowey*, and the *Tamar* patrolled the waters from the St. Lawrence River to the Florida Keys. Long before the first shots were fired at Lexington and Concord, the Royal Navy had been involved in the struggle between the colonies and the Crown, with Boston the flash-point. In order to pay for the tea damaged during the Boston Tea Party on 17 December 1773, Parliament passed the Boston Port Act on 1 June 1774, which forbade goods from passing in or out of Boston Harbor, with the exception of provisions for troops garrisoned there and humanitarian supplies. Otherwise, any ship that violated the act would be confiscated. The enforcement of the Boston Port Act fell to the Royal Navy and, in particular, the North American Squadron. Rear-Admiral John Montagu stationed eight warships to seal up Boston Harbor and later placed full responsibility of enforcing the Boston Port Act on Graves.

At the beginning of the war, Graves had under his command thirty warships, which were spread across the Atlantic coastline from Nova Scotia to Florida. In the opening months of the conflict, New England was the main focus of British operations for both the land and naval forces. Graves deployed the North American Squadron to procure supplies from Nova Scotia and convey them to the West Indies, while keeping Boston blockaded. The first naval engagement with the Americans consisted of raids by American whaleboats and schooners along Boston Bay. On 31 July 1775, such a raid resulted in the destruction of Boston Lighthouse and the capture of forty British Marines. British logistical support was also vulnerable to American raids. On 29 August, Graves assumed the offensive by launching attacks on New England ports to prevent attacks on British supplies, but he did not have ground support. On 8 October, Lieutenant Henry Mowat received orders to destroy the northern towns of Cape Ann, Marblehead, Salem, Newburyport, Portsmouth, Ipswich, Saco, Falmouth, and Machias. He took with him the *Canceaux*, the *Halifax*, the *Symmetry*, and the *Spitfire*. On 17 October, having bypassed Cape Ann after finding it unsuitable for a naval bombardment, he proceeded to Falmouth, where he ordered the colonists to surrender or face destruction. After the colonists indicated their refusal to surrender, he ordered his ships to fire on Falmouth, destroying the town. He seized four American vessels and destroyed eleven others. The plan to destroy the towns on the north shores of Massachusetts and Maine was abandoned because of disagreements between Graves and Lieutenant-General William Howe on the question of army support. Graves then fell back to the plan of blockading the ports along Massachusetts Bay, which was both ineffective in neutralizing American attacks and hazardous due to the inclement New England weather during the winter of 1775–1776.

The newly established Continental Navy gained distinction for its harassment of British shipping. The *Alfred* (24 guns), under the command of Commodore Esek Hopkins, served as the flagship of the Continental Navy. On 5 January 1776, the Naval Committee ordered Hopkins to dispatch a force of seven ships consisting of the *Alfred*, the *Columbus*, the *Andrew Doria*, the *Providence*, the *Hornet*, the *Fly*, and the *Wasp* to Chesapeake Bay to destroy whatever British vessels he found there and to undertake the same in the Carolinas and in Rhode Island. In addition, Hopkins was to seize transports and supply vessels. The fleet set sail for the first time on 17 February. Hopkins, however, departed from his instructions, and instead of attacking Virginia and the Carolinas, he ordered his captains to sail for the island of New Providence in the Bahamas. Hopkins captured the city of Nassau without bloodshed and acquired large quantities of guns and ammunition. Thus, in its first year of existence, the Continental Navy proved to be an effective fighting force that could inflict damage on the enemy, notwithstanding the great discrepancy between American and British naval forces.

By 1776, it became apparent to the British that they were not facing an insurrection in one province of the British Empire but rather a widespread revolution throughout its thirteen American colonies. More significant, however, were the wider diplomatic implications of a protracted civil war within the empire. France, which had improved its army and navy after the Seven Years' War, was seeking an opportunity to avenge its losses resulting from that conflict, and Spain longed to recover Gibraltar and Minorca. The combined fleet resulting from an alliance between both countries could outnumber the Royal Navy. By the end of 1775, the North American Squadron had grown to fifty-one warships and 7,555 men, totaling a third of the Royal Navy. Thus, London's attention was divided, looking with one eye toward suppressing the Revolution and the other eye looking toward Europe.

In 1776, the Royal Navy missed opportunities to bring the war to a rapid conclusion. While the British hoped that a coastal blockade would bring the colonies to submission,

USS *Alfred*, a 30-gun former merchantman commissioned in Philadelphia in December 1775, took part in the raid on Nassau and captured numerous prizes in European waters before being captured by the British ships *Adriane* and *Ceres* in March 1778. (National Archives and Records Administration)

the Admiralty's decision not to commit ships of the line to that theater of operations ensured the failure of its blockade policy. Still, the Royal Navy achieved a significant success with the capture of New York. Situated at the mouth of the Hudson River, the city was strategically important for the transport of troops and as a source of supplies. The capture of New York would cut off New England from the rest of the colonies. The British had hoped that the occupation of the city would demoralize the Americans into surrendering. As early as 12 July 1776, the *Phoenix*, the *Rose*, and the *Trial* sailed up the Hudson and exposed the weaknesses of American forces in New York. On 22 August, British ships provided cover for an amphibious landing on Long Island, which outflanked the Americans at Brooklyn Heights. New York City lay next.

On 15 September, the British, under the command of General Sir Henry Clinton, attacked Manhattan with the *Renown*, the *Repulse*, the *Pearl*, and the *Trial*. This barrage was followed one hour later by fire from the *Roebuck*, the *Phoenix*, the *Orpheus*, and the *Carysfort*. These bombardments drove the Americans away from the shore, paving the way for a landing party at Kips Bay. In pausing to wait for their entire army to regroup, the British inadvertently allowed the Americans to escape. As a result, the British lost an opportunity to annihilate General George Washington's army and prolonged the conflict. After a month of consolidating their forces in lower Manhattan, the British sent warships up the Hudson to capture Fort Washington and planned another amphibious landing in the east Bronx. On 9 October, they broke through the defenses at Fort Washington and continued their offensive through the Tappan Zee. On 16 November, Fort Washington fell, with the British taking 2,000 prisoners; two days later Fort Lee followed suit. Even though the British had taken New York, the city's occupation did not constitute a decisive victory, as Washington's army simply retreated into the countryside to avoid a pitched battle that might lead to its annihilation. While the British captured 140 American vessels, for their part American cruisers seized 342 vessels, resulting in the loss of commerce and valuable military supplies.

The first American cruiser to sail in European waters was the privateer *Rover* on 31 August 1776, resulting in the capture of four British merchant ships. The Continental Navy began sending cruisers to capture and destroy British shipping, to divert British naval vessels away from American waters, and to escalate tensions between Britain and France by using French ports as sanctuaries. One American captain who took advantage of the deteriorating conditions between Britain and France was Captain Gustavus Conyngham. Conyngham was a commerce raider who harassed British shipping throughout 1777 and used French ports as havens. The Royal Navy thus diverted ships in pursuit of commerce raiders, often yielding little results and exacerbating the shortage of ships. In the course of the year, American cruisers captured more than 300 British merchant ships.

After the surrender of British forces at Saratoga, France intervened on the side of the Americans, a development that inevitably expanded the conflict into the West Indies, the Mediterranean, and even the English Channel. The British had been reduced to waging a defensive war, as Saratoga had drastically reduced the likelihood of a decisive victory. By 1778, there were ninety-two ships stationed in America, of which half were deployed to protect Philadelphia, New York City, Newport, Halifax, and Quebec. Seven ships carried dispatches and escorted military convoys, and the rest were thinly spread in an attempt to blockade the Atlantic coastline.

By 1779 the war had expanded to become a general European conflict, with Spain and Holland joining the side of the Americans, leaving Britain completely isolated and potentially outnumbered. In June of that year, France and Spain attempted an invasion of Britain itself. The plan was to assemble a fleet large enough to destroy the Channel Fleet that protected the British Isles. The invasion fleet would consist of twenty-five French ships of the line sailing from Brest and twenty Spanish ships sailing from Corunna on the northwest coast of Spain. After destroying the Channel Fleet, an army would land on the Isle of Wight, the Channel Islands, or at Plymouth. The plan ultimately collapsed due to poor planning and sickness on the part of the French and Spanish crews. In the same year, to avenge the loss of Gibraltar in 1704, the Spanish laid siege to the fortress in a prolonged engagement that was ultimately unsuccessful. In September 1779, John Paul Jones achieved his famous victory over the *Serapis* off the Yorkshire coast. As neither France nor Spain was able to gain a decisive victory, Britain emerged in an advantageous position during the negotiations that ended in the Treaty of Paris in 1783.

The ingenuity of the Americans in turning a small force to limited advantage, coupled with the very significant benefits to be gained through alliances with nations possessing substantial naval forces, unquestionably influenced the outcome of what might otherwise have been a one-sided conflict in which the colonists would have stood little chance of ultimate victory.

DINO E. BUENVIAJE

See also

Adams, John; *Bonhomme Richard* vs. *Serapis;* Boston Port Act; Boston Tea Party; Continental Navy; Conyngham, Gustavus; Fort Lee; Fort Washington, New York, Fall of; Gibraltar, Siege of; Hopkins, Esek; Jones, John Paul; Marines, British; Marines, Continental; Privateering; Quincy, Josiah, Jr.; Royal Navy; Saratoga Campaign; Washington's Navy

References

Allen, Gardner W. *A Naval History of the American Revolution*. 1913. Reprint, New York: Russell and Russell, 1962.

Conway, Stephen. *The War of American Independence, 1775–1783*. London: Arnold, 1995.

Gardiner, Robert, ed. *Navies and the American Revolution, 1775–1783*. London: Chatham, 1996.

Kennedy, Paul. *The Rise and Fall of the Great Powers: Economic Change and Military Conflict from 1500 to 2000*. New York: Random House, 1987.

Mahan, Alfred Thayer. *The Major Operations of the Navies in the War of American Independence*. Boston: Little, Brown, 1913.

Miller, Nathan. *Sea of Glory: The Continental Navy Fights for Independence, 1775–1783*. New York: David McKay, 1974.

Paullin, Charles Oscar. *The Navy of the American Revolution: Its Administration, Its Policy, and Its Achievements*. New York: Haskell House, 1971.

Syrett, David. *The Royal Navy in American Waters, 1775–1783*. Brookfield, VT: Gower, 1989.

———. *The Royal Navy in European Waters during the American Revolutionary War*. Columbia: University of South Carolina Press, 1998.

Tilley, J. A. *The Royal Navy in the American Revolution*. Columbia: University of South Carolina Press, 1987.

Naval Operations, British vs. French

Toward the end of February 1765, Étienne François de Choiseul, who had been the secretary of state for foreign affairs from 1758 to 1761 before becoming secretary of state for the navy and the colonies, shared his premonition to Louis XV: a war with Britain was inevitable, and the American colonies would secede. Choiseul, therefore, through a regulation of 25 March 1765, proceeded to reform the navy. Older officers were retired, and a large contribution of funds resulted in the construction of a dozen naval vessels. The French navy

The French 90-gun *Languedoc* under fire from the British 50-gun *Renown*, 13 August 1778, an unlikely encounter resulting from the dispersal by a gale of the fleets under Admirals Jean-Baptiste d'Estaing and Richard Howe off Rhode Island. The French vessel, being utterly crippled, might have fallen easy prey to its smaller opponent, but when the *Renown* suspended fighting as darkness approached, it lost the opportunity to capture its stricken adversary, which was rescued the following morning by other French vessels. (Library of Congress)

favored new and more powerful ships of the line, of eighty, seventy-four, and sixty-four guns, as well as large frigates armed with 12-pounder guns.

In 1775, many French men-of-war were ten years old. Admiral d'Orvilliers, commander of the Brest fleet, estimated that of thirty-eight vessels, only thirteen would be ready for operations in six months. On the other hand, Britain had refitted sixteen ships of the line, twenty-two frigates, and thirty-two corvettes and had sent 12,000 soldiers to the colonies. The navy minister at this time, Gabriel de Sartine, emphasized the need for increased supplies of wood for ship construction and masts (the latter coming from Russia) as well as the need for naval training of officers. France had a reputation of having well-educated officers who nevertheless lacked sailing experience. In 1776, a naval squadron committed to maneuvers and commanded by the comte Du Chaffault was created to train officers and crew. The number of sailors called up reached 10,616 in December and 13,946 a year later. After refitting the ships already built, France, starting in 1778, launched ships of the line of 110-guns and frigates armed with 18-pounders.

France knew that it could only equip sixty ships to oppose the one hundred that Britain maintained. An alliance with Spain was therefore essential. In the days following the British capitulation at Saratoga, Foreign Minister Charles Gravier, the comte de Vergennes, sought such an alliance, but the Spanish government absolutely refused to support the American rebels for fear of encouraging revolt in its own American colonies. This explains the volte-face in the three phases of French strategy during the war: the pursuit of an alliance with Spain in 1778, the setback in small-scale operations in 1779; and recourse to a wider strategy encompassing all the world's oceans in 1780–1783.

In 1778, Britain could not hope to catch France unawares as it had in August 1755. At that time—in the middle of a state of peace—Admiral

Edward Boscawen had captured the French cod fishing fleet and numerous colonial vessels, which had deprived the French navy of 10,000 of its best sailors. Now, in this new conflict, it was France, and then Spain, who chose the moment to open hostilities. To support the rebels and to secure the assistance of Spain, Sartine sent a fleet from Toulon to cruise from Philadelphia to Boston and kept the Brest fleet in home waters so that it could engage the Royal Navy's Channel Fleet.

This was a skillful strategy. By sending ships to North America, France forced Britain to divide its forces. The Brest fleet, in turn, had another purpose: to achieve a substantial naval victory, for Spain was only willing to go to war if the French could demonstrate their ability to beat the British. Off Ushant on 27 July 1778, with ships carrying a total of 1,934 guns against 2,288 British guns, and after four days of skillful maneuvering, d'Orvilliers forced Admiral Augustus Keppel to break off hostilities and return in disgrace to friendly waters. The French victory at Ushant was more than a tactical success; it was a diplomatic victory, though in naval terms it was not exploited by further action.

Meanwhile, Louis XVI had charged Admiral Jean-Baptiste d'Estaing's twelve ships with taking the offensive in North American waters, though d'Estaing lost precious time crossing the Atlantic, a journey that took him eighty days. British Admirals Richard Howe and John Byron, alerted by a frigate, were able to combine their force of twenty ships. D'Estaing declined to force his way through the Narrows below New York and instead focused his efforts on Newport, Rhode Island, where 6,000 British troops were based, though the allied siege there failed. On 27 August, d'Estaing joined battle with the British, but a storm dispersed the opposing fleets. The British, having numerical superiority, tried to blockade the French around Boston. The latter escaped toward the Antilles on 3 November, to the great displeasure of the rebels, who thereafter held the French in very low esteem.

In the Antilles, the British resumed the offensive, with Byron seizing the French island of St. Lucia on 15 December. The capture of this island was of no great economic importance but occurred in response to the capture of Dominica by François Bouillé in September. From January to March 1779, the British and French fought over various West Indian islands. The French, for instance, retook St. Martin, then St. Vincent. In the face of these French naval successes, Spain agreed to join France against Britain, and concerns over the presence of d'Estaing's squadron forced the British to evacuate Philadelphia, the very center of the rebellion.

In 1779, proponents of an amphibious landing in Britain, headed by Admiral Charles Pierre Claret, the comte de Fleurieu, received the approval of Louis XVI and Vergennes. On the Spanish side, the foreign minister, José Moñino, the comte de Floridablanca, wanted a short war and the securing of a French pledge that Gibraltar would be returned to Spain. Vergennes secured Spanish support for the landing project, a plan thought feasible since the British had dispersed their fleets. For the first time in the eighteenth century, the Royal Navy suffered from numerical inferiority in European waters, with only forty-five ships at its disposal. The Spanish pledged

Captain Lord Robert Manners falls mortally wounded aboard his 74-gun ship, the *Resolution*, during the Battle of the Saintes, in the West Indies. The Saintes, a clear British victory, was the last major fleet action of the American Revolutionary War. (Library of Congress)

thirty ships, and 20,000 men were concentrated at Le Havre and St. Malo, with the purpose of landing in southern England and marching on London. Because of delays in the Spanish dockyards, the joining of the two fleets did not take place until 22 July, off the Spanish coast. There were to be no more small squadrons or far-flung expeditions. As far as the French were concerned, all force was to be concentrated for a single decisive battle at sea.

Fate then crippled the French fleet. The French troops who were accompanying the sailors on board ship brought an intestinal flu with them, a kind of typhus that decimated the crews. On 16 August, the combined fleet appeared off Portsmouth, expecting to engage Admiral Sir Charles Hardy's fleet. The British commander, with forty ships, declined an engagement, dragging the combined fleet after him in pursuit out of the Channel, having the advantage of speed due to the copper sheathing on his ships. Even though the Channel was temporarily free of British ships, d'Orvilliers refused to give the order for a landing without having first beaten Britain's main force. The best opportunity for a short war was therefore lost, especially since the British had neither fortifications nor any army in the southern Channel. On 3 September, the French fleet, being unable to continue its pursuit, returned to Brest with 8,000 men sick and hundreds of dead, including d'Orvilliers' only son. The epidemic had saved Britain.

In the autumn, a Spanish squadron of ten ships blockaded Gibraltar but Rodney, with eighteen ships, managed to reprovision the fortress. The limited war had failed. France needed to adopt a long-term worldwide naval strategy that depended on the success of convoys and on victory on all the seas. This new strategy required a good system of resupply overseas and the means to control epidemics. The paradox of the American Revolutionary War was that the only naval epidemic that struck the French navy at that time took place in the Channel in 1779. Neither d'Estaing's forces in 1778–1779 nor those of his successors suffered from any epidemics in spite of long stretches of one to two years away from European ports.

On 4 July 1779, d'Estaing landed on Grenada and seized the initiative from the British. Two days later, Byron, with twenty-one ships, took up battle but was repulsed, leaving the island to the French. D'Estaing tried a landing at Savannah in September but failed, sustaining heavy losses. He then returned to Brest. In spite of the failure at Savannah, the capture of Grenada boosted d'Estaing's fortunes in the naval service.

The Antilles and the West Indian colonial trade then became each side's principal objects. Starting in February 1780, the Spanish decided to send twelve to fourteen ships to the Antilles to protect Cuba. Luc-Urbain du Bouexic Guichen left for the Antilles with a mission to escort supply convoys and to protect the French islands. The British sent Rodney, who had achieved fame through his exploits at Gibraltar. Three times, on 17 April and on 15 and 18 May, Rodney and Guichen faced off. These three engagements, considered by some to be masterpieces of tactical combat, illustrated the fact that the line of battle employed by both fleets and the equal skills of the two admirals resulted in a draw. Rodney and Guichen then returned to Europe, each protecting a convoy loaded with colonial products, neither having achieved a decisive advantage. The war was dragging, to the ire of the French public, who witnessed a very rapid increase in the cost of the war and the size of the national debt.

War was proving very costly to the French but even more so to the British. Because of the rise of the public debt, Jacques Necker, the general comptroller of finance, secured Sartine's departure from the cabinet and his replacement by the Marquis de Castries. Sartine was a very skilled navy secretary, but his talents were more administrative than military. Castries would combine these two qualities. He was primarily a land soldier, but with his victory at Kloster-Kamp in 1760 he had shown himself to be one of the few good leaders of the Seven Years' War.

From a global perspective, the differences in the distribution of French and British ships across the seas in 1780–1781 were negligible. Castries, however, shifted eight ships from the European theater and allocated them to American waters and the Indian Ocean. The difference between the number of French and British vessels outside of Europe was worthy of note. The superiority of the allies on the American side of the Atlantic was due to the assignment of Spanish ships to Havana. Castries did not expect a victory in Europe. He kept a combined fleet there to immobilize the British in the English Channel and at Gibraltar, but he was counting on a victory in America and secondarily in the Indies, thanks to his aggressive new admirals, François de Grasse, Jacques Barras, and Pierre-André de Suffren. For the first time in the eighteenth century, the decisive theater of operations was outside of Europe, proof of the importance attached to the colonies.

After the naval encounter off the Chesapeake between Commodore Destouches and Admiral Marriot Arbuthnot on 16 March 1781, the British combined all their forces from the Carolinas and Virginia on the Yorktown peninsula. This British victory was a testimony to the British Army's absolute confidence in its navy. On 22 March, de Grasse left Brest with 21 ships as an escort for a convoy of 156 vessels. Castries had ordered him to secure decisive victories and to take the initiative while, at the same time, protecting commerce. Using naval vessels to tow commercial ships, de Grasse managed, on 29 April, to surprise Samuel Hood, who was in the process of blockading Martinique. Six British ships were damaged. On 1 May, after another engagement, Hood, whose flagship *Pocahantas* had been dismasted by French cannon fire, declined to continue the fight, which allowed de Grasse to resupply the French islands. French forces then directed themselves toward the Dutch island of Tobago, which had been seized by the British. Troops commanded by Bouillé landed on 30 May and captured the place, at the cost of fifty-six dead and fifty wounded.

On 1 June, the British governor surrendered the island, together with 1,000 soldiers. On 1 May 1781, La Motte-Picquet, commanding a squadron of six ships of the line and three frigates, had intercepted the British convoy that was bringing back to Britain the spoils that Rodney had taken from the Dutch island of St. Eustatius. On 9 May, five French and ten Spanish ships captured Pensacola, as a result of which Florida, once more, became a Spanish colony. At Porto Praya on 16 April 1781, Suffren saved the Spanish possessions at the Cape Verde Islands by attacking and immobilizing Commodore George Johnstone in an action that gave the French the initiative in the Indian Ocean. However, the British fleet had not been destroyed. With Pensacola, Tobago, and Porto Praya, the Franco-Spanish strategy of engagement on a worldwide basis was achieving its first victories, though none had been decisive.

In the course of the American Revolutionary War, the quality of the construction of naval vessels and, conversely, the relative weakness of naval gunfire (almost entirely limited to the use of round shot) made it almost impossible for either side to achieve a decisive victory. Combined land and naval operations were needed. D'Estaing had understood this in his operations at Grenada and Savannah. De Grasse also appreciated its importance, for the capture of neither Pensacola nor Tobago was decisive enough as long as Jean-Baptiste Vimeur, the comte de Rochambeau, remained at a standstill around New York and George Washington continued in a desperate situation, with American troops deserting in large numbers.

Everything depended on de Grasse taking the initiative. Rochambeau suggested to him that he leave the Antilles for New York or, especially, Yorktown, Virginia. De Grasse understood the enormous military error that the British had made in establishing themselves on the Yorktown peninsula, where all help depended on unimpeded access to the sea. He therefore devised an extraordinary plan of combined operations. He took advantage of the large distances by sea that separated the different theaters of operations, seeking to bring decisive force against an enemy who did not expect it. The troops under Rochambeau would leave Newport and by forced march reach Annapolis, Maryland, where French frigates would transport them across the Chesapeake to Yorktown, while the Marquis de Lafayette's and Anthony Wayne's small force of cavalry would go to Williamsburg. Everything would come by sea: siege artillery, American troops, French soldiers aboard transports, money, ammunition, and supplies.

De Grasse pretended to steer a course for New York but instead passed through the Bahamas straits. This fooled Rodney, who left the Chesapeake undefended. On 30 August, the twenty-four French naval vessels appeared off Yorktown. At Jamestown, they landed 3,400 soldiers from the Antilles regiment, who then proceeded immediately to encircle British General Charles Cornwallis. In addition, de Grasse landed 1,800 sailors, supported by 90 Marines. He then had the foresight to organize a river fleet composed of small vessels, frigates, and corvettes. These were to transport across the Chesapeake (a distance of 120 nautical miles) Rochambeau's men, who were expected at Annapolis.

Admiral Thomas Graves, who had succeeded Rodney, appeared at the Chesapeake on 5 September with nineteen ships and tried to take the twenty-four French vessels by surprise. De Grasse's force left its 2,500 troops ashore and engaged the British as each vessel got under way. Graves lost the fight: the *Ajax* and the *Terrible* were put out of action, the *Shrewsbury* was dismasted, and the *Intrepid*, the *Princesa*, and the *Montagu* sustained severe damage to their rigging. The French lost 3 officers killed and 18 wounded and 209 other men out of action; the British had 90 dead and 246 wounded.

After spending four days watching the French, the British fleet scuttled the *Terrible* and sailed to New York to undertake repairs. On 6 September, French transports started to embark Rochambeau's and Washington's men at the mouth of the Elk River and transported them by sea to Yorktown. Pounded by naval and siege artillery brought up by Barras, the besieged Cornwallis, realizing that he had been abandoned, surrendered on 17 October after a few skirmishes. Yorktown was not merely a victory on land but rather the result of brilliant combined naval and land action. As the historian Samuel Eliot Morrison pointed out, without de Grasse's naval victory, it would not have been Cornwallis's but Washington's surrender that history would have recorded. Britain had unquestionably lost the war at the Chesapeake but was not yet ready to admit it.

De Grasse left Rochambeau in America and returned to the Antilles in order to protect an enormous colonial convoy. De Grasse took advantage of his victory to send two convoys to France without sustaining any losses. Then, in spite of tired crews and ships requiring repairs, he landed 6,000 men on St. Kitts (also known as St. Christophers) on 11 January 1782. He fought two violent actions on 25 and 26 January against Hood, who had appeared with twenty-two ships to rescue the garrison besieged on Brimstone Hill. Hood's intervention failed to save the island, and the British surrendered the place on 17 February 1782.

In Europe, the Spanish were able to combine the Brest fleet with that of Cadiz. Guichen and nineteen French ships came under the command of Admiral Cordova on 6 July. The combined fleet then escorted a convoy charged with the seizure of Minorca. On 9 August, under the command of the Duc de Crillon, troops landed and captured the town of Mahon, followed by the fall of the fortress at St. Philip, which surrendered on 4 February 1782.

Following this success, in 1782 the Spanish requested that the French attack Gibraltar and Jamaica. Castries therefore ordered de Grasse to send an expedition against Jamaica in conjunction with Spanish ships carrying troops based on Cuba under Bernardo de Gálvez, who was put in command of the land forces. De Grasse, however, never got the expected reinforcements, receiving only 2 ships instead of the expected 10. Moreover, his fleet only consisted of older vessels, half of which were not sheathed in copper. It was with this force that he was expected to complete his mission. On 12 December 1781, off Ushant, Rear-Admiral Richard Kempenfelt surprised Guichen's squadron and captured 19 merchant ships laden with supplies for the Antilles fleet. Meanwhile, de Grasse had to convoy to Santo Domingo 150 merchant ships loaded with colonial goods as well as to transport troops who were destined to defend Martinique and Guadeloupe. He was pursued by Rodney, fought his first action with him on 9 April 1782, won the advantage, and consequently guaranteed the convoy's safety.

De Grasse tried the same maneuver on 12 April at the Saintes, off Guadeloupe, but his captains' hesitation led them into poor dispositions during the initial stages of the battle. Then the winds failed him. His fleet divided by becalmed conditions, de Grasse found himself defeated by Rodney, with the loss of five French vessels, including the flagship *Ville de Paris*. Nevertheless, the convoy reached Santo Domingo without loss. This French defeat, albeit a notable one, did not change the course of the conflict, but it permitted Britain to initiate peace negotiations from a stronger position, bolstered by the failure of the allied attack on Gibraltar later in the year.

After the fight at Porto Praya, Suffren led a brilliant campaign in the Indian Ocean in support of Hyder Ali, the Mysorean leader then at war with the British, and secured victories at Sadras, Providien, Negapatam, Trincomalee, and Cuddalore. This separate theater of operations, as a judicious addition to the war being conducted in the Atlantic and the Mediterranean, posed a serious threat to British commercial interests in India and served to accelerate peace negotiations.

PATRICK VILLIERS

See also

Barras, Jacques Melchoir, Comte de; Bougainville, Louis-Antoine de; British West Indies; Cape St. Vincent, Battle of; Chesapeake, First Battle of the; Chesapeake, Second Battle of the; Cuddalore, Battle of; Dogger Bank, Battle of; Dominica, First Battle of; Dominica, Second Battle of; Estaing, Jean-Baptiste, Comte d'; French Navy; French West Indies; Gibraltar, Siege of; Grasse, François-Joseph-Paul, Comte de; Graves, Thomas; Guichen, Luc-Urbain du Bouexic, Comte de; Hood, Samuel; Martinique, Battle of; Monte Cristi, Actions off; Negapatam, Battle of; Newport, Rhode Island, Naval Operations against; Porto Praya, Battle of; Providien, Battle of; Rodney, George; Royal Navy; Sadras, Battle of; Savannah, Georgia, Operations against; St. Lucia, Naval and Military Operations against; Suffren, Pierre-André de; Trincomalee, Battle of; Ushant, First and Second Battles of; West Indies; Yorktown Campaign

References

Cavaliero, Roderick. *Admiral Satan: The Life and Campaigns of Suffren*. London: Tauris, 1994.

Clowes, William Laird. *The Royal Navy: A History from the Earliest Times to 1900*. Vol. 3 of 7. London: Chatham, 1996.

Dull, John R. *The French Navy and the American Revolution: A Study of Arms and Diplomacy, 1774–1787*. Princeton, NJ: Princeton University Press, 1975.

Gardiner, Robert, ed. *Navies and the American Revolution, 1775–1783*. London: Chatham, 1996.

James, William. *The Naval History of Great Britain: During the French Revolutionary and Napoleonic Wars*. 4 vols. Mechanicsburg, PA: Stackpole, 2003.

Jenkins, Ernest H. *A History of the French Navy, from Its Beginnings to the Present Day*. London: Macdonald and Jane's, 1973.

Villiers, Patrick. *Le commerce colonial atlantique et la guerre d'indépendance des États-Unis d'Amérique, 1778–1783*. New York: Arno, 1977.

Naval Operations, British vs. Spanish

When Spain entered the war, it entered into alliance with France by the Treaty of Aranquez in April 1779. Spain had little interest in providing direct aid to the American colonists but was keen to recover Gibraltar and assist the French in the West Indies.

Major naval encounters between Britain and Spain (and there were many insignificant ship-to-ship actions) were confined to three distinct episodes: first, the joint attempt by Spain and France to seize control of the English Channel as a prelude to an invasion of Britain; second, the engagement fought between Admirals Rodney and Langara near Cadiz; and last, the operations connected with the siege of Gibraltar.

Spain's resources being fairly limited, it could not sustain a long war. The most direct harm to be inflicted on Britain, it was felt, would be to cooperate with the French in clearing the English Channel of British ships in preparation either for a full-scale invasion of Britain or to enable more limited operations to be directed against the Isle of Wight and the dockyards on the southern coast, particularly at Portsmouth. The second option, though obviously much more limited in scale, nevertheless held the prospect of achieving the same results as the first. A successful raid, or series of raids, against the southern coast could imperil Britain's trade, causing its credit to collapse and obliging it to sue for peace.

For operations in the Channel, Spain dispatched thirty-six line of battle ships that, when joined by thirty French ships, brought overwhelming superiority to bear against the Royal Navy's fleet in home waters, which consisted of only forty vessels under Admiral Sir Charles Hardy. Nevertheless, the French put to sea weeks late and without a full complement of supplies; even then the Spanish, under Admiral Cordova, did not leave port for another seven weeks. When at last the two forces combined and entered the Channel, they outnumbered the British by three to two, but after sustaining heavy losses through sickness and death, and with the ships themselves in poor condition, this otherwise enormous force proved itself unfit to provoke a general action, much less provide protection for an amphibious invasion. Hardy, on the other hand, with fewer but better ships, was intact and to windward. Worst of all for the Spanish and French allies, they faced the real possibility that in late summer a southerly gale might force their fleet, practically unseaworthy as it was and already ravaged by disease, onto the English coast.

British strategy was meant to compensate for weaker numbers. Hardy had been stationed westward so that when the allies made a westerly course in order to open an engagement, Hardy, with copper-bottomed ships capable of outrunning his decrepit opponents, sailed past them into the Channel and took on supplies at Portsmouth. Even had Hardy been obliged to confront

The Battle of Cape St. Vincent, 16 January 1780. Fighting on a stormy, moonlit night, Admiral George Rodney's numerically superior British fleet defeated the Spanish under Admiral Don Juan de Langara. (Library of Congress)

the opposing fleet while it covered an actual invasion attempt, he would have held the advantage over less-maneuverable vessels burdened with the responsibility of protecting innumerable transports. This, however, was now all superfluous. With Hardy back in the Channel, the Franco-Spanish fleet could do no more and returned to friendly ports.

Their attempt at invasion having failed, Franco-Spanish forces were soon directed to one of Britain's vital overseas bases: Gibraltar. By the end of 1780 Rodney, with seventeen ships of the line and a large convoy, was sent out to relieve the garrison. During his journey south, he first captured a Spanish supply convoy and then, on approaching Cadiz, made contact with a Spanish squadron under Langara off Cape St. Vincent. In foul weather and beneath a dramatic moonlit sky, Rodney engaged the Spanish rear, taking six vessels and causing a seventh to blow up. Two more ships were driven ashore, and Rodney captured another two a few days later. To cap his achievement, shortly thereafter he sailed safely into Gibraltar, to the delight of the besieged garrison, whose stocks were replenished for another year.

Notwithstanding this success, British naval resources were by this point severely stretched between home waters, the West Indies, North America, the Baltic, and elsewhere, thus enabling a combined Franco-Spanish fleet, in support of troop transports, to enter the Mediterranean unhindered in the summer of 1781 and land troops on Minorca. The British garrison, badly afflicted by scurvy, capitulated in February 1782. When the combined fleet returned to the Atlantic in late summer of that year, with most of the vessels bound for Brest, Admiral Darby, in command of the Channel Fleet, had only twenty-seven ships to oppose more than forty under Cordova. The British admiral was therefore fortunate that his Spanish counterpart ordered his ships to their respective home ports. Thus, the Franco-Spanish allies squandered yet another opportunity to wrest control of the Channel from the Royal Navy, already stung by its stunning failure to support Charles Cornwallis at Yorktown the previous autumn.

By this time there was also a renewed and urgent need to relieve Gibraltar, still under siege by combined Franco-Spanish land and naval forces. No assistance could be made available before the allied assault, launched on 13 September 1782 and involving ten floating batteries specially designed to withstand artillery fire. Notwithstanding the novelty of these vessels, the Spanish deployed them badly, and by a twist of irony these innovative craft were themselves destroyed by a British "secret weapon" employed on this occasion: hot shot, heated round shot that set alight targets whose principal constituents, wood and canvas, were highly combustible.

Upon his arrival, Admiral Lord Richard Howe, Britain's greatest naval commander, with thirty-four ships of the line and an immense supply convoy, proved too threatening to Cordova's besieging force of thirty-five ships that, though numerically about equal, were in a poor state and consequently refused to fight on two occasions. Once again Gibraltar was saved, and when the preliminaries of peace between Britain, France, and Spain were concluded in January 1783, the Rock remained in British possession.

GREGORY FREMONT-BARNES

See also
Cape St. Vincent, Battle of; Gibraltar, Siege of

References
Clowes, William Laird. *The Royal Navy: A History from the Earliest Times to 1900.* 7 vols. London: Chatham, 1996.
Gardiner, Robert, ed. *Navies and the American Revolution, 1775–1783.* London: Chatham, 1996.
Syrett, David. *The Royal Navy in European Waters during the American Revolutionary War.* Columbia: University of South Carolina Press, 1998.

Navigation Acts
(1651–1764)

Britain's seventeenth- and eighteenth-century trade and navigation laws were rooted in the economic doctrine of mercantilism, which had as its objective the creation of a largely self-sufficient commercial empire centered on its founding nation, or mother country, such as Great Britain. Such an empire sought to keep control of its gold and silver, to protect the industries and the manufacturing jobs in its central nation, and to direct the flow of raw materials from all of its colonies directly to the central nation in order to reduce the costs of production, and of consumption, at the center. Laws written under the influence of a mercantilist view of international economics discouraged or prohibited the export of certain raw materials from a nation's colonies to nations outside the empire whenever the central nation could productively convert those materials into manufactured products or consume them directly, and mercantilist regulations also prohibited the direct importation of manufactured products by a nation's colonies from nations outside the empire. Mercantilism, in short, shaped the economy to benefit the empire as a whole by benefiting the mother country.

England's first Navigation Act was passed during Oliver Cromwell's Interregnum in 1651. Dutch trade with English North America had grown rapidly, and Parliament responded by prohibiting all foreign ships from trading in the English colonies and by requiring that all cargoes shipped from America to England or Ireland be brought on ships commanded and crewed by Englishmen. These laws, however, were difficult to enforce. Parliament relied upon colonial governors to assist in this regulation, but few colonial governors had the interest or the capacity to do so.

Yet in spite of the difficulties of enforcement, Charles II and the Restoration Parliament saw the value of continuing the Navigation Acts, and in 1660 and 1663, Parliament began constructing a comprehensive Navigation Act system. These first laws restricted most shipping to the English colonies to English- and colonial-built, -owned, and -manned ships and, for the first time, created a list of enumerated goods produced in the colonies that had to be unloaded in Great Britain before they could be shipped to other countries. At the outset, the list included three of the most important colonial commodities: tobacco, sugar, and indigo.

Over the next three decades, Parliament passed two more important Navigation Acts. In 1673, Parliament demanded that duties be paid on enumerated goods that were shipped from plantation to plantation before they could cross the Atlantic. More importantly, this measure provided for the appointment of customs commissioners to collect the duties on enumerated goods. Finally, in 1696, Parliament under William III confined all colonial trade to transportation on English ships; granted customs officials in the colonies the same powers possessed by customs officials in England, including the authority to make forcible entries during searches; required bonds to be posted on enumerated goods; enlarged the work of the colonial naval officers; and voided all colonial law contrary to the Navigation Acts.

Soon thereafter, England's Navigation Acts moved beyond creating a more integrated imperial system of trade to regulating the production of certain colonial commodities and manufactures. In 1699, Parliament restricted the production of wool in the colonies and tightly controlled its exportation to England, and by 1705 new legislation had expanded the list of enumerated articles to include rice, molasses, and vital naval stores. Over the next fifty years, Parliament, now legislating for Scotland as well as England, continued its policy of protecting nearly all British commerce from colonial competition. This mercantilist arrangement was, however, to some degree reciprocal. Parliament was willing to grant the colonies monopolies in producing certain raw materials and to protect such monopolies. Perhaps the best-known example was Parliament's prohibition against growing tobacco in England; thereafter, virtually all British tobacco leaf was produced in Maryland, Virginia, and North Carolina.

Britain also continued to expand the list of enumerated goods that could only be shipped within the empire. In 1721, Parliament added beaver skins, furs, and copper to the list. In the next decade, Britain attempted to regulate the colonial hat industry to protect London felt makers and sought to protect British West Indian planters from heavy competition from French West Indies planters in the molasses trade to New England. These laws, however, proved to be nearly unenforceable.

In the decade preceding the outbreak of hostilities between the colonies and Great Britain, Parliament regulated the production of iron in the colonies (the Iron Acts of 1750 and 1757). In the Revenue (Sugar) Act of 1764, Parliament further restricted the importation of West Indian molasses by New England and again expanded the enumerated list. More importantly, the Sugar Act became the first act passed by Parliament primarily for the purpose of raising revenue in the colonies. In this sense, the Sugar Act was both the last important Navigation Act and the first of a decade of revenue acts—including the Stamp Act, Townshend Acts, and Tea Act—that had as their goal not trade regulation but the taxation and political control of British North America. When the First Continental Congress began massive colonial resistance to British policies in October 1774, Parliament's revenue acts of 1764–1773 were, along with the Coercive Acts of 1774, its principal targets. By 1776, however, the pre-1764 Navigation Acts were also seen as a burden, and freedom from those regulations was an eagerly anticipated benefit of independence.

CHRISTOPHER N. FRITSCH

See also
British Parliament; Sugar Act; Trade

References

Barrow, Thomas C. *Trade and Empire: The British Customs Service in Colonial America, 1660–1775.* Cambridge: Harvard University Press, 1967.

Dickerson, Oliver M. *The Navigation Acts and the American Revolution.* New York: A. S. Barnes, 1963.

McCusker, John J., and Russell Menard. *The Economy of British North America, 1607–1789.* Chapel Hill: University of North Carolina Press, 1985.

Negapatam, Battle of
(6 July 1782)

The Battle of Negapatam was the third naval action fought between British and French squadrons under Admirals Sir Edward Hughes and Pierre de Suffren in the Indian Ocean during 1782. Following his contest with Hughes off Providien on 12 April, Suffren made for Ceylon, taking several British transports en route. In early July, Hughes, then at Negapatam—formerly Dutch but then under British control—received intelligence that Suffren was only a few miles away off Cuddalore, which had fallen to Hyder Ali on 4 April. At about 1:00 P.M. on 5 July, Hughes, with eleven ships, sighted the French squadron of twelve vessels, and two hours later he weighed anchor and proceeded south, taking advantage of southerly winds produced by a monsoon. At dawn on 6 July, he sighted Suffren at anchor, about 8 miles to leeward. The French made sail about 6:00 A.M., with one of their vessels, the *Ajax* (64 guns), remaining out of line, having lost its main and mizzen topmasts in a severe squall the previous afternoon. This therefore left equal numbers of vessels on both sides.

Action began just before 11:00 A.M., with both squadrons heading southsoutheast on the starboard tack, with the British to windward. This enabled the British to bear up together in preparation for an attack, thus duplicating Suffren's maneuver at Providien three months earlier. The British van reached its appointed position sooner than the rear, and soon the fourth ship in Suffren's line lost its mainmast and was obliged to drop to leeward of the line. At 12:30 P.M. the wind suddenly shifted to south-southeast, moving the vessels on both sides slightly on the port bow. Most ships consequently separated from their opponents—the British going to starboard and the French to port. However, between the opposing lines, which were temporarily in disarray as a result of the rapid change in wind and their maneuvers, four British and two French ships were caught, having turned in the wrong direction. From Hughes's force these were the *Sultan* (74 guns) and the *Burford*, the *Worcester*, and the *Eagle* (all 64 guns). In Suffren's force they were the *Severe* and the *Brilliant* (both 64 guns), which had been dismasted either by the *Sultan* or the *Burford*. These maneuvers resulted in a brief but sharp encounter between the *Severe* and the *Sultan* as well as the other two British vessels.

On seeing the remaining ships of the French squadron moving off, the *Severe* hauled down its flag, but when the ships opposing it ceased fire and one hauled off, the *Severe* realized that it would not be boarded and, with a fresh breeze, resumed fire and rejoined the squadron. The *Sultan* consequently wore to resume its place in the main line and was raked by the *Severe* while in this process. Meanwhile, the dismasted *Brilliant*, also caught between the lines, came under fire from the *Worcester* and the *Eagle*. The *Brilliant* also certainly would have been captured had not Suffren himself come to its assistance, but not before it had lost 47 killed and 136 wounded, a staggering loss well exceeding a third of its complement.

Seeing these individual contests taking place between ships trapped inside the main lines, Hughes decided to wear and start a general chase. However, on learning that two of his vessels had suffered serious damage, he countermanded his orders and at 1:30 P.M. formed his line on the port tack and ordered the four engaged ships to rejoin the main body. By 6:00 P.M. both squadrons stood in shore and at anchor, with Hughes near Negapatam and Suffren about 10 miles north. The next day, Suffren made for Cuddalore. The British lost 77 killed and 233 wounded, while the French suffered 178 killed and 601 wounded.

GREGORY FREMONT-BARNES

See also
Cuddalore, Battle of; Hughes, Edward; India, Operations in; Porto Praya, Battle of; Providien, Battle of; Sadras, Battle of; Suffren, Pierre-André de; Trincomalee, Battle of

References
Cavaliero, Roderick. *Admiral Satan: The Life and Campaigns of Suffren*. London: Tauris, 1994.

Clowes, William Laird. *The Royal Navy: A History from the Earliest Times to 1900*. Vol. 3 of 7. London: Chatham, 1996.

Gardiner, Robert, ed. *Navies and the American Revolution, 1775–1783*. London: Chatham, 1996.

James, William. *The Naval History of Great Britain: During the French Revolutionary and Napoleonic Wars*. 4 vols. Mechanicsburg, PA: Stackpole, 2003.

Nelson, Horatio
(1758–1805)

Although Horatio Nelson is of course most often associated with his naval triumphs during the French Revolutionary and Napoleonic Wars (1792–1815), he first saw active service during the War for American Independence.

The son of a Norfolk rector, Nelson joined the Royal Navy in 1771 at the age of twelve through the influence of his uncle, Maurice Suckling, commander of the *Raisonnable* (64 guns). As a midshipman, in 1773 Nelson accompanied an expedition to the Arctic aboard the *Racehorse* during a search for a northern route to the China Sea and the Pacific, and he later served in the East Indies, where he contracted malaria. Sickness was, in fact, to plague him throughout his life. At the end of 1775, for instance, he was at Bombay and during his journey home was not expected to live. By the time he reached Britain, his uncle had been made comptroller of the navy, responsible for administration of the dockyards and the appointment of most of the navy's warrant officers. With war in the colonies now well in earnest and his health restored, Nelson saw the prospect of active service.

In September 1776 Nelson became an acting lieutenant aboard the *Worcester* (64 guns), convoying merchant vessels to and from Gibraltar and into the North Sea. Although two years short of the required age of twenty (he falsified his birth certificate), he passed the exam for second lieutenant after the *Worcester* returned to Portsmouth in April 1777, and Suckling found a new ship, the frigate *Lowestoffe* (32 guns), for his newly commissioned nephew. Nelson sailed on the *Lowestoffe* to the West Indies, where he transferred onto a schooner, the *Little Lucy*, with himself in command, capturing an American schooner after an eight-hour chase. In 1778 he transferred, again through his uncle's favor, to the *Bristol*, the flagship of the commander in chief of the Jamaica station, Sir Peter Parker. Later Nelson was promoted to first lieutenant.

When France joined the war against Britain in February 1778 the Royal Navy expanded in size, giving the ambitious and now experienced Nelson the opportunity for independent command. In December he was appointed

Horatio Nelson, who would become the greatest naval commander in British history during the French Revolutionary and Napoleonic Wars, was a young naval captain operating against the Spanish in Central America during the American Revolutionary War. (Archibald Alison, *History of Europe from the Commencement of the French Revolution to the Restoration of the Bourbons in MDCCCXV*, 1860)

commander of the brig *Badger* and was sent to protect British settlers and traders along the Mosquito Coast and in the Bay of Honduras against American privateers. He was then transferred to Jamaica, which the French were expected to attack. In June 1779, at the age of twenty, Nelson learned of his promotion to post captain of the frigate *Hinchinbrooke*, which was en route to Jamaica, where he was then commanding the batteries at Fort Charles, part of the defenses of Port Royal. The expected French descent on Jamaica never materialized and, in September, he resumed his patrol of the Central American coast, now aboard ship. As Spain had by this time entered the war on the allied side, Nelson now found himself in hostile waters.

In September 1779 a British expedition, in which Nelson played no part, was sent against the coast of Honduras and captured the fort of Omoa and $3 million from the Spanish treasury there. The success of that venture encouraged the governor of Jamaica, Major-General John Dalling, to launch another, much more ambitious, expedition, this one to cut Spanish possessions in Central America in two by sending an expedition up the San Juan River in Nicaragua, across Lake Nicaragua to Granada, and then on to the Pacific coast. The main obstacle would be Fort San Juan, 65 miles upriver.

The expedition embarked in March 1780 under an army major but with Nelson in charge of the boats conveying the troops. The climate, however, proved extremely unhealthy, and during the two weeks it took to reach Fort San Juan, the men experienced great hardships struggling against difficult terrain, tropical rainstorms, and shallow water that often obliged the men to carry the boats. On reaching their first objective, the attackers captured an island battery in a surprise night attack and then laid siege to the fort, Nelson landing four guns for the purpose. At this point, however, he was gripped by stomach pains, and for the subsequent two weeks he suffered from dysentery and malaria. Reinforcements arrived and took the fort by assault on 29 April, just as Nelson was being evacuated downriver by canoe in a frantic effort to save his life. On reaching the coast, he gave command of the *Hinchinbrooke* to another officer and was sent to Jamaica to recover. Nelson's recovery was slow, and though he had been given command of the *Janus*, a frigate larger than his previous vessel, he was still too weak for service and in September returned to Britain.

Nelson did not fully recover until the summer of 1781, when he was given command of the frigate *Albemarle* (28 guns), which he sailed in October, together with two other frigates, to escort a convoy of merchant ships from the Baltic back to Britain. In April 1782 he accompanied a convoy bound for Newfoundland and Quebec, capturing an American fishing schooner off the Canadian coast, escaping from three French ships of the line, and briefly fighting a French frigate, the *Iris*. In October, while at Quebec, he protected troop transports bound for New York and came to the notice of two important patrons: Lord Hood and the seventeen-year-old son of George III, Prince William, the future King William IV.

From New York, Nelson formed part of the main fleet proceeding south to Jamaica in February 1783. During this journey with the *Albemarle* and several other vessels, on his own authority he put ashore a party of sailors and marines to assault the fortified French post on Turks Island, a minor station at the southeastern extremity of the Bahamas. The attack was repulsed, and after withdrawing and bombarding the fort from offshore, Nelson was obliged to sail off. The preliminaries of peace soon followed, and with them ended his part in the American Revolutionary War.

Nelson's career prospects at the end of the war were bright. Notwithstanding his illness in the expedition to Fort San Juan, he had distinguished himself and come to the attention of important patrons. Indeed, after accompanying Prince William on a visit to Havana shortly after the war, Nelson returned to Britain and had an audience with the king. He soon returned to the West Indies, where he tried to prevent the flourishing illegal American trade with Britain's Caribbean possessions. Ten years passed before Britain was again at war, but when hostilities with France resumed in 1793—on a far greater scale than ever before—the potent combination of Nelson's irrepressible ambition and considerable experience could at last come to the fore, establishing him by the time of the Battle of Trafalgar in 1805 as Britain's greatest naval commander.

GREGORY FREMONT-BARNES

See also

Omoa, Honduras, Capture of; Privateering; Royal Navy

References

Clowes, William Laird. *The Royal Navy: A History from the Earliest Times to 1900*. 7 vols. London: Chatham, 1996.
Gardiner, Robert, ed. *Navies and the American Revolution, 1775–1783*. London: Chatham, 1996.
Pocock, Tom. *The Young Nelson in the Americas*. London: Collins, 1980.

Nelson, Thomas
(1738–1789)

The merchant, planter, commander of Virginia militia, and wartime governor Thomas Nelson was born in Yorktown, Virginia, the eldest son of William Nelson and Elizabeth Burwell. William Nelson was a prosperous merchant-planter who became one of the more powerful political figures in the colony. His son was first educated at home and at a nearby private school before going to England in 1753 to complete his education. Nelson attended a private school near London and in 1758 entered Christ College, Cambridge. He completed his residence at Cambridge in 1761 and returned home. Almost

Thomas Nelson, a Virginia delegate to the Second Continental Congress from 1775 to 1777 and again in 1779. He signed the Declaration of Independence in 1776 and became governor of Virginia in 1781. He was also a brigadier general of his state's militia. (Library of Congress)

immediately, he was elected to represent York County in the House of Burgesses, was appointed to the county court, and was soon made a colonel of the county militia.

Nelson married Lucy Grymes (1743–1834) in 1762. The union produced thirteen children, eleven of whom lived to maturity. In the years following his marriage, Nelson became acquainted with his father's business and estates. But he also developed a characteristic, common among the Virginia elite, of not being able to live within his income. A visitor in 1768 reported that Nelson lived "like a prince."

Nelson's father died in 1771, and his bequests made his eldest son a very wealthy man. Among other things, Nelson inherited 20,000 acres of land and 400 slaves. The mercantile firm was left to him and his brother Hugh (b. 1750). Unfortunately, Nelson was not a good businessman, and this coupled with deteriorating economic conditions led him to confess in 1775 that his business affairs were in a sad state.

Nelson was deeply involved in the protest movement against British policies from the late 1760s onward. He was a signer of the Virginia nonimportation agreement of 1769. And in 1774, after the Boston Tea Party and the closure of the port of Boston, he told the voters of York County that British actions threatened not only their lives but something more important, their liberty. By this time, Virginia's royal governor, Lord Dunmore, had dissolved the House of Burgesses, and Nelson and his colleagues met in August, formed an association forbidding the importation of British goods after 1 November, and elected delegates to the First Continental Congress. Nelson was not among those elected, and Lord Dunmore said that this was because he was "too violent."

Nelson did indeed support vigorous resistance to British authority, and in November 1774 he led a group that dumped tea from an English merchant vessel into the York River. The following March, he supported Patrick Henry's plan to raise and arm men for the defense of the colony. In July 1775, Nelson was elected a delegate to the Second Continental Congress and was a signer of the Declaration of Independence. He served intermittently, because of ill health, in Congress through 1779 and was a member of Virginia's new House of Delegates when not in Congress. Despite his lack of military experience, he also commanded the Virginia militia in 1777 and 1778 and in 1780–1781 when British forces threatened the state. Nelson, as well as others, solicited loans for the support of the war effort and collected £62,000 by pledging his own security.

In June 1781, with a massive British army under Lord Charles Cornwallis occupying the center of Tidewater, Virginia, Nelson was elected governor to replace Thomas Jefferson. The legislature granted Nelson extensive powers, which had to be exercised with the consent of the Council of State. He proved to be a good administrator, vigorous, decisive, and evenhanded. But ultimately, he exceeded the broad powers granted him when he acted without the consent of the council to raise supplies for the American and French armies that had Cornwallis penned up in Yorktown. Nelson also took personal command of the Virginia militia at Yorktown.

Cornwallis surrendered on 19 October, and Nelson played an important role in bringing about that outcome. But again his health declined, and he resigned in late November to be replaced by Benjamin Harrison. In December, Nelson's administration was severely criticized in the House of Delegates, primarily because he had acted without the advice of the Council of State. But after his appearance before the House to defend his actions, the delegates passed a bill legalizing the measures he had taken while governor.

During the final years of his life, Nelson returned to the legislature in 1782, 1783, and 1786–1788, but private affairs occupied most of his time. He was deeply in debt, and his situation was made more difficult by the money he had raised, pledging his own security, during the loan drives of 1780. His creditors were pressing for payment. In 1784 he petitioned to have the state repay some £10,000 that he had raised in the loan drives, but the legislature, for unknown reasons, did not appropriate the money. He reopened his mercantile firm and did considerable business, but this did not solve his money troubles, which were made worse by the fact that, unlike many Virginians, he began to try to repay his prewar British debts. All of this took its toll on him mentally and physically.

During the 1780s, Nelson was a hard-money advocate and believed that the Articles of Confederation did not provide the central government with enough powers. He favored the move to revise the Articles of Confederation, but he declined to serve as a delegate to the Philadelphia convention, and in the end he opposed Virginia's ratification of the proposed Constitution. By that time, however, Nelson was a very sick man. He signed his will in December 1788 and died on 4 January 1789. He was buried in the parish churchyard in Yorktown.

EMORY G. EVANS

See also

Cornwallis, Charles; Henry, Patrick; Jefferson, Thomas; Murray, John, Lord Dunmore; Virginia

References

Evans, Emory G. "Executive Leadership in Virginia: Henry, Jefferson and Nelson." In *Sovereign States in an Age of Uncertainty*. Edited by Ronald Hoffman and Peter J. Albert. Charlottesville: University of Virginia Press, 1981.
———. *Thomas Nelson of Yorktown: Revolutionary Virginian*. Charlottesville: University of Virginia Press, 1975.

Netherlands

On 16 November 1776, the armed brig *Andrew Doria* sailed into the harbor of St. Eustatius, one of the Windward Isles under the control of the Dutch West India Company. The brig flew a banner containing seven red and six white stripes and saluted the colors of the United Provinces. The guns of Fort Oranje replied. Though this was not the first military post to make this salute—the Danes at St. Croix had done so a few days before—this was the first time that officers of the Dutch Republic made an act of acceptance to the flag of the United States. In honor of "brave little Holland," a portrait of the governor of St. Eustatius was placed in the State House of New Hampshire.

The sequel to this salute was more cautious and noncommittal. By saluting the *Andrew Doria*'s flag, the Dutch seemed to have acknowledged the sovereignty of a republic that Great Britain viewed as a mere gang of rebels, and the British government protested. St. Eustatius's governor was recalled but then exonerated because, so the Dutch argued, he had saluted the American ship not with the full complement of eleven shots but with nine. Therefore, his action did not constitute the recognition of the United States as a sovereign power. The Dutch thus took the sting out of the matter, circumventing the issue on technical grounds.

In the same vein, in 1775 when King George III requested that the Dutch Republic place the Scots Brigade, a British unit in Dutch service, at his disposal for service in America, the States General refused, but not until after the Prince of Orange had attempted to have the request retracted, pleading practical considerations, to avoid a diplomatic incident. However reluctant they were in this instance to assist Britain (and in a similar case concerning two German regiments in Dutch service in 1777), the Dutch were most complaisant in another matter. They allowed the German mercenaries hired by Britain for service in America to be transported through Dutch territory, mustered at Dordrecht, and embarked at Hellevoetsluis and even made Dutch troops available to prevent desertion.

Such maneuvering was characteristic of the Dutch Republic's relations with Great Britain and the United States during the American Revolution. The Dutch Republic was caught between the naval superpower Britain and the military giant France, neither of whom it wanted to antagonize. The British fleet could easily suffocate Dutch overseas trade, for the Dutch navy was only a mere shadow of its former self. And the French army could easily invade the tiny Dutch Republic, whose military might was decidedly weak compared to its glorious past.

Furthermore, the country was internally divided. William V, the Prince of Orange, who held certain monarchical powers as stadtholder and was closely connected to the British royal house, strongly opposed the rebellion of the American colonists against their—in his opinion—rightful ruler. Diametrically opposed to the prince were citizens who were strongly influenced by the ideals of the Enlightenment. They wanted to reform the Dutch Republic into an efficient, modern state and would soon become known as Patriots.

More powerful yet less extreme than the Patriots were the regents of the Province of Holland. The regents were the hereditary merchant elite who, if not effectively in control of the Dutch Republic, were extremely influential in its economy and magistracy. The influence of the regents in the respective provincial states differed by region, but the regents of Holland completely dominated the States of Holland (its provincial legislature) and were very influential in the States General, the federal legislature of the Dutch Republic. Hardly friendly to the Patriots, the regents traditionally opposed both the House of Orange and the stadtholderate as an institution and therefore were in natural opposition to the prince, and by extension to the British. Their main motive, however, was to preserve economic stability and prosperity.

The British prohibited trade with its North American colonies to any merchantman not sailing under the British flag, and smuggling was thus endemic, a trade that became much livelier when the colonies revolted. Because of Britain's mercantile restrictions and the rural character of North America, Britain's colonies had not developed an industry of any importance, and most goods needed by the insurgents, both civilian and military, had to be imported, a task that the Dutch, among others, gladly took upon themselves. Moreover, if the revolutionaries succeeded in winning independence, the British lock on trade would be broken, opening up American harbors for Dutch commerce.

Opposing the regents of Holland were a mixture of Orangists, mainly commoners who supported the prince—but hardly shared his love for the British—and some more cautious members of the propertied classes, mainly from provinces other than Holland. Having little to win by fresh commerce and with other vested interests to lose, they saw no advantage in antagonizing Britain.

William V, prince of Orange. The Netherlands was officially neutral during most of the war but provided supplies and weapons to the Americans and eventually recognized the independent United States in April 1782. (Library of Congress)

The Dutch Republic had always been a center of political discussion, and the question of American independence produced a variety of pamphlets. Some tracts were outright propaganda, while others were purely informative. Some were strongly politically motivated, touching both on the situation overseas and on that in the Dutch Republic, while others were highly pragmatic in tone. Both local authors and foreigners in translation contributed to the exchange. Prominent participants were Isaäc de Pinto, a Sephardic Jew and staunch Orangist who supported the British; the flamboyant Joan Derk van den Capellen tot den Pol, a thoroughly anti-Orangist knight from Overijssel who strongly sympathized with the Americans and wrote a fiery pamphlet against King George III's request to use the Scots Brigade in America; and Jean Luzac, a personal acquaintance of John Adams and the publisher of the French-language *Gazette de Leyde* (officially the *Nouvelles Extraordinaires*

Distant view of Oranjestad on St. Eustatius in the Netherlands Antilles, circa 1777. The island offered American ships a safe port of call and served as a base of supply for the Continental Army. After the Netherlands entered the war on the American side, the British were quick to seize its West Indian possessions, occupying St. Eustatius in February 1781. (Library of Congress)

de Divers Endroits), a newspaper that supported the Revolution not so much with fiery articles as with arduous, constant, and accurate coverage, using a variety of sources. In one instance, American involvement was even more direct. *Le Politique Holandais* was a French-language newspaper that Adams published from 1781 to 1783 in concert with Antoine Cérisier.

Notwithstanding these spirited interchanges and the obvious sympathy of many Dutchmen for the Americans, enthusiasm was cautious and slow to develop. Often at least partially motivated by economic interests and anti-British sentiment rather than by ideology, Dutch merchants proved initially reluctant to take financial risks, asking for very high guarantees for any support and biding their time until a republican victory became within reach. This was deeply frustrating for Adams, who came to the Dutch Republic as an American envoy in 1780 but did not succeed in procuring either a loan or official support for America for almost two years.

Dutch fears of involvement in the conflict were not imaginary. Dutch trade with the rebelling colonies was a thorn in Britain's side, especially the trade out of St. Eustatius, which was the main harbor through which both legal goods and contraband were transported to America. The British demanded that the Dutch stop this trade and backed their demands by threats, by boarding and capturing Dutch merchant vessels, and by a display of arrogance rarely matched in European diplomacy. In the responding surge of public indignation, William V could not maintain his pro-British position and ordered the Dutch fleet to prepare to protect Dutch merchant ships.

In 1779 the British fired on a Dutch convoy and forcibly escorted it to Plymouth. British boardings of vessels and obstructions of Dutch trade became set policy, and in 1780, 200 British Marines landed on St. Martin, a Dutch island opposite to St. Eustatius, captured any American ships they found, and took their crews prisoner, thus provoking another diplomatic incident. In the same year, the British captured the *Mercury,* a ship on which the American envoy Henry Laurens was sailing to Holland. Laurens unsuccessfully attempted to sink his briefcase with classified documents, and from his papers the British soon publicized the fact that in 1779 a delegation of Amsterdam regents had agreed to the so-called Treaty of Aachen, a treaty of commerce with the United States modeled on the treaty between America and France. In this agreement, the Dutch freely acknowledged the sovereignty of the newly born American republic. Britain saw its chance. Notwithstanding the fact that neither the Amsterdam delegation nor its American counterpart was either official or had any legitimate mandate, Britain declared war on the Dutch Republic on 20 December 1780.

The fourth Anglo-Dutch War was a disaster for the Dutch Republic. During the first month of the war, the Dutch lost more than 200 vessels to the Royal Navy and privateers. On 3 February 1781, Admiral George Rodney captured St. Eustatius without encountering any resistance. The harbor held some 150 vessels, and the British kept Dutch colors flying to lure even more enemy ships into their grasp. On 15 August 1781, off Dogger Bank, the British attacked Dutch warships that were protecting a convoy heading for the Baltic. The Dutch fended off their adversaries, but it was a pyrrhic victory. Their vessels were so severely damaged that the strategic advantage went to the British. In the same year, Britain seized Dutch possessions in Guyana and the East Indies, including Negapatam on the Coromandel Coast. And in 1782 the British captured all Dutch forts on the West African coast except Fort Elmina.

Yet permanent damage to the Dutch Republic and real advantage to Great Britain were limited. The French assisted in protecting Dutch interests in the East, and they reconquered Guyana for the Dutch Republic as well as St. Eustatius, where they confiscated a large portion of the goods that the British had captured from the Dutch. In addition, Rodney and Great Britain both paid dearly for their initial capture of St. Eustatius. Several of the merchant ships seized there belonged, in fact, to British traders, who were caught red-handed attempting to sell their wares to Congress. Yet these merchants, far from being embarrassed into silence, now relentlessly sued Rodney for capturing their ships.

Far more important, however, was the fact that in focusing his attention on St. Eustatius, Rodney assigned only a small squadron to the North American coast and then allowed the French fleet under François de Grasse to sail north from the Caribbean Sea without following them. This blunder outnumbered the British navy in American waters, and the French fleet was able to close off Chesapeake Bay, thereby allowing the combined Continental and French armies in Virginia to force Lord Charles Cornwallis to surrender at Yorktown.

The Americans also profited from the Anglo-Dutch War in the political and financial arenas. Once they were at war with the British, the Dutch had

The Netherlands became the second country in Europe to recognize the United States.

no reason to placate them, and on 19 April 1782 the Netherlands became the second country in Europe to recognize the United States as an independent republic. The Netherlands now accepted Adams, the man who had been working to this end since 1780, as America's minister. In his efforts, Adams had been assisted by Charles Guillaume Fréderic Dumas, a Swiss-born Frenchman who had moved to Holland in the 1750s and had been strongly impressed by the Americans since 1766, when he had met Benjamin Franklin during the latter's visit to the Netherlands. In June 1782, Adams convinced Dutch bankers to loan 5 million guilders to the United States, and in October 1782 the Dutch signed a treaty of commerce and friendship with the United States. The first loan was not large, and Dutch investors were slow to subscribe to it, but enthusiasm rose over time, the Americans contracted new loans, and by 1794 the Dutch held the full American foreign debt, amounting to 30 million guilders.

M. R. VAN DER WERF

See also

Adams, John; Demerara and Essequibo, Dutch Guiana, Seizure of; Diplomacy, American; Diplomacy, British; Diplomacy, French; Dogger Bank, Battle of; German Mercenaries; India, Operations in; Laurens, Henry; Rodney, George; Royal Navy; Yorktown, Virginia, Siege of; Yorktown Campaign

References

Carter, Alice Clare. *Neutrality or Commitment: The Evolution of Dutch Foreign Policy, 1667–1795*. London: Edward Arnold, 1975.

Hutson, James. *John Adams and the Diplomacy of the American Revolution*. Lexington: University Press of Kentucky, 1980.

Israel, Jonathan. *The Dutch Republic: Rise, Greatness, and Fall, 1477–1806*. Oxford: Oxford University Press, 1995.

Madariaga, Isabel de. *Britain, Russia, and the Armed Neutrality of 1780: Sir James Harris's Mission to St. Petersburg during the American Revolution*. New Haven, CT: Yale University Press, 1962.

Morris, Richard B. *The Peacemakers: The Great Powers and American Independence*. New York: Harper and Row, 1965.

Schulte Nordholt, Jan Willem. *The Dutch Republic and American Independence*. Translated by Herbert H. Rowen. Chapel Hill: University of North Carolina Press, 1982.

Van Wijk, F. W. *De Republiek en Amerika, 1776–1782*. Leiden: Brill, 1921.

New England Army
(19 April–3 July 1775)

The New England Army, also known as the Army of Observation, was the precursor of the Continental Army. The term refers to the military force that coalesced outside Boston immediately after the battles at Lexington and Concord. In practical terms, the New England Army launched the siege of the British Army in Boston, then under the command of General Thomas

Gage. On 17 June 1775, it fought the Battle of Bunker Hill, shortly before learning of its adoption by the Continental Congress as the Continental Army on 14 June 1775. Its transformation into the broader force was symbolically completed when General George Washington took command of the Continental Army on 3 July 1775 at Cambridge, Massachusetts. A number of commanders who later figured prominently in the War for American Independence gained their first military experiences serving in this force, which evolved out of a plan devised by Massachusetts's Revolutionary leaders.

It is often assumed that the militiamen who gathered around Boston beginning on the evening of 19 April 1775 assembled there on their own initiative. In fact, they were following a contingency plan that had been developed over the winter and early spring by the Massachusetts Provincial Congress. Once the shooting started at Lexington and Concord, the plan went into effect. Along with raising local troops, it included calling on neighboring colonies for military assistance and assigning quotas of men from each of the various towns in Massachusetts for active duty. After the fighting on 19 April, however, the Massachusetts authorities adopted the expedient, suggested by General Artemas Ward, of surveying the men gathered outside Boston and asking them to stay in the environs of the city. Ward became the head of this force, with John Whitcomb, William Heath, and Ebenezer Frye as his subordinates. The Provincial Congress then called for the formation of a New England Army of 30,000 men, with Massachusetts furnishing 13,600 of these troops. The other New England colonies—Connecticut, New Hampshire, and Rhode Island—were to supply the remainder of the force. Each of these colonies followed the organizational pattern developed by the Massachusetts Provincial Congress, with slight variations.

Organizationally, each infantry regiment was to consist of just under 600 men, including a colonel, a lieutenant colonel, a major, an adjutant, a quartermaster, a chaplain, a surgeon, two surgeon's mates, and ten companies of soldiers. Each company, in turn, would include a captain, two lieutenants, an ensign, and 55 enlisted men. The Massachusetts Committee of Safety, the province's executive arm, approved this plan on 25 April 1775. Although much of this plan was devised months earlier, putting these directives into practice took some time, and it was May before order began to emerge out of the chaos around Boston.

A great deal of the disorder arose from the coming and going of various contingents of troops and individual soldiers seemingly at random. Adding to the confusion, many of the units from more distant towns and from neighboring colonies arrived piecemeal as the states completed their respective quotas. Troops marched up to 100 miles or more over rough roads. As they arrived outside Boston, they were positioned and given duties according to the military necessities of the moment. By July 1775, however, there were twenty-six infantry regiments from Massachusetts, along with three each from Connecticut, New Hampshire, and Rhode Island, ringing the city. This made for a grand total, on paper, of thirty-five infantry regiments with up to 21,000 soldiers.

The New England Army also had several artillery companies. On 13 April, six days before Lexington and Concord, the Massachusetts Provincial Congress had completed the organizational plan for the artillery units. The plan called for six companies, each with four officers, four sergeants, four corporals, a drummer, a fife player, and thirty-two matrosses, or privates. Again, the other New England colonies followed this plan in its essentials. Henry Knox, who later became the chief of the Continental Army artillery, first came to prominence while serving in the Massachusetts artillery.

Several other officers who would soon rise to prominence in the War of Independence also served in the New England Army. Nathanael Greene led the Rhode Island contingent to Boston. Joseph Trumbull, who came with Connecticut's troops as their commissary general, would soon be tapped by Washington for the same role in the Continental Army. Some troops from New Hampshire headed toward Boston as individuals on hearing the first news of hostilities; these were organized by their home colony and designated the 1st New Hampshire regiment. Their commander, John Stark, a veteran of Rogers's Rangers in the 1750s, would later command the victorious Patriot forces at the Battle of Bennington.

The artillery and infantry from the four New England colonies who gathered outside Boston never came close to reaching the total of 30,000 troops set out in Massachusetts's grand plan. Yet the recruiting in 1775 was markedly better than in the later years of the War of Independence. Much of the ease of filling the ranks can be attributed to what historian Charles Royster has called the "rage militaire." This military spirit was at its highest in the spring and summer of 1775. Whatever its deficiencies in numbers or organization, the New England Army provided a strong immediate defense while all of the colonies, under the leadership of Congress, organized for further military action. And this army repulsed two determined British attacks on Breed's (Bunker) Hill before finally relinquishing the ground, giving America's Patriot leaders a vital early propaganda victory.

JAMES R. MCINTYRE

See also

Boston, Massachusetts; Boston, Siege of; British Army; Bunker Hill, Battle of; Continental Army; Gage, Thomas; Greene, Nathanael; Heath, William; Knox, Henry; Lexington and Concord; Putnam, Israel; Ward, Artemas; Washington, George

References

Martin, James Kirby, and Mark E. Lender. *A Respectable Army: The Military Origins of the Republic, 1763–1789.* Wheeling, IL: Harlan Davidson, 1982.

Royster, C. *A Revolutionary People at War: The Continental Army and the American Character.* Chapel Hill: University of North Carolina Press, 1979.

Wright, Robert K. *The Continental Army.* Washington, DC: Center for Military History, United States Army, 1989.

Passed by Parliament less than a month before the outbreak of war at Lexington and Concord, the New England Restraining Act was a direct response to the Continental Association that had been adopted by the American colonists during the First Continental Congress.

The act prohibited the colonists of New England (specifically those in the province of Massachusetts Bay) from engaging in trade with any European nation or colonial possession except Britain, Ireland, and the British West Indies. It also denied colonial fishermen access to the fisheries of the North Atlantic. The scope of the legislation was extended in April 1775 to include five more colonies. Parliament stipulated that the trade provisions of the legislation would remain in place until "Peace and Obedience" had returned to the region and commerce with Britain had been restored.

The New England Restraining Act can be seen as a link in a chain of legislation that began with the passage of the Coercive Acts by Parliament in the spring of 1774. The colonial response to the Coercive Acts was the enactment of a comprehensive economic boycott by the First Continental Congress in October 1774, in the form of the Continental Association. The association was comprised of three main elements: (1) the nonimportation of British goods starting on 1 December 1774, (2) the nonconsumption of British goods beginning on 1 March 1775, and (3) the nonexportation of American products to Britain beginning on 30 September 1775. It also contained pledges to promote the growth of American industry, encourage frugality, and discontinue the slave trade in all of the colonies. The target of the association was the British merchant class. Colonial leaders believed that cessation of commerce would force British merchants to put pressure on Parliament to dissolve the Coercive Acts and work to restore trade in North America.

The Continental Association, however, had the opposite effect on Parliament. The New England Restraining Act was designed to deny access by the colonial merchants to any market other than the mother country and its possessions. Parliament viewed the legislation as a means to reinforce British authority in North America and as a warning sign to the rest of the colonies. Instead, it served as another symbol of British indifference to American rights and helped to advance the cause of rebellion.

KIRK WATSON

See also

Coercive Acts; Congress, First Continental; Continental Association

References

Ammerman, David. *In the Common Cause: American Response to the Coercive Acts of 1774.* New York: Norton, 1975.

Van Tyne, Claude H. *The Causes of the War of Independence.* New York: Peter Smith, 1951.

New Hampshire

New Hampshire was one of only two states where no major battles were fought.

The northernmost of the thirteen colonies that rebelled from Britain, New Hampshire was first settled by the English in 1623 and became a royal province in 1679. While British taxation without representation angered New Hampshire's inhabitants as deeply as it did other colonists, they were slower than many to rebel. The fundamental alteration in their loyalties came in 1774, when Britain began to mass troops in Boston. While no major Revolutionary War battles were fought in New Hampshire, the province sent troops to fight at Bunker Hill and fielded regiments in the Continental Army. New Hampshire soldiers were instrumental in blocking General John Burgoyne's invasion from Canada in 1777, especially at the Battle of Bennington. In June 1788, New Hampshire became the ninth state to ratify the Constitution of the United States.

From 1679 until 1775, New Hampshire was a royal province. The government consisted of a royal governor appointed by the British Crown, a Council appointed by Britain on the recommendation of the governor, and a popularly elected Assembly. By midcentury, this government was an oligarchy, with most of the power from 1741 to 1775 revolving around the mercantile friends and family of the Wentworths. The family's leaders, Benning Wentworth and then his nephew John Wentworth, were both competent governors who were generally liked by the people.

The seat of power and the only well-populated area, with roughly half of the province's inhabitants, was a fairly narrow strip of land along New Hampshire's 18-mile seacoast, with just one major port, Portsmouth. Most of the courts and government offices, most mercantile firms, and the province's only newspaper, the *New Hampshire Gazette*, were all located in this modest-sized town. The rest of the province had only two quite sparsely populated areas: the Merrimack Valley and the Connecticut River Valley, which was considered the frontier.

The movement from royal province to independent state began slowly. At first, the people of New Hampshire protested the infringements on their rights as Englishmen in a respectful and cautious way, and always from the perspective of aggrieved subjects of the king, not as rebels or radicals. But gradually, the actions of Britain became more controlling and more threatening. And New Hampshire's reactions became more radical and more violent.

In May 1763, the *New Hampshire Gazette* reported that Britain would soon levy a series of taxes to defray the costs of quartering British troops in America. The first of these, the Sugar Act, was passed in 1764. New Hampshire reluctantly accepted this new tax partly because it had no strong economic impact on the province. Most of New Hampshire's economy revolved around agriculture, fishing, lumber, and shipbuilding, not on sugar and molasses refining. Then Parliament passed the Stamp Act and the Quartering Act. The Stamp Act of 1765 aroused greater concern in New Hampshire where, as in other colonies, it was seen as a direct tax on the people rather than as a regulation of trade. Massachusetts called for a Stamp Act Congress, which met in New York City in October 1765. New Hampshire declined to send a representative to the congress, but its popular Assembly respectfully petitioned to repeal the Stamp Act. This official restraint didn't keep a rowdy mob in Portsmouth from intimidating New Hampshire's official stamp distributor, George Meserve, and, in effect, forcing him to resign. And in 1766, Britain did indeed repeal the Stamp Act.

When Britain enacted a new set of taxes and regulations, known as the Townshend Acts, in 1767, the Massachusetts Assembly sent out a circular letter to the assemblies of other colonies asking for united action. The New Hampshire Assembly reacted by writing another petition to Britain but did not send it for two years. In 1768, most of the major mercantile colonies began a boycott against British imports, but Portsmouth, New Hampshire's only significant port, refused to participate. In 1770 Britain repealed the Townshend Acts, except for the duty on tea, but in 1773 enacted the Tea Act, which gave overwhelming competitive advantages to East India Company tea. This cut into the colonies' ability to consume other tea, even untaxed smuggled tea, and led to the Boston Tea Party. But New Hampshire had a less violent approach. The citizens of Portsmouth refused to accept the tea but paid to have it shipped to Halifax, Nova Scotia.

In 1774, however, sympathy for Boston, whose port was now shut up and blockaded by British warships, pushed New Hampshire closer to rebellion. Boston was now run by a military governor, General Thomas Gage, who as commander of the British Army in America was gathering British troops there. It was finally becoming clear to nearly all of Britain's North American colonies that a united defense against British policy was needed, and that summer New Hampshire agreed to send two representatives, Nathaniel Folsom and John Sullivan, to the First Continental Congress.

In December 1774, New Hampshire's Revolutionary leaders learned that a ship carrying British troops was on its way to reinforce Fort William and Mary in Portsmouth Harbor. Over a two-night period, John Langden and John Sullivan raided the fort (which was held by only six British soldiers) for powder and arms, including sixteen cannon. This is considered the first armed attack in the rebelling colonies against the British Army. At news of the fighting at Lexington and Concord in April 1775, New Hampshire began sending troops to the Boston area. There, under the leadership of John Stark and James Reed, New Hampshire's soldiers made a significant contribution at the Battle of Bunker Hill. In August 1775, New Hampshire's last royal governor, John Wentworth, left New Hampshire for good. New Hampshire's Revolutionary leaders set up a wartime government in January 1776, and in June they declared the province independent. On 18 July, the Declaration of Independence of the United States was "published by beat of drum in all the shire towns of New Hampshire."

John Sullivan, a delegate from New Hampshire to the Second Continental Congress, became a brigadier general in the Continental Army. He served in the invasion of Canada and in the battles at Trenton, Princeton, Brandywine, and Germantown. In 1779 he led an expedition against the Six Nations but resigned his commission later that year to return to politics. (Library of Congress)

In 1777, Burgoyne attempted to crush the American rebellion by invading the state of New York from Canada. Stark led some 1,500 troops, primarily made up of New Hampshire militia, into the New Hampshire Grants (later Vermont) and then into eastern New York. There, on 16 August 1777, his men played the central role in defeating a major detachment from Burgoyne's army at the Battle of Bennington. Burgoyne's army soon thereafter came to a halt and in October surrendered to the Continental Army at Saratoga.

While New Hampshire was one of only two states (along with Maryland) where no major battles were fought and that suffered no occupation forces during the Revolutionary War, the state contributed three regiments to the Continental Army, and Sullivan earned the rank of brigadier general. New Hampshire troops fought in many of the most important battles of the Revolutionary War, including Trenton, Princeton, Monmouth, and Yorktown, and they suffered at Valley Forge along with General George Washington's other troops from several states.

At the end of the war, New Hampshire adopted a new constitution in 1783. And on 21 June 1788, it became the ninth state to ratify the Constitution of the United States, an approval that technically put the new frame of government into effect.

WILLIAM TOTH

See also

Bartlett, Josiah; Bennington, Battle of; Bunker Hill, Battle of; Burgoyne, John; Constitution, United States; Constitutions, State; Declaration of Independence; Langdon, John; Nonimportation Agreements; Stamp Act; Stamp Act Congress; Stark, John; Sugar Act; Sullivan, John; Townshend Acts

References

Belknap, Jeremy. *The History of New Hampshire*, Vol. 1. Dover, NH: S. C. Stevens and Ela and Wadleigh, 1831.

Upton, Richard Francis. *Revolutionary New Hampshire*. New York: Octagon, 1971.

New Jersey

In the American Revolution, New Jersey was often called the "Crossroads State" or the "Cockpit State" because it was situated between two important Revolutionary cities: New York and Philadelphia. But it could also be called the "Battleground State" since there were nearly one hundred battles and skirmishes fought in New Jersey during the Revolutionary War. Beginning in 1764, its citizens resented what they considered to be Britain's denial of their rights, especially through taxation without representation. The colony participated in most of the protests and boycotts leading up to the Revolution but was more likely to follow than to lead the larger colonies. Once America broke with Britain, New Jersey became the site of many important battles. After the war, the people of New Jersey were critical of the Articles of Confederation, and the state's spokesmen proposed several important features of the U.S. Constitution, most importantly an equal representation of all the states in the Senate. On 18 December 1787, New Jersey unanimously ratified the Constitution, the third state to do so.

New Jersey's early history shaped its participation in the Revolution. Originally a Dutch appendage to New Netherlands (later New York), it was organized after the English conquest as a proprietary colony in the 1660s but was immediately divided into two parts, East Jersey and West Jersey (a distinction that survives to this day, in altered form, as North and South Jersey). From the 1670s, West Jersey was a Quaker stronghold and inclined to pacifism. The earliest white settlers of East Jersey were primarily Puritans from New England. But the colony was always a mixture of nationalities: Dutch, German, Swedish, French, Scottish, Welsh, Irish, and English. Diverse nationalities brought in diverse religions. There were Baptists, Presbyterians, Dutch Reformists, German Lutherans, Swedish Lutherans, Methodists, and Scottish Calvinists as well as Quakers and Puritan Congregationalists. Despite the potential differences between people and between the two halves of the colony, and despite the anti-Revolutionary pacifism of the Quakers, the majority of the colony would end up backing the Revolution. But its historical divisions also helped create one of the largest and most active Loyalist minorities of all thirteen rebelling colonies.

In 1703 New Jersey became a royal province, and the two halves were united. Its government included a royal governor; a governor's council, which was generally conservative in nature; and an elected assembly, which controlled the money. As a throwback to its bisectional proprietary history, the provincial capital alternated between two cities: East Jersey's Perth Amboy and West Jersey's Burlington.

In 1763, when the French and Indian (Seven Years') War came to an end, Britain appointed a new governor for New Jersey, William Franklin, son of Benjamin Franklin. Talented and charming, he would take a radically different position in the Revolution from his father and from his own son. But New Jersey itself followed a pattern typical of the colonies, going from protest to resistance to rebellion. Protest often centered on the famous phrase "no taxation without representation."

The first of Britain's new taxes was the Sugar Act of 1764. This had little economic impact on New Jersey and caused no real protest. Most of the population was engaged in agriculture, with winter wheat the major cash crop. There were also some cattle raising, lumbering, fishing, and whaling. The main industrial activity was iron mining. Little of New Jersey's commercial activity directly involved Britain. Most of its exports went to New York, Philadelphia, and Rhode Island, and New York and Philadelphia supplied most of New Jersey's need for imports.

The Stamp Act of 1765 had more impact and created both protest and resistance in New Jersey, though like most of colonial America, New Jersey's citizens protested as aggrieved British subjects, not as revolutionaries. When New Jersey received a circular letter from Massachusetts calling for an intercolonial meeting to plan a common resistance, the colony at first declined. But the general population soon let its disfavor be known. By September, a

> There were nearly one hundred battles and skirmishes fought in New Jersey.

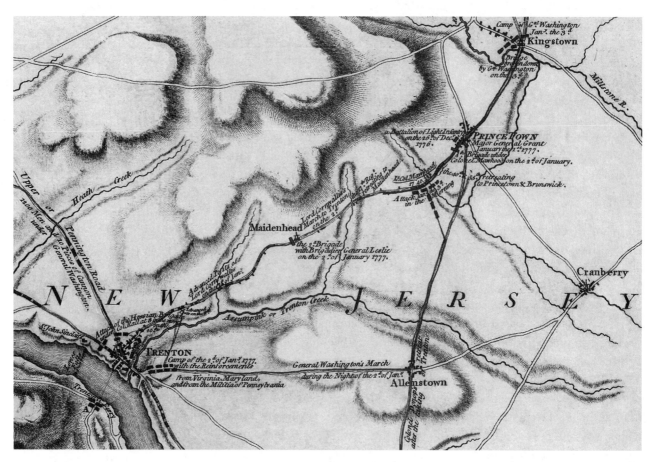

Map of military engagements during the American Revolution in New Jersey, circa 1777. (Library of Congress, Geography and Map Division)

group of the colony's lawyers met and agreed not to buy the stamps. In October the Assembly met and, in a change of mind, selected representatives to send to the Stamp Act Congress in New York City. There the New Jersey contingent (except for Robert Ogden, who was later burned in effigy) agreed to condemn taxation without representation and to petition the king and Parliament. In 1766, Parliament repealed the Stamp Act.

New Jersey, like its colonial neighbors, celebrated its victory, but not for long. In 1767, England levied new taxes, the Townshend duties. This sparked another circular letter from Massachusetts calling for the colonies to write petitions to the king and to boycott British goods. The New Jersey Assembly agreed to these actions and to economic pressure on Britain through nonimportation. This gradually had its intended effect, and in 1770 Britain lifted all the duties except that on tea. From 1770 to 1773, tensions between New Jersey and Britain decreased, but they quickly revived in 1773 with the implementation of the Tea Act. This led to the Boston Tea Party in December of that year, and, more importantly, to Britain's reaction to it: a series of measures that became known among the colonists as the Coercive or Intolerable Acts. Events now began to move from protest and resistance to rebellion.

Following an exhortation by Virginia's House of Burgesses to all the colonies, the New Jersey Assembly set up a Committee of Correspondence in February 1774. The goal was intercolonial communication in case of the need for mutual defense against the British. In June and July, in response to Britain's Coercive Acts, New Jersey's counties, imitating Massachusetts's towns, also set up committees of correspondence. For New Jersey, these county committees were the beginning of an extralegal political structure— a government within the royal provincial government. On 21 July 1774, a convention of counties assembled at New Brunswick, where they picked five delegates to attend the First Continental Congress, to meet in Philadelphia in September. The delegates were James Kinsey, William Livingston, John DeHart, Stephen Crane, and Richard Smith. This First Continental Congress recommended a policy of nonimportation and nonexportation, to which New Jersey agreed. In January 1775, the same five men were picked to attend the Second Continental Congress.

The event that transformed New Jersey into a Revolutionary community, however, was the open conflict between British regulars and American militia at Lexington and Concord. This motivated New Jersey to convene its first Provincial Congress at Trenton on 23 May 1775. At this congress, New Jersey set up a militia system and levied a tax to support it. In November 1775, Governor Franklin held a last meeting of the royal provincial government in New Jersey. Franklin, who now found himself in an environment that was increasingly hostile to Loyalists, showed great courage and managed to retain his full loyalty to the British Crown. He refused to flee or to be intimidated. In June 1776, he was arrested and sent to appear before the Continental Congress. Congress sent him to Connecticut, where he remained a prisoner until 1778. Freed that year in a prisoner exchange, he remained in New York City until 1782, when he left for England, never to return.

In June 1776, another Provincial Congress decided to draft a new constitution for the independent state of New Jersey. A ten-man committee drafted the document, which was adopted on 2 July 1776. An unusual feature of this constitution was its inclusion of property-owning women among its voting citizens, an anomaly in early American republicanism for a quarter of a century, until the state rescinded its pioneering initiative. On 30 August, Livingston was elected the first governor of the State of New Jersey and served from 1776 until his death in 1790. The Provincial Congress also picked five men to return to the Continental Congress with orders to vote for independence: Richard Stockton, John Hart, Francis Hopkinson, Abraham Clark, and John Witherspoon, the president of the College of New Jersey (today Princeton University).

By now the Revolutionary War was well under way. General George Washington had driven the British out of Boston in March 1776, but they returned in much greater force to New York in the summer, with the intention of putting down the rebellion once and for all. Between August and November, Washington's Continental Army suffered a string of defeats all around New York City and was forced to retreat into New Jersey in the fall. The British followed them and pushed the Continental Army across the state and then, in early December, across the Delaware River into Pennsylvania.

Washington's retreat had a demoralizing effect upon many New Jersey citizens. In November 1776 the British commander, General Sir William Howe, offered amnesty to anyone in the state who would pledge allegiance to the Crown, and almost 3,000 people complied. But many New Jersey militiamen doggedly harassed the British Army and played a crucial role in wearing down the enemy, both during the initial invasion in November–December 1776 and for several years thereafter. Determined not to lose West Jersey completely, Washington recrossed the ice-filled Delaware River (the celebrated crossing) late on Christmas Day and marched all night to attack Trenton, held by Hessian mercenaries fighting for Britain. The success of this battle on 26 December 1776, of the Battle of Assunpink Creek (the Second Battle of Trenton) on 1 January 1777, and of the Battle of Princeton on 2 January, followed by Washington's march to safe winter quarters in Morristown, New Jersey, reenergized the spirits of both the Continental Army and the militia and citizens of New Jersey. The British fell back to New Brunswick and never again controlled the western part of the state.

But despite this victorious campaign, there would be intermittent and often intense warfare in the state until 1781 involving not only British regulars, their Hessian allies, and the Continental Army but also New Jersey militia, well-organized Loyalist legions, and some combatants who were little more than brigands and thieves. Several naval engagements occurred throughout the war, both on the state's Atlantic coast and along the lower Delaware River. Major battles, in addition to those at Trenton and Princeton, occurred at Red Bank (Fort Mercer) in October 1777, Monmouth in June 1778, Paulus Hook in 1779, and Springfield and Connecticut Farms in 1780. Even when the major armies were quiet or absent from New Jersey, outbursts of partisan warfare between local Loyalists and Patriots caused both many casualties and great damage to property, and hungry soldiers from both sides often pillaged the countryside for food. Fortunately, during all this turmoil New Jersey had, in Livingston, one of the strongest and most resourceful governors of the Revolutionary era.

After the war, New Jersey made several changes in its government and public policy. The legislature banned the further importation of slaves but wouldn't agree to end slavery—despite Quaker agitation to do so—until 1804, and then by a gradual emancipation. And the legislature made needed changes in monetary policies. On the federal level, New Jersey insisted on changes in the Articles of Confederation. This insistence helped move the Confederation toward the creation of the U.S. Constitution. First, New Jersey insisted on a stronger federal government, especially one that could raise money to pay creditors through revenues from duties and land sales of the western territories. And the state insisted that lands to the west of the Appalachian Mountains not be owned exclusively by a few large states (as they were at that time) but instead by the nation itself. New Jersey began to force these issues as early as 1783 by refusing to contribute any more money to the Confederation. In May 1787, New Jersey leaders were finally gratified to attend a convention in Philadelphia to consider the necessary changes in the national government.

New Jersey's delegates to this convention included Livingston, David Brealy, Jonathan Dayton, William Churchill Houston, and William Paterson. One of the issues taken up at the convention was the question of how to determine the number of representatives to Congress from each state. It was Paterson who fought strongly against any system of representation that would be totally determined by the several states' respective populations. This, he felt, would be unfair to the smaller states. He presented the New Jersey Plan, a plan for equal representation, that Connecticut and other small states strongly supported. A compromise was struck. Each state would be equally represented in the Senate, and the House of Representatives would be based on representation by population.

After the Constitution was published in September 1787, New Jersey quickly held an election to choose delegates to vote for or against the new federal Constitution. The delegates met on 11 December 1787, and on 18 December they unanimously approved the Constitution of the United States.

WILLIAM TOTH

See also

Assunpink Creek, New Jersey, Action at; Articles of Confederation; Boston Tea Party; Boycotts; Coercive Acts; Congress, First Continental; Congress, Second Continental and Confederation; Constitution, United States; Constitutions, State; Correspondence, Committees of; Declaration of Independence; Fort Mercer, New Jersey, Assault on and Capture of; Franklin, Benjamin; Franklin, William; Hopkinson, Francis; Livingston, William; Loyalist Units; Loyalists; Monmouth, Battle of; Morristown, New Jersey, Continental Army Winter Quarters; New Jersey, Operations in; Paterson, John; Paulus Hook, New Jersey, Action at; Princeton, Battle of; Stamp Act; Sugar Act; Tea Act; Townshend Acts; Trenton, Battle of; Witherspoon, John

References

Dwyer, William M. *The Day Is Ours! An Inside View of the Battles of Trenton and Princeton, November 1776–January 1777.* New Brunswick, NJ: Rutgers University Press, 1998.

Fischer, David Hackett. *Washington's Crossing.* Oxford and New York: Oxford University Press, 2004.

Gerlach, Larry R. *Prologue to Independence: New Jersey in the Coming of the American Revolution.* New Brunswick, NJ: Rutgers University Press, 1976.

Kemmerer, Donald L. *Path to Freedom: The Struggle for Self-Government in Colonial New Jersey, 1703–1776.* Princeton, NJ: Princeton University Press, 1940.

Lefkowitz, Arthur S. *The Long Retreat.* Metuchen, NJ: Rutgers University Press, 1998.

Lundin, Leonard. *Cockpit of the Revolution: The War for Independence in New Jersey.* 1940. Reprint, New York: Octagon, 1972.

McCormick, Richard P. *New Jersey from Colony to State: 1609–1789,* Vol. 1, *The New Jersey Historical Series.* Princeton, New Jersey: D. Van Nostrand, 1964.

Miers, Earl Schenck. *Crossroads of Freedom: The American Revolution and the Rise of a New Nation.* New Brunswick, NJ: Rutgers University Press, 1971.

New Jersey, Operations in
(1776–1783)

New Jersey, the "Cockpit of the Revolution," experienced almost continuous warfare between American and British forces in some form or other from early 1776 to 1783. The Continental Army, commanded by General George Washington, was stationed intermittently in New Jersey for long periods of time. During much of that time, it was actively campaigning against British troops. Even when the British army was not conquering New Jersey territory or fighting the Americans there, it was in garrisons in New Jersey cities or occupying New York City and Philadelphia, near the state's borders. Patriot-Loyalist warfare was also an issue during the first months of 1777.

In November 1775, the New Jersey Provincial Congress, which had supplanted the colonial assembly as the colony's political authority, organized two battalions (or regiments) of militia to defend New Jersey. Colonels William Alexander (Lord Stirling) and William Maxwell were appointed commanders, with Stirling given overall command. Shortly thereafter, Stirling and Maxwell were appointed officers in the Continental Army, and their regiments were incorporated into the national military structure. While most of the New Jersey troops were quickly dispatched to shore up the defenses of New York City, Stirling employed his time in recruiting and supplying more troops, suppressing Loyalists, and enforcing the American embargo against British goods. On 21 January 1776, he seized a British transport ship, the *Blue Mountain Valley*, that was laden with military stores. Actual bloodshed did not commence until 19 June, after Stirling had joined the New Jersey soldiers at New York City. At that time, six British men-of-war ran the American brig *Nancy* ashore off Cape May. One New Jersey soldier was killed as American troops unsuccessfully attempted to thwart British seizure of the ship and cargo.

Beginning in July 1776, an Anglo-German army of 32,000 men, led by General William Howe, attacked Washington's smaller army of 20,000 soldiers in and around New York City. In a series of battles over the next four months, Washington was swept off Long Island and Manhattan and crossed the Hudson River into New Jersey. He and Lord Stirling made their headquarters at Hackensack as Howe completed consolidation of his grip on New York City. On 20 November, Howe led 4,500 soldiers in an assault on Fort Lee, on the New Jersey side of the Hudson River opposite Manhattan. Forced to flee, the Americans abandoned quantities of military stores, and Washington's army began retreating westward across New Jersey, pursued by the British forces. On 28 November, Washington abandoned Newark and fell back to New Brunswick. With his depleted army of 3,400 men, he retreated across the Raritan River on 1 December and five days later began ferrying his army across the Delaware River into Pennsylvania. On 13 December one of his officers, Major General Charles Lee, was captured by the British at Basking Ridge.

To the Americans' advantage, Howe was not aggressive in his pursuit of Washington's army across New Jersey. Nor did Howe attempt to follow his enemies across the Delaware River. Instead of constructing rafts to ferry his

General Charles Cornwallis lands in New Jersey, 1776. (National Archives and Records Administration)

army to Pennsylvania, he withdrew the bulk of his troops to New York City on 13 December, leaving only isolated garrisons at Princeton, Trenton, Bordentown, Perth Amboy, and New Brunswick. Although Washington commanded only 4,707 Continentals and 2,000 militiamen by 20 December, he felt compelled to attempt a surprise attack against the enemy in New Jersey in order to restore American confidence. Hence, he and his officers decided on a three-pronged assault against Trenton, designed to encircle the town and force the surrender of a Hessian garrison commanded by Colonel Johann Rall. On the morning of 26 December, after ferrying his army across the ice-choked Delaware, Washington routed Rall's men at Trenton and captured more than 900 prisoners.

On 27 December, Washington returned to the west bank of the Delaware, but he worried that Howe might launch an assault into Pennsylvania should the river freeze over. To avert this possibility, Washington launched a spoiling attack back into New Jersey on 30 December. With his army, which numbered only 1,600 men, he recrossed the ice-clogged Delaware River and slogged through bitter cold and deep snow to Trenton. There he gathered a force of about 5,000 men. He was opposed by 6,000 British troops in New Jersey, most of whom were stationed at New Brunswick and Princeton. Although he was almost cut off at Trenton by Charles Cornwallis on 2 January, Washington maneuvered around the British general and arrived in Princeton the following day. In the Battle of Princeton, Washington was attacked by three British regiments and was almost overwhelmed when Lieutenant-Colonel Charles Mawhood's regiment charged with fixed bayonets. But Washington, personally restoring order, drove off the British regulars. He then withdrew his forces into the hills at Morristown and established winter quarters there. Howe fell back to New Brunswick and other eastern New Jersey towns for the winter.

For the next few months, New Jersey was ravaged by Patriot and Loyalist irregular bands that looted and carried on a general partisan conflict. Washington ordered out patrols to harass British supply columns, and before long his strategy yielded some success. As spring arrived, both Continental and British officers increased their spoiling attacks on each other. On 12 April, Cornwallis and Major General James Grant set out with 4,000 troops to attack Major General Benjamin Lincoln's 500 men at Bound Brook. In a successful assault the following day, the British generals routed Lincoln's men and almost captured Lincoln. On 25 May, Brigadier General Anthony Wayne and 500 Pennsylvania troops got into a firefight with 700 British soldiers led by Grant. In driving off the enemy, Wayne's artillerists decapitated Grant's horse and toppled the general into the mud.

In June 1777, Howe began a series of maneuvers to withdraw his army from New Jersey back to New York City. His plan was to embark his army, sail southward to Chesapeake Bay, and drive on Philadelphia from that direction. If he could maneuver Washington's army out of the sheltering hills around Morristown, however, he would willingly give the Continentals battle. On 14 June, he tried to lure Washington into a fight, but when the American general would not take the bait, Howe marched to Perth Amboy with his army of 11,000 men, intending to cross to Staten Island. On 26 June, Howe reversed directions. Still in hopes of bringing on a battle, he marched two columns toward Washington's army, which had taken station about 5 miles northwest of Perth Amboy. Washington quickly withdrew his troops into the protective hills at Middlebrook. But Stirling, at Woodbridge, did not move fast enough and got into a small but sharp battle before successfully disengaging and joining Washington. Howe then evacuated New Jersey and implemented his plan of attacking Philadelphia from the south.

New Jersey was only peripherally involved in Howe's operations over the next few months. On 11 September, Brigadier-General John Campbell, British commander on Staten Island, conducted a raid against Elizabeth Town to forage and to create a diversion in support of Howe's operations in southeastern Pennsylvania. After Howe captured Philadelphia on 26 September, he began operations to clear the Delaware River for British shipping. Supported by General Sir Henry Clinton, who led British troops from New York City in ravaging East Jersey, Howe concentrated on Fort Mifflin on Mud Island below Philadelphia. Although the Americans defended the fort for a time, it fell, as did Fort Mercer, and Howe gained control of the Delaware River. The Americans escaped by rowing over to Red Bank, New Jersey.

With much of New Jersey now firmly back in the hands of the Patriots during the winter of 1777–1778, the Loyalists suffered from severe suppression. In the southern counties to the east of occupied Philadelphia, however, the Patriots came in for abuse from Loyalists and their British Army allies in the city. British authorities arrested Patriot families, seized or destroyed their property, and foraged at will to support the army in Philadelphia. As the military campaigning season of 1778 approached, Americans were outraged by a Loyalist atrocity at Hancock's Creek. During a raid, Loyalists bayoneted all their Patriot prisoners, thus setting off a series of reprisals against Loyalists. The British also enjoyed a similar victory at Bordentown, but it too tended to anger the Patriots and prepare them for the upcoming campaign.

In early June 1778, Clinton, who had replaced Howe as British commander in chief, began evacuating Philadelphia and marching to New York City across New Jersey. Although in the long run the state would benefit from this contraction of British territory, the immediate problem was to deal with the movement of the enemy's army across its very center. Washington, wary of engaging the British Army but not wanting it to reach New York unmolested, finally decided to launch a limited attack against its rear guard. He sent Lee, who had been released in a prisoner exchange, with 6,000 Continental troops to carry out the operation, and on 28 June, Lee attacked at Monmouth. In the battle, the Americans were thrown back in confusion. When Washington arrived on the field to take personal command, he quickly restored order and stopped the American retreat. That night, the British continued their march to New York City, finally evacuating New Jersey on 5 July. Lee was court-martialed and suspended from the Continental Army for a year.

American General Charles Lee was taken prisoner by the British at Basking Ridge, New Jersey, in December 1776. (Library of Congress)

For almost two years after the Battle of Monmouth, there were no major military operations in New Jersey. In February 1779, British forces raided Elizabeth Town in search of Maxwell's corps, which was stationed there but at the time was serving at Morristown. On the coast, privateers operated from Toms River and Little Egg Harbor against British shipping. From time to time the British sent retaliatory forces against pirates and other perceived enemies, and the forces burned, looted, and ravaged coastal towns.

In 1779, former Royal Governor William Franklin organized the Associated Loyalists in New Jersey. During the next two years, the Associated Loyalists cooperated with Colonel John Simcoe's Queen's Rangers and a black irregular officer, Colonel Titus Tye, in raiding Patriot areas in Monmouth County with impunity. On 19 August 1779, Major Henry "Light-Horse Harry" Lee attacked Paulus Hook, New Jersey, a strategic British post across from southern Manhattan that guarded the lower Hudson River. Leading a special corps of 400 troops, he operated against a British garrison of 300 men, commanded by Major William Sutherland. In a successful early-morning assault, Lee's elite Virginia and Maryland troops drove into the enemy position, killing 50 men and capturing 158 others.

In another spoiling attack, on the bitterly cold morning of 15 January 1780 Stirling led 2,700 Continentals against the British on Staten Island. Advancing across frozen Newark Bay, he accomplished little and withdrew the following day. British forces retaliated on 25 January by raiding Elizabeth Town and Newark, capturing some American soldiers and citizens and burning the courthouse and Presbyterian meetinghouse in Elizabeth Town. On 6 June, General Wilhelm von Knyphausen, a Hessian officer in British service, landed an assault force of 5,000 soldiers at Elizabeth Town in hopes of cooperating with Tye and the Associated Loyalists in recapturing New Jersey for the Crown. Knyphausen marched to Connecticut Farms, looted and burned the town, then advanced on Springfield. There he was stopped by American forces and retreated back to Elizabeth Town. On 23 June he advanced again, and in an action at Springfield he was once more turned back. Finally, he evacuated New Jersey. Trying to turn the tables on the British, Wayne conducted a raid on 20–21 July against a British blockhouse at Bull's Ferry. He led 2,000 troops against only 70 enemy soldiers but was unsuccessful and had to retreat.

Tye continued his raids in the summer of 1780. He was wounded in an attack on the home of Captain Joshua Huddy, an American militia officer, at Monmouth on 1 September 1780, and died of tetanus shortly thereafter. Although regular warfare between British and American troops around New York ceased after Cornwallis surrendered at Yorktown on 19 October 1781, fratricidal fighting between Loyalists and rebels continued. On 12 April 1782, a New Jersey Associated Loyalist, Captain Richard Lippincott, hanged Huddy, and an angry Washington demanded that Clinton, commander at New York, turn Lippincott over to him for punishment. When Clinton refused, Washington chose by lot a young British prisoner, Captain Charles Asgill, to die in Lippincott's place.

Clinton court-martialed Lippincott for murder on 13 June, but nine days later the captain was found not guilty. Finally, General Sir Guy Carleton, Clinton's replacement as commander in New York City, promised Washington that the matter would be settled amicably. Governor Franklin, anticipating that Carleton was less supportive of the Loyalists than Clinton had been, sailed for England a thoroughly disillusioned man. Washington then wrote to Congress on 19 August that he had no desire any longer to retaliate by hanging Asgill. Nevertheless, Congress dallied for two months while Asgill's mother, the wife of a former lord mayor of London, used her influence to get the French government to intercede on behalf of her son. Congress, finally realizing the diplomatic implications of the matter, voted to release Asgill.

At the same time, Congress instructed Washington to remind Carleton of the need to bring Lippincott and the Associated Loyalists under control. Carleton reiterated his promise that justice would be done. He curbed the Associated Loyalists and in December 1782 disbanded them altogether. Although all hostilities between Britain and America officially ceased in

April 1783, a few Loyalist refugees continued plundering raids in the Hackensack Valley through the spring of 1783.

PAUL DAVID NELSON

See also

Alexander, William; Elizabeth Town, New Jersey, Raids on; Huddy-Asgill Incident; Monmouth, Battle of; New Jersey; Paulus Hook, New Jersey, Action at; Princeton, Battle of; Trenton, Battle of

References

Bill, Alfred H. *The Campaign of Princeton, 1776, 1777*. Princeton, NJ: Princeton University Press, 1948.

———. *New Jersey and the Revolutionary War*. New Brunswick, NJ: Rutgers University Press, 1992.

Duer, William Alexander. *The Life of William Alexander, Earl of Stirling: Major General in the Army of the United States, during the Revolution*. New York: Wiley and Putnam, 1847.

Fleming, Thomas J. *The Battle of Springfield*. Trenton: New Jersey Historical Society, 1975.

———. *The Forgotten Victory: The Battle for New Jersey, 1780*. New York: Reader's Digest, 1973.

———. *1776: Year of Illusions*. New York: Norton, 1975.

Ketchum, Richard M. *The Winter Soldiers*. Garden City, NY: Doubleday, 1973.

Leiby, Adrian C. *The Revolutionary War in the Hackensack Valley: The Jersey Dutch and the Neutral Ground, 1775–1783*. New Brunswick, NJ: Rutgers University Press, 1962.

Lossing, Benson J. *The Pictorial Field Book of the Revolution*. 1951. Reprint, Rutland, VT: Tuttle, 1972.

Lundin, Leonard. *Cockpit of the Revolution: The War for Independence in New Jersey*. 1940. Reprint, New York: Octagon, 1972.

Nelson, Paul David. *William Alexander, Lord Stirling*. University: University of Alabama Press, 1987.

Ryan, Dennis P. *New Jersey in the American Revolution, 1763–1783: A Chronology*. Trenton: New Jersey Historical Commission, 1974.

Stryker, William S. *The Battle of Monmouth*. 1927. Reprint, Port Washington, NY: Kennikat, 1970.

———. *The Battles of Trenton and Princeton*. Boston: Houghton Mifflin, 1898.

Ward, Christopher. *War of the Revolution*. 2 vols. New York: Macmillan, 1952.

Ward, Harry M. *Between the Lines: Banditti of the American Revolution*. Westport, CT: Praeger, 2002.

New London, Connecticut, Raid on
(6 September 1781)

In early September 1781 the traitor Benedict Arnold, a native of Connecticut now wearing the uniform of a British brigadier-general, conducted a bloody and destructive raid on New London, Connecticut, and nearby Fort Griswold. The citizens of Connecticut had been more fortunate than some of their neighbors in the American Revolution, for they were not victimized by

Benedict Arnold, who in September 1780 burned more than a hundred buildings and a dozen ships in a raid on New London, Connecticut. (National Archives and Records Administration)

widespread warfare. The state did, however, experience considerable damage from four British forays against important towns. On 21–28 April 1777, Major-General William Tryon conducted destructive operations against Danbury, then fought his way back to British warships on the coast. He carried out another raid on Horseneck (Greenwich) on 25–27 February 1779 to eliminate salt-works and military supplies. Tryon's most extensive and destructive operations took place on 3–12 July 1779, when he attacked in turn the coastal towns of New Haven, Fairfield, and Norwalk, inflicting much property damage. Norwalk was particularly hard-hit, losing a large number of churches, shops, houses, and barns. And New London was threatened on 3 September 1778 when Major-General Charles Grey, while conducting amphibious operations in Long Island Sound, seriously considered an attack on the town. At the last minute, however, Grey decided instead to attack New Bedford, Fairhaven, and Martha's Vineyard, all in Massachusetts.

On 6 September 1781, however, New London's time for destruction had come. Arnold was serving under Sir Henry Clinton in New York after returning from his command of a successful incursion into Virginia the previous winter. Arnold had hoped during the summer that Clinton would order him to assault West Point, New York, which he had tried to deliver to the British by treachery the previous September, or even Philadelphia. Instead, he found himself given command of an expedition against New London, an attractive military target because it contained a considerable quantity of Continental Army stores, was easily reachable by water from New York City, and was familiar to Arnold, who had been raised in the vicinity. But the expedition also had another purpose: to draw the attention of General George Washington and his Franco-American army away from General Charles Cornwallis, who was already beleaguered on Virginia's York peninsula. It is likely that Arnold himself devised the plan and proposed it to Clinton. The troops assembled for the expedition, 1,700 in all, were in two divisions. The first, under the command of Lieutenant-Colonel Edmund Eyre, was composed of the British 40th and 54th Regiments, the 3rd Battalion of New Jersey Volunteers, a detachment of Hessian jaegers, and some cannon. The second, under Arnold's direct command, was made up of the British 38th Regiment, the Loyal Americans under Colonel Beverly Robinson, Arnold's own American Legion Refugees, and another small detachment of Hessian jaegers.

New London was situated on the west bank of the broad, tidal Thames River, about 5 miles from Long Island Sound and equidistant between New Haven and Newport, Rhode Island. The river was actually a bay defended by two forts, Trumbull on the west bank and Griswold on the east. Fort

Trumbull's battery was designed to overlook the harbor, so the fort was weak on the land side. It was commanded by Captain Adam Shapley and garrisoned with a company of 24 Connecticut troops. Fort Griswold, on a high bluff above Groton, across the Thames from New London, was a square structure with stone walls twelve feet high, and was defended by a ditch and outer works. Lieutenant Colonel William Ledyard, its commander, had a garrison of 124 militiamen.

Arnold set forth from New York on 4 September and by the next evening was approaching New London Harbor. He had hoped to land at midnight, but his plans were foiled when the wind shifted to northward, and he did not reach the Thames and commence unloading the infantry until 9:00 A.M. on 6 September. His own division landed on the west side of the river and proceeded toward New London, while four companies of the 38th Regiment threatened Fort Trumbull. The defenders, hugely outnumbered, fired one round of grapeshot, then spiked the fort's guns, took to waiting boats, and rowed across the Thames to join the garrison of Fort Griswold. Other reinforcements also joined them. Arnold marched on toward a small redoubt on Town Hill, called Fort Nonsense, which he seized after a brisk but futile fire from its defenders. He then brushed aside a group of citizens who fired an old 6-pound cannon at him before fleeing and captured New London, which he devastated with fire. Groton suffered the same fate. More than 140 buildings were burned, and a dozen ships were consumed by fire.

Meanwhile, Arnold ordered the first division under Eyre to attack Fort Griswold. Later discovering the strength of the post, Arnold attempted to countermand his order, but it was too late. Eyre approached the fort and demanded that Ledyard surrender, but Ledyard refused. Eyre then divided his troops and attacked the fort from two directions. Met with scathing fire, Eyre was killed and his soldiers thrown back. On a third desperate charge, they finally broke the garrison's stubborn defense. When Ledyard tried to surrender, he was killed with his own sword by a Loyalist attacker. The rest of the garrison was then set upon, and an indiscriminate slaughter occurred, with Americans being killed by sword, bayonet, and musket. Before the massacre, only 6 men were dead and 18 wounded, but when the carnage ceased, 85 were dead, 60 wounded, and 70 captured. The British lost 48 killed and 145 wounded in the entire expedition. Arnold, having achieved nothing but the further alienation of his former countrymen, reembarked his troops and returned to New York, thus ending the last military engagement of the Revolutionary War in the North.

PAUL DAVID NELSON

See also
Arnold, Benedict; Cornwallis, Charles; Grey, Charles; Robinson, Beverly; Tryon, William; West Point, New York

References
Arnold, Isaac. *The Life of Benedict Arnold: His Patriotism and His Treason*. Chicago: Jansen, McClurg, 1880.

Commager, Henry S., and Richard B. Morris, eds. *The Spirit of 'Seventy-Six: The Story of the American Revolution as Told by Participants.* 1958. Reprint, New York: Bonanza, 1995.

Kwasny, Mark V. *Washington's Partisan War, 1775–1783.* Kent, OH: Kent State University Press, 1990.

Lossing, Benson J. *The Pictorial Field Book of the Revolution.* 1951. Reprint, Rutland, VT: Tuttle, 1972.

Middlekauf, Robert. *The Glorious Cause: The American Revolution, 1763–1789.* 1981. Reprint, Oxford: Oxford University Press, 2005.

Wallace, Willard M. *Traitorous Hero: The Life and Fortunes of Benedict Arnold.* New York: Harper and Row, 1954.

New Orleans, Louisiana

New Orleans, capital of the Spanish province of Louisiana, served as a major supply depot for the Continental Army during the American Revolutionary War, both before and after Spain declared war on Britain in 1779.

Founded by the French in 1718, the city of New Orleans enjoyed a strategic location near the mouth of the Mississippi River that, in the era of waterway transport, provided it with great commercial significance. By the 1760s, the city formed a vital link in the chain of river-borne communication that tied the western Pennsylvania backcountry at Fort Pitt to the Gulf of Mexico and the Caribbean by way of the Ohio and Mississippi Rivers. With the outbreak of the Revolution, New Orleans became an important trading center from which the rebel armies received supplies from Europe, especially badly needed goods and materials sent by Spain itself. Gunpowder used at the Battle of Saratoga by the army of General Horatio Gates came from New Orleans via the inland waterways.

New Orleans had passed to the sovereignty of Spain at the Treaty of Paris in 1763, and by the time of the battles at Lexington and Concord, it had become home to several wealthy British North American merchants who supported the American cause. Oliver Pollock, a former resident of Pennsylvania, proved to be the most important of these supporters. He pledged his fortune and his personal support to the Continental Congress and received an official appointment as Congress's agent at New Orleans. Pollock superintended the shipping of many boatloads of supplies up the river system to Pennsylvania while he worked closely with the governor of Spanish Louisiana, Bernardo de Gálvez, who was a strong supporter of the American cause.

In 1777, Gálvez offered the city as refuge to the Mississippi River expedition of the American Captain James Willing, who led a detachment of rebel troops in an attack against settlements and posts in West Florida, a British province that bordered Spanish Louisiana. During 1778 and 1779, Pollock made New Orleans a primary supply center for George Rogers Clark's expedition into the Illinois Country. The American conquest of the Northwest, and Clark's ability to hold this region, was accomplished in large measure because of the supplies shipped northward from New Orleans. When Spain entered the war as a belligerent in June 1779, New Orleans became the military staging area for Gálvez's conquests of British posts in West Florida. The Spanish victories at Baton Rouge in 1779, Mobile in 1780, and Pensacola in 1781 all originated in New Orleans. By the end of the Revolutionary War, New Orleans had become a bustling city that served as governmental headquarters for Spanish Louisiana and West Florida, an extended geographic region that included the entire lower Mississippi Valley and the Gulf Coast from the Sabine River on the Mexican (later the Texan) border eastward to the Apalachicola River near the Florida peninsula. Moreover, New Orleans's importance as a trading center for the entire Mississippi Valley began attracting into Spanish territory a number of American merchants and settlers who would be a vanguard for the substantial American population at the time of the Louisiana Purchase twenty years after the end of the Revolutionary War.

LIGHT TOWNSEND CUMMINS

See also

Florida, East and West; Gálvez, Bernardo de; Pensacola, West Florida, Operation against; Spain

References

Caughey, John. *Bernardo de Gálvez in Louisiana*. Berkeley. University of California Press, 1934.

Chavez, Thomas. *Spain and the Independence of the United States: An Intrinsic Gift*. Albuquerque: University of New Mexico Press, 2002.

Cummins, Light Townsend. *Spanish Observers and the American Revolution, 1775–1783*. Baton Rouge: Louisiana State University Press, 1992.

James, James Alton. *Oliver Pollock: The Life and Times of an Unknown Patriot*. New York. Appleton-Century, 1937.

From 1775 to 1783, the state of New York was a center of military operations of one kind or another. Both the British and Americans viewed New York as strategically important. In early May 1775, less than a month after the war began at Lexington and Concord, Massachusetts, Captain Benedict Arnold of Connecticut and Colonel Ethan Allen, leader of the Green Mountain Boys of Vermont, began operations against British-held Forts Ticonderoga and Crown Point. These bastions were captured on 10 and 12 May, respectively, and supplied the Americans with 110 cannon for use against the British in Boston.

In June 1775, Congress voted to send a Patriot army against Montreal and Quebec in an attempt to win that territory's French residents to the American cause. Two New Yorkers, Major General Philip Schuyler and Brigadier General Richard Montgomery, were appointed commander and second in command, respectively. By late August, they had organized an army of 500 men at Fort Ticonderoga and in early September began siege operations against St. John's and Chambly on the Sorel River. Montgomery

New York, Operations in
(1775–1783)

Triumphant British troops march down the street in New York City. General William Howe's army of more than 30,000 troops arrived off the city in June 1776 and, after a series of actions, forced the Americans to evacuate the place in September. Several hundred buildings burned in the fire that consumed much of the city on 25 September. (Library of Congress)

was killed at Quebec on 31 December while attempting to storm the city, and in the spring of 1776 the American army retreated back to Fort Ticonderoga.

Although the Patriots expected General Guy Carleton, governor-general of Canada, to drive south and capture Fort Ticonderoga, he paused at the north end of Lake Champlain during the summer of 1776 and began construction of an invasion fleet. Schuyler, assisted by now General Arnold and General Horatio Gates, responded with a shipbuilding program of his own. In early October, Carleton's fleet was ready for battle. He sailed up Lake Champlain in the company of troop transports carrying his army, seeking contact with the American vessels, which were commanded by Arnold. The two flotillas met on 11 October, and in a three-day running battle that began near Valcour Island and continued for many miles southward, the Americans were swept off the lake.

On 17 March 1776, a British army commanded by General William Howe evacuated Boston and withdrew temporarily to Halifax, Nova Scotia. General George Washington, commander in chief of the Continental Army at Boston, foresaw that Howe would assault New York City in the coming summer. In fact, the British plan was to capture New York City and seize control of the Hudson River, while Carleton was pushing southward to Albany. Washington first sent Major General Charles Lee to organize the defenses of the city, then arrived himself with his army on 13 April. Despite his best efforts, Washington was unable to prepare an adequate defense with the 20,000 troops under his command. In July, Howe and his brother, Admiral Lord Richard Howe, arrived with a vast armada of 500 ships and an army of 32,000 British and Hessian regulars.

On 22 August, General Howe landed his army on Long Island to attack Washington's prepared defenses around Brooklyn. Washington, who remained in New York City because he feared that Howe might also attempt an assault on Manhattan, ordered General Israel Putnam to take command of the American forces in Brooklyn, about 9,000 troops. Putnam stationed half his men outside the town to the south under Generals John Sullivan and William Alexander, Lord Stirling. On 27 August, Howe launched a two-pronged attack against the Americans. He sent General James Grant to engage Sullivan and Stirling in a frontal assault, while Generals Sir Henry Clinton and Lord Charles Cornwallis led a flanking attack around their left. The Americans were routed and fell back on Brooklyn Heights. Washington withdrew his army to Manhattan on the night of 29–30 August, hoping to stave off the loss of New York City to the enemy.

On 15 September, Howe landed troops at Kips Bay, overcoming Washington's defenses and capturing New York City. As he evacuated Manhattan, he left behind at a garrison of 3,000 men at Fort Washington, commanded by Colonel Robert Magaw. Washington withdrew to White Plains, staying just ahead of Howe's advance, and encamped in a strong defensive position. On 28 October, Howe attacked the American army at White Plains, seizing Chatterton's Hill on the British left but accomplishing nothing more. Shortly thereafter, Washington retreated to a defensible position at North Castle. Howe then turned his back on the American army and besieged Fort Washington. It was bombarded and captured on 15 November, with the loss of almost 3,000 American prisoners. Washington's army, which had crossed the Hudson River into New Jersey, was soon in retreat across New Jersey toward the Delaware River. For the remainder of the war, until December 1783, New York City was under British occupation.

In the spring of 1777, General John Burgoyne replaced Carleton as commander of British forces in Canada and prepared to reinvade upstate New York. With 7,000 troops, he was to capture Fort Ticonderoga and push on to Albany. Lieutenant-Colonel Barry St. Leger would assist him by marching up the Mohawk Valley from Oswego on Lake Ontario with 875 soldiers and almost 1,000 Indians, meeting him at Albany. On 15 June, Burgoyne embarked his army at St. John's on the Richelieu River and advanced toward Ticonderoga. He surrounded the fort on 30 June, and on 5 July he forced the defenders to retreat southward. During the next month, Schuyler, the American commander, carried out a retreat toward the Hudson River while building up his own forces. He also sent Arnold to Fort Stanwix, in the Mohawk Valley, to halt St. Leger's advance toward Albany.

On 16 August, two detachments of Burgoyne's army, commanded by Colonels Friedrich Baum and Heinrich von Breymann, were defeated by a New England militia army under General John Stark at Bennington, Vermont. Advancing to Fort Stanwix by 2 August, St. Leger besieged an American garrison of 750 men commanded by Colonel Peter Gansevoort. Four

American and British flotillas under Benedict Arnold and Guy Carleton, respectively, engage one another at the Battle of Valcour Island, 11 October 1776. The American ships are, from left to right, the *Washington*, the *Congress*, the *Revenge*, and the *Enterprise*. The British ships are the *Carleton*, the *Inflexible*, and the *Maria*. (Naval Historical Society)

days later, St. Leger sent 250 men to attack a column under General Nicholas Herkimer in a ravine near Oriskany. Herkimer marched blindly into a trap, lost half his men, and was forced to retreat. During the next two weeks, St. Leger and Gansevoort continued to face off against each other. Gansevoort sent his second in command, Colonel Marinus Willett, on a successful raid against the British besiegers, and St. Leger continued to close the ring on Fort Stanwix.

Meanwhile, Arnold was marching westward to Gansevoort's relief with 950 soldiers. Deciding to trick St. Leger's Indians, he sent among them Han Yost Schuyler, a halfwit with whom they were familiar, to spread outrageous stories about the size of the American force. The Indians abandoned their British allies and departed for home. St. Leger had no choice but to call off the siege of Fort Stanwix and retreat toward Oswego. He departed on 22 August, pursued by Arnold. Leaving 700 men to garrison Fort Stanwix, Arnold marched eastward with his remaining 1,200 troops to rejoin the American army that was retreating before Burgoyne's forces.

Despite these American triumphs, Schuyler's command was being challenged in Congress. New England politicians, dismayed by his loss of Fort Ticonderoga and Schuyler's subsequent retreat, claimed that he was both incompetent and disloyal. On 4 August, Congress voted to replace him with

Gates. Fifteen days later, Gates took control of the American army, which was encamped about 10 miles above Albany at the mouth of the Mohawk River. When Arnold appeared with his troops, Gates marched northward and occupied high ground called Bemis Heights. He employed the Polish engineer Colonel Thaddeus Kosciuszko to construct formidable defensive works on this strategic bottleneck on Burgoyne's path of advance. Burgoyne gave the Americans ample time to prepare their defenses, for he was collecting supplies for thirty days before he marched forward.

On 19 September, Burgoyne advanced against Gates's position, and the Battle of Freeman's Farm followed. Burgoyne's troops converged on the American left, while Gates waited quietly in his fortifications. Finally, Gates ordered Colonel Daniel Morgan and Major Henry Dearborn to advance and halt Burgoyne's attempt to turn the American left flank. At nightfall, after a successful defense, the Americans withdrew back into their lines. Although the British held the field, they had suffered 556 casualties to Gates's 280. During the next few days, Burgoyne lingered near the American fortifications, while Gates and Arnold quarreled and the latter almost left the camp for Philadelphia. On 21 September, Burgoyne received word from Clinton in New York that he was soon to lead a force up the lower Hudson River Valley against the Highland forts. Clinton delayed until he received reinforcements from England and did not commence operations until 3 October. Within three days, he had captured Forts Clinton, Montgomery, and Constitution. Although he then returned to New York City, he ordered Major-General John Vaughan to advance farther up the Hudson River.

By 4 October, Burgoyne's situation was becoming desperate. His stores of food were low, and he had heard no good tidings from Clinton. Burgoyne decided on 7 October to attempt another breakthrough on Gates's left toward Albany. At the Battle of Bemis Heights, Gates unleashed Morgan's men and other troops against Burgoyne, and Arnold dashed into the fray without orders. The British were stopped cold, and Burgoyne ordered a withdrawal into his own fortified lines. Two days later, Burgoyne began a retreat northward toward Fort Ticonderoga, but on 13 October he was cut off by Stark's militia forces. Compelled to call for terms, Burgoyne parleyed with Gates for the next four days, hoping against hope that Vaughan would rescue him. On 15 October, Vaughan captured and burned Kingston, only 45 miles below Albany, but Burgoyne's luck had run out. He surrendered to Gates on 17 October, agreeing to liberal terms that would allow his men to return to England.

Although the failure of Burgoyne's expedition marked the end of major British attempts to defeat the American colonies by conquering New York, warfare continued in the state until 1783. Around New York City, in the no-man's-land between the British lines and Washington's Continental encampments on the Hudson River, a particularly vicious type of conflict broke out between irregular Loyalist partisans and Patriot militiamen. In numerous raids, Loyalist bandits perpetrated the most savage kinds of murder, rape, pillage, and illegal executions. Claudius Smith and his Loyalist gang of Highlands desperadoes were the best known and most hunted of the bandit

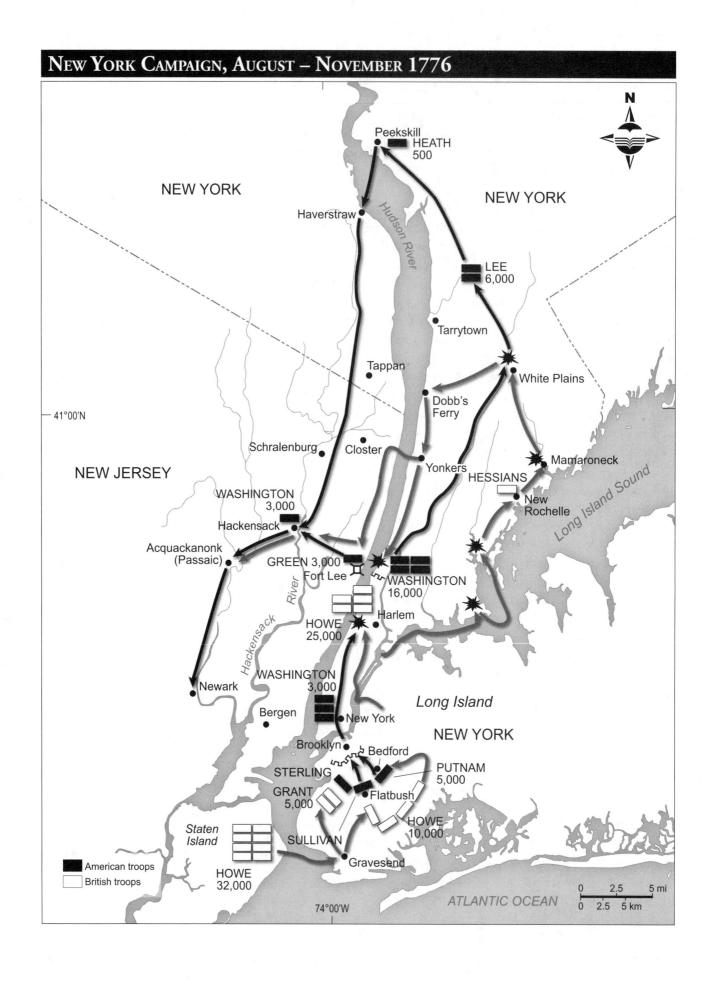

NEW YORK CAMPAIGN, AUGUST – NOVEMBER 1776

N

Peekskill
HEATH
500

NEW YORK

Haverstraw

Hudson River

NEW YORK

LEE
6,000

Tarrytown

Tappan

White Plains

Dobb's
Ferry

—41°00'N

Schralenburg

Closter

Yonkers

Mamaroneck

HESSIANS

New
Rochelle

Long Island Sound

NEW JERSEY

WASHINGTON
3,000

Hackensack

Acquackanonk
(Passaic)

Hackensack River

GREEN 3,000
Fort Lee

WASHINGTON
16,000

Harlem

HOWE
25,000

WASHINGTON
3,000

Newark

Bergen

New York

Long Island

NEW YORK

Brooklyn
Bedford

STERLING

PUTNAM
5,000

GRANT
5,000

Flatbush

*Staten
Island*

SULLIVAN

HOWE
10,000

Gravesend

HOWE
32,000

■ American troops
□ British troops

ATLANTIC OCEAN

74°00'W

0   2.5   5 mi
0 2.5 5 km

raiders, but they were by no means the only ones. They created headaches for both Washington and British commanders in New York, although the Loyalists probably received tenuous support from British authorities in New York City.

The British in Canada continued to harass Americans around Lake Champlain. In October 1778, Governor-General Frederick Haldimand appointed Major Christopher Carleton to conduct a raid against American settlements on the lake. In command of a small flotilla of warships and 454 soldiers and Indians, he departed Île-aux-Noix in the Richelieu River on 24 October. With near impunity, he raided blockhouses, destroyed supplies, and captured Americans until he returned to Canada on 12 November.

In October 1781, Barry St. Leger began another operation on Lake Champlain, pushing southward toward Fort Ticonderoga in hopes of encouraging Vermonters to secede from the United States and join the British Empire. To counter this threat, General William Heath, American commander in New York, ordered Stirling to take command at Albany and stymie British plans. On 23 October, before Stirling could mobilize his forces, St. Leger occupied Fort Ticonderoga and seemed to be threatening to move on Lake George. Two days later, Stirling learned that Major John Ross, at the head of another British force, was threatening the Mohawk Valley. But Ross was defeated in a skirmish with Willett's forces at Johnstown on 25 October and withdrew. Five days later, Stirling took command of American troops at Saratoga and began preparing defenses to counteract an expected attack by St. Leger. The assault never materialized, for when St. Leger learned in early November of the recent surrender of Cornwallis at Yorktown, he withdrew back into Canada. Except for minor, sporadic skirmishes that gradually ceased over the next two years, the War for American Independence in New York was at an end.

PAUL DAVID NELSON

See also

Alexander, William; Allen, Ethan; Arnold, Benedict; Bennington, Battle of; Brant, Joseph; Brodhead, Daniel; Burgoyne, John; Butler, John; Canada, Operations in; Carleton, Christopher; Carleton, Guy; Chambly, Quebec, Action at; Clinton, Henry; Clinton, James; Cornwallis, Charles; Fort Clinton, New York; Fort Montgomery, New York, Assault on; Fort Stanwix, New York; Fort Ticonderoga, New York; Fort Washington, New York, Fall of; Gansevoort, Peter; Gates, Horatio; Grant, James; Green Mountain Boys; Harlem Heights, Battle of; Heath, William; Herkimer, Nicholas; Howe, Richard; Howe, William; Hudson River and the Hudson Highlands; Johnson, Sir John; Kips Bay, New York, Action at; Kosciuszko, Thaddeus; Lake Champlain, Operations on; Lee, Charles; Long Island, Battle of; Montgomery, Richard; Morgan, Daniel; New York, Province and State; New York City; Oriskany, Battle of; Putnam, Israel; Quebec, Siege of; Saratoga Campaign; Schuyler, Philip; St. John's, Actions against; St. Leger Expedition; Stark, John; Sullivan Expedition; Valcour Island, Battle of; White Plains, Battle of; Willett, Marinus

References

Commager, Henry S., and Richard B. Morris, eds. *The Spirit of 'Seventy-Six: The Story of the American Revolution as Told by Participants*. 1958. Reprint, New York: Bonanza, 1995.

Mintz, Max M. *The Generals of Saratoga: John Burgoyne and Horatio Gates.* New Haven, CT: Yale University Press, 1990.

Nelson, Paul David. *General Horatio Gates: A Biography.* Baton Rouge: Louisiana State University Press, 1976.

———. *William Alexander, Lord Stirling.* University: University of Alabama Press, 1987.

Ranlet, Philip. *The New York Loyalists.* Knoxville: University of Tennessee Press, 1986.

Swiggett, H. *War Out of Niagara: Walter Butler and the Tory Rangers.* 1933. Reprint, Port Washington, NY: I. J. Friedman, 1963.

Wallace, Willard M. *Traitorous Hero: The Life and Fortunes of Benedict Arnold.* New York: Harper and Row, 1954.

Ward, Christopher. *War of the Revolution.* 2 vols. New York: Macmillan, 1952.

Ward, Harry M. *Between the Lines: Banditti of the American Revolution.* Westport, CT: Praeger, 2002.

Wertenbaker, Thomas J. *Father Knickerbocker Rebels: New York City during the Revolution.* New York: Scribner, 1948.

New York, Province and State

At the beginning of the American Revolution, New York ranked in the second tier of colonies. By the end of the war, it was on its way to being the Empire State. Revolutionary New Yorkers challenged and transformed most aspects of their lives, and the price they paid was very high. At the heart of it all was a wartime experience that lasted longer and proved more wrenching than any other state's.

Colonial New Yorkers knew war very well. Warfare transformed Dutch New Netherlands into British New York. Thereafter, New York City always had a resident British company of soldiers. The late-seventeenth-century war that the Iroquois fought against the French and their Indian allies established New York's western land claims, on the supposed ground that the Iroquois belonged to New York. During the French and Indian (Seven Years') War (1754–1763), New York City was the main British headquarters, and northern New York was a major theater of fighting. By that war's end, New Yorkers were used to the presence of sailors and soldiers and to the money that they and their suppliers spent.

After 1763, New York City continued to serve as the British headquarters. Enough troops remained permanently on station to require accommodation both at Fort George, near the Battery, and at the Upper Barracks, roughly on the site of City Hall. But the free-spending policies of William Pitt's wartime British administration ended, and a sharp downturn in New York's trade was the result. From the Sugar Act of 1764 to the Tea Act of 1773, British policy was to raise money within the colonies in order to support civil government and the military. For New Yorkers, the results included a sharp commercial depression, conflict between their own government and the British authorities, and outright hostility between troops and civilians. That hostility merged with conflicts among the New Yorkers themselves.

During the independence crisis (1774–1776), New York's leaders won a reputation for caution. But they and their people were among the leaders of earlier resistance. Unlike most of its counterparts, New York's Provincial Assembly passed a resolution against the Sugar Act. New York City hosted the Stamp Act Congress in August 1765. The city's Stamp Act uprising at the end of October made the act unenforceable in both New York and in Maryland, whose stamp distributor resigned when Long Islanders caught him. A crowd came close to assaulting Fort George, where the stamps were being kept. It did sack the elegant house of the British officer who had ordered the fort's guns to be trained on the city. The Sons of Liberty in Albany wrote a formal constitution. Their New York City counterparts worked out a mutual aid agreement with the Sons of Liberty in Connecticut. In the spring of 1766, however, British troops equipped with artillery suppressed rebellious Hudson Valley farmers. The province's leaders approved.

In 1767, those same leaders made a show of refusing to comply with Parliament's Quartering Act, which ordered them to supply the troops. John Dickinson praised their refusal in his widely read *Letters from a Farmer in Pennsylvania* (1767–1768). When a newly elected Assembly did comply with the Quartering Act in 1769, an anonymous broadside, "To the Betrayed Inhabitants of the City and Colony of New-York," condemned it. By that time ordinary city people and resident troops were locked in ongoing street combat. One reason was ideological: the widespread belief that any standing army showed their rulers' desire to crush their subjects' liberty. Another was the symbolic question of whether or not there should be a liberty pole to honor American resistance. Underpinning both was the very real problem of off-duty soldiers taking scarce jobs away from civilians. All these came to a violent head during a week of street brawls between soldiers and workingmen in January 1770. No lives were lost, but otherwise this so-called Battle of Golden Hill prefigured the Boston Massacre in March.

Between the summer of 1770 and Boston's destruction of East India Company tea in December 1773, the conflict between the colonies and Britain seemed to ease. But New York political life remained intense. One issue was conflict between one group of politicians centered on the urban De Lancey family, who had made their fortunes as transatlantic merchants and who had strong connections to the British elite, and another led by the landowning Livingstons of the middle and upper Hudson Valley. After winning the election of 1769, the De Lancey group complied with Britain's Quartering Act so that the governor would not dissolve the Assembly. When the Assembly learned that Alexander McDougall had written "To the Betrayed Inhabitants," it jailed him. The son of an immigrant milkman, McDougall had risen to modest prosperity as a sea captain, wartime privateer, and coastal merchant. His imprisonment became a well-publicized martyrdom.

The McDougall affair helped both to revive the Sons of Liberty among ordinary city people, particularly mechanics (master and journeyman artisans), and to solidify their alliance with the Livingston faction. In 1773 the artisans established their own committee, bought a building to serve as their headquarters, and named it Liberty Hall. They were becoming an independent political force, acting in concert with like-minded elite politicians but learning "to think and to reason" for themselves. One such politician, Gouverneur Morris, used that phrase with "fear and trembling" as he likened "the mob" to "poor reptiles" that would "strike" before noon. Unlike many of his sort, including most De Lancey politicians and several members of his own family, Morris did not drift fearfully toward the supposed safety of supporting the British. But he did find kindred spirits among other elite leaders, such as Robert R. Livingston Jr., John Jay, and Philip Schuyler, who sought to guide and delay popular politics.

Independent of the crisis with Britain, another movement was developing in the newly created counties of Gloucester and Cumberland (present-day Vermont). New York's colonial boundaries were nothing like the familiar modern shape of New York. One supposedly authoritative British map, drawn about 1775 but published in 1779, asserted New York's title to much of New England west of the Connecticut River. That map presented the country of the Six Nations of the Iroquois in the same way it presented New England east of the river, as white space not belonging to New York at all. About the same time, Governor William Tryon asserted to London that the province's relationship to the Iroquois gave it title at least as far west as Lake Michigan.

Although the Board of Trade upheld New York's Green Mountain (Vermont) claim in 1764, New Hampshire had made many land grants in the region. Most passed to Connecticut people, whose own province was overcrowded after four or five generations of long lives and large families. After the French withdrew from Canada in 1763, these people began taking up their claims. Some, such as Ethan Allen and his brothers, were land speculators, though not on the scale of the great New York families. Most of the New Englanders, however, were yeoman farmers who wanted to transplant their village-centered way of life northward. New York, however, proposed to establish its Hudson River model of great estates worked by tenant farmers.

Allen had grown up along the actual New York–Connecticut border and loathed the New York system. Beginning in the late 1760s and gathering force during the early 1770s, he led a movement to resist New York's political authority in the region and nullify its land grants. By 1773 his Green Mountain Boys were closing New York courts, destroying the villages and farmsteads of New York grantees, and establishing their own informal government. Eighteenth-century America saw many such rural insurrections. One of the most notable was the great tenant uprising in the Hudson Valley in 1766. But the Green Mountain movement was the only one that put the rioters in a position to shape exactly the society they wanted. In 1774, New York's Assembly passed an Act of Attainder that outlawed the Green Mountain leaders by name, authorized their killing on sight, and imposed the death penalty for many offenses committed in the region. The act had no real effect. Allen himself rode from Bennington into Albany to proclaim his defiance and rode out again safely.

By then, Bostonians had destroyed the East India Company tea that was consigned to their merchants. They expected a British retreat, just as in 1766 when Parliament repealed the Stamp Act and in 1770 when it revoked all but one of the Townshend duties on imported goods. But led by a stable ministry under Lord North, Parliament chose to punish the town and its province with the four Coercive (Intolerable) Acts. New York City turned its first tea ship around at Sandy Hook in April 1774. But when a second vessel tied up shortly afterward with East India Company tea on board, a crowd came aboard and dumped the cargo. Unlike Boston, this New York Tea Party took place with no attempt at negotiations or disguise. And also unlike Boston, New York suffered no direct punishment.

During the tense summer that followed, the people of Massachusetts prepared to overturn their royal government rather than accept the changes that Parliament imposed upon them. By midautumn, the power of Governor Thomas Gage, who also was commander in chief in North America and who had moved his headquarters to Boston, extended only to Boston itself. Elsewhere a provincial congress and informal committees ruled. New Yorkers moved more slowly in 1774. Governor Tryon continued in office. The Assembly met to legislate. The mayors and councils of New York City and Albany governed their respective cities. Crown courts decided cases.

But a movement was assembling that pointed toward destroying royal authority and creating new centers of power. The first step was creating committees of correspondence to share information and direct aid for Boston, whose port was closed. In May 1774, city people elected a Committee of Fifty-One at a tumultuous meeting. Committees elsewhere assembled more quietly, most often by simple self-selection rather than popular election. In Tryon County, where New York abutted Iroquois country and where the family of Sir William Johnson, Britain's Indian agent, exercised great power, the committee met in secret.

In the autumn, matters began to change. The First Continental Congress called for committees of inspection to enforce its boycott of British commerce, known as the Continental Association. The name suggested voluntary compliance, but these new committees would wield real power. New York City chose a committee of sixty members to enforce the Continental Association, but street radicals such as McDougall and fellow former sea captain Isaac Sears were anxious to follow New England's lead toward a more forceful resistance. They found their moment on 23 April 1775, when news arrived of the battles at Lexington and Concord, Massachusetts. Sears led a crowd that burst into the city arsenal, seized weapons and ammunition, and paraded through the streets. A mass meeting elected a new Committee of Safety, composed of one hundred members, and open meetings picked similar committees in most other counties. These were much larger than their predecessors, and they began taking on real governing power, most especially by creating a militia that would not obey royal authorities.

The first of five provincial congresses also assembled that spring. At every level from local government to continental affairs, a countergovernment was taking shape. Even the Green Mountain Boys forgot their differences with New York for a time, and Allen accepted a colonel's commission from the provincial congress. The old authorities did, however, hang on. By coincidence, Governor Tryon returned from England on the same day in

June 1775 that George Washington passed through New York City on his way to Boston. Tryon delayed disembarking until Washington was gone. Crowds cheered both men. But the governor had to establish his headquarters on a ship in the harbor, under the protection of a man-of-war's guns. When he tried to convene a new assembly in December 1775, confident Revolutionary leaders called for a counterelection to "awe a corrupt assembly . . . from interfering with political subjects."

New York City got its first taste of war on 23 August 1775, when HMS *Asia* fired a broadside to stop revolutionaries taking cannon from the Battery. Real warfare came in July 1776. The British Army had withdrawn from Boston, regrouped at Halifax, and linked up with fresh redcoats and hired German Hessian regiments transported from England and Europe to form the largest seaborne force the world had seen. Its target was New York City. The first warships and transports began passing through the unfortified Narrows on the same day that Congress voted for independence, 2 July 1776. Joint commanders General Sir William Howe and Admiral Lord Richard Howe took their time disembarking their troops on Staten Island, while Washington positioned the Continental Army along Bay Ridge on the Brooklyn side of New York Harbor. Washington was, relatively speaking, still a military amateur, and his troops were undisciplined and ill-equipped. Crossing the Narrows in August, the British nearly trapped him and most of the army at Brooklyn Heights when they took an undefended pass near modern Prospect Park. But a northerly wind that kept British ships out of the East River and possible hesitation by the Howe brothers enabled the Americans to escape to Manhattan.

By September 1776, the city had become indefensible, so the Americans retreated into Westchester County, standing off the British at White Plains in October before crossing to relative safety in New Jersey. Sizable forces remained at Forts Washington and Lee, roughly where the ends of the present-day George Washington Bridge now stand. In November, British forces captured both strongholds and took the large body of Americans at Fort Washington prisoner. The British would remain in control of Manhattan, Staten Island, Long Island, and lower Westchester County until the end of 1783.

Many people in the conquered zone were glad to see the British return, even if it was as military rather than civil rulers. New York probably had a larger Loyalist problem than any other state. In the unconquered Hudson Valley, whole militia units were disarmed because of their members' disaffection. Although both sides urged the Six Nations to stay neutral, the Mohawks, Onondagas, Cayugas, and Senecas sided with the British. The Oneidas and Tuscaroras chose the Americans. Their Mohawk Valley settler neighbors also split. The Johnson family had been good landlords, and most of their tenants followed Sir William's heirs into Loyalism. But nontenant farmers and small traders chose the American side. In June 1775, Sir John Johnson, flailing his horsewhip, broke up a meeting to elect a militia captain. When he fortified the family seat at Johnson Hall with light artillery, a Patriot crowd besieged the house. A civil war was erupting that would lay the Mohawk Valley, the upper Delaware and Susquehanna Valleys, and the Lake

Ontario Plain in flames until 1782. That war would destroy the centuries-old power of the Iroquois Confederacy.

The Green Mountain Boys seized the moment to break with New York, declaring Vermont's independence early in 1777. The new State of New York was a bare remnant of the former province. Its leaders called the Vermonters "revolted subjects" and described their new state as "pretended," but any claim to western New England was gone. On the contrary, Massachusetts was asserting its own claim to the land between Seneca Lake and Lake Erie. The Southern District was under military occupation. The final Provincial Congress renamed itself the Convention of the People and started to write a state constitution. Constantly retreating in the fall of 1776, it shifted from New York City to White Plains for safety and finished its work at Kingston (Esopus).

The convention proclaimed the new constitution on 25 April 1777. There would be a two-house legislature, with a broad electorate for the Assembly and a narrower one for the state Senate and the governorship. The governor would hold office for three years and would be significantly more powerful than his counterparts in other states. A strong independent judiciary completed the structure, setting an institutional model that the federal convention of 1787 would imitate. Men such as Livingston, Jay, Morris, and Schuyler expected to take control of the new state government. But Schuyler lost the governorship to George Clinton of Ulster County. Clinton was an astute politician whose plain ways contrasted with Schuyler's air of command. Clinton would hold the governorship until 1795 and return to it from 1801 to 1804. His kind of men began to enter the legislature, although they were slow to recognize themselves as a distinct political group. Colonial-era family factions were yielding to party politics. It was a major change.

First, however, the new government had to take control of its state. The legislature assembled at Kingston on 10 September 1777, but it broke up almost immediately when British forces sailed up the Hudson, seized the town, and burned it. Popular committees continued to meet until well into 1778. In some places, courts could not open and taxes could not be collected because of disaffection. Worst of all, British strategy for 1777 planned a major assault on what remained of independent New York, with troops converging toward Albany from the north, west, and south.

The plan belonged to General John Burgoyne, who had returned from occupied New York City to London and secured an independent command based in Montreal. He would lead his own army south along Lake Champlain and the upper Hudson River Valley. Lieutenant-Colonel Barry St. Leger would take a smaller force west to Oswego on Lake Ontario, join Loyalists and pro-British Indians, and head south and east to the Mohawk Valley. Burgoyne counted on General Howe, in New York City, to cooperate from the south, but Howe had other ideas and took the main body of his own army to capture Philadelphia, traveling the long way through Chesapeake Bay. He did capture the American capital, but had he remained in New York City and given serious aid to Burgoyne, all of New York might have fallen under British control.

The strategy failed. General Clinton's October raid on Kingston was a feint. St. Leger's forces ambushed Mohawk Valley militia in a ravine at

Oriskany, in Oneida Indian territory, and besieged Fort Stanwix, on the Oneida carrying place where the upper Mohawk River comes closest to Wood Creek, flowing toward Lake Ontario. But Fort Stanwix's garrison resisted, and an American force hurried west under General Benedict Arnold and used a ruse to break the siege. Burgoyne himself started out successfully, driving Americans out of Fort Ticonderoga and then moving down the Hudson River toward Albany. But the British started to run short of supplies, and New Englanders defeated Hessians who tried a foraging raid toward Bennington. Overextended and exhausted, Burgoyne allowed himself to be trapped at Saratoga by American regulars and militia under General Horatio Gates and surrendered to Gates in October 1777. The two generals knew each other; they had begun their careers as junior officers in the same British regiment.

The worst was over for most New Yorkers. But irregular warfare continued in Westchester County, and the western frontier remained aflame. That conflict was brutal. Indian and Loyalist raids in the Cherry and Schoharie Valleys in 1778 were particularly brutal. Those raids provoked Washington to send a major expedition into Indian country in 1779, under Generals John Sullivan and James Clinton. The Americans pillaged and burned, but the Indians and Loyalists simply fled west. The major result was that Americans, particularly New Englanders, saw and began to covet the rich lands of Iroquoia. Even after the Americans and French defeated General Charles Cornwallis at Yorktown in 1781, the war did not end for New Yorkers. Washington returned to the Hudson Valley and began planning an assault on the final prize, New York City. The Mohawk Valley and Indian country continued to see sporadic conflict. Instead of abruptly ending, war in New York slowly dwindled away.

Neither the preliminary treaty of peace (1782) nor the final agreement (1783) brought tranquility to New York. Redcoats remained in control of the southern district until the end of 1783, and they would hold Fort Niagara and control some of the surrounding frontier until 1795. And the pro-British Iroquois had no idea that they were defeated for several years. The handover of New York City went smoothly, but Patriots disgraced their new liberty by boarding British transports to recapture former slaves who claimed freedom under the Union Jack. Despite the terms of peace, the legislature continued passing anti-Loyalist laws. As early as 1779, it charged Loyalist leaders with treason, confiscated their land, and declared Loyalists "outside the protection of the laws." It forgave "zealous Friends to the Freedom and Independence of the United States" for whatever they might have done "with intent to further the Common Cause," protected Patriots against Loyalist creditors, let them sue Loyalists who had used their property, disqualified former Loyalists from political life, and imposed punitive taxation on the southern district. Radicals led by Sears and McDougall won New York City's first free election. Loyalists who had hoped to stay began packing for Halifax and London.

A split, however, was opening within the top leadership. Governor Clinton had spent the war years seeking cooperation rather than conflict among Patriots. But in 1779 he endorsed both confiscating Tory property and a popular though cumbersome tax system according to "circumstances and abilities . . .

collectively considered." At the war's end, Clinton was still corresponding with conservative leaders such as Jay and Alexander Hamilton. But Clinton was also building his own support through patronage and state-oriented policies on taxation, Loyalists, and land. Hamilton lumped him with other "rulers of this state" as not fit for power. In 1784 and again in 1786, Clinton opposed granting taxing power to Congress. He stood firm against recognizing Vermont.

One major issue was a wild card: slavery. Both Hamilton and Clinton joined the Manumission Society, established in 1784. The legislature debated gradual abolition in 1785, and the votes cut across all other divisions. That bill failed in the Council of Revision, composed of the governor and the state's highest judges. Their objection was not to ending slavery but to the second-class status that the bill would impose on former slaves. Not until 1799 would New York begin slavery's demolition.

The state also jostled with Congress over Indian relations. New York claimed control over Indian tribes as heir to colonial powers, sanctioned in the state constitution. Congress claimed control as heir to the British Crown. Not until 1790 would the federal government declare its supremacy on Indian matters. By then, New York had negotiated its own land treaties. One, in 1788, reduced the territory of the pro-American Oneidas from roughly 5 million acres to about 250,000. At the same time, agreements with New Jersey and Pennsylvania were establishing the state's modern borders. A treaty with Massachusetts gave that state ownership of land from Seneca Lake nearly to the Niagara River, but not sovereignty over it. As land passed out of Indian control, speculators began acquiring it in large parcels. The largest, Alexander McComb's purchase, was more than 3 million acres.

For all these reasons, New York figured large in the thinking of the men who created the new U.S. Constitution. Hamilton was among the foremost of these leaders. He understood the economic importance of New York City. Insisting on the supremacy of the peace treaty, he opposed the persecution of the Loyalists. He rallied merchants and lawyers, founded the Bank of New York, and in correspondence and essays argued for a continental view of every issue. Even on a matter such as granting a divorce, he wanted regular, predictable laws that courts would administer rather than ad hoc decisions by state legislatures. Hamilton entered New York's legislature in 1787 so that he could be a delegate to the Philadelphia Convention. He joined James Madison and John Jay to write the Federalist Papers, addressed to New York's "considerate people." Hamilton sought the support not only of merchants but also of city workingmen, who wanted the commercial stability and large markets that the Constitution promised. But rural New Yorkers overwhelmingly opposed a strong central government, believing that the state served their own interests well. When the ratifying convention gathered at Poughkeepsie in June 1788, forty-five delegates were Antifederalists. Governor Clinton led them. Only nineteen delegates joined Hamilton.

Had the convention voted immediately, a triumph by New York's Antifederalists might have encouraged the many Antifederalists in Virginia and New Hampshire and stopped ratification altogether. But as the delegates in Poughkeepsie deliberated, those two states did ratify the document,

New York City became the nation's first capital.

changing the question from whether the Constitution would take effect at all to whether New York would join the new nation. That bare fact, together with the possibility that New York City would secede from the state and ratify on its own, tipped the balance. New York City became the nation's first capital when Congress assembled and Washington assumed the presidency there in 1789. In certain ways the Revolution had begun in New York, and in important ways it had been fought there. If the new government marked the Revolution's end, it can also be said that the Revolution ended in New York.

EDWARD COUNTRYMAN

See also

Clinton, George; Constitutions, State; Correspondence, Committees of; Hamilton, Alexander; Loyalists; Native Americans; New York, Operations in; Oriskany, Battle of; Saratoga Campaign; Vermont

References

Becker, Carl L. *The History of Political Parties in the Province of New York, 1760–1776.* Madison: University of Wisconsin Press, 1909.

Bonomi, Patricia U. *A Factious People: Politics and Society in Colonial New York.* New York: Columbia University Press, 1971.

Champagne, Roger J. *Alexander McDougall and the American Revolution in New York.* Schenectady: New York State American Revolution Bicentennial Commission and Union College Press, 1975.

Countryman, Edward. *A People in Revolution: The American Revolution and Political Society in New York, 1760–1790.* Baltimore, MD: Johns Hopkins University Press, 1981.

———. "From Revolution to Statehood, 1776–1825." Pp. 227–304 in *The Empire State: A History of New York.* Edited by Milton M. Klein. Ithaca, NY: Cornell University Press, 2000.

Dangerfield, George. *Chancellor Robert R. Livingston of New York, 1746–1813.* New York: Harcourt, Brace, 1960.

East, Robert A., and Jacob Judd, eds. *The Loyalist Americans: A Focus on Greater New York.* Tarrytown, NY: Sleepy Hollow, 1975.

Gilje, Paul A. *The Road to Mobocracy: Popular Disorder in New York City, 1763–1834.* Chapel Hill: University of North Carolina Press, 1987.

Graymont, Barbara. *The Iroquois in the American Revolution.* Syracuse, NY: Syracuse University Press, 1972.

Howard, Ronald W. "The English Province, 1664–1776." Pp. 111–225 in *The Empire State: A History of New York.* Edited by Milton M. Klein. Ithaca, NY: Cornell University Press, 2000.

Kaminski, John P. *George Clinton: Yeoman Politician of the New Republic.* Madison, WI: Madison House, 1993.

Kelsay, Isabel T. *Joseph Brant, 1743–1807: Man of Two Worlds.* Syracuse, NY: Syracuse University Press, 1984.

Kierner, Cynthia A. *Traders and Gentlefolk: The Livingstons of New York, 1765–1790.* Ithaca, NY: Cornell University Press, 1992.

Mintz, Max M. *The Generals of Saratoga: John Burgoyne and Horatio Gates.* New Haven, CT: Yale University Press, 1990.

Potter, Janice. *The Liberty We Seek: Loyalist Ideology in Colonial New York and Massachusetts.* Cambridge: Harvard University Press, 1983.

Schecter, Barnet. *The Battle for New York: The City at the Heart of the American Revolution*. New York: Walker, 2002.

Tiedemann, Joseph S. *Reluctant Revolutionaries: New York City and the Road to Independence, 1763–1776*. Ithaca, NY: Cornell University Press, 1997.

Wallace, Anthony F. C. *The Death and Rebirth of the Seneca*. New York: Knopf, 1970.

White, Shane. *Somewhat More Independent: The End of Slavery in New York City, 1770–1810*. Athens: University of Georgia Press, 1991.

Young, Alfred F. *The Democratic Republicans of New York: The Origins, 1763–1797*. Chapel Hill: University of North Carolina Press, 1967.

New York City

New York City and its immediate surrounding area were occupied by the British Army and the Royal Navy throughout the American Revolutionary War, and the city was the major stronghold for American Loyalists.

Heavily populated with military, administrative, and clerical officials throughout the eighteenth century, New York's support for royal government always exceeded that of other cities. The commercial class, too, supported close ties with Britain, as merchants, shopkeepers, and farmers relied on contracts with the government, army, and navy as well as on trade from throughout the British Empire. In May 1775, however, royal government in the city collapsed when officials abandoned Manhattan and the military withdrew to ships in the harbor. By January 1776, close to 10,000 of the city's 25,000 people had fled from the Revolutionary government.

The British, however, had no intention of leaving New York City in the hands of the revolutionaries. Strategically located, its superb harbor provided an ideal base of operations ranging up and down the Atlantic seaboard. The Loyalist population was an asset that would provide support for the troops and a safe haven. General George Washington had hopes of holding New York City for the purpose of denying these benefits to the British, but his army of some 23,000 inexperienced, badly led, and poorly equipped soldiers was inadequately prepared for the task. General William Howe, commanding 32,000 British soldiers and German mercenaries, began landing his force on Staten Island in June 1776. Hundreds of Staten Island and northern New Jersey farmers flocked to the British, enlisting in the army and joining Loyalist militia companies. Howe began his attack in August, defeating Washington at the Battle of Long Island. The British invaded Manhattan at Kips Bay in September and swiftly occupied the city itself, accompanied by much looting. By November 1776, American forces had been completely cleared out of the New York City area and never again seriously threatened the British hold on the city, despite Washington's deep desire to recapture it.

Howe used New York City as a base for his 1777 campaign directed at the capture of Philadelphia, but his successor, Sir Henry Clinton, abandoned Pennsylvania and returned to New York the following year. The city remained the British headquarters for the rest of the war but saw little military action. Clinton feared losing his citadel to the Americans and only

View of New York from Long Island, circa 1776. The city fell to the British in September of that year and remained in their hands until the end of the war. (Library of Congress)

launched small operations. The British successively drained Clinton's forces to support the southern campaign of Lord Charles Cornwallis and the defense of its Caribbean islands. Militarily, New York served mainly as the base of Loyalist militia who operated on Long Island and northern New Jersey and in the lower Hudson River Valley while mounting attacks on the Connecticut coast. Ships stationed in the harbor housed American prisoners of war, and more than 11,000 died there in the atrocious conditions. The British also used New York City as a base of clandestine operations ranging from espionage to counterfeiting Continental currency. The only Loyalist newspapers in America were printed in New York City and provided a voice in opposition to the Revolution and a valuable source of propaganda.

The British governed New York City through martial law. Loyalists by the thousands flocked from throughout the province and from other colonies to the city. Numerous blacks, too, made their way to New York after they were promised their freedom by Clinton in 1779 if they stood by the king. By that year, some 50,000 civilians and 2,500 military dependents lived in the city, along with anywhere between 4,000 and 20,000 troops. There were generally at least 10,000 soldiers camped on Manhattan and Staten Island.

The rapid population growth created many problems. Fires in 1776 and again in 1778 exacerbated the housing shortage by destroying more than one-quarter of the housing supply. When the army seized houses belonging to revolutionaries and used them to billet troops, many civilians were forced to live in a squalid tent city called Canvas Town. Unsanitary and cramped conditions provided ideal circumstances for outbreaks of cholera, smallpox, and yellow fever. Venereal disease, spread by a large number of prostitutes, presented a particular problem. There were chronic shortages of food and fuel (Manhattan was shaved bare of trees by 1783), and both essential items had to be imported from other parts of the empire. Crime and corruption were rampant, and the police court established in 1780 did little to prosecute soldiers and sailors. Reliance on civilian patrols created numerous gangs and protection rackets. The British did battle poverty with regulations on food-stuffs, rent and economic controls, almshouses, and a vestry that distributed money to the poor, but skyrocketing inflation and the constantly rising population undercut much of their efforts to alleviate destitution.

Hard times, however, were not shared by all. The British military brought lucrative contracts that allowed some citizens to prosper. Others made a small fortune by smuggling scarce items in and out of the city. Military officers lived well and often maintained mistresses. Royal officials held lavish parties and dances in their houses and in exclusive clubs and even entertained Prince William Henry (later King William IV) in 1781.

Although Cornwallis surrendered at Yorktown in October 1781, it was another two years before the last British troops pulled out of New York City. The army remained until the British were satisfied that all Loyalists who wanted to leave had done so. Martial law was eased and a civilian government reinstituted, but constant friction and fights between Americans and the British continued. In the meantime, more than 40,000 Loyalist civilians from throughout America fled through New York City, including 4,000 blacks. Most of the Loyalists relocated to Canada. On 25 November 1783, the last British troops evacuated New York City.

GREGORY DEHLER

See also

British Army; Clinton, Henry; Continental Army; Cornwallis, Charles; Howe, William; Long Island, Battle of; Loyalist Exiles; Loyalist Units; Loyalists; Militia, Patriot and Loyalist; New York, Operations in; New York, Province and State; Philadelphia Campaign; Slaves and Free Blacks; Tryon, William; Washington, George

References

Barck, Oscar. *New York City during the War for Independence*. New York: Columbia University Press, 1931.

Burrows, Edwin G., and Mike Wallace. *Gotham: A History of New York City to 1898*. New York: Oxford University Press, 1999.

Flick, Alexander. *Loyalism in New York during the American Revolution*. New York: Arno, 1969.

Gerlach, Larry, ed. *The American Revolution in New York as a Case Study*. Belmont, CA: Wadsworth, 1972.

Klein, Milton, and Ronald Howard, eds. *The Twilight of British Rule in America: The New York Letterbook of General James Robertson, 1780–1783*. Cooperstown: New York State Historical Association, 1983.

Van Buskirk, Judith L. *Generous Enemies: Patriots and Loyalists in Revolutionary New York*. Philadelphia: University of Pennsylvania Press, 2002.

Newburgh Addresses

(March 1783)

The Newburgh Addresses were several speeches given to Continental Army officers at the army's winter quarters at Newburgh, New York, in March 1783, just as the American republic was about to achieve its formal independence from Great Britain. The opposing orators, General George Washington versus certain army officers, were responding to escalating unrest among both the officers and soldiers, which almost resulted in a military coup d'état.

In 1781, Washington was forced to reorganize the Continental Army. A major cause for this reorganization was fear of an impending financial collapse of Congress. The latter years of the war, with declining contributions to Congress from several states—Congress's only major source of revenue—forced severe financial cuts. The Continental Army soon experienced an increase in chronic shortages of food, clothing, and pay. In 1781 and 1782, the financial shortages alienated many—officers and soldiers alike—within the Continental Army. Even the victory of Washington and Jean-Baptiste Vimeur, the comte de Rochambeau, over Lord Charles Cornwallis at Yorktown, Virginia, in October 1781 could not quiet their unrest.

By late 1781, Washington and his top officers decided on a military reorganization plan to make the army more efficient, but in April 1782, Congress reversed an important part of the reorganization. As a cost-cutting measure, the delegates ordered the elimination of three lieutenants from each regiment. In addition, company officers were directed to perform functions previously assigned to adjutants, quartermasters, and recruiters. The Continental Army was now forced into an even more severe streamlining of its operations, which soon alienated many officers.

Throughout 1782, Congress continued to reduce the army's support structure. Robert Morris, Congress's superintendent of finance, along with Benjamin Lincoln, its new secretary of war, spearheaded this radical reorganization of the army. Lincoln, a former general, reduced most staff agencies in the War Office and filled many remaining positions with line officers who were to perform their new administrative duties on a part-time basis. The reforms even eliminated many positions that were crucial to supporting the army in the field. These reforms angered Washington, who protested that the changes weakened the army's mobility in their actions against the British Army, which was then quiet but still garrisoned in force in New York and Charleston.

By early 1783, America was in a more favorable military and diplomatic position. The British Army had evacuated Charleston and concentrated nearly all its forces in New York. The British Parliament was in the last, futile stages of postponing a final peace treaty granting American independence. Given Congress's still straitened circumstances, however, America's stronger position threatened to place the Continental Army in a weaker position.

In Congress, pressure mounted to reduce military expenditures by dismantling the army. One group of delegates made this demand in the hope of giving the states a stronger position in government policy. Another group, composed mostly of ardent nationalists, sought a stronger central government.

They viewed the army as an ally in their labors to force the stubborn Congress to adopt a taxation program. And the army, both at the officer and enlisted levels, concluded that it must secure congressional action on its own bread-and-butter issues, specifically arrears in pay, before the war formally ended.

In Newburgh, the Continental Army's winter headquarters, officer discontent mounted over Congress's refusal to meet its obligations. Washington sympathized with his officers but feared that the hungry and impoverished troops might become rebellious. He warned Congress that the mood of the army was threatening. But even as he issued this caution, rumors began circulating that Congress would rescind its promises of half pay to the army's officers. This prompted General Alexander McDougall, accompanied by Colonel John Brooks and Colonel Matthias Ogden, to transmit a petition to Congress in January 1783 that stated the officers' complaints.

This petition symbolized the critical political situation because, unlike earlier officer protests, it claimed to speak for the entire army. Fearing a general mutiny, Washington urged Congress to confront the crisis. He privately wrote to several delegates, who were committed to a stronger central government, favoring the claims of the petitioners. In response, a congressional committee reported favorably on the petition, but the whole Congress resoundingly defeated a resolution offering the officers a sum equal to five years' pay as commutation for their pensions.

On 12 March 1783, angry officers addressed the assembled army, stating their grievances. Washington reacted swiftly by calling for a general assembly of officers in which he would address the issue. Although he hoped that he could delay precipitate action by the officers to allow tensions to decrease, he warned Congress that swift congressional action on the pay issue was needed to alleviate the underlying problems.

Washington dominated the next officers' meeting, on 15 March, in a dramatic fashion. After fumbling through the first paragraph of a prepared speech, the venerable general, just fifty-one years old, put on a pair of glasses and muttered that not only had he grown gray in the service of his country but now he was also going blind. He then proceeded to condemn the officers' Newburgh addresses as a call to military mutiny and even suggested the secret authorship of a British agent. His speech moved several of his comrades in arms to tears. Following the emotional appeal by their leader, the officers quietly adopted an extraordinarily moderate petition to Congress.

In the aftermath of the crisis, Congress agreed to make a lump sum payment to the officers in lieu of half-pay pensions, and Washington, working with Lincoln, fashioned a plan to disband the Continental Army gradually. On 23 April 1783, Congress adopted a demobilization resolution, which was a compromise between those who argued for a swift disbandment to reduce expenses and those who favored gradual demobilization until the British Army had evacuated its last posts in America. Washington, as acting general in chief, was given the authority to recall the army if final peace negotiations with Britain collapsed.

On 26 May 1783, Congress ordered demobilization to begin. All soldiers were to march home under the direction of their officers but were allowed to keep their arms as a bonus. The process continued for several months, with Washington, several of his officers, and a core of troops remaining in service long enough to march into New York City in November 1783, just as the last British forces boarded ships in the harbor for their return home.

JAIME RAMÓN OLIVARES

See also

Armstrong, James; Congress, Second Continental and Confederation; Continental Army; Lincoln, Benjamin; Morris, Robert; Washington, George

References

Corning, Amos Elwood. *Washington at Temple Hill.* Newburgh, NY: Lanmere, 1932.

Kohn, Richard H. *Eagle and Sword: The Beginnings of the Military Establishment in America.* New York: Free Press, 1975.

Martin, James Kirby, and Mark E. Lender. *A Respectable Army: The Military Origins of the Republic, 1763–1789.* Wheeling, IL: Harlan Davidson, 1982.

Rakove, Jack. *The Beginnings of National Politics: An Interpretive History of the Continental Congress.* New York: Knopf, 1979.

Newcastle, Duke of

See Pelham-Holles, Thomas, 1st Duke of Newcastle

Newport, Rhode Island, Naval Operations against
(1776–1781)

From 1776 to 1781, Rhode Island, and Newport in particular, was the focus of British and French naval activities as part of the War for American Independence. Rhode Island came to the attention of the British in late 1776, when General William Howe, commander in chief of British forces in North America, decided to seize it after he had captured New York City. Newport and Providence were important commercial ports, and Narragansett Bay offered a fine winter anchorage for the fleet of Admiral Lord Richard Howe, brother of General Howe and commander of the British fleet in American waters. The task was given to General Sir Henry Clinton and Commodores William Hotham and Sir Peter Parker. Hotham was assigned the task of escorting the transports, fifty-one vessels, carrying 6,000 British regulars and Hessian mercenaries. Parker was given command of a squadron of warships, which would support the troops during the landing. In all, the admirals commanded a dozen warships.

The fleet sailed into Narragansett Bay on 7 December, led by the *Experiment* (50 guns), commanded by Captain James Wallace, who was familiar with the geography and defenses of Rhode Island. Next in line was Parker's flagship, the *Chatham*, with Clinton and his second in command, Lord Hugh Percy, on board. All the other ships followed in single file. American vessels

A French fleet commanded by Admiral Jean-Baptiste d'Estaing attempts to enter the bay at Newport, Rhode Island, in August 1778. A British fleet arrived from New York and fought an inconclusive action, but the intervention of a storm that scattered the two fleets convinced d'Estaing of the need to withdraw to Boston to make repairs. (Library of Congress)

commanded by Captain Esek Hopkins immediately withdrew up the bay toward Providence, moving as far as possible out of harm's way. On the following day, the Anglo-German army was landed on Aquidneck (or Rhode) Island without opposition, under the precautionary covering fire of British warships, and seized Newport. The people of the town, many of them Quakers, welcomed Clinton's forces with enthusiasm. Clinton also occupied Conanicut Island but left the remaining twelve islands in the bay, all uninhabited, devoid of troops. For the next eighteen months, a number of American privateers trapped in upper Narragansett Bay attempted to flee to the open sea, while British ships attempted to keep them bottled up. Some privateers were captured or driven ashore, but probably an equal number escaped and sailed to other ports in Massachusetts and Connecticut.

On 6 February 1778, the United States and France signed a treaty of recognition and alliance, and two months later the French foreign minister, Charles Gravier, the comte de Vergennes, dispatched Admiral Jean-Baptiste d'Estaing and the Toulon fleet to North American waters. This fleet, comprised of twelve ships of the line, five frigates, some smaller vessels, and transports loaded with 4,000 French soldiers, sailed from Toulon in mid-May. D'Estaing was accompanied on his flagship, the *Languedoc* (90 guns), by Conrad Gérard, France's first foreign minister to America. D'Estaing arrived off the Delaware Capes some eighty-seven days later, only to discover that he was ten days too late to intercept a British fleet under Admiral Howe proceeding from Philadelphia toward New York. D'Estaing sailed on to New York, intending to assist General George Washington's army, and arrived off Sandy Hook on 11 July. There he discovered that his ships could not safely cross the bar at Sandy Hook and that Howe had positioned his own outnumbered warships to take advantage of his lack of maneuvering room.

After consultations with Washington and Congress, d'Estaing learned that the Americans wanted him to sail to Rhode Island, where he would cooperate with a land army commanded by General John Sullivan in an attack on the British garrison at Newport. Agreeing with this plan, d'Estaing weighed anchor on 22 July for Rhode Island. Seven days later he reached his destination and on 30 July devised a plan of operations with Sullivan. D'Estaing would sail up the Middle Passage on 8 August, bombarding Newport as he passed. A day later, Sullivan would land troops on the northern end of Aquidneck Island. On 10 August, d'Estaing would land French troops on the western shore of the island, whereupon the combined armies would attack General Robert Pigot's army of 6,700 men in the lines around Newport. Preparatory to these maneuvers, d'Estaing wanted to resupply his fleet with water and food and allow his soldiers and sailors to recuperate on land. He also wanted to probe British naval defenses to determine what enemy warships he would face as the Franco-American campaign developed.

On 5 August, d'Estaing sent Admiral Pierre de Suffren with two frigates up the Seakonnet, or East, Passage and ordered two ships of the line up the Middle Passage in support of this operation. The British defenders were thrown into disarray. They withdrew their troops from Conanicut Island, and their senior naval officer, Captain John Brisbane of the *Flora* (32 guns) scattered his warships. The frigate *Cerberus* (32 guns), which ran aground while attempting to reach Newport, was set on fire and exploded. Also run aground and destroyed were the frigates *Lark*, *Juno*, and *Orpheus* (all 32 guns); the *Kingfisher* (16 guns); and the galley *Pigot*. The *Flora*, the *Falcon* (18 guns), and a number of transports were scuttled and sunk in front of Newport Harbor to block French warships from entering. These ships' crews went ashore to augment Pigot's forces defending Newport. With all British warships in Narragansett Bay destroyed, the French gained control of the waters surrounding Aquidneck Island.

Persuaded that Narragansett Bay was now safe to enter, d'Estaing sailed his fleet up the Middle Passage on 8 August and landed 4,000 sailors and soldiers on Conanicut Island. On the following day, he learned that Sullivan was crossing to Aquidneck Island, a day earlier than the plan called for. Although irked that the Americans had not consulted him before this action, he recognized that it made tactical sense and made plans to support Sullivan with French troops. But that same day Admiral Howe, anxious for a fight, arrived from New York off Rhode Island with his fleet: eight ships of the line, five ships of fifty guns, two of forty-four guns, four frigates, two sloops, an armed transport, two bomb ketches, three fireships, and four galleys. D'Estaing quickly reembarked his troops, despite Sullivan's pleas that he leave them to assist the Americans against Newport, and on 10 August sailed out to do battle. When Howe saw the French ships, he sent his galleys back to New York and ordered his fleet to weigh anchor and steer south-southeast. He was waiting for a change in the wind that would give him the weather gauge and

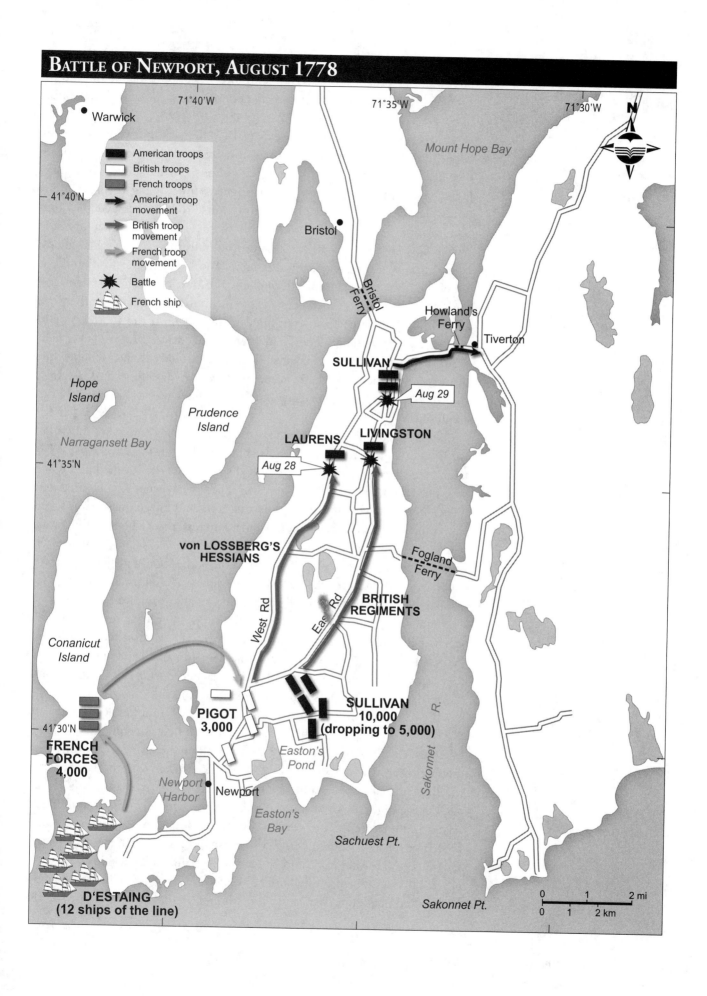

BATTLE OF NEWPORT, AUGUST 1778

Legend:
- American troops
- British troops
- French troops
- American troop movement
- British troop movement
- French troop movement
- Battle
- French ship

Warwick

71°40'W 71°35'W 71°30'W

41°40'N

Mount Hope Bay

Bristol

Bristol Ferry

Howland's Ferry

Tiverton

Hope Island

Prudence Island

Narragansett Bay

SULLIVAN

Aug 29

41°35'N

LAURENS **LIVINGSTON**

Aug 28

von LOSSBERG'S HESSIANS

Fogland Ferry

West Rd

East Rd

BRITISH REGIMENTS

Conanicut Island

Sakonnet R.

PIGOT 3,000

SULLIVAN 10,000 (dropping to 5,000)

41°30'N

Easton's Pond

FRENCH FORCES 4,000

Newport Harbor

Newport

Easton's Bay

Sachuest Pt.

D'ESTAING (12 ships of the line)

Sakonnet Pt.

0 1 2 mi
0 1 2 km

allow him to use his fireships to counteract the heavier guns that the French possessed. His main intention was to protect Newport, not to engage the French at a disadvantage. For the moment, d'Estaing's twelve ships of the line were satisfied to follow in Howe's wake.

For twenty-four hours, Howe and d'Estaing warily eyed each other, with the two fleets about 8 miles apart. Finally, the British gained an advantageous wind from the south, and Howe began to maneuver for a more favorable position. At 1:30 P.M. on 11 August, Howe changed course to the northwest. D'Estaing, instead of altering course to keep his favorable position relative to the wind, closed with the rear of the British line and began slipping to the southeast. Late in the afternoon, Howe had almost gained the weather gauge from d'Estaing. But by then, the wind and sea, which had been intensifying throughout the day, became so violent that both the British and French fleets began to combat the weather rather than each other. The great gale continued unabated until the morning of 14 August, and by then both fleets had been damaged and dispersed over hundreds of miles of ocean. The British fleet reassembled at Sandy Hook, while the French rendezvoused 75 miles east of Cape May. Five of d'Estaing's ships of the line were damaged, and Howe's fleet was not in much better condition.

After the storm, there were a few individual actions between French and British ships. The *Renown* (44 guns) happened upon the *Languedoc*, d'Estaing's flagship, which had been totally dismasted by the storm. The French ship was saved by nightfall and the arrival of several other French warships. The *Tonnant* (80 guns), which had lost its fore- and mizzenmasts, was saved from capture by the *Preston* under similar circumstances. The *Isis* (50 guns), commanded by Captain John Raynor, and the *César* (74 guns) fought each other, with the French ship finally breaking off action and fleeing. Howe caught up with the French fleet off Cape May on 15 August, but seeing that d'Estaing's ships were badly damaged and unable to undertake offensive operations any time soon, he sailed to New York in order to refit. D'Estaing reached Rhode Island on 20 August but two days later sailed for Boston, leaving a disgusted Sullivan and his American army engaged in siege operations against Pigot at Newport. D'Estaing reached Boston on 28 August, and Howe arrived off that port with his fleet on 30 August.

Realizing that d'Estaing was unassailable in Nantasket Road and that the French admiral would be busy repairing his fleet for some time, Howe sailed to Rhode Island to assist Pigot. By the time he arrived, Sullivan's disintegrating army had been attacked by Pigot's garrison, with the assistance of the British sloops *Sphynx* and *Vigilant*, the galley *Spitfire*, and the brig *Privateer*. On the night of 30–31 August, Sullivan had withdrawn from Aquidneck Island and retreated to Providence. Clinton had reinforced Pigot with 5,000 fresh troops on 1 September. The British position in Rhode Island was secure, and the Americans and French were temporarily at odds with each other. This situation prevailed until 25 October 1779, when Clinton, the new British commander in chief, and Vice-Admiral Marriot Arbuthnot, the newly appointed commander of the British fleet in American waters, ordered the British garrison at Newport, under General Richard Prescott, to demolish all defensive works and withdraw to New York in preparation for a campaign in the South. Newport was left in shambles.

On 10 July 1780, French Admiral Charles Louis d'Arsac, Chevalier de Ternay, sailed into Rhode Island in command of a dozen French warships, convoying a fleet of transports carrying 5,500 troops under Jean-Baptiste Vimeur, the comte de Rochambeau. Belatedly, the British Admiralty sent a naval reinforcement of six ships of the line, commanded by Rear-Admiral Thomas Graves, in pursuit. The hope was that Graves would unite with Arbuthnot at New York in time to deal with Ternay. Even though the French admiral beat Graves to America and Rochambeau established his headquarters at Newport, the British navy still had an excellent opportunity to attack the French. Its preponderance of power increased for a time when Admiral Sir George Rodney put in temporarily at New York with a detachment of his West Indian squadron. But a feud between Clinton and Arbuthnot doomed any chance that Ternay would be assaulted off Rhode Island. Nevertheless, his fleet was contained by British sea power at Newport until well into 1781, as he awaited the buildup of French sea power in American waters.

PAUL DAVID NELSON

See also

Estaing, Jean-Baptiste, Comte d'; Graves, Thomas; Gravier, Charles, Comte de Vergennes; Hopkins, Esek; Howe, Richard; Naval Operations: American vs. British; Pigot, Robert; Rhode Island, Battle of; Rodney, George; Suffren, Pierre-André de; Sullivan, John; Vimeur, Jean-Baptiste, Comte de Rochambeau

References

Clowes, William Laird. *The Royal Navy: A History from the Earliest Times to 1900.* 7 vols. London: Chatham, 1996.

Dull, John R. *The French Navy and the American Revolution: A Study of Arms and Diplomacy, 1774–1787.* Princeton, NJ: Princeton University Press, 1975.

Gardiner, Robert, ed. *Navies and the American Revolution, 1775–1783.* London: Chatham, 1996.

Gruber, Ira D. *The Howe Brothers and the American Revolution.* New York: Norton, 1972.

———. "Richard Lord Howe: Admiral as Peacemaker." Pp. 232–259 in *George Washington's Opponents: British Generals and Admirals in the American Revolution.* Edited by George Athan Billias. New York: Morrow, 1969.

Mahan, Alfred Thayer. *The Major Operations of the Navies in the War of American Independence.* Boston: Little, Brown, 1913.

Stinchcombe, William C. *The American Revolution and the French Alliance.* Syracuse, NY: Syracuse University Press, 1969.

Syrett, David. *The Royal Navy in American Waters, 1775–1783.* Brookfield, VT: Gower, 1989.

Tilley, J. A. *The Royal Navy in the American Revolution.* Columbia: University of South Carolina Press, 1987.

Nicholas, Samuel
(1744–1790)

Samuel Nicholas, the first commandant of the U.S. Marine Corps, led the Marines through the entire Revolutionary War. In March 1776, he commanded America's first Marine landing, and in December of that year he led the first Marine detachment to serve under the direct command of an army officer. With the British evacuation of Philadelphia in June 1778, he returned to the city to reestablish the Marine's barracks and resume recruiting, serving there until the end of the war.

Nicholas was born in Philadelphia in 1744 into a local merchant family and may have served aboard a merchant ship before the war. In November 1775 the Continental Congress authorized the raising of two battalions of Marines and commissioned Nicholas a captain in the new service. By tradition, he is recognized as the senior officer in the Continental Marines and is therefore considered the first commandant of the U.S. Marine Corps.

Nicholas began recruiting men for Marine service at Tun's Tavern, which he owned, in Philadelphia. In January 1776, the first detachments of Marines were assigned to Continental Navy ships then in Philadelphia, with Nicholas in command. The naval force was under the command of Commodore Esek Hopkins, who had orders to raid British shipping. Setting out that January, the flotilla sailed to the Bahamas. Arriving at New Providence (Nassau) on 2 March, Hopkins ordered the capture of the port and the supplies there. Nicholas led the landing party made up of Marines and sailors in the attack on the forts protecting the town. After they captured one of the forts with little effort, the town surrendered. Unfortunately for the Americans, the British had already removed most of their military supplies. After leaving Nassau in April, Nicholas's Marines were involved in the sea battle between the squadron and the British warship *Glasgow.*

In June 1776, Nicholas was ordered to return to Philadelphia and was promoted to the rank of major. He was now ordered to recruit more Marines to serve on ships then under construction. When the British Army overran New Jersey in November and early December, however, the Continental Marines, with Nicholas in command, were sent to join the Continental Army under General George Washington. Although they were not involved in the fighting at Trenton, the Marines did serve at Princeton, where they fought well. In March 1777, they returned to Philadelphia and were assigned to various ships. Nicholas served out the remainder of the war administering the nation's Marine Corps.

After the war, Nicolas resumed his trade as a merchant and then as an innkeeper in Philadelphia until his death on 27 August 1790.

DALLACE W. UNGER JR.

See also
Continental Navy; Hopkins, Esek; Marines, Continental; Naval Operations, American vs. British; Princeton, Battle of; Trenton, Battle of

References

"Major Samuel Nicholas, Continental Marines (Deceased)." *Who's Who in Marine Corps History*. United State Marine Corps, History and Museums Division. http://hqinet001.hqmc.usmc.mil/HD/Historical/Whos_Who/Nicholas_S.htm.

Purcell, L. Edward. *Who Was Who in the American Revolution*. New York: Facts On File, 1993.

Ninety-Six, Fort

See Fort Ninety-Six, South Carolina, Sieges of

Nixon, John
(1727–1815)

John Nixon, a Continental Army officer, rose from humble origins to become one of Massachusetts's more important military commanders during the Revolutionary War. The son of a farmer, he first experienced military life in 1744–1745 during Sir William Pepperell's expedition against the French citadel of Louisbourg on Cape Breton Island. Nixon volunteered for duty in a regiment commanded by Pepperell as colonel and in Captain Ephraim Baker's company. Although the fortress fell on 17 July 1745, the New Englanders lingered during the winter, suffering from scanty clothing, smallpox, unsanitary conditions, drinking, and immorality. Nixon, only eighteen years old, deserted as a result of the influence of older men, was captured, and was sentenced to death by firing squad. Because of the intervention of his captain, the firing squad was secretly ordered to miss. He fainted during this ordeal but recovered, and for the duration of his duty he remained in the care of Baker.

On 7 March 1755 during the French and Indian War, Nixon enlisted as a lieutenant in the company of Captain Newell Roxbury. Later Nixon transferred to Captain Jonathan Hoar's company and on 8 September succeeded him as captain. Nixon then commanded a company in Colonel Timothy Ruggles's regiment, taking part in the Crown Point expedition and fighting in a battle on 8 September 1756. In July 1758, Nixon was with Ruggles's regiment during General James Abercromby's disastrous campaign against Fort Ticonderoga. The following year, Nixon served again with Ruggles, then transferred to the regiment of Colonel John Jones and fought under Lord Jeffrey Amherst in Canada. Nixon commanded his company a final time from 18 April 1761 to 18 July 1762. In all these years, he was deeply influenced by the example of Ruggles, a brave soldier, able lawyer, good scholar, wit, and misanthrope. It was Ruggles who supplied Nixon with the education that he had been denied in his youth.

As tensions grew between America and Britain in late 1774, Nixon, a prosperous farmer, organized a large company of minutemen from Sudbury, Massachusetts. He led them to Concord as their captain on 19 April 1775.

John Nixon, who in 1775 was president of the provincial Committee of Public Safety during Benjamin Franklin and Gouverneur Morris's absence. Nixon made the first public reading of the Declaration of Independence and led troops at Trenton and Princeton. (Collections of the University of Pennsylvania Archives)

Pursuing the British Army back to Boston, where he joined the siege, he was commissioned colonel of Massachusetts militia on 24 April and given command of a regiment. He served under General Artemas Ward and in May took part in a foray to Noodle's Island and Hog Island. He was at the Battle of Bunker Hill on 17 June, arriving with his regiment just in time to take position near a rail fence. After repulsing one British assault, he was severely wounded in a second attack and had to be carried from the field. After recovering, he served with his regiment on Winter Hill as part of General John Sullivan's brigade. On 1 January 1776, Nixon was commissioned colonel of the 4th Continental Infantry, and in March, after the British evacuated Boston, he accompanied General George Washington to New York. Nixon was promoted to brigadier general on 9 August 1776 and given command of a brigade on Governor's Island. In the following months, he was with Washington's army as it retreated from New York across New Jersey. On 26 December 1776, Nixon led a division during Washington's victory at the Battle of Trenton but was unable to cross the Delaware River in time to take part in the fighting.

In the first half of 1777, Nixon's brigade was stationed at Peekskill, New York, as part of Major General Israel Putnam's division. In early July, Putnam dispatched Nixon to join General Philip Schuyler's army in upstate New York to oppose an invasion by John Burgoyne. Nixon was posted at Fort Ann, under orders to scout Burgoyne's army, impede its advance by felling trees across roads and navigable streams, and remove all cattle, draft animals, and forage from its line of advance. For several weeks Nixon successfully carried out his orders, slowing Burgoyne's advance to a snail's pace. In mid-September, Nixon marched to Bemis Heights, a commanding fortified position near Stillwater, and joined Major General Horatio Gates, who had replaced Schuyler as commander in upstate New York. Nixon led his brigade in the battles at Freeman's Farm on 19 September and Bemis Heights on 7 October. Ordered by Gates to pursue the retreating enemy, he crossed Saratoga Creek in a thick fog on 11 October and suddenly ran into Burgoyne's entire army. Quickly retreating under fire, Nixon's unit suffered a number of casualties. A cannonball passed so close to his head that his sight and hearing were permanently impaired.

After Burgoyne surrendered on 17 October 1777, Nixon was ordered to Albany. From there, he escorted Burgoyne's army to Cambridge, Massachusetts, then took an extended leave to care for his family. In July 1778, he joined his brigade at White Plains, New York, and in September sat on a court-martial that acquitted Schuyler of any responsibility for the loss of Fort Ticonderoga the previous year. Nixon took another leave in the winter of 1778–1779, this time because of his health, rejoining the army in February

1779 for further service at White Plains and West Point. On 12 September 1780, compelled by poor health, he resigned his commission and reluctantly departed the Continental Army. He returned to farming, became a Mason, and spent the last years of his life in Framingham, Massachusetts, and Middlebury, Vermont, as a respected old veteran of numerous military campaigns.

PAUL DAVID NELSON

See also

Bunker Hill, Battle of; Burgoyne, John; Fort Ticonderoga, New York; Gates, Horatio; Lexington and Concord; New Jersey, Operations in; New York, Operations in; Putnam, Israel; Saratoga Campaign; Schuyler, Philip; Sullivan, John; Trenton, Battle of; Ward, Artemas; West Point, New York

References

Massachusetts Secretary of the Commonwealth. *Massachusetts Soldiers and Sailors of the Revolutionary War*, Vol. 11. Boston: Wright and Potter, 1903.

Merriam, John H. *Five Framingham Heroes of the American Revolution*. Framingham, MA: Lakeview, 1925.

———. "The Military Record of Brigadier General John Nixon of Massachusetts." *Proceedings of the American Antiquarian Society* 36 (April 1926): 38–70.

Nelson, Paul David. *General Horatio Gates: A Biography*. Baton Rouge: Louisiana State University Press, 1976.

Nonimportation Agreements
(1768–1770 and 1774–1775)

In the contentious decade before the outbreak of the American Revolutionary War, the nonimportation agreement was British North America's most potent weapon in opposing Britain's new imperial policies, and it ultimately played a crucial role in building Revolutionary leadership at the community level and in forging intercolonial unity. Yet the power of these agreements was always limited. The first use of nonimportation, from 1768 to 1770, failed to achieve its full objective—the repeal of all new import taxes in America—and led to disunity and recriminations between America's leading commercial ports. The second agreement, the Continental Association of October 1774, was more successful, especially in uniting the thirteen colonies. But this nonimportation effort also failed to achieve its stated purpose, the full redress of a decade of grievances by Great Britain. By early 1775 the British ministry, faced with a powerful and seemingly unbreakable commercial combination, instead chose war, and arms rather than commerce ultimately settled the Anglo-American conflict.

The idea of a broad, coordinated agreement not to import British goods had a natural relationship, especially in Calvinist New England but also in the middle colonies and the Chesapeake region, to a long moral and religious tradition that a community could gain deliverance from affliction by denying itself luxuries and thereby demonstrating its virtue. In a less moral vein, material self-denial was regarded as a sound preparation for facing even

Advertisement.

THE Subscribers to the Non-Importation Agreement, are desired to meet at the Exchange To-morrow Morning, precisely at 11 o'Clock, to consider of a Letter received from Philadelphia, relative to the Non-Importation Agreement; and as it is a Matter of great Consequence, it is hoped that every Subscriber will punctually attend.

Advertisement calling for a meeting of New Yorkers to reconsider the nonimportation agreement of 1768. (Library of Congress)

greater economic or military difficulties that might arise. Finally, of course, any kind of a boycott—a refusal to patronize or have any dealings with a particular merchant or community leader or with an entire community or nation—was a satisfying and often effective means of expressing political disapproval. All of these feelings came into play in British North America's nonimportation movements of 1768–1770 and 1774–1775.

The use of nonimportation agreements among America's import merchants, however, was initially a response to a particular tactic of British imperial policy. For more than a century before the Revolution, the British government had occasionally implemented policies that displeased some colonists, and by the mid-eighteenth century certain British measures, whether edicts of the Board of Trade or the Privy Council or statutes of Parliament, caused such distress that colonial leaders had to take some action. Colonial governors, whether appointed by the British Crown or by the proprietary families of Maryland, Pennsylvania, and Delaware, were generally unwilling to protest British policies, and this role fell to the lower, elected houses of the colonial legislatures. To make their case, most assemblies appointed agents, whether British or American, to represent them and their colonies in London. Until the 1760s, this strategy was often effective, and in any event both the legislators and their constituents found that they could live with whatever burdens Britain placed upon them.

Britain's great victory over France and its acquisition of vast new lands in North America, filled with many Native American tribes, all acquired at great cost to the British treasury and all needing additional administration and defense, changed everything. To control and pay for this new empire, the British government issued its Proclamation of 1763 forbidding new settlement in the American West, and Parliament passed the Revenue (Sugar) Act of 1764, providing for the strict collection of customs duties, and finally the Stamp Act in 1765, which aimed at collecting substantial new revenue. The colonists and their agents in London quickly discovered that they could not block or even alter any of these policies. Individual settlers could, and did, ignore the Proclamation Act, and individual merchants could, and did, try to smuggle or bribe their molasses past the customs inspectors. And for a brief time, many colonists evidently believed that the imperial relationship had not fundamentally changed but had just become a little more frustrating.

The Stamp Act could not be so easily evaded. Colonial courts would not recognize unstamped documents and, as would be the case in the nonimportation movement of 1768–1770, colonial leaders were not confident that every colonist would sacrifice his interest by boycotting the stamped paper and postponing his legal business indefinitely. Here, however, they were fortunate. Because the stamps were to be distributed by just a few individuals in each major city, they could block the act's implementation simply by intimidating the stamp agents to resign their commissions. They then persuaded the courts to conduct business as usual, as no stamps were available. The act, Britain's first—and only—internal tax in North America, had been nullified by North America's first collective defiance of British rule. As the law was unenforceable, Parliament quickly repealed it.

Both British and American leaders drew lessons from the Stamp Act crisis. The British ministry concluded that while Britain could not collect an internal tax in America, it could collect new and more comprehensive external taxes, that is, import duties. One such duty, levied under the Molasses Act of 1733, had been nominally in effect for three decades although never effectively collected. But the reform of this act had already begun with the Sugar Act of 1764, and certain Americans, notably Benjamin Franklin, had led British ministers to believe that Americans would pay external taxes imposed by Parliament.

American leaders drew a different lesson from the Stamp Act crisis: that collective action, involving pamphlets and speeches, but also the threat, or the reality, of mob action could stop new British taxes at their most vulnerable point. In 1765, that point had been the stamp agents. From 1768 to 1770, in response to the Townshend duties, it would be America's major import merchants.

The British lost little time in pursuing external taxes. In 1766 they revised the Sugar Act, setting the duty on West Indian molasses so low that it was no longer worth the effort for merchants to smuggle their cargoes to American distillers and sugar bakers. At the same time, they completely reorganized the customs commissioners in America to ensure the strict collection of all duties. And in 1767, Parliament gave the commissioners more to do by passing the Townshend duties on several products imported from Britain, including paper, lead, paint, and tea.

The colonial response was initially more gradual than it had been to the Stamp Act but steadily gained strength. In 1767, John Dickinson wrote *Letters from a Farmer in Pennsylvania*, which declared that all parliamentary taxation passed to gain revenue in North America violated the British Constitution because the colonists were not represented in Parliament. This pamphlet quickly became more popular in America than any tract written against the Stamp Act, and Dickinson's position, that internal and external taxes were equally unconstitutional, quickly became American orthodoxy.

By 1768, the colonists were ready to take action. Their targets were now more numerous than they had been in 1765. To avoid paying any of the new duties and to put pressure on English merchants and manufacturers to support them in their struggle with Parliament, they had to pressure all import merchants in every important colonial port to stop importing any British merchandise.

The leaders who accomplished this were generally not public officials, either in port cities or colonial legislatures, but rather members of new clubs and organizations that sprang up in every seaport to defend colonial rights. They went under several names, and some cities, notably Boston, had several such organizations, but the name taken by several radical Patriots in every city was the Sons of Liberty. Their principal leaders, all well-established opponents of British policy by 1768, included Isaac Sears of New York City, Charles Thomson of Philadelphia, Christopher Gadsden of Charleston, and the most prominent of them all, Samuel Adams of Boston. The small radical gatherings that they mobilized included small-scale merchants, artisans, and minor public officeholders who spanned the social spectrum, in terms of income, from the moderately affluent to those of quite modest fortune.

The first step taken by each of these groups was to call for public meetings to protest the Townshend duties and consider how to oppose them. At these meetings they secured the election of a committee consisting primarily of merchants, and in some cities they created a second committee of artisans or brought a few artisans into the merchant committee. These bodies then pressured all major import merchants, who were the wealthiest inhabitants in every seaport, to stop importing any goods from Britain. They used every means at their disposal: reason and exhortation, the fear of public embarrassment, and, if needed, the threat that artisans and dockworkers would do no work for merchants who did not agree to cease importing British goods. Once the committees had secured a comprehensive nonimportation association, they closely monitored the merchants' compliance with its terms.

The committees benefited in their work from broad public support. They had many allies in their colonies' legislative assemblies and among the general population, both in the cities and in the surrounding countryside. Some individual merchants did, of course, oppose nonimportation. Several resisted any halt in their lucrative businesses, and many merchants felt more hostility toward the radical Patriots than they did toward the British government. But these recalcitrant merchants were too few to halt nonimportation, and in bringing them into line the nonimportation committees had the advantage that, in most colonies, no substantial numbers opposed their principles or their strategies. Gradually, the committees persuaded the merchants of every major port to enter into agreements that they would halt all imports from Great Britain until Parliament repealed all the Townshend duties.

The nonimportation movement against the Townshend duties began in Boston, preceded by an effective nonconsumption pledge that Boston had circulated among the towns of eastern Massachusetts. Boston's merchants agreed to nonimportation in March 1768, and New York City followed suit with an even stricter association in April. Philadelphia and Charleston delayed but entered associations in 1769, the high point of the movement's success. By the end of the year, a mixed pattern of parallel but not identical nonimportation and nonconsumption agreements covered every colony except New Hampshire.

The following year, however, saw the nonconsumption movement begin to unravel, just as it was earning its first triumph in Parliament. In March, as civilians and British soldiers clashed in the Boston Massacre, the new ministry of Lord North took up the issue of repealing the Townshend duties in direct response to the harm inflicted on British merchants and manufactures by nonimportation. In April 1770, Parliament passed a general repeal, but North persuaded Parliament to keep the tax on tea, which, he observed, was not a British manufacture but a luxury good. This tax, he believed, would both maintain Parliament's claim of a right to tax America and produce enough revenue to support several civil officeholders in America, thereby making them more independent of the rebellious colonists. North did, however, pledge that his ministry would seek no further tax on America. Partly in response to repeal but also for local reasons, the colonists' commitment to nonimportation now began to wane. New York's merchants, distrustful of Boston with its less restrictive association, were the first to abandon the movement. Philadelphia, now resentful of New York, followed suit, and by the end of 1770 the nonimportation movement had ended everywhere.

Parliament's repeal of all the Townshend duties except that on tea and the subsequent collapse of the nonimportation movement left America in an uncertain state. The government of Lord North had succeeded in levying one external tax without bringing American commerce to a halt, its customs commissioners were now as efficient as ever, and the tea tax revenue, after the end of nonimportation, was sufficient to support several civil officers in America. But Britain's revenue from the tea tax was small and would not have been large even if many colonists had not resorted to drinking smuggled Dutch tea to evade paying the duty. And to achieve even this much, the British had been forced to send troops to America's seaports, setting off the Boston Massacre and further alienating their colonial subjects.

Between 1770 and 1773, however, colonial opposition leaders were in an equally uncertain state. They had succeeded in forcing the repeal of most of the Townshend duties, but at the cost of bitter recriminations between Patriot leaders in the different seaports as well as personal and class antagonisms within several communities. And Britain was collecting some revenue in America and with that revenue appeared to be gaining more control over its colonial officials. It was clear to many colonial leaders that intercolonial unity, such as they had briefly achieved in the Stamp Act Congress of 1765, had been sadly lacking in the nonimportation movement. And they did not know whether they could achieve this unity against any future British policies that they found abhorrent.

The crisis presented by the Tea Act of 1773 only partially answered this question. In one respect, the problem of 1773 was like that of 1765, as the British again entrusted the success of a new taxation strategy to just a few men, now the tea agents, in each port city. As in 1765, these men could be intimidated by direct action, with the ultimate threat of mob violence, so nonimportation agreements were not needed to block the tea. What was different in 1773–1774 was the determination of one colonial governor, Massachusetts's Thomas Hutchinson, not to allow this intimidation and the determination of Lord North, after the Boston Tea Party and several less violent but equally effective actions against the tea imports in other cities, not to back down as Parliament had in 1766.

The Coercive Acts of 1774 did not include any taxes and were nominally not even about taxes. But when Parliament announced these punitive measures in the spring of 1774, the colonists could not think of any way to resist them other than a massive nonimportation agreement. This time, to be successful, every American seaport and every community in every colony must act together and resolve to maintain their boycott until the acts were rescinded. In the spring of 1774, Americans still did not know whether they could do this.

By October, their leaders discovered that they could achieve this unity. Meeting in the First Continental Congress in Philadelphia, they passed a comprehensive, open-ended nonimportation agreement, the Continental Association, that included an additional pledge of nonexportation by the fall of 1775 if the Coercive Acts had not been repealed. To make sure every North American colonist took the Continental Association seriously, Congress directed that every community create committees of observation, inspection, and correspondence to monitor compliance. What in 1768–1770 had been a set of agreements between major merchants in half a dozen cities now became something more like a single covenant between hundreds of thousands of inhabitants in every community in a dozen colonies.

The Continental Association, America's last nonimportation agreement before independence, had two great successes and one failure. As a nonimportation agreement, it was spectacularly successful. The amount of leakage of imports from Britain after 1 December 1774 and of exports to Britain after 1 September 1775 was negligible. Neither Britain's mercantile community nor its government could ignore this action, which threatened to ruin the British economy. Of equal importance over the next two years, the Continental Association's vast committee movement effectively disciplined Americans for the difficult war ahead while recruiting thousands of men to Revolutionary politics and providing the civil manpower that the Revolution would need.

The Continental Association's failure, of course, was its inability to achieve the one objective that any boycott is supposed to achieve: to persuade the target of the boycott to alter its behavior and become a good economic partner on the boycotters' terms. In the case of America and Britain in the winter of 1774–1775, however, it appears that there was no real chance of reaching such a settlement, at least not by a coercive boycott. America hoped that Britain would see its choice as accommodation or economic ruin and choose the former. Britain, however, saw its choice as political ruin or war and chose the latter.

RICHARD ALAN RYERSON

See also

Adams, Samuel; Boston, Massachusetts; Boston Tea Party; Boycotts; Coercive Acts; Congress, First Continental; Continental Association; Correspondence, Committees of; Dickinson, John; Gadsden, Christopher; Hutchinson, Thomas; New York City; North, Lord Frederick; Philadelphia; Sears, Isaac; Sons of Liberty; Stamp Act; Sugar Act; Tea Act; Thomson, Charles; Townshend, Charles; Townshend Acts

References

Ammerman, David. *In the Common Cause: American Response to the Coercive Acts of 1774.* New York: Norton, 1975.

Barrow, Thomas. *Trade and Empire: The British Customs Service in Colonial America, 1660–1775*. Cambridge: Harvard University Press, 1967.

Chaffin, Robert J. "The Townshend Act Crisis, 1767–1770." Pp. 126–145 in *The Blackwell Encyclopedia of the American Revolution*. Edited by Jack P. Greene and J. R. Pole. Oxford, UK: Blackwell, 1991.

Conroy, David W. "Development of a Revolutionary Organization, 1765–1776." Pp. 223–230 in *The Blackwell Encyclopedia of the American Revolution*, ed. Jack P. Greene and J. R. Pole. Oxford, UK: Blackwell, 1991.

Countryman, Edward. *A People in Revolution: The American Revolution and Political Society in New York, 1760–1790*. Baltimore, MD: Johns Hopkins University Press, 1981.

Maier, Pauline. *From Resistance to Revolution: Colonial Radicals and the Development of American Opposition to Britain, 1765–1776*. New York: Knopf, 1972.

Nash, Gary B. *The Urban Crucible: Social Change, Political Consciousness and the Origins of the American Revolution*. Cambridge: Harvard University Press, 1979.

Ryerson, Richard Alan. *The Revolution Is Now Begun: The Radical Committees of Philadelphia, 1765–1776*. Philadelphia: University of Pennsylvania Press, 1978.

Schlesinger, Arthur M. *The Colonial Merchants and the American Revolution, 1763–1776*. New York: Atheneum, 1968.

Weir, Robert M. *"A Most Important Epoch": The Coming of the Revolution in South Carolina*. Columbia: University of South Carolina Press, 1970.

North, Lord Frederick
(1732–1792)

Frederick, Lord North, the son of a peer, sat for most of his political career in the House of Commons, was active in British politics for his entire adult life, and served as first lord of the Treasury (prime minister) from 1770 to 1782. North, with his ministry, became increasingly involved in the imperial crisis in America and then in attempting to put down the rebellion.

North was born on 13 April 1732 to Francis North, the 1st Earl of Guilford, and Lady Lucy Montagu and was related to several prominent English political leaders, including the Duke of Newcastle. He was given a classical education at Eton and Trinity College, Oxford, and left a favorable impression on the faculty because of his great memory. North entered the House of Commons in 1754, where he represented his family's borough, Banbury, for thirty-six years.

In his late twenties, North began his service in a succession of governing ministries. He was a junior lord of the Treasury (1759–1765), first under William Pitt the Elder and the Duke of Newcastle, then under the Earl of Bute, and finally under George Grenville; a joint paymaster-general (1766–1767) in the Chatham (Pitt the Elder) ministry; and chancellor of the Exchequer in 1767 under the Duke of Grafton. King George III invited North to form his own ministry as prime minister in 1770, and North held this office while continuing as chancellor of the Exchequer until 1782.

Politically, North remained unattached to factions. While admittedly conservative, he was not reactionary. His participation in the debates to expel John Wilkes from the House of Commons, however, earned him the

Lord Frederick North, first lord of the Treasury (prime minister) from 1770 to 1782. He resigned shortly after hearing news of Charles Cornwallis's surrender at Yorktown. (Library of Congress)

reputation, in some circles, of a minister who favored tyranny over liberty. North's avoidance of factions made him attractive to the king's court and made him more acceptable to the Opposition faction. Consequently, North was able to keep a divided Parliament unified beyond ordinary expectations during the troubled years leading up to and through the American Revolution.

After taking his first government post as a junior lord of the Treasury during the French and Indian (Seven Years') War, North continued in the Grenville ministry (1763–1765), where he supported the Stamp Act. The extreme colonial hostility toward this act, which most directly affected the well-educated and professional members of the colonial populace, helped bring about the fall of Grenville's government.

North viewed the formation of the inexperienced and disorganized Rockingham ministry (1765–1766) as an opportune time to become an articulate member of the Opposition to the government. During Rockingham's short ministry, North voted against the repeal of the unpopular Stamp Act and in favor of the Declaratory Act. In this, he was consistent in his conservative views of making only moderate revisions in government policy while upholding the constitutional right of Parliament to govern the colonies.

Following the fall of Rockingham, George III brought William Pitt the Elder back into government. Pitt convinced North to join his ministry as joint paymaster-general, but Pitt's effective ministry was also short-lived. Pitt accepted a peerage as the Earl of Chatham but soon fell into a mental depression, leaving the duties of prime minister to the Duke of Grafton and the office of chancellor of the Exchequer to the questionable handling of Charles Townshend. North later claimed that he opposed the Townshend duties, but as a member of the ministry was unable to publicly criticize the act.

In 1767, the declining British economy, questions of affairs in India, Pitt's continued ill health, and Townshend's sudden death brought about another change in George III's ministry, now headed by Grafton. North was offered, and eventually accepted, the position of chancellor of the Exchequer. Three years later, in 1770, George III asked North to assume the office of first lord of the Treasury. North accepted and continued to hold both positions for the following twelve years.

North used his skills in public finance to reduce the national debt without imposing new taxes. Perceiving the empire to be at peace, he underfunded the armed forces. He was accused by the Opposition of sacrificing national security, but the reduction in spending to support the military during a time of peace was applauded by England's country faction and contributed to three quiet years in America. The decision to reduce military spending, however, later haunted North's ministry during the American Revolutionary War, especially with regard to the Royal Navy.

By 1773, with the support of George III, North pushed three measures concerning the ailing East India Company through Parliament. The Tea Act established a monopolistic arrangement in the tea trade in the American colonies between the company and a small number of designated merchants in major American ports and refunded the stiff British import duty on all tea destined for America to facilitate the movement of the company's staggering surplus of tea. The import duty on tea that was collected in America remained in place. North asserted that tea was a luxury item and therefore was properly taxed to reduce the national debt. His second measure, the Loan Act, required the company to use its profits to pay outstanding debts before making other expenditures. The Regulating Act increased government oversight by establishing government approval of the appointments of the company's governor-general and council members.

North's stubborn insistence on retaining the tea import duty in America, however, infuriated the colonists. Some colonists had personal motives—smuggled tea to sell—for opposing the tea monopoly. Others viewed the retention of the import duty as a tax that North was determined to make the colonists pay as a way of asserting parliamentary authority. He consistently used the tea tax, along with taxes on other luxury items, to help reduce the national debt, arguing that only the rich and opulent bore this burden. As the years passed, however, the list of so-called luxury items increased to include items commonly purchased by rich and poor alike.

Print from 1781 shows George III and Lord Frederick North standing in a kitchen, both wearing aprons. George III has his back to the fireplace. Between them, on the floor, is an overturned kettle of fish, each fish labeled with the name of a colony. George III says, "O Boreas, the loss of these fish will ruin us forever." North replies, "My honored liege never fret. Minden & I will cook 'em yet." On the wall behind North is a map labeled "Plan of North America." (Library of Congress)

When North sought to use the American colonies to help alleviate the problems with the East India Company and the British economy, however, he failed to comprehend either colonial opinion or the effects upon the American economy. Similarly, when the Sons of Liberty organized the Boston Tea Party to block the collection of the tea tax, North failed to perceive how a strong parliamentary reaction, and the largely coincidental but untimely passage of the Quebec Act, might further alienate the colonists. In light of parliamentary outrage over the Boston Tea Party and the increasing tumult within British society over economic issues, North's ministry chose to react with extraordinary firmness. The ministry struggled throughout much of 1774 to frame an appropriately repressive response, and particularly to make an example of the rebellious colony of Massachusetts, through the closing of the port of Boston and the passage of the Coercive Acts.

In 1775, North vacillated between rigid enforcement of parliamentary authority and conciliation toward the colonies. He helped shut down the Earl of Chatham's motion for "settling the troubles in America" and received wide support for demanding colonial obedience to Parliament and the

Lord North's ministry was initially divided over the use of force to subdue the colonies.

monarchy. As the tensions and hostilities increased, however, North's verbal support for the king's demand of total colonial submission was offset by limited military support and by the limited provisioning that he authorized for the colonial governors. These divergent positions and actions were evident throughout North's cabinet. Legge, who was secretary for the colonies, pushed for offering an olive branch to the colonies in 1775. That same year, however, Dartmouth instructed General Thomas Gage in Boston to adopt more aggressive tactics with the rebels, while simultaneously warning Gage that he was responsible for the outcome of such tactics. With little organized opposition and the king pushing North for action, the government issued a Proclamation of Rebellion on 23 August 1775.

North's ministry was initially divided over the use of force to subdue the colonies, and the division resulted in cabinet changes. Grafton was removed from holding the office of Privy Seal to make way for Dartmouth, who had yielded the office of secretary for the colonies to the more vigorous Lord George Germain. The king, meanwhile, remained involved in the appointments of military commanders in America despite ministerial misgivings. Over time, Germain resisted many of the king's appointments. Sir Guy Carleton, who served both as commander of the forces on the Great Lakes and as governor of Canada, was constantly undermined by Germain, eventually resulting in Carleton's recall to England. Sir William Howe experienced similar treatment by Germain, resulting in his eventual return to London in 1778.

When General John Burgoyne surrendered at Saratoga in October 1777 and French interests in America became known a few months thereafter, North deflected the Opposition by declaring his willingness to resign if such action would bring peace. He then continued the order of business for the day, supporting more war provisions. By June 1778, the war broadened into an international conflict, in part due to British foreign policy but also in part due to North's political schemes.

The loss of the British at Saratoga brought a realization that the conflict in America could end in disaster, but this realization failed to improve consistency on the part of North's ministry. In early 1778, North supported the forming of the Carlisle Peace Commission to offer a peaceful resolution (without independence) to the colonies. The commission reached Philadelphia in late spring of 1778 and was immediately informed of General Sir Henry Clinton's impending withdrawal of the occupying army to New York. The British departure from Philadelphia in June 1778 signaled the colonists of British weakness and stiffened the Americans' resolve to reject the commission without even giving it a hearing.

The year 1778 saw North preoccupied with political matters close to home. He repeatedly requested to resign his post as prime minister, and the king repeatedly convinced him to remain. North was forced to deal with renewed Irish complaints as well as the recruitment of several volunteer units to help protect the British Isles from a potential invasion by France. In 1779, the Spanish threw their support to France in a naval war against England. This low point in North's ministry was accompanied by increased frustration on the part of the king toward his prime minister. North became increasingly indecisive, his cabinet became more divided, and his own spirits were low.

The year 1780 saw a further deterioration of Britain's position, especially at home. The Gordon Riots in London that summer shook the government's confidence. Moreover, British foreign policy during North's ministry depended heavily upon naval supremacy, and interruptions in the naval supplies trade, the destruction of the Portsmouth dockyards, and poor administration hindered British naval capacity. North's several years of underfunding the navy exacerbated these problems. Germain's decision to conduct a southern campaign in America did temporarily bolster British confidence when Clinton captured Charleston, South Carolina, in May.

Despite British successes in the South, General Charles Cornwallis's defeat at Yorktown on 19 October 1781, spelled defeat for North's ministry. Opposition demands for investigations into the handling of the war and into corruption eventually resulted in a vote of no confidence, and George III finally accepted North's resignation on 20 March 1782. North's ministry was briefly replaced by another Rockingham ministry. But Rockingham died in July and was succeeded by the Earl of Shelburne, who agreed to negotiations in which Britain recognized the independence of the United States. North returned to office in April 1783, holding the position of home secretary in a coalition government that included Charles James Fox, the king's staunchest critic, with William Cavendish Bentinck, the 3rd Duke of Portland, as its titular head. The Portland ministry promised to renegotiate better peace terms for Britain, but it soon accepted the terms that Shelburne had negotiated with the United States the previous November, and in September 1783 Britain signed the Treaty of Paris.

The Portland ministry, an unlikely combination of disparate views and talents, fell in December 1783, to be replaced by the first ministry of William Pitt the Younger, who would be the dominant figure in Parliament for the next two decades. North immediately went into the Opposition, where he remained until 1790 when, nearly blind, he succeeded his father as the 2nd Earl of Guilford and entered the House of Lords. He died in London on 5 August 1792.

REBECCA SEAMAN

See also

Boston Port Act; Boston Tea Party; British Parliament; Carlisle Peace Commission; Coercive Acts; Fox, Charles James; George III, King of England; Germain, Lord George; Great Britain; Petty-Fitzmaurice, William, 2nd Earl of Shelburne; Pitt, William, the Elder; Tea Act; Townshend, Charles

References

Cornwallis, Charles. *Correspondence of Charles, 1st Marquis Cornwallis.* Edited with notes by Charles Ross. London: John Murray, 1859.

Donne, W. Bodham, ed. *The Correspondence of King George the Third with Lord North, 1768 to 1783*, Vols. 1 and 2. New York: Da Capo, 1971.

Extracts from the Journals of the House of Lords: The Campaign in Virginia. 1st Series. London: Trafalgar Square, Charing Cross, 1888. [Individual titles on microfilm.]

Guedalla, Philip. *Fathers of the Revolution*. New York and London: Putnam and Knickerbocker, 1926.

Scott, H. M. *British Foreign Policy in the Age of the American Revolution*. New York: Oxford University Press, 1990.

Smith, Charles Daniel. *The Early Career of Lord North the Prime Minister*. Rutherford, Madison and Teaneck: Fairleigh Dickenson University Press, 1979.

Syrett, David. *The Royal Navy in European Waters during the American Revolution*. Studies in Maritime History Series. Edited by William N. Still Jr. Columbia: University of South Carolina Press, 1998.

Thomas, Peter D. G. *Lord North*. New York: St. Martin's, 1976.

Thoughts on the Present Wars. With an Impartial Review of Lord North's Administration in Conducting the American, French, Spanish and Dutch War and in the Management of Contracts, Taxes, the Public Money, Etc. London: Microfilmed for Goldsmiths' Kress Library on Economic Literature, No. 12540.8 suppl., 1783.

Valentine, Alan. *Lord North*. Norman: University of Oklahoma Press, 1967.

Walpole, Horace. *Memoirs of the Reign of King George the Third*, Vol. 4. 2nd ed. Edited with notes by Sir Denis Le Marchant. London: Richard Bentley, Publisher in Ordinary to Her Majesty, 1851.

Whiteley, Peter. *Lord North: The Prime Minister Who Lost America*. London and Rio Grande: Hambledon, 1996.

North Carolina

At the time of the American Revolution, North Carolina was one of the fastest-growing British colonies. A recent influx of people down the Great Wagon Road brought settlers, including many recent British and European immigrants, from Virginia, Maryland, and Pennsylvania into the Piedmont. Large numbers of Scottish settlers were already living in the Cross Creek area, near present-day Fayetteville. By the 1770s, the majority of North Carolina's 270,000 settlers lived in the Piedmont, where small farms predominated. Major planters on the coastal plain, however, still controlled the colonial assembly at New Bern.

North Carolina was an important source of supplies for the Royal Navy. The colony's economy was tied to exporting tar, pitch, and lumber from the coastal plain. North Carolina's ports, principally Wilmington, Edenton, and New Bern, were small but active centers of trade. The colony did not have a central port like South Carolina's Charleston or even a predominant one like Virginia's Norfolk.

In the eighteenth century, differences between North Carolina's eastern and western regions finally led to the violent Regulator movement of the 1760s and early 1770s. The western region held most of the population but had little power. Representatives from the eastern counties dominated the Assembly and were reluctant to create new counties or to open new courthouses in the western counties. When the legislators did create a new western county, they often divided an eastern one, which partly accounts for the many small counties along the coast. Sheriffs and judges appointed by the Assembly were often corrupt. The combination of high taxes and unfair representation led to violence.

Western settlers organized themselves into Regulators, taking justice into their own hands. The Regulator movement was strongest in present-day Orange, Bladen, and Alamance Counties. Royal Governor William Tryon called out the militia from the eastern counties to restore order. At Alamance Creek in 1771, Tryon crushed the Regulators, and the movement largely disintegrated. After its decline, however, the Regulator movement still left much of the colony in turmoil. When the Revolution broke out a few years later, many North Carolinians saw the chance to take revenge for earlier atrocities. Former Regulators fought with both the Loyalists and Patriots in a larger, more violent civil war.

Royal Governor William Tryon angrily suppressing the Regulator revolt in North Carolina in 1771. (North Wind Picture Archives)

Tensions first mounted in North Carolina over its relationship with Britain during the Stamp Act debate. A mob led by local Sons of Liberty prevented the stamps from being unloaded at Wilmington in 1765. Although the crisis passed, other British taxes, and a new local dispute, soon followed. Josiah Martin, who had replaced Tryon as governor in August 1771, soon clashed with his Assembly over the funding of the colonial court system. By 1772, the colony's courts had ceased functioning. That same year, however, the colony did settle a border dispute with South Carolina, establishing the boundary at its present location.

In the fall of 1774, North Carolina responded to the imperial crisis by sending delegates to the First Continental Congress in Philadelphia. Martin tried to prevent the Assembly from appointing these delegates, but the legislators defied him, and he dissolved the Assembly. In May 1775, when news of the fighting at Lexington and Concord reached North Carolina, a group of citizens meeting in Charlotte took more extreme action; just how extreme has been the subject of debate for decades. In the nineteenth century, a local antiquarian published what has become known as the Mecklenburg Declaration, supposedly approved at Charlotte that May, that called for the state to formally break its relationship with Great Britain. This powerfully worded document espoused independence many months before any other community in America dared raise this issue. Its authenticity has never been definitively affirmed or denied.

All over North Carolina in May 1775 local militiamen began to drill, and members of the Assembly began to discuss joining in the rebellion. Realizing that he was losing control of the colony, Martin fled to an English warship and called on Loyalists to rise up and crush the rebellion. With the Loyalists and the British fleet, Martin hoped to reestablish royal authority. But the Loyalists met a crushing defeat in late February 1776 at Moore's Creek Bridge, northwest of Wilmington.

With the colony firmly in Patriot control, the Loyalists had to lie low. North Carolina's legislators now began functioning as a provincial congress, recruiting soldiers for the Continental Army and debating the question of independence. On 12 April 1776, delegates in Halifax adopted the Halifax Resolves, which instructed North Carolina's representatives in Congress to vote for independence. North Carolina was the first state to issue such instructions (although it was Virginia's Richard Henry Lee who would first propose independence in Congress).

In the early years of the war, with the Loyalists thoroughly cowed, North Carolina was free of military activity. The state sent troops north to join George Washington's defense of Philadelphia in 1777. And with its long coastline, North Carolina was an important entry for smugglers who eluded British warships to bring in vital supplies during the war.

In December 1776, the first postindependence legislature in North Carolina drafted both a constitution and a bill of rights. Their new government had a two-house legislature and a governor, and to fill the executive chair, they elected Richard Caswell, the Patriot commander who had defeated the Loyalists at Moore's Creek Bridge. The first meeting of the state's new General Assembly took place in April 1777. Huge problems immediately faced the new government, including the threat of civil war, a severe lack of money, and the need to raise troops and organize military supplies.

Encouraged by the British, Cherokee warriors began raiding the exposed settlements in western North Carolina and what would become eastern Tennessee in July 1776. Retaliatory campaigns crushed the Cherokees in 1777, but warfare again broke out on the frontier in 1779. By then, the British army was turning its attention to the southern states. In late 1778, the British seized Savannah, and in early 1780 they captured Charleston. With the fall of the South Carolina low country, the British Army began moving toward North Carolina in the late summer of 1780.

North Carolina's Loyalists, who had suffered for years under Patriot rule, did not wait for the British Army to arrive. A month after the fall of Charleston, they rose up more than 100 miles from the coast, but they repeatedly met with failure in the state. At Ramseur's Mill in June 1780, Patriot militia crushed a Loyalist force that was just organizing. Loyalists also met defeat at Pyle's Massacre, in which they initially mistook the Patriot troops for British soldiers. Unable to organize effectively, few Loyalists joined the British that summer and fall, to the disappointment of General Lord Charles Cornwallis. The general did briefly occupy Charlotte in September, but in October he drew back into South Carolina when a force of combined militias from Virginia and both Carolinas defeated and captured nearly 1,000 Carolina Loyalists, under the command of Major Patrick Ferguson, at Kings Mountain, South Carolina.

In January 1781, the British felt ready to move north again. A small force captured the port of Wilmington, while Cornwallis marched his main army back to the Charlotte area. But at Cowpens, South Carolina, a large detachment from the Continental Army, under General Daniel Morgan, defeated and captured most of a large detachment from Cornwallis's army, commanded by Colonel Banastre Tarleton. Cornwallis, determined to recover the British prisoners, chased General Nathanael Greene's main Continental Army across central North Carolina in February but could not cross the Dan River into Virginia to catch him. Greene soon returned to North Carolina to face Cornwallis in the largest battle in the state, at Guilford Courthouse on 15 March 1781. The British won a hard-fought victory, but they lost so many troops and were so short of supplies that they turned south and east to their secure supply base at Wilmington.

At this point, in late April, Cornwallis moved into Virginia, while Greene moved south into South Carolina. This left North Carolina's Loyalists and Patriots to struggle for control of the eastern and central regions of the state for the next four months. Up to this point, the Loyalists had not been successful, but from April to August 1781, working with the small British garrison at Wilmington, they were quite effective. The Loyalist David Fanning organized a raid on the state capital at Hillsborough, where he seized Governor Thomas Burke and took him back to Wilmington. And in August the British raided the old colonial capital, New Bern.

The larger movements of the war, however, were going against the British by the summer and early fall of 1781. In South Carolina, Greene was slowly driving the British back to Charleston, while in Virginia, Cornwallis's invasion ended in disaster at Yorktown in October. This virtually ended active fighting in North Carolina, and the British evacuated Wilmington, their last possession in North Carolina, in November 1781.

Although they were not as famous as the partisan leaders of South Carolina, North Carolina's militia members did include such as Benjamin Cleveland, Griffith Rutherford, Charles McDowell, Francis Locke, and Isaac Shelby as well as John Sevier, who lived in the Overmountain settlements to the west. North Carolina contributed ten Continental regiments to the American cause, about 7,000 men, as well as nearly 10,000 militiamen.

With the war virtually over in 1782, North Carolina began the difficult process of rebuilding its shattered economy. Several communities were still divided by the hatred between the Patriots and Loyalists, and the state was heavily in debt. Throughout the 1780s, most North Carolinians were deeply suspicious of any strong and distant government, and opposed strengthening the Articles of Confederation. They sent delegates to the Philadelphia convention, but their spokesmen made only slight contributions to the crucial debates. And in August 1788, North Carolina's ratifying convention rejected the U.S. Constitution, which its members said they could not approve without a bill of rights. In November 1789, however, once a functioning federal Congress had passed a bill of rights, North Carolina approved the Constitution, the second to last state to ratify the document.

Robert M. Dunkerly

See also

References

Historic Halifax Guidebook. Raleigh: North Carolina Department of Archives and History, n.d.

Lutz, Donald S. *Popular Consent and Popular Control: Whig Political Theory in the Early Constitutions.* Baton Rouge: Louisiana State University Press, 1980.

Main, Jackson Turner. *The Sovereign States, 1775–1783.* New York: New Viewpoints, 1973.

Powell, Walter. *North Carolina: A History.* Chapel Hill: University of North Carolina Press, 1977.

Rankin, Hugh. *North Carolina in the American Revolution.* Raleigh, NC: Division of Archives and History, 1959.

Taylor, Dale. *Everyday Life in Colonial America.* Cincinnati: Writer's Digest Books, 1997.

Trenholme, Louise Irby. *The Ratification of the Federal Constitution in North Carolina.* New York: Columbia University Press, 1932.

Northwest Territory

The territory north and west of the Ohio River, the Northwest or Old Northwest, was a strategically important and politically contested region from the time of the great struggle for North American empire between Great Britain and France in the French and Indian (Seven Years') War (1756–1763) and through the Revolution, the subsequent American campaigns against the Ohio Indians in the 1790s, and the admission of the new state of Ohio to the union in 1803.

The Revolution had a more profound, transformative effect on the Northwest than on any other region recognized as part of the United States at the Peace of Paris in 1783. This vast border zone remained at the heart of Indian territory until the late-eighteenth- and early-nineteenth-century wars demolished the traditional balance of power and opened the way for a surge of American settlement. Within a few short decades, the new states of the Northwest constituted the most demographically dynamic and rapidly developing region of the United States. As Indians were forcibly removed or voluntarily departed, only a few traces of their presence remained, most notably in the famous burial mounds and other artifacts of precontact native civilizations.

Though the Americans' northwestern frontier remained exposed and vulnerable throughout the war, it did not loom large in British strategic thinking. Instead, commanders such as Henry Hamilton, the infamous "Hair Buyer General" at Fort Detroit, sought to maximize a minimal British investment in the West by fomenting irregular Indian assaults on scattered American settlements. But, as George Rogers Clark's brilliantly successful campaign of 1778–1779 demonstrated, Britain's control of the region did not extend beyond a few fortified places, and inadequately supported Indian allies were not prepared to offer sustained resistance. With only a small expeditionary force of three militia companies (approximately 170 men), Clark was able to capture Vincennes (and Hamilton), neutralize the French settlements in the Illinois Country, and even threaten the British stronghold at Detroit. Clark enjoyed such great success because Britain was unwilling to commit major resources to prosecuting the war in the region.

Although the Northwest was only a secondary theater during the Revolution, it had great political importance before and after the war. In the years leading up to independence, however, Britain began to govern Indian country directly, limiting colonial settlement under the Proclamation of 1763; establishing northern and southern Indian superintendencies under William Johnson and John Stuart, respectively; and finally, in the Quebec Act of 1774, annexing the entire northwestern region to the formerly French province of Quebec. In the emerging Revolutionary ideology, Britain's apparent solicitude for the Indians and its determination to control and limit settlement under the aegis of the old colonial governments were portrayed as degrading assaults on American liberty. In effect, Patriots demanded a return to the jurisdictional status quo prior to 1763 and the elimination of the apparatus of imperial rule—and, by logical extension, the elimination of Britain's Indian clients.

Yet this geopolitical vision, the conception of the Northwest as a terra nullius, a great empty space liberated from British despotism and Indian savagery, could not resolve conflicts among landed states or between landed and landless state advocates of congressional claims. Territorial claims in the Northwest were arbitrary, overlapping, open-ended, and politically nonsensical. The Massachusetts and Connecticut claims, overleaping New York and Pennsylvania, were discontinuous with those states' established boundaries, and both covered territory simultaneously claimed by New York and Virginia. The sensible

George Rogers Clark leads his western campaign across the Wabash River toward the village of Vincennes (in what is today Indiana). Clark's campaign against the British Army and its Loyalist and Indian allies on the American frontier secured huge tracts of land for the United States. (National Archives and Records Administration)

solution to this problem was for these landed states to cede their claims to Congress, acting on behalf of the United States as a whole. But each state's proposed cession proved controversial, whether because of conditions attached to its cession, because it sought congressional recognition for claims it did not cede, or because its offer was linked to some other controversial subject of interstate diplomacy.

Though Congress issued a call for cessions on 6 September 1780, the first cession, New York's, was only completed after extended negotiation on 29 October 1782, and skeptics doubted that New York, whose claims in the region were at best secondhand, really had anything to cede. Meanwhile, Virginia's first cession offer, in 1781, was refused, despite the fact that the Old Dominion had a strong claim under its 1609 charter to the contiguous hinterland and had established rudimentary governance in the Illinois Country in the wake of the Clark expedition. From the perspective of Maryland and

Colonel George Rogers Clark confers with Native Americans at Cahokia (near present-day St. Louis) in the Illinois territory. The group surrendered to Clark and his men in 1778, and Clark continued with his successful attempt to acquire immense tracts of land for the United States. (National Archives and Records Administration)

other small landless states, the Virginia cession would consolidate its preeminent position in the union: the unceded Kentucky District south of the river had been incorporated into the state through the traditional device of new county formation and land grants, while Virginia retained extensive property rights in the cession (the Virginia Military District) for distribution to Revolutionary War veterans.

The landless bloc argued that cessions were unnecessary in any case, for it was only by the military efforts of the states collectively that any state could gain the benefits of independence, including recognized territorial jurisdiction. This argument for national supremacy and for an original national title to territory beyond the bounds of any state—in other words, to Indian country—was, of course, all too reminiscent of British imperial claims in the trans-Appalachian region to enjoy broad support. Furthermore, Congress was in no position to enforce a national title without Virginia's cooperation. Landless state agitation thus underscored the need for landed state cessions, however encumbered they might be with conditions and reservations. While these cessions remained outstanding, congressional impotence was guaranteed, both by its continuing stalemate on cessions and because the absence of a national domain meant that it had no lands to distribute and could not deal effectively with disaffected Indians on the frontiers. (Under the Articles, Congress only had jurisdiction over Indian affairs beyond the limits of the states, where its domain was uncontested.)

Virginia, however, also had a strong interest in a comprehensive territorial settlement. The same vast jurisdiction that filled its smaller neighbors with foreboding was, as a practical matter, a potential drain on the state's limited resources and made Virginia vulnerable to separatist movements as well as external threats. Effective control over the Illinois French was at best nominal, and Virginia would be in no position to mobilize effectively against another pan-Indian mobilization. Far better to cede the responsibilities and costs of the northwestern empire to the United States collectively, particularly given the likelihood that the region would be settled largely by Virginians who would be drawn into their native state's political and commercial orbit. Thomas Jefferson and other geopolitical visionaries believed that Virginia's central and dominant position in the union would be guaranteed by its propinquity to the Mississippi-Ohio river system, enhanced by improvements to the navigation of the Potomac. Turning landless state logic on its head, Jefferson and other advocates of Virginia's northwestern cession—finally completed on 1 March 1784—thus saw the state's relinquishment of its charter claims not as a sacrifice but rather as the best possible guarantee of its future greatness.

The Virginia cession was followed in short order by cessions of the more dubious charter claims of Massachusetts (1785) and Connecticut (1786), thus clearing the Northwest of conflicting state claims and creating the national domain. Proceeding on the premise that the United States had secured its title to the region in the Treaty of Paris of 1783 following its victory over Britain—and the conquest of the Indians—in the Revolution, Congress planned for the political and economic development of the Northwest as if it were a blank slate. Congress decided that public lands would be sold for the benefit of the United States as a whole and that settlements would eventually be formed into new states.

The first ordinance for territorial government, approved by Congress on 23 April 1784, invited settlers to form temporary governments that would adopt the "constitution and laws" of one of the existing states; when the new region gained a population of 20,000 free inhabitants, it would be entitled to draft its own constitution and claim admission to the union "on an equal footing with the . . . original states." The 1784 ordinance stipulated the boundaries of sixteen new states, including ten north of the Ohio River that were supplied with fanciful names by committee chair Jefferson. But none of its provisions could be implemented until public land sales opened the way for legal settlement. The outlines of congressional land policy were sketched out in a companion ordinance proposed to Congress by Jefferson and Hugh Williamson of North Carolina on 30 April 1784. Under the proposed scheme, the national domain would be surveyed prior to settlement in the now familiar grid system. The ordinance eventually adopted by Congress, on 20 May 1785, incorporated the prior surveying principle, dividing the national domain into 6-mile-square townships, beginning with seven ranges running north from the Ohio to Lake Erie. When the first surveys were completed, the townships would be sold in fractional units at a price of $1 per acre. Sluggish land sales made Congress receptive to overtures from land companies, most notably the Ohio Company, purchasers of 1.5 million acres of land west of the seven ranges at a much reduced price.

Implementation of congressional land policy precipitated changes in territorial government and new state formation. The establishment of the land system and of a military presence in the region sufficient to drive off illegal squatters and to defend settlements against the depredations of the Ohio Indians (who, understandably, resisted encroachments on their ancestral lands) called for a much stronger and more elaborate "temporary" government. The greatest pressure for revision of the 1784 ordinance came from prospective settlers themselves: because their first concern was with law and order—and secure land titles—they pressed Congress to set up a court system under its own authority before providing for territorial self-government. It was no coincidence that the Ohio Company purchase was completed on 14 July 1787, the day after enactment of the Northwest Ordinance.

Congress made the key move in abandoning the 1784 ordinance when it adopted the report of a new committee on western government headed by James Monroe of Virginia on 13 July 1786. Monroe urged Congress to create a "colonial" system for the Northwest and, based on his own observations of

> The Revolution had a greater effect on the Northwest than on any other region.

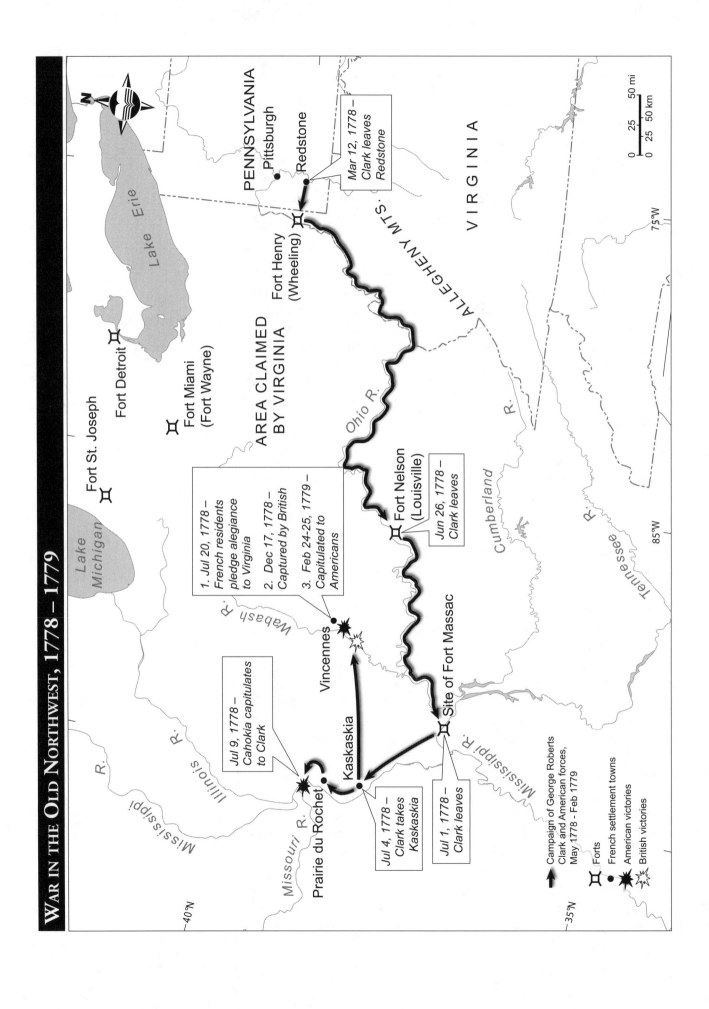

WAR IN THE OLD NORTHWEST, 1778 – 1779

Lake Erie

Lake Michigan

PENNSYLVANIA

Pittsburgh

Redstone

Mar 12, 1778 – Clark leaves Redstone

Fort Henry (Wheeling)

AREA CLAIMED BY VIRGINIA

ALLEGHENY MTS.

VIRGINIA

Fort Detroit

Fort St. Joseph

Fort Miami (Fort Wayne)

Ohio R.

Fort Nelson (Louisville)

Jun 26, 1778 – Clark leaves

Wabash R.

1. Jul 20, 1778 – French residents pledge alegiance to Virginia

2. Dec 17, 1778 – Captured by British

3. Feb 24-25, 1779 – Capitulated to Americans

Vincennes

Site of Fort Massac

Cumberland R.

Jul 9, 1778 – Cahokia capitulates to Clark

Illinois R.

Missouri R.

Mississippi R.

Prairie du Rochet

Kaskaskia

Jul 4, 1778 – Clark takes Kaskaskia

Jul 1, 1778 – Clark leaves

Mississippi R.

Tennessee R.

Campaign of George Roberts Clark and American forces, May 1778 - Feb 1779

Forts

French settlement towns

American victories

British victories

40°N

35°N

75°W

85°W

0   25   50 mi
0   25   50 km

the region's potential development, concluded that it should ultimately be divided into "not more than five nor less than three" new states. These principles were incorporated in the territorial government ordinance, the Northwest Ordinance, finally adopted on 13 July 1787. In the first stage of territorial government prescribed by the new ordinance, Congress governed through an appointed governor, a secretary, and three judges. The governor appointed all subordinate civil officers. Settlers would gain legislative representation in the second stage, when there were 5,000 free adult males in the territory, and admission to the union was guaranteed when "any of the said States shall have sixty thousand free inhabitants." The ordinance also included provisions for the inheritance of estates as well as "articles of compact" guaranteeing settlers' legal rights and civil liberties and securing the status of the new territories and their successor states in the union. The most famous compact article, the sixth, provided that "there shall never be Slavery nor involuntary Servitude in the said territory." Responding to settlers' demands, Congress eventually dispensed with colonial rule in the first stage of territorial government, and the ban on slavery was quietly dropped in federal territories south of the Ohio (beginning with the Southwest Territory in 1790). Nor were other specific provisions of the ordinance, including the new state boundaries sketched out in the fifth compact article, faithfully observed in practice. Nonetheless, the Northwest Ordinance assumed a quasi-constitutional status in the developing territorial system and particularly in the new states formed in the Old Northwest.

Although Congress's policy initiatives were designed to create political order in the Northwest, the influx of white settlers led to violent confrontations with local Indian tribes. Congress's campaign against the Ohio Indians constituted the final and bloodiest chapter in the history of the Revolution in the Northwest. An ill-equipped and poorly led expeditionary force under the direction of General Arthur St. Clair, the first governor of the Northwest Territory, suffered a devastating defeat in a surprise attack on 4 November 1791, with 900 casualties in a force of approximately 1,400 men. St. Clair's debacle demonstrated the new federal government's weakness and vulnerability and the need for a more massive show of force. Congress thus authorized the mobilization of a 5,000-man regular army, and Revolutionary War General Anthony Wayne took command in Ohio. Wayne systematically devastated Indian villages en route to his definitive victory over the Ohio Indians at Fallen Timbers (20 August 1794). The Indians discovered that expected British support would not be forthcoming. Instead, the United States and Britain moved toward settlement of their outstanding differences. Under the terms of the Jay Treaty (ratified by the Senate on 24 June 1795), Britain finally agreed to evacuate its northwestern posts. Now dealing from strength, the United States rolled back the Indian boundary in the Treaty of Greenville (3 August 1795), thus opening up much of present-day Ohio to development and setting the precedent for a series of treaties that effectively removed Indians from the region within a half-century.

PETER S. ONUF

See also

Clark, George Rogers; Jefferson, Thomas; St. Clair, Arthur; Wayne, Anthony

References

Abernethy, Thomas Perkins. *Western Lands and the American Revolution.* New York: Russell and Russell, 1958.

Cayton, Andrew L. *The Frontier Republic: Ideology and Politics in the Ohio Country, 1790–1825.* Kent, OH: Kent State University Press, 1986.

Eblen, Jack Ericson. *The First and Second United States Empires: Governors and Territorial Governments, 1784–1912.* Pittsburgh: University of Pittsburgh Press, 1968.

Onuf, Peter S. *The Origins of the Federal Republic: Jurisdictional Controversies in the United States, 1775–1787.* Philadelphia: University of Pennsylvania Press, 1983.

———. *Statehood and Union: A History of the Northwest Ordinance.* Bloomington: Indiana University Press, 1987.

Philbrick, Francis. *The Laws of the Illinois Territory, 1809–1818.* Springfield: Illinois State Historical Library, 1950.

Sosin, Jack M. *The Revolutionary Frontier, 1763–1783.* New York: Harper and Row, 1967.

Waller, George M. *The American Revolution in the West.* Chicago: Nelson-Hall, 1976.

White, Richard. *The Middle Ground: Indians, Empires, and Republics in the Great Lakes Region, 1650–1815.* 1991. Reprint. New York: Cambridge University Press, 1999.

O

The American privateer Jeremiah O'Brien was the victor in the first naval encounter between American and British forces and continued as a successful commander of several privateer vessels during the Revolutionary War.

O'Brien was born in 1744 in Kittery, Maine, to Irish immigrant parents. Around 1760 the O'Briens moved east to Machias, Maine, where they built and operated sawmills. Young O'Brien became a town leader and an outspoken critic of British policy by the early 1770s.

O'Brien's privateering began on 2 June 1775 with the arrival of two lumber sloops and the British armed schooner *Margaretta* in Machias. With the British Army in Boston in short supply of timber for fortifications, Admiral Samuel Graves sent the Loyalist trader Ichabod Jones to Machias to trade provisions for pickets and planks. When the townspeople expressed their reluctance to trade with Jones, he refused to trade with anyone who opposed his presence. Resentful at Jones's actions, O'Brien and others planned to seize all three vessels on 11 June. The schooner's commander eluded the mob and escaped aboard his vessel, but locals captured Jones's timber sloops. On the morning of 12 June, O'Brien and a party of Machias inhabitants pursued the *Margaretta* in Jones's sloops and captured the British vessel after a sharp fight, thus winning the first sea battle of the American Revolution. Having rechristened one of the lumber sloops *Machias Liberty*, O'Brien cruised the Bay of Fundy in July 1775 and captured the British sloop *Diligence* and its tender, the *Tapanagouche*. In grateful appreciation, the Massachusetts Provincial Council appointed O'Brien as captain of marine of the province of Massachusetts and ordered him to employ this first American naval "flying squadron," comprised of the *Machias Liberty* and the *Diligence*, against British shipping. Over the next eighteen months, O'Brien successfully preyed on British transports until his squadron was paid off in October 1776.

The decisive action of O'Brien and the citizens of Machias, combined with similar resistance elsewhere along New England's coast, virtually shut down New England's naval stores industry and deprived the British navy of a vital source of masts and spars. Graves retaliated with the burning of Falmouth, Maine, in October 1775. The victories of O'Brien and other early privateers also forced the Massachusetts Provincial Congress and the Continental Congress to consider the organization of a formal naval force to legitimize the privateers' actions, protect the colonies' coastlines, and procure military stores for George Washington's army.

Between 1777 and 1779, O'Brien commanded several privateers, including the *Resolution*, the *Cyrus*, the *Little Vincent*, and the *Tiger*. While ashore in 1779, he served as captain of the Ranging Company of Machias, formed to counter rumored attacks against coastal Maine by Robert Rogers. As commander of the privateer *Hannibal* in 1780, O'Brien was captured and imprisoned for two years, first aboard the notorious prison hulk *Jersey* in New York Harbor, and then in Mill Prison near Plymouth, England, before returning home in 1782.

O'Brien lived out the rest of his life in Machias, serving in various civil posts and enduring the British occupation of the town in 1814. He died on 5 September 1818.

DAVID M. CORLETT

See also
Continental Navy; Naval Operations, American vs. British; Prisoners of War; Privateering; Royal Navy; Washington's Navy

References
Fowler, William M. *Rebels Under Sail: The American Navy during the Revolution*. New York: Scribner, 1976.

Sherman, Andrew M. *Life of Captain Jeremiah O'Brien*. Morristown, NJ: George W. Sherman, 1902.

Oconostota
(1710?–1783)

The Cherokee Chief Oconostota earned the title of "great warrior" long before the American Revolution. Born around 1710, he first appeared on the historical stage in 1736 when he and other Cherokees met with French negotiators. His activities centered on Chota, the diplomatic, ceremonial, and political town where the Cherokees traded for European cloth, guns, and alcohol.

Great warriors, who ruled the Cherokees in periods of strife, recruited followers for parties to strike against enemies and to strengthen their hand at diplomacy. To affirm an alliance with South Carolina and support the embattled Chickasaw tribe, Oconostota led war parties against the Choctaws in 1753. Two years later, he attacked the Creeks and then led expeditions against the French and Indians of the Wabash, Ohio, and Mississippi River Valleys. Yet despite the fact that the Cherokees sided with the British, Virginians in the Shenandoah Valley attacked Oconostota's returning warriors and scalped them for bounties. Seeking revenge, mourning relatives of the murdered Cherokees attacked enclaves of squatters in the Carolina backcountry. Governor William Lyttleton of South Carolina demanded the surrender of the attackers, even taking Oconostota hostage briefly in 1759. After his release, he led an ambush against Lieutenant Richard Coytmore, the commanding officer at Fort Prince George, then led a siege against Fort Loudoun and forced its commanders into submission on 8 August 1760. After the British ravaged a number of Cherokee towns, the chiefs came to terms with them in 1761.

Thereafter, Oconostota became a mediator of peace in Indian country. In 1767, he attended a council at Fort Stanwix, New York, and concluded an accord with the Iroquois that endured until the outbreak of the American Revolution. He refused, however, to join an Indian confederacy to strike against white encroachment. Ostensibly, he became the principal chief of the Cherokees in 1768. He requested a trip to London to meet King George III and embraced the goal of education among his people. In 1773, he even became a member of the Saint Andrew's Society of Charleston, a club of expatriate Scots. His efforts culminated in 1775 when he agreed to the Treaty of Sycamore Shoals, in which the Cherokees ceded 20 million acres of land in Kentucky and Tennessee to Richard Henderson's Transylvania Company in exchange for trade goods worth approximately £10,000. Aged, emaciated, and nearly blind, Oconostota claimed that he had only accepted rent for the hunting grounds, not absolute sale. Some Cherokees claimed that Henderson forged Oconostota's signature.

As the American Revolution erupted, Oconostota failed to maintain the neutrality of all the Cherokees. Led by Dragging Canoe, the chief of Big Island Town, a younger generation of warriors rejected the leadership of the chiefs at Chota, declared their own war on the "Long Knives," and organized war parties to attack American frontier settlements. Militia from Georgia, South Carolina, North Carolina, and Virginia retaliated and devastated Cherokee towns throughout Indian country. Now wearing spectacles, Oconostota traveled to Fort Patrick Henry in 1777 and signed the Treaty of Long Island that resulted in more land cessions by the Cherokees. In July 1782, he passed the mantle of leadership to his son, Tuckese. That year, Oconostota made his last public appearance at the signing of the Treaty of Chota. He died in the spring of 1783 and was buried in an old canoe made into a coffin, with a string of white wampum, some vermilion, an iron sheath knife, two siltstone pipes, and a pair of eyeglasses.

Oconostota, chief of the Cherokees. In the course of the war, the Cherokees conducted numerous raids against Patriot settlements between Georgia and Virginia, in return for which the Americans waged campaigns against them in 1776 and 1782. (National Archives of Canada)

BRAD D. LOOKINGBILL

See also

Cherokees, Operations against; Native Americans

References

Calloway, Colin G. *The American Revolution in Indian Country: Crisis and Diversity in Native American Communities.* Cambridge: Cambridge University Press, 1995.

Hoig, Stanley W. *The Cherokee and Their Chiefs: In the Wake of Empire*. Fayetteville: University of Arkansas Press, 1998.

Kelley, James C. "Oconostota." *Journal of Cherokee Studies* 3 (1978): 221–238.

King, Duane H. "Oconastota." *Encyclopedia of North American Indians*. Edited by Frederick Hoxie. Boston: Houghton Mifflin, 1996.

Odell, Jonathan
(1737–1818)

The Loyalist physician, clergyman, and poet Jonathan Odell served as a spy for the British Army. Between May 1779 and September 1780, he helped encode and decode secret ciphers and letters containing messages written in invisible ink that were being passed between General Benedict Arnold and Major John André.

Odell was born in New Jersey, the grandson of Reverend Jonathan Dickson, the founder and first president of the College of New Jersey (now Princeton University). Odell graduated from the college in 1754 and obtained an MA in medicine there in 1757. He served briefly as a surgeon with the British Army in the West Indies, but in 1763 he prepared for the priesthood in the Anglican Church under the sponsorship of Benjamin Franklin's son William, who had just been appointed the royal governor of New Jersey. It was Odell's desire to be appointed the first Anglican bishop in America. He was soon licensed as a minister in New Jersey and took the pastorate at St. Mary's, a less than prosperous congregation in Burlington.

Odell's strong Loyalist convictions became evident in October 1775 when the New Jersey Committee of Safety intercepted two of his letters to England expressing disapproval of affairs in the American colonies, and he was compelled to appear before the New Jersey Provisional Congress. In June 1776, he penned a "Birth-day Ode" in honor of King George III, which delighted several British officers. When General William Howe's army marched on and captured Philadelphia in September 1777, Odell went with them and was charged in absentia with high treason. Howe appointed Odell chaplain to the 1st Battalion of Pennsylvania Loyalists and superintendent of the printing presses and periodical publications in the city. In the spring of 1778, when Sir Henry Clinton replaced Howe and abandoned Philadelphia, Odell left with the British Army and moved to New York City. Although he was not part of Clinton's inner circle, Odell was a friend of André, whom he had met in Burlington while André was briefly a prisoner of war.

In the spring of 1779, Arnold secretly offered his services to Clinton through Joseph Stansbury, the owner of a china shop in Philadelphia where Arnold was residing. Although instructed by Arnold to act alone, Stansbury immediately involved his friend Odell, who introduced Stansbury to André, then serving as Clinton's aide-de-camp. Fellow conspirators John Rattoon and other unnamed couriers carried many of Arnold's and André's letters between Odell and Stansbury. Numerous pseudonyms appeared in this clandestine correspondence. André was called Joseph Andrews, Lothario, and John Anderson. Arnold had the monikers A. G., Monk, Moore, and Gustavus. Odell referred to himself as Yoric, James Osborne, and Jasper Overhill. Stansbury was called Jonathan Stevens.

Initially, it appears that Odell was to serve merely as a conveyor, moving the letters between Stansbury and André. In the course of this transmission there were a few mishaps, as some letters were lost and confusion arose over which edition of selected works was to be used as a base for encryption. Early in the conspiracy, Odell attempted to decipher a dispatch on his own instead of passing it to André. Odell likely was responsible for damaging the letter, which he tried to explain away:

Odell to André
New York, 31 May 1779

My Dear Sir,

I am mortified to death—having just received (what I had been so anxiously expecting) a Letter from S[tansbury] and, by a private mark agreed on between us, perceiving it contained an invisible page for you, I assay'd it by the Fire, when to my inexpressible vexation, I found that the paper, having by some accident got damp on the way, had spread the Solution in such manner as to make the writing all one indistinguishable Blott, out of which not the half of any one line can be made legible.

Despite Odell's bungling, André gave him permission to handle all future cryptography. In addition to supporting communications, Odell did his best to keep the conspiracy going by encouraging the participants to remain steadfast and patient. When Arnold read a letter encoded in Odell's hand, however, he became concerned that the British had brought another party into the plot. Confronted by Arnold, Stansbury lied by denying that Odell knew the true identity of the American general.

In July 1780, Arnold had begun communicating information about West Point to André through Odell, who deciphered the correspondence. Like many other cautious eighteenth-century correspondents, the Arnold circle used coded transmissions keyed to specific editions of books that the conspirators held in common. The sender would encrypt a message with each coded word comprised of whole numbers delimited by periods. The first number represented the page number, the second the line number, and the third the word on the line counting from the left margin. For example, "57.9.7" in the coded message below represents the word "command." Often, common words were interspersed among the numbers. The recipient would decode the message using the same key. The conspirators also used invisible ink to write secret messages between the lines of innocuous correspondence. The letter "A" signified to decode with acid, while the letter "F," for fire, instructed the decoder to apply heat. The following is from a letter dated 12 July 1780 from Arnold to André:

Coded message	Decoded message
I 105.9.5. soon to 57.9.7 .at 288.9.8, 198.9.26, and most . 230.8.12. by --- / 291.8.27 an 149.8.27 with ---255.9.11 . 148.8.22, 182.4.28 in whom a 175.9.12 / 67.8.28 could be .196.9.16	I expect soon / to command W[est] P[oin]t and most seriously wish an interview with some / intelligent officer in whom a mutual confidence could be placed.

Arnold penned the coded message, and Odell, likely using a small dictionary, decoded it for André. Note that some codes were undecipherable, and some words were ignored.

By September 1780, the conspiracy had progressed to the point where Arnold was about to betray West Point to the British, but the meeting of André and Arnold that sealed the final arrangements left André exposed behind the American lines, and his capture led to Arnold's sudden and dramatic escape and the public discovery of the entire plot. Odell, however, was safely behind British lines and survived the war.

G. L. Donhardt

See also
André, John; Arnold, Benedict; West Point, New York

References
Edelberg, Cynthia Dubin. *Jonathan Odell, Loyalist Poet of the American Revolution.* Durham, NC: Duke University Press, 1987.

Flexner, James Thomas. *The Traitor and the Spy: Benedict Arnold and John André.* 1953. Reprint, Syracuse, NY: Syracuse University Press, 1992.

"July 12, 1780—Benedict Arnold to John André (Code): From the Clinton Collection." *Spy Letters of the American Revolution: From the Collections of the Clements Library.* Ann Arbor, University of Michigan. http://www.si.umich.edu/spies/ letter-1780july12-code.html.

Van Doren, Carl. *Secret History of the American Revolution: An Account of the Conspiracies of Benedict Arnold and Numerous Others from the Secret Service Papers of the British Headquarters in North America.* New York: Viking, 1941.

Wallace, Willard Mosher. *Traitorous Hero: The Life and Fortunes of Benedict Arnold.* New York: Harper and Row, 1954.

Ogden, Aaron
(1756–1839)

Soldier, lawyer, and public official, Aaron Ogden is most remembered for *Gibbons v. Ogden*, the steamboat monopoly case he lost in 1824 in the U.S. Supreme Court. A descendant of pioneer settlers, he was born in Elizabeth Town, New Jersey. He graduated in 1773 from the College of New Jersey (later Princeton University), a year behind his friend Aaron Burr. In January 1776, after three years spent teaching, Ogden joined with Elias Dayton and other Elizabeth Town volunteers in the capture of the *Blue Mountain Valley*, a

British merchant ship that had run aground off the coast of Sandy Hook. Encouraged by the ship's capture, the Continental Congress authorized privateering to encourage the seizure of enemy vessels.

In November 1776, Ogden entered the 1st New Jersey Regiment of the Continental line, of which his brother Matthias ultimately became colonel. Ogden served until 1783, rising from the rank of first lieutenant to major. He and his regiment fought in the Battle of Brandywine in September 1777 and at the Battle of Monmouth in June 1778. In the summer of 1779, he participated in John Sullivan's expedition against New York and Pennsylvania Indians. Ogden served at the action at Springfield, New Jersey, in June 1780, and at Yorktown in October 1781 he led the van of Colonel Alexander Hamilton's regiment in storming a redoubt high on the riverbank in a celebrated assault involving few American casualties. In addition to his Revolutionary combat, Ogden was a witness in the court-martial of General Charles Lee on charges of misconduct for ordering his troops to retreat from Monmouth. Ogden also served as George Washington's emissary to General Sir Henry Clinton in the attempt to exchange General Benedict Arnold for Major John André in the fall of 1780.

Aaron Ogden, who served in the New Jersey Continental line, fought at Brandywine and Monmouth, in Sullivan's expedition against the Iroquois, and at the siege of Yorktown, where he was wounded while storming a redoubt. (Library of Congress)

After the war, Ogden studied law and was admitted to the New Jersey bar in 1784. A prominent Federalist of the era, he held numerous public offices in the new nation. He was selected U.S. Senator in 1801, serving two years of an unexpired term, and in 1807 he sat on the commission that studied the boundary between New York and New Jersey. The legislature elected Ogden governor of New Jersey in 1812, but he was replaced a year later by William S. Pennington. Ogden married Elizabeth Chetwood, the daughter of a prominent judge, in 1787, and the couple had seven children.

Ogden is most remembered for his participation in the steamboat monopoly case *Gibbons v. Ogden*, decided by the U.S. Supreme Court in 1824. In 1811, at a time of transportation entrepreneurship, Ogden had built a steamer, the *Seahorse*, for service between Elizabeth Town Point and New York City. The New York legislature, which in 1798 had promised entrepreneur Robert Livingston a monopoly over steamboat traffic in the state's waters as an incentive to develop faster service, refused to allow the *Seahorse* to cross over to New York. After failing to obtain concessions in the courts or the legislature, Ogden purchased a ten-year exclusive license to operate the steamboat service from Livingston's brother and successor in 1815. The next year, however, Thomas Gibbons, who had once been in business with Ogden, obtained a federal coasting license and started a competing steamer service between New Jersey and Manhattan.

Following years of litigation between Gibbons and Ogden in state courts over who was authorized to run steamers, the case reached the Supreme

Court. In 1824, in an opinion by Chief Justice John Marshall, the Court held that under the Supremacy Clause of the U.S. Constitution, the New York monopoly was invalid because it conflicted with the federal licensing law. Gibbons could therefore operate his steamship. Read by every law student, *Gibbons v. Ogden* stands as an early landmark case on the powers of the federal government to regulate interstate commerce.

For Ogden, the Supreme Court case was a financial disaster. Deep in debt, he was imprisoned in New York City in 1830 and released only after Burr, his old friend, prompted the New York legislature to prohibit debt imprisonment for Revolutionary War veterans. Ogden then became a federal customs collector in Jersey City and worked in that capacity until his death in 1839.

JASON MAZZONE

See also

André, John; Arnold, Benedict; Brandywine, Battle of; Dayton, Elias; Hamilton, Alexander; Lee, Charles; Monmouth, Battle of; Ogden, Matthias; Privateering; Sullivan Expedition; Yorktown, Virginia, Siege of

References

Baxter, Maurice G. *The Steamboat Monopoly: Gibbons v. Ogden, 1824*. New York: Knopf, 1972.

Harrison, Richard A. "Ogden, Aaron." Pp. 328–334 in *Princetonians, 1769–1775: A Biographical Dictionary*. Princeton, NJ: Princeton University Press, 1980.

Wheeler, William Ogden. *The Ogden Family in America*. Philadelphia: Lippincott, 1907.

Ogden, Matthias
(1754–1791)

Matthias Ogden left college after the Battle of Bunker Hill to join the Patriot army at Boston. He was part of Benedict Arnold's march on Quebec and was wounded. Ogden then returned to New Jersey to take command of one of the state's regiments. He led his unit at the Battle of Brandywine, through the winter at Valley Forge, and at the Battle of Monmouth. He was captured in 1780 but exchanged in 1781, when he resumed command of the same regiment until it was disbanded in 1783.

Ogden was born in 1754 in Elizabeth Town, New Jersey, where his father, Robert Ogden, was a prominent colonial official who became a leading Patriot. Matthias and his brother Aaron were also devoted to the American cause. When the war began, Ogden was enrolled in college at Princeton, but after the Battle of Bunker Hill (17 June 1775), he and fellow student Aaron Burr set out to join the American army besieging Boston. Both men volunteered to join Arnold's expedition to capture Quebec. Ogden had the privilege of being the first to ask the British garrison at Quebec to surrender. The British response was to fire at Ogden and send him scurrying back to the American lines. During the unsuccessful assault on Quebec on 31 December 1775, Ogden was wounded. Soon thereafter, he left Canada and returned to New Jersey.

Upon his return, Ogden was commissioned the lieutenant colonel of the 1st New Jersey Regiment on 7 March 1776. He assumed command of the regiment on 1 January 1777, when the enlistments expired for the regiment and it had to be reconstituted. His regiment was part of General William Alexander's division at the Battle of Brandywine on 11 September 1777, where they were posted at Plowed Hill and helped slow the British advance. Ogden's regiment then spent the winter at Valley Forge and participated in the Battle of Monmouth on 28 June 1778 as part of General Charles Lee's command. When Lee suddenly pulled back his division at Monmouth, Ogden, reports claim, was very angry at the general's conduct, especially since Lee's withdrawal probably cost the Americans a decisive victory.

Ogden was captured at Elizabeth Town in the fall of 1780 but was exchanged in April 1781, when he resumed command of the 1st New Jersey regiment. In late September 1781, the Patriots learned that Prince William Henry, the future King William IV of England, was in New York City. They also learned where he was staying. Ogden submitted a plan to capture the prince, which Washington approved. Ogden then selected a group of forty officers and men for the mission, but the plan was compromised and had to be abandoned.

In April 1783, the 1st New Jersey was disbanded and Ogden was given a leave of absence. He traveled to France, where he was received by the royal court. In September 1783, during his absence, he was breveted to the rank of brigadier general and mustered out of the army. When he returned to the United States, he lived in Elizabeth Town until his death in 1791.

DALLACE W. UNGER JR.

See also
Brandywine, Battle of; Burr, Aaron; Canada, Operations in; Lee, Charles; Monmouth, Battle of; Ogden, Aaron; Valley Forge, Pennsylvania

References
Boatner, Mark. *Encyclopedia of the American Revolution.* Mechanicsburg, PA: Stackpole, 1994.
Mays, Terry M. *Historical Dictionary of the American Revolution.* Historical Dictionaries of War, Revolution, and Civil Unrest Series, no. 7. Lanham, MD: Scarecrow, 1999.
Purcell, L. Edward. *Who Was Who in the American Revolution.* New York: Facts On File, 1993.

O'Hara, Charles
(1740?–1802)

The illegitimate son of the second Lord Tyrawley, Charles O'Hara went to Westminster School and joined the British Army in 1752. In 1756 he received a captaincy in the Coldstream Guards, of which his father was colonel, and served as aide-de-camp to the Marquis of Granby during the campaign in Germany. With the rank of lieutenant-colonel, O'Hara was quartermaster-general of the forces led by Lord Tyrawley during the expedition to Portugal in 1762. From October 1780 O'Hara commanded the brigade of Guards in the American War of Independence. He served with distinction during the crossing of the Catawba River in February 1781 and was twice severely wounded at Guilford Courthouse. It was O'Hara who had the misfortune to surrender the troops at Yorktown on behalf of the ailing Lord Charles Cornwallis.

In 1792 O'Hara became lieutenant governor of Gibraltar. The following year he was promoted to lieutenant-general and left Gibraltar for Toulon, there to supercede General Henry Phipps, Lord Mulgrave, in command of the British forces besieging that port. O'Hara was wounded, captured, and taken to Paris, where he remained throughout the Reign of Terror, before being exchanged for General Jean-Baptiste Vimeur, the comte de Rochambeau, in August 1795. After his release, O'Hara was given the governorship of Gibraltar and became a full general in 1798. He died in 1802 at the Rock from problems arising from old wounds. He left a great sum of money to two women, by whom he had illegitimate children, and to his servant.

GREGORY FREMONT-BARNES

See also
Cornwallis, Charles; Guilford Courthouse, Battle of; Vimeur, Jean-Baptiste, Comte de Rochambeau; Yorktown, Virginia, Siege of

References
Fortescue, John. *The War of Independence: The British Army in North America, 1775–1783*. London: Greenhill, 2001.
Wickwire, Franklin, and Mary Wickwire. *Cornwallis: The American Adventure*. Boston: Houghton Mifflin, 1970.

Ohio

See Fort Laurens, Ohio; Northwest Territory

Olive Branch Petition
(8 July 1775)

Written by John Dickinson and adopted by the Second Continental Congress in July, the final American petition to George III, generally known as the Olive Branch Petition, was the colonists' last attempt to avert a war with Great Britain. It was approved just two days after Congress's Declaration of the Causes and Necessity of Taking Up Arms (6 July), which was addressed to a much wider audience in America, Britain, and Europe. The Olive Branch Petition asked the king to redress America's grievances and assured him of the colonists' continued loyalty. Yet despite the petition's conciliatory tone, the king and his ministers completely ignored the appeal. Instead, in late August 1775, George III declared that the colonists were in rebellion.

This declaration played a part in the rapid development of colonial sentiment in favor of independence from the late fall of 1775 until the formal break with Britain in July 1776.

Following the outbreak of hostilities at Lexington and Concord in April 1775, the Second Continental Congress met in Philadelphia to decide whether to try to negotiate with Britain or to continue the war to compel the British to recognize America's rights. Led by Dickinson, moderate congressmen who hoped to avoid conflict argued that now was not the time to adopt radical measures. They deplored the idea of war with Great Britain, remained open to reconciliation, and sought to send a petition directly to the king asking for a settlement. In late May, Dickinson submitted to Congress four resolutions, including one that eventually became the Olive Branch Petition, that had as their goal reconciliation with England. Although Dickinson hoped to find a peaceful solution to the impasse, he also viewed the petition as a political gesture that could ultimately strengthen America's military effort. If the king rejected it, then hesitant Americans would abandon hopes of reconciliation and be more willing to fight.

Radical congressmen, such as John Adams, disagreed with these views but decided to support the petition. They believed that in light of Great Britain's recent actions, further negotiation was not just futile but also dangerous because it would delay making preparations for war. Some were even ready to argue that immediate independence was America's only viable option. This position, however, was not popular in a Congress that still hoped to find a peaceful solution to the crisis. Therefore, the radicals supported the petition because they believed that the king would reject it, which would convince the moderates that reconciliation was no longer possible and that independence was the only available course of action.

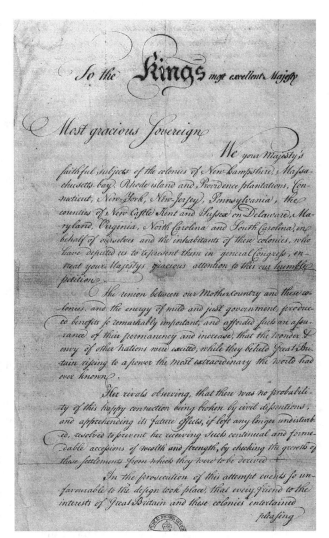

Front page of the Olive Branch Petition to King George III (July 1775), an attempt by America's moderate Patriots in Congress to prevent armed resistance from becoming a war for independence (HIP/Art Resource, New York)

After ten days of debate, Congress voted to send a petition to the king and appointed a committee to write the document. The committee consisted of Dickinson, John Jay, Benjamin Franklin, and two other members. Both Dickinson and Jay wrote drafts. The less-cautious Jay draft concluded by threatening independence. In the end, Dickinson wrote the final petition, eliminating any wording that might anger the king.

The Olive Branch Petition was courteous, conciliatory, and respectful and sought to explain why the colonists had taken up arms. The document began by praising the "union between our mother country and these colonies" and acknowledging the benefits gained from "the energy of mild and just government" provided by Great Britain. After the French and Indian War, Americans had hoped to enjoy the blessings of peace and victory but "were alarmed by a new system of statutes and regulations adopted for the administration of the colonies." Dickinson blamed the king's ministers for enacting, enforcing, and refusing to repeal these various laws. As a result, Dickinson claimed that the ministers "have compelled us to arm in our own defense."

The petition then assured George III of the colonists' loyalty, aversion to conflict, and desire for reconciliation and asked him to find a peaceful solution to the crisis. Though forced to take up arms in self-defense, the colonists hoped to stop "the further effusion of blood" and to avert "the impending calamities that threaten the British empire." Dickinson appealed to the king's "magnanimity and benevolence" and assured him of the colonists' continued loyalty to him and their "tender regard" for Great Britain. He asked the king "to procure us relief . . . and to settle peace through every part of your dominions." The petition concluded by promising the king that if he accepted reconciliation, established peace, and helped secure the repeal of the offensive statutes, the Americans would become "the most dutiful subjects and the most affectionate colonists."

Adopted and signed on 8 July, the petition was sent to London under the care of Richard Penn, who was to join Arthur Lee in presenting it. Penn arrived in England on 14 August, and a week later the two emissaries sent a copy of the document to William Legge, the Earl of Dartmouth, who was the king's secretary for the American colonies. On 1 September, Penn personally gave the original to Dartmouth and asked the secretary to obtain the king's reply. Dartmouth promised to present the petition to George III, but soon thereafter he informed Penn that there would be no answer because the king refused to formally accept the document. Although he never officially rejected it, George III essentially renounced the Olive Branch Petition and all attempts at reconciliation on 23 August, when he issued a proclamation declaring the American colonies to be in open rebellion. On 9 November, the Continental Congress was informed that the king had refused to receive the petition.

The failure of the Olive Branch Petition was not surprising, but the contempt with which it was treated played a role in the move toward independence. Its rejection ended all hopes of reconciliation or a negotiated settlement of the conflict and helped to push many moderates toward radical measures. In the spring of 1776, one of the prominent grievances listed in the many distinctive declarations of independence issued by various American colonies, cities, and towns was the contempt with which George III had received the Olive Branch Petition.

DAVID WORK

See also

Adams, John; Congress, Second Continental and Confederation; Dickinson, John; George III, King of England; Jay, John

References

Davies, K. G., ed. *Documents of the American Revolution, 1770–1783*, Vol. 11, *Transcripts, 1775, July–December*. Dublin: Irish University Press, 1979.

Flower, Milton E. *John Dickinson: Conservative Revolutionary*. Charlottesville: University of Virginia Press, 1983.

Jacobson, David L. *John Dickinson and the Revolution in Pennsylvania, 1764–1776.* Berkeley: University of California Press, 1965.

Maier, Pauline. *American Scripture: Making the Declaration of Independence.* New York: Knopf, 1997.

Oriskany, Battle of
(6 August 1777)

Despite being ambushed en route, Tryon County, New York, militia and their commander, Nicholas Herkimer, helped to raise the siege of Fort Stanwix by Barry St. Leger's forces during General John Burgoyne's campaign of 1777.

Even before Burgoyne's army left Canada in the summer of 1777, word had reached Congress that a second British force might attempt to attack Albany via the Mohawk Valley. As well as sending Peter Gansevoort to speed up the rebuilding of Fort Stanwix, at the western end of the valley, the commander of the Northern Department, Philip Schuyler, also alerted the local authorities and ordered them to assist where and when they could. At the beginning of July, Herkimer, one of the leaders of the Palatine German community and a brigadier general in the Tryon County militia, tried to negotiate the neutrality of Joseph Brant, the Iroquois chief, but failed after a meeting that almost led to bloodshed. Two weeks later, Herkimer tried to mobilize a force of militia to assist in the defense of Fort Stanwix but had to abandon the project when only 200 men turned out.

On 30 July, a friendly Oneida warrior warned Herkimer that St. Leger's force was about to cross Lake Oneida. Herkimer promptly ordered all males between sixteen and sixty years of age to gather at Fort Dayton. Five days later, he had 800 men, organized into four regiments: the 1st (Canajoharie), commanded by Ebenezer Cox; the 2nd (Palatine), commanded by Jacob Klock; the 3rd (Mohawk), commanded by Frederick Fischer (or Visscher); and the 4th (Kingsland/German Flats), commanded by Peter Bellinger. With these troops and a convoy of ox wagons, Herkimer left Fort Dayton on 4 August, covering 12 miles before halting for the night at Stirling Creek. The following day, the column crossed the Mohawk River and was just 8 miles from Fort Stanwix by nightfall.

Meanwhile, on the evening of 5 August, St. Leger had been informed that a relief force was within striking distance of the fort. It was imperative that it be stopped well short of the fort so that the garrison could not join in the fighting. If the latter happened, with more than half of St. Leger's force composed of Indians, the imbalance in regular troops would probably be fatal to the British. St. Leger promptly dispatched Brant and Sir John Johnson with 150 Loyalists and 400 Iroquois to ambush Herkimer's column before it could reach Fort Stanwix and link up with Gansevoort.

For his part, Herkimer was aware that defeat would leave both the fort and the communities of the Mohawk Valley defenseless, and he voiced this concern—and doubts over the safety of the route they were taking—at a council of war on the morning of 6 August. However, his four colonels

At the Battle of Oriskany on 6 August 1777, some 30 Loyalists and 400 Indians under Joseph Brant ambushed a Patriot militia force of 800 men under Colonel Nicholas Herkimer that was marching to relieve the besieged Fort Stanwix. In a bloody battle characterized by hand-to-hand combat, the Patriots lost 150 to 200 men killed, including Herkimer, and another 200 captured, but the Indians lost 150 men and withdrew after several hours of fighting. General Benedict Arnold, leading a force of Continentals, later relieved Fort Stanwix. (John Grafton, ed., *The American Revolution: A Picture Sourcebook*, 1975)

demanded an immediate advance, and at least two of them reputedly accused him of cowardice and even treason (it being well known that he had a brother in St. Leger's force). Against his better judgment, and perhaps feeling more confident after the arrival of 60 Oneida warriors and 50 rangers who could provide scouts and flank guards, Herkimer gave in to the colonels' demands. He ordered the men to march off and, possibly to allay suspicions as to his bravery or loyalty, rode at the head of the column. At some point that morning, he also sent four messengers ahead to the fort to inform Gansevoort of his approach and to ask him to carry out a sortie against the British lines. The signal that the message had been received was to be three cannon shots.

By 9:00 A.M., Herkimer's column had reached a point where the military road (made of logs laid across the track at right angles, often called a corduroy road) was intersected by two steep-sided ravines. The first was 700 feet wide and 50 feet deep, and the second was narrower but still deep enough to hide men from view; both were heavily shaded by tall trees growing within a few feet of the track. As Herkimer's leading regiment, commanded by Cox, emerged from the second ravine, the men heard three whistle blasts.

Johnson had planned the ambush and had chosen the site well. His own regiment, the King's Royal Regiment of New York (also known as the Royal Yorkers or Royal Greens), blocked the road and lined the sides of the second ravine. The rest of the trail was flanked by Iroquois under Brant and some Loyalist rangers under John Butler. (Butler's troops were an ad hoc unit, probably composed of spare officers from the Indian Department, and not the famous Butler's Rangers, which was only raised in 1778.) The plan was to allow the leading militia to enter the smaller ravine, by which time the wagons and rear guard would be inside the larger ravine and then spring the trap. Around 10:00 A.M., Johnson's men fired the first volley, wounding Herkimer, killing Cox, and throwing the head of the column into confusion. Unfortunately, the Iroquois attacked the rear guard, commanded by Fischer, too soon and ended up having to chase them eastward, back toward Fort Dayton. (Skeletons of militiamen were later found up to 2 miles away.) While this destroyed Fischer's regiment as a fighting unit, it left a gap in the Indian line through which the other units could fight their way off the road and onto higher ground in small groups. As the militia rallied in a large circle, Herkimer was propped against his saddle under a beech tree. There he dispensed orders, calmly smoking a pipe in full view of the enemy but unable to move because of his shattered leg.

About an hour after the fighting began, the area was hit by a thunderstorm that lasted for about forty-five minutes but halted the fighting for more than an hour, as both sides were forced to allow time for their muskets and powder to dry out. The lull gave Herkimer time to reorganize his defenses. In particular, he had noticed that once a man fired, one or more Indians would be on him with their knives and tomahawks before he could reload. Herkimer ordered his men to operate in pairs, with at least one having a loaded weapon at any moment to prevent these deadly rushes by the enemy. The plan worked, and as Indian casualties began to mount, the Iroquois became restless. Around noon, the Loyalists attempted to break the deadlock by subterfuge. Major Stephen Watts had his men turn their coats (which were green with gray-white facings and lining) inside out and approached the enemy as if they were a relief party coming from Fort Stanwix. The ruse might have worked had not Captain Jacob Gardenier of Fischer's regiment not recognized a neighbor. As one of his men rushed out to greet these "friends," he was captured. At this, Gardenier, armed only with a spontoon and a sword, rushed forward and killed the man's captor and another man. He then wounded a third Loyalist before three others knocked him to the ground. Two immediately bayoneted him—one through each thigh—while the third (an officer named McDonald) went to bayonet him in the chest. Gardenier caught the bayonet in his left hand, cutting himself badly, and then, as two comrades distracted the other two Loyalists, killed McDonald with his spontoon, calling to the rest of his company, "They are not our men, they are the enemy. Fire away!"

SIEGE OF FORT STANWIX AND BATTLE OF ORISKANY, 6 AUGUST 1777

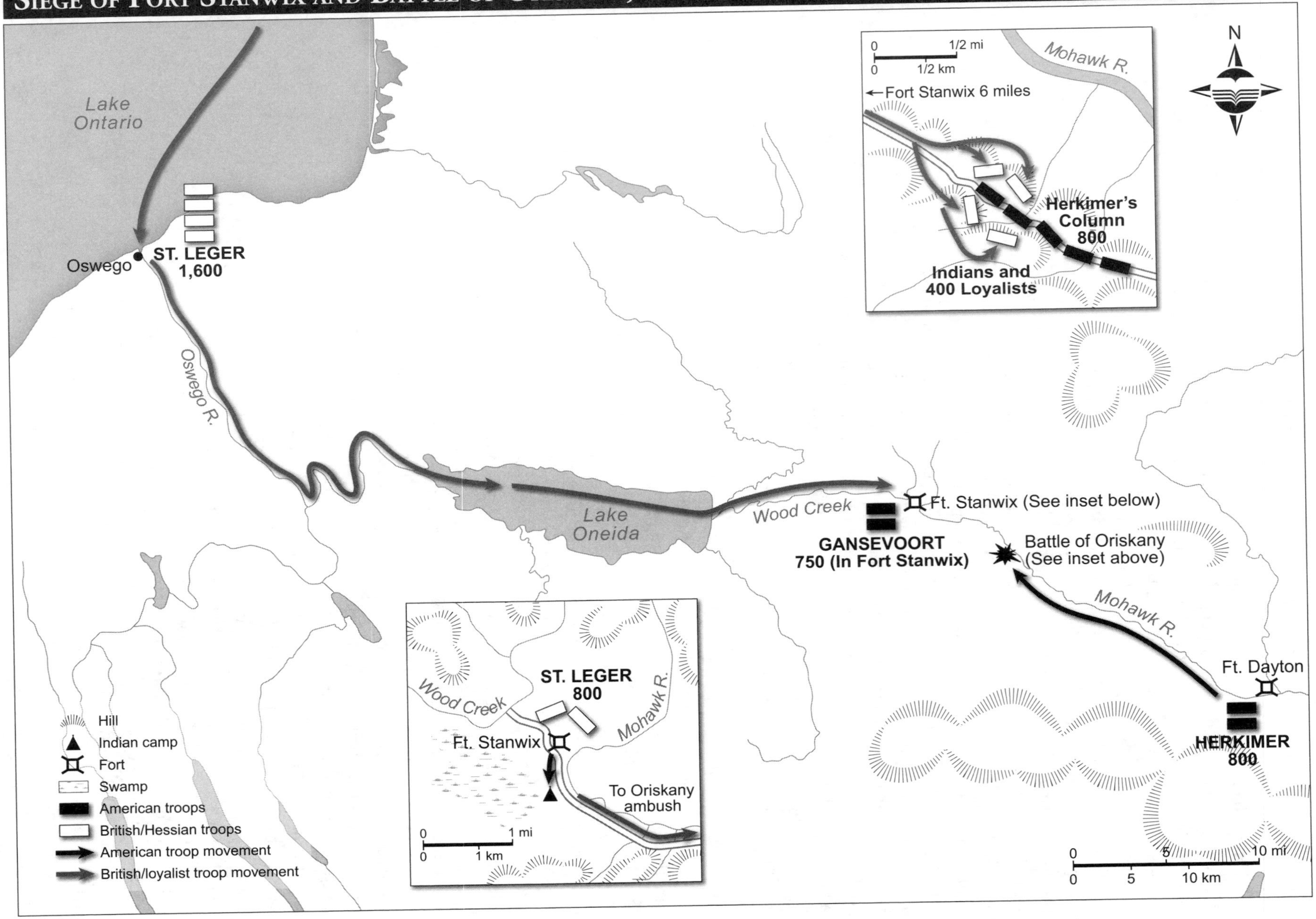

N

Mohawk R.

Herkimer's Column 800

Fort Stanwix 6 miles

Indians and 400 Loyalists

1/2 mi
1/2 km

Ft. Dayton

HERKIMER 800

10 mi

10 km

5

5

Mohawk R.

Ft. Stanwix (See inset below)

Battle of Oriskany (See inset above)

GANSEVOORT 750 (In Fort Stanwix)

Ft. Stanwix

Wood Creek

Mohawk R.

ST. LEGER 800

To Oriskany ambush

Ft. Stanwix

Wood Creek

1 mi
1 km

Lake Oneida

Oswego R.

Lake Ontario

Oswego

ST. LEGER 1,600

Hill
Indian camp
Fort
Swamp
American troops
British/Hessian troops
American troop movement
British/loyalist troop movement

Fierce hand-to-hand fighting followed, and as both sides withdrew to recover, three cannon shots were heard. Herkimer and his men knew instantly what they meant; their enemies found out soon enough as messengers arrived to tell Brant that the camp was being sacked. Already demoralized by heavy losses, the threat to their possessions persuaded the remaining warriors to leave. Unable to fight on unaided, Johnson and Butler also withdrew.

Herkimer's messengers had arrived at the fort around 10:00 A.M., almost at the same time as the ambush was sprung (St. Leger's men saw them entering and realized their purpose). By the time a sortie had been planned, the garrison was forced to wait for the same storm that later soaked the combatants at Oriskany to pass over. As the weather cleared, 250 men led by Marinus Willett, second in command at the fort, attacked the Loyalist and Indian camps and removed twenty-one wagonloads of supplies and matériel without losing a single man. Their haul included flags (probably camp colors, rather than regimental standards), papers, weapons, and, perhaps most important of all, the blankets and cooking utensils of Brant's warriors. On top of their casualties at Oriskany, this loss infuriated the Indians, who promptly sacked the camps of their allies in frustration.

As the enemy withdrew, Herkimer ordered his surviving troops to fall back to Fort Dayton. Little more than one-quarter of the 600 men from his three leading regiments were unhurt (Fischer's losses went unrecorded), and with insufficient healthy men to carry the dead and wounded, runners had to be sent to bring up bateaux to collect them. St. Leger claimed to have taken 200 prisoners, which seems highly unlikely; however, two captured officers were sent into the fort the next day to inform Gansevoort of the disaster and encourage him to surrender. The combined Loyalist and Indian losses were probably around 150; figures of 160 dead for the Indians seem unlikely, given their reputation for leaving bloody battles before losses became too severe. How the Oneida scouts and rangers failed to detect the ambush before it was sprung has never been established, but it is possible that either Herkimer's subordinates were too eager to press on to use them properly or the nature of the terrain forced them to keep so close to the column that they could not fulfill their role.

Herkimer died ten days later when surgeons failed to stop the bleeding after his leg was amputated. Despite the massive loss among his militia, he gave Gansevoort the opportunity to attack the British camp. The material losses of that raid, combined with the combat losses in the battle, removed Brant's warriors—half of St. Leger's force—from the enemy order of battle (to the point that they turned against their allies). While the siege went on officially until 21 August, St. Leger's chances of capturing the fort effectively ended fifteen days earlier at Oriskany.

BRENDAN D. MORRISSEY

See also

Brant, Joseph; Burgoyne, John; Butler, John; Fort Stanwix, New York; Gansevoort, Peter; Herkimer, Nicholas; Johnson, Sir John; Saratoga Campaign; Schuyler, Philip; Siege Warfare; St. Leger Expedition; Willett, Marinus

References

Carrington, Henry B. *Battles of the American Revolution, 1775–1781.* 1876. Reprint, New York: Promontory, 1974.

Foote, Alan. *Liberty March: The Battle of Oriskany.* Utica, NY: North Country Books, 1998.

Scott, John. *Fort Stanwix and Oriskany.* Rome, NY: Rome Sentinel, 1927.

Wood, W. J. *Battles of the Revolutionary War, 1775–1781.* Chapel Hill, NC: Algonquin, 1990.

Oswald, Eleazer

(1750?–1795)

Eleazer Oswald served with distinction at the capture of Fort Ticonderoga in May 1775 and with the Continental Army at Quebec that fall and winter, in both instances under the command of Benedict Arnold. Then, after more than a year as a prisoner of war, he served as an artillery officer repelling the British raid on Danbury, Connecticut, and at the Battle of Monmouth. After leaving the army in 1779, Oswald resumed his career in newspaper publishing as founder and editor of Philadelphia's *Independent Gazetteer,* which became a leading Antifederalist newspaper. Within its pages, Oswald contentiously opposed the adoption of the Constitution while simultaneously publishing articles and essays that were important contributions to the debate to establish the limits of freedom of the press in the emerging nation.

Oswald was born in 1750 or 1751 in Falmouth, England, and immigrated to New York City in 1770, where he was apprenticed as a printer to John Holt, the publisher of the *New-York Journal, or General Advertiser.* An early supporter of the rights of the British colonies, Oswald joined Arnold's expedition of May 1775 that captured the British forts at Ticonderoga and Crown Point and helped seize two British vessels on Lake Champlain. Rising to the rank of captain, Oswald served as secretary to Arnold during the Quebec expedition and, along with artillery captain John Lamb, joined an advance squad in the unsuccessful attack on the fortified city. Captured on 31 December 1775 by the British during that attack, Oswald was held as a prisoner of war until May 1777.

Upon his release, Oswald returned to duty in the 2nd Continental Artillery with the rank of lieutenant colonel. He became skilled in estimating the origin of British cannon fire from its trajectory and successfully returning fire, and he drew praise for his checking of the British artillery at Campo Hill during the British raid on Danbury in 1777 and at the Battle of Monmouth in June 1778. Always protective about his rights, Oswald by then felt

Eleazer Oswald, an officer in the Continental Army, was wounded and captured during the storming of Quebec in December 1775. After being exchanged, he took part in the Danbury raid and the Battle of Monmouth. (Library of Congress)

that he had been denied the proper seniority of his rank, and in 1779 he resigned from the army.

Oswald returned to journalism, first in Maryland and then in Philadelphia, where in 1782 he established the Antifederalist *Independent Gazetteer*. Fearing that the proposed federal Constitution would dangerously centralize power, the newspaper led the opposition to the document, publishing at least twenty-four of the "Centinel" essays by Pennsylvania politician Samuel Bryan that served as counterparts to the Federalist Papers and are credited with helping to win the concession to add a Bill of Rights to the Constitution. Prompted partially by his own legal entanglements, Oswald also published some of the first American arguments against seditious libel, in which he vigorously defended the right to criticize the government or government officials without fear of punishment.

While settling his legal affairs in England in 1792, Oswald was drawn to the French Revolution and briefly volunteered as an artillery officer before returning to the United States in 1793. He died in New York City of yellow fever on 30 September 1795.

SUE BARKER

See also

Arnold, Benedict; Federalist Papers; Fort Ticonderoga, New York; Monmouth, Battle of

References

Tweeter, Dwight L., Jr. "Eleazer Oswald." Pp. 818–820 in *The American National Biography*, Vol. 16. Edited by John A. Gerraty and Mark C. Carnes. New York: Oxford University Press, 1999.

———. "Eleazer Oswald." Pp. 334–338 in *Dictionary of Literary Biography*, Vol. 43, *American Newspaper Journalists, 1690–1872*. Edited by Perry J. Ashley. Detroit: Gale Group, 1985.

Wheeler, Joseph Towne. "Eleazer Oswald, Lieutenant-Colonel in the Revolution, Printer in Baltimore and Philadelphia, Soldier of Fortune in the French Revolution." Pp. 19–36 in *The Maryland Press, 1777–1790*. Baltimore: Maryland Historical Society, 1938.

Oswald, Richard
(1705–1784)

The Scotsman Richard Oswald lived for several years in Virginia but returned to England before the American Revolutionary War. His knowledge of America was sought by several leading men in the British government, which finally led to his selection as the first representative of the British government in its preliminary peace negotiations with the Americans in 1782.

Oswald was born in Scotland in 1705. In 1750 he married Mary Ramsay, who had inherited lands in North America and the West Indies. He used these lands to build a profitable trading business, based primarily in the slave trade between Africa and both the West Indian and the North American

The British diplomat Richard Oswald, discussing the preliminary Treaty of Paris with Benjamin Franklin. (Library of Congress)

colonies. During the Seven Years' War, he also helped supply the British Army. In the course of his slave trading business in South Carolina, he met Henry Laurens, and the two would become friends during their twenty years of corresponding and working together. Oswald moved to London before the American Revolutionary War.

Both before and during the war, Oswald's council was valued because of the time he had spent in the colonies and his connections with important persons there. Lord Frederick North and Lord George Germain particularly sought out his advice. With the downfall of North's government in March 1782, brought about by General Charles Cornwallis's surrender at Yorktown the previous fall, Charles Watson-Wentworth, Lord Rockingham, the new leader of the British government, selected Oswald to start negotiations with the Americans. Oswald first helped secure the release of his friend Laurens, who had been captured while sailing to Europe in 1780, from the Tower of London. This was especially significant because in 1781, while still in prison, Laurens had been named to the American peace delegation by the Continental Congress.

Oswald arrived in Paris in April 1782 and began talks with Benjamin Franklin, who wanted to wait for the other American commissioners, especially John Adams and John Jay, before starting formal negotiations with the British. Franklin did agree, however, to start preliminary negotiations with Oswald. The sudden death of Rockingham in July and the need for William Petty-Fitzmaurice, Lord Shelburne, to form a new British government delayed this process, but in September, Shelburne authorized Oswald to begin formal negotiations with the Americans. Oswald, who had returned to England, went again to Paris, and by the end of November he had worked out a preliminary treaty with the Americans. This agreement, with no significant changes, would eventually become the final peace treaty that representatives of Great Britain and the United States signed in Paris on 3 September 1783.

Following the resignation of Shelburne as prime minister in February 1783, however, Oswald was recalled from Paris by the succeeding government. The House of Commons then censured Oswald on the grounds that he had given the Americans too many concessions, and he was barred from signing the treaty that he had negotiated for the British. Following his censure, Oswald retired from public life and died the following year.

DALLACE W. UNGER JR.

See also

Diplomacy, American; Diplomacy, British; Franklin, Benjamin; Germain, Lord George; Laurens, Henry; North, Lord Frederick; Petty-Fitzmaurice, William, 2nd Earl of Shelburne

References

Boatner, Mark. *Encyclopedia of the American Revolution*. Mechanicsburg, PA: Stackpole, 1994.

Faragher, Jack Mack. *The Encyclopedia of Colonial and Revolutionary America*. New York: Facts On File, 1990.

Morris, Richard B. *The Peacemakers: The Great Powers and American Independence*. New York: Harper and Row, 1965.

Purcell, L. Edward. *Who Was Who in the American Revolution*. New York: Facts On File, 1993.

Otis, James, Jr.
(1725–1783)

The Massachusetts lawyer, orator, and resistance leader James Otis Jr. was born in West Barnstable, Massachusetts. His father, James Otis Sr., was the leading political figure of Barnstable County (Cape Cod), and his sister became the prominent historian Mercy Otis Warren. The younger Otis graduated from Harvard College in 1743 and studied law in Boston with Jeremiah Gridley before setting up practice for himself. In 1755, Otis married the wealthy heiress Ruth Cunningham. She sympathized with the Loyalists during the Revolution, and their three children reflected their parents' political differences: their first daughter married a British Army officer, their son died in a British prisoner of war camp, and their second daughter married the son of Patriot General Benjamin Lincoln.

The elder Otis was one of the leaders of the Massachusetts House of Representatives in the 1750s, and owing to his connections with Governors William Shirley and Thomas Pownall, the younger Otis became deputy advocate general of the vice-admiralty court. He was an impressive lawyer, and both Thomas Hutchinson and John Adams praised him for winning cases on their merits rather than through chicanery or the technical manipulation of legal points.

In 1760 the Otis family switched from the court faction that favored the governor to the Country Party, which opposed him. The elder Otis had been promised the next vacancy on the superior court by Pownall, but Pownall's successor, Francis Bernard, chose Hutchinson instead. The Otises believed that Hutchinson had offered his assistance to them and then double-crossed them. Hutchinson claimed to have accepted the post only when Bernard stated that he would never appoint a politician such as Otis, who did "low, dirty things." Hutchinson also claimed that the younger Otis then swore revenge, saying that he would set the province in a flame or perish in the attempt. Otis denied this charge.

Hutchinson and Otis clashed again in 1761 over writs of assistance. These were search warrants that allowed Boston customs officials to look anywhere for illegal imports, and the writs were considerably hindering the city's trade. When a number of merchants brought suit to have the writs declared illegal, Otis resigned his position at the admiralty court to take up the merchants' cause. He argued before Hutchinson and the other members of the court that the writs were "the worst instrument of arbitrary power, the

From 1761 to 1769, James Otis Jr. was a prominent spokesman of the American cause. It is thought that he coined the phrase "no taxation without representation." (Library of Congress)

most destructive to English liberty and the fundamental principles of law." At this point, Otis was grasping at straws, because it was difficult to deny that an act of Parliament had binding force. Hutchinson sent a message to England, found out that the courts there issued such writs, and assumed that a like power resided in colonial courts. Ironically, when in 1766 the British attorney general ruled on the issue, he ignored both Hutchinson's and Otis's arguments and simply noted that the act authorizing the writs did not extend to the colonies.

By then, however, the damage had been done. The customs officers continued their seizures, and Otis, according to Adams, who was present at the trial, had raised in the public sphere the question of whether acts of Parliament could violate the fundamental rights of British subjects and thereby be lawfully resisted: "Otis was a flame of fire! . . . American independence was then and there born; the seeds of patriots and heroes were then and there sown."

Two months later, in May 1761, Otis joined his father in the Massachusetts House of Representatives as a member from Boston. He won election each year until 1769 and then again in 1771. Throughout the 1760s he was noted for his powerful public speaking against British measures. He also wrote a series of important pamphlets. *A Vindication of the Conduct of the House of Representatives* (1762) strongly criticized Bernard for making a trivial expenditure without the House's consent, insisting that "a House of Representatives here, at least, bears an equal proportion to the governor, as the House of Commons to the King," who could not spend a shilling without their consent. *The Rights of the British Colonies Asserted and Proved* (1764) denied Parliament's right to tax the colonies in any way whatsoever, stating that it "depriv[ed] them of one of their most essential rights as freemen; and if continued, seems to be in effect an entire disfranchisement of every civil right." Otis here advanced one of the main reasons for the Revolution: any British infringement of a colonial right was a foot in the door that signaled an approaching end to all rights. And in *A Vindication of the British Colonies* (1765), written as the Stamp Act was under discussion, Otis denied that Parliament could "virtually" represent colonies that in Britain had "no more share, weight or influence than the Hottentots have in China . . . or the Ethiopians . . . in Great Britain."

Yet while Otis laid out the American case against British policy earlier than any other thinker, he also struggled with the implications of his positions more than almost anyone else. He wrote in *A Vindication* that "God forbid these colonies should ever prove undutiful to their mother country! . . . Were these colonies left to themselves tomorrow, America would be a mere shambles of blood and confusion." His critics also charged that he contradicted himself and from time to time would change sides, along with his father, when the elder Otis received lucrative government offices. In any event, Otis's inconsistent political stances, coupled with a drinking problem and developing insanity, perhaps brought on by a savage beating he received from Customs Commissioner John Robinson in 1769, ensured that by the early 1770s he was finished as a politician. As judge of probate, Hutchinson remanded Otis to the custody of his relatives after he had shot off guns at random and broken the windows of the province house, now Boston's Old State House. He even charged into the midst of the Battle of Bunker Hill but somehow survived. Otis died, as he both predicted and desired, when a bolt of lightning struck him in 1783. Well before his death, however, he was true to his word, as Hutchinson noted in a 1771 letter to General Thomas Gage after Otis's insanity had set in: "He set the province in a flame and perished [politically] in the attempt."

WILLIAM PENCAK

See also

Adams, John; Boston, Massachusetts; Hutchinson, Thomas; Massachusetts; Stamp Act; Warren, Mercy Otis

References

Benson, James A. "James Otis and the 'Writs of Assistance Speech'—Fact and Fiction." *Southern Speech Journal* 34 (1969): 256–263.

Breen, T. H. "Subjecthood and Citizenship: The Context of James Otis's Radical Critique of John Locke." *New England Quarterly* 77 (1998): 378–403.

Ferguson, James R. "Reason in Madness: The Political Thought of James Otis." *William and Mary Quarterly*, 3rd ser., 34 (1979): 194–214.

Tudor, William. *The Life of James Otis*. Boston: n.p., 1823.

Waters, John J., Jr. *The Otis Family in Provincial and Revolutionary Massachusetts*. New York: Norton, 1968.

> James Otis Jr. laid out the American case against British policy earlier than any other thinker.

Otto, Bodo
(1711–1787)

A Continental Army physician and surgeon, Bodo Otto was born in Hanover, Germany, and immigrated to Pennsylvania with his second wife, Catherina Dorothea Dahncken, and their children after his father's death in 1752. He arrived in Philadelphia in October 1755 and shortly thereafter opened a medical practice with Reimer Landt. In 1756 the partnership ended, and Otto relocated to Germantown, Pennsylvania. From 1756 to 1773, he practiced medicine in several locations in Pennsylvania and New Jersey. In 1773, Otto permanently settled in Reading, Pennsylvania, where he took over Adam Simon Kuhn's apothecary shop and became an active member of the community and the Lutheran Church. In September 1776, Otto married his third wife, Maria Margaretta Paris.

A supporter of the Revolutionary movement in America, Otto joined the Berks County Committee of Safety in 1775. The group, one of several committees organized county by county, was established to help prepare for a

British attack. On 24 June 1776, he represented Berks County at the Pennsylvania Provincial Conference, where he supported a resolution for independence. That same year, the Berks County Committee of Safety chose him, at age sixty-five, as the surgeon for the county's battalion in Pennsylvania's Flying Camp. He served in this capacity at the Battle of Long Island on 27 August 1776. During the winter of 1776–1777, he was stationed at the Bettering House, a commandeered hospital in Philadelphia. On 17 February 1777, in response to General George Washington's directive that all Continental troops be inoculated against smallpox, Otto went to Trenton, New Jersey, and established an inoculation hospital. Following additional transfers to medical facilities in Bethlehem, Pennsylvania, and then to a site near Valley Forge, he was assigned to the hospital at Yellow Springs, Pennsylvania, in 1778. Also located near Valley Forge, the Yellow Springs hospital provided care for chronically ill or severely wounded soldiers in need of extensive rehabilitation. The hospital was continually short of food, clothing, and medical provisions, and Otto successfully wrote, on several occasions, to the Continental Congress and to Quartermaster General Timothy Pickering asking for relief. Even under these conditions, Otto operated a clean and efficient facility. In recognition of his abilities, when the Continental Congress reorganized the army's medical department in 1780, it appointed him to the rank of hospital physician and surgeon for the Continental Army. Attempting to reduce spending in 1781, however, Congress closed several hospitals, including the one at Yellow Springs. Left without an assignment, Otto honorably retired from military service in February 1782. After briefly practicing medicine in Philadelphia and then Baltimore, he returned to Reading in 1784 and continued to work as a physician with his son, John, until his death in June 1787.

BERNADETTE ZBICKI HEINEY

See also

Continental Army; Long Island, Battle of; Pennsylvania; Smallpox

Reference

Gibson, James E. *Dr. Bodo Otto and the Medical Background of the American Revolution.* Baltimore, MD: Charles C. Thomas, 1937.

P

William Paca practiced law, worked with Samuel Chase in support of the Patriot cause, represented Maryland in Congress, signed the Declaration of Independence, held several offices in Maryland during and after the Revolutionary War, and finally served as a U.S. district court judge.

Born in Hartford County, Maryland, Paca attended the College of Philadelphia, from which he graduated in 1759. In 1762 he began the study of law at the Middle Temple in London, where he passed the bar two years later. Paca then returned to Annapolis, Maryland, where he started a prosperous law practice. Because of his wealth, he quickly became one of the most important and influential Patriots in Maryland. He opposed the Stamp Act in 1765 and condemned any British attempt to collect it. He also allied with Chase, and the two of them worked to get Maryland to support the Revolution. From 1771 to 1774, Paca was a member of the Maryland legislature, and as the Revolution began, he joined the local Committee of Correspondence. As a lawyer before the war, he often defended Patriots in the courts.

Paca and Chase were as responsible as any leaders for bringing Maryland into the Revolutionary War. Paca represented Maryland at both the First and Second Continental Congresses, and in 1776, after playing a leading role in persuading the Maryland convention to support the break with Great Britain, he signed the Declaration of Independence. While continuing to serve in the Continental Congress until 1779, he also held several different offices in Maryland's new government.

In August 1776, Paca helped write the new Maryland Constitution. He then served in the Maryland Senate from 1777 until 1779, and in 1778 he was appointed chief judge of the Maryland General Court. Two years later, in 1780, he became the chief justice of the Court of Appeals created by Congress to try admiralty and prize cases. In 1782, he was elected governor of Maryland and was reelected to the position twice, serving until 1785.

In 1788, Paca attended the Maryland convention called to ratify the federal Constitution. He was not happy with the document and proposed twenty-eight amendments to it, but he finally agreed to vote for it as it was

Paca, William
(1740–1799)

in 1788. President George Washington appointed Paca to the federal district court in 1789, a position he held until his death on 13 October 1799.

Dallace W. Unger Jr.

See also
Chase, Samuel; Congress, First Continental; Congress, Second Continental and Confederation; Constitution, United States; Correspondence, Committees of; Declaration of Independence; Stamp Act

References
Barthelmas, Della Gray. *The Signers of the Declaration of Independence.* Jefferson, NC: McFarland, 1997.

Boatner, Mark. *Encyclopedia of the American Revolution.* Mechanicsburg, PA: Stackpole, 1994.

Purcell, L. Edward. *Who Was Who in the American Revolution.* New York: Facts On File, 1993.

Paine, Robert Treat
(1731–1814)

The prominent Massachusetts Revolutionary leader Robert Treat Paine was born in Boston, the son of Thomas Paine, a minister-turned-merchant, and Eunice Treat. He traced his Massachusetts ancestry from the *Mayflower* on his mother's side and from the 1630s on his father's. Paine attended Boston Latin School, graduated from Harvard College in 1749, and prepared for the ministry, a traditional calling of men in his family. But his father's business failure about the time of his graduation discouraged him, and he engaged instead in a number of commercial ventures in North Carolina, Spain, and the Azores, concluding with a whaling voyage to Greenland. He finally turned to the law, studying first in Lancaster, Massachusetts, and then with Benjamin Prat in Boston from 1755 to 1757. Paine also served briefly in 1755 as a chaplain to a Massachusetts force during the French and Indian War. After being admitted to the bar, he moved first to Portland (now in Maine) and then to Taunton, the seat of Bristol County. There he married Sally Cobb, daughter of an iron manufacturer (and sister of David Cobb, the Revolutionary War general), by whom he had eight children. Their son Robert Treat Paine Jr. (1773–1811), who became a poet of some note, was named Thomas at birth but changed his name to avoid confusion with the famous Thomas Paine, whose radical political and religious ideas both he and his father detested.

Paine first came to the attention of the general public during the crisis over the Stamp Act, which he vigorously opposed. In 1768, he served as a delegate to the convention that met to protest Governor Francis Bernard's dissolution of the Massachusetts Assembly, which had sent a circular letter to the other colonies requesting that they cooperate to resist British infringements on their traditional liberty. Paine gained even more attention during the Boston Massacre trials in 1770. Hired by the Town of Boston to prosecute the British soldiers charged with firing on innocent civilians, he raised an underlying constitutional issue, denying that Parliament had the right to quarter a standing army among a civilian population in peacetime. The opposing counsel, John Adams and Josiah Quincy Jr., however, gained even greater celebrity for their successful defense of the soldiers.

With the exception of 1776, Paine was annually elected by Taunton as its representative in Massachusetts's House of Representatives from 1773 to 1778. Assuming a prominent role in the resistance to Britain, he was elected to both the First and Second Continental Congresses. Often fearing that Congress would go too far, however, he became known as "the Objection Maker" to most of the measures that the other delegates proposed. He played a prominent role in obtaining cannon, gunpowder, and saltpeter for the Continental Army. Originally opposed to independence and a supporter of Congress's 1775 Olive Branch Petition, he was nevertheless reelected to Congress and signed the Declaration of Independence, as instructed by the Massachusetts legislature.

In 1777, Paine was elected Speaker of the Massachusetts House of Representatives, and later that same year he became the first attorney general of the newly independent state, a position he held until Governor John Hancock appointed him associate justice of the Massachusetts Supreme Court in 1790. Paine had twice turned down this position and only accepted it after Adams, with whom he had never gotten along, refused to help him obtain a federal judicial post in the new nation. Paine remained on the bench until 1804, when he resigned due to increasing deafness and the tedious requirement of riding circuit throughout the province (which then included Maine).

Paine's most notable service as attorney general included his prominent role in drafting the state's constitution of 1778, which the towns failed to ratify. He also helped revise state laws to conform with the Massachusetts Constitution of 1780 (drafted by his old rival, Adams), which was implemented. A conservative document reflecting both men's political attitudes, the new constitution provided for increasing property requirements for service as assemblyman, senator, and governor. In contrast to most new state constitutions, which minimized executive power, Massachusetts's constitution granted the governor the power to appoint judges and exercise a veto over legislation. Paine also made vigorous efforts to confiscate Loyalist property, but these came to little. More important was his active and successful prosecution of those involved in Shays's Rebellion in 1787; the blacklists of rebels are included in his papers. Although only six of the Shaysites were sentenced to death, and these men had been involved in looting that was only tenuously connected to the rebellion's major actions, Paine's historical reputation has suffered for his vigorous support of James Bowdoin's administration,

Robert Treat Paine, delegate from Massachusetts to the First and Second Continental Congresses. He signed both the Olive Branch Petition and the Declaration of Independence and became the first attorney general of his state. (Library of Congress)

which disfranchised the so-called rebels and refused to pardon their leaders. Nevertheless, the hard work, intelligence, legal skill, and overall fairness that Paine demonstrated in this, as in all the public offices he held, ensured that he retained that office even when the more conciliatory Hancock replaced Bowdoin as governor in 1787. Paine was also noted for his exceptional wit.

Paine moved to Boston in 1780, and that year his interest in science, especially astronomy, led to his election to the newly established American Academy of Arts and Sciences. Like many upper-class Bostonians who were conservative Federalists in politics, he became a Unitarian and religious rationalist. (He was once fined for traveling on the Sabbath to fulfill his judicial duties, even though he himself had drafted the state's Sabbatarian laws.) He died in Boston in 1814 and is buried in the Old Granary Burial Ground.

WILLIAM PENCAK

See also
Adams, John; Boston, Massachusetts; Boston Massacre; Hancock, John; Olive Branch Petition; Shays's Rebellion

References
Hanson, Edward W. "'A Sense of Honor and Duty': Robert Treat Paine (1731–1814) and the New Nation." PhD diss., Boston College, 1992.

Riley, Stephen T., and Edward W. Hanson, eds. "Robert Treat Paine, Papers." *Collections of the Massachusetts Historical Society*, Vols. 87 and 88. Boston: Massachusetts Historical Society, 1992.

Paine, Thomas
(1739–1809)

Thomas Paine was the quintessential Revolutionary propagandist. John Adams, an erstwhile opponent, said that, as a writer, Paine had more influence than any other person during the last quarter of the eighteenth century.

Paine was born in Thetford, Norfolk, England. His father was a Quaker, and his mother an Anglican. After only five years of grammar school education, he was apprenticed to his father as a stay maker for women's corsets. Despite objections from his father, he enlisted on privateers during the Seven Years' War. In 1762 he was appointed an excise tax collector but was dismissed three years later for certain improprieties. In 1768 he was reappointed to the excise service but was again dismissed six years later when he led fellow tax collectors in an unsuccessful unionizing movement that sought increased pay. Facing bankruptcy in a grocery business and divorce from his second wife (his first wife had died in childbirth), he left England for America.

Paine arrived in Philadelphia in November 1774 and almost immediately embraced the American cause against Parliament's new imperial policies. Printer Robert Aitken hired him to edit the monthly *Pennsylvania Magazine*, which Paine increasingly politicized, personally writing about 40 percent of the copy. He became closely associated with other Philadelphia revolutionaries, and on 10 January 1776 he published his electrifying pamphlet *Common Sense*. When other writers such as Adams, Benjamin Franklin, and Benjamin Rush were thought to be the pamphlet's author, Paine quickly claimed credit for the publication and henceforth regularly signed his essays "Common Sense" so that there would be no doubt of his authorship.

In *Common Sense*, Paine drew the distinction between society and government: the former promotes happiness, while the latter restrains vices. Society is always a blessing, but government is at best a necessary evil and "in its worst state an intolerable one." Paine demonstrated the irrationality of monarchy, especially hereditary monarchy. He proclaimed the cause of America to be "the cause of all mankind." The struggle was not for a province or a country but for a continent—not for a day, a year, or an age but for all of posterity. Americans had the opportunity "to begin the world over again. . . . The birthday of a new world is at hand," and a race of men was about "to receive their portion of freedom." Reconciliation was impossible. "We are already greater than the king wishes us to be." Paine called for a manifesto declaring independence and explaining to the world why Americans were "driven to the necessity of breaking off all connection" with Britain. Such a declaration would bind the colonies together and promote foreign assistance. Perhaps, most importantly, Paine argued that Americans could succeed in the arduous military struggle that was expected.

The author of the extremely popular pamphlet *Common Sense*, Thomas Paine probably did more to inspire Americans to seek their independence from Britain and to endeavor to spread the principles of the American Revolution to Europe than any other writer. (Library of Congress)

At the end of *Common Sense*, Paine outlined plans for both state and confederation governments. The new state constitutions should provide single-house assemblies elected annually and unfettered with governors or upper legislative houses. The state legislatures would, however, be subservient to Congress in continental matters. Pennsylvania and Georgia adopted constitutions along Paine's model. Adams and several other Revolutionary leaders, however, denounced such uncontrollable democracy, proposing instead balanced state governments with separate legislative, executive, and judicial powers.

In July 1776, Paine joined the Continental Army and soon became aide-de-camp to General Nathanael Greene as the British chased the American forces out of New York, across New Jersey, and into Pennsylvania. Paine left the army in December and wrote the first essay of his "American Crisis" series, which was read to George Washington's troops on the banks of the Delaware on 23 December 1776, two days before the perilous attack on Trenton. The essay began with great passion: "These are the times that try men's souls. The summer soldier and the sunshine patriot will, in this crisis, shrink from the service of their country; but he that stands it *now*, deserves the love and thanks of man and woman."

In January 1777, Congress appointed Paine to a five-man delegation to meet with leaders of the Iroquois Confederacy in an attempt to secure their support for the American cause. Three months later, he was appointed secretary to Congress's Committee for Foreign Affairs, but within two years he was forced to resign because of his public statements, based on secret documents, acknowledging French assistance to America before the formal alliance between the two countries, concluded in February 1778, had been announced. In November 1779, he became the clerk of the Pennsylvania Assembly. In this capacity he wrote the preamble of the first legislative act providing for the gradual but complete emancipation of slaves in that state.

As the fiscal crisis of the Revolutionary War deepened, Paine repeatedly wrote essays boosting American morale and encouraging the wealthy to create a bank and contribute financially to the war effort. In December 1780 he wrote *Public Good*, a pamphlet arguing that Virginia's huge land holdings west of the Appalachians rightly belonged in the national domain. Although many prominent Virginians promptly denounced him, their state's legislature ceded to Congress all of its land claims northwest of the Ohio River in 1781. *Public Good* also called for a national convention that would instill new confidence in Congress by increasing its powers.

Throughout most of 1780, Paine formulated a plan for him to return clandestinely to England and undermine its war effort from within. The American capture and execution of British Major John André in the fall of 1780 for his involvement in Benedict Arnold's treason, however, convinced Paine that such a daring plan might be foolhardy and end in his own execution. Instead, he proposed a mission to Versailles to request additional funds from the French. Congress appointed John Laurens of South Carolina as its official envoy to perform this task, and Paine's enemies were able to prevent his appointment as secretary to the delegation. Paine, however, accompanied Laurens as an unofficial, unpaid advisor. The delegation arrived in France on 9 March 1781, and the French people warmly received the illustrious author of *Common Sense*. With the assistance of Franklin, the delegation obtained French government loans and gifts amounting to 25 million livres.

As the war wound down Paine returned to America, where he was secretly employed by Superintendent of Finance Robert Morris, Secretary for Foreign Affairs Robert R. Livingston, and General Washington as a propagandist to write "in support of the measures of Congress and their Ministers." Paid $800 annually from secret service funds, Paine was to lobby for more powers for Congress, prepare the minds of the people for more taxes, and comment favorably on military activities.

When word arrived from Europe that a preliminary peace treaty had been signed, Paine readied his last essay of the "American Crisis" series for publication. Designating it as essay number thirteen (three other essays in the series were unnumbered), this last essay was printed on 19 April 1783, the eighth anniversary of the battles at Lexington and Concord. The essay began "'The times that tried men's souls,' are over—and the greatest and compleatest revolution the world ever knew is gloriously and happily accomplished." Paine now encouraged Americans to maintain and strengthen the

Union and increase the powers of Congress. Throughout the next few years, he wrote similar essays as well as political and economic pieces in the employ of Morris, favoring not only the establishment of the Bank of North America (1784) but the policies of Pennsylvania's Republican Party in opposition to his former political allies, the state's Constitutionalist Party, who denounced him as an unprincipled propagandist who let his pen out for hire.

Much of Paine's time after the Revolutionary War, however, was devoted to designing an iron bridge capable of spanning the Schuylkill and other wide rivers. He left America in April 1787 to seek endorsements for his bridge design from European scientific communities. An expected year or two absence turned into more than fifteen years, during which time he became embroiled in the politics of the French Revolution. While in England, he wrote his two-volume *Rights of Man* (1791), which denounced Edmund Burke's criticism of the French Revolution and again attacked monarchy. This British equivalent of *Common Sense* provoked a firestorm in Britain for which Paine, who fled the country, was tried and convicted in absentia for seditious libel.

In August 1792, Paine was made an honorary French citizen and was elected to the French National Convention, one of only two foreigners to serve in that body. He aligned himself with the moderate Girondists, and in 1793 he argued unsuccessfully against the execution of King Louis XVI. When the radical Jacobins took control of the convention, they instituted their Reign of Terror, revoked Paine's French citizenship, and incarcerated him for almost a year in Luxembourg Prison in Paris. Only through the private efforts of James Monroe, America's new minister to France, was Paine released. In a public letter to Washington, Paine bitterly denounced the president for failing to use his influence to gain his release, declaring, "He has acted towards me the part of a cold blooded traitor." While in prison, Paine also began his last great work, the two-volume *Age of Reason* (1794–1795), which espoused Deism and critically attacked orthodox religions, especially Christianity. The Bible, Paine wrote, was not the word of God; that was to be found only in the creation of the universe visible every day in nature.

Paine returned to America in 1802, during a brief respite in the twenty-year struggle between Britain and France. Disembarking in Baltimore, he was welcomed in Washington, D.C., at the Executive Mansion by President Thomas Jefferson, who on various occasions sought his old friend's advice on such matters as the American navy and the purchase of the Louisiana Territory. Paine left Washington in February 1803 and met with both praise and criticism on his journey to New York City, where he was welcomed as a hero. To many Americans, however, he was vilified as the devil incarnate, both for his anti-Christian *Age of Reason* and for his harsh attack on Washington. During his last years, Paine lived in poverty and despair outside New York City while suffering from the effects of alcoholism. He died on 8 June 1809. A decade later, his exhumed body was sent to Britain for a special honorary burial, but his remains were lost and have never been recovered.

Paine's talent for writing was remarkable. Rush, who suggested to Paine the title *Common Sense*, observed that "he possessed a wonderful talent of

"I am a farmer of thoughts."
—Thomas Paine

writing to the tempers and feelings of the public. . . . His compositions, though full of splendid and original imagery, were always adapted to the common capacities." In a 1778 letter to Henry Laurens, then president of Congress, Paine wrote that he was "neither farmer, manufacturer, mechanic, merchant nor shopkeeper." Rather, he said, "I am a *Farmer of thoughts*." In his will, written five months prior to his death, Paine wrote that "I have lived an honest and useful life to mankind; my time has been spent in doing good, and I die in perfect composure and resignation to the will of my Creator, God."

JOHN P. KAMINSKI

See also
Adams, John; Jefferson, Thomas; Morris, Robert; Pennsylvania; Rush, Benjamin

References
Foner, Eric, ed. *Thomas Paine: Collected Writings*. New York: Library of America, 1995.
———. *Tom Paine and Revolutionary America*. London and New York: Oxford University Press, 1976.
Fruchtman, Jack, Jr. *Thomas Paine: Apostle of Freedom*. New York: Four Walls Eight Windows, 1994.
Hawke, David Freeman. *Paine*. New York: Norton, 1974.
Kaminski, John P., ed. *Citizen Paine: Thomas Paine's Thoughts on Man, Government, Society, and Religion*. Lanham, MD: Rowman and Littlefield, 2002.
Keane, John. *Tom Paine: A Political Life*. Boston: Little, Brown, 1995.

Paoli, Battle of
(20–21 September 1777)

On the night of 20–21 September 1777, a division of 1,500 Continental soldiers commanded by Brigadier General Anthony Wayne was surprised in camp near Paoli, Pennsylvania, by Major-General Charles Grey at the head of a British force of 5,000 men. After the clash of American and Anglo-German armies in the Battle of Brandywine on 11 September, General George Washington had fallen back to Reading Furnace. The British commander, General William Howe, had encamped at Swede's Ford, between Washington's Continentals and Philadelphia, thus posing a threat to the city. All that Washington could do in response was to send Wayne, Brigadier General William Maxwell, and Brigadier General William Smallwood in separate units to harass the rear of Howe's army as it continued to advance. Perhaps they could delay Howe long enough to allow the main American army to rest and again challenge the British drive on Philadelphia.

Wayne was pleased with this assignment. On the evening of 18 September, he marched with his men south and east around the British rear and encamped between Paoli and White Horse Tavern, near the Lancaster Road. He was stationed only 4 miles from the British Army and was outnumbered ten to one. But he was undaunted, believing that his presence was unknown to the enemy. His intention was to unite his force with Maxwell's and carry out a joint operation against Howe. Wayne requested that Maxwell join him,

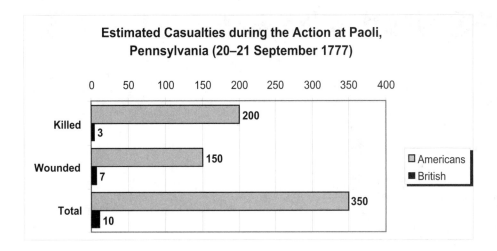

Estimated Casualties during the Action at Paoli, Pennsylvania (20–21 September 1777)

but on the morning of 19 September, Maxwell had not appeared. On his own, Wayne conducted a reconnaissance with his troops but learned that the British Army remained in its cantonment and was too concentrated to assault.

Wayne therefore drew his men back to their camp and wrote to Washington, urging him to attack Howe immediately while Wayne and Maxwell struck the British from two directions. Washington's army did not arrive, however, and by the evening of 20 September, Wayne prepared his troops for the night, posting a routine number of pickets and mounted patrols around his encampment. He intended to attack the British the following morning as his orders called for, whether or not he received support from Washington or Maxwell. At about 9:00 P.M., he learned from a local citizen that the British were aware of his presence and intended to attack him that night. Immediately, Wayne bolstered the number of guards and pickets around his camp, placing one on the Swedesford Road, the one that the enemy would use to advance against him that night.

Indeed, Howe was apprised of Wayne's presence and had pinpointed the position of his camp. Obviously, he could not allow Washington's detachments to lurk about his flanks and rear as he resumed his march toward Philadelphia. Hence, on the afternoon of 20 September, Howe ordered Grey to conduct a surprise assault on Wayne's camp during the coming night, thereby also scaring off other enemy detachments. For this service, Howe chose the 2nd Light Infantry Battalion, the 42nd and 44th Regiments, and a squadron from the 16th Dragoons. He ordered another detachment, consisting of the 40th and 55th Regiments, commanded by Lieutenant-Colonel Thomas Musgrave, to cooperate with Grey by blocking Wayne's retreat should he attempt to escape along the Lancaster Road. Grey ordered his men to remove the flints from their muskets, in order to avoid alerting the enemy, and to rely on their bayonets as they attacked. Hence, he earned the nickname of "No Flint Grey."

As Grey's men approached Wayne's camp, they ran into the American sentries and pickets, and shots were fired. Instantly, Wayne was alert to the enemy presence, and he ordered his men to arms. Within ten minutes his soldiers were firing at the attacking British on his right, where the artillery was parked. Not knowing the size of the enemy force, he ordered a general withdrawal

ACTION AT PAOLI, 20–21 SEPTEMBER 1777

Fagleysville

Limerick

Skippack

Parker's Ford

WASHINGTON
Evansburg

Royer's Ford

Gorden's Ford

Pauling's Ford

Whitemarsh

Flatland's Ford

Yellow Springs

Valley Forge

King of Prussia

Swede's Ford

Schuylkill R.

Valley Store

Guelph

Battle of the Clouds

Paoli

WAYNE

HOWE

PENNSYLVANIA

Darby Creek

Turk's Head
(West Chester)

CORNWALLIS

Philadelphia

Darby

HOWE
12,000

WASHINGTON
9,000

Ft. Mifflin

Ft. Mercer

Chester

Billingsport

Brandywine Creek

Delaware R.

NEW JERSEY

DELAWARE

Wilmington

Newport

■	American troops
□	British troops
→	American troop movement
→	British troop movement
	Hill

0   3   6 mi

0   3   6 km

westward along White Horse Road and directed his light infantry and 1st Regiment of cavalry to oppose Grey's assault. After firing at the British, Wayne's men were compelled to give way to the weight of the enemy attack. In an attempt to save his cannon and continue his withdrawal, Wayne formed the 4th Regiment for another volley, but Grey chose not to attack. Finally, behind the protective shield of the 4th Regiment, the Americans got their cannon on the road to White Horse Tavern, and the other troops also withdrew.

About 1,000 yards up White Horse Road, Wayne attempted in vain to rally his demoralized men to oppose Grey's triumphant troops. The British infantry, overtaking many of the fugitives, stabbed them in great numbers and pressed on their rear until Grey decided to call an end to the carnage. At last Wayne reached the Red Lion Tavern, where he united his men with Smallwood's, halted his withdrawal, and reported the action to Washington. Just before daybreak on 21 September, Grey returned in triumph to Howe's camp. When the results of the carnage were assessed, it was learned that Grey's bayonets had killed about 200 Americans and wounded 150 more. Grey had lost only 3 men killed and 7 wounded. Grey's reputation among the British was enhanced by this action, but among Americans he became a monster who had perpetrated a massacre. Wayne's reputation was also damaged, although a court-martial later exonerated him of any responsibility. Ironically, Wayne insisted on calling the action a battle because he wanted to escape responsibility for such a lopsided enemy triumph.

PAUL DAVID NELSON

See also
Brandywine, Battle of; Grey, Charles; Maxwell, William; Philadelphia Campaign; Smallwood, William; Wayne, Anthony

References
Nelson, Paul David. *Anthony Wayne: Soldier of the Early Republic.* Bloomington: Indiana University Press, 1985.
———. *Sir Charles Grey, First Earl Grey: Royal Soldier, Family Patriarch.* Madison, NJ: Fairleigh Dickinson University Press, 1996.
Reed, John F. *Campaign to Valley Forge: July 1 to December 19, 1777.* Philadelphia: University of Pennsylvania Press, 1965.
Stillé, Charles J. *Major-General Anthony Wayne and the Pennsylvania Line in the Continental Army.* Philadelphia: Lippincott, 1893.

Paris, Treaty of
(1763)

Along with the Treaty of Fontainebleau (signed between France and Spain) and the Treaty of Hubertusburg (signed among Prussia, Austria, and Saxony), the Treaty of Paris marked the end of the Seven Years' War (including its North American component, the French and Indian War) in Europe, India, Africa, and the Americas. Signed on 10 February 1763 at Paris, the treaty bound Kings George III of Great Britain, Louis XV of France, Charles

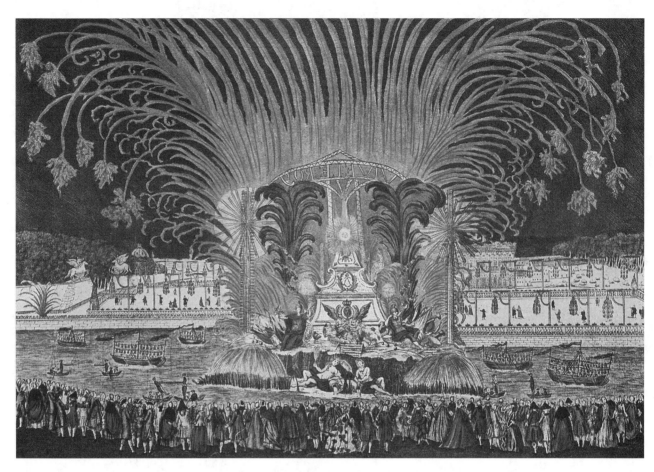

Fireworks display at Place Louis XV, celebrating peace after the Seven Years' (French and Indian) War, and the dedication of an equestrian statue to the king on 22 June 1763. (Giraudon/Art Resource, New York)

III of Spain, and Joseph I of Portugal through their respective ambassadors, the Duke of Bedford, the Duc de Choiseul, the Marquis Grimaldi, and Martin de Mello and Castro.

The treaty marked a great victory for the British, as France ceded to Britain all of Canada and all other French-held territory in North America east of the Mississippi River (except the city of New Orleans), Grenada and the Grenadine Islands in the West Indies, and all French possessions, including lucrative slave fortresses, on the Senegal River in West Africa. The French also agreed not to garrison any territory they had recovered from the British in India, a provision that gave Britain preeminence there. Additionally, Spain gave up all of Florida to Great Britain, including St. Augustine and Pensacola, and the island of Minorca in the Mediterranean Sea and allowed the British logging rights in Honduras. France and Spain both agreed to a border running down the center of the Mississippi River and to free navigation of the river for all parties. For their part, the British agreed to allow Catholics in all former French and Spanish colonies to practice their faith to the degree permitted under British law. The acquisitions gave Great Britain a formidable overseas empire and important advantages in the Atlantic slave trade and the Indian fur trade.

France, which lost most of its American empire in the treaty, did retain the islands of St. Pierre and Macquilon, south of Newfoundland, as fishing bases but was forbidden to fortify them, and the British returned Guadeloupe and Martinique in the West Indies to French rule. The French agreed to abide by a significant offshore boundary for fishing off the coast of Canada; to return all land seized in Europe during the course of the hostilities, including parts of Hanover, Hesse, and Brunswick; and to replace any artillery taken from them during the occupation. Spain received Cuba and the Philippines back from Britain in exchange for Florida and an agreement allowing British admiralty courts to judge prize cases for ships seized after the peace treaty went into effect but before it could be communicated to the theaters of war. Through the Treaty of Fontainebleau, concluded shortly before the Treaty of Paris, France ceded Louisiana and New Orleans to Spain in compensation for its loss of Florida to Britain.

The Treaty of Paris signaled a significant shift in the power of European colonial empires, with France reduced to a shadow of its former possessions and Britain in command of nearly all of North America and in virtual possession of India and key points in West Africa. Britain had to deal with the colonization of West Florida, the management of French Native American allies in North America, and the problem of a majority French Catholic population in Quebec. These stresses, combined with the war debt incurred in the course of the war, for which the treaty offered no indemnity, proved a major political issue for the British government and soon led to British policies that alienated its older North American colonies. These new policies, in turn, led to the imperial crisis of the 1770s, culminating in the American Revolution.

MARGARET SANKEY

See also

Diplomacy, British; Diplomacy, French; France; Great Britain; Native Americans; Spain

References

Anderson, Fred. *Crucible of War: The Seven Years' War and the Fate of Empire in British North America, 1754–1766*. London: Vintage, 2001.

Nester, William. *The First Global War: Britain, France, and the Fate of North America, 1756–1775*. Westport, CT: Praeger, 2000.

Rashed, Zenab Esmat. *The Peace of Paris, 1763*. Liverpool: Liverpool University Press, 1951.

Paris, Treaty of
(1783)

The Treaty of Paris of 1783 was the Anglo-American peace settlement that ended the American War of Independence. The definitive peace treaty was signed in Paris on 3 September 1783, but it was virtually identical to the provisional peace treaty signed on 30 November 1782. The peace settlement made generous provisions for the United States, recognizing the new nation's independence and awarding it liberal concessions in terms of boundaries, fisheries, and other interests.

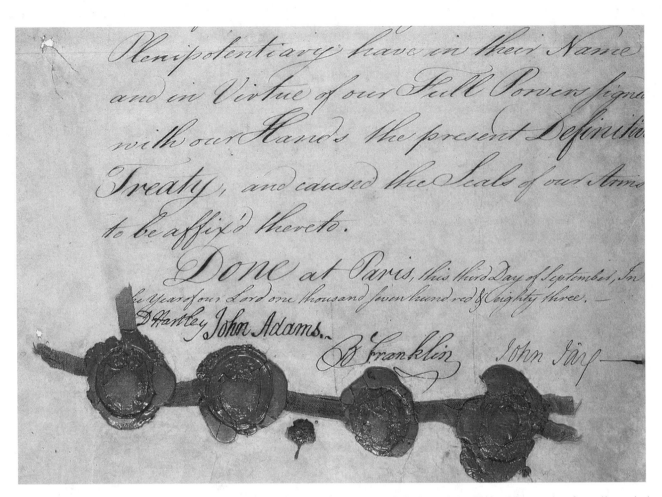

Signature page of the Treaty of Paris, 3 September 1783, between Great Britain and the United States that formally ended the Revolutionary War. (National Archives and Records Administration)

American independence had become inevitable when war weariness and the British defeat at the Battle of Yorktown prompted the House of Commons to renounce offensive warfare in America in February 1782. The ministry of Lord Frederick North fell in March, and the treaty recognizing American independence was, in all essential respects, framed during the ministry of William Petty-Fitzmaurice, Lord Shelburne (July 1782–February 1783). Shelburne decided to offer generous terms to America in an attempt to break the Franco-American Alliance, to revive American goodwill toward Britain, and to reestablish Anglo-American trade on its former footing.

Shelburne was concerned that were America to move permanently into France's orbit, Britain's traditional enemy would be strengthened unacceptably. An Anglo-American peace would enable Britain to pressure the other belligerents—France, Spain, and the Netherlands—to lower their own peace terms. Shelburne was also motivated by a desire for Anglo-American reconciliation. Writing to Richard Oswald, whom he had sent to Paris in July 1782 to begin negotiations with Benjamin Franklin (who was both an American peace commissioner and America's minister to France), Shelburne noted that although he had hoped for reunion between Britain and its colonies, since America would settle for nothing less than independence, "if it is given up, . . . it shall be done *decidedly,* so as to avoid all future Risque of Enmity, and lay the Foundation of a new Connection better adapted to the present Temper and Instincts of both Countries."

In entering this treaty, Shelburne hoped that Britain and America could resume trading on much the same basis as before the war. America would remain an expanding market for British manufactures and reexports and would continue to be an important source of raw materials for British industry and commerce. The prime minister's domestic political difficulties (he lacked a firm base of support in the House of Commons) provided further motivation to conclude a peace settlement as quickly as possible. Shelburne believed that since Parliament had demanded peace with America, he needed to obtain this during Parliament's summer adjournment to shore up his ministry.

Yet despite Shelburne's willingness to settle a quick and generous peace, negotiations were delayed through July and August 1782. The arrival in Paris of John Jay, who was both an American peace commissioner and America's envoy to Spain, to assist Franklin in the peace negotiations slowed down those negotiations. Suspicious of Shelburne, who had opposed American independence when he was in opposition (believing reconciliation was still possible if war was abandoned), Jay demanded that Britain recognize American independence before any serious negotiations commenced. By September, Shelburne had decided to concede the point if needed, but this was avoided when Jay reversed himself on hearing that the French foreign minister, Charles Gravier, the comte de Vergennes, had sent his undersecretary, Gérard de Rayneval, to hold secret discussions with Shelburne. Fearing that Britain and France were preparing their own settlement at the expense of America, Jay dropped his demand for an immediate recognition of American independence, agreeing instead that an amendment to Oswald's commission would suffice (whereby the American peace commissioners were described as acting for the "thirteen United States of America").

During the two months that negotiations were delayed, Britain successfully defended Gibraltar against Spain, France sent Rayneval to Britain and commenced serious negotiations of their conflict, and in the British cabinet dissatisfaction with Shelburne's policy of generosity to America had time to fester. By the time the two parties began to negotiate in earnest in early October 1782, Britain had raised its demands in almost all areas. In September, Oswald had been authorized, if needed, to waive the claims of American Loyalists whose properties had been seized by America's Revolutionary governments and of British merchants for debts incurred before 1775. In October, he was instructed to revive the claims of British creditors and Loyalists and to press the king's right to the "western lands" (situated between the Appalachian Mountains and the Mississippi River) should America decline to compensate the Loyalists. American demands to dry fish along Newfoundland's coasts were rejected (on the grounds that it would lead to disputes), together with Jay's proposal for reciprocal free trade (this being a matter for Parliament to determine). And Henry Strachey, an undersecretary at the home office, was sent to Paris to strengthen Oswald's resolve.

Despite Britain's new determination to defend its interests, the negotiations were completed relatively quickly. John Adams, America's ranking peace commissioner who had also represented American interests in the Netherlands, arrived in Paris in late October to join Franklin and Jay. Adams reinforced Jay's suspicions of the French and his belief in the need to settle with Britain before Britain settled with France, and the two persuaded Franklin to risk alienating the French to gain a peace quickly. Henry Laurens, whom Congress had also named to the peace commission, only joined the other American envoys the day before the provisional treaty was signed. On the British side, it was Shelburne's vision that dominated the Anglo-American peace settlement. The United States obtained extensive boundaries allowing considerable room for expansion, its fishermen retained considerable fishing rights in British North America, and Shelburne accepted minimal guarantees of compensation for the Loyalists.

The United States received, in addition to the Atlantic seaboard of its thirteen states, all the territory between the Appalachians, the Mississippi, and the Great Lakes. Shelburne had refused an earlier overture by Franklin for the cession of Canada but had been willing to cede the Nipissing Country (present-day southern Ontario) as originally proposed by Jay. Shelburne was able to avoid doing so when the Americans failed to press for it. The treaty provided for free navigation of the Mississippi River to its mouth, but this provision was unenforceable once the Anglo-Spanish peace settlement of 1783 conferred East and West Florida upon Spain, giving it control of the mouth and both banks of the lower river.

Adams partially succeeded in protecting the fishing interests that were so important to his native New England. Americans were given the right to take fish from the Newfoundland and Gulf of St. Lawrence fishing banks and the liberty (but not the right) to take fish from the British area of the Newfoundland coast. Americans were denied the right to dry and cure fish in the bays or creeks of Newfoundland but were allowed to do so on the shores of Nova Scotia, the Magdalen Islands, and Labrador for as long as those areas remained unsettled.

Insofar as British creditors were concerned, the Americans declared that they had no intention of cheating anyone and that all American debts, contracted both before and after 1775, would be made recoverable. The American envoys said that they were not authorized to offer any compensation for the losses of the Loyalists, and Franklin insisted that any such claim would be met by a demand for British reparation for damage to American property. Shelburne pressed the necessity to satisfy the Loyalists to achieve a true reconciliation (and so that he could satisfy the popular clamor to support those who had remained loyal to Britain). The end result was a compromise fashioned by Oswald, namely that Congress would "earnestly recommend" to the states that they restore the Loyalists' property. While the Americans exceeded their instructions on this point, Britain failed to obtain any meaningful guarantee that the Loyalists would in fact be compensated. Nevertheless, as Shelburne later noted to Parliament, Britain could always recompense them itself and would find this to be less expensive than continuing the war.

The provisional Anglo-American peace treaty upset the calculations of Vergennes. In June 1781, Congress had instructed the American peace commissioners to keep France informed of their negotiations and to follow French advice. Vergennes had been willing to countenance separate negotiations but expected these to coalesce in a general peace. The Franco-American Alliance (1778) prohibited either party from making peace with Britain without the consent of the other. While the treaty of 30 November 1782 was provisional and would only take effect upon the conclusion of an Anglo-French peace, in reality it removed America from the war. It placed pressure on both France and Spain to accept lesser terms than they might have achieved and conclude a peace settlement promptly or face the danger of renewed warfare with a Britain that was no longer pinned down in America. Nevertheless, France had achieved its primary war aim. Vergennes had gone to war for American independence and the heavy blow this would deliver to British prestige, trade, and political power.

The American commissioners' suspicion of France was accompanied by their strong dislike of Spain. Although Spain had provided America with some money and matériel and had diverted British men and resources to Florida, the West Indies, and the Mediterranean, Jay had been offended by Spain's refusal to ally with or recognize America and by its rejection of American claims to the western lands and the free navigation of the Mississippi. Jay took up one of Oswald's ideas and secretly encouraged Britain to attack Spain in West Florida. The Anglo-American treaty included a secret article granting Britain a more favorable boundary should it hold West Florida at the end of the war.

Britain signed preliminary peace treaties with France and Spain on 20 January 1783. But Shelburne's handling of the peace negotiations was immediately attacked in Parliament, and he resigned in February 1783 after the House of Commons censured the peace treaties. The new government (the Fox-North coalition) appointed David Hartley to replace Oswald and to negotiate both a commercial treaty and the definitive peace with America. While Hartley, like Shelburne, proposed allowing Americans to continue sharing in free trade with Britain and its colonies, the Fox-North government was much less friendly. An order-in-council on 14 May 1783 allowed free access to Britain for American raw materials but made it clear that both American manufactures and American ships carrying goods from other countries would be denied entry to British ports. An order-in-council on 2 July 1783 substantially restricted American access to the British West Indies.

Preoccupied with European concerns, Britain's foreign secretary, Charles James Fox, paid little attention to the American negotiations and took almost four weeks to inform Hartley of the order-in-council of 2 July. On 4 August 1783, Fox instructed Hartley to put commercial arrangements aside and to conclude a definitive treaty on exactly the same terms found in the preliminary treaty of the past November. The Anglo-American definitive peace treaty was signed in Paris on 3 September, several hours before the Anglo-French and Anglo-Spanish definitive treaties were signed at Versailles. The British and American ratifications of the treaty were exchanged on 12 May 1784, thus formally ending the American Revolutionary War.

Almost in spite of Fox, Anglo-American trade revived and entered a boom period by the end of the 1780s. Common ties of language, religion, customs, and habit meant that American trade abandoned the French and returned to British merchants. Political relations between Britain and America, however, remained distant. Shelburne's policy of generosity and reconciliation ended with his departure from office. During the 1780s Britain became increasingly critical of American state governments, several of which continued to persecute Loyalists and refused to facilitate the collection of money owed to British creditors. (Scarcity of money and depreciation of assets, however, meant that many small debtors, and in the South even many large debtors, were in fact unable to pay.) Britain in return refused to vacate nine forts in the Northwest and continued its exclusionary policy in the West Indies. A settlement of several of these issues was only reached in 1794. The so-called Jay Treaty of that year provided for British withdrawal from the forts by 1796, the opening of the West Indies trade to small American vessels, and the establishment of a commission to provide compensation for British creditors (£600,000 was finally awarded in 1802). Disputes over the exact boundaries with Spanish Florida and British Canada continued well into the nineteenth century, and conflicting interpretations over American fishing rights off Newfoundland went on even longer. But the Treaty of Paris held and has proved enduring.

ANDREW STOCKLEY

See also

Adams, John; Fox, Charles James; Franklin, Benjamin; Gravier, Charles, Comte de Vergennes; Hartley, David; Jay, John; Laurens, Henry; Loyalists; Oswald, Richard; Petty-Fitzmaurice, William, 2nd Earl of Shelburne; Versailles, Treaty of

References

Dull, Jonathan R. "Diplomacy of the Revolution, to 1783." Pp. 352–361 in *A Companion to the American Revolution*. Edited by Jack P. Greene and J. R. Pole. Malden, MA: Blackwell, 2000.

———. *A Diplomatic History of the American Revolution*. New Haven, CT: Yale University Press, 1985.

Fitzmaurice, Lord Edmond. *Life of William, Earl of Shelburne*, Vol. 3. London: Macmillan, 1876.

Harlow, Vincent T. *The Founding of the Second British Empire, 1763–1793*, Vol. 1, *Discovery and Revolution*. London: Longmans, Green, 1952.

Hoffman, Ronald, and Peter J. Albert, eds. *Peace and the Peacemakers: The Treaty of 1783*. Charlottesville: University of Virginia Press, 1986.

Hutson, James. *John Adams and the Diplomacy of the American Revolution*. Lexington: University Press of Kentucky, 1980.

Morris, Richard B. *The Peacemakers: The Great Powers and American Independence*. New York: Harper and Row, 1965.

Scott, H. M. *British Foreign Policy in the Age of the American Revolution*. New York: Oxford University Press, 1990.

Stockley, Andrew. *Britain and France at the Birth of America: The European Powers and the Peace Negotiations of 1782–1783*. Exeter, UK: University of Exeter Press, 2001.

Commander of the Lexington Minutemen, Captain John Parker's actions on 19 April 1775 helped to start the American Revolutionary War. Contrary to legend, he had no intention of actually confronting the British at Lexington and instead hoped to uphold his town's honor while avoiding a fight.

Born and raised in Lexington, Massachusetts, Parker came from one of the town's influential families, a family that had lived in Lexington for four generations and played a prominent role in the community's politics. He gained military experience in the French and Indian War, where he served as a member of Rogers's Rangers. Following this conflict, he returned to Lexington and became a successful farmer, supporting a wife and seven children, and a respected member of the community. In the winter of 1774–1775, Lexington established a company of minutemen and elected Parker captain.

Shortly after midnight on 19 April, Parker was warned of an approaching British force and ordered his company to gather on the Lexington Common. He had never received instructions explaining how to proceed if the British actually marched into Lexington, so he adopted the militia custom of conferring with his men to decide on a course of action. The company agreed not to oppose the British but rather to allow them to pass through the town unmolested. Parker then dismissed the men, ordered them to remain ready, and sent out several scouts to ascertain the location of the British.

At 4:30 A.M., one of the scouts galloped into Lexington and informed Parker that the British were coming up the road on their way to Concord. Parker immediately ordered the alarm sounded. He placed his company of seventy-seven men on the Common but made sure not to block the road to Concord, intending to "maintain the honor of the company and the town" while not provoking an engagement. As the British approached, Parker ordered his men to move farther away from the road, clearly seeking to avoid a fight. At that moment, an unknown individual fired a shot, and the battle began, concluding quickly as the British routed Parker's command.

Following the engagement, Parker reassembled his company and, assuming that the British would retreat from Concord through Lexington, set up an ambush. The British, harassed by other minutemen companies, walked into Parker's trap. Though his command was routed again, Parker's troops managed to inflict several casualties and delay the British, allowing other minutemen companies to get in front of the British column. In May, Parker and his company participated in the siege of Boston, but four months later he died of tuberculosis.

DAVID WORK

See also

Lexington and Concord; Militia, Patriot and Loyalist; Minutemen

References

Galvin, John R. *The Minute Men: The First Fight; Myths & Realities of the American Revolution.* 2nd ed. New York: Pergamon-Brassey's, 1989.

Tourtellot, Arthur Bernon. *Lexington and Concord: The Beginnings of the War of the American Revolution.* New York: Norton, 1963.

Parker, John
(1729–1775)

Parker's Ferry, South Carolina, Action at

(30 August 1781)

The engagement at Parker's Ferry occurred southwest of Charleston as the British forces based there were attempting to raise Loyalist militia south of the city in the late summer of 1781. The battle prevented them from rallying the support they needed to sustain their faltering southern campaign.

British Major Thomas Fraser led approximately 200 British dragoons from Charleston to provide moral support to Loyalist militia south of the Edisto River. Patriot militia General Francis Marion (the "Swamp Fox") learned of Fraser's movement from Continental General Nathanael Greene and rode to the area with 200 men to join Colonel William Harden, the Patriot militia commander in the Edisto River area. Marion's men rode quickly and at night in order to mask their arrival in the area south of Charleston. South Carolina Patriots were especially eager to engage Fraser following his arrest of Isaac Hayne, a local Patriot leader. Hayne had been accused of violating his parole from an earlier capture by British forces and was executed under questionable circumstances after being seized by Fraser.

Knowing that Fraser's men were south of the Edisto River, Marion opted to set an ambush at Parker's Ferry on the main road to Charleston. On 30 August 1781, he dispatched a small detachment to lure the dragoons onto a causeway leading toward the ferry while the rest of his men waited in the swamp. After feigning surprise, his detachment turned toward the causeway with Fraser's dragoons in close pursuit. As the dragoons rode past the swamp, Marion's concealed men rose and opened fire at close range with buckshot. The first volley from the Patriot troops spread panic among the British force when the buckshot brought down men and horses. As Fraser attempted to rally his dragoons for a charge into the Patriot position, a second and then a third volley from Marion's men shattered the British ranks. But a large band of Loyalist militia (some estimates place the total at over 400) was following Fraser's men. As his troops were low on ammunition, Marion opted to withdraw from the area upon seeing the Loyalist militia approaching his position.

Approximately 200 British dragoons had entered the ambush zone and met quick defeat at the hands of the Patriots under Marion. Sources differ as to the number of casualties, but some place the British losses as high as one half of their total force. There were no reported casualties among the Patriot militia. The engagement at Parker's Ferry helped to prevent the British from raising large numbers of Loyalist militia in the Edisto River area. The battle is also significant in that it is seen as a measure of revenge for the execution of Hayne.

Terry M. Mays

See also
Marion, Francis

References
Bass, Robert. *Swamp Fox: The Life and Campaigns of General Francis Marion.* 1959. Reprint, Orangeburg, SC: Sandlapper, 1989.
Lumpkin, Henry. *From Savannah to Yorktown: The American Revolution in the South.* New York: Paragon, 1981.

**Parsons,
Samuel Holden**
(1737–1789)

Samuel Holden Parsons served as a major general in the Continental Army and played a major role in recruiting soldiers. After the war, he played a prominent role in Connecticut affairs and in western settlement and served briefly as chief judge of the Northwest Territory until his untimely death by drowning in the Ohio Country.

Parsons was born at Lyme, Connecticut, on 14 May 1737. His father was a minister who married a daughter of Judge John Griswold, one of the wealthiest men in town. This background helped ensure young Parsons's early and rapid political advancement, as his mother's family had many men of prominence in Connecticut, including both judges and governors. His family moved to Massachusetts when he was quite young, and he entered Harvard at age fifteen and graduated in 1756, receiving both a bachelor's and a master's degree. Among his college acquaintances were John Hancock, Jonathan Trumbull, and John Adams. Parsons would later receive honorary degrees from Yale. After his graduation, he returned to Lyme to study law under his uncle, Matthew Griswold. In 1759 Parsons was admitted to the bar of New London County, and in 1761 he married Mehetable Mather, the daughter of Richard Mather of Lyme. In 1762 Parsons was elected a member of the General Assembly of Connecticut and was continuously reelected until he moved to New London in 1774. He also received several appointments of civil responsibility, including in 1773 appointment as the king's prosecuting attorney for New London County and later for the entire colony.

By this date, however, Parsons was becoming thoroughly disenchanted with British policy. In a letter of 3 March 1773 to Samuel Adams, Parsons became one of the first persons to suggest assembling a congress of all the colonies to consider American grievances, an idea that became a reality in Philadelphia in 1774. And as an active member of the local committee of correspondence, he roused his countrymen to resist British authority.

Parsons was named a colonel in the Connecticut militia on 20 April 1775, the day after the clashes at Lexington and Concord. He served for seven months in his state's forces during the siege of Boston and fought at Bunker Hill before joining the Continental Army in the fall. Congress appointed the thirty-nine-year-old Parsons a brigadier general on 9 August 1776, almost a month after the promotion of his fellow Connecticut officer, Benedict Arnold of New Haven, at age thirty-six the youngest of the appointees of Congress from Connecticut to this rank.

Parsons commanded forces at some important battle sites, including the disastrous American rout at Kips Bay in Manhattan in September 1776, but his great contribution to the war was in recruiting, organizing, and maintaining the

> Samuel Parsons became one of the first persons to suggest assembling a congress of all the colonies.

Connecticut line and protecting the state against invasion. This task, however, was not without its problems. Parsons was particularly concerned about his lack of authority to make contracts to supply his troops. Whatever he might do without such authority must be his individual responsibility, as was the expedition to capture Fort Ticonderoga that he helped organize in May 1775. Other generals had been given this authority, but not the commandant of that fort, and Parsons's brigade was lacking in essential clothing because of this oversight.

In the spring of 1778, Parsons, depressed by his failing health, frustrated by Congress's failure to send promised supplies to his suffering troops, and burdened with anxiety at the depreciation in currency and the rise of prices that left his own family without vital support, decided to resign from the army. He wrote to John Jay, the president of Congress, but Congress took no action, and Parsons remained in the service. He also had friction with his superior, Arnold, who, unwilling to work with Parsons and with a secret agenda, requested a transfer to the command of the fort at West Point (which Parsons had earlier commanded). There Arnold's treachery was discovered in September 1780.

At the end of the war Connecticut's soldiers returned home, and Parsons became a director of Connecticut's Ohio Land Company, which provided a way for the officers and soldiers of the Connecticut line to convert their almost worthless pay certificates into valuable land warrants. He also sat on a committee composed of the ablest men in Connecticut that supported Governor Jonathan Trumbull in asserting Connecticut's ultimately unsuccessful claims, under its seventeenth-century charter, to the Wyoming Valley lands in Pennsylvania. Parsons was a member of the Connecticut convention that ratified the U.S. Constitution in January 1788, and he served on a commission to extinguish by treaty the Indian titles to the Connecticut reserve lands in Ohio.

After several years in these Connecticut pursuits, however, Parsons resumed his service to the nation when Congress appointed him a judge for the Northwest Territory in 1787. In 1788, he headed west to the Ohio Country and began the survey of the part of the Western Reserve east of the Cuyahoga River that summer. The region was still an unbroken wilderness without even a military post except for one small blockhouse. Parsons left the blockhouse on 8 November 1789 and set out on the Big Beaver River near Salt Springs in a canoe with a man with a broken leg. Several days later, probably on 17 November, while running the rapids his canoe was wrecked, and both he and the injured man drowned. Parsons's body was not found until May, and his face was badly disfigured. He was buried along the south bank of the Beaver Creek near its confluence with the Ohio River. His family wanted the body removed to Pittsburgh, but there is no proof that it was. In the old cemetery in Middletown, Connecticut, where Parsons lived before heading west, is a marble monument that records his death but marks an empty grave.

Parsons lived his life according to high moral principles and had outstanding intellectual abilities. He was one of the earliest and most strenuous colonial opponents of British imperial policy. He negotiated a treaty with the Indians in the Northwest Territory, and under Congress's Ordinance of 1787 it became his duty as a chief judge of the territory to frame and enact a code of laws for its government. His untimely death was a great loss to the territory.

LINDA MILLER

See also

Arnold, Benedict; Connecticut; Northwest Territory; Trumbull, Jonathan

References

Blanco, Richard L. "Parsons, Samuel Holden." P. 1281 in *The American Revolution, 1775–1783: An Encyclopedia*, Vol. 2. Edited by Richard L. Blanco. New York: Garland, 1993.

Hall, Charles S. *Life and Letters of Samuel Holden Parsons.* 1905. Reprint, Binghamton, NY: Otseningo, 1968.

Purcell, L. Edward. *Who Was Who in the American Revolution.* New York: Facts On File, 1993.

Paterson, John
(1744–1808)

General John Paterson served in the Continental Army throughout the War for Independence, and after the conclusion of peace he had an active public career as a lawyer, local public official, congressman, and judge in western Massachusetts and upstate New York.

Paterson was born in 1744 in Newington, Connecticut. He attended Yale College, graduating in 1762, and returned to New Britain to the home of his parents, not far from his birthplace. His neighbors included Oliver Elsworth, later chief justice of the United States. Paterson's father died soon after his return home, and young Paterson managed his father's estate while studying law. He began his legal practice in New Britain while still teaching in the public school part of the year and soon thereafter was appointed a justice of the peace. In 1766, he married Elizabeth Lee, the only child of Josiah and Hannah Lee of Farmington.

In 1774, Paterson and his family moved to Lenox, Massachusetts, where he practiced law and became deeply involved in resistance to British authority. He participated in the Massachusetts Provincial Congresses of 1774 and 1775, and when fighting broke out between British regulars and Massachusetts militiamen at Lexington and Concord on 19 April 1775, he responded immediately. On 22 April, at sunrise, Paterson marched for Cambridge with a militia regiment fully armed and equipped. His unit, one of the first forces from outside eastern Massachusetts to join in the siege of Boston, would soon become the 15th Continental Infantry Regiment. Paterson's men built a fort near the town of Somerville and remained to guard the left flank of the army until the British evacuation of Boston in March 1776. On 10 November 1775, during the siege of Boston, General George Washington complimented Paterson in his general orders of the day.

On 13 April 1776, Paterson's regiment was ordered to Canada, but before it could join the American army on the St. Lawrence River, Colonel Benedict

Arnold had begun his retreat from Quebec City to Montreal. Paterson's regiment, like America's entire Canadian army, suffered from smallpox during the retreat that spring and summer, but they fought at the Battle of the Cedars against the British and Indians. In that engagement, they suffered many casualties, and sixty-seven members of the regiment were captured. In September 1776, Paterson was in command at Fort George, New York, and was recommended by General Horatio Gates for promotion.

In November 1776, Paterson's regiment was ordered to rejoin Washington's army. Paterson and his men shared in the crossing of the Delaware River on 25 December 1776 and the brilliant victories at Trenton and at Princeton. For his conduct, he was promoted to brigadier general in February 1777 and was ordered to Fort Ticonderoga. His brigade took part in nearly every engagement of the Saratoga Campaign in 1777, where they suffered heavy losses, and Paterson's horse was shot from under him and killed. Paterson later fought in the Battle of Monmouth in June 1778, and his image, next to that of the Marquis de Lafayette, was included in the bas-relief monument to that event.

After Monmouth, Paterson was ordered to take command of the fort at West Point, which his brigade held until their replacement by Arnold in 1780, just before Arnold's treason. Paterson was a member of the court-martial that tried Major John André and was the youngest member of the court except for Lafayette. Paterson and his brigade continued their service, both in the South and again at West Point; saw action in most of the decisive battles of the Revolution; and remained in the Continental Army during the entire war.

Peace with Britain was formally proclaimed on 19 April 1783, and soon thereafter the Continental Army began to disband, but Paterson and his brigade stayed at West Point until December 1783. In June 1783, he presided when Massachusetts officers organized their state's unit of the Society of the Cincinnati and later served as its vice president. In September, he was promoted to major general. He was one of just a handful of major generals holding command at the close of the war and, with the exception of Lafayette, was the youngest officer of his rank in the army. Paterson also took part in many courts-martial, being selected not only for his character as a soldier but also for his knowledge of law and his judicial ability. By the war's end, he had seen as much active service and done as much actual fighting—at the siege of Boston, during the Canada Campaign, in two major New Jersey campaigns (1776–1777 and 1778), and during the victory over John Burgoyne at Saratoga—as any Continental general.

On his retirement from the army, Paterson returned to Lenox, where he purchased a considerable piece of land. He became a leader of the successful effort to make Lenox the county seat of Berkshire County and served in several local offices, including moderator, selectman, and assessor, and was chosen one of the school committee members to provide schoolmasters. From 1785 to 1786 he served as a legislator from Berkshire County in the General Court at Boston, and in December 1785 he was appointed major general of the 9th Division of Militia by the State of Massachusetts.

Paterson's military services did not end with the Revolutionary War. Deep political and economic discontent in Massachusetts led to open acts of rebellion by poor debtors and farmers under the leadership of a Revolutionary War veteran, Captain Daniel Shays. At the request of Governor James Bowdoin, Paterson commanded the Berkshire militia in the suppression of Shays's Rebellion and selected as his staff several men who served with him during the war. Those who suppressed the rebellion, such as Paterson, believed that Shays's uprising threatened both law and order in Massachusetts and the idea of orderly self-government for which the Revolutionary War had been fought. Shays's men were soon defeated at Springfield, but there were still other insurgents who had to be put down as well. Paterson raised 500 men to defeat them. When order was restored, Paterson resumed his legal practice.

In 1790, Paterson and his family moved again, to Broome County in upstate New York, where he continued in public service as a representative to the state legislature from the new county, as a judge (until his death), and as a member of the convention to amend the constitution of the State of New York (1801). He was also elected to the U.S. Congress in 1802, serving until 1805. The $6'1\frac{1}{2}''$ judge would often walk 18 miles to the court in Binghamton rather than ride a horse.

Paterson died suddenly at Lisle, New York, on 19 July 1808 at the age of sixty-four. He was first buried in an obscure location, and his grave was neglected. He and his wife were later reburied, and a monumental tablet to his memory was erected in Trinity Church in Lenox by his great-grandson, Thomas Egleston, in 1887. Paterson was among the foremost of Massachusetts's Revolutionary Patriots and soldiers and became one of the most trusted of Washington's officers, serving continuously during eight and a half years of war at considerable cost to his personal fortune.

LINDA MILLER

See also
Boston, Siege of; Canada, Operations in; Monmouth, Battle of; Princeton, Battle of; Saratoga Campaign; Society of the Cincinnati; Trenton, Battle of

References
Egleston, Thomas. *The Life of John Paterson Major-General in the Revolutionary Army.* New York: Putnam, 1898.
Purcell, L. Edward. *Who Was Who in the American Revolution.* New York: Facts On File, 1993.
Ward, Harry M. "Paterson, John." Pp. 118–119 in *American National Biography*, Vol. 17. Edited by John Garraty. New York: Oxford University Press, 1999.

Paulus Hook, New Jersey, Action at
(19 August 1779)

On 19 August 1779, Major Henry "Light-Horse Harry" Lee and a special corps of Continental soldiers successfully stormed Paulus Hook, New Jersey, an important British post across from the southern tip of Manhattan that guarded the lower Hudson River. Lee had led his partisan corps in Brigadier

Capture of Paulus Hook, New Jersey, by Americans under Major Henry Lee in 1779. (North Wind Picture Archives)

General Anthony Wayne's brilliant operation against Stony Point on the night of 15–16 July but had played a relatively inactive and unnoticed part. Now serving in the division of Major General William Alexander, Lord Stirling, and jealous of the adulation heaped upon Wayne by General George Washington and Congress, Lee was determined to emulate Wayne's success. While scouting the west bank of the Hudson River, he had observed the isolated British post at Paulus Hook, and he suggested to Washington that he be allowed to attack it. Washington approved the idea after making some suggestions to Lee as to how the operation should be conducted. The plan called for an operation that would draw upon Lee's special skills for stealth, thoughtful planning, and hit-and-run operations against the enemy. He would seize the post by surprise in a night operation, take the men of the garrison prisoner, then withdraw before British power could be brought to bear against him.

Paulus Hook, a low-lying point of land projecting into the Hudson River, was an island at high tide connected to the mainland by a long causeway. It was cut off from the mainland by a creek, fordable in only two places, and a deep ditch, across which a drawbridge, protected by a heavy gate, was constructed. Protected by a double row of abatis, breastworks, two blockhouses, ten cannon mounted to defend the approaches, a sloop offshore with 50 marines aboard, and British troops available as reinforcements from Manhattan, the position appeared unassailable. The garrison, commanded by Major

William Sutherland, numbered about 300 men and consisted of British regulars and New York provincial troops. Lee's attacking force was to consist of about 400 men. Major Jonathan Clark was to lead 100 Virginia troops on the right; Captain Levin Handy, at the head of two companies of Maryland regulars, would compose the center; and Lee himself would command 100 Virginia Continentals and some dismounted dragoons under Captain Allan McLane on the left. Preceding each of these columns would be forlorn hope troops, men chosen for the dangerous task of cutting through the abatis and clearing the way for the main assaults. There would also be a reserve force, led by Captain Nathan Reid of the 10th Virginia Infantry.

Before commencing operations, Lee learned from McLane's scouts of the size and disposition of enemy forces at Paulus Hook. Lee stationed Captain Henry Peyton at Douwe's Ferry on the Hackensack River with boats so that Lee would not be trapped should British forces pursue him as he withdrew after the action. In addition, Stirling stationed a covering party of 300 men at New Bridge, 14 miles away, in case Lee needed to retreat in that direction. On the morning of 18 August, Lee marched from Paramus with Handy's Marylanders, and at the Hackensack River he met up with the Virginians. As they marched toward their objective, they were misled by their guide and floundered about for three hours before getting back on their way. Also, Clark began to complain about having to serve under Lee, whose commission was of a later date than his own. Soon, half the Virginians abandoned the operation, although Clark did not, and the remainder of Lee's command was harassed by the unfortunate march. Although Lee had intended to reach the edge of the marshy area north of Paulus Hook by 12:30 A.M. on 19 August, he did not arrive until 4:00 A.M.

Lee's entire enterprise was now endangered by a rising tide, which would render the ditch impassable, as well as by the coming daylight, which would expose his troops to detection by the enemy. Nevertheless, he persevered. He sent Lieutenant Michael Rudulph of the dragoons forward to reconnoiter the British positions, and when Rudulph reported that the ditch was still fordable, Lee ordered his troops forward. With bayonets fixed and muskets loaded but not primed, the soldiers were ordered to maintain complete silence and keep their weapons shouldered until directed to remove them. To ensure that no muskets were fired prematurely, each man was ordered to hold his hat in his right hand by his side until the attackers had crossed the ditch. Because of the desertion of the Virginians, Lee decided to send forward two attacking columns instead of three. Clark, with part of the remaining Virginians, was to advance on the right; Captain Robert Forsyth of Lee's corps, with McLane's dragoons and the rest of the Virginians, would attack on the left. Handy's Marylanders would be held in reserve, while the forlorn hope would be led by Lieutenant Archibald McAllister of Maryland on the right and Rudulph on the left.

Across 2 miles of swampy morass Lee's troops slogged in silence, sometimes wading up to their chests in water and reaching the ditch before British sentries detected them. Then the forlorn hope troops came under sporadic fire from the enemy's blockhouses and outer works. Charging forward, the Patriots tore their way through the abatis and penetrated one of the redoubts. McAllister quickly lowered a British flag, while both American

ACTIONS AT STONY POINT AND PAULUS HOOK, 1779

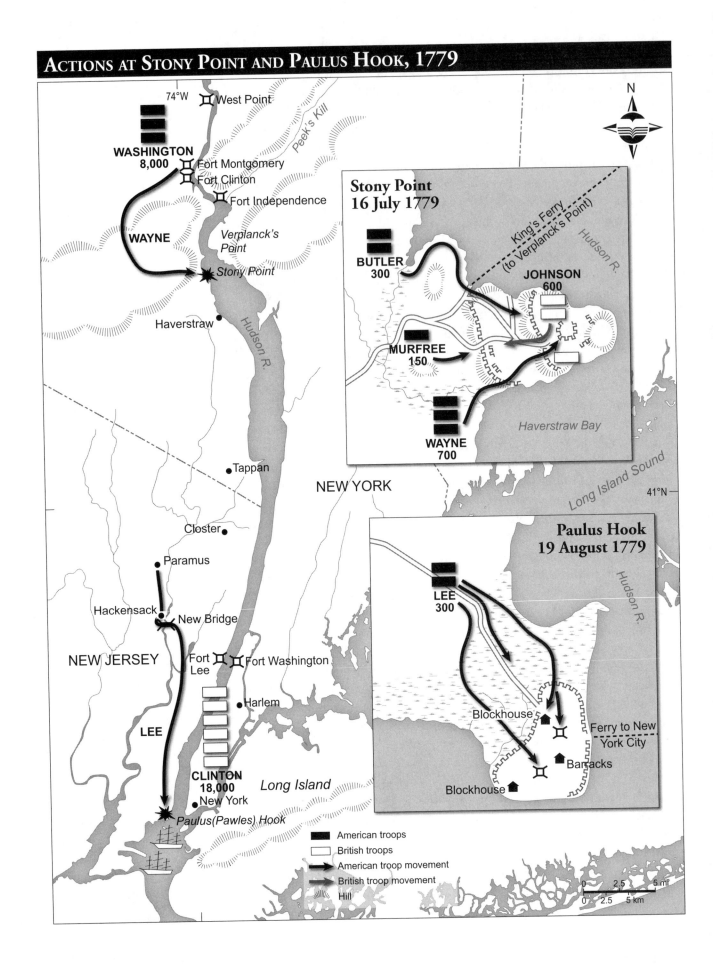

West Point

74°W

WASHINGTON
8,000

Fort Montgomery
Fort Clinton
Fort Independence

Peek's Kill

WAYNE

Verplanck's
Point

Stony Point

Haverstraw

Hudson R.

Stony Point
16 July 1779

BUTLER
300

King's Ferry
(to Verplanck's Point)

Hudson R.

JOHNSON
600

MURFREE
150

WAYNE
700

Haverstraw Bay

Tappan

NEW YORK

41°N

Long Island Sound

Closter

Paramus

Paulus Hook
19 August 1779

Hackensack

New Bridge

LEE
300

Hudson R.

NEW JERSEY

Fort
Lee

Fort Washington

LEE

Harlem

Blockhouse

Ferry to New
York City

CLINTON
18,000
New York

Long Island

Barracks

Blockhouse

Paulus (Pawles) Hook

■ American troops
□ British troops
→ American troop movement
→ British troop movement
⟋⟋⟋ Hill

N

0   2.5   5 mi
0   2.5   5 km

columns surged through the British position, capturing a blockhouse and all the soldiers quartered there. Within half an hour, Lee's forces had captured 158 prisoners and killed 50 British soldiers with their bayonets. Not one American had fired a shot. Sutherland, however, was not among the British casualties, for he and about 50 Hessians had taken refuge in a second blockhouse and refused to surrender. Keeping up a fire against their attackers, they managed to kill two Americans and wound three others. Lee had no time to deal with Sutherland and the Hessians, for the British in New York City were aroused, and he was in danger of being cut off before he could reach the Hackensack River and safety.

Hence, Lee quickly withdrew with his British captives, not even taking time to spike the guns of the post or to collect much enemy booty. He had intended to burn the captured barracks but changed his mind when he learned that they housed a number of sick soldiers, women, and children. Directing his line of march toward Douwe's Ferry on the Hackensack River, he spurred his exhausted men and reluctant British prisoners forward on a 5-mile march to his destination, realizing that if he was attacked on the march his men's ammunition would be useless because it had been soaked earlier. He detached a small party of men under Captain Forsyth to move forward and occupy heights overlooking his line of retreat. Finally reaching the ferry, Lee was chagrined to learn that Peyton, believing that the expedition was canceled, had withdrawn with the boats hours earlier. By now, a party of thirty Loyalists commanded by Lieutenant-Colonel Abraham Van Buskirk was closing in on Lee's desperate troops.

Undaunted, Lee sent word to Stirling to send a relief expedition toward him and turned his own men toward New Bridge. After he had passed Weehawken, he was reinforced by 50 Virginians with dry ammunition, under Captain Thomas Catlett, and shortly after that by a detachment of 200 men from Stirling, commanded by Colonel Burgess Ball. The relief forces arrived none too soon, for Lee's right flank was immediately assaulted by Van Buskirk and his small Loyalist force at Liberty Pole Tavern (Englewood). A small contingent of British regulars commanded by Colonel Cosmo Gordon also got into the fray. Facing his rear guard about, Lee prepared for action, directing a party of soldiers under Rudulph to take post in a stone house. When Van Buskirk and Gordon confronted this situation, they quickly retired, taking with them three American prisoners. Lee then resumed his march to New Bridge, arriving there safely with all the prisoners at 1:00 P.M.

Although Lee's operation against Paulus Hook had little military value beyond the capture of the British prisoners, it inspired the American army and brought adulation to Lee. Congress responded with a vote of thanks for Lee and his men and congratulations and a gold medal for Lee himself. Rudulph and McAllister were promoted to captain by brevet for their brave exploits in leading the forlorn hope, and the soldiers were given $15,000 in Continental money to be divided among them. Of far greater importance to the glory-seeking Lee, his military colleagues also praised him, and he reveled in his martial splendor. Ironically, however, he was also court-martialed because jealous Virginia officers charged that he had taken unwarranted liberties with precedent in commanding the expedition. These disgruntled officers ignored the fact that Lee was acting on the direct authority and command of Washington. On 29 September 1779 Lee was acquitted with honor, and in 1781 he went on to distinguish himself as a cavalry leader in the South.

Paul David Nelson

See also

Alexander, William; Hudson River and the Hudson Highlands; Lee, Henry; New Jersey, Operations in; Stony Point, New York, Capture of; Wayne, Anthony

References

Boyd, Thomas. *Light-Horse Harry Lee*. New York: Scribner, 1931.

Gerson, Noel B. *Light-Horse Harry: A Biography of Washington's Great Cavalryman, General Henry Lee*. Garden City, NY: Doubleday, 1966.

Greene, Francis V. *The Revolutionary War and Military Policy of the United States*. New York: Scribner, 1911.

Hartley, Cecil B. *Life of Major General Henry Lee, Commander of Lee's Legion in the Revolutionary War, and Subsequently Governor of Virginia*. New York: Derby and Jackson, 1859.

Nelson, Paul David. *William Alexander, Lord Stirling*. University: University of Alabama Press, 1987.

Royster, Charles. *Light-Horse Harry Lee and the Legacy of the American Revolution*. New York: Knopf, 1981.

Templin, Thomas E. "Henry 'Light Horse Harry' Lee: A Biography." PhD diss., University of Kentucky, 1975.

Ward, Christopher. *War of the Revolution*. 2 vols. New York: Macmillan, 1952.

Peace Commissions

See Carlisle Peace Commission; Howe Peace Commission

Peale, Charles Willson
(1741–1827)

The American painter, inventor, politician, soldier, and naturalist Charles Willson Peale is best known for his portraits of famous figures of the American Revolution and for founding America's first art institution and its first museum of natural history.

Peale was born in Queen Anne's County, Maryland, the eldest son of Charles Peale, a native of England, and Margaret Triggs Matthews of Annapolis, Maryland. As a boy, Peale excelled in Latin and mathematics and showed a keen interest in drawing. His formal education ended abruptly in 1750, however, when his father died, leaving the family destitute. In 1754, at the age of thirteen, Peale was apprenticed to a local saddle maker and remained in his service until 1760. In January 1762, Peale married Rachael Brewer and immediately opened his own saddle shop. He supplemented his meager income by taking on upholstery, metalworking, watch repair, and harness making.

Peale's early interest in art was revived when he saw some poorly executed oil paintings and thought he could do better. His earliest efforts at painting earned him praise and commissions for other works. He immediately saw the lucrative potential of painting and devoted himself to it. He began consulting art books and taking lessons from a local artist. Eventually, he met the painter John Singleton Copley, who taught him how to paint miniatures and encouraged his growing skills by offering him a portrait to copy. Peale's artistic training, however, received its greatest boost in December 1766, when his friends collected enough money to send him to London to study with Benjamin West. Peale returned to the colonies in 1769 and received many commissions for paintings, including one in 1772 to paint George Washington in his military uniform. This painting, the only extant portrait of Washington known to be executed before the Revolution, is the first of some sixty portraits that Peale would paint of the general.

In June 1776, Peale moved his family to Philadelphia as the city was busily preparing for war. Deeply patriotic, he soon enlisted as a common soldier in the Philadelphia Militia. He was shortly promoted to the rank of lieutenant, and in December 1776 he marched his eighty-one recruits to New Jersey, where he saw but did not participate in Washington's famous crossing of the Delaware River. Peale and his men, however, did play a crucial role in the Battle of Princeton, during which they charged a British regiment and weakened it enough to secure a victory for Washington's men.

In the summer of 1777, Peale, now a captain of infantry, reenlisted in the militia, and in the fall he participated in the battles at Germantown and Whitemarsh. That winter, he paid numerous visits to Valley Forge, where he dined occasionally with Washington, made the acquaintance of the Marquis de Lafayette, and painted more than forty miniatures of officers encamped there, including General Nathanael Greene and General Henry Knox. It was at this time that Peale conceived the idea of creating a portrait gallery of distinguished individuals, both American and foreign, who participated in the Revolution.

Peale's second military stint ended after the British evacuated Philadelphia in June 1778, but he remained active in the war effort by serving on numerous military and civilian committees. In January 1779 the Supreme Executive Council of Pennsylvania commissioned him to paint a full-length portrait of Washington to hang in the council chamber. Peale obliged, and the work was a great success. That same year, he represented Philadelphia in the Pennsylvania Assembly, serving on no fewer than thirty committees. He was defeated in the election the following year and effectively retired from politics.

Throughout the rest of the war, Peale never stopped painting, and in 1782 he achieved his long-anticipated goal of opening the nation's first portrait gallery. In 1786 he broadened his achievements by opening the

Charles Willson Peale, one of the outstanding painters of the early American republic, painted more than a thousand portraits, mostly of Revolutionary War leaders. He also founded the nation's first museum and first art school. (Library of Congress)

Philadelphia Museum, America's first museum of natural history. This collection offered the public the rare opportunity to see fossilized bones, Indian artifacts, and many specimens of indigenous mammals, insects, and fish.

In 1790 Peale's wife, Rachel, died from complications from her eleventh pregnancy (only seven of her children lived to adulthood), and Peale wasted no time in finding a new spouse—Elizabeth de Peyster, whom he married in May 1791. Twenty-four years his junior, she bore Peale seven more children (two died in infancy), and like his other children, he named them all in honor of famous painters or natural historians. In 1801 Peale added the reconstructed skeleton of an excavated mastodon to his museum collection, and this attraction drew large crowds of visitors. By this time, his collection had grown so extensive that he needed larger accommodations. He found them in the vacant state house in Philadelphia (Independence Hall) and moved his collection there in March 1802.

In 1804 Peale's second wife died in childbirth, and he married his last wife, Hannah Moore, the following year. Around this time, Peale resumed painting, and his renewed interest in art prompted him to help found the Pennsylvania Academy of the Fine Arts in 1805. He served as director of that institution until 1810, when he retired and relinquished control of his natural history museum to his son Rubens. In 1821 Peale's third wife succumbed to yellow fever. He did not remarry, but he remained active in farming, painting, writing, and scientific pursuits until his death in Philadelphia in 1827.

LARRY SEAN KINDER

See also
Art; Copley, John Singleton; Philadelphia; Princeton, Battle of; Valley Forge, Pennsylvania; Washington, George

References
Friedrich, Otto. "The Peales: America's First Family of Art." *National Geographic* (December 1990): 98–121.

Miller, Lillian B., Sidney Hart, and David C. Ward, eds. *The Selected Papers of Charles Willson Peale and His Family.* 5 vols. New Haven, CT: Yale University Press, 1983–2000.

Richardson, E. P., Brooke Hindle, and Lillian B. Miller, eds. *Charles Willson Peale and His World.* New York: Harry N. Abrams, 1982.

Sellers, Charles C. *Charles Willson Peale.* 1947. Reprint, New York: Scribner, 1969.

Pelham-Holles, Thomas, 1st Duke of Newcastle
(1693–1768)

Thomas Pelham was born in London to Sir Thomas Pelham and Lady Grace Holles. Educated at Cambridge, he adopted the surname of his uncle, John Holles, from whom he inherited vast estates in ten counties and his title, the Duke of Newcastle, in 1711. In 1717, Newcastle married Lady Harriet Godolphin and entered politics as Lord Chamberlain. He furthered his political career and numerous causes with the assistance of his grandfather-in-law, the Duke of Marlborough, and by dispensing patronage to potential supporters.

Newcastle served as secretary of state for the Southern Department for twenty-four years, beginning in 1724. His many duties included overseeing the North American colonies, which provided him with the opportunity to shape colonial policy under the powerful government of Robert Walpole. In 1748 Newcastle's position shifted to control of the Northern Department until 1754. Then, he succeeded his younger brother, Henry, as first lord of the Treasury (prime minister) during the turbulent Seven Years' War. Newcastle resigned his post in 1756 only to return to leading the government the next year, thanks to the assistance of William Pitt. Forced out of office in 1762 by imperialists led by John Stuart, the Earl of Bute, Newcastle's last political position was Lord Privy Seal under the Marquis of Rockingham. Newcastle suffered a stroke in 1768 and died in Surrey.

Often portrayed as an inept administrator and faulted for his lack of prodigious control over the North American colonies, Newcastle was overly burdened by his duties rather than incompetent. Above all, he should be credited as the chief architect of Britain's policy of salutary neglect toward the colonies. As secretary of state for the Southern Department, Newcastle upheld Whig principles that the colonies worked best when left alone, and his policies contributed to prosperous and harmonious colonial relations.

Throughout his career, Newcastle sternly opposed imperialist tendencies among the supporters of George II and George III. Newcastle relented to their pressure after becoming prime minister on the stance that if war with France must come, he preferred a limited war on the European continent rather than an unlimited war in North America. He condemned the war as creating a "mountain of expense" and unsuccessfully resisted its expansion at the hands of imperialists. His resignation as prime minister in 1762 made way for the Earl of Bute to remove all of Newcastle's appointed supporters from the government in the so-called Massacre of the Pelhamite Innocents. But the collapse of Newcastle's strength invigorated younger Whigs already rallying to Rockingham's side.

CAREY M. ROBERTS

See also
George III, King of England; Pitt, William, the Elder; Stuart, John, 3rd Earl of Bute

References
Henretta, James A. *"Salutary Neglect": Colonial Administration under the Duke of Newcastle*. Princeton, NJ: Princeton University Press, 1972.

Middleton, Richard. *The Bells of Victory: The Pitt-Newcastle Ministry and the Conduct of the Seven Years' War, 1757–1762*. Cambridge: Cambridge University Press, 1985.

Rothbard, Murray. *Conceived in Liberty*. Auburn, AL: Mises Institute, 1999.

Pennsylvania

Pennsylvania witnessed the most radical revolution of any colony that rebelled from Great Britain in 1776, and this political and social fact shaped its experience in the Revolutionary War. The colony had begun to shed its longtime pacifist heritage after 1750, and by the 1770s it was ready to plunge into the armed struggle with Britain. It overturned two generations of hard-won political stability to embrace practical but risky experiments with democratic self-government and social change. The same geographical accident that made Philadelphia a central meeting place for delegates from the North and South made Pennsylvania a transition zone between more traditional, European-style combat arenas in New England and New York and the more fluid and irregular theaters of war of the plantation societies below the Potomac River. Pennsylvania also illustrated the complex divisions between the long-settled and socially mature coastal plain and the dynamic new frontier districts that were developing everywhere from Maine to Georgia.

The Quaker colony lost its military innocence during the French and Indian (Seven Years') War. Both General Edward Braddock's shocking defeat and death and the beginning of George Washington's march to fame occurred in 1755 in the Monongahela Valley, on the ragged edges of terrain contested between Pennsylvania and Virginia. The arrival of Connecticut Yankee settlers in the Wyoming Valley of northeastern Pennsylvania showed that the province's sovereignty was threatened there, too. From 1755 until 1763, Delaware Indians attacked settlers from the Dutch-populated Minisink Country on the upper Delaware River through German communities in Northampton, Berks, and Lancaster Counties and ethnically diverse townships on the lower Susquehanna River to Scots-Irish enclaves in the Juniata Valley. As these attacks began, the Pennsylvania government, lacking even a militia, was defenseless.

Facing frontier outrage and imperial threats from London, members of the strict Quaker majority in the provincial assembly yielded power to a coalition of coreligionists who could bring themselves to authorize defense measures and selected non-Quakers who were allies of the Society of Friends. Under the leadership of Benjamin Franklin, the new Assembly Party made concessions to imperial military demands. Philadelphians now competed with Virginians to promote their city as a base for expeditions to dislodge the French from the Ohio Valley. In 1758, General John Forbes led a campaign against Fort Duquesne across Pennsylvania. Philadelphia merchants profited from defense contracting, the province got a road to the Monongahela Valley that shaped the settlement of the western region, and its government dodged problems with Parliament. Before Forbes reached the Allegheny front, however, an intercolonial treaty with the Indians convened at Easton. The army waited while civilian leaders—including some Quakers who had left public life and were now working as members of the private Friendly Association—persuaded the Indians to abandon the French. This caused Fort Duquesne (at the site of Pittsburgh) to fall almost without a shot being fired and helped to tie the colony back together by

The Battle of Germantown, in which General George Washington attacked the British army under General William Howe encamped outside of Philadelphia, 4 October 1777. Although a narrow American defeat, Germantown emboldened the Patriot cause and impressed the still neutral French with the fighting prowess of Washington's forces. (National Archives and Records Administration)

repairing some of the damage of the Virginia and Yankee territorial intrusions. Once peace was restored, several members of the Quaker establishment quietly reclaimed political power in the 1760s.

Resuming power was not the same thing, however, as regaining political preeminence. Backcountry settlers never again trusted the government in Philadelphia. In 1763, during another round of Indian raids along the frontier precipitated by Pontiac's Rebellion, settlers from Paxton township on the east bank of the Susquehanna murdered a group of peaceful Indians to avenge their own sufferings and then marched on Philadelphia, threatening to treat its Quakers and other inhabitants almost as roughly. The town was spared largely because Franklin organized an informal militia to meet the Paxton Boys in Germantown and persuaded them to return to their homes. A more stable internal peace was restored by 1765, but the regional, ethnic, religious, and socioeconomic fractures revealed by the events of 1755–1764 loomed ominously over a society now threading its way through the growing imperial crises. The seeds of a colony-wide militia tradition were belatedly sown during the French and Indian War, but local militia organizations—especially in Philadelphia—became custodians of popular alienation from the old political establishment.

After the outbreak of armed conflict at Lexington and Concord in the spring of 1775, the colony overtook several of its neighbors in its military zeal. Hastily recruited companies of eager but inexperienced Pennsylvanians converged on Cambridge, Massachusetts, that summer, where Washington was molding New England's Army of Observation into the new Continental Army. A few Pennsylvanians joined Benedict Arnold's heroic late-autumn trek through the Maine wilderness to the St. Lawrence River to besiege Quebec. More Pennsylvanians followed General Richard Montgomery into Canada to attack Quebec from the west. After the failure of both the attack and the following siege, remnants of the invasion force conducted a stubborn rearguard action along the Richelieu River and Lake Champlain during the summer and fall of 1776, forcing British strategists to delay plans to invade America directly from Canada until the following year.

Other Pennsylvanians left the colony in 1776 to defend their hearths closer to home. As General William Howe transferred the war from intensely hostile New England to the supposedly friendlier middle colonies by seizing New York City, Washington called for the creation of a flying camp, a reserve force of 10,000 provincial forces from Pennsylvania, Maryland, and Delaware to defend New Jersey's seacoast, suppress Loyalist activity west of the Hudson River, and reinforce the Continental Army. The auxiliary force never reached this number, but 2,000 members of Pennsylvania's new militia crossed the Delaware River in June and July 1776 to serve as a core of the projected flying camp. The overthrow of the provincial Assembly and the drafting of a radical new constitution by radical forces, known to historians as Pennsylvania's internal revolution, was under way during these same months and complicated the state's mobilization.

With Whigs from the interior counties preferring to remain at home to defend the frontier, most of Pennsylvania's contribution to the flying camp came from the self-created Philadelphia militia organization known as the Associators. These men, mainly artisans, mechanics, and laborers, were eager to fight the British in New Jersey to avoid having to fight them at home. They were also politically sophisticated, avowedly radical, and insistent that military burdens be fairly shared among the state's localities and social classes. They demanded that their own families should not suffer from rising prices or from their own absences from work. When their tour in New Jersey proved to be a time of anxious waiting for Howe to strike, they became restless. In August 1776, Philadelphia troops showed that Pennsylvanians would be among the most mutiny-prone soldiers by challenging their officers and winning concessions. In November and December 1776, however—with the redcoats at hand in New Jersey and the Continental Army retreating into Pennsylvania—the Associators valiantly attempted to cross the ice-choked Delaware River below Trenton to give decisive support to Washington's regulars in their campaign against the Hessians at that town. Some succeeded, and others crossed later to drive the last British units out of western New Jersey.

Except for these few young and adventurous men, most Pennsylvanians experienced the first year of the Revolution in the isolated tranquility that their ancestors had become used to as part of their Quaker inheritance. It was not until Continental resistance nearly collapsed in late 1776 that the reality of the war dawned on them. As the Continental Army began to crumble in early December, Philadelphians began to flee (as did the Continental Congress, to Baltimore). The town was largely empty when Washington struck back across the Delaware on Christmas night. It was early 1777 before the city's population reached its prewar level. Some returnees seemed to have vowed not to repeat the futile retreat. When Pennsylvania was invaded for real the next summer, the reaction of the civilian population was much more orderly and in some ways almost calculating.

The 1777 invasion came from the south, through Chesapeake Bay, rather than across the Delaware. In August, Howe and 14,000 regulars landed at the head of the Elk River and began moving toward Philadelphia. Washington marched 10,000 mostly new and untested Continental troops through the city and deployed them behind Brandywine Creek in Chester County. Howe outmaneuvered Washington, crossed the Brandywine above Chadds Ford early on 11 September 1777, and crumpled the American right flank. But Washington quickly realigned his army, and the soldiers fought bravely and fiercely enough to turn a potentially destructive defeat into a mere embarrassment.

Choosing to protect Continental supply facilities in the Schuylkill Valley, Washington allowed the British to enter Philadelphia unopposed on 26 September 1777. Congress fled to York, Pennsylvania, while the weak and badly divided state government found refuge in Lancaster. On 4 October, Washington counterattacked at Germantown, a suburb of Philadelphia, in a move reminiscent of the Trenton surprise. His troops drove the enemy outposts before them for several miles before his complex battle plan unraveled in fog and the confusion of combat. The Continentals retreated 20 miles up the Schuylkill Valley, saddled with their second defeat of the campaign. The ensuing weeks brought a third defeat, as the Americans failed to maintain control of fortifications on the lower Delaware River. The British then brought their fleet up to Philadelphia, ensuring that they could use that town as a winter garrison. Washington's aggression, however, reinforced Howe's inclination to be cautious and occasionally even passive. This denied the British many of the political fruits of their capture of Philadelphia and their rout of the state and national governments.

The autumn 1777 campaign involved dispersed operations in a politically ambiguous countryside. The State of Pennsylvania, operating with a weak government and a new militia law, failed to mobilize enough of its population to contribute effectively to its own defense. This inevitably became a political issue. After the Battle of Germantown, Continental officers were frustrated by their loss, but they still expected to wage a series of successful engagements against the enemy. They were shocked by the abrupt collapse of the supply organizations that immobilized the army at Whitemarsh in early November. The October defeat of British General John Burgoyne at Saratoga, New York, by a technically autonomous Northern Continental Army under General Horatio Gates boosted American morale and greatly improved America's diplomatic prospects in France, but it also contributed to a serious rivalry between Gates and Washington. The integration of thousands of triumphant northern

A meeting of the Society of Friends. Members of the religious sect became known as Quakers due to the way they trembled with emotion during their meetings. (North Wind Picture Archives)

troops—mostly Yankees from New England and upstate New York—into the main Continental Army, just as the Pennsylvania Campaign stagnated, was difficult. These Northerners had never seen farms as richly prosperous or a social landscape as confusingly diverse as they saw in Pennsylvania. Their reaction to abrupt material hardships in a land of plenty was to blame everything on the supposed treachery of "Quakers," by which they meant all Pennsylvanians.

In December 1777, Washington brokered a compromise plan for the army's winter disposition between political pressures to maintain active resistance to the British invasion and the genuine weaknesses of his force. This brought the army to Valley Forge, where its winter encampment was more complex and less melodramatic than American tradition suggests. The army stoically endured brief and occasional periods of hunger, muddled through a comparatively mild winter, and struggled to keep Pennsylvania's eastern civilians isolated from their British invaders. Friedrich von Steuben's training of the troops made real, but hardly miraculous, improvements in their military capabilities and readiness. The news late in the spring of 1778 that France had granted diplomatic recognition to the United States and joined the war against Britain gratified most revolutionaries and made the winter and the Pennsylvania Campaign seem worthwhile.

On 18 June 1778, the British Army left Philadelphia to return to New York and prepare for the new challenges of what was becoming a world war. The next day, six months after arriving there, the Continentals marched from Valley Forge to chase the enemy across New Jersey. On 28 June, the two sides fought a sharp but inconclusive action at Monmouth Court House, New Jersey. Military action then veered into the southern states and toward the sea, but important political and military activity continued in the North. Washington deployed his main army in a vast arc around New York City, from Long Island Sound to the New Jersey shore, and soon demonstrated that the previous winter he had learned important lessons about managing a police action among a diverse and divided civilian population.

In Pennsylvania, the Valley Forge winter purged local communities of thousands of avowed Loyalists, many of whom first moved to Philadelphia and then left the state with the retreating British Army. It also tempered the conflict between radical and moderate revolutionaries, who gradually came to conduct their battles within the framework of electoral politics. The Pennsylvania militia remained a work in progress. Western counties preferred to protect their frontiers from the Indians, most of whom were hostile to the Revolution. The Philadelphia Associators remained behind when the seat of war first moved north to New York and then south to the Carolinas. Their attraction to radical politics and their willingness to use their youth, arms, and combat experience as political resources were tangible outcomes of the winter of occupation. In late 1779, a fierce conflict between radical and moderate forces in Philadelphia over monetary inflation, price controls, and economic Toryism brought pitched battles to the city streets between the Associators and a company of militia drawn from and allied to the merchant elites. The latter's victory broke the back of active radicalism in the Continental capital and helped conservative forces in Pennsylvania politics to rally behind their agenda.

But Pennsylvania's civilians continued to believe that their communities were exposed to an invasion. Every seaborne deployment of troops or supplies between the British headquarters in New York and the combat theaters in the South conjured fears that redcoats might materialize out of the Delaware or Chesapeake Bays. Frontier inhabitants knew that they were vulnerable. On 3 July 1778, a makeshift army of Iroquois warriors and Loyalists attacked the mostly Yankee settlements in the Wyoming Valley of northeastern Pennsylvania, killing more than 200 local militia members. A year later, Washington sent a retaliatory force under General John Sullivan to disrupt the communities of Iroquoia that sustained such raiding. Assembling his men in the Lehigh Valley, Sullivan proceeded to Wyoming, near modernday Scranton and Wilkes-Barre, and launched a devastating march into the Finger Lakes region of New York. The expedition was specifically aimed at the ecological and communal infrastructure that supported Indian raiding, and it sowed the seeds for the removal of many Native Americans from New York and much of northern Pennsylvania after the war.

During the last years of the Revolution, Pennsylvania became synonymous in the public imagination with war weariness and the supposed decline of republican virtue. This reputation was unfair, but it was embedded in

Pennsylvania became synonymous in the public imagination with war weariness.

attributes of the colony's historical experience. In addition to its violent struggle over Revolutionary economics, Pennsylvania acquired an indirect tie to the traitor Benedict Arnold. After being wounded at Saratoga in 1777, Arnold was unfit for a field command. Washington named him the interim military commander of postoccupation Philadelphia, responsible for overseeing its transition back to civil government. There Arnold met and married Margaret Shippen, the daughter of a prominent merchant family that was perceived to have been close to the British occupiers. In 1779, he joined Margaret's old acquaintance, British Major John André, in an intrigue that led to his effort to betray West Point in September 1780. But Philadelphia, which had endured Arnold's profitable provisioning activities in 1778 and 1779, left no doubt about its opinion of the traitor. Within weeks of his exposure, the city staged a parade in which a two-faced Arnold figure was carted through the streets, tempted by an effigy of the Devil.

Pennsylvania troops also lived up to the rowdy-to-mutinous reputation that they established in the flying camp of 1776. At Morristown, New Jersey, in 1780, members of the Pennsylvania line were only one of three state units that rose up against tribulations of bad weather, food shortages, and missing pay that made Valley Forge seem like an easy posting. But only they abandoned the camp and headed toward the Delaware River. Many were interested only in going home, but their march was toward Philadelphia, and it badly rattled Congress. They were met near Trenton by a delegation of congressional leaders who made concessions to them to defuse the uprising. When the New Jersey troops rose up at Morristown a few weeks later, Washington responded with selective but brutal force, and mutiny declined in the army.

In 1783, with the war over and Congress struggling to demobilize the army, however, a group of Pennsylvania troops garrisoned at Lancaster again marched on Philadelphia to demand back pay. They got all the way to the yard of Independence Hall, where their loud antics persuaded Congress to adjourn to Princeton. This event was at most a noisy coda to the Revolution, but it may have cost Pennsylvania any chance to become the permanent capital of the new nation.

Pennsylvania's experience with the Revolutionary War reflected the processes that brought the colony into the Revolution itself and that would shape its emergence as a state. In 1776, Pennsylvania left behind a tradition of pacifist exceptionalism and, in some respects, resistance to the processes of state (or at least empire) formation that had characterized the seventeenth- and eighteenth-century Atlantic world to plunge headlong into a struggle for political power. It did not, however, abandon its equally long-standing commitment to social experimentation that only began to be normative in that Atlantic world as the eighteenth century ended. Pennsylvanians adopted the gradual emancipation of its slaves in 1780, continued to embrace diversified immigration, and turned their century-old commitment to market agriculture into a platform for the emergence of industrial capitalism. More than any other state before about 1820, Pennsylvania constituted the gateway between the Atlantic basin and the trans-Appalachian west. And its Quakers, involuntarily freed from the burdens of having to govern any specific piece of territory, turned their considerable energies and imaginations to becoming the reform conscience of early nineteenth-century America as a whole.

In 1800, Philadelphia again surrendered the national capital, not to an invading army but to a new conception of the meaning of federal sovereignty, and not before providing the stage on which partisan political battles unanticipated in the new Constitution were worked out. Before this, in 1794 (the Whiskey Rebellion) and 1798 (Fries's Rebellion), conflicts pitting national interests against those of western Pennsylvania corn growers and whiskey distillers and Delaware Valley ethnic groups established the principle that while taxation with representation was scarcely more tolerable than taxation without representation, the people as sovereign needed to, and when necessary would, govern. Pennsylvania, in other words, was a place that anticipated many contours of the American Revolution decades before the event and that continued experimentally to work on its unresolved problems generations thereafter.

WAYNE BODLE

See also

Arnold, Benedict; Brandywine, Battle of; Congress, Second Continental and Confederation; Constitutions, State; Dickinson, John; Galloway, Joseph; Germantown, Battle of; Howe, William; Paoli, Battle of; Philadelphia; Philadelphia Campaign; Reed, Joseph; Thomson, Charles; Valley Forge, Pennsylvania; Washington, George; Whitemarsh, Pennsylvania, Action at; Wilson, James

References

Bodle, Wayne. *The Valley Forge Winter: Civilians and Soldiers in War.* University Park, PA: Penn State University Press, 2002.

Brunhouse, Robert. *The Counter-Revolution in Pennsylvania, 1776–1790.* Harrisburg: Pennsylvania Historical and Museum Commission, 1942.

Maier, Pauline. *From Resistance to Revolution: Colonial Radicals and the Development of American Opposition to Britain, 1765–1776.* New York: Knopf, 1972.

Nash, Gary B. *The Urban Crucible: Social Change, Political Consciousness and the Origins of the American Revolution.* Cambridge: Harvard University Press, 1979.

Rosswurm, Steven. *Arms, Country, and Class: The Philadelphia Militia and the "Lower Sort" during the American Revolution.* New Brunswick, NJ: Rutgers University Press, 1987.

Ryerson, Richard A. *The Revolution Is Now Begun: The Radical Committees of Philadelphia, 1765–1776.* Philadelphia: University of Pennsylvania Press, 1978.

Selsam, J. Paul. *The Pennsylvania Constitution of 1776: A Study in Revolutionary Democracy.* 1936. Reprint, New York: Octagon, 1971.

Slaughter, Thomas. *The Whiskey Rebellion: Frontier Epilogue to the American Revolution.* New York: Oxford University Press, 1986.

Smith, Billy G. *The "Lower Sort": Philadelphia's Laboring People, 1750–1800.* Ithaca, NY: Cornell University Press, 1990.

Penobscot Expedition

(July–August 1779)

The Americans suffered their worst naval defeat of the war in Penobscot Bay as they attempted to dislodge the British from the coast of present-day Maine, which was a district of Massachusetts until 1820.

On 30 May 1779, British general Francis McLean and 800 soldiers sailed from Halifax, Nova Scotia, aboard a squadron commanded by Captain Henry Mowat. They landed on the Bagaduce Peninsula in Penobscot Bay on 16 June. McLean began constructing Fort George, while Mowat deployed three sloops in Bagaduce Harbor. This advance post was intended to buffer Nova Scotia from American incursions, disrupt the numerous privateers operating along the Maine coast, and become a refuge for Loyalists.

The Massachusetts government quickly dispatched an expedition to eliminate this threat. Continental Navy Captain Dudley Saltonstall headed the naval force that eventually included forty-six warships, privateers, transports, and supply vessels. General Solomon Lovell and approximately 1,000 militiamen, 500 fewer than authorized, accompanied Saltonstall, with Colonel Paul Revere in command of the artillery train. The Americans left Boston on 19 July and arrived at Penobscot Bay six days later. Saltonstall immediately attacked Mowat's ships but only inflicted light damage. The next day, 200 American Marines landed on nearby Banks' Island and captured a battery overlooking the British ships, which sailed deeper into the harbor. On 27 July, Lovell's troops, supported by Marines and naval gunfire, surprised McLean by landing on the Bagaduce Peninsula and scaling its precipitous heights but failed to seize the unfinished fort. Meanwhile, Saltonstall again attacked Mowat's sloops, but the square-rigged American vessels had difficulty maneuvering in the harbor's narrow waters. The American effort then bogged down. Lovell believed that he lacked the strength to capture the fort until Mowat's ships were destroyed. Saltonstall, however, thought that the fort had to be seized before his ships could successfully confront Mowat. Repeated councils of war failed to overcome this impasse, and attempts to launch a simultaneous attack on the fort and ships failed to materialize.

This stalemate ended on 14 August when Commodore Sir George Collier's powerful squadron arrived at Penobscot Bay to relieve the beleaguered fort. Now trapped in the bay, Saltonstall and Lovell frantically embarked the troops and fled up the Penobscot River with Collier in pursuit. The entire American fleet was scuttled by their crews or captured, and the survivors marched back to Massachusetts. The Americans lost approximately 500 men and forty-six ships, while the British suffered only 13 casualties. The British remained at Bagaduce for the rest of the war, ending American efforts to capture Nova Scotia. They were not, however, able to stop American privateering in the area.

A Massachusetts committee of inquiry blamed Saltonstall, a Continental officer, for the Penobscot fiasco, which cost the Commonwealth of Massachusetts nearly £1.6 million. The committee was partly influenced by a desire to assess a portion of the cost to the Continental Congress.

MICHAEL P. GABRIEL

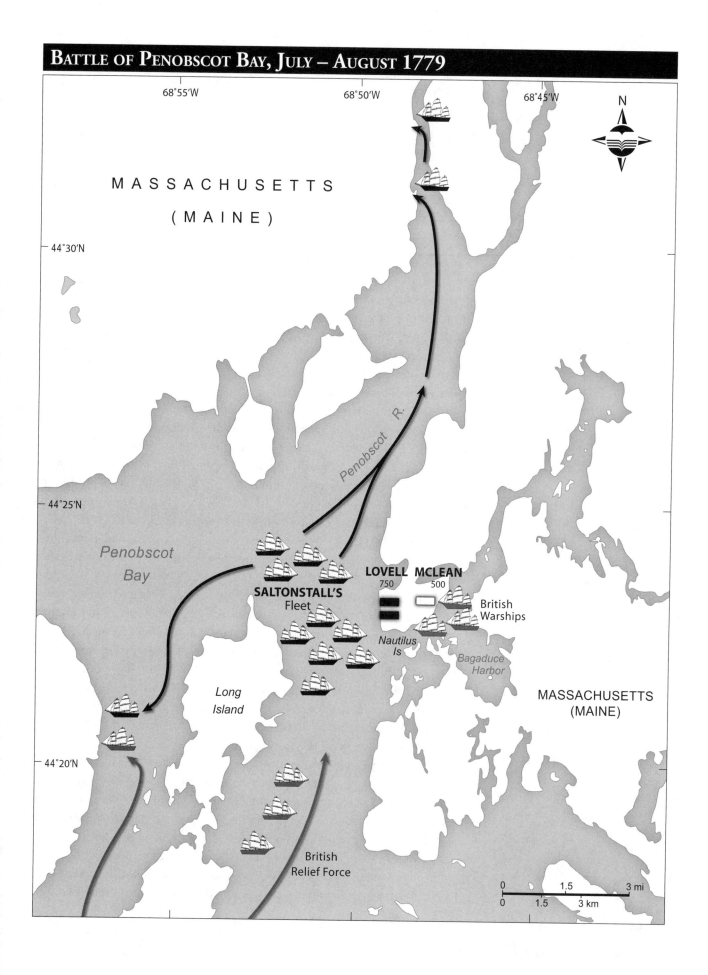

68°55'W

68°50'W

68°45'W

N

MASSACHUSETTS

(MAINE)

44°30'N

Penobscot R.

44°25'N

Penobscot
Bay

SALTONSTALL'S
Fleet

LOVELL
750

MCLEAN
500

British
Warships

Nautilus
Is

Bagaduce
Harbor

MASSACHUSETTS
(MAINE)

Long
Island

44°20'N

British
Relief Force

0   1.5   3 mi

0   1.5   3 km

See also

Marines, Continental; Massachusetts; Privateering; Revere, Paul; Saltonstall, Dudley

References

Buker, George E. *The Penobscot Expedition: Commodore Saltonstall and the Massachusetts Conspiracy of 1779*. Annapolis, MD: Naval Institute Press, 2002.

Faibsiy, John D. "Penobscot, 1779: The Eye of a Hurricane." *Maine Historical Society Quarterly* 19(2) (1979): 91–117.

Pensacola, West Florida, Operation against

(February–May 1781)

The Spanish victory at Pensacola in May 1781 swept the British from the entire northern coast of the Gulf of Mexico, thereby giving Spain complete control of the British province of West Florida, which extended from the east bank of the lower Mississippi River south of Natchez almost to New Orleans and then eastward along the Gulf Coast from Lake Ponchartrain to the Apalachicola River, just west of the Florida peninsula. This victory was one of the last great military accomplishments for Spain in the Americas. It permitted the creation of a Spanish province that included both the area that would later become the Louisiana Purchase and the northern coastline of the Gulf of Mexico. The Spanish military campaigns in the lower Mississippi watershed that culminated in the Battle of Pensacola also significantly assisted the armies of George Washington by providing a timely and effective drain on the British capability to wage war from 1779 to 1781.

Bernardo de Gálvez, the governor of Spanish Louisiana, had established himself as a supporter of the American rebel cause from the moment he assumed office at New Orleans in January 1777. His desire to assist the Americans did not arise from sympathy for them but rather from his long-standing hatred of the British as Spain's traditional international enemy. Gálvez permitted the American merchant Oliver Pollock to use New Orleans as a supply center for the army of George Rogers Clark in its conquest of the Illinois Country during 1778 and 1779. Spain, however, delayed entry into the conflict as a belligerent until June 1779, when King Charles III issued a declaration of war against Great Britain, and he did not formally ally his nation with the United States or indeed even recognize the new nation until well after the end of the Revolution.

Gálvez had received advance notice of Spain's declaration and was immediately ready to attack Britain's southwesternmost post in North America at Baton Rouge, which he did successfully in September 1779. When his troops took the British garrison at Mobile the following spring, Pensacola was left as the last remaining military bastion for Great Britain in West Florida. As the capital of the province, Pensacola was well defended by an army under the command of General John Campbell, whose forces were entrenched at Fort George, a major post overlooking Escambia Bay and its outlet to the Gulf of

Mexico. This fortification and its naval roadstead presented one of the major British military positions in the Gulf of Mexico and the Caribbean Sea during the era of the American Revolution.

Gálvez organized a joint army and navy expedition in two large units—one departing from New Orleans, the other from Havana—to converge on Pensacola during the late winter of 1781. They arrived in early March at Santa Rosa Island, which forms a land barrier between Escambia Bay and the Gulf of Mexico. Pensacola was located several miles north on the bay's northern shore, to the east of Fort George. Gálvez deployed his army onto the island as a base camp and ordered his naval commander to sail his ships of the line across the shallow bar into Escambia Bay for an attack on the main British positions. The heavy guns of Fort George, however, looked directly down on the Santa Rosa bar, and the Spanish naval commander refused to comply with Gálvez's order to move the fleet inside the bay. Outraged at this insubordination, Gálvez boarded the flagship, took personal command, and sailed across the bar into the safety of Escambia Bay beyond the range of the British guns at Fort George. Other ships of the fleet quickly followed, which allowed the Spanish to establish a well-protected camp from which to assault the fort.

The attack on Fort George began in late April as the sizable Spanish army and its Native American allies surrounded the British position on the land side. The British defenses, however, proved to be formidable. Gálvez and his troops were unable to breach them, and a siege quickly ensued. Fighting came to a quick and unanticipated end on the afternoon of 8 May 1781, when a Spanish cannon fired a round that penetrated, apparently without the gunner's intent, directly into the main British ammunition supply dump located inside Fort George. The ensuing explosion proved to be a spectacular one, with more than one hundred men and tons of material being thrown into the sky. This event so disheartened the stunned British that Campbell quickly surrendered his entire command to Gálvez.

The following day witnessed the formal surrender of Pensacola to Gálvez's army and the signing of a capitulation that delivered all of British West Florida to the control of Spain. Gálvez received custody of more than 1,000 British troops whom he paroled, permitting them to return to the British Isles. He joined the province of West Florida to that of Spanish Louisiana. Pensacola would remain a Spanish possession until the Transcontinental Treaty of 1819 (also known as the Adams-Onis Treaty), when it passed to the territorial sovereignty of the United States. Gálvez emerged from this victory as Spain's greatest military hero of the War of American Independence.

LIGHT TOWNSEND CUMMINS

Spanish troops under Bernardo de Gálvez storm Fort George, Pensacola, 9 May 1781, during operations in West Florida. (U.S. Army Center of Military History)

See also

Florida, East and West; Gálvez, Bernardo de; Spain

References

Caughey, John. *Bernardo de Gálvez in Louisiana.* Berkeley: University of California Press, 1934.

Chavez, Thomas. *Spain and the Independence of the United States: An Intrinsic Gift.* Albuquerque: University of New Mexico Press, 2002.

Cummins, Light Townsend. *Spanish Observers and the American Revolution, 1775–1783.* Baton Rouge: Louisiana State University Press, 1992.

Percy, Hugh
(1742–1817)

Hugh Percy, the 2nd Duke of Northumberland, was an aristocratic British officer who served with distinction during the American Revolutionary War. On 1 May 1759, he entered the British Army with a brevet commission as ensign in the 24th Regiment. He exchanged into the 85th Regiment as captain on 6 August. During the Seven Years' War, he served under Prince Ferdinand of Brunswick on the Continent and distinguished himself in the battles at Bergen and Minden. On 15 April 1762, he was promoted to lieutenant-colonel commandant of the 111th Regiment, and later that year he joined the Grenadier Guards as captain and lieutenant-colonel. He was elected a member of Parliament for Westminster in May 1763 and was subsequently reelected until he succeeded to the peerage in 1776. On 24 October 1764, he was promoted to colonel and appointed aide-de-camp to King George III. He married Lady Anne Stuart, the Earl of Bute's daughter, on 3 July 1764 and thus became one of the so-called king's friends in Parliament. After a divorce in 1779, he married Frances Julia Burrell the same year. He was appointed colonel of the 5th Regiment in November 1768 and was accused of gaining the position because of his first marriage. When his mother died on 5 December 1776, he succeeded as Baron Percy, with the courtesy title of earl because his father was a duke.

As tensions rose between Britain and America during the early 1770s, Percy openly opposed the government's colonial policies, thus loosening his connections with the court. Despite this opposition, he volunteered to command British troops in America. Promoted to brigadier-general in America, he embarked for Boston in the spring of 1774. There, General Thomas Gage gave him command of the army camp. On 19 April 1775, after the actions at Lexington and Concord, Percy led a brigade, consisting of the Welsh fusiliers and four other regiments, to the relief of the retreating British column. Although his troops were under constant harassing fire, he brought the column back to Charlestown, perhaps saving them from annihilation. His 5th Regiment was almost cut to pieces in the Battle of Bunker Hill on 17 June, but he was not leading them, either because of illness or because of a disagreement with General William Howe. On 11 July 1775, Percy was promoted to major-general in America and on 29 September to permanent major-general. He was promoted to general in America and was made a permanent lieutenant-general on 29 August 1777. He was slated by Howe to lead an attack on Dorchester Heights in March 1776, but the attack was called off, and Howe instead evacuated Boston.

On 27 August 1776, at New York, Percy commanded the British Army's right wing in the Battle of Long Island, and he approved of Howe's decision not to attack Brooklyn Heights afterward. Percy led a division during the assault on Fort Washington on 16 November and was first to enter the American lines. In December, he accompanied General Sir Henry Clinton on an expedition to capture Rhode Island and assumed command there when Clinton returned to Britain on leave. In January 1777, Percy received a letter from Howe requesting that forage be sent to New York. He waited six weeks to reply, then informed Howe that he had no forage to spare. In reply, Howe delineated a number of criticisms of Percy's command, and in early March Percy asked for and was granted leave to resign and return home. Throughout his tenure in America, Percy had difficulty getting along with Howe, and matters finally had come to a head. In June 1777, Percy returned to Britain.

Portrait of Hugh Percy, 2nd Duke of Northumberland (1742–1817), who relieved the British soldiers as they were retreating from Concord through Lexington on 19 April 1775. (Library of Congress)

It was curious that Percy and Howe could not cooperate, for Percy had a reputation as a capable and likeable soldier. Horace Walpole described him as a man totally devoid of ostentation, with simple habits. Percy was popular with the public, the press, and his regiment. He opposed corporal punishment and paid more than usual attention to his men's personal welfare. The widows of his soldiers killed at Bunker Hill were sent home at his own expense and given money in Britain. Because of his kindnesses, the 5th Regiment requested and was given permission to call itself the Northumberland Fusiliers. On 2 November 1784, he was made commander of the 2nd troop of Horse Grenadier Guards, which was transferred in June 1788 to the 2nd Life Guards. When he succeeded his father as Duke of Northumberland on 6 June 1786, he achieved a reputation as a benevolent and paternal landlord. He also became lord-lieutenant and vice-admiral of Northumberland. He became a Knight of the Garter on 9 April 1788.

In the 1780s, Percy's politics led him into opposition against the policies of William Pitt the Younger and of King George III. Percy joined the Prince of Wales's circle of friends and was courted by the parliamentary opposition but refused proffered cabinet posts. On 17 October 1793, he was promoted to general, and in 1798 he became commander of the Percy Yeomanry Regiment. He was made colonel of the Horse Guards on 30 December 1806. But his political views kept him from attaining any important military commands.

PAUL DAVID NELSON

See also

Boston, Siege of; Bunker Hill, Battle of; Dorchester Heights, Massachusetts; Fort Washington, New York, Fall of; Gage, Thomas; George III, King of England; Howe, William; Lexington and Concord; Long Island, Battle of; Pitt, William, the Younger; Rhode Island, Battle of

References

Clinton, Henry. *The American Rebellion: Sir Henry Clinton's Narrative of His Campaigns, 1775–1782, with an Appendix of Original Documents.* Edited by William B. Willcox. New Haven, CT: Yale University Press, 1954.

Gruber, Ira D. *The Howe Brothers and the American Revolution.* New York: Norton, 1972.

Ward, Christopher. *War of the Revolution.* 2 vols. New York: Macmillan, 1952.

Willcox, William B. *Portrait of a General: Sir Henry Clinton in the War of Independence.* New York: Knopf, 1964.

Petersburg, Virginia, Action at

(25 April 1781)

At Petersburg, Virginia, 1,000 militiamen commanded by Generals Friedrich von Steuben and John Muhlenberg fought a stubborn and effective delaying action against 2,500 British and Loyalist soldiers under the command of Generals William Phillips and Benedict Arnold. After pushing the Americans out of Petersburg, Phillips conducted raids into the countryside to capture and destroy rebel supplies and equipment.

Since the late fall of 1780, Arnold had commanded a small British contingent in Virginia attempting to interdict the flow of rebel men and supplies southward into the Carolinas. When General Charles Cornwallis moved into North Carolina in early 1781, Sir Henry Clinton decided to send a stronger force to Virginia to support the effort in the South more effectively. He appointed Phillips, a highly experienced artillery officer, to lead the expedition to gain control of the Chesapeake region and raid rebel supply bases. In April 1781, Phillips invaded Portsmouth, Virginia, with almost 2,500 men and began a methodical campaign by moving up the James River toward Petersburg, a supply storage area and vital link in the American line of communication.

Unfortunately, the Americans had no Continental force in Virginia to defend against the British invasion. There was only a contingent of a little more than 1,000 militiamen under the overall command of Steuben. To confront Phillips's regular and Loyalist troops, Steuben had five regiments of infantry, three companies of cavalry, and two 6-pound artillery pieces. With these men, he was determined to hold out as long as he could to allow expected reinforcements led by the Marquis de Lafayette to reach Richmond and prepare defenses for that town. Steuben ordered Muhlenberg to shadow the British advance by moving south of the James River. On 24 April, Steuben confirmed that Petersburg was indeed Phillips's next target and ordered Muhlenberg's force to defend the town.

During the evening of 24 April 1781, Phillips landed 2,500 troops near City Point, at the confluence of the James and Appomattox Rivers. At 10:00

the next morning, Phillips's army began a 12-mile march from City Point to Petersburg along the south bank of the Appomattox River. At about noon the British column sighted the Americans deployed for battle. Muhlenberg exercised tactical command of the defending militia infantry in a position east of the small settlement of Blandford, which was separated from Petersburg by a wide valley cut by a small creek called Lieutenant's Run. Here Muhlenberg placed two regiments as the forward elements, overlooking another stream called Poor's Creek, to meet the British advance from the east. He took full advantage of the series of small hills cut by recently swollen streams to hinder the British advance.

Phillips deployed his army with a battalion of light infantry on his right flank and the 76th and 80th Foot regiments on his left. Before his army could get within musket range of the enemy, the men had to cross marshy low ground and then advance up a steep grade. Observing that Muhlenberg had not positioned any units south of Blandford, Phillips ordered the Loyalist Queen's Rangers and a battalion of light infantry to conduct a wide movement around the American right. If they could get behind the main American line, they might cut off the Americans' escape route across the Appomattox River.

As the British light infantry attacked Muhlenberg's left along the river road, heavy musket fire demonstrated that the American militia stood firm on well-chosen ground. The 76th and 80th Regiments attacking Muhlenberg's right flank also failed to make much headway. Phillips turned to his artillery detachment, with two 6-pounder and two 3-pounder guns, to fire into the American line to break up the stout defense. Muhlenberg reacted by ordering his troops to fall back through Blandford and join his main line on the high ground east of Petersburg.

As Phillips's men pursued the Americans through Blandford, his troops came under fire from Steuben's artillery, located on the heights north of the Appomattox overlooking Petersburg. Steuben had also deployed three companies of cavalry and a militia regiment to cover any enemy approaches north of the river. He had developed an effective defense that could react to any British move and yet, if necessary, make a safe escape from the superior British forces.

After the British moved through Blandford, they found themselves facing a valley filled with marshy ground beyond which, on the opposite summit, were four regiments of Virginia militia. As the British struggled to move across the low ground and close with the enemy above, they came under enfilading fire from Steuben's artillery. By this time, the Queen's Rangers had completed their flanking movement and were driving north into the American rear. Phillips ordered his artillery moved opposite to the American right flank where they could fire directly into Muhlenberg's line.

As the British struggled to advance, however, the American militia began to run low on ammunition. By about 4:00 P.M., Steuben was convinced that his defense had done all it could and ordered Muhlenberg to withdraw north of the Appomattox. The militia conducted an orderly retreat as they moved through Petersburg and across the Pocahontas Bridge, but the narrow bridge limited their movement, so Steuben ordered his cavalry and infantry north of the bridge to provide covering fire to protect the units making the crossing. As the battle for Petersburg came to a bloody close at about 6:00 P.M., the Americans removed the planks from the bridge to prevent any British pursuit.

Total American casualties during the battle were about 150 killed and wounded, while the British suffered 25 to 30 casualties. In spite of the overwhelming odds, the determined and disciplined Virginia militia had withstood the British attack on Petersburg. Following the American withdrawal, the British searched Petersburg for supplies. The largest cache they found contained 4,000 hogsheads of fine tobacco, which Phillips ordered burned.

Two days after the battle, Phillips led his army north toward Chesterfield Court House, where he burned a military barracks and destroyed several ships in the James River at Osborne's Landing. Meanwhile, the Continentals led by Lafayette had arrived at Richmond in time to prevent Phillips from taking the capital. Phillips decided that his expedition had been successful and ordered his army back to Portsmouth. He returned to Petersburg in May to rendezvous with Cornwallis, who was coming into Virginia from North Carolina. But by the time Phillips reached Petersburg, he was already ill with typhoid fever and died within a few days. He was buried in an unmarked grave somewhere on the battlefield of Petersburg.

STEVEN J. RAUCH

See also

Arnold, Benedict; Lafayette, Marquis de; Muhlenberg, John Peter Gabriel; Phillips, William; Southern Campaigns; Steuben, Friedrich von; Virginia

References

Davis, Robert P. *Where a Man Can Go: Major General William Phillips, British Royal Artillery, 1731–1781*. Westport, CT: Greenwood, 1999.
Johnston, Henry. *The Yorktown Campaign and the Surrender of Cornwallis*. 1881. Reprint, New York: Eastern Acorn, 1981.

Petty-Fitzmaurice, William, 2nd Earl of Shelburne
(1737–1805)

William Petty-Fitzmaurice, the 2nd Earl of Shelburne and later the 1st Marquis of Landsdowne, served as Britain's prime minister from July 1782 to February 1783 and oversaw the preliminary peace negotiations with the United States that ended the American Revolutionary War.

Fitzmaurice, generally referred to as Lord Shelburne, was born in Dublin, the son of John Fitzmaurice, the scion of a powerful County Kerry family and the 1st Earl of Shelburne, and his wife Mary, a cousin and descendant of Sir William Petty of High Wycombe. In his youth, Shelburne was educated at Christ Church, Oxford, and briefly pursued a military career. Having distinguished himself at both Minden in 1759 and Kloster Kampen in 1760, he was appointed an aide-de-camp with the rank of colonel to the young King George III. The death of his father in May 1761 would redirect Shelburne's life and transform his prospects, for he began a twenty-year political career as a member of both the Irish and the British House of Lords.

Despite his immense wealth, ambition, ability, and intellectual curiosity, or perhaps because of these advantages, Shelburne was highly distrusted by his parliamentary colleagues and disliked by George III. His rapid rise in British politics would perhaps have aroused envy in any event, but Shelburne generated intense hostility among his contemporaries. David Hartley, one of the British peace commissioners in 1782, told John Adams that as an Irishman, Shelburne "has all the impudence of his nation. He is a palaverer beyond all description . . . and has no sincerity." The same year, one of his political opponents, Dennis O'Bryen, charged that every motion of Shelburne's body, "every motion of his face, are accompanied with a design either to invite the indifferent, to conciliate the hostile, or to flatter the friendly."

Shelburne's early unpopularity may also have owed partly to the fact that he was groomed for office by his unscrupulous distant relative, Henry Fox, and in addition that he served his early political apprenticeship under the widely hated Lord Bute. While Shelburne's reputation for insincerity would continue to damage his standing and limit his career, it has also baffled historians. Nonetheless, that this British political antihero became prime minister at all is a tribute to the fact that in reality Shelburne was a superb political in-fighter.

Shelburne's political debut occurred in December 1762, when he moved for the acceptance of the preliminaries of the Peace of Paris in the House of Lords. Although he refused to accept office in the Bute administration, Shelburne was forced upon a reluctant George Grenville by Bute, who engineered his appointment as president of the Board of Trade in April 1763. Shelburne's performance in this position not only gave him his first opportunity to familiarize himself with American affairs but also established his pattern of ignoring his political colleagues and preferring to work privately with a few trusted subordinates, especially his long-serving private secretary, Maurice Morgann. Feeling aggrieved by his lack of real political power, Shelburne largely ignored the formation of colonial policy under the Grenville administration. Yet his rather routine correspondence with the secretary of state for the Southern Department, Lord Egremont, on the future of the newly acquired American territories resulted in the important Board of Trade report of 8 June 1763. Ambition and private concerns, rather than differences with his colleagues over American policy, led to Shelburne's resignation in September 1763. And private concerns, including his marriage to

William Petty, 2nd Earl of Shelburne, the British prime minister from 1782 to 1783. His ministry oversaw the final negotiations for peace and recognized the independence of the United States. (Bettmann/Corbis)

Lady Sophia Carteret in February 1765, continued to blind him to the potential dangers of Grenville's colonial policy.

In opposition, Shelburne forged a lasting alliance with William Pitt the Elder (later the Earl of Chatham), and although Lord Rockingham offered Shelburne his old position at the Board of Trade in July 1765, he declined it. In early 1765, Shelburne was forewarned by Morgann of American opposition to the Stamp Act and consequently followed Pitt's lead in believing that abstract constitutional questions endangered the harmony of the empire. Shelburne spoke in favor of the repeal of the Stamp Act in February 1766 and was strongly opposed to the passage of the Declaratory Act in March of that year. When Pitt was ennobled as Lord Chatham and formed his second ministry in July 1766, Shelburne was appointed the secretary of state for an enlarged Southern Department, with full control of American affairs.

Although Shelburne was viewed as a friend to America, the continued colonial opposition to imperial regulation led him to suggest firm measures to uphold British authority when the New York Assembly refused to comply with the 1765 Quartering Act. Yet within an administration that gradually moved politically to the right on colonial matters, Shelburne nonetheless supported continued westward expansion, the extension of full civil rights to the French inhabitants of Quebec, and the end to military rule in that province while opposing the introduction of the Townshend duties in June 1767. Characteristically, Shelburne's answer to his increasing political isolation in the cabinet, even after the death of Charles Townshend in September 1767, was to merely stop attending its meetings.

At the same time, Lord Chatham's strange physical and mental malady soon began to weaken the whole administration and kept him from preventing the Duke of Grafton from reducing Shelburne's supervision of American affairs by creating the new American Department under Lord Hillsborough in January 1768. Mistakenly believing that Shelburne had been dismissed in September 1768, Chatham resigned, an action that prompted Shelburne's own resignation from office in October 1768. When the Grafton administration finally fell apart the following year, George III sent for Lord Frederick North, not the Earl of Chatham, to form a new administration. Shelburne would not return to office until the news of the defeat of Yorktown brought down North's long-lived administration in March 1782.

During these years of opposition, from 1768 to 1782, Shelburne's estate at Bowood became a center for some of the most advanced thinkers of their day, many of whom were prominent friends to America. Shelburne's small parliamentary following included Colonel Isaac Barré and John Dunning as well as Shelburne's librarian for eight years, the Reverend Joseph Priestley. Following the outbreak of the War of Independence, Shelburne cultivated a growing friendship among the radical politicians of London, and Dr. Richard Price, Jeremy Bentham, and the leader of the Yorkshire Association, the Reverend Christopher Wyvill, all became associated with Shelburne, though none of them seem to have completely trusted him. Eventually all of these associates became disillusioned with what they perceived as Shelburne's insincerity and intellectual pretensions, and only Morgann, who served Shelburne for more than twenty years, remained loyal to him. Following the death of his first wife in January 1771, Shelburne undertook a Continental tour on which he met a number of French philosophes, including Turgot and Morellet, and became interested in the doctrine of free trade. Several historians have suggested that this interest influenced his direction of the peace negotiations with the Americans in 1782.

As the constitutional impasse of the British Empire worsened, Shelburne continued to adhere to the Chathamite position that constitutional differences between Britain and its colonies were little more than irrelevant abstractions that blinded both sides of the transatlantic community to their real economic interest, a mutually beneficial trade. Following the imperial crisis generated by the Boston Tea Party in December 1773, Shelburne continued to oppose the coercion of the colonies. In January 1775 he supported Chatham's motion that British troops ought to be withdrawn from Boston, and in February 1775 he supported Chatham's call for a plan of reconciliation with the colonies. In March 1776, Shelburne supported the Duke of Richmond's motion that German troops ought not to be employed in the king's dominions, and he was present when Chatham collapsed in the House of Lords on 7 April 1778 while advocating a negotiated peace with America. Chatham's death three weeks later elevated Shelburne to the leadership of the Chathamites in Parliament, where he continued to be a vocal friend to America. Nevertheless, he refused to accept the possibility of American independence. Throughout the war, he continued to advocate the necessity of an eventual reestablishment of the transatlantic relationship, vaguely based upon economic self-interest.

Shelburne's small parliamentary following precluded him from forming an administration following the collapse of the North ministry in March 1782, so he entered a coalition government as secretary of state for home affairs under Lord Rockingham. Divisions over the political status of Ireland, the need for parliamentary and economic reform, and the issue of American independence would all bedevil Rockingham's brief second administration. His followers, especially his other secretary of state, Charles James Fox, believed that American independence should be recognized as a prelude to peace negotiations. Shelburne, whose position was supported by the king, believed that independence should be a topic for negotiation. As both Shelburne's and Fox's peace envoys haggled in Paris, Shelburne dispatched Morgann to New York City to try to persuade the American leadership to return to their old family affections. This peace commission was ill-conceived, as both General George Washington and Congress refused to accept Morgann as an envoy, and in May 1782 Morgann informed Shelburne that the "fancy of independence" was so deep in America that it could not be denied them.

Rockingham's unexpected death in July 1782 led to the formation of Shelburne's own short-lived administration from July 1782 to February 1783. Aided by the fact that Parliament was in recess, Shelburne, a late convert to the idea of an independent United States, closely supervised the preliminary peace negotiations that finally concluded an agreement on 30 November 1782. While there can be no doubt that he hoped that the generous boundaries granted to the United States would conciliate the new republic, there is little evidence to suggest that Shelburne, as asserted by a number of historians, including Vincent Harlow, was systematically working toward a preconceived plan guided by the principles of free trade.

Blind to domestic political realities, his own personal unpopularity, and the hostility generated by his failure to secure adequate compensation for the Loyalists or assurances for Britain's Native American allies from the American negotiators, Shelburne faced an angry Parliament in the winter of 1783. Although his peace preliminaries scraped through the House of Lords, they were narrowly defeated in the House of Commons by 224 votes to 208 on 18 February. The peace preliminaries would eventually be accepted, but Shelburne resigned from office on 24 February 1783. Although only forty-five years old, he would never hold office again, and he was soon overshadowed in his own party by the rising career of William Pitt the Younger. In November 1784, Pitt secured for Shelburne an aristocratic promotion to the marquessate of Landsdowne.

An able speaker and an aristocratic leader who was intellectually superior to most of his contemporaries, Shelburne never came to understand his political eclipse or his unpopularity. His personality continues to baffle scholars, and if his advocacy of domestic political reform and a more conciliatory attitude toward America has commended him to some nineteenth- and early-twentieth-century historians, it won him few friends among his contemporaries. The research of more recent scholars has suggested that Shelburne's liberal vision of empire differed only in degree from that of his political opponents and was not, in reality, a distinctive alternative to the then accepted political orthodoxy. Shelburne died in London on 7 May 1805 and is buried at High Wycombe.

RORY T. CORNISH

See also

Barré, Isaac; Fox, Charles James; George III, King of England; North, Lord Frederick; Oswald, Richard; Paris, Treaty of (1783); Price, Richard; Priestley, Joseph; Pitt, William, the Elder; Pitt, William, the Younger; Proclamation of 1763; Smith, Adam; Versailles, Treaty of; Watson-Wentworth, Charles, 2nd Marquis of Rockingham

References

Brown, Peter. *The Chathamites*. London and New York: Macmillan, 1967.
Cornish, R. T. "Maurice Morgann (c. 1725/26–1802)—A British Undersecretary of State Revisited." *Proceedings of the South Carolina Historical Association* (2004): 1–12.
Gould, Eliza H. *The Persistence of Empire: British Political Culture in the Age of the American Revolution*. Chapel Hill: University of North Carolina Press, 2000.
Harlow, Vincent *The Founding of the Second British Empire*. London: Longmans, Green, 1952.
Langford, Paul. "Old Whigs, Old Tories and the American Revolution." *Journal of Imperial and Commonwealth History* 8 (1980): 106–130.
Norris, John. *Shelburne and Reform*. London: Macmillan, 1963.

O'Bryen, Dennis. *A Defense of the Rt. Hon. The Earl of Shelburne*. London: J. Stockdale, 1782.

Ritcheson, Charles K. "The Earl of Shelburne and Peace with America, 1782–1785: Vision and Reality." *International History Review* 3 (1983): 322–329.

Walsh-Atkins, P. "Shelburne and America, 1763–1783." Unpublished PhD diss., Oxford University, 1971.

Philadelphia

Philadelphia was at the center of the American Revolutionary War, with a few brief interruptions, from the convening of the First Continental Congress in 1774 until the conclusion of peace with Great Britain in 1783. Thereafter, it remained America's principal city and was usually its capital until the federal government moved to Washington, D.C., in 1800. Yet as a community, this capital and its surrounding state did not consistently play a leading role in either the politics of the Revolution or the war. The early Revolutionary movement developed more slowly in Philadelphia, and in Pennsylvania, than in several other cities, notably Boston and New York City, and in several other colonies, especially Massachusetts, Connecticut, and Virginia. Once the Revolution triumphed in Philadelphia, however, it brought about a more radical transformation in government than in any other city. Yet once the war itself had begun, Pennsylvania supplied a relatively moderate amount of supplies and number of soldiers, given its large agricultural economy and population, and produced few Continental Army officers of great distinction.

On the eve of the American Revolution, Philadelphia, with about 30,000 residents, was the largest city in British North America and was one of the largest cities in the British Empire. In population and trade it even rivaled several major cities in the British Isles, such as Bristol, Dublin, Edinburgh, and Glasgow, although it was a small fraction of the size of London. Two forces drove the city's strong growth from its founding in 1682. The first was Pennsylvania's easy tolerance of all religions and nationalities and its great abundance of land, which made Philadelphia North America's preferred port of entry for every European nationality from the 1720s to the Revolution. The second was its position as the major port for the largest wheat- and grain-producing area in North America, and by the 1770s, wheat and flour were North America's second largest export, trailing only tobacco.

With such advantages, Philadelphia began to rival both Boston and New York as a cultural and medical center by midcentury, when it founded three institutions that had no counterpart elsewhere in British North America: the Philadelphia Library Company, the American Philosophical Society, and the Pennsylvania Hospital. It also had a lively and increasingly sophisticated press, headed by Benjamin Franklin's *Pennsylvania Gazette*. By 1776, Philadelphia had more newspapers than any other American city. And it enjoyed the greatest variety of peoples and faiths, after New York, of any American city, with large numbers of English, Welsh, Scottish, and Irish settlers as well as many Germans and a few Dutch, Swedes, Finns, and French

View of the Philadelphia State House, circa 1778. The First and Second Continental Congresses met in Philadelphia, which was occupied by British forces from September 1777 to June 1778. Following the American Revolution, Philadelphia was America's principal city and capital until 1800. (Library of Congress)

Huguenots and a moderate number of Africans, both slave and free. These peoples worshiped in Quaker, Anglican, Presbyterian, German and Dutch Reformed, German and Swedish Lutheran, Baptist, and Roman Catholic churches, and in one of British North America's five Jewish synagogues.

When the North American colonies began openly protesting British policy in response to the Stamp Act, Philadelphia's response was nearly as strong as that of Boston, New York, and Charleston. And the Philadelphia-based lawyer John Dickinson, most often remembered for his series of newspaper articles collectively known as "Letters from a Farmer in Pennsylvania" (1768), became one of the Revolutionary movement's great penmen. But during America's extended response to the Townshend revenue duties, from 1768 to 1771, Pennsylvania's deeply conservative assembly and Philadelphia's powerful Quaker merchants worked to modify the commitment of city and province to the cause of resistance. Philadelphia's radical leaders, headed by Dickinson and Charles Thomson, had to struggle to bring the city to oppose the Tea Act in 1773 and then to support Massachusetts against the Coercive Acts in 1774, and the provincial assembly remained cool to the First Continental Congress.

When Pennsylvania conservative Joseph Galloway failed to control Congress in 1774 and lost his position as Speaker of the provincial assembly, Pennsylvanians began looking to his rival, Dickinson, who supported both Congress and, with some misgivings, armed conflict the following year. Philadelphia itself, meanwhile, was finally radicalized by the Revolutionary movement. In the course of electing committees of observation, inspection, and correspondence to enforce Congress's Continental Association of October 1774, the city brought many new men into public roles, particularly Joseph Reed, who would remain a powerful figure in Philadelphia and then Pennsylvania politics for the next decade. The first committee of sixty-six members, chosen in November 1774, was succeeded by bodies of one hundred members, the first elected in August 1775, and the next (and last) in February 1776. In each case secret ballot elections, employing printed tickets, chose the more radically resistant candidates, drawing in scores of new men at each turn. And in May 1775, in response to Lexington and Concord, Philadelphians formed large militia units, the first seen in Pennsylvania in nearly twenty years. Philadelphia's militia, called the Associators, quickly elected several new and often even more radical leaders who promptly began feuding with the provincial assembly, which was reluctant to support a militia effectively.

In the spring of 1776, Dickinson and the Pennsylvania Assembly, who were prepared to resist Britain but not to chance a full revolution in government, fought a rearguard action against independence. Most Philadelphians, and most rural Pennsylvanians, reacted with fury by drafting America's most radically democratic constitution in September 1776 and electing a very different legislature immediately thereafter. The new Pennsylvania Constitution of 1776 continued the state's one-house legislature, created a Supreme Executive Council, and granted every freeman who paid any taxes or served in the militia the right to vote. Thereafter, the state had what was probably the broadest voting franchise enjoyed by any large area and population on the face of the globe.

For the remainder of the Revolutionary War, a radicalized Pennsylvania and its capital city supported independence, but often with less zeal than several other states and cities, both to the north and the south. There were two main reasons for this relative lack of firm popular support, which particularly distressed the thousands of New York and New England soldiers of the Continental Army camped at Valley Forge (December 1777–June 1778). First, both the city and the countryside contained thousands of persons who opposed the Revolutionary War. Many were Loyalists, but many more—especially English Quakers and German Mennonites and Amish—were committed pacifists who both deplored the war and resented the harsh claims in money and military service that the aggressive new government tried to impose on all inhabitants. When these groups resisted paying taxes or bearing arms, Pennsylvania's new leaders responded with Test Acts, which required the people to take loyalty oaths in order to vote and hold office. This had little effect on the Mennonites and Amish, who had generally not been politically active, but it quickly drove all remaining Quakers, the denomination that had dominated colonial Pennsylvania, from public life.

Second, in September 1777, General William Howe invaded southeastern Pennsylvania, defeated General George Washington in battles at Brandywine and Germantown, and seized Philadelphia. For nearly nine

> Philadelphia had more newspapers than any other American city.

months the city was securely in British hands, and its appointed civilian administrator was Galloway, the former Speaker of the Pennsylvania Assembly who had since become an ardent Loyalist. For these months, as during a brief earlier period (December 1776–February 1777) when the British Army had approached Philadelphia across New Jersey and Congress fled to Baltimore, Philadelphia lost its important role as America's capital. During the British occupation, Loyalist merchants briefly became the city's leading citizens. But in June 1778, the British Army evacuated Philadelphia for New York, and Congress soon returned. Congress would remain in the city for several more years, with a brief sojourn in Annapolis in 1783 and a long stay in New York from 1785 to 1790 before again returning to make Philadelphia the capital of the new federal nation for the next decade.

But the later years of the war were difficult for Philadelphians. In 1778, General Benedict Arnold was appointed the chief administrator in charge of supplying the city as it recovered from the British occupation. During his stay in Philadelphia, Arnold not only married Peggy Shippen, daughter of a merchant of strong Loyalist sympathies but also abused his office by profiting from supplying the city with provisions and soon ran afoul of Joseph Reed, president of Pennsylvania's Supreme Executive Council. And Reed himself quickly became embroiled in arguments over the high price of food between the city's merchants, whom he supported, and the radicalized Associators who demanded price controls. This dispute even resulted in an armed clash at James Wilson's house (the so-called Fort Wilson Incident) in the fall of 1778. Philadelphia's economic crisis eventually eased as the city's trade, which had been repeatedly disrupted and then reoriented from the fall of 1776 through the end of 1778, gradually recovered and, in the last years of the war, regained its old vigor. And Philadelphians were able to take sweet revenge on Arnold in the fall of 1780 when his treason at West Point offered them the chance to cart a two-faced masked figure through the streets, with a devil figure behind him, offering gold to the general to betray his country.

The larger political battles in Pennsylvania, however, did not end. Both city and state had divided between two sharply defined political parties, the Constitutionalists, who defended the radical state constitution of 1776, and the Republicans, who opposed it. Both parties remained powerful until 1790, when the Constitutionalists, weakened by their opposition to the new U.S. Constitution in 1787, finally lost their battle to defend their own unicameral, weak-executive constitution, and the state framed a new document along the bicameral, strong-executive model that predominated in the new nation. This fourteen-year struggle had dominated virtually every annual election to the legislature, generated the widely hated Test Acts against Loyalists and pacifists, and divided both city and state along class, ethnic, and religious lines. Militia Associators, artisans and laborers in Philadelphia, and Scots-Irish Presbyterian and German Reformed voters everywhere rallied to the Constitutionalists, while city merchants, Anglicans, and most men of Quaker background who remained politically active formed the core of the Republican faction. During the war itself, the Constitutionalists generally predominated, but during the nation's economic difficulties of the 1780s the Republicans gained ground and finally used their support of the U.S. Constitution during the ratification struggle in the fall of 1787 to seize control of the state.

Pennsylvania also had to endure the embarrassing behavior of its Continental Army troops. Both in 1780 and 1782, whole regiments of the Pennsylvania line mutinied for more pay and a postwar settlement for service and marched on Philadelphia to intimidate Congress. This rebellious behavior may have damaged Philadelphia's chances to become America's permanent capital a decade later, although larger political considerations were decisive in the selection of the Potomac River, rather than the Delaware River, as the site for a new federal city.

In other respects, however, Philadelphia fared well after the Revolutionary War. Both its economy and population continued to grow rapidly in the 1780s and 1790s, with an enormous new influx of immigrants from Ireland, its robust grain and flour export trade with Western Europe and the Mediterranean nations, and the firm establishment of its import trade with Britain. The city flourished during its decade as the federal capital and continued to grow after 1800, remaining the nation's first city until New York surpassed it, in population and trade, in the 1820s. Philadelphia's institutional life as a city, which had been virtually extinguished when the colonial City of Philadelphia was abolished in 1776, was restored in the 1790s with new powers and control over an increased geographical area.

Overall, the American Revolution probably helped Philadelphia considerably more than it hurt the city. Despite the anxiety of dealing with the threat of the invading British Army in 1776 and 1777, the lengthy British occupation in 1777–1778, and the chaotic year following the occupation, Philadelphia's role as America's capital for most of the period from 1774 to 1800 brought great economic and cultural benefits to the city. At the end of the Revolutionary War, just as on the eve of that event, Philadelphia was the most important city in America.

RICHARD A. RYERSON

See also

Arnold, Benedict; Congress, First Continental; Congress, Second Continental and Confederation; Constitution, United States; Constitution, United States, Ratification of; Continental Army; Dickinson, John; Franklin, Benjamin; Galloway, Joseph; Nonimportation Agreements; Paine, Thomas; Pennsylvania; Ross, Betsy; Thomson, Charles; Valley Forge, Pennsylvania; Wilson, James

References

Bodle, Wayne. *The Valley Forge Winter: Civilians and Soldiers in War.* University Park, PA: Penn State University Press, 2002.

Brunhouse, Robert L. *The Counter-Revolution in Pennsylvania, 1776–1790.* Harrisburg: Pennsylvania Historical and Museum Commission, 1942.

Foner, Eric. *Tom Paine and Revolutionary America.* London and New York: Oxford University Press, 1976.

Nash, Gary B. *The Urban Crucible: Social Change, Political Consciousness and the Origins of the American Revolution.* Cambridge: Harvard University Press, 1979.

Olton, Charles S. *Artisans for Independence: Philadelphia Mechanics and the American Revolution.* Syracuse, NY: Syracuse University Press, 1975.

Rosswurm, Steven. *Arms, Country, and Class: The Philadelphia Militia and the "Lower Sort" during the American Revolution.* New Brunswick, NJ: Rutgers University Press, 1987.

Ryerson, Richard Alan. *The Revolution Is Now Begun: The Radical Committees of Philadelphia, 1765–1776.* Philadelphia: University of Pennsylvania Press, 1978.

Selsam, J. Paul. *The Pennsylvania Constitution of 1776: A Study in Revolutionary Democracy.* 1936. Reprint, New York: Octagon, 1971.

Smith, Bill G. *The "Lower Sort": Philadelphia's Laboring People, 1750–1800.* Ithaca, NY: Cornell University Press, 1990.

Philadelphia Campaign

The Philadelphia Campaign lasted from 25 August to 19 December 1777. Senior British commanders intended the campaign to be decisive, though they failed to achieve this aim. While the British were successful in defeating the Continental Army in two major battles and a series of skirmishes, they were unable to crush their opponents once and for all. In any case, the Continental Army was able to regroup and threaten British positions in the Philadelphia area throughout the course of the campaign. The British achieved a degree of success by seizing the colonial capital, but a decisive military victory nevertheless eluded them. American forces remained in the field, bolstered by their resilience and by the defeat of General John Burgoyne's army during the Saratoga Campaign in New York.

Throughout June and July 1777, the British commander in chief, General Sir William Howe, headquartered in New York City, attempted to draw General George Washington into battle. Howe wished to move against Philadelphia, while Washington aimed to protect the land approaches to Philadelphia through New Jersey. Washington was unsure of Howe's plans; he thought that Howe might advance north toward Albany to link up with British forces coming from Quebec.

Both sides maneuvered around northeastern New Jersey, each side attempting to gain the advantage. Howe eventually realized that he could not bring Washington to battle in New Jersey and in late July embarked his army of 12,000 men and sailed south from New York. Washington advanced on Philadelphia, still intending to defend the city. He left behind a small corps in Morristown to deal with any British move to the north. He still feared that Howe might return to New York and march north toward Albany.

On 30 July, the British fleet was sighted near the Delaware Capes. Washington, with most of his army committed to the defense of Philadelphia, continued to worry about Howe's next move. It was not until 10 August, when Washington received news that the British fleet had been sighted off the coast of Maryland, that he finally determined that the British must be planning to land somewhere to the south.

Howe had avoided landing along the Delaware River for fear of a strong American presence in the region. He had failed to gather proper intelligence; in reality he could have safely landed at Chester, about 30 miles south of Philadelphia. Instead, he decided to land his troops at the northern end of Chesapeake Bay, at a place called Head of Elk. After Washington received news that the British fleet had been sighted off Maryland, he moved his 12,000 troops south from New Jersey and Pennsylvania, marching through Philadelphia on 24 August.

On the following day, after six weeks at sea, Howe's force landed at Head of Elk. Washington, meanwhile, was advancing south toward Wilmington, Delaware. He thought that Howe was planning to make a direct attack on Philadelphia. Howe took his time to move out after disembarking, knowing that his men were tired and in need of reinforcements and supplies. He moved his forces a short distance due east of the landing area, making Washington suspicious that Howe was planning to move against Wilmington.

Rested and ready for the march, the British moved out in early September. A series of small skirmishes took place as each side tried to gain intelligence on the whereabouts and movements of the other. As they had done during the previous campaign in New Jersey, the British looted and pillaged their way across the countryside to compensate for their lack of supplies. Howe decided to proceed due north, as his scouts had reported a large American build-up to the east, in and around Wilmington.

British surprise attack on Continental forces at Paoli during the night of 21 September 1777. The British success, in which large numbers of prisoners were taken, prevented Anthony Wayne from attacking Charles Cornwallis's baggage train. (Library of Congress)

On 3 September, the first major skirmish occurred between the two armies at Cooch's Bridge. Troops in the American vanguard, under the command of Brigadier General William Maxwell, had been deployed to ambush the enemy advance guard under the command of Lieutenant-General Lord Charles Cornwallis. Light troops on both sides became heavily engaged. Maxwell was under orders only to inflict damage and then retreat. After his troops expended most of their ammunition, the British launched a bayonet attack. The Americans were forced back, with each side losing about forty men killed and wounded.

Following this skirmish, Howe consolidated his force, sending his wounded men and extra baggage back to the landing area at Head of Elk. Both sides settled down in the area, sending out more scouts to gather intelligence. Meanwhile, the supporting Royal Navy fleet prepared to depart, which Washington interpreted as a sign that Howe was readying himself for an advance on Philadelphia.

On 8 September, Howe sent forward a few units that, deploying themselves in front of the American positions, screened Howe's troops so as to conceal the commander's true intentions. He then moved his main body westward in an attempt to outflank the Americans. Washington, alerted to the ruse, began to shift his forces northward toward Chadds Ford and Brandywine Creek. The Americans had the shorter march, since they were marching on interior lines. The positions of both armies were ideal: one to defend and the other to attack in the direction of Philadelphia.

Washington began to build up his defenses near Brandywine and Chadds Ford on the morning of 10 September. British forces had reached Kennett Square, 5 miles to the east of Chadds Ford, late on the previous day. Washington deployed Maxwell with his light infantry to the east of Chadds Ford to report on the movements of the British.

On the morning of 11 September, the Battle of Brandywine began in earnest. The Americans were deployed in a line stretching north-south for 5 miles along Brandywine Creek, with the main defense resting on Chadds Ford. Smaller units were positioned to the north to report on any movement by the British. Howe's plan consisted of a flanking attack to the northeast. He deployed a third of his force along the main road to Chadds Ford; these proceeded to attack and drive back the Americans toward the creek. This attack was, however, merely a feint. The British and Hessian troops had been ordered to advance and execute the main attack.

Meanwhile, a second force, comprising the remainder of the army, was marching under Howe and Cornwallis in an 18-mile flanking movement to the northeast. Their movements were mostly undetected, and Washington and his staff did not realize the threat to their right flank until it was almost too late. Washington therefore shifted part of the American line to repel the British attack, and heavy fighting ensued. Howe's flanking movement proved successful, but the units that composed it did not enter into action until 4:00 P.M. The Americans were defeated but were not routed, and Howe was thus unable to inflict a decisive blow. The Americans lost close to 1,000 men killed, wounded, and captured; the British lost half that number.

Following the battle, Washington and his army withdrew to Chester, due east of Chadds Ford, and on 12 September, realizing that his position at Chester was precarious, he decided to withdraw northwest of Philadelphia. There he replenished his troops and received reinforcements. He then moved south again, crossing the Schuylkill River at Swede's Ford in an attempt to block the British advance on Philadelphia that he was convinced would ultimately materialize.

The British were slow to advance after Brandywine; they had marched only 10 miles north of Chadds Ford by 16 September. Realizing that Howe's forces were marching in dispersed columns, Washington moved to engage a British column at Warren Tavern, until weather forced the abandonment of his plans. His ammunition supplies were ruined by rain, and he was forced to withdraw to the west to acquire more supplies. Nevertheless, he left a brigade of militia under the command of Brigadier General Anthony Wayne in the forests near Paoli to oppose any British movements in the area.

With Washington's second withdrawal, there was virtually nothing to stop Howe from taking Philadelphia. He decided, however, to move against Wash-

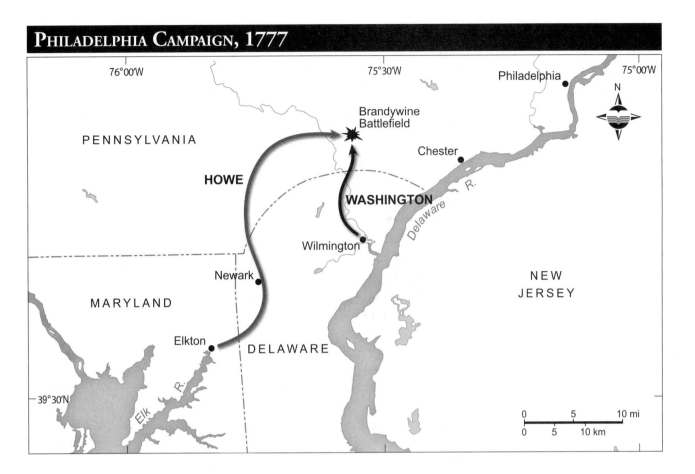

ington's army and destroy it if he could. Howe marched slowly toward the northwest, where Washington's troops were concentrated. In the meantime, Washington had been resupplied and began to march his forces toward Howe. The presence of Wayne and his troops was reported to Howe on 19 September. Howe decided to destroy Wayne's forces and dispatched a column of 5,000 men under the command of Major-General Charles Grey. Part of this force was sent to the south of Paoli to confront any escaping American forces.

The action that followed, sometimes known as the Paoli Massacre, took place in the early hours of 21 September. Grey, who was aware of Wayne's defensive position and wanted to surprise the Americans, deployed half his force with orders to attack without firing a shot. The battle was swift: the Americans were decisively defeated, thanks partially to Wayne's failure to construct proper defenses. The Americans suffered 500 men killed, wounded, and captured; the British counted only 7 wounded. After their success at Paoli, word spread quickly of British skill in the use of the bayonet. Many of Washington's militia troops, fearful of encountering them, failed to report for duty. He urgently requested reinforcements to replace them.

Howe decided to launch another feint attack to keep Washington off balance and dispatched a force toward the west to threaten Washington's supply depots. Washington began to move to the west to intercept Howe, who shifted the main force of his army toward Philadelphia. The British crossed the Schuylkill River on 22 September, and by 26 September they had occupied Philadelphia.

Howe was already experiencing major supply problems when he entered the nearly deserted city. He therefore sent 3,000 troops southward to help the Royal Navy clear American defenses along the Delaware River, which would open the way for waterborne supplies. He moved another 8,000 troops northwest to Germantown to oppose any movement Washington might make with the main body of his army. Finally, Howe left Cornwallis with 3,000 men to hold Philadelphia and to serve as a reserve and a potential threat to any rebel operations in New Jersey.

Over the course of three days in late September, Washington received reinforcements of both Continental and militia troops. In early October, he devised a bold plan. He would advance toward the British camp at Germantown, seeking to inflict a devastating blow on the forces there. This would mark the first attack by the main American army on its British counterpart over open terrain. Washington's plan called for four columns—two militia and two Continental—to advance in a coordinated fashion during the evening hours so as to surprise the British camp at dawn. As planned, the Americans attacked in the early hours of 4 October. However, the plan quickly began to unravel when the militia columns failed to advance at the proper time and attack the British lines with vigor. The two Continental brigades advanced in two different stages. Further complications arose when the Americans discovered that the British had established an unexpectedly strong position at Chew House, when one militia column got lost, and when fighting became confused because of heavy fog. Despite this, by 8:00 A.M. the Americans were close to victory, as the British center began to waver under the American attack. However, when two American brigades mistook one another for the enemy and fired on each other, the British seized their chance and immediately counterattacked. Beset by lack of discipline and dwindling ammunition, the Americans began to fall back. As at Brandywine, they withdrew in fairly good order and once again denied Howe a decisive victory. Washington withdrew to the northwest, while the British remained in the area around Germantown for two weeks.

On 19 October, Howe withdrew from Germantown to Philadelphia to shorten his supply lines. He built a series of redoubts to protect the approaches to Philadelphia, a strategy that was eventually to backfire on him. As a result of these withdrawals, Washington was left in command of the countryside, enabling American raiding parties to deny enemy foragers all access to supplies much beyond the confines of Philadelphia. This forced Howe to confront the problem posed by American defenses on the Delaware once and for all, for he now would have to depend on the Royal Navy's ability to convey supplies to his army by water. The American strongholds of Fort Mercer, on the New Jersey bank of the river, and of Fort Mifflin, on Mud Island in the middle of the Delaware, had to be captured. Howe had already ordered the bombardment of Fort Mifflin, but the Americans had thus far not surrendered.

The British attacked Fort Mercer on 22 October. The garrison, under Colonel Christopher Greene, totaled just under 500 men. Howe gave orders for Colonel Carl von Donop and 2,000 Hessians to attack the position, which would be supported by a Royal Navy ship of the line, three frigates, and a floating artillery battery.

The Hessian brigade was transported to the eastern bank of the river and marched toward Fort Mercer. The attackers retired in the face of American artillery fire, but at 4:00 P.M. they demanded the surrender of the fort. When that failed, they threatened the slaughter of the entire garrison on its eventual capture. When this threat was ignored, the Hessians resumed their artillery fire and advanced in two columns, which were repulsed after forty minutes of continuous musket fire. British ships offered heavy supporting fire throughout, but the attack failed, and more than 400 Hessians lay dead or wounded. The Royal Navy vessels had suffered as well. Two ships, including the ship of the line, had run aground on the mud banks. The next day, the guns from both forts pounded these ships. The ship of the line caught fire, and the frigate was destroyed by its crew to avoid capture.

The British next decided to subdue both forts through prolonged bombardment. Redoubts were constructed to fire on Fort Mifflin, and the intense bombardment lasted from 10–15 November, eventually killing or wounding some 200 men—more than half the garrison. The Royal Navy provided additional support, and on 16 November the survivors of the garrison were withdrawn by American ships. With the destruction of Fort Mifflin, Howe turned his attention once again to Fort Mercer. He deployed another force of 2,000 men, compelling the Americans there to withdraw on 22 November. At last Howe had successfully cleared the Delaware of American defenses.

Washington had remained throughout November with his forces at Whitemarsh, a few miles from Germantown. His army was depleted as a result of casualties and the expiration of enlistment contracts. He lacked supplies to rearm units and feed his troops. When he requested reinforcements, many militia officers in New Jersey refused to march for fear of a British strike across the Delaware into New Jersey or from New York City. Washington was in no position to attack the defenses around Philadelphia.

Howe, after clearing the Delaware, decided to march out to seek a battle with Washington at Whitemarsh. The American defenses were strong, but their numbers had dwindled. Howe arrived opposite Washington's positions on 4 December, and a short but sharp skirmish quickly ensued. Realizing, however, that his opponent's defenses were in fact too strong to breach, Howe soon decided to withdraw, and he returned with his forces to Philadelphia to establish winter quarters there. Washington also decided that the time was right to withdraw to winter quarters. He marched his depleted forces northwest to Valley Forge, arriving on 21 December.

The Philadelphia Campaign was over. The British had been successful at Brandywine and Germantown, but they had not been able to prevent the main American army from making orderly retreats and regrouping in order to fight another day. Howe's last bid to draw the Americans into battle at

Whitemarsh had also failed. British forces had succeeded in occupying Philadelphia, but they had still not managed to destroy Washington's army.

DANIEL PATRICK MARSTON

See also

Brandywine, Battle of; Burgoyne, John; Cooch's Bridge, Delaware, Action at; Cornwallis, Charles; Fort Mercer, New Jersey, Assault on and Capture of; Fort Mifflin, Pennsylvania, Siege and Capture of; German Mercenaries; Germantown, Battle of; Grey, Charles; Howe, William; Maxwell, William; Morristown, New Jersey, Continental Army Winter Quarters; Paoli, Battle of; Saratoga Campaign; Valley Forge, Pennsylvania; Washington, George; Wayne, Anthony; Whitemarsh, Pennsylvania, Action at

References

Black, Jeremy. *War for America: The Fight for Independence*. Stroud, Gloucestershire, UK: Alan Sutton, 1991.

Clinton, Henry. *The American Rebellion: Sir Henry Clinton's Narrative of His Campaigns, 1775–1782, with an Appendix of Original Documents*. Edited by William B. Willcox. New Haven, CT: Yale University Press, 1954.

Conway, Stephen. *The War of American Independence, 1775–1783*. London: Arnold, 1995.

Ewald, Johann. *Diary of the American War: A Hessian Journal*. New Haven, CT: Yale University Press, 1979.

Ford, Worthington C., ed. *Defenses of Philadelphia in 1777*. N.d. Reprint, New York: Da Capo, 1971.

Higginbotham, Don. *The War of American Independence: Military Attitudes, Policies, and Practice, 1763–1789*. New York: Macmillan, 1971.

Mackesy, Piers. *The War for America, 1775–1783*. 1965. Reprint, Lincoln: University of Nebraska Press, 1993.

Pancake, John S. *1777: The Year of the Hangman*. University: University of Alabama Press, 1977.

Reed, John F. *Campaign to Valley Forge: July 1 to December 19, 1777*. Philadelphia: University of Pennsylvania Press, 1965.

Thompson, Ray. *Washington at Whitemarsh: Prelude to Valley Forge*. Fort Washington, PA: Bicentennial Press, 1970.

Wood, W. J. *Battles of the Revolutionary War, 1775–1781*. Chapel Hill, NC: Algonquin, 1990.

Pickens, Andrew

(1739–1817)

Andrew Pickens, a South Carolina militia officer during the War for American Independence, rose to prominence because of his notable abilities as a leader of citizen soldiers. Although not an educated man, he was eloquent in his use of language. A devout Presbyterian and devoted Patriot, his personality and actions were molded by these basic characteristics.

Pickens was born in Paxton Township, Pennsylvania, and spent his childhood in Virginia and North Carolina before his parents finally settled in the Waxhaws area of South Carolina in 1752. As an adult, he was of medium height, lean in physique, and robust. His father died in 1757. Four years later, Pickens took part in Lieutenant-Colonel James Grant's campaign against the Cherokee Indians in the western Carolinas, serving as a company officer in a South Carolina regiment and getting his first taste of what he later called the brutish cruelty of war. On a more positive note, Pickens met a number of important low-country South Carolinians during his service, forming acquaintances that would be useful to him in the future.

In 1763 or 1764, Pickens moved to the Long Canes settlement on the South Carolina frontier. This area was deeply divided during the next two decades over political issues leading to the American war against Britain. Many leaders of both the Patriot and Loyalist factions sprang from the Long Canes region. On 19 March 1765, Pickens married Rebecca Calhoun, niece of Patrick Calhoun, an ardent Patriot, thereby establishing close ties with a number of Whig families in the South Carolina up-country. The couple had ten children. Soon Pickens was a settled landowner in the Abbeville area, an Indian trader, and a justice of the peace. His close associations with Patriots inclined him to favor the cause of America when fighting with Britain broke out in 1775. As a volunteer captain, he served under Andrew Williamson in suppressing Loyalists such as Thomas Fletchall, Joseph Robinson, Moses Kirkland, and Robert, Patrick, and William Cunningham. On 19 November 1775, near Ninety-Six, Pickens took part in dispersing Loyalists in the first action of the war in South Carolina. His early activities against the king's friends were perhaps his most important contribution to the war, for the Patriot defeat of Loyalism in South Carolina was a body blow to British plans to restore the colony to subordination to the Crown.

A stern Presbyterian, Andrew Pickens was one of the most successful guerrilla leaders during the American Revolutionary War. In concert with Francis Marion and Thomas Sumter, Pickens conducted several small-scale actions that confounded the British, harassed the Loyalists and Cherokees, and kept the Patriot cause alive in South Carolina. (Library of Congress)

Pickens was also active in the crucial suppression of Britain's Cherokee allies. Promoted to major of militia in 1776, he took part in a Patriot campaign in August–September against the Cherokees that utterly devastated the Lower, Middle, and Upper Towns. On 12 August, he and 35 other men were surrounded by Cherokee warriors at Tamassee and won a desperate contest at close range. In 1778, he joined a South Carolina expeditionary force in an abortive attack on British East Florida, but when Georgia fell to British forces under Lieutenant-Colonel Archibald Campbell in December, Pickens turned his attention to defending his home state. Promoted to colonel and given command of the Upper Ninety-Six Regiment, he decided in early 1779 to oppose Lieutenant-Colonel John Hamilton and his 200 mounted Loyalist partisans in backcountry Georgia. Pickens joined Colonel John Dooley in early February and, taking command of a combined force of 350 men, crossed the Savannah River on 10 February to attack Hamilton.

Just then Pickens learned that a body of North Carolina Loyalists, chiefly Scotsmen, were marching through western South Carolina to join up with Hamilton. About 700 in number, these soldiers were commanded by a shadowy figure, Boyd, whose first name was perhaps James and whose rank was perhaps colonel. Pickens immediately decided that Boyd's force was of more importance than Hamilton's and started after it. Pickens recrossed the Savannah River into South Carolina near Fort Charlotte, only to discover that Boyd was marching westward toward Cherokee Ford, which was 10 miles north of Fort Charlotte. Boyd was stopped at Cherokee Ford by 8 Patriot militiamen with two swivel guns in a redoubt and then moved farther upstream, crossed on rafts into Georgia, and marched downriver. Pickens, meanwhile, marched upstream on the South Carolina side, crossed the river, and followed Boyd downstream. Unaware that he was being followed, Boyd encamped on the evening of 13 February on the north side of Kettle Creek.

Pickens quietly approached the enemy encampment during the night and on the morning of 14 February came upon Boyd's men slaughtering stolen cattle while their horses grazed. Pickens deployed his men in line of battle, with himself commanding the center, Lieutenant Colonel Thomas Clark the left, and Dooley the right. Pickens then fell upon the unsuspecting Loyalists, quickly driving Boyd's pickets back into their camp. The two wings of Pickens's attacking force swung around the camp, attacking simultaneously with the center. Boyd, proving to be an able soldier, rallied his men, fell back, and fought the Patriots for almost an hour. After Boyd fell with a mortal wound and 40 of his soldiers were killed, many more wounded, and 75 captured, the remainder broke and ran. Boyd died that night, but 300 of his men reached Augusta to join the British occupying forces. Pickens lost 9 killed and 23 wounded.

Pickens's triumph in the action at Kettle Creek was a severe blow to British attempts to capture the backcountry and a tonic for the Americans, who needed a military victory. Serving again under Williamson, Pickens and his regiment covered the retreat of American forces after their defeat in the action at Stono Ferry, South Carolina, on 20 June 1779. In August and September, he took part in another expedition against the Upper Towns of the Cherokees. He also cooperated with Georgia militia in keeping a band of Creek Indians from uniting with the British in Savannah. In early 1780, he took part in a raid against British lines at Savannah, then was given command of a fort in the Ninety-Six district with a garrison of 300 men. After the American surrender of Charleston to General Sir Henry Clinton on 12 May 1780, South Carolina fell under the sway of British and Loyalist forces. Pickens, bowing to the will of his men, surrendered and was allowed to remain at home under the category of notoriously disaffected.

Despite his being under British protection, Pickens was harassed in subsequent months by Loyalists, and his plantation was plundered by a Tory band commanded by Captain James Dunlap. Considering himself released from his parole, Pickens renounced protection in December 1780 and rejoined the Patriots. On 16 January 1781, with 70 North Carolina riflemen, he joined Brigadier General Daniel Morgan at Cowpens, in northern South Carolina. Morgan, who had been retreating before Lieutenant-Colonel Banastre Tarleton, decided to take a stand at Cowpens and fight. On 17 January, Morgan arranged his troops in three defensive lines on a gentle slope, with militia forces in the first two lines and Continental regulars in the third line. He gave Pickens command of the second line, composed of 300 North and South Carolina militiamen, under instructions to fire two shots before retiring to the left and behind the Continentals in an orderly fashion. When Tarleton's soldiers charged, Pickens's men waited patiently until the enemy was within killing distance, fired twice with deadly accuracy, and withdrew. Morgan then ordered the Continentals to charge with bayonets while he unleashed his mounted troops on Tarleton's flanks in a double envelopment. Tarleton's men fled in terror, suffering 110 killed, 200 wounded, and 527 captured. Morgan lost only 12 killed and 60 wounded. For his role in this victory, Pickens received a sword and a vote of thanks from Congress.

Serving under General Nathanael Greene in February 1781, Pickens was detached on 18 February with Henry Lee's cavalrymen and two companies of militia to suppress Loyalists in North Carolina. Near Alamance five days later, Pickens surprised 400 Loyalists under Colonel John Pyle, killing 90 and wounding most of the others. He lost only a single man. Promoted to brigadier general of South Carolina militia, Pickens raised a regiment of regulars to plunder Loyalists, helped capture Augusta on 5 June, and participated in an unsuccessful siege of Ninety-Six later in the month. He rejoined Greene's army near the Congaree River in August and on 8 September took part in the Battle of Eutaw Springs. In this fight, Greene posted Pickens's men with other militia troops in his first line, with the Continentals in a second line. The militia fought gallantly, firing seventeen rounds before weakening and being supported by the regulars. Although the Americans almost carried the day, the British finally prevailed, and Greene was compelled to retreat. Pickens's troops had performed well, and Pickens had been wounded. After his recovery in 1782, he campaigned again against the Cherokees, unsuccessfully attempting to end Cherokee-Loyalist raids against frontier settlements. In March, he led 300 men against the Cherokees, burning thirteen towns and killing 40 warriors, and again in September, as the American Revolution drew to a close, he carried out another foray.

After the war, Pickens was a popular hero and an active politician. In 1783, the South Carolina legislature voted him thanks and a gold medal for his military service. He was elected to the state assembly in 1783 and served six terms between then and 1813. He was elected to one term in the state senate in 1790 and two years later to a term in Congress. He organized a company in 1784 to trade with the Indians and a year later was appointed a federal commissioner to negotiate peace treaties with the Cherokee, Chickasaw, and Choctaw tribes. In 1796, he also negotiated a treaty with the Creeks. He and Benjamin Hawkins surveyed a southern boundary line between American and Indian lands in 1797. Four years later, Pickens helped draw up new treaties with the Chickasaw, Choctaw, and Cherokee Indians. He declined a command in a newly expanded American army in 1792, but in 1794 he accepted appointment as senior major general of the South Carolina militia.

Pickens moved to the Hopewell region in 1787, and in 1805 he moved to his plantation, Tamassee, in the Pendleton district. There he lived in retirement, devoting himself to the encouragement of law, order, and the establishment of schools, churches, and a legal system for the backcountry. At the beginning of the War of 1812 with Britain, he was touted as a candidate for governor but declined to run. He did, however, allow himself to be elected to the legislature for a final term, spending the next two years urging South Carolinians to prepare for and support America's "Second War for Independence." He died suddenly in 1817 and was buried in the graveyard of Old Stone Church, which he had helped found and of which he had served as an elder.

PAUL DAVID NELSON

See also
Augusta, Georgia, Operations at; Campbell, Archibald; Charleston, South Carolina, Expedition against (1780); Cherokees, Operations against; Cowpens, Battle of; Eutaw Springs, Battle of; Fort Ninety-Six, South Carolina, Sieges of; Grant, James; Greene, Nathanael; Kettle Creek, Battle of; Lee, Henry; Loyalist Units; Morgan, Daniel; Southern Campaigns; Stono Ferry, South Carolina, Action at; Tarleton, Banastre

References
Ferguson, Clyde R. "Functions of the Partisan-Militia in the South during the American Revolution: An Interpretation." Pp. 239–258 in *The Revolutionary War in the South: Power, Conflict, and Leadership.* Edited by W. Robert Higgins. Durham, NC: Duke University Press, 1979.
———. "General Andrew Pickens." PhD diss., Duke University, 1960.
Lambert, Robert Stansbury. *South Carolina Loyalists in the American Revolution.* Columbia: University of South Carolina Press, 1987.
McCrady, Edward. *The History of South Carolina in the Revolution, 1775–1780.* 1901. Reprint, New York: Russell and Russell, 1969.
Pickens, Andrew Lee. *Skyagunsta, the Border Wizard Owl, Major-General Andrew Pickens (1739–1817).* Greenville, SC: Observer Printing Company, 1934.
Ward, Christopher. *War of the Revolution.* 2 vols. New York: Macmillan, 1952.
Waring, Alice Noble. *The Fighting Elder: Andrew Pickens, 1739–1817.* Columbia: University of South Carolina Press, 1962.

Pickering, Timothy
(1745–1829)

An American officer who distinguished himself for his administrative talents and rose to become the quartermaster general of the Continental Army, Timothy Pickering later served in a variety of executive and legislative positions in the post-Revolutionary American government.

Pickering was born into a prominent Salem, Massachusetts, family and attended Harvard College. He became a lawyer in 1766, but with little aptitude for or interest in the law, he turned his attention to a variety of local political offices and soon became well known as an anti-British pamphleteer. Pickering was commissioned a lieutenant in the Massachusetts militia in 1766 and became fascinated with the military. Over the next decade, the young officer waged a largely unsuccessful campaign to reform the province's militia and increase its efficiency, but he did write an influential infantry manual, *An Easy Plan of Discipline for a Militia*, which the Massachusetts militia adopted. Pickering's manual would later be used by the Continental Army, until General George Washington replaced it with Baron Friedrich von Steuben's manual.

In 1775, Pickering was elected a colonel of the Essex County militia because of his strong opposition to British rule and his military experience. He commanded the county's regiment during the early period of the war, and his organizational abilities soon attracted Washington's attention. In 1777, Washington appointed Pickering adjutant general of the Continental Army. Later in the year, Pickering was also named to the Continental Congress's Board of War. He served in both posts until 1778, when Washington chose a new adjutant general because he believed that Pickering could best serve the American cause by concentrating his energies on the vital duties of the Board of War. On 5 August 1780, Pickering was appointed quartermaster general of the Continental Army and was tasked to reform its supply and logistics system. He continued as a consultative member of the Board of War, but his board privileges and powers were suspended so as not to conflict with his new duties.

A Federalist and early follower of George Washington, Timothy Pickering held many offices in the new government of the United States. (Library of Congress)

The new quartermaster general discovered that the army was constrained by a variety of financial problems. The most pressing issue was a lack of both ready funds and credit. To meet this need, Pickering persuaded Congress to issue specie bonds. These were credit certificates issued in lieu of cash for goods and services. They promised the recipient future payment, but if the government could not make payment on the specified date, then the certificate accrued interest at an annual rate of 6 percent. Although specie bonds were not popular and did not provide the amount of supplies Pickering had hoped for, they did allow the quartermaster general to furnish enough materials for Washington to conduct the war. Nonetheless, Pickering consistently complained to Congress about chronic underfunding of the army.

Pickering's greatest single success was in providing strong support for the Yorktown Campaign. Working closely with the Board of War, he was able to secure the money and supplies necessary to transport Washington's army from its base in New York to Virginia in the fall of 1781. The final victory of the combined American and French forces over Lord Charles Cornwallis that effectively ended the war owed much to Pickering's efforts.

One factor that differentiated Pickering from most other prominent Americans during the war was his efforts on behalf of America's Loyalists. He actively tried to gain support for legislation to safeguard their property because he did not want the new country to lose influential and talented citizens whose loyalty to the Crown might drive them into exile.

As the war drew to a close, Pickering attempted to settle the growing debts of America's military forces and secure continued funding for them. Congress, however, was faced with a variety of heavy debts and Pickering had little success. He was able to enact new reforms at the quartermaster general's office and reduce waste and fraud. He also proposed the establishment of a facility to train future officers for the military, which would eventually result, some two decades later, in the creation of the United States Military Academy at West Point.

Pickering, however, now confronted his own personal debts, which had accumulated during the course of the war. His salary was inadequate to his needs, and he occasionally had to use personal funds in the pursuit of his duties. His efforts to settle his debts extended well beyond the end of the Revolutionary War. But he continued as quartermaster general until July 1785, when Congress abolished the office. He left government service with a growing family and still considerably in debt.

Pickering subsequently held a variety of posts in both state and national government and played a role in negotiating treaties with Native American tribes in the Northwest. He also became active in a variety of agricultural societies along with other luminaries such as Benjamin Franklin and endeavored to promote improved farming techniques. When Washington became president in 1789, he appointed Pickering postmaster general. Pickering went on to serve Washington as secretary of war and then succeeded Edmund Randolph as secretary of state. President John Adams retained Pickering as his secretary of state but abruptly fired him in May 1800 after Pickering sharply opposed Adams's diplomatic reconciliation with France. Pickering went on to serve in both the House of Representatives and the Senate and was most noted for his opposition to the War of 1812. He retired from public life in 1817 and died in 1829.

Tom Lansford

See also

Adams, John; Congress, Second Continental and Confederation; Continental Army; Franklin, Benjamin; Massachusetts; Northwest Territory; Randolph, Edmund Jennings; Steuben, Friedrich von; Washington, George; West Point, New York; Yorktown, Virginia, Siege of; Yorktown Campaign

References

Clarfield, Gerald. *Timothy Pickering and American Diplomacy, 1795–1800*. Columbia: University of Missouri, 1969.

Lansford, Tom. *The Lords of Foggy Bottom: The American Secretaries of State and the World They Shaped*. New York: Encyclopedia Society, 2001.

McLean, David. *Timothy Pickering and the Age of the American Revolution*. New York: Arno, 1982.

Varg, Paul. *Foreign Policies of the Founding Fathers*. East Lansing: Michigan State University, 1963.

Sir Robert Pigot, baronet, was a brave and competent British Army officer who served in two wars and culminated his active career as commander of the garrison at Rhode Island during the Revolution. He first saw service in the 31st Regiment during the War of the Austrian Succession, fighting at the Battle of Fontenoy in 1745. In the next few years he also saw duty on Minorca and in Scotland, and on 31 October 1751 he was promoted to captain in the 31st Regiment. In 1758, his battalion was transferred to the 70th Regiment, and he was promoted to major of the 70th on 5 May. He became lieutenant-colonel of the 38th Regiment on 1 October 1764. After service in the West Indies, he was ordered to Boston in July 1774. He was involved in the fighting at Lexington and Concord on 19 April 1775. At the Battle of Bunker Hill on 17 June, holding the local rank of brigadier-general, he was given command of the army's left wing by General William Howe. Fighting gallantly, Pigot and his soldiers assaulted an American redoubt on Charlestown Heights under intense fire and finally broke the Americans' resistance, but with enormous losses. For his distinguished service and bravery, he was promoted by King George III to the colonelcy of the 38th Regiment on 11 December.

When the British Army evacuated Boston in March 1776, Pigot accompanied Howe to Halifax, Nova Scotia. In the Battle of Long Island on 27 August he commanded the 2nd Brigade, and when the Americans evacuated New York, Howe appointed him commandant of the city's garrison. Upon the death of his brother, Sir George Pigot, on 11 May 1777, Pigot inherited the baronetcy and a considerable fortune. On 15 July, he took command of the British garrison at Rhode Island and was promoted to major-general on 29 August. Although he missed the social life of New York, he was kept busy defending Newport against combined operations by John Sullivan's American army and a French fleet commanded by Jean-Baptiste d'Estaing. Although hard-pressed by Sullivan on land and threatened by French warships, Pigot held firm and refused to panic. On 8 August he was rescued by the arrival of a British fleet commanded by Admiral Lord Richard Howe. Three weeks later, Pigot received reinforcements from Sir Henry Clinton in New York. Pigot fought a sharp engagement with Sullivan at Butt's Hill on 29 August, as Sullivan withdrew from Newport, and was repulsed with considerable losses. Pigot relinquished his command in October to Richard Prescott, returned to Britain in 1779, and was promoted to lieutenant-general on 20 November 1782. Pigot died at Patshull in 1796 after a long and painful illness.

PAUL DAVID NELSON

See also

Bunker Hill, Battle of; Estaing, Jean-Baptiste, Comte d'; Howe, Richard; Lexington and Concord; Long Island, Battle of; Newport, Rhode Island, Naval Operations against; Rhode Island, Battle of; Sullivan, John

References

Ketchum, Richard. *Decisive Day: The Battle for Bunker Hill.* 1974. Reprint, New York: Henry Holt, 1999.

Willcox, William B. *Portrait of a General: Sir Henry Clinton in the War of Independence.* New York: Knopf, 1964.

Pinckney, Charles
(1757–1824)

Charles Pinckney, a South Carolina congressman, was a tireless advocate of increased federal power both before and at the Constitutional Convention. Though his nationalist vision was not fully realized, he helped shape the terms of debate as well as the final form of the U.S. Constitution.

Pinckney's youth was overshadowed by the outbreak of the Revolutionary War, which prevented him from studying law in England as his family had planned. He spent the war years in South Carolina, where he read law, served as a militia officer, and was elected to the state legislature in 1779. He was captured during the fall of Charleston in May 1780 but was soon paroled. Later he was briefly confined on a British prison ship. He also suffered financially because of the war, as the estate he inherited from his nominally Loyalist father in 1782 was subject to a punitive fine by the South Carolina legislature.

In 1784 Pinckney's political career began in earnest. He was again elected to the South Carolina legislature, which in turn elected him to Congress. As a congressman (1784–1787), he concentrated on frontier policy and on the national effort to create a stronger federal government. He published pamphlets urging that Congress be granted broader powers to regulate commerce and raise internal revenue. In 1786 he chaired a committee that proposed several amendments to the Articles of Confederation, addressing both financial matters and the balance between state and federal authority.

Pinckney's pamphlets and congressional activities had begun to earn him a national reputation by 1787, and he quickly emerged as a leading delegate to the Constitutional Convention. Like James Madison, Pinckney prepared a detailed proposal for a new federal government. His plan is not extant, but it both anticipated and influenced the final shape of the U.S. Constitution in several ways. Pinckney favored a federal government consisting of a single executive and a bicameral legislature, which would exercise power over interstate commerce. His sympathies lay with the established political elite; he believed that officers of the federal government should be indirectly elected and should meet high property qualifications. He also advocated the federal protection of slavery and the transatlantic slave trade.

Back in South Carolina, Pinckney led the state campaign to ratify the U.S. Constitution. His subsequent career, however, lay more in state rather than in national politics. He married Mary Eleanor Laurens, a daughter of the American diplomat Henry Laurens, in 1788. Between 1789 and 1808, Pinckney served four terms as South Carolina's governor. Initially a Federalist in national politics, he became a Jeffersonian Republican and supported public education, a broader suffrage, and the expanded representation of western districts in the state legislature. He also served, at various times, as a federal congressman, senator, and ambassador to Spain.

DARCY R. FRYER

See also

Congress, Second Continental and Confederation; Constitution, United States; South Carolina

References

Bailey, N. Louise, and Elizabeth Ivey Cooper. "Pinckney, Charles." Pp. 555–560 in *Biographical Directory of the South Carolina House of Representatives*, Vol. 3, *1775–1790*. Columbia: University of South Carolina Press, 1981.

Weir, Robert M. "Pinckney, Charles." *American National Biography* 17 (1999): 533–536.

The Continental Army officer and Federalist politician Charles Cotesworth Pinckney rose to prominence as a South Carolina legislator in the 1770s and served with distinction in several military campaigns during the Revolutionary War. He emerged as a national politician at the Constitutional Convention of 1787, helped secure ratification of the U.S. Constitution in South Carolina, and was a prominent candidate for president in the election of 1800.

Pinckney spent his youth (1753–1769) in England, but his experiences as an American student at Westminster School, Oxford University, and the Middle Temple intensified rather than weakened his American identity. His patriotic ardor even prompted him to commission a portrait of himself decrying the Stamp Act. Shortly after his return to South Carolina, he was elected to the provincial legislature, where he became an active member of the Revolutionary faction. In the spring of 1775, he participated in a local offensive to seize British military stores, and in 1776 he chaired the committee that wrote South Carolina's first independent state constitution.

Pinckney was commissioned lieutenant in a South Carolina regiment in 1774 and had risen steadily to the rank of brigadier general by 1783. Early in the war, he served as aide-de-camp to George Washington and fought in the battles at Brandywine and Germantown. When the locus of fighting shifted southward, Pinckney returned to the South and fought in several major campaigns, including the expedition to East Florida and the unsuccessful defenses of Savannah (December 1778) and Charleston (May 1780). He was captured in the fall of Charleston and held prisoner at Snee Farm, the captured plantation of his cousin Charles Pinckney, until his exchange in 1782.

After the war, Pinckney returned home to practice law and rebuild his fortune. He served in the South Carolina legislature almost continuously

Pinckney, Charles Cotesworth
(1746–1825)

Charles Cotesworth Pinckney, the South Carolina Patriot, signer of the U.S. Constitution, and Federalist leader. (National Archives and Records Administration)

from 1769 to 1790. In the 1780s, his overriding concern was fostering the economic and political stability of South Carolina. He was one of several low-country politicians who urged the new state government to adopt conciliatory policies toward Loyalists who remained in the state after independence. Pinckney also sought to promote the public welfare through commercial projects such as canals and educational projects such as a state college.

Concern for the economic and political stability of his home state also prompted Pinckney to support the drive for a stronger federal government. He was an active member of South Carolina's delegation to the Constitutional Convention of 1787, but most of his proposals were unsuccessful. When northern and southern delegates disagreed over whether to permit the continuance of the transatlantic slave trade, Pinckney proposed that the slave trade be protected until 1808; this provision was adopted. He subsequently led the fight for ratification of the U.S. Constitution in South Carolina. He later served as ambassador to France (1796–1798) and ran unsuccessfully for president in the elections of 1800, 1804, and 1808.

DARCY R. FRYER

See also

Charleston, South Carolina, Expedition against (1780); Constitution, United States; South Carolina

Reference

Zahniser, Marvin R. *Charles Cotesworth Pinckney: Founding Father.* Chapel Hill: University of North Carolina Press, 1967.

Pinckney, Thomas

(1750–1828)

The South Carolina lawyer, army officer, and politician Thomas Pinckney served with distinction in Florida, Savannah, Charleston, and other southern theaters of combat between 1778 and 1781. After the war, he was briefly governor of South Carolina, chaired the South Carolina convention that ratified the U.S. Constitution, and served as U.S. minister to Great Britain, and special envoy to Spain.

Pinckney spent his childhood not in South Carolina but rather in England. He traveled there with his parents and siblings, including his elder brother Charles Cotesworth Pinckney, in 1753, and remained abroad for more than twenty years. His education at Westminster School, Oxford University, and the Middle Temple, however, failed to dull his American sensibilities. His Westminster schoolmates teasingly dubbed him "little rebel" on account of his opposition to British policies in North America. He also traveled on the Continent and studied briefly at a French military academy in Caen. After qualifying for the English bar, he returned to Charleston at the end of 1774 and established a law practice.

Pinckney continued to defend American rights vociferously after his return to South Carolina. He was commissioned lieutenant of a ranger company in 1775 and captain soon thereafter. From 1776 to 1779 he was stationed at Fort Moultrie, guarding the entrance to Charleston Harbor, but spent much of his time on recruiting missions in the southern backcountry and as far north as Virginia. He drew on his French military training in drilling his own troops, who were said to be among the most disciplined soldiers in the American army.

In 1778 Pinckney was promoted to major. In the three years that followed, he saw action in several locales. He participated in the abortive American invasion of Florida (1778) and won praise for his leadership at Stono Ferry (1779). At the siege of Savannah (1779), Pinckney, who spoke French, acted as a liaison between the American forces under General Benjamin Lincoln and the French forces under Jean-Baptiste d'Estaing. Once again, Pinckney won acclaim for his calmness under fire and his ability to maintain order among his troops. The Americans failed to recapture Savannah, however, and Pinckney's home

Thomas Pinckney, an officer in the Continental Army, fought at Stono Ferry, Savannah, and Charleston and served as aide-de-camp to Horatio Gates. Pinckney later negotiated an important treaty with Spain. (Library of Congress)

state was rendered increasingly vulnerable to attack. Pinckney himself suffered severe financial losses when British troops raided and burned his plantation on the Ashepoo River in May 1779.

When the British Army and Royal Navy laid siege to Charleston in the spring of 1780, Pinckney commanded part of the city's defenses. Lincoln sent him out of Charleston a few days before the city fell, however, so he evaded capture by the British. Pinckney made his way northward and served as aide-de-camp to General Horatio Gates. At the Battle of Camden in August 1780, Pinckney was severely wounded and captured. After his exchange in the spring of 1781, he returned to active duty as a recruiting officer in Virginia. There he became a close friend of the Marquis de Lafayette and was present at the British surrender at Yorktown in October 1781.

Pinckney was of a gregarious disposition, and in spite of the war, he found time to enjoy a lively social life. His wartime letters to his mother and sister are dotted with requests for goods as various as limes and sugar (presumably for making punch), his cello, and a book of cotillions. In 1777 he pressed them to attend a turtle feast at Fort Moultrie. During his service at Fort Moultrie, he courted Elizabeth Motte, whom he married in the summer of 1779. Pinckney's extensive kinship ties to other low-country planter families shaped his political attitudes and, in particular, fostered his commitment to rebuilding the state's plantation economy and to reabsorbing former Loyalists into South Carolina society.

In addition to his military service, Pinckney served eight consecutive terms in the South Carolina legislature between 1776 and 1791, representing the Charleston parish of St. Philip and St. Michael. His sixth term in office was interrupted by a stint as governor of South Carolina (1787–1789). As governor, Pinckney chaired the state convention that ratified the U.S. Constitution. Although as chair he did not cast a vote, he undoubtedly agreed with his brother Charles, one of the state's leading advocates of ratification. Otherwise, Pinckney's gubernatorial term was dominated by conflicts between frontier settlers and Native Americans residing in the interior.

After the ratification of the U.S. Constitution, Pinckney gradually emerged as a force in national as well as state politics. In 1791, George Washington appointed him U.S. minister to Great Britain. Pinckney's mission was marred by continuing tensions between Britain and the United States. Despite his position, he played little role in the negotiation of the Jay Treaty (1794), the landmark event in British-American diplomacy of the 1790s. But during his term as a special commissioner to Spain in 1795, he negotiated the Treaty of San Lorenzo (better known as Pinckney's Treaty), which determined the U.S.–Spanish West Florida border and secured the right of American citizens to navigate the Mississippi River. After returning to the United States in 1796, he ran unsuccessfully for vice president as a Federalist and served two terms in the U.S. House of Representatives.

DARCY R. FRYER

See also
Camden Campaign; Charleston, South Carolina, Expedition against (1780); Lafayette, Marquis de; Pinckney, Charles Cotesworth; Savannah, Georgia, Operations against; South Carolina

References
Bailey, N. Louise, and Elizabeth Ivey Cooper. "Pinckney, Thomas." Pp. 561–565 in *Biographical Directory of the South Carolina House of Representatives*, Vol. 3, *1775–1790*. Columbia: University of South Carolina Press, 1981.

Cross, Jack L., ed. "Letters of Thomas Pinckney." *South Carolina Historical Magazine* 58 (1957): 19–33, 67–83.

Pinckney, Charles Cotesworth. *Life of General Thomas Pinckney*. Boston: Houghton Mifflin, 1895.

Reuter, Frank T. "Pinckney, Thomas." *American National Biography* 17 (1999): 539–540.

Pitt, William, the Elder
(1708–1778)

The parliamentary leader William Pitt the Elder, the Earl of Chatham, first became a hero to both Britons and Americans for leading the nation to victory over the French in the Seven Years' War. In the 1760s and early 1770s, he became even more widely admired in America for his support of their opposition to imperial taxation, although he always opposed American independence.

Pitt was born in London to an aristocratic family. His father, Robert Pitt, was a member of Parliament and son of Thomas Pitt, who made his fortune as governor of the East India Company's factory in Madras, India. Pitt's mother was Lady Harriet Villiers, daughter of Viscount Grandison. Pitt received a classical education at Eton College before attending Trinity College, Oxford, for one year and then attending the University of Utrecht in the Netherlands. He became friends with Lord Cobham and his nephews Richard Grenville and George Lyttelton, spending a great deal of time at Cobham's country estate at Stowe. In 1735, after a brief trip to Europe, Pitt entered Parliament, and in 1737 the Prince of Wales named him the groom of the bedchamber. Pitt, Grenville, and Lyttelton became known in Parliament as Cobham's Cubs. It was during this time that Pitt discovered his talent for oratory. In 1744, King George II appointed Pitt a joint vice-treasurer of Ireland and later the same year made him paymaster general. In 1754, he became ill and retired to his new house in Bath to recover his health. In November 1754, at the age of forty-six, he married Lady Hester Grenville, sister of Earl Temple and George Grenville. They enjoyed a happy marriage and had two daughters and three sons, including William Pitt the Younger, who became prime minister of Britain following the American Revolutionary War.

In 1756, Britain became involved in the Seven Years' War, and Pitt returned to government with renewed vitality. After Britain suffered several military failures, the Duke of Newcastle resigned as prime minister, and in the new government Pitt was appointed secretary of state. His successful involvement in the strategy of the war on every level led to his nickname, "the Great Commoner." Pitt strengthened the Royal Navy and concentrated on driving the French from North America. He helped consolidate the empire while annexing territory in Africa and the West Indies as well. By 1760, however, following France's loss of Canada, George II was determined to have peace, and after failing to persuade Parliament to declare war on a hostile Spain, France's principal ally, Pitt resigned in October 1761. He retired to home and family and was politically inactive for several years, but his leadership during the Seven Years' War ended French power in North America, a British victory formalized in the Treaty of Paris in 1763.

When Parliament began having problems with its American colonies, Pitt's expertise in foreign policy and his triumph in the Seven Years' War made him a desirable commodity. In January 1766 he addressed Parliament in a passionate speech entreating them to repeal the Stamp Act on behalf of the troubled American colonists. In July 1766, when Charles Watson-Wentworth, Lord Rockingham, was dismissed as prime minister, Pitt was called to the office, now as the Earl of Chatham and Lord Privy Seal. In 1767 and 1768, however, Pitt suffered from severe depression, and the members of his government, including Charles Townshend and the Earl of Hillsborough,

William Pitt the Elder, Earl of Chatham, one of the most dynamic eighteenth-century British statesmen, served as prime minister during the Seven Years' War (known in America as the French and Indian War). In a moving speech in the House of Lords in April 1778, he opposed the Duke of Richmond's proposal for peace with the American colonies in order to forestall French intervention in the conflict. Rising to speak for a second time, Pitt collapsed and died the following month. (Library of Congress)

William Pitt the Elder waged his own political war against the oppression of American rights.

whose policies were so unpopular with Americans, largely went their own ways until he resigned his office in October 1768.

Although he was now regarded by his peers as a retired elder statesman, Pitt continued to speak occasionally in Parliament whenever his health intermittently improved. He sought reconciliation with the American colonists and admired their love of liberty, but he did not support granting them independence, believing, like virtually every member of Parliament, that Britain's colonies must remain subordinate and fully subject to the British Crown, especially in matters of navigation and trade. He also feared that the French might obtain the American colonies if Britain loosened its grip. Yet he admired the Americans' first intercolonial governing body, describing the Continental Congress as "the most honourable assembly of statesmen since those of ancient Greeks and Romans, in the most virtuous of times." In 1774, Pitt sought both information and opinion on the crisis from a few Americans residing in London at the time, including Stephen Sayre, William Lee, and Benjamin Franklin. From these contacts he concluded that the Americans' primary objection to British rule was Parliament's attempt to force revenue from the colonies. In a speech of 20 January 1775, Pitt defended the right of the Americans not to be taxed without their consent.

In February 1775, Pitt continued to wage war against the oppression of American rights. He introduced a bill designed to utilize the Continental Congress to estimate the fiscal contribution that each colony made to the Crown. Lord Frederick North, however, continued to hold the majority in Parliament in support of taxing America. Pitt's foreign policy now began to anger King George III, who referred to Pitt as a "trumpet of sedition." On 18 November 1777, Pitt delivered a speech to the House of Lords opposing the use of American Indians in the war against the colonists. On 7 April 1778, however, in his last address to Parliament, he dramatically opposed the Duke of Richmond's motion to give the American colonies their independence. Richmond responded, and Pitt rose again and began to reply but soon collapsed and was carried from the House of Lords to his home at Hayes Place in Kent. He died there on 11 May 1778 at the age of sixty-nine. He was buried with great ceremony in Westminster Abbey. Pitt's collapse in Parliament was the subject of John Singleton Copley's painting *The Death of Chatham*, regarded by some critics as the most important history painting ever done in England.

KATHLEEN HITT

See also
Copley, John Singleton; George III, King of England; Grenville, George; Hill, Wills; North, Lord Frederick; Paris, Treaty of (1763); Pitt, William, the Younger; Stamp Act; Stamp Act Congress; Townshend, Charles; Townshend Acts; Watson-Wentworth, Charles, 2nd Marquis of Rockingham

References
Black, Jeremy. *Pitt the Elder.* New York: Cambridge University Press, 1992.
Commager, Henry S., and Richard B. Morris, eds. *The Spirit of 'Seventy-Six: The Story of the American Revolution as Told by Participants.* 1958. Reprint, New York: Bonanza, 1995.
Peters, Marie. *The Elder Pitt.* New York: Longman, 1998.

Second son of William Pitt the Elder, 1st Earl of Chatham and one of Britain's great prime ministers, William Pitt the Younger would also distinguish himself as prime minister a generation later (1783–1801 and 1804–1806). When the American Revolutionary War broke out, Pitt was studying at Cambridge, having matriculated in 1773, under his tutor George Pretyman, the junior fellow at Pembroke College. There, Pitt became adept at translations to and from Latin and Greek and was highly skilled in mathematics. He took his Master of Arts degree without an examination in 1776, a privilege open to the sons of noblemen. He made friends with many men who would later hold prominent positions in government.

Pitt keenly followed the course of the war like his father, a man by then in his declining years who had remained out of politics for several years but who then made three historic visits to the House of Lords to oppose British government policy in dramatic terms. In 1775, the elder Pitt demanded conciliation toward the colonies in a speech at which his son was present. The younger Pitt often traveled to London from Cambridge to listen to the debates in the House of Commons, where he was introduced to Charles James Fox, his future parliamentary nemesis. Pitt was not unnaturally entranced by his father's eloquence, as was Parliament generally.

In his second speech to the House of Lords, the elder Pitt warned that the conflict would soon include France and Spain, a prospect that required immediate peace with the rebellious colonies. The ministry took no notice of his advice, yet Lord Frederick North hoped to approach him to discuss the terms under which Pitt might form a new government with himself as prime minister. This possibility was rejected by the king, who despised Pitt for his opposition to the war and was also concerned about the earl's rapidly declining health.

Ignoring the advice of his doctors, Pitt attended the House of Lords debate on 7 April 1778, supported by his son and his son-in-law, Lord Mahon. In a faltering voice and almost unable to stand, the elder Pitt once again thundered against the government before sitting down amid cries of support and condemnation. On trying to rise for a second time, he fell back exhausted and died on 11 May. His son was chief mourner at his funeral.

The younger Pitt left Cambridge that year, fully convinced that the war was both immoral and unwinnable. He became a strong supporter of parliamentary reform—a movement intended to reduce the power of the king and to increase the number of members of Parliament in areas of greatest population density. Pitt was also opposed to the system of patronage connected with Crown-appointed offices, his object being to reduce the number of sinecures and other positions.

By 1780, Pitt was studying law at Lincoln's Inn in London. He had little in the way of income, for his father's immense debts, though partly covered by a vote of Parliament, had left Pitt with no immediate inheritance and an annual income of only £600, a sum provided to him by his elder brother, John. Notwithstanding further support from his mother, Pitt began borrowing from

William Pitt the Younger was not only the youngest prime minister of Great Britain but also one of its longest-serving and most able. A great parliamentarian, he came to power immediately after the end of the Revolutionary War and was responsible for the India Act (1784) and the Act of Union with Ireland (1801). (Library of Congress)

bankers and friends, embarking on a habit of indebtedness that would plague him for the rest of his life.

Pitt was called to the bar on 12 June 1780, but his preferences drew him to politics rather than to the law at a time when parliamentary opposition to North's government was growing ever stronger. Pitt hoped to become one of the two members of Parliament for Cambridge University, a position he sought to attain without the help of a patron. He was determined not to beholden himself because of undue outside influence or the purchase of a rotten borough—a corrupt practice in the eighteenth century by which constituents' votes were effectively paid for in the form of bribes or promises of political or ecclesiastical posts.

Pitt continued to attend debates in the House of Commons and greatly admired Edmund Burke's attacks on the North ministry in the form of appeals for the abolition of special royal jurisdictions in England and Wales and calls for the reduction of the Civil List (a substantial parliamentary subsidy voted by Parliament from public funds and paid directly to the sovereign). Pitt, like Burke, also backed the abolition of various costly sinecures and irrelevant Crown offices.

In the general election of September 1780, Pitt failed to win either seat for Cambridge University, though at the age of only twenty-one he was elected the member for Appleby through the influence of Sir James Lowther, who controlled a number of boroughs in the north of England. Having cast aside his scruples on the inequities of patronage in order to reach Parliament, Pitt took up his seat in the House of Commons on 23 January 1781. Burke and Fox formed one of the principal opposition factions, with William Petty-Fitzmaurice, Lord Shelburne, leading the other. Pitt belonged to the latter.

In his maiden speech, delivered on 26 February, Pitt spoke spontaneously and without notes to a packed House on an important motion, introduced by Burke, on the reduction of spending on the Civil List. The occasion was of particular importance for Pitt, who, already well known as the son of the great Earl of Chatham, that day established himself as a skilled orator and respected politician from the very outset of his parliamentary career—a career that was to stretch until his death in January 1806. Although the Opposition failed in the vote, Pitt's eloquence—acknowledged by Burke, Fox and even North—was so impressive that thereafter his reputation no longer rested on the legacy of his father. He spoke next on 12 June, supporting Fox's motion for peace with the American colonies, and then again on 28 November, condemning, in the wake of Charles Cornwallis's surrender at Yorktown, the government's speech, delivered by George III.

Pitt's boldness grew rapidly. On 8 March 1782 he declared in the House, perhaps unintentionally, that if a new government were formed he would not accept a minor post. This constituted an extraordinary example of presumption for a new and inexperienced member of Parliament. Still, he meant what he said. When the North ministry fell a few days later and was replaced by the ministry of Charles Watson-Wentworth, Lord Rockingham, Pitt declined the vice-treasurership of Ireland, though he continued to offer his support to the government. He continued on the back benches, and on 7 May he brought forth a motion for electoral reform, which was narrowly defeated.

When Rockingham died, he was succeeded by Shelburne, who, on 6 July, finding that the resignations of Fox and Burke now denied him sufficient support in Parliament, offered Pitt the post of chancellor of the Exchequer. Pitt accepted, and in the winter in that capacity he argued, albeit unsuccessfully, against the signature of the preliminaries of peace with the American colonists on the basis that if a definitive peace was not concluded, Britain would have already formally recognized the independence of the United States. When Shelburne sought to bolster his strength in Parliament, he authorized Pitt, on Pitt's recommendation, to invite Fox to join his cabinet. When Fox declined to serve in a government in which Shelburne would continue to hold the premiership, Pitt withdrew the offer, as he refused to be the instrument of his own patron's dismissal from office. Thereafter, Pitt and Fox were sworn political adversaries. Shelburne's period in office was, in any event, rapidly coming to an end, and as the Opposition gathered its forces, on 21 March 1783 Pitt made one of his most eloquent speeches. Although this failed to secure the life of the ministry, which fell two days later, Pitt was invited by the king to retain office in the new government. He refused, announcing himself to be free of political connection to any party or faction.

The Duke of Portland formed a coalition government on 2 April. A month later, Pitt once again raised the issue of parliamentary reform, attacking the practice of electoral bribery and the system of rotten boroughs and advocating the redistribution of the franchise among the more populous regions of the country. The motion failed to gain a majority. On 2 June his bill for the checking of abuses in government-appointed posts won a majority in the House of Commons but failed to secure one in the House of Lords. The Portland ministry, meanwhile, proceeded to conclude a definitive peace with the United States in September 1783.

Pitt's fortunes, however, soon took a dramatic turn, for the debate on Fox's India bill, proposed on 18 November, proved the death knell for Portland's ministry. The bill, which Pitt attacked in very strong terms, passed the House of Commons but was rejected by the House of Lords, and with the fall of the government on 19 December, the king asked Pitt—only twenty-four years old—to form a new one in the capacity of prime minister, a post in which Pitt would distinguish himself, apart from the brief period out of office from 1801 to 1804, for more than twenty years.

GREGORY FREMONT-BARNES

See also
British Parliament; Burke, Edmund; Fox, Charles James; George III, King of England; Great Britain; North, Lord Frederick; Petty-Fitzmaurice, William, 2nd Earl of Shelburne; Pitt, William, the Elder

References
Duffy, Michael. *The Younger Pitt*. New York: Longman, 2000.
Ehrman, John. *The Younger Pitt: The Years of Acclaim*. New York: Dutton, 1969.
Reilly, Robin. *William Pitt the Younger*. New York: Putnam, 1979.
Turner, Michael. *Pitt the Younger: A Life*. London: Hambledon and London, 2002.

Pontiac
(1720?–1769)

The Native American leader Pontiac is remembered for his role in the struggle against the British occupation of the Great Lakes region during and after the French and Indian (Seven Years') War. He rose to fame during the conflict known as Pontiac's Rebellion (1763–1766). The facts about his life, however, are scarce and often based on oral tradition or sheer speculation.

Pontiac was commonly called the chief of the Ottawas by white contemporaries and several subsequent historians. Modern scholars do not believe that Ottawa leaders had the authority that Pontiac was depicted as wielding over his tribe, but his rise to prominence led British officials to negotiate with him as if he spoke for all the Ottawas. Pontiac took pleasure in this inflated role, causing tensions with other Indian leaders that ultimately led to his downfall.

There is little reliable information about Pontiac before the rebellion of 1763. He was probably born sometime between 1712 and 1720, perhaps at an Ottawa village on the Detroit or Maumee Rivers. His father was an Ottawa and his mother an Ojibwa. By 1755, Pontiac had become a prominent war leader among the uneasy confederacy of Ottawas, Potawatomis, and Ojibwas, called the Council of Three Fires. He was an ally of France and possibly took part in the July 1755 victory over General Edward Braddock near the forks of the Ohio River.

Following the French and Indian War, Indian allies of the defeated French found themselves increasingly dissatisfied with the trading practices of the British. The originator of British Indian policy in the Northwest was General Jeffrey Amherst, who decided to cut back on the provisions customarily distributed to the Indians from the various forts. The French had made gunpowder and ammunition readily available to the Indians, who needed these items to hunt food for their families and skins for trade. Amherst did not trust his former Indian adversaries and restricted the distribution of gunpowder and ammunition. Pontiac, like other Indian leaders, was certain that the British intended to starve, disarm, and destroy them. Taking advantage of general Indian dissatisfaction with the British as well as a native religious revival, Pontiac and others began planning their resistance. On 27 April 1763, he held a council 10 miles below Fort Detroit. The siege of Fort Detroit that shortly followed became the heart of what Europeans came to call Pontiac's

A conclave between Ottawa Chief Pontiac and Rogers's Rangers. Pontiac led a rebellion against the British in the western territories ceded by the French at the end of the French and Indian War in 1763. British troops took three years to subdue the revolt. (Library of Congress)

Rebellion, but the rebellion was hardly the work of Pontiac alone. His attack on Fort Detroit was only one of several synchronized attacks ranging throughout the Great Lakes and Ohio River regions. British reinforcements arrived to end the siege of Fort Detroit, and Colonel John Bradstreet, thinking that Pontiac was defeated, initially refused to negotiate with him.

Pontiac retreated to the Illinois Country, where he continued to encourage militant resistance to British occupation. The British military position on the frontier was weak, and eventually British leaders sought negotiations with the Ottawa leader. Pontiac met with Sir William Johnson on 25 July 1766 at Oswego, New York, and formally ended hostilities. But the attention paid to Pontiac by British officials served to encourage his sense of self-importance and increased his attempts to influence other Indian leaders. Local rivalries flared up, and in 1768 he was forced to leave his Ottawa village on the Maumee River. Upon returning to the Illinois Country, Pontiac was murdered on 20 April 1769 at the French village of Cahokia by a Peoria Indian, perhaps in retaliation for an earlier attack.

Pontiac seemed to aspire to a kind of chieftainship that was never really a possibility in Ottawa society. It was only after the rebellion that he sought to unite the villages and towns of Native Americans and backcountry French settlers into a single confederation under a single leadership, which in the end cost him his life.

CLARA HUDSON

See also

Amherst, Jeffrey; Johnson, Sir William; Native Americans; Northwest Territory; Pontiac's Rebellion

References

Jennings, Francis. *Empire of Fortune: Crowns, Colonies & Tribes in the Seven Years' War in America*. New York: Norton, 1988.

Keller, Allan. "Pontiac's Conspiracy." *American History Illustrated* 12(2) (1977): 4–9, 42–49.

Parkman, Francis. *The Conspiracy of Pontiac and the Indian War after the Conquest of Canada*. Boston: Little, Brown, 1898.

Peckham, Howard Henry. *Pontiac and the Indian Uprising*. Princeton, NJ: Princeton University Press, 1947.

Pontiac's Rebellion
(1763–1766)

Pontiac's Rebellion was the name given to a major Indian uprising in the Northwest that extended from 1763 to 1766. With the end of the French and Indian War in North America, Great Britain gained control of vast lands west of the Appalachian Mountains. The new administration of the territory sparked tensions, first with the former French-allied Indian tribes and later with frontier settlers from Britain's North American colonies south of Canada.

When French forces in Canada surrendered to the British in 1760, British troops were sent to occupy the French forts at Detroit and other strategic points along the Great Lakes. The troops were given orders to accept the surrender of the French forces in the region, meet with various Indian chiefs, and explain that Great Britain had taken control of the area. The soldiers were warned not to give offense to any one group; peace was to be maintained at all costs. The French had maintained several forts, a small settler presence, and an active trade with the Indians in the region but had infringed very little upon the Indians' independence or their control of their hunting lands. With the British now in control of the region, however, many settlers from Britain's Atlantic coast colonies wished to push west and open up the interior for settlement. The Indians who were already living in the area naturally objected to this white expansion, but many white settlers were determined to carry on regardless of any opposition.

These incursions not only alarmed Indians who had been allied with the French but also created problems with the Senecas, one of the tribes of the British-allied Six Nations (the Iroquois), who believed that the British had failed to keep promises made during the war with the French. To persuade Iroquois warriors to side with them, the British had signed agreements promising that lands west of the Allegheny Mountains would only be used by Indians for hunting. In return for this promise, however, Iroquois leaders pledged not to move west into territory formerly belonging to the French. This proscription irked many Indians, who felt that they had scores to settle with the French-allied tribes, and who wanted access to the hunting grounds in the Ohio River Valley.

Given the size of the area that British troops had to patrol, white settlers were able to elude them without great difficulty, slip into the prohibited areas, and carry out large-scale hunting west of the Appalachians. The Indians in the region grew increasingly restless about these incursions, and clashes between Indians and white settlers began to occur. By 1761, the Senecas were holding meetings with members of the Delaware and Miami tribes to discuss attacks on Britain's frontier forts. They agreed, however, that they were not ready for an all-out rebellion.

The purpose of the Indian uprising is still somewhat unclear. Its principal military objective seems to have been the seizure of all British forts and posts, but even this strategy was not implemented with any consistency. Particularly at first, the Indian effort was not a coordinated onslaught but rather a series of seemingly unrelated attacks on various forts by various groups of warriors.

One prominent indication of the fact that the Indian uprising was not as widespread or organized as it could have been was the conduct of one Indian chief, Pontiac. Pontiac was an Ottawa chief who only commanded a local village near Fort Detroit. He agreed with other Indian chiefs about the state of affairs under British governance, but instead of acting in conjunction with others, he set up a campaign against Fort Detroit by himself. Pontiac did not participate in any other actions, but Fort Detroit was such an important outpost that the British hailed him as the leading war chief, and the entire uprising became known as Pontiac's Rebellion.

The Indian uprising began in late 1762, when Seneca warriors killed two white settlers and sent war belts to the western tribes as the signal to begin a war. While extremely dangerous to those in the frontier region, the uprising was not a unanimous effort. Members of the Senecas, Ottawas, Hurons, Delawares, and Miamis participated, but no tribe used all of its warriors.

Native Americans attack a ship during Pontiac's Rebellion. This uprising covered a large sweep of country, from the northern Great Lakes to Ohio and Pennsylvania. (North Wind Picture Archives)

By late 1762, however, British troops on the frontier were in a difficult position, caught between white settlers and Indian tribes. Colonel Henry Bouquet, commander of the 60th Regiment of Foot, the unit that was deployed in the west, recognized the potential for even greater trouble and attempted to reinforce the various forts, preparing them for a possible outbreak of violence. Bouquet also advised General Jeffrey Amherst, commander in chief of the British Army in North America, of the rising tension on the frontier and asked for further reinforcements.

In early April 1763, Pontiac gathered various Indian warriors near Fort Detroit and called for action against the British fort. On 1 May, Pontiac arrived at Fort Detroit with a small reconnaissance party to assess the British defenses and troops. He was greeted and entertained by the British commander, a Major Gladwin, after which the Indian party left, promising to return at a later date. The British, although they were aware of the possibility of attack, still did not want to aggravate the situation. Pontiac met with another party of Indian warriors on 5 May and called for the extermination of the British at Fort Detroit. Other Indian warriors decided to join in as word reached Pontiac that other forts were also going to be attacked. On 7 May, a select group of warriors marched toward Fort Detroit with weapons hidden and a plan to storm the fort.

Gladwin, who had one hundred men under his command, had received information that an attack was imminent. He decided to close the gates and put white traders in the area under arms to boost his defense. Pontiac acted surprised when he came up to the fort and was not received with open gates. On 8 May, other chiefs attempted to meet with Gladwin to promise that the Indians had no intention of seizing the fort. Gladwin dismissed these claims and prepared for an armed encounter. On 9 May, an armed flotilla of Indian canoes arrived. Gladwin continued to refuse to speak with the Indians, and on 10 May the siege of Fort Detroit formally began. A relief force of ninety-five soldiers marching toward the fort was surrounded and overwhelmed on 29 May, but the British garrison managed to hold on.

The remaining forts along the Great Lakes and in the Ohio River Valley were subsequently attacked by other Indian tribes, and other Indian war parties attacked small white settlements on the frontier. Some British forts were immediately seized by a surprise attack, while in others the garrisons were able to repel the Indians and slip away during the evening. At Fort Venango, a Seneca war party was received into the fort as allies, only to turn and massacre the garrison, destroying relations between the British and the Senecas. By the end of June, all of the British forts along the frontier and in the newly claimed territories had been seized except for Forts Pitt, Detroit, and Niagara. Indian war parties also headed east toward Fort Bedford but were not able to capture it. Fort Pitt was surrounded in late June but not attacked until late July. The British managed to repulse the Indian attack when it came, knowing that it was critical to hold Fort Pitt as well as Forts Niagara and Detroit, all strategic positions from which to reconquer the Ohio River Valley and secure the Great Lakes region. Bouquet and his headquarters received word of the attacks by late May.

On 28 July, a relief column arrived at Fort Detroit. This force numbered 200 men drawn from regular and ranger units but was carrying few supplies or provisions for the fort. On 31 July the column, commanded by Captain James Dalyell, marched to destroy the Indian camp and lift the siege but was ambushed and all but destroyed at a creek named Bloody Run. The Indians killed more than 20 British soldiers, wounded 30 more, and captured 100. Dalyell was killed in the battle, and the siege of Detroit continued.

To the east, all available troops were sent to Philadelphia to stage an expedition to relieve Fort Pitt. Bouquet gathered a force of about 500 men from the 42nd, 77th, and 60th Regiments of Foot as well as from the rangers to open the road to Fort Pitt. His force marched to Carlisle and moved out toward Fort Pitt on 18 July. The Indians besieging Fort Pitt received word of Bouquet's movement and moved east to ambush his force. The two groups met at Bushy Run, 25 miles from Fort Pitt. On the morning of 5 August, Bouquet's forward units skirmished with Indian warriors. Realizing that his force was in a potential ambush situation, he deployed his troops in a circular defensive position and awaited the Indian attack. It came shortly after noon and lasted into the evening. His circle held out but took many casualties. On the morning of 6 August, the Indians advanced again, undertaking coordinated attacks. When Bouquet recognized that he was in danger of a breach, he decided to shorten his lines, and two light companies were ordered to fall back. The Indians saw this, mistook it for a retreat, and launched a disorganized attack. Unbeknownst to the Indians, the British had already pulled back four other companies, and the right flank of the British circle began to pour heavy fire into the attacking Indian mass, then rushed them with bayonets. The British left flank attacked the Indian mass next. The Indians attempted to withdraw but were cut down. The remainder of the Indian force managed to withdraw from the field of battle.

Bouquet's force relieved Fort Pitt on 10 August, after which the colonel, deciding that his force needed rest, postponed further advances into the Ohio River Valley. Small detachments were sent out to Forts Bedford and Ligonier, and provincial troops arrived at Fort Pitt in early September. Bouquet then marched toward Fort Detroit, while a second column of regulars retook Presque Isle. Colonel William Johnson, meanwhile, had been meeting with members of the Six Nations concerning the Senecas' treachery at Fort Vendango. The Six Nations officially remained allied with the British throughout the crisis and vowed to deal with the traitors. The Senecas, however, kept fighting, first ambushing a relief column heading out to Fort Niagara and then ambushing and destroying another column of ninety British regulars sent out to attack the Indians.

The Ottawas negotiate with Colonel Henry Bouquet, a Swiss officer in British service, at a council fire near the British camp on the Muskingum River in October 1764. Ottawa Chief Pontiac led his tribe, as well as the Potawatomis and Hurons, in a rebellion against the British from 1763 to 1766. (Library of Congress)

The tension in the region that provoked the Indian uprising eventually forced the British government to announce a proclamation concerning the newly conquered territories. The Proclamation of 1763 was an attempt to resolve several outstanding issues in the region conclusively, but it was still somewhat ambiguous. The principal conditions of the proclamation were that the French settlements north of New York and New England were to become known as the new colony of Quebec; that Florida was to be divided into two new colonies, East and West Florida; that all three new colonies were to operate under English law; and that all other land not encompassed by the three new colonies was to belong to the Indians. Only Crown representatives could negotiate with Indians over the sale of land. No whites were to settle the region, and any whites already present in the region were ordered to withdraw east of the Appalachian Mountains. White traders were allowed to cross into Indian territory but were required to carry a license from the commander in chief.

Amherst was replaced as commander of British forces on 17 November 1763 by Major-General Thomas Gage but had developed the strategy for regaining control of the Northwest before he left. Provincials and regulars would be raised in New York to lift the siege of Fort Niagara and under the command of Colonel John Bradstreet would be sent to subdue the Indians on the Great Lakes. Bouquet and his troops would march into the Ohio River Valley and subdue the Indian tribes there. Assuming these campaigns were successful, Johnson would negotiate a treaty with the Indians and settle the uprising. Intelligence reports indicated that the Indians were growing tired of the situation. The siege of Detroit, in particular, had carried on longer than they had expected, and the British success at the Battle of Bushy Run had broken the back of the Indians' resolve. Johnson and Bradstreet arrived at Fort Niagara in early July to meet with a number of tribal chiefs who wished to discuss peace terms. Johnson conducted the negotiations and managed to reach agreement with all but three of the tribes in attendance. The terms of the treaty were not as harsh as might have been expected under the circumstances. The Indians were given several concessions, including the right to lodge complaints at Fort Detroit and a schedule for setting values on the European goods and American animal skins used in trade.

By this point the Indian uprising had ended, although Pontiac continued to lead attacks until 1766. The Proclamation of 1763 and its enforcement by British troops, however, helped to lay the foundation for animosities between the thirteen Atlantic coast colonies and the British government that would contribute to the open conflict between them in 1775.

DANIEL PATRICK MARSTON

See also
British Army; Gage, Thomas; Johnson, Sir William; Native Americans; Proclamation of 1763

References
Dowd, Gregory. *War under Heaven: Pontiac, the Indian Nations & the British Empire.* Baltimore, MD: Johns Hopkins University Press, 2002.
Nester, William. *"Haughty Conquerors": Amherst and the Great Indian Uprising of 1763.* Westport, CT: Praeger, 2000.
Parkman, Francis. *The Conspiracy of Pontiac.* London: Dent, 1908.
Peckham, Howard. *Pontiac and the Indian Uprising.* Princeton, NJ: Princeton University Press, 1947.
Quaife, Milo Milton. *The Siege of Detroit in 1763: Journal of Pontiac's Rebellion.* Chicago: R. R. Donnelley, 1958.

Popular Culture

The development of American popular culture during the Revolutionary era suggests that the American Revolution marked a radical departure from the more hierarchical British social order that had dominated British colonial life. Social constraints were loosened as common people expressed their freedom in their everyday lives. In journalism and all publishing as well as in the nascent American theater, the political ferment of the period encouraged dra-

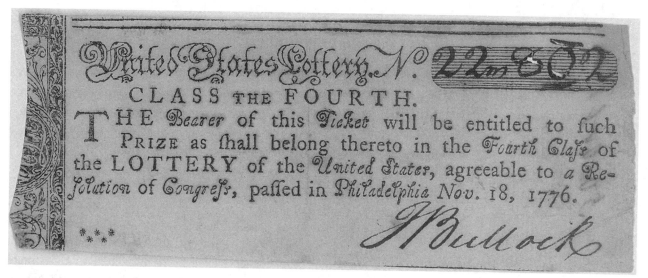

An early U.S. lottery ticket, issued according to a 1776 act of Congress. (Library of Congress)

matic change, while in music and painting British influences remained somewhat more important.

Many cultural developments, while accelerated by the Revolution, were well under way by the early 1760s. During the French and Indian (Seven Years') War, both British and French troops had poured into the colonies, and many of them stayed, expanding the population and introducing new customs and ideas on the eve of the Revolution. This expanding population contributed to urbanization and commercial activity, but most colonists continued to earn their livelihood by farming. The isolation of rural life in colonial America focused cultural life on the family. Due to the low population density of the predominant rural population, marriages between cousins or among in-laws were not unusual. Socialization among young people in small communities occurred during holidays, on Saturday evenings, or on Sundays after church.

On the eve of the Revolution, however, some social restraints upon courtship appeared to be in flux. The conventional moral standards of colonial America included the expectation that couples would abstain from sexual activity until marriage. In the seventeenth century, the overwhelming majority of first children born arrived at least nine months after marriage, yet between 1720 and 1760, this majority began to diminish, indicating an increase in premarital sexual relations. The acceptability of this behavior was made somewhat easier because many couples had publicly announced their betrothal well before marriage. The apparent growth in premarital intercourse may also be reflective of social changes that became more evident following the Revolution, in which marriage partners were more often selected according to mutual emotional attachment rather than by arrangements made by parents. Although divorce remained rare in early America, the increased emotional expectations for the institution, and perhaps the disruptions of the Revolutionary War, may have contributed to an increase in the divorce rate. In Massachusetts, one-third of the divorces granted between 1692 and 1786 occurred after 1774.

Weddings (like funerals) were primarily conducted in the home rather than in churches. Women were especially socially isolated in the scattered agricultural settlements of the colonial South, as travel distances limited the establishment of churches. Harvesting events and quilting bees offered some exception to women's social isolation. Men, on the other hand, enjoyed more opportunities for social interaction. They gathered frequently for buying and selling goods and crops, voting, observing court proceedings, and mustering in the militia. These occasions often provided opportunities for playing games, gambling, and drinking. Indeed, civic occasions often involved more frivolity than public virtue.

Play was certainly important for the hardworking colonists. Fox hunting was popular among the upper class, and organizations such as the Gloucester Fox Hunting Club in Pennsylvania emulated the rituals of English aristocrats. The common people engaged in less ostentatious activities. Team sports such as cudgels, a British game using a ball and clubs, and lacrosse, which the colonials learned from Native Americans, were less popular in rural America than more individual contests in foot races, marksmanship, wrestling, and boxing. These male sports offered opportunities for relaxation and letting off steam during service in the Revolutionary cause. The southern backcountry developed a reputation for no-holds-barred combat in which activities such as eye-gouging were not uncommon.

Cards and dice were also important diversions almost everywhere and were mostly, but not entirely, for men. The lack of gambling houses generally kept the stakes small, and simple gambling was not usually considered an example of moral laxity. Wagering often focused upon one of colonial America's most popular pastimes: horse racing. The most common example of this sport was the quarter race, matching two riders over a straight course measuring a quarter mile. In these contests the riders were allowed to jostle and bump their rivals. The colonial upper class often imported English thoroughbreds for more structured racing on circular tracks in New York City, Charleston, and Williamsburg. The popularity of horse racing was evident among enthusiasts of all social classes who ignored the efforts by the Continental Congress to suspend the sport in an effort to promote public virtue in anticipation of the coming armed struggle with Britain. The boisterous and unrestrained nature of colonial play was also evident in the fervor surrounding cockfighting in the South. Initially, cockfighting was considered an appropriate diversion only for lower-class white males, free blacks, and slaves. After 1720, this bloody sport became a favorite of the Southern gentry, who placed large wagers on their favorite birds.

Many common folk could not afford to bet on horse races and cockfights, but they could at least purchase a lottery ticket. There was little religious condemnation of lotteries, which were licensed by colonial assemblies for the benefit of churches, schools, entrepreneurs seeking to finance such projects as turnpikes, and even debtors hoping to raise money to erase their financial obligations. Internal improvements by many local governments were also financed by lotteries. While such wagering was popular across social classes in the colonies, the British government, which maintained a monopoly over lotteries in the mother country, ordered that all royal governors should ban lotteries unless they were authorized by London. This measure was another example of British regulations that colonists believed unduly restricted their freedoms.

The consumption of alcohol, both in more social and in everyday settings, was another pastime enjoyed by all social classes in the colonial and Revolutionary eras. Continental soldiers were provided a daily ration of four ounces of rum or whiskey. The average American, aged fifteen or older, consumed approximately forty gallons of hard cider, wine, or distilled spirits per year between 1770 and 1800. The most popular alcoholic beverage was rum, which provided an inexpensive calorie supplement in cold winter weather for hardworking laborers. Although Quakers and Methodists condemned liquor distilled from grain or molasses, alcohol consumption was generally tolerated everywhere. Public drunkenness was not considered a major problem, perhaps because the great level of colonial consumption produced a high physical tolerance for alcohol. Drinking was not reserved for festive occasions (although it was nearly always part of such events) but rather was an integral part of everyday colonial life.

Thus in several ways, Americans of the Revolutionary era were a people who resisted restrictions placed upon their behavior. In areas as diverse as sexual relations, sports, gambling, and drinking, the popular culture of the era embodied the ideology of the American Revolution: that the prosperity and happiness of ordinary people should be the goal of society. This perspective was also evident in popular literature and the arts. The scope and number of newspapers in colonial America grew rapidly during the Revolutionary era and increased further in the early national period. Between 1770 and 1780, the number of colonial newspapers rose from twenty-nine to thirty-eight, while subscribers increased from approximately 23,000 to nearly 54,000. About 10 percent of adult white males were subscribers, a rate slightly higher than that in England. But readership was more numerous, because many inns and taverns subscribed so that their patrons could read the latest news, and still more Americans listened to papers read aloud in the same places.

Before 1770, most newspapers were established primarily as advertising auxiliaries to printing shops. As Revolutionary ferment swept the colonies, newspapers became vehicles for political causes, and the great majority rallied support for independence from Britain. This trend continued into the political debates of the 1790s between Federalists and Democratic-Republicans. The literacy rate for the colonial population in 1760, which has been estimated at as high as 75 percent for men and 40 percent for women, also provided a foundation for growing newspaper circulation. Between 1783 and 1801, seventy-five magazines also appeared in the United States, although many were short-lived. The first periodical designed for women, *Gentlemen and Ladies' Town & Country Magazine*, appeared in 1784.

The political discourse of the Revolutionary era directly fostered the growth of the American publishing industry. The number of print shops in the colonies grew from thirty-eight in 1764 to fifty-six in 1775, with Boston,

> Continental soldiers were provided a daily ration of four ounces of rum or whiskey.

New York, and Philadelphia dominating the publishing industry. Printers produced government documents, almanacs, schoolbooks, religious tracts, and, increasingly, political pamphlets, including America's first best-seller, Thomas Paine's *Common Sense* (January 1776), which may have reached 100,000 copies.

Between 1765 and 1785, American publishers issued few novels, and there was a general prejudice against reading for enjoyment as opposed to self-improvement, especially for men. In the last decade of the eighteenth century Americans did produce thirty-five novels, with William Hill Brown's sentimental *Power of Sympathy*, aimed at young female readers, typical of the genre. But American readers of fiction continued to rely primarily upon British titles until the emergence of a national literature with James Fenimore Cooper and Washington Irving in the early nineteenth century.

Themes of Revolutionary virtue and the new nation's territorial and economic expansion dominated America's slight poetic output. In 1785, Timothy Dwight published *The Conquest of Canaan*, in which he compared George Washington to the Biblical Joshua. In his *Vision of Columbus* (1787), Joel Barlow perceived America as continuing the era of progress initiated by the explorer. Patriotism also provided inspiration for "To His Excellency George Washington" by Phillis Wheatley, an African American poet whose master freed her from enslavement.

Several American painters were acclaimed in England, but not necessarily for their Revolutionary proclivities. Pennsylvania Quaker Benjamin West set up a London studio in 1763, gained fame for his *Death of General Wolfe* (1771), and became court painter to George III in 1772. London also celebrated the paintings of John Singleton Copley and the sculptures of Patience Wright. Other American artists, such as Charles Willson Peale and Gilbert Stuart, studied in London but returned to America and became the leading portrait painters of America's Revolutionary heroes. John Trumbull earned a reputation for celebrating the Revolution in works such as *The Battle of Bunker's Hill* (1785) and *The Declaration of Independence* (1794). All of these artists were greatly influenced by British art and less so by American culture. Several less-celebrated painters, however, recorded everyday American life in cruder portraitures of popular folk art.

In popular music, English folk traditions and songs, such as "Chevy Chase," "Children in the Woods," and "Spanish Lady," continued to exercise a major influence upon Americans throughout the eighteenth century. William Billings, however, declared his independence from European tradition in church and folk hymns and in the patriotic march "Chester," which was popular with the Continental Army. And in the slave quarters of the American South, an African American musical tradition was being formed that would culminate more than a century later in jazz, spirituals, and the blues.

The Revolution, which broadened the definitions of acceptable political and social behavior, also helped make drama more accessible to the general population. Royall Tyler's *The Contrast* (1787) celebrated the triumph of its simple but honest American character over more aristocratic British foils. Mercy Otis Warren produced a series of plays written anonymously—*The Adu-*

lateur (1772), *The Defeat* (1773), and *The Blockheads* (1776)—that mercilessly satirized both Loyalists and British politicians and soldiers. Washington's enthusiastic attendance at plays after the war increased their acceptance in American popular culture.

Revolutionary Americans increasingly embraced a popular culture that extolled the virtue and equality of the common people and the achievements of their Revolution while encouraging emerging popular art forms, particularly in journalism but also in literature, music, painting, and the theater.

RON BRILEY

See also

Art; Barlow, Joel; Copley, John Singleton; Music; Paine, Thomas; Peale, Charles Willson; Stuart, Gilbert; Trumbull, John; Warren, Mercy Otis; Wheatley, Phillis

References

Fliegelman, Jay. *Prodigals & Pilgrims: The American Revolution against Patriarchal Authority, 1750–1800.* New York: Cambridge University Press, 1982.

Grabo, Norman S. "The Cultural Effects of the Revolution." Pp. 578–588 in *The Blackwell Encyclopedia of the American Revolution.* Edited by Jack P. Greene and J. R. Pole. Oxford, UK: Blackwell, 1991.

Greene, Jack P. *Pursuits of Happiness: The Social Development of the Early Modern British Colonies and the Formation of American Culture.* Chapel Hill: University of North Carolina Press, 1988.

Nye, Russell P. *The Cultural Life of the New Nation, 1776–1830.* New York: Harper and Row, 1960.

Silverman, Kenneth. *A Cultural History of the American Revolution: Painting, Music, Literature, and the Theatre in the Colonies from the Treaty of Paris to the Inauguration of George Washington, 1763–1789.* New York: Crowell, 1976.

Porto Praya, Battle of
(16 April 1781)

The Battle of Porto Praya was the first of many naval victories won by Admiral Pierre de Suffren during the American Revolutionary War, presaging his later string of successes in the Indian Ocean in 1782–1783. When Holland entered the war in 1781, the British government decided to send an expeditionary force to southern Africa to capture the Dutch colony of the Cape of Good Hope. The squadron dispatched, commanded by Commodore George Johnstone, consisted of the *Hero* and the *Monmouth* (both 74 guns); the *Romney*, the *Jupiter*, and the *Isis* (all 50 guns); the *Diana*, the *Jason*, and the *Active* (all 32 guns); eight smaller vessels of the navy; and another ten East Indiamen (all 26 guns). Johnstone departed on 13 March, taking a large number of troops in his convoy and accompanied by the Channel Fleet under Vice-Admiral George Darby, who was then en route for Gibraltar to aid in its relief.

Aware of the British plan, the French took measures to upset it and sent the able Suffren in command of a squadron of five vessels, consisting of the *Héros* and the *Annibal* (both 74 guns) and the *Artésien*, the *Sphinx*, and the

The Battle of Porto Praya, 16 April 1781, took place off the Cape Verde Islands between a French squadron of five ships under Admiral Pierre-André de Suffren and Commodore George Johnstone with an equal British force. (Art Archive/Musée de la Marine Paris/Dagli Orti)

Vengeur (all 64 guns). Suffren left Brest on 22 March, together with a fleet under the comte François de Grasse. This combined force also carried troops.

On 11 April Johnstone arrived at Porto Praya, in the Cape Verde Islands, whose bay opens to the south and extends from west to east about 1.5 miles. Here Johnstone anchored, although aware that he was being followed and that, while at a neutral port, he could expect no protection from Portuguese authorities. Johnstone's dispositions were faulty: his flagship, the *Romney*, stood in a cluster of other vessels, severely restricting its field of fire. At 9:30 A.M. on 16 April, the *Isis* sighted a squadron to the northeast and signaled its approach. This was Suffren's force. Johnstone was caught completely unawares: 1,500 of his men were on shore collecting food, livestock, and water and relaxing.

Suffren had arrived at Porto Praya merely to collect water and did not expect to find the British squadron there. Nevertheless, he immediately decided to engage Johnstone's squadron, maneuvering in column around the east point of the bay with his own ship, the *Héros*, in the lead, flying the signal for attack. Suffren dropped anchor 500 feet to starboard of the *Hero*, at which Suffren began to fire. Immediately astern of the *Héros* stood the *Annibal*, but when this ship proceeded ahead of the flagship, it passed so close that the *Héros* was obliged to drop astern, taking it closer to the *Monmouth*.

The *Annibal* failed to clear for action and consequently contributed little to the fight. The *Artésien*, the third in line, reached its appointed position, but when its captain was killed, the next in command neglected to anchor. The vessel fouled with one of the East Indiamen, and the wind pulled the two vessels out to sea. The *Sphinx* and the *Vengeur*—the last two ships in Suffren's force—did nothing more than fire their broadsides as they sailed past the mouth of the bay, unaccountably finding no position from which to engage Johnstone's ships.

Under these circumstances the battle could only prove indecisive, and of Suffren's ships only the *Annibal* and the *Héros* played any effective part. Finally, after nearly four hours, Suffren appreciated that nothing further could be achieved, and he made for the open sea. Despite having lost all its masts, the *Annibal* succeeded in following the flagship. Considering his failure to take adequate measures of defense, Johnstone came out of the action well. Having assessed the damage his ships had sustained, he directed them to pursue. All but the *Isis* could do so, for its captain, Evelyn Sutton, claimed that damage sustained by the spars and rigging would not bear up against the wind. Johnstone nevertheless insisted, with the result that soon after the ship's fore topmast tumbled overboard.

Johnstone faced a host of problems: the injury to the *Isis* left him unable to keep pace with Suffren; night was approaching; the *Isis* and the *Monmouth* were lagging astern at least 2 miles; the sea was growing heavier; and Johnstone himself had failed to assign a point to which the convoy should sail in order to rejoin the squadron. He therefore decided that he should not attempt a night engagement. On the other hand, if he allowed Suffren to escape, the French might reach the Cape first. Such a dilemma caused Johnstone much anguish and eventually led him to call off the pursuit and return to Porto Praya. There he stayed in the harbor for a fortnight and ordered the arrest of Sutton.

Suffren made all sail for the Cape, which he reached ahead of Johnstone, and disembarked his troops, rendering the colony effectively safe from British conquest. When Johnstone eventually appeared, he judged further action futile and made for nearby Saldanha Bay, where he captured five Dutch East Indiamen. Then, having detached the *Hero*, the *Monmouth*, and the *Isis* for service in Indian waters under Rear-Admiral Sir Edward Hughes, Johnstone returned to Britain with the remainder of his force.

Sutton was acquitted before a court-martial, but little favorable can be said of Johnstone's conduct during the battle, notwithstanding his lack of experience. Whatever the explanation for his failure, he was at least fortunate that his adversary did not show a more intrepid nature. Indeed, although Suffren began the action against Johnstone, both commanders were equally surprised at the other's presence. The British commander was fortunate, in spite of himself, to be anchored and numerically superior.

In the end, Johnstone's losses were only 9 killed and 47 wounded. These numbers rose to 36 killed and 130 wounded when the losses sustained aboard the ships of war were added to those suffered aboard the convoy, which was struck by stray fire. French losses, according to their records, were 105 killed and 204 wounded, virtually all of these aboard the *Héros* and the *Annibal*. Suffren spent the next two months near the Cape. Having ensured that the colony was safe from attack, he proceeded to Île de France (Mauritius), where he arrived on 25 October. On 17 December his squadron, now under Commodore d'Orves, headed for the Coromandel coast.

GREGORY FREMONT-BARNES

See also

Gibraltar, Siege of; Howe, Richard; Johnstone, George; Suffren, Pierre-André de

References

Cavaliero, Roderick. *Admiral Satan: The Life and Campaigns of Suffren*. London: Tauris, 1994.
Clowes, William Laird. *The Royal Navy: A History from the Earliest Times to 1900*. Vol. 3 of 7. London: Chatham, 1996.
Gardiner, Robert, ed. *Navies and the American Revolution, 1775–1783*. London: Chatham, 1996.
James, William. *The Naval History of Great Britain: During the French Revolutionary and Napoleonic Wars*. 4 vols. Mechanicsburg, PA: Stackpole, 2003.

Pownall, Thomas
(1722–1805)

Thomas Pownall began his career, and his connection to British North America, as a clerk for the Board of Trade in 1743. In 1753 he resigned this position to accompany Sir Danvers Osborne, governor designate of New York, to America as Osborne's personal secretary. The two men arrived in October 1753. Two weeks later Osborne committed suicide, leaving Pownall without employment.

Pownall spent the next two years traveling around the colonies, documenting his observations and writing his contemporaries and his patron, the Earl of Halifax, about what he saw, heard, and experienced. Keenly interested in cartography and in the American Indians, Pownall corresponded with Cadwallader Colden and Lewis Evans about the topography of America and the location of various Indian communities. Eventually Pownall submitted a map of North America to the Board of Trade. He also sent a remarkable essay titled "Considerations on the Means, Method and Nature of Settling a Colony on the Lands South of Lake Erie" to his brother John, then a secretary in the office of the British government's secretary of state for the Southern Department, who was responsible for the governance of British North America. In his essay, Pownall considered how the settlement of the American interior ought to occur. At its core was a belief that the prospect of vast lands west of the Appalachian Mountains tempted British settlers to look westward and not toward the established seaboard towns or across the Atlantic to London. This fact, he argued, should make the British government take more interest in the future development of the American interior. Such an interest soon came to pass in the years following the Seven Years' (French and Indian) War in America (1756–1763).

Besides exploring the future of the development of Britain's colonies, Pownall spent considerable time investigating Britain's Indian affairs. Though only a guest at the Albany Congress of 1754, he submitted a proposal to the delegates suggesting that the colonies had two choices when it came to controlling North America: either fighting the French everywhere or dominating the Great Lakes to control maritime access to the American interior. He followed up his public proposal with a private proposal to his brother, who had become the most important secretary to the Board of Trade in the mid-eighteenth century. Many of Pownall's proposals for the settlement of the American interior were integrated into the Proclamation of 1763, a document that his brother helped draft.

Thomas Pownall, a member of Parliament during the American Revolution. In May 1780 the House of Commons rejected his proposal for peace with the rebellious colonies. (Library of Congress)

In 1756, Pownall returned to London, where he was soon named governor of Massachusetts. Serving in this post from 1757 to 1759, he extended British garrisons along the northern frontier. He then lost his post in Massachusetts but in 1760 was named governor of South Carolina. Rather than accept his new position, he returned to England. Though he was then elected to Parliament, he chose to serve in the British Army on the European continent until 1763, before returning to England and writing his most influential work, *The Administration of the Colonies*, that established his reputation as an expert on British North America. He was soon reelected to Parliament and served there from 1767 to 1780.

Because Pownall was one of the few members of the House of Commons who had spent considerable time in America, several politicians sought his advice during the imperial crises of the 1760s and 1770s. In parliamentary sessions, he opposed the Townshend duties of 1767 but approved the Boston Port Act (although not the other Coercive Acts) in 1774. He opposed Edmund Burke's reconciliation bill of 1775 but by December 1777 was arguing that Britain had permanently lost control of the colonies and would have to grant independence to regain influence in America. In 1780 Pownall published *A Memorial, Most Humbly Addressed to the Sovereigns of Europe, on the Present State of Affairs, between the Old and New World*, which proposed that Britain grant America independence and arrange new commercial relations with the former colonies. This work so impressed John Adams (who, as America's peace commissioner in Paris, was hoping to persuade the British of exactly this policy) that he produced an anonymous *Translation*, really a considerable reduction and revision, of Pownall's work in 1780 under a pseudonym. Pownall also introduced a resolution in the House of Commons seeking an end to the Revolutionary War in 1780 but soon thereafter left Parliament and spent the remainder of his career writing and traveling.

MICHAEL MULLIN

See also
Adams, John; Albany Congress; Massachusetts; Proclamation of 1763; Trade, Board of

References
Christie, Ian R. "Thomas Pownall." Pp. 768–769 in *The Blackwell Encyclopedia of the American Revolution*. Edited by Jack P. Greene and J. R. Pole. Oxford, UK: Blackwell, 1991.

Schutz, John A. *Thomas Pownall, British Defender of American Liberty: A Study of Anglo-American Relations*. Glendale, CA: A. H. Clark, 1951.

Prescott, Oliver
(1731–1804)

Oliver Prescott, a citizen of Massachusetts, was a physician and soldier during the Revolution. A kind and gentle man, he was appreciated by his fellow citizens for his medical knowledge, military bearing, and pleasant manners. He was born in Groton in 1731, and after graduation from Harvard College in 1750, he studied medicine with Dr. Ebenezer Robie of Sudbury and earned a master's degree from Harvard in 1753. Prescott returned to Groton and practiced medicine there for the rest of his life. During the Seven Years' War, he served in the Massachusetts militia, and he was town clerk and selectman in Groton for many years. During the Stamp Act crisis in 1765, he was chairman of a local committee that opposed British taxation. In 1774, he was clerk of Groton's Committee of Correspondence in opposition to the Coercive Acts.

In 1775, Prescott was appointed brigadier general of Middlesex County militia by the Revolutionary government of Massachusetts. He also was appointed justice of the peace and of the quorum. He was put in charge of four cannon evacuated from Concord on 17 April, and two days later he gave medical attention to militiamen wounded at Lexington and Concord. He also tended the wounded after the Battle of Bunker Hill on 17 June. On 30 October, he was elected to the Board of War but declined to serve. Instead, he remained with his militiamen at the siege of Boston, guarding bridges to keep Loyalists from joining British troops in the town. In 1777, he began a three-year term on the Massachusetts Executive Council. He was also a member of the Harvard College Board of Overseers. In 1778 he was appointed major general of Massachusetts militia, and a year later he began a life term as probate judge in Middlesex County. He was an original founder of the American Academy of Arts and Sciences in 1780, and in 1781 he helped found the Massachusetts Medical Society. Later he became an honorary member of the New Hampshire Medical Society. He was also president of the Middlesex Medical Society and the Western Society of Middlesex Husbandmen.

Prescott was interested in education. He was among the first trustees of Groton Academy and was the first president of Groton's board of trustees. He conducted a thriving medical practice, which covered an extensive area and required him to spend a great deal of time on horseback. He was recognized for his contributions to the medical practice in 1791 when Harvard College awarded him an honorary doctorate in medicine. During Shays's Rebellion in 1786, he served a final stint in the military, acting as a militia recruiter to suppress unrest in Middlesex County. Portly and deaf in his old age, he practiced medicine and cultivated his many other interests until his death in 1804.

PAUL DAVID NELSON

See also
Boston, Siege of; Bunker Hill, Battle of; Coercive Acts; Lexington and Concord; Stamp Act

References
Butler, Caleb. *History of the Town of Groton*. Boston: T. R. Marvin, 1848.
Thacher, James. *American Medical Biography*, Vol. 1. Boston: Richardson and Lord, 1828.

Prescott, William
(1726–1795)

In June 1775, Colonel William Prescott commanded a regiment of minutemen from Pepperell, Massachusetts, and played a crucial role in the Battle of Bunker Hill. He fortified Breed's Hill rather than Bunker Hill, decided to hold the fort instead of retreating, and capably defended against the British attack.

Born in Groton, Massachusetts, Prescott acquired substantial military experience as a young man. In 1745 he participated in the campaign that captured the French fortress at Louisbourg on Cape Breton Island, and in 1755 he served as a lieutenant in the expedition that captured Fort Beausejour, another maritime French stronghold. Prescott's excellent service during the latter operation was recognized when he was offered a commission in the British Army, but he declined and returned home to Pepperell. There he devoted himself to his family and farming while remaining active in the colonial militia and reading all available books on military affairs.

As the crisis with Britain escalated, Prescott led Pepperell's preparations for war. In 1774, he was elected colonel of the town's minutemen. He also sent forty bushels of grain to Boston and a letter that urged the people of Boston "to stand firm in the common cause" and promised that "we heartily sympathize with you, and are always ready to do all in our power for your support, comfort, and relief." On 19 April 1775, Prescott led his regiment to join the fighting at Lexington and Concord but arrived too late to participate in the engagement. He then proceeded to Cambridge and served in the siege of Boston.

On 13 June 1775, Prescott was among the group of officers who debated whether or not to fortify Bunker Hill in Charlestown, just north of Boston.

William Prescott, supervising the construction of the redoubt on Breed's Hill on the Charlestown peninsula opposite Boston. (North Wind Picture Archives)

He argued in favor of such an action, agreeing with Israel Putnam that a fort on Bunker Hill would force the British to come out from Boston and engage the Americans. Three days later, General Artemas Ward, commander of the Patriot troops, ordered Prescott to take three regiments and fortify Bunker Hill. Upon arriving in Charlestown, however, Prescott built the fort on Breed's Hill, primarily because this would place guns in range of the British fleet in Boston Harbor and thus more effectively force the British to attack the position to eliminate the threat to their navy. Whether Prescott or Putnam made this decision is not known.

During the night, Prescott's troops constructed the fort on Breed's Hill. On two occasions, he walked along the harbor shore listening for the sound of oars, certain that a British attack was imminent. At dawn on 17 June, he realized that the British could easily outflank his position and ordered the construction of breastworks on his left flank. By this time, the British had opened an artillery bombardment on the Patriots. The fire rattled the inexperienced militia, and to steady the men, Prescott, with drawn sword, jumped onto the fort's parapet and walked back and forth. This action settled his troops, and they finished constructing the bastion.

It was clear that the British were preparing to attack, and Prescott called a council of war to decide whether to stay and fight. Nearly all of his officers argued that the troops were in no condition to fight; they were exhausted, hungry, fearful, and beginning to desert in small numbers. But Prescott refused to retreat, eagerly seeking an opportunity to engage the British and prove "that Americans could stand up to British regulars." He agreed to request reinforcements and supplies, but none arrived. In fact, he actually lost troops, because Putnam ordered him to provide soldiers from Breed's Hill to construct fortifications on Bunker Hill.

When the British finally attacked, Prescott maneuvered his troops to maximize his firepower. He first shifted soldiers from the south to the north wall to repel a British assault against the north side and then moved his forces to the south end of the fort and blunted another British advance. At the same time, he carefully controlled his men's rate of fire, reminding them: "you are all marksmen; do not any of you fire until you can see the whites of their eyes." Such tactics, at first highly effective, eventually proved insufficient when the Patriots ran low on ammunition and the British launched a three-sided assault with 1,500 men. With their powder and ammunition exhausted and the British pouring into the fort, Prescott ordered his men to retreat. He refused to run, however, and walked out of the bastion while fending off bayonet thrusts.

Immediately after the engagement, an angry Prescott confronted Ward and asked for three regiments with which to launch a counterattack, but Ward refused. Prescott then charged that Ward's failure to send reinforcements and supplies had cost the Patriots the battle. For the rest of his life, Prescott believed that the Patriots would have won the Battle of Bunker Hill if he had received proper support.

Following the battle, Prescott remained in the service for about two years. He fought in the engagements around New York City, commanding the garrison on Governor's Island and receiving a commendation from George Washington for safely abandoning the position when the American army was compelled to retreat from the city. At the end of 1776, he left the army because of physical infirmities, though in 1777 he served briefly in the Saratoga Campaign. He then permanently withdrew from the war. Following the Revolution, he served as a local magistrate and selectman, was elected to the Massachusetts General Court, and participated in the suppression of Shays's Rebellion in Middlesex County.

DAVID WORK

See also
Boston, Siege of; Bunker Hill, Battle of; Lexington and Concord; Militia, Patriot and Loyalist; Minutemen; New York, Operations in; Putnam, Israel; Saratoga Campaign; Ward, Artemas

References
Birnbaum, Louis. *Red Dawn at Lexington*. Boston: Houghton, Mifflin, 1986.
Fleming, Thomas J. *Now We Are Enemies: The Story of Bunker Hill*. New York: St. Martin's, 1960.
Ketchum, Richard M. *The Battle for Bunker Hill*. Garden City, NY: Doubleday, 1962.
Winthrop, Robert C. *Address at the Unveiling of the Statue of Colonel William Prescott, on Bunker Hill, June 17, 1881*. Cambridge, MA: John Wilson and Son, 1881.

Prevost, Augustine
(1723–1786)

A skillful and professional Swiss general in the British Army, Augustine Prevost commanded British forces in the southern theater during the American Revolutionary War and was noted for his successful defense of Savannah against the American siege in 1779.

Born in Geneva, Switzerland, in 1723, Prevost began his military service with the British 60th Foot (Royal American Regiment) in North America. Promoted to major in 1756, he served in the French and Indian War (1754–1763) and was severely wounded during the Battle of the Heights of Abraham in September 1759. He recovered from his injuries and was promoted to lieutenant-colonel in 1761 and then to colonel in the early 1770s. He commanded British forces in East Florida at the outbreak of the war in 1775 and was later given command of all British forces in the southern theater in

December 1778. He captured Fort Morris, Georgia, after a brief siege in January 1779 and was rewarded with a promotion to major-general in February. Advancing toward Charleston in April, he defeated a smaller American force under the command of General William Moultrie at Coosawhatchie River on 3 May. Prevost pursued Moultrie to Charleston but was finally driven off by a larger American force under the command of General Benjamin Lincoln and Casimir Pulaski. Prevost returned to Savannah and later successfully defended it against besieging Franco-American forces under Lincoln and Admiral Jean-Baptiste d'Estaing in September–October 1779.

Savannah was Prevost's last military victory. He returned to England after the engagement and died peacefully in 1786. An extremely skilled, intelligent, and professional soldier, he soundly defeated his adversaries time and again under very difficult conditions. His son, Sir George Prevost, would later fight American forces in the War of 1812 and achieve great fame.

ANDREW B. GODEFROY

See also

Estaing, Jean-Baptiste, Comte d'; Florida, East and West; Fort Morris, Georgia; Lincoln, Benjamin; Moultrie, William; Pulaski, Casimir; Savannah, Georgia, Operations against; Southern Campaigns

Reference

Dupuy, T., and G. Hammerman, eds. *People and Events of the American Revolution.* New York: Bowker, 1974.

Priestley, Joseph
(1733–1804)

Joseph Priestley was an English-born dissenting minister, philosopher, and chemist. His many writings were wide-ranging and well received in Revolutionary America where they were often reprinted, making Priestley's a household name. The controversy that arose because of his move to America in 1794, however, was illustrative of both his growing international fame and the political tensions he encountered in America.

Born in Yorkshire, Priestley attended a nonconformist academy at Northampton, and by 1758 he was preaching at Nantwich, where he also taught school and experimented in natural philosophy. By 1766 he had been elected a member of the Royal Society, and in 1767 he published his *History and Present State of Electricity with Original Experiments*, a book that is notable, in part, for its detailed account of Benjamin Franklin's kite experiment of 1752. Franklin and Priestley were also friends, having met in London where the two moved in similar circles. In 1768 Priestley published *An Essay on the First Principles of Government, and on the Nature of Political, Civil, and Religious Liberty*, a book that was read by many in the colonies for its Lockean-inspired ideas about freedom of religion and thought.

Priestley was a Unitarian and believed that human society was perfectible, a theory that he espoused in *Hartley's Theory of the Human Mind* (1775). He viewed the French Revolution as a significant step toward a more perfect world. Because of that view, his life became increasingly uncomfortable in England during the early 1790s. In 1791, rioters destroyed his home and laboratory in Birmingham. In the spring of 1794, he decided to move to the United States, following his three sons.

Priestley landed in New York, traveled to Philadelphia, and then settled at Northumberland, Pennsylvania. His arrival in New York was celebrated with addresses from the Democratic Society of the City of New York and the Tammany Society, among others. It also drew attention in newspapers, such as the *American Daily Advertiser,* and even occasioned pamphlets, such as William Cobbett's critical *Observations on the Emigration of Dr. Joseph Priestly, and on the Several Addresses Delivered to Him on His Arrival at New-York* (1794). While many Republicans thought of Priestley as a kindred spirit, many Federalists loathed him. Even President John Adams, who had known and liked Priestley in England in the 1780s, had become cooler toward him. And Adams's secretary of state, Timothy Pickering, seriously considered having Priestley deported under the Alien Act.

Priestley continued his chemical experiments, publishing some findings in the *Transactions of the American Philosophical Society.* In particular, having been the first chemist to identify oxygen as an independent element in the 1770s, Priestley now debated with James Woodhouse, professor of chemistry at the University of Pennsylvania, about the older phlogiston theory. In 1797 Priestley published *An Address to the Unitarian Congregation at Philadelphia.* In 1799 he published *A Comparison of the Institutions of Moses with Those of the Hindoos,* a book that helped to popularize his other writings by including "A catalogue of books, written by Dr. Priestley." Also in 1799, he published *Letters to the Inhabitants of Northumberland and Its Neighbourhood, on Subjects Interesting to the Author and to Them,* a book praised by Thomas Jefferson, among others. Priestley died in 1804 and is buried in the Quaker Meeting Ground at Northumberland.

Dr. Joseph Priestley, the dissenting British minister and scientist, befriended many Americans in England during the Revolutionary War and moved to America after the war in search of greater political freedom. (Library of Congress)

MARK G. SPENCER

See also

Franklin, Benjamin; Locke, John; Pickering, Timothy; Price, Richard

References

Gibbs, F. W. *Joseph Priestley: Adventurer in Science and Champion of Truth.* London, UK: Nelson, 1965.

Graham, Jenny. *Revolutionary in Exile: The Emigration of Joseph Priestley to America, 1794–1804.* Philadelphia, PA: American Philosophical Society, 1995.

Smith, Edgar Fays. *Priestley in America, 1794–1804.* Philadelphia, PA: P. Blakiston's Son and Company, 1920.

Princeton, Battle of
(3 January 1777)

The Battle of Princeton was part of a larger campaign that pitted the forces of General George Washington and Lieutenant-General Lord Charles Cornwallis against each other in New Jersey. Both the battle and the larger campaign followed, and to a degree resulted from, Washington's smashing triumph against Colonel Johann Rall's Hessian soldiers at Trenton on 26 December 1776. Immediately after this victory, Washington had intended to march toward Princeton and New Brunswick, but his fear of Colonel Carl von Donop's 2,000 German troops at Bordentown had caused him to withdraw across the Delaware River to Pennsylvania during the night of 26–27 December. Nonetheless, the "dire necessity" that had compelled him to attempt the hazardous operation against Trenton had not abated in late December. On the last day of the month, enlistments for the vast majority of his soldiers would expire, and he would be left with only the skeleton of a military force.

Mitigating Washington's concern was the fact that General Sir William Howe, British commander in chief, had ceased military operations for the winter of 1776–1777 and therefore posed no immediate threat to his army's existence. But Washington's fighting blood was up. Although he had been compelled early in the war with Britain to adopt a defensive strategy, he was by temperament an aggressive general, itching to take the fight to his enemies whenever possible. Soon he received a dispatch from Lieutenant Colonel John Cadwalader, serving as a temporary brigadier general in New Jersey at the head of a small army consisting of 900 Rhode Island Continentals and 1,000 Pennsylvania and Delaware militiamen. Cadwalader was supposed to have supported Washington's attack on Trenton on 26 December but had not gotten his troops across the Delaware until the following day. He reported to Washington that as a result of the Battle of Trenton, the Hessians had abandoned all their posts along the river and had fallen back to Princeton. He urged Washington to recross the Delaware, join forces with him, and continue with his original plan to march farther into New Jersey.

Washington needed little encouragement. He was already planning a return to New Jersey to recapture part of that state from Howe's Anglo-British forces before his army disintegrated at the end of the year. Starting to cross the Delaware River on 29 December, he completed the operation the following day and marched his soldiers to Trenton. The weather was bitterly cold, with snow on the ground and ice floes clogging the Delaware. His force numbered only 1,500 men, for many of his soldiers, incapacitated by their recent marches to and from Trenton, had been left in their camps in Pennsylvania. Once across the Delaware, he was joined by a Pennsylvania militia unit of 1,500, raised by General Thomas Mifflin and already in New Jersey, and Cadwalader's troops, numbering 2,100 soldiers with militia reinforcements. Still, Washington had to deal with the fact that enlistments of most of his Continental regulars would expire on 31 December. He, Mifflin, and Brigadier General Henry Knox made speeches to the troops, offering them a bounty of $10 if they would remain in the service for six more weeks. About half the

George Washington personally leads an American attack at the Battle of Princeton, 3 January 1777. His victory served to boost Patriot morale and proved that American regulars could match the discipline and fighting skills of their British counterparts in the field. (National Archives and Records Administration)

soldiers accepted; the other half, including Colonel John Glover's Marblehead Mariners, went home. As Washington had acted entirely upon his own authority without consulting the Continental Congress, he asked Robert Morris in Philadelphia to borrow money to pay the bounties. Morris quickly raised $50,000 on his own recognizance and sent the money to Washington.

With about 5,000 soldiers and forty pieces of artillery serving under his immediate command by 2 January, Washington turned to face a British army of 8,000 British and German troops under Cornwallis rapidly approaching from Princeton, 12 miles away, to contest the Continentals' return to New Jersey. Many of Washington's men were untrained, inexperienced militia, and his Continentals were half-starved, unclad, footsore, and bone-weary from poor food, lack of sleep, and overexertion. Cornwallis, on the other hand, commanded the flower of General William Howe's army in America. Before Rall's defeat, Cornwallis had been preparing to return to England for the winter. Afterward, he was ordered by Howe to replace Major-General James Grant as commander in New Jersey for the duration of the crisis. Grant remained in New Jersey and accompanied Cornwallis on his march toward Trenton. American forces under General Matthias Fermoy and Colonel Edward Hand skirmished with and delayed, but did not halt, the British Army in its advance.

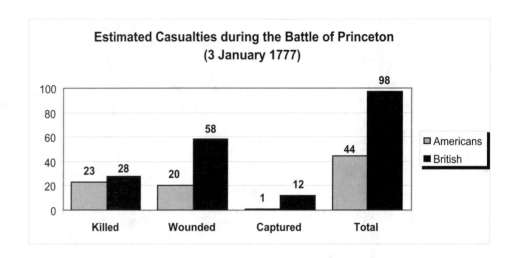

**Estimated Casualties during the Battle of Princeton
(3 January 1777)**

Washington positioned his troops on a ridge to the south of Trenton, on the bank of Assunpink Creek, with his line extending about 3 miles. From behind quickly constructed earthworks, his men watched Cornwallis's army approach at about 5:00 P.M. and begin to probe the American lines. Cornwallis and Grant had expected to find that Washington and his rebel band had scampered back across the Delaware River to safety. Instead, to their delight, they discovered the general encamped with his ragtag army and ready for battle. The British officers attempted to send a party of Hessians across the creek at a ford, but they were driven off by the fire of well-entrenched Rhode Island Continentals, commanded by Major Israel Angell. After an exchange of cannon fire, both armies gradually allowed the fighting to abate. Although Cornwallis now was urged by General Sir William Erskine to assault Washington's army in the darkness, the British commander decided to wait until morning to deliver the coup de grâce to his American foe. Convinced that he had entrapped Washington's army against the Delaware River, Cornwallis felt certain that he would "bag the fox" at his leisure on the morrow.

Washington realized the peril his army was in on the evening of 2 January and called his officers together to discuss American options. Fighting seemed out of the question to them. Their most obvious hope was to escape southward, seeking a place to get across the Delaware River to safety. But with Cornwallis hounding them, the retreat might become a rout, and in any case there were no boats available to rescue them. Then someone, perhaps Washington himself, made a remarkable suggestion that later was claimed by many. The new proposal was to march the army surreptitiously around Cornwallis's left flank during the early morning hours of 3 January, attack and defeat the British rear guard at Princeton before Cornwallis could react, then assault the important British post at New Brunswick. The council quickly adopted this audacious plan, which was aided by a drop in temperatures during the night that froze the roads and made movement easier. Creating diversions to delude the British and wrapping the wheels of their gun carriages in rags to deaden noise, the American army slunk away and marched rapidly toward Princeton.

Just as the sun rose, Washington's soldiers began crossing Stony Brook, 2 miles south of Princeton. Here the commander divided his army. He sent

General Hugh Mercer's 350-man brigade and Cadwalader's militia to the left to seize and destroy Stony Brook bridge on the direct road to Trenton, in case Cornwallis was pursuing him. General John Sullivan, in command of Lieutenant Colonel Edward Hand's Pennsylvania riflemen, the 7th Virginia Continentals, and Angell's Rhode Island Continental regiment, was to march to the right and enter Princeton from the east. Washington accompanied the latter detachment. British forces in Princeton, 1,700 strong, were commanded by Lieutenant-Colonel Charles Mawhood. They consisted of the 17th, 40th, and 55th Regiments and three troops of light dragoons. Mawhood was under orders from Cornwallis to march that day with most of his troops to Maidenhead, join there with General Alexander Leslie's contingent of 1,200 men, and proceed to Cornwallis's assistance at Trenton. Leaving the 40th Regiment at Princeton to guard British stores, Mawhood set out on the morning of 3 January toward Trenton. As he crossed Stony Brook bridge, he was surprised to discern Mercer's troops just emerging from the woods to the south.

Quickly sending out dragoon patrols, Mawhood learned that not only Mercer's soldiers but also Sullivan's were maneuvering against Princeton. These rebels, surprisingly, were not merely stragglers from a battle with Cornwallis the day before but organized units under Washington's command. Mawhood withdrew his troops back across the bridge and rushed to deploy them on rising ground nearby in order to defend Princeton. Mercer, with equal speed, reached an open field below Mawhood's line and formed his men behind a hedge for a fight. At a distance of forty yards, both sides opened fire, the Americans with rifles and the British with muskets; each side also had two cannon each. Mercer's horse was wounded, but he continued to fight on foot. After Mawhood's troops had fired one volley, he ordered them to charge with bayonets, and the Americans broke and retreated in confusion. Mercer was killed in the melee, stabbed seven times by bayonets. When Cadwalader's militiamen joined the fight, Mawhood withdrew a short distance and re-formed his soldiers. When they fired upon Cadwalader's advancing troops, this entire corps in its turn broke and ran.

At this moment Washington arrived with his staff officers and viewed the scene of chaotic disarray. Riding a white horse, exposing himself to the volley fire of Mawhood's troops, he attempted without success to rally Mercer's and Cadwalader's terrified men. Finally, Sullivan's three brigades also arrived, and the defeated American troops rallied. A line of battle was formed, consisting of the new arrivals as well as Cadwalader's troops and a part of Mercer's. These soldiers advanced against Mawhood's position, relieving in the process a two-gun battery, commanded by Captain Joseph Moulder, that had continued to fire grapeshot into the enemy even after being abandoned during the American retreat. Hand's riflemen assaulted Mawhood's right, while the rest of Sullivan's soldiers attacked the British center and left. The British line, under intense fire from Washington's troops, broke and retreated. The 40th Regiment, cut off in Princeton from the fight, could provide no assistance.

Almost surrounded, Mawhood refused to surrender; instead, he ordered his soldiers to charge in the direction of Trenton with bayonets. Breaking

Battle of Princeton, 2 January 1777

N
NEW JERSEY
Washington's route to Morristown
Kingston
MAWHOOD 1,200
Princeton
Stoney Creek
MERCER
Mawhood's retreat
Pennington
Stoney Creek
American pursuit
Jacob's Creek
LESLIE 1,200
Eight Mile Creek
Quaker Road
Lawrenceville
Bear Swamp
Five Mile Creek
Shabakonk
Post Road
Birmngham
Creek
CORNWALLIS 5,500
Assunpink R.
Miry Run
Sandtown
Hamilton Square
MERCER
Trenton
CADWALADER
GREENE
WASHINGTON 5,000
PENNSYLVANIA
American Camp
Delaware R.
0 1 2 mi
0 1 2 km

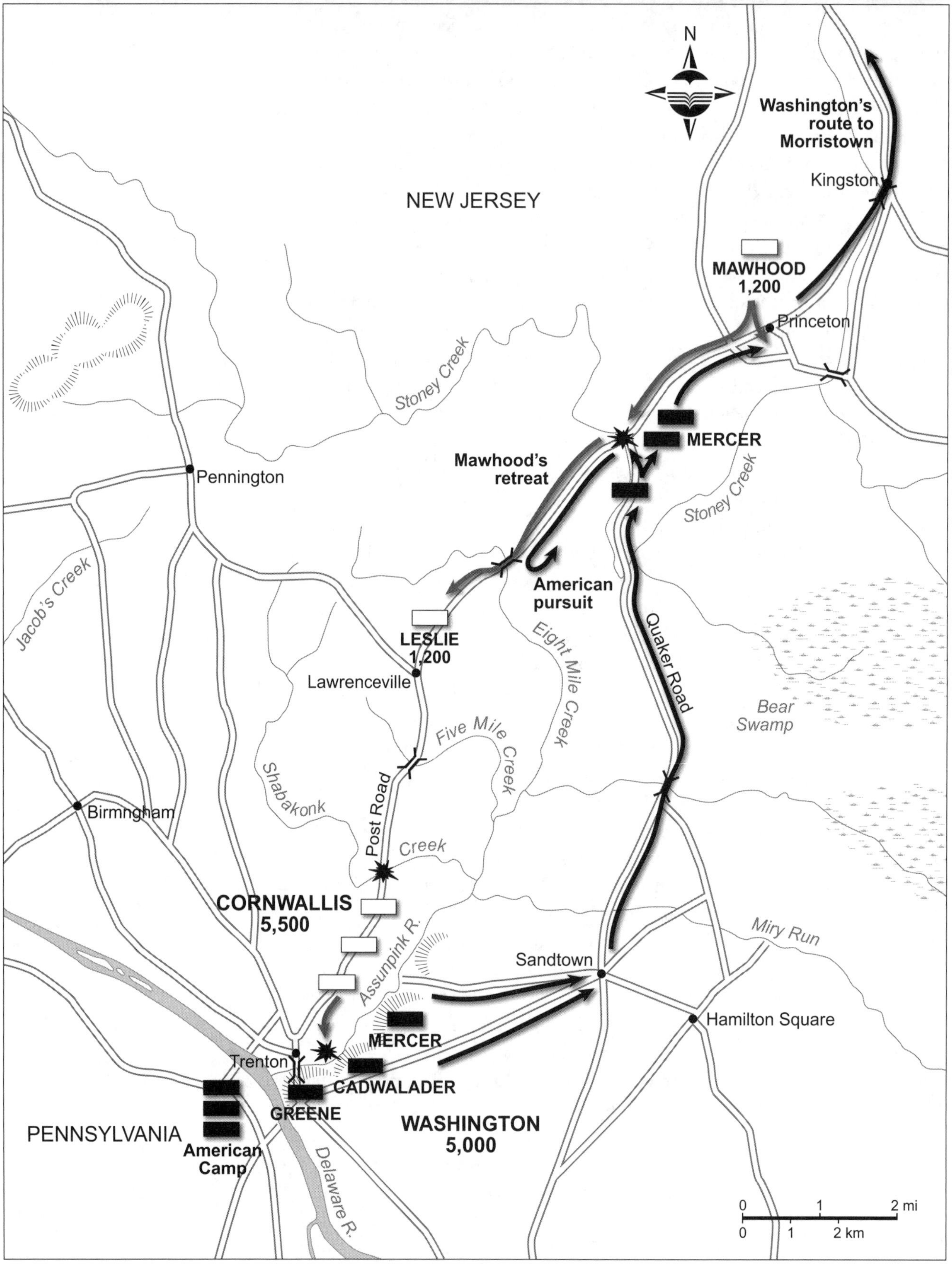

through the American lines, he and his remaining troops retreated rapidly toward Cornwallis's army, with the dragoons covering his withdrawal. Washington, leading a squadron of Philadelphia light horse, pursued the fleeing enemy, killing many British soldiers and capturing 50 others. The pursuit was called off when Mawhood's dragoons turned and made a stand to allow their comrades to escape. Meanwhile, Sullivan was leading an attack against the British 40th and 55th Regiments just outside Princeton. When the Americans threatened to outflank these regiments, they too fled. Part of the 40th Regiment, 194 men in all, took refuge in Nassau Hall, on the campus of the College of New Jersey (later Princeton University). Most of them were compelled to surrender when Captain Alexander Hamilton, an American artillery officer, fired one cannonball into the front doors of the building. The few soldiers who escaped fell back with the remainder of the British troops to New Brunswick.

Washington's smashing victory at Princeton, coming only days after his triumph at Trenton, was accomplished with practically a different army. Only about 20 percent of the soldiers who had fought with him in the first battle were still available for the second. His accomplishments in these few days were perhaps more important than any others during the entire war. Coming as they did at a time of crisis in the American fight for independence, they reinvigorated the Revolutionary cause and chastened the enemy. American casualties were 23 killed, about 20 wounded, and 1 captured; the British suffered 28 killed, 58 wounded, and 129 or more captured. After the battle, his men exhausted and debilitated, Washington had to abandon his plan to attack New Brunswick. Cornwallis and Grant were moving rapidly toward him from Trenton, and he barely had time to get his army out of Princeton before they entered from the southwest.

Washington marched his men to Morristown, deep into the hills of New Jersey, where he was safe from a British attack. There he went into winter cantonment, thus threatening British communications in New Jersey. Consequently, Cornwallis and Grant had to contract their lines and abandon British posts in that state. Ultimately, they held only New Brunswick and Amboy, and even these posts were not totally secure. For the remainder of the winter, Washington sent out militia raiders to harass British communications between these towns, thus making life miserable for their enemies. In utter frustration, Grant finally declared that his present military situation was the "most unpleasant" that he had ever experienced.

PAUL DAVID NELSON

See also
Cadwalader, John; Cornwallis, Charles; Fermoy, Matthias Alexis; Glover, John; Grant, James; Hand, Edward; Knox, Henry; Leslie, Alexander; Mercer, Hugh; Mifflin, Thomas; New Jersey, Operations in; Sullivan, John; Trenton, Battle of; Washington, George

References
Bill, Alfred Hoyt. *The Campaign of Princeton, 1776–1777.* Princeton, NJ: Princeton University Press, 1948.

Dwyer, William M. *The Day Is Ours! An Inside View of the Battles of Trenton and Princeton, November 1776–January 1777.* New Brunswick, NJ: Rutgers University Press, 1998.

English, Frederick. *General Hugh Mercer: Forgotten Hero of the American Revolution.* New York: Vantage, 1975.

Fleming, Thomas. *1776: Year of Illusions.* New York: Norton, 1975.

Ketchum, Richard M. *The Winter Soldiers.* Garden City, NY: Doubleday, 1973.

Lundin, Leonard. *Cockpit of the Revolution: The War for Independence in New Jersey.* 1940. Reprint, New York: Octagon, 1972.

Nelson, Paul David. *General James Grant: Scottish Soldier and Royal Governor of East Florida.* Gainesville: University Press of Florida, 1993.

Smith, Samuel Stelle. *The Battle of Princeton.* Monmouth Beach, NJ: Philip Freneau, 1967.

Stryker, William S. *The Battles of Trenton and Princeton.* Boston: Houghton Mifflin, 1898.

Ward, Christopher. *War of the Revolution.* 2 vols. New York: Macmillan, 1952.

Wood, W. J. *Battles of the Revolutionary War, 1775–1781.* Chapel Hill, NC: Algonquin, 1990.

Prisoners of War

Prisoners of war are soldiers and officers taken captive by enemy forces. Both American and British forces—including American militia, Loyalist units, and German mercenaries—took and were taken as prisoners of war during the American Revolution. These captives often overburdened the supplies of the unprepared armies who seized them, and were sometimes a hindrance, and sometimes a benefit, to the civilian communities that hosted them.

General procedures, conditions, and numbers. The American Revolutionary War was a conflict for which neither American nor British forces were fully prepared in several respects, including caring for prisoners of war. Both sides lacked adequate housing facilities and supplies and the organization to properly handle their captives. As the war progressed, however, both American and British forces developed methods to manage their captives. While holding, transporting, and feeding prisoners were costly in time and resources for both sides, the benefits of taking prisoners of war generally outweighed the costs. By taking prisoners, armies prevented these enemies from bearing arms for as long as they held them, and sometimes they recruited prisoners for their own forces.

The experiences of officers and soldiers as prisoners of war were quite different. Because officers were respected as gentlemen they were afforded more privileges, including a trust in their word. They were usually released on their honor after signing a parole statement. Often held in the homes of privileged civilians, captive officers escaped the spoiled rations, inhumane treatment, and other deplorable conditions that captive soldiers regularly faced. Additionally, officers received medical attention, including treatment for smallpox that regularly swept through camps of captive soldiers.

Food rations provided by the American and British armies to their captive soldiers were usually contaminated and of poor quality, and the captives were

Interior of the *Old Jersey* prison ship during the Revolutionary War. Thousands of American captives died of disease and malnutrition aboard such vessels, usually hulks moored in ports like New York. (Library of Congress)

often forced to sell personal belongings, including their clothing, for food. The quality of food, however, was not a problem exclusively for captives; both the American and British armies often had difficulty providing adequate food for their own soldiers. Captors were also expected to provide medical treatment for their prisoners, although in reality there were often not enough doctors, hospitals, and medical supplies available to treat everyone.

Each army was also expected to supplement the supplies they provided their prisoners with a stipend. The size of the supplement depended on each captive's rank, with high-ranking officers receiving substantially larger supplements compared to their lower-ranking subordinates, who often did not receive a supplement in any form.

The British, who initially held far more prisoners than the Americans, seized more than 4,300 prisoners during the New York Campaign in 1776 and briefly held as many as 5,000 prisoners in America, mostly on prison ships. This number rapidly declined, however, due in part to the high death rate of prison ship inmates, which totaled at least 7,000, and perhaps more than 10,000, during the course of the war. It has in fact been estimated that more American soldiers died on British prison ships than were killed by British guns in all the battles of the war. In addition, the British captured large numbers of American sailors and held as many as 5,000 prisoners at one time in England, Ireland, and America. The Americans, after a slower start, also held thousands of British and German prisoners, taking 900 Hessians at Trenton, more than 5,000 soldiers at Saratoga, and an even larger number at Yorktown.

American and other captives of British forces. The British imprisonment of Americans was often particularly harsh, although not necessarily by design. Yet scholars estimate that a minimum of 8,500 American prisoners of war died of disease, with the greatest mortality among those held on British prison ships. And numerous diseases, including smallpox, spread rapidly through prison camps. When diseased prisoners were released, they often spread smallpox and other communicable diseases to their fellow soldiers if they returned to military service, as well as to civilians, including their own families, thereby creating new epidemics in widely scattered locations.

Because the British often captured and occupied heavily populated areas, especially seaports, they imprisoned American civilians as well as soldiers and officers. They arrested these civilians on a number of charges linked to their political principles. At the time of the Battle of Brooklyn in late August 1776, many local citizens were arrested for their general support of American independence. The British also seized and imprisoned civilians from France, Spain, and Holland in various locations after those nations became involved in the conflict. These non-American captives, however, generally received substantially better treatment than American prisoners.

American prisoners of war seized by British forces were held in quite varied facilities in North America, Britain, and the West Indies and aboard ships. The British regularly took as prisoners wounded American soldiers who were left behind on the battlefield. Therefore, many prisoners who entered British captivity were in poor health before their exposure to the harsh conditions of captivity. Large numbers of prisoners were held on British ships and in jails, homes, sugarhouses, and even barns claimed by British forces.

American soldiers held captive by British forces often faced many hours of boredom. Literate prisoners with access to paper and writing utensils often chose to write. Common themes found in these writings by soldiers include isolation, boredom, and the ghastly conditions. Writings of American officers being held prisoner reveal a quite different situation. They received better treatment, were not subjected to as vile conditions, and were offered more outlets to socialize, so they did not face the isolation of captive common soldiers. Competitive activities, including gambling, wrestling, and foot races, became popular among numerous groups of prisoners. Groups of American soldiers held in prisons also tended to develop forms of self-government and often sought to use warrants and threats of physical punishment to enforce discipline among fellow captives. In addition to providing order in the prisons, self-government promoted loyalty to the American cause.

American prisoners of war taken to England were generally held captive for longer periods of time than those held in America. These captives were primarily soldiers and sailors in American naval forces. Most American

More American soldiers died on British prison ships than were killed by British guns.

prisoners sent to England were held in Old Mill Prison in Plymouth and Forton Prison in Portsmouth, on England's south coast; a few were incarcerated in Dartmoor Prison. Even in England, however, prisoners were often given spoiled food, and when they were given meat they usually ate it raw because they had no facilities for cooking. At Old Mill Prison the inmates received one meal a day, but they did have access to a marketplace held at the prison gates where they could trade their personal possessions for additional rations. Prisoners resorted to a number of creative ways to earn money to buy food. Some created souvenirs to sell to British tourists who visited the prison gates daily.

Benjamin Franklin, in Paris, became alarmed by Britain's treatment of American prisoners and began lobbying for their exchange. As the best-known American public official in Europe, he was an obvious correspondent for the prisoners, who were generally allowed to send letters from their jail cells. After being made aware of the American prisoners' plight, he energetically pursued two primary goals: developing exchange agreements for the prisoners' release and improving the conditions of those remaining in prison. After continued failures in negotiating exchange agreements, he resorted to assisting prisoners in their escape attempts.

American prisoners in England faced a relatively lenient policy toward escapees. Prison guards were ordered not to fire at escaping prisoners, and should an attempted escapee be caught, his punishment was relatively lax. Common punishments included closed confinement with partial rations and the forfeiture of their turn for exchange. Tunneling attempts were most often tried. But it was difficult for American escapees to return to America without special support from friends or American officials. And prisoners who were officially released from English jails discovered that reaching America was not much easier for them than it was for escapees.

The British also detained American prisoners at Kinsale, in southern Ireland. These prisoners faced the same fate as those held in England with little chance of a quick return. Like prisoners held in Old Mill and Forton Prisons, the captives at Kinsale were poorly clothed, and some were detained without any clothing.

Many American prisoners of war were taken to Nova Scotia. From there some were sent on to Sumatra and forced to serve as soldiers in the British military. Facing this situation, some captives attempted to escape, but captured escapees, now classed as British soldiers, faced the possibility of being sentenced to death.

In North America, British forces used at least sixteen prison ships during the war. Most of these vessels were anchored at Wallabout Bay, off Brooklyn, New York. A few prison ships were anchored near Charleston, South Carolina. Conditions encountered by those held on the British prison ships were among the most horrid of the war. Individuals held on ships were often kept for extended periods of time and received as little as one pint of rice, often contaminated with worms, a day. Unlike prisoners held elsewhere, those on ships had no alternative sources of food or water. They also did not have sufficient access to fresh air. Disease easily spread among prisoners already weakened by the extreme conditions they endured, and the unsanitary con-

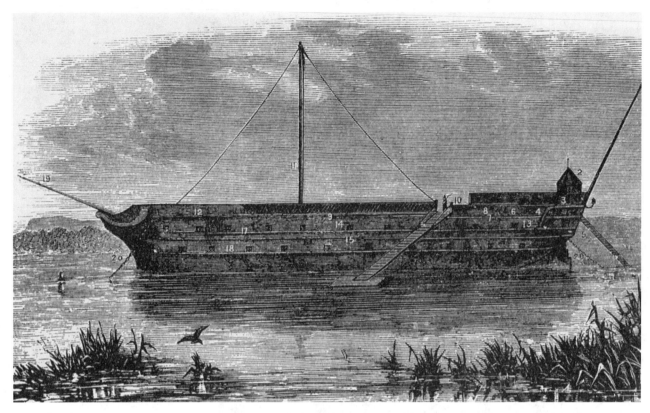

The *Old Jersey* prison ship, a decommissioned 74-gun vessel moored in New York Harbor, housed American prisoners during the Revolutionary War. Thousands of captives in British hands died of disease and poor diet aboard overcrowded and filthy hulks such as this one. (North Wind Picture Archives)

ditions further aided in the spread of disease. Prisoners confined to the holds of these prison ships did not have a method to dispose of waste, which posed further health problems. This situation led to the death of perhaps 80 percent of those held on the prison ships.

Yet the relationship between prisoners and their captors was not always adversarial. A number of prisoners formed close relationships with those detaining them. Some prisoners and their captors later became business partners. And several incidents have been recorded in which prisoners warned their captors of uprisings that fellow prisoners were planning.

British and other captives of American forces. The arrival of prisoners of war in American communities was first documented before the Declaration of Independence and quickly grew in number. Beginning with more than 900 prisoners taken at Trenton, the Americans eventually seized entire armies at Saratoga and Yorktown.

During the war, American forces took English, Scottish, Irish, Canadian, Hessian, and Native American prisoners. All were detained within the thirteen rebelling colonies and, later, states, and a high proportion were held in just a few locations in Massachusetts, Connecticut, New York, Pennsylvania, Maryland, and Virginia. Most prisoners were sent to communities, such as Lancaster in Pennsylvania, Frederick in Maryland, or Charlottesville in Virginia, that were a comfortable distance from the British Army and any

British forces on the seacoast yet were well connected by road to major routes of travel.

Although the Americans often had difficulty supplying their captives, the large number of prisoners of war they held were also valuable to the Revolutionary cause. The captives helped replace labor lost to the war effort. Prisoners were paroled to local farmers and assisted in the planting of crops and the production of food to feed the American public and the military. Paroled prisoners received room and board from the contracting farmers. Prisoners were also used in towns, as artisans and craftsmen, and in other areas needing labor. These prisoners, however, were often seen as menacing, and towns had to use improvise security forces.

After the war, most British prisoners of war returned to their home nations. Several, however, especially among the German mercenaries, remained in or near such communities as Lancaster and Frederick (both situated in areas with many German Americans), where they had been detained as prisoners of war.

Prisoner exchanges. The process of exchanging prisoners of war was a critical issue for both British and American forces. Often desperate for men, both American and British forces wanted the return of prisoners of war so that they could reenter service to their nation.

An early example of this is the correspondence between General George Washington and General Thomas Gage during the siege of Boston, in which the two generals attempted to reach an agreement regarding the treatment and handling of prisoners of war. After hearing of the harsh conditions that American prisoners of war were experiencing, Washington became increasingly flexible in meeting British demands. Exchange agreements often included standards of treatment and conditions for captives. These issues became increasingly important because prisoners who received poor treatment in extreme conditions were less valuable to their army after their release.

Throughout the war, officer exchanges were more easily arranged, and officers were more quickly freed. Warfare in previous centuries in Europe set customs that both American and British forces observed. These customs dictated that officers of similar rank were to be exchanged for each other.

The process of prisoner exchange did, however, encounter many problems. One problem hindering the smooth exchange of prisoners was that the British government did not view the American colonies as a foreign nation. They were seen as rebels against the British government. This made formal agreements impossible. In fact, at the beginning of the American Revolution, some British soldiers refused to even identify their captives as prisoners of war because that would recognize the prisoners' military status, and they instead labeled them as rebels. Yet treating prisoners as rebels, who were commonly charged with treason, was impractical due to the large number of prisoners. Therefore, most American captives were treated like prisoners of war, even if the British government refused to recognize their status officially.

To deal with this situation, commanders made informal agreements for the exchange of prisoners, beginning in the fall of 1775. The agreements followed conventions developed in traditional European warfare. As the Revolutionary

War progressed, the American captives were more generally recognized as prisoners of war by British soldiers and eventually by the British government. In early 1776, British military leaders were given permission to make deals with the American forces to exchange prisoners. In 1782, the British Parliament voted to allow formal cartels, which expedited prisoner exchanges.

Cartels were complex and formal bargaining agreements for prisoner exchanges that set specific values for each rank. Soldiers were commonly exchanged in larger groups, which caused their time as captives to be extended significantly longer than that of higher-ranking officers. Cartels were in effect used well before 1782, but because the British government would not acknowledge these agreements as formal cartels, Washington had to settle for informal and partial prisoner exchanges in New Jersey, Pennsylvania, and New York from 1777 to 1782.

Additionally, the American Congress often interfered in exchange agreements. Without clear provisions for prisoner exchanges in the American Articles of War, Congress often dealt with exchanges on a case-by-case basis. But Congress was not the only entity to interfere with prisoner negotiations; the New England state governments also intruded in the process. The Continental Congress controlled only prisoners of the Continental Army. Repeatedly, after negotiations for the exchange of prisoners were complete, New England state governments refused to release prisoners under their control, thereby causing prolonged imprisonment for both British and American prisoners.

Finally, a particular challenge to prisoner exchanges was posed by the practices of war of the two sides' Native American allies. Traditional warfare of Native Americans included holding prisoners for ransom. Most Native American tribes viewed prisoners as part of the spoils of war and did not treat officers any differently than they treated common soldiers. The hostile attitudes held by American and British forces toward Native American tribes also prevented a speedy exchange of prisoners. Many British and American officers did not consider Native Americans worthy of their customary practices in regard to prisoner exchanges.

Only with the signing of the preliminary articles of peace in Paris in late 1782 could a comprehensive prisoner exchange take place. In May 1783, at Tappan, New York, Washington was able to negotiate a true and comprehensive cartel with the British commander, General Guy Carleton. This agreement covered nearly all prisoners held by each side, and their exchange was virtually completed in the summer of 1783.

KRISTIN WHITEHAIR

See also

British Army; Carleton, Guy; Congress, Second Continental and Confederation; Continental Army; Continental Navy; Convention Army; German Mercenaries; Royal Navy; Washington, George

References

Becker, Ann M. "Smallpox in Washington's Army: Strategic Implications of the Disease during the American Revolutionary War." *Journal of Military History* 68 (2004): 381–430.

Becker, Laura L. "Prisoners of War in the American Revolution: A Community Perspective." *Military Affairs* 46(4) (1982): 169–173.

Blanco, Richard L., ed. *The American Revolution, 1775–1783: An Encyclopedia.* New York: Garland, 1993.

Boatner, Mark. *Encyclopedia of the American Revolution.* Mechanicsburg, PA: Stackpole, 1994.

Cogliano, Francis D. *American Maritime Prisoners in the Revolutionary War: The Captivity of William Russell.* Annapolis, MD: Naval Institute Press, 2001.

———. "'We All Hoisted the American Flag': National Identity among American Prisoners in Britain during the American Revolution." *Journal of American Studies* 32 (1998): 19–37.

Cohen, Sheldon W. *Yankee Sailors in British Gaols: Prisoners of War at Forton and Mill, 1777–1783.* Newark: University of Delaware Press, 1995.

Cox, Caroline. *A Proper Sense of Honor: Service and Sacrifice in George Washington's Army.* Chapel Hill: University of North Carolina Press, 2004.

DeWan, George. "The Wretched Prison Ships." *Corrections Forum* 7 (2) (1998): 58–59.

Knight, Betsy. "Prisoner Exchange and Parole in the American Revolution." *William and Mary Quarterly* 48 (1991): 201–222.

Lindsey, William R. "Treatment of American Prisoners of War during the American Revolution." *Emporia State Research Studies* 22(1) (1973): 5–32.

Moyne, Ernest J. "The Reverend William Hazlitt: A Friend of Liberty in Ireland during the American Revolution." *William and Mary Quarterly* 21(2) (1964): 228–297.

Prelinger, Catherine M. "Benjamin Franklin and the American Prisoners of War in England during the American Revolution." *William and Mary Quarterly* 32(2) (1975): 261–294.

Privateering

Privateering is the cruising against an enemy's commerce in privately owned and manned armed vessels. Both the Americans and the British made extensive use of privateering during the Revolutionary War. The Americans resorted to it first because they entered the conflict without a formal navy. Later in the war, Britain supplemented its overtaxed naval resources with privateers. Privateering failed to confer decisive advantage to either side.

Congress authorized the states to commission privateers in March 1776, three months before formal independence. The privately armed vessels that General George Washington used during the last months of 1775 to seize British supply vessels differed from subsequent privateers in that they were restricted to seizing ships directly supporting British military operations rather than all British vessels indiscriminately. During the war every state fitted out privateers, but New England responded with special enthusiasm to Congress's authorization. The region's commerce had been restrained by British edicts and the Royal Navy before that of the other colonies, and its proximity to the Gulf of St. Lawrence as well as to the principal sea route from the Caribbean to Europe advantageously positioned it for commerce raiding. The tonnage of prizes libeled in Massachusetts admiralty courts by privateers at the beginning of the war exceeded that libeled by them at any other time throughout the conflict.

Privateering ventures involved the pooling of diverse resources. A syndicate of investors, led by a small number of principals who usually sold shares of their initial stake to other investors, provided the vessels and outfitted them with cannon, ammunition, rigging, spars, chandlery, sails, and provisions. The sponsoring syndicate also posted bond with the commissioning authority that the privateer would prey only on enemy shipping and would have their captures condemned by an admiralty court before disposing of the proceeds. In exchange, the investors were entitled to half the value of the prizes seized. The other half went to those manning the vessel. In addition, a few shares were reserved for distribution to those who preformed meritorious service.

The success of American cruisers in the early stages of the conflict made privateering very attractive to men of military age, especially after it became clear that Britain would treat captured privateersmen as prisoners of war rather than as pirates. Privateering was relatively safe because there was no disgrace in a privateer avoiding enemy craft of superior force. Since privateers also had an interest in preserving the value of their prospective prizes, they preferred to attack by boarding rather than cannonading. Enemy merchant vessels of inferior armament usually surrendered without resisting, especially where there was a good chance of recapture before they made a hostile port. Besides offering the prospect of monetary gain, privateering involved a shorter time commitment than enlistment in the army or navy. American privateering competed with maintaining the force levels of both the Continental Army and Navy after 1776.

British authorities initially discouraged Loyalist privateering. During 1777 the Admiralty authorized the issuance of a few commissions to syndicates based in the Channel Islands, Bermuda, and Nova Scotia, but the British government regarded Loyalist manpower in North America as a resource for replenishing its army and navy. Such a policy was appropriate during the initial years of the conflict when Britain's overwhelming naval supremacy made American commerce more vulnerable to the Royal Navy than British commerce was to American privateers. But once France entered the war in 1778, Britain found its naval power stretched to the limit and responded to the new circumstance by issuing commissions to mainland Loyalists. Beginning in 1778, Loyalist privateers made two significant contributions to the British war effort.

Before 1778 the Patriots had relied on their smaller fast-sailing vessels to maintain a limited commerce in military supplies with the foreign West Indies. Beginning in 1778, speed, shallow draft, and apparent insignificance no longer conferred the protection it had previously afforded, and those wishing to undertake such voyages had to arm to counter the Loyalist threat. Since the return on privateering in American waters was also declining, the vast majority of American privateers transformed themselves from private vessels of war into ships sailing with letters of marque. Letters of marque licensed a vessel to take enemy shipping as occasion permitted while pursuing

Recruiting privateersmen in New London, Connecticut, to serve the Patriot cause. Privateers captured hundreds of British merchant vessels in the course of the war. (North Wind Picture Archives)

commercial voyages. Because prizes were easier to come by in distant seas where American privateers had not previously been active, letters of marque gave new life to cruising for prizes. Thus Loyalist privateering helped diminish the access of the Revolutionaries to overseas imports and perpetuated the imbalance that the war created between the high cost of foreign goods relative to the low price that American produce fetched on the domestic market.

Loyalist privateering also shaped the Franco-American commercial relationship. Both France and the United States initially entertained high expectations for the economic benefits of the alliance. French entrepreneurs had begun positioning themselves to take advantage of the American market in 1777, and many attempted to establish direct contact with North America during the summer of 1778 on the assumption that Admiral Jean-Baptiste d'Estaing's expeditionary force would establish naval supremacy in the western Atlantic. But the Royal Navy quickly neutralized d'Estaing's advantage in American waters, while Loyalist privateers wreaked havoc among the many French commercial ventures. By the end of the year, French underwriters in Europe were refusing to insure vessels heading for North America.

Though some French entrepreneurs persisted, the vast majority lost their enthusiasm for the Franco-American trade.

Yet American privateering was, overall, quite successful. Britain lost more merchantmen to privateering than the United States and its allies did on the high seas, despite enjoying a recapture rate thirty times greater than its adversaries. The disparity in recaptures highlights the effectiveness of American privateers even with the absence of a naval shield. Shelter provided by the French and Dutch islands in the Caribbean enabled the Americans to prey on British shipping in the Lesser Antilles well before the Franco-American Alliance. America's most successful privateer, the Philadelphia-based *Holker*, owed this distinction to its speed and the skill of its men in getting its many prizes into safe harbors. Beginning in 1779, Benjamin Franklin issued commissions to American privateers in France. These vessels, manned largely by French crews, inflicted heavy losses on British commerce in European seas and collected naval prisoners whom Franklin hoped to exchange for American seamen imprisoned in Britain. Spain's entry into the war in June 1779 and the threat of invasion that the allied fleets posed to Britain during that year contributed to their success. But American privateers persisted in their operations even after the allies' naval superiority had dissipated. In 1780 several New England privateers managed to seize a sizable portion of a Quebec fleet after a French frigate took out the convoy's escort in the mid-Atlantic. American privateers even occasionally elected to fight superior enemy forces. Jonathan Haraden of Salem earned a place for himself in the nation's seafaring lore by engaging in several such actions as well as by bluffing a British vessel of superior armament into surrendering.

These triumphs, however, conferred little lasting advantage for Americans compared to the toll that British privateering exacted on their commerce. Britain's losses to American privateers had less of an impact on Britain than America's losses had on the United States because the British had more that they could afford to lose. The communities of New Bedford, Massachusetts, and New London, Connecticut, attracted British raids because of their privateering. On 5–6 September 1778, Major-General Charles Grey led a British force onto the Acushnet River (present-day New Bedford and Fairhaven), burning seventy vessels, mostly privateers and their prizes, in the process. Three years later almost to the day, Benedict Arnold attacked New London, burning the town and slaughtering the garrison at Fort Griswold. Most Americans, however, experienced the downside of privateering in the deprivations sustained by the estimated 70,000 individuals who either invested in or served on privateers. By the end of the war, privateering had come to resemble a lottery in which the losses of the many dwarfed the good fortunes of the few.

Privateering did play a creative role in jump-starting the regional grain economy centered in Philadelphia after 1778. The city's merchants had little choice but privateering between 1778 and 1780, when embargoes throttled the city's commerce. But Philadelphia's economic recovery owed more to Spain opening up the Cuban market to American grain in 1780 than it did to cruising for prizes. Philadelphia managed to convert the capital that its

**Average Distribution of Prize Money on Worships
and Privateers during the American Revolution**

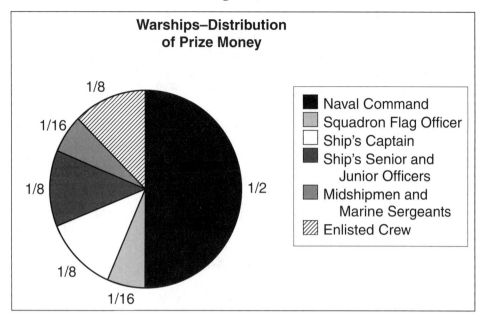

**Warships–Distribution
of Prize Money**

■ Naval Command
□ Squadron Flag Officer
□ Ship's Captain
■ Ship's Senior and
   Junior Officers
▨ Midshipmen and
   Marine Sergeants
▨ Enlisted Crew

1/8
1/16
1/8
1/8
1/16
1/2

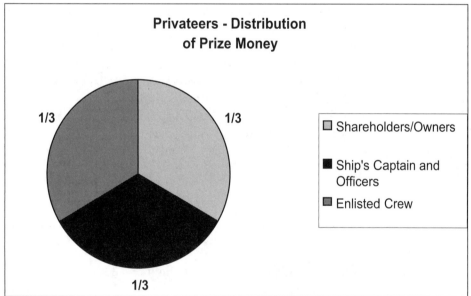

**Privateers - Distribution
of Prize Money**

1/3
1/3
1/3

□ Shareholders/Owners

■ Ship's Captain and
   Officers

▨ Enlisted Crew

armed vessels had seized into a lucrative commerce with Havana in 1781 because of the peculiar resources of its hinterland and the Royal Navy's pre-occupation with other challenges that it confronted. As a consequence, Philadelphia emerged from the war without relinquishing its prewar role as the leading trade center of the continent, while Boston failed to recover the comparable prominence it had enjoyed prior to 1740.

RICHARD BUEL JR.

See also

Bedford and Fairhaven, Massachusetts, Raid on; Boston, Massachusetts; Continental Navy; Estaing, Jean-Baptiste, Comte d'; Franco-American Alliance;

Haraden, Jonathan; Loyalists; New London, Connecticut, Raid on; Penobscot Expedition; Philadelphia; Prizes and Prize Money

References

Allen, Gardner W. "Massachusetts Privateers of the Revolution." *Massachusetts Historical Society, Collections* 77 (1927): 3–331.

Broker, Marshall. "Privateering from the Bay, Including Admiralty Courts and Tory as well as Patriot Operations." Pp. 261–282 in *Chesapeake Bay in the American Revolution*. Edited by Ernst M. Eller. Centreville, MD: Tidewater, 1981.

Buel, Richard Jr. *In Irons: Britain's Naval Supremacy and the American Revolutionary Economy*. New Haven and London: Yale University Press, 1998.

Clark, William B. *Ben Franklin's Privateers: A Naval Epic of the American Revolution*. Baton Rouge: Louisiana State University Press, 1956.

———. *George Washington's Navy, Being an Account of His Excellency's Fleet in New England Waters*. Baton Rouge: Louisiana State University Press, 1960.

———. "That Mischievous *Holker:* The Story of a Privateer." *Pennsylvania Magazine of History and Biography* 79 (1955): 27–62.

Fowler, William H. "The Business of War: Boston as a Navy Base, 1776–1783." *American Neptune* 42 (1982): 25–35.

Howe, Octavius. "Beverly Privateers in the American Revolution." *Colonial Society of Massachusetts, Transactions* 24 (1922): 318–435.

Jamieson, Alan G. "American Privateers in the Leeward Islands 1776–1778." *American Neptune* 43 (1983): 20–30.

McKey, Richard H., Jr. "Elias H. Derby and the American Revolution." *Essex Institute Historical Collections* 97 (1961): 166–196.

Middlebrook, Louis F. *History of Maritime Connecticut during the American Revolution, 1775–1783*. 2 vols. Salem, MA: Essex Institute, 1925.

Miller, Nathan. *Sea of Glory: A Naval History of the American Revolution*. 1974. Reprint, Charleston, SC: Nautical and Aviation Publishing Company, 2000.

Morgan, William J. "American Privateering in America's War for Independence, 1775–1783." *American Neptune* 36 (1978): 79–87.

Proclamation of 1763

Britain's Proclamation of 1763 set a temporary limit on all settlement west of the crest of the Appalachian Mountains, thereby reserving the entire Ohio and eastern Mississippi Valleys for Native Americans and the Indian trade. This measure angered a wide range of British North American colonists and, combined with new British taxes in America, alienated them from British rule.

The 1763 Treaty of Paris ended the Seven Years' War (known in America as the French and Indian War) and gained an empire for Great Britain. The British government now had to deal with a host of problems concerning its new acquisitions. George Grenville, George Montagu Dunk (Lord Halifax), and William Wyndham (Lord Egremont) headed the administration in an unusual three-way coalition, while a nervous young king, George III, fretted about their ability to retain control of Parliament. Most of the postwar decisions, both in the treaty settlements concluded by the three major belligerents and those made thereafter by British officials, involved North

America: the disposition of the former French continental colonies of Canada, which Britain kept, and Louisiana, which France ceded to Spain; the former Spanish colony of Florida, which Britain acquired; the enlargement of Nova Scotia by the addition of Prince Edward and Cape Breton Islands; three new governments, for Quebec and East and West Florida; and a policy for regulating Indian trade in the eastern Mississippi Valley.

The task facing the triumvirate was all the more formidable because Egremont, the secretary for the Southern Department, who was responsible for American affairs, knew practically nothing about America. In October 1761, he had replaced the man who thought he knew everything about America, the architect of Britain's victory over France, William Pitt the Elder. Fortunately for Egremont, Henry Ellis, the former governor of Georgia, had recently arrived in England. During his four years in Georgia, Ellis had thoroughly informed himself about conditions in America. Ever since he had made his reputation as a scientist and explorer of Hudson's Bay in 1749, he had the attention and favor of Halifax. Halifax now introduced Ellis to Egremont as an authority on America. Ellis's advice proved invaluable in the last stage of the war, notably in his recommendation that Britain should seize Cuba from Spain and then during treaty negotiations exchange Cuba for Florida, which had been a perennial threat to his former colony, Georgia.

At Egremont's request, however, Ellis went further and wrote memoranda touching on all aspects of North American policy. He advised creating new governments in Quebec, East and West Florida, and Nova Scotia based on the instructions that Halifax, then president of the Board of Trade, had drawn up for Georgia in 1754. These instructions guaranteed representative governments and the usual rights of Englishmen, even for Quebec and the two Floridas, which had few English inhabitants. He drew a new boundary for Georgia, extending that colony's territory to the south and west. He recommended disbanding the forts in the former Louisiana Territory but establishing garrisons in the unsettled Northwest Territory. And he advocated the creation of an Indian reserve and the strict regulation of Indian trade, a measure that seemed all the more necessary after receiving word that an Indian uprising known as Pontiac's Rebellion had broken out in the Ohio Country.

In the curious bureaucracy of British government, the Board of Trade was supposed to advise the secretary about American affairs but could not offer advice unless and until asked to do so by the secretary. Therefore, Egremont sent Ellis's memoranda to the board, headed in 1763 by William Petty, Lord Shelburne, and asked for comment. Shelburne or John Pownall, his secretary, approved most of Ellis's suggestions but inserted a clause throwing open the Indian trade to all licensed persons, regardless of the colony in which they were licensed. The board also recommended establishing a line beyond which settlement by Britons and Europeans would be prohibited, with the understanding that the prohibition would be temporary.

After Ellis concurred with the board's report, Egremont secured royal approval for the new arrangement. On 6 August, he notified his friend Grenville, who had recently become Britain's prime minister, that he had finally settled his American affairs. But Egremont did not live to implement

90°W 80°W 70°W 60°W 50°W

50°N

Hudson
Bay

LABRADOR

NEWFOUNDLAND

RUPERT'S LAND
HUDSON'S BAY
COMPANY

Gulf of
St. Lawrence

St.-Pierre
(FRANCE)

Miquelon
(FRANCE)

NOVA
SCOTIA

QUEBEC

MAINE
(MASSACHUSETTS)

40°N

L. Superior

L. Ontario

L. Michigan

L. Huron

NEW
YORK

NEW HAMPSHIRE

MASSACHUSETTS

RHODE ISLAND

CONNECTICUT

L. Erie

PENNSYLVANIA

NEW JERSEY

INDIAN

COUNTRY

DELAWARE

MARYLAND

VIRGINIA

LOUISIANA

NORTH
CAROLINA

30°N

SOUTH
CAROLINA

ATLANTIC

OCEAN

GEORGIA

WEST
FLORIDA

EAST
FLORIDA

British territory
Indian country (British territory)
Spanish territory
French territory
Proclamation Line of 1763

Gulf of
Mexico

0   150   300 mi
0   150   300 km

20°N

his policy; he suffered a stroke and died on 21 August. Halifax replaced him as secretary of the Southern Department and finished the business. He delivered the final report to the Board of Trade on 19 September for approval. As a matter of course, the Privy Council ratified the policy, and on 7 October 1763 it received the royal signature. The Proclamation of 1763 transformed the North American frontier and set in motion a chain of events that helped bring on the American Revolution.

The proclamation immediately ran into difficulties. The prohibition on western settlement angered land-hungry pioneers and profit-minded speculators alike and only delayed rather than prevented their encroachment upon Indian lands. The Indian trade suffered as hundreds of unscrupulous characters invaded the Indian reserve, claiming trading licenses from one colony or another. The promise of government by elected representatives to populations that had no experience with such governments led to political turmoil in Quebec and the Floridas.

The British government eventually drafted a creative and generous solution to Quebec's problems: the Quebec Act of 1774. But this measure quickly alienated many Protestant inhabitants of the older British colonies, especially in New England, who feared the rise of Roman Catholicism in Canada. The need to garrison forts in the Northwest Territory required more troops to be quartered in the colonies, which they resented. And the removal of the French threat from North America made this military expense and the colonists' whole dependence upon Britain seem less necessary. Finally, the Grenville government had to find a way to pay for the costs of the war and of the expanded peacetime military presence on North America, and its new revenue measures—a cider tax in Britain and a stamp tax in America—fomented further unrest.

Ironically, one American province prospered under the terms of the Proclamation of 1763. Ellis's former colony of Georgia became a more secure imperial domain, with vast unsettled lands extending to its new southern boundary, a boundary that now ran from the St. Marys River near the Atlantic Ocean to its western terminus at the Mississippi. Many westward-migrating pioneers, deterred temporarily from crossing the Appalachians, moved down the piedmont roads into Georgia.

EDWARD J. CASHIN

See also
Florida, East and West; Georgia; Grenville, George; Northwest Territory; Pontiac's Rebellion; Stuart, John

References
Alden, John Richard. *John Stuart and the Southern Colonial Frontier: A Study of Indian Relations, War, Trade, and Land Problems in the Southern Wilderness, 1754–1775.* 1944. Reprint, New York: Gordian, 1966.

Cashin, Edward J. *Governor Henry Ellis and the Transformation of British North America.* Athens: University of Georgia Press, 1994.

Juricek, John T. *Georgia Treaties, 1733 to 1763.* Frederick, MD: University Publications of America, 1989.

Prohibitory Act
(1775)

The Prohibitory Act was Britain's last legislative attempt to control the colonies and obtain their compliance in the pursuance of British political and economic policy. The bloodshed of the battles at Lexington and Concord and the British retreat to Boston set the stage for the 22 December 1775 passage of the act. The Prohibitory Act contained three main provisions. First, all trade was to be prohibited during the "present rebellion." Second, all colonial commerce was beyond the Crown's protection, and any ships seized would be forfeited. Third, the unlimited impressment of American crews was allowed.

The Prohibitory Act was the British response to colonial requests for mutual discussion. British intransigence to compromise mirrored anger and frustration on both sides of the Atlantic. Congress dispatched its Olive Branch Petition to King George III on 8 July 1775, in time for Parliament to consider colonial concerns before committing to increased military efforts. Congress expressed its admonitions in a conciliatory tone and asked in the petition for an immediate cease-fire in Boston, the repeal of the Coercive Acts, and negotiations on the establishment of American rights.

George III, however, refused to receive the Olive Branch Petition, and the government never took any notice of it. The failure of the Olive Branch Petition indicated that the Crown's government was united in its intent to reduce the colonies to abject submission. Rather than mollify the colonials, the Prohibitory Act marked the beginning of the end of British rule in America.

ARTHUR STEINBERG

See also
George III, King of England; Legge, William, 2nd Earl of Dartmouth; Olive Branch Petition

References
Donoughue, Bernard. *British Politics and the American Revolution: The Path to War, 1773–1775.* New York: St. Martin's, 1964.

Marston, Jerrilyn Greene. *King and Congress: The Transfer of Political Legitimacy, 1774–1776.* Princeton, NJ: Princeton University Press, 1987.

Propaganda

Propaganda campaigns, the competition for what John Adams called "minds and hearts," are crucial in civil struggles such as the American Revolution. In that contest the British appealed to traditional loyalties and the merits of remaining in their empire. Rebels had to justify their reasons for abandoning those loyalties while stirring up and maintaining resistance. Love of the mother country and the king had to be transformed into love of America, and then of the United States of America, as a tax revolt evolved into full-blown rebellion. Two developments made propaganda decisive to the war's outcome. First, during the taxation controversies of the 1760s, American protestors effectively reduced dry constitutional debates to simple slogans, pictures, and rallying cries. During the relatively quiet period from late 1770 to early 1773, these symbols sustained an image of Americans as victims, nourishing the idea of a British conspiracy aimed at usurping the colonists' freedoms. Second, after 1775 the American rebels' home field advantage and the British public's relative apathy canceled out the British military's financial and technical superiority, thereby forcing each side to rally its core supporters and enlist the aid of interested third parties: Indians, slaves, Canadians, mercenaries, and Europeans. Although this struggle was a difficult one, the rebels eventually outfoxed the British and Loyalists in clarifying their message and in neutralizing or gaining support from outside groups.

Adams believed that the colonists' "minds and hearts" were changed between 1763 and 1775, before the war began. In an easily overlooked masterstroke, the rebels adopted the term "Patriot" for what became a treasonous cause. The term might seem more appropriate for Loyalists, who saw themselves as defending the existing social order of their country, but its natural adoption underscored the shift in mentality that Adams described, as did the unifying term "American." Patriots also signed their writings with classical pseudonyms to legitimize their claims within a familiar historical context. They identified with radical English Whig writers such as John Wilkes, publisher of the newspaper *North Britain*, whose defamation of the king's ministers in the forty-fifth issue got him jailed and expelled from Parliament. In Wilkes's honor, Patriots hung forty-five lanterns on liberty trees, made forty-five toasts, and even consumed forty-five pounds of beef from a forty-five-month-old bullock. The British found themselves in the more difficult position of defending imperial authority and never effectively countered the underdog rebels' manipulation of language, history, and symbols.

Patriot symbols translated readily into pamphlets, illustrated broadsides, and bar songs. Children learned jingles that emphasized Whig virtue and Tory evil. Religious symbolism connected the self-determination inherent in democratic rule to the Protestant Reformation. Beginning with the 1764 Sugar Act, patriotic newspapers and pamphleteers galvanized and disseminated this political and religious propaganda, while mobs intimidated Loyalist writers. Benjamin Franklin noted that the press could present truths in different lights and "strike while the iron is hot" but also "heat it continually by striking."

The most effective antitax pamphlet was lawyer John Dickinson's "Letters from a Farmer in Pennsylvania," which first appeared serially in the *Pennsylvania Chronicle* in opposition to the 1767 Townshend duties. Dickinson argued that taxation without consent was unconstitutional, knowing full well

Paul Revere's sensational illustration of the Boston Massacre, a skirmish on 5 March 1770 in which British soldiers fired on and killed five townspeople. Revere's historic print, released within a month, publicized the event and was hugely influential in stoking anti-British sentiment in the years before the American Revolution. An interesting example of Revere's emphasis on impact over accuracy is the depiction of one of the victims, Crispus Attucks, an African American, as a white man. (National Archives and Records Administration)

that America's relatively small population would translate into little power in Parliament if they *had* been awarded proportional representation. His title also cleverly drew attention to agricultural and working-class grievances in a debate argued mainly by merchants and lawyers.

Other leaders took more direct action. Boston's radical elite was especially adept at mobilizing street mobs. Their behavior aggravated the British, whose reciprocating occupations of the town and occasional retaliations fueled propagandist fires. Paul Revere, a member of Samuel Adams's Sons of Liberty, produced engravings that portrayed the 1765 Stamp Act as a dragon, and his print *A Warm Place—Hell* (1768) denounced Loyalist legislators who voted to rescind Massachusetts's circular letter, which called for colonial-wide protest against the Townshend duties. In 1770, redcoats (British Army regulars whom the local population called "bloodybacks" or "lobsters") shot into an unruly mob in self-defense. The event was christened the Boston Massacre and immortalized in a Revere engraving and poem so melodramatic that jurors at the ensuing trials had to be warned against "wings of fancy."

The city strategically honored the Boston Massacre in annual rituals of oratory, poetry, and mourning. The anniversary of the Stamp Act's 1766 repeal was more celebratory, including booming cannon, chiming bells, and parades. And while the 1773 Boston Tea Party was initially discredited by many critics outside the city as juvenile vandalism, the subsequent British crackdown on Massachusetts—in the Coercive (or Intolerable) Acts of 1774—enabled Bostonians to forge ties with sympathetic middle and southern colonies, leading to the First Continental Congress. The Coercive Acts were widely resisted with days of fasting, originally a religious practice that was first employed politically to sanctify boycotts against the Townshend duties.

By the mid-1770s, sloganeering aimed at restoring America's pre-1763 economic rights began to be redirected toward a broader ambition of colonial autonomy and finally toward independence. The use of the phrase "no taxation without representation" by such leaders as Dickinson, James Otis Jr., and Patrick Henry gave way in March 1775 to Henry's "give me liberty or give me death." Samuel Adams brilliantly exploited the same patriotic choice in the broadside he produced to announce the news of the battles at Lexington and Concord in April 1775. And in January 1776 Thomas Paine's *Common Sense* spelled out the logic of independence in straightforward prose and challenged the loyalty that subjects felt toward their king. Combining the religious and secular, Paine argued that in the Old Testament the Jews initially rejected monarchy but later accepted it as God's punishment for their sins. He thereby inspired God's new "chosen people" to choose a more virtuous form of government. Maryland Loyalist James Chalmers answered Paine in *Plain Truth*, emphasizing the lack of successful democratic precedents and arguing that independence would disrupt America's Atlantic trade.

Paine's arguments carried the day over Chalmers and several other critics. On 4 July 1776, Congress approved the most famous propaganda tract of the war, the Declaration of Independence, that explained the rebel cause to the world (especially potential ally France) and personalized a list of imperial legalities by charging King George III with a tyrannical abuse of power.

The British even prepared special silver handcuffs for Jefferson, but failed twice to catch him.

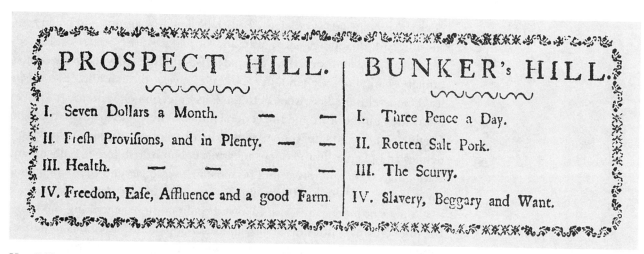

Handbill, meant to entice British soldiers to desert, was distributed during the winter of 1775–1776. (John Grafton, ed., *The American Revolution: A Picture Sourcebook*, 1975)

The Declaration was a culmination of earlier political tracts both by its author, Thomas Jefferson, and many other writers and incorporated the essence of similar pronouncements and constitutional preambles written elsewhere. The colonists enjoyed relative freedom and low taxation under British rule, but Jefferson's excessive use of "tyranny," "oppression," and "slavery"—contrasted with "liberty" and "freedom"—effectively underscored the rollback of rights that colonists experienced between 1763 and 1775. Conscious of Jefferson's hypocrisy on a key point, Virginia Governor John Murray, Lord Dunmore, offered slaves freedom in exchange for joining the British Army, but his proclamation, and those of other "negro thieves" such as Sir Henry Clinton, further infuriated the colonists. Patriot organs such as the *Boston Gazette* stressed the rebels' enslavement to Britain while ignoring writers, both black and white, who tried to connect emancipation with the Revolutionary cause.

After the Continental Congress unified the rebellion in 1776, it became the formal source of patriotic propaganda. As early military losses mounted, patriotic fervor was critical to maintaining political support and recruiting soldiers who were hesitant to die or even to leave their farms for a season. The sloganeering of tax revolts and independence carried over into the war. During General George Washington's retreat from Manhattan in September 1776, the captured American spy Nathan Hale was famously (but perhaps falsely) quoted as proclaiming on the gallows that he "regretted he had but one life to give to his country," a well-known line from early eighteenth-century British patriotic literature. The first number of Thomas Paine's *The Crisis* (December 1776), with its opening declaration "These are the times that try men's souls," turned the Continental Army's early New York defeats into an inspirational call to arms. Cued by a drum roll, the passage was read to Washington's troops before the Battle of Trenton.

In addition to the normal exaggerations of propaganda, each side in the conflict employed accepted modes of treachery and deceit, including kidnappings, bribery, and misinformation. Since Washington himself was a powerful propaganda symbol, the British desired his capture, and he, in turn, considered kidnappings and poisonings of major British leaders. The redcoats even prepared special silver handcuffs for Jefferson, who had become a primary symbol of independence, but failed twice to catch him. The rebels used General Benedict Arnold's treasonous defection of September 1780 as motivation for the army and the general public to defeat the British troops he fought with. Each side spread rumors (and solid news) of smallpox epidemics and plagues in the opposing armies. The British forged a document stating that rebel soldiers would be forced to serve beyond their appointed times and published it in Philadelphia's Loyalist *Evening Post.*

American propaganda also followed tradition in exaggerating the number of enemy casualties in victory and their opponents' atrocities in defeat. American leaders embellished their figures and issued reports that gangs of redcoats had raped both women and young girls. As in other wars, of course, lootings, desecrations, and rapes were common enough, but it is very hard to separate fact from fiction. American leaders did not, however, claim that atrocities were perpetrated by the British on prisoners of war because they wanted to assure recruits that they would be treated humanely if they were captured.

The 30,000 German mercenaries employed by the British were subjected to propaganda of a different sort when they became prisoners of the Americans. Hessian soldiers captured at Trenton and Saratoga were sent out on work-release details among Pennsylvania's German population as farmers, lumberjacks, and even musicians. Washington knew that the region's soil, religious tolerance, and mild government were attractive, and many prisoners became interested in local women and defected after being offered land and livestock. German Americans even placed similar offers in tobacco pouches and smuggled them to active mercenary troops. And for higher ranks, the Americans offered higher rewards. Jefferson entertained captured Hessian officers at Monticello to spread America's view of the conflict. Bribery leaflets were also wrapped around bullets at Bunker Hill and tossed to the Royal Irish Regiment. On the British side, Sir William Howe enticed more than 1,000 rebels to "gain over" with bribes, but Patriot deserters usually had better alternatives than joining the redcoats.

Overseas, the "blood money" that King George III offered the Prince of Hesse for mercenaries provided diplomatic propaganda. Many Europeans envied or detested British imperialism, and Franklin, America's minister to France, made sure that intercepted Hessian letters critical of Britain were translated and published in Belgium and Holland. In early 1776, Chalmers had argued that the French and Spanish would unite with Britain to crush American independence, but Franklin exploited French jealousy of Britain and their resentment over their defeat in the Seven Years' War to solicit covert aid. Like Washington on a horse, Franklin in a coonskin cap was human propaganda, playing to the Paris intelligentsia's infatuation with the frontier philosopher. When news of America's victory at Saratoga reached Paris, the United States secured a formal alliance with France that brought about eventual victory. Franklin also made overtures to rebels in Ireland that helped force moderate concessions to the Irish from the British, though it was implausible for the Americans to offer serious assistance there beyond John Paul Jones's popular sea raids.

For their part, the British attained several alliances with interior Indians, particularly the Iroquois, because of their established connections. The best rebels could hope for from most Indians was neutrality, so they made threats to Indian leaders to stave off the sort of frontier attacks that plagued them during the French and Indian War. Jefferson relayed a message to the Shawnees that if they did not stay neutral, Virginia would wage war on them until they had exterminated them. Subtler diplomacy was conducted in the Ohio Country, where each side sought Indian allies by proving its military power. The British took Indian leaders to Quebec to show them their fleet, and George Rogers Clark designed his exploits in Illinois partly for Indian eyes. Congress signed an agreement with the Delawares in 1778 that formally denied the British claim that Americans would someday threaten the Indians' autonomy. Overall, however, Britain's use of threats of Indian attacks on the frontier, like their proposals for freeing and using slaves, backfired, encouraging many civilians to join the rebel cause.

CAMERON ADDIS

See also

Adams, John; Adams, Samuel; Art; Atrocities; Boycotts; Hale, Nathan; Henry, Patrick; Jefferson, Thomas; Music; Paine, Thomas; Public Opinion, American; Public Opinion, British; Religion

References

Berger, Carl. *Broadsides & Bayonets: The Propaganda War of the American Revolution*. San Rafael, CA: Presidio, 1976.

Bradley, Patricia. *Slavery, Propaganda and the American Revolution*. Jackson: University Press of Mississippi, 1998.

Davidson, Philip. *Propaganda and the American Revolution*. Chapel Hill: University of North Carolina Press, 1941.

Fischer, David Hackett. *Washington's Crossing*. Oxford and New York: Oxford University Press, 2004.

Miller, John C. *Sam Adams: Pioneer in Propaganda*. 1936. Reprint, Stanford, CA: Stanford University Press, 1960.

Schlesinger, Arthur M., Sr. *Prelude to Independence: The Newspaper War on Britain, 1764–1776*. New York: Knopf, 1958.

Providien, Battle of
(12 April 1782)

The Battle of Providien was the second of five remarkable engagements fought between Admirals Pierre de Suffren and Sir Edward Hughes in the Indian Ocean in 1782–1783. Following the naval confrontation at Sadras on 17 February 1782, Hughes proceeded to Trincomalee, on the coast of Ceylon, to refit, while Suffren sailed to Pondicherry. On 12 March, Hughes returned to Madras but later that month made sail once again for Trincomalee, bearing supplies and reinforcements. Reinforcements for him arrived in the form of the *Sultan* (74 guns) and the *Magnanime* (64 guns) from home ports. In order to provide moral support to the French ally, the Mysorean leader Hyder Ali, then at war with the British, Suffren maintained a presence near the coast. Then, on 22 March, he disembarked troops to aid in the siege of Cuddalore, a town of strategic importance on the Coromandel coast of India, before putting to sea and the following day steering south with the intention of intercepting the *Sultan* and the *Magnanime* off the south coast of Ceylon.

On 9 April, however, he sighted Hughes to the southwest. Hughes saw his primary duty as reinforcing Trincomalee, whether this involved a renewed fight with Suffren or not. He therefore carried on toward Trincomalee until, on the morning of 12 April, when about 50 miles to the northeast of his destination, Hughes realized that he must form a line of battle to confront Suffren, who was then capable of overtaking the rear British ships. With the French to windward, Hughes steered westward, moving on the starboard tack, with two cable intervals between his ships and with the wind north by east. Suffren also formed his line on the starboard tack, his ships parallel to Hughes. At 11:00 A.M. the French began their attack, approaching together west-southwest, each ship making for an opponent in the opposing line. As Suffren possessed twelve ships to Hughes's eleven, the extra vessel was directed to confront the rearmost vessel in the British line.

As the French approached, their van came within range before their rear, and as the British opened fire the leading French vessels hauled up in order to reply. Suffren, himself in the center of the line, signaled his vessels closest to Hughes to hold back, enabling his ship to bear down on Hughes's flagship at point-blank range. He was not alone, however, being supported by his next ship ahead and the two immediately astern. Meanwhile, Suffren's rear, comprised of three ships, although technically in action remained so distant as to have little effect on the fighting.

The four vessels comprising the French van also remained somewhat distant, while Suffren, in the *Héros*, and the three other ships of the center fought at extremely close quarters, with the French line formed in a curve. As a consequence, the brunt of the fire was directed against Hughes's flagship, the *Superb* (74 guns) and the next ahead, the *Monmouth* (64 guns).

The *Héros* sustained considerable damage to its rigging, largely from the fire of the *Superb*, and could not shorten sail but bore up beside the *Monmouth*, heavily engaged against another vessel. Under the weight of such combined fire, the *Héros* eventually lost its main and mizzen masts and at 3:00 P.M. had to maneuver out of the line. The *Superb*, meanwhile, engaged the *Orient* (74 guns), which had replaced the position once held by the *Héros*. The *Orient* was supported by the *Brilliant* (64 guns), and with the *Monmouth* outgunned and keeping some distance, the two French ships were assisted by the fire from the *Héros*, which, having drifted into Hughes's line, could employ its stern chasers against the bows of the *Superb*.

The action between these two British and three French ships proved extremely costly—one of the costliest in the age of sail. The *Superb* lost 59 killed and 96 wounded, while the *Monmouth* suffered 45 killed and 102 wounded. The combined losses of the French vessels were 52 killed and 142 wounded. In addition, the *Sphinx* (64 guns), against which the *Monmouth* was first engaged, lost 22 killed and 74 wounded. Total British losses were 137 killed and 430 wounded. The French lost 137 killed and 357 wounded.

At about 3:40 P.M., concerned that if he maintained his course west he would run ashore, Hughes wore his vessels. The French did the same and sought to take the *Monmouth*, which remained between the opposing lines. A tow rope from the *Hero*, however, pulled the *Monmouth* from this precarious situation, and at 5:40 P.M. Hughes anchored. Suffren followed suit at 8:00 P.M. Both sides, worn out from this vicious action, remained anchored at sea for a week, with only 2 miles separating them, while they undertook repairs. The French sailed on 19 April and made a demonstration, but as the *Monmouth* was in no condition to engage, Hughes did not rise to the bait. Suffren declined to initiate an attack and instead headed for Batacolo, on the Ceylonese coast. On 22 April, Hughes reached Trincomalee, where he stayed for two months before proceeding to Negapatam.

GREGORY FREMONT-BARNES

See also
Cuddalore, Battle of; Hughes, Edward; India, Operations in; Negapatam, Battle of; Sadras, Battle of; Suffren, Pierre-André de; Trincomalee, Battle of

References
Cavaliero, Roderick. *Admiral Satan: The Life and Campaigns of Suffren.* London: Tauris, 1994.
Clowes, William Laird. *The Royal Navy: A History from the Earliest Times to 1900.* 7 vols. London: Chatham, 1996.
Gardiner, Robert, ed. *Navies and the American Revolution, 1775–1783.* London: Chatham, 1996.
James, William. *The Naval History of Great Britain: During the French Revolutionary and Napoleonic Wars.* 4 vols. Mechanicsburg, PA: Stackpole, 2003.

See Loyalist Units

Provincial Military Units

Public Opinion, American

The general attitude of the many peoples who made up the thirteen rebelling colonies toward either the justice of the American cause or the wisdom of seeking independence at any given point is difficult to estimate and impossible to quantify with any precision. But a few patterns of opinion seem fairly clear, and the means used by each side to influence public opinion to their position are well known.

Crowd of Patriots pull down the statue of George III in New York, July 1776. (Library of Congress)

More than three decades after the Revolutionary War, John Adams estimated that some two-thirds of the people in the thirteen colonies had either been firmly committed to the cause of independence or not actively opposed to it and that as many as one-third either remained firmly loyal or sympathetic to Great Britain. Both Adams and Alexander Hamilton thought that in New York City, fully half the population was motivated by Tory sympathies in 1776. More recent estimates, however, suggest that probably no more than 300,000 colonials were Loyalists, perhaps one-sixth of the free white population.

In fact, public expressions of opinion often shifted according to who was in military control of a given territory at a given time. In November 1776, as the British under General William Howe invaded New Jersey in pursuit of George Washington's retreating army, thousands of residents took the oath of allegiance to the king, but thousands of these renounced their oaths in 1777 as the Americans gradually regained control of the area. In March 1781, with the Continental Army at a low ebb from desertion and lack of new enlistments, Lord George Germain, Britain's secretary of state for the colonies, proclaimed that Americans fighting under British command were "more in number than the whole of the enlisted troops in the service of Congress." That statement, which was probably not even briefly accurate in that or any other month and would be far from reality just a few months later, left out the substantial Patriot state militias. Yet Germain's boast does reflect the fact that the American Revolutionary War was in many states a civil war between Americans as well as a war against the British Crown.

In the 1770s Americans had divided into Whigs and Tories, but not with quite the same meaning that these names had in England. There were differences in each faction from one colony to another, and neither label meant anything to backcountry farmers. An overwhelming majority of Americans professed loyalty to the Crown while firmly opposing taxation of the colonies by the British Parliament until just a few months before the Declaration of Independence. Leading Tories were generally wealthy, conservative in their political and social views, and often affiliated with the Anglican Church. Several held appointments from the British government. When new colonial and state governments committed to independence were formed at the call of the Second Continental Congress, between May and July 1776, colonists who remained faithful to King George III and the British Empire were universally branded as Tories or Loyalists.

Many Whigs were also major landowners, such as Washington, Thomas Jefferson, and New York's Livingston family, or wealthy merchants, such as John Hancock, but they consistently opposed British policy and favored imperial reform. As leaders, they received the support of most farmers, shop owners, and craftsmen and even of laborers who owned little or no property.

The Sons of Liberty was, in every city, the radical wing of the Whigs, the first to agitate, and the most extreme in its demands and methods. Presbyterians, Congregationalists, and Baptists were predominantly Whigs in nearly every colony, while Anglicans were more divided. Some active Whigs, such as Peter Van Schaak of New York, balked at the actual separation from Great Britain and became last-minute Loyalists. And some Loyalist exiles, including Van Schaak, became disillusioned with England or Canada in the 1780s and returned to America.

One difficulty in determining the true division of public opinion is that local leaders on each side of the conflict intimidated their opponents with threats of violence. When Britain closed the port of Boston in retaliation for the Boston Tea Party, the Sons of Liberty made it dangerous to refuse to sign the Solemn League and Covenant, an agreement not to buy British-made goods. They also sent large squads of men to the homes of Governor Thomas Gage's newly appointed councilors and persuaded most of them to resign from their positions. When areas came under British military control, however, long-suffering Tories took immediate revenge on their rebel neighbors, and direct reprisals by the British Army were common as well.

Several dramatic indicators of public sentiment do stand out. Two thousand men turned out in Worcester, Massachusetts, to escort a Crown nominee for the Council to announce his resignation. When justices appointed by Gage took their seats, they found none who would take the oath to serve as jurors. And when judges in Worcester approached the courthouse, they found the streets lined for a quarter mile with militiamen in six ranks. Clearly, there was a large body of people determined to resist the exercise of British authority.

But this was not true everywhere. The committee formed in Westchester, New York, to enforce the First Continental Congress's resolution to boycott all trade with Britain called on Congress to provide protection against assault by angry local Tories. Bergen County, New Jersey, and Orange County, New York, elected Loyalist delegations to their colonies' provincial congresses. During the course of the Revolutionary War, 23,500 New Yorkers served in Loyalist units with the British Army. An organization called the Loyal Ladies of New York engaged in civic projects such as raising funds to finance the Loyalist privateer *Fair American* so that it could raid the coast of New England. After the war, as many as 35,000 Loyalists emigrated from New York alone to Canada or England, although many of these émigrés had fled to British-occupied New York City during the war from other colonies.

Both Loyalists and Patriots fielded skilled writers to present their views to the American public. "Massachusettensis," a pen name for Daniel Leonard, presented the Loyalist view of the First Continental Congress in a series of newspaper essays, which were answered by Adams, writing under the name "Novanglus." In his last published letter, in early 1775, Leonard, while admitting "that the collective body of the people . . . have an inherent right to change their form of government," denied that "the inhabitants of a single province or of a number of provinces, or any given part under a majority of the whole, have such a right." Having affirmed that the British Empire was a single body from which one part could not secede, he added that the colonists could not hope to win a full-scale war with Great Britain.

John Boucher, an Anglican priest in Annapolis, Maryland, preached fervently in 1775 that obedience to existing government was commanded by God. Human beings, Boucher insisted, are "so disorderly and unmanageable" that God did not leave government up to "the guidance of their own unruly wills." But his sermons were not published at the time, due, he said, to radical control of the local press, and he was soon forced to flee to England.

There were Tory newspapers in several colonies up to 1775, but only one important Loyalist paper was able to publish after 1776, James Rivington's *New-York Gazette* in New York City. The outbreak of open war in 1775 eventually forced Rivington to leave New York. But after Howe occupied the city in 1776, Rivington returned and resumed publishing his paper, now called *Rivington's Royal Gazette*.

The swing of colonial public opinion toward favoring armed resistance to British authority happened rather quickly, in response to events in Massachusetts. In most colonies, the Boston Port Act of 1774 was greeted with expressions of mourning and resolutions of protest at mass meetings, proceeding to the collection of food for the citizens of the closed port. The outbreak of fighting at Lexington and Concord led to the assembling of militia companies in every rebelling colony in May 1775 and then to Congress's formation of the Continental Army in June, which set off a new round of enlistments.

From 1774 to 1776, many New York legislators voted against participating in the Continental Congresses, where the province's delegates were consistently among the most conservative members. Political leaders in New York continued to recognize the authority of the British Crown until well into 1776, and many wavered in their allegiance up to the writing of the Declaration of Independence. Some legislators who were ultimately arrested as Loyalists, such as Frederick Philipse, had been elected to the New York Committee of Correspondence as recently as 1774. Future Loyalists and Patriots joined in adopting a Declaration of Grievances in March 1775 to uphold "that system of Rights and Priviliges on which the Government of the colonies hath been established." But New York, faced with the choice of joining the other colonies or standing against them by itself, did not ratify the Declaration of Independence until 9 July 1776. Philipse, for one, broke with George Clinton, Philip Schuyler, Philip Livingston, and others who declared for independence to affirm his loyalty to the British government and in doing so drew the attention of New York's Committee of Public Safety.

New Jersey, a middle state geographically, was also a swing state in terms of public opinion. Demographically it has been described as a mix of "liberal western Quakers, conservative eastern gentry, and thousands of riot-prone Scotch-Irish squatters," to which must be added the descendants of the Swedish and Dutch colonists of the seventeenth century. New Jersey's royal governor, William Franklin (Benjamin Franklin's son), remained loyal to the

Crown and in 1775 convened the colonial assembly to secure a resolution opposing independence as a "horrid measure." And New Jersey's delegates to the Second Continental Congress were instructed to vote against independence, favoring legal petitions to King George III. But in 1776, New Jersey's Provincial Congress ordered Franklin arrested when he summoned the colonial assembly to consider negotiation on terms communicated from London. Deported as a prisoner to Connecticut and then exchanged in 1778, he spent the rest of the war in British-occupied New York City among 15,000 Loyalist refugees, of whom he became a leader. Loyalists still in New Jersey made regular trips to British positions on Staten Island to provide intelligence on the position of the Continental Army and the condition of the state government that had deposed Franklin.

America was a patchwork of conflicting loyalties in many places. While the owners of New York's manorial estates were mostly Loyalists and their tenants tended to support the Revolutionary cause, when a proprietor such as the Livingston family supported independence, their tenants became resolute Tories. New York was the scene of tenant uprisings throughout the 1760s, leaving bitterness that could drive tenants to either side of the Revolution.

A larger portion of landed gentry supported independence in Virginia than in any other colony, but it was the riflemen from the western counties who set the cultural style in the first months of independence. The wealthy Landon Carter complained to Washington that many Virginia farmers who supported independence expected that they would become independent of rich men and able to do whatever they pleased. Carter, long used to the lower orders of free men being politically and financially dependent on his patronage, did not share this view of independence.

In the Carolinas, many backcountry farmers were loyal to the king. North Carolina had been through an upheaval in 1770–1771 when the Regulator movement of disenfranchised western farmers closed the corrupt local courts. An army led by soon-to-be Patriot leaders defeated the Regulators at Alamance Creek and hanged several on the spot. Many Regulators later received a pardon from George III, so they were disposed to think well of him and indisposed to follow their recent persecutors in a war against him. In South Carolina, where the Regulator movement had filled in the void caused by the complete absence of backcountry government, farmers pointed out that they had been denied the liberty of voting in the last elections in the colony, so how could they be said to be represented, and how could they be taxed by the legislature? Protesting tenant farmers in New York, who looked for support to the Sons of Liberty in the city, instead saw leading Whig judges condemn their leader, William Prendergast, to be hanged, drawn, and quartered, but he was also pardoned by the king.

A host of local contradictions such as these, between Whig rhetoric and Whig behavior, could have been fatal to the Revolutionary cause, dooming both the drive for independence in 1776 and the war effort to secure that independence. But the Patriots had three great advantages in the war for public opinion.

First, Congress itself made skillful use of appeals to the people of America and Britain and of petitions to the king in 1774 and 1775 and finally of the Declaration of Independence itself to set out its case and make America seem to be the fair and reasonable party and Britain the heartless aggressor. Second, in Thomas Paine the Patriots had one of the most effective propagandists found in any revolution. Not only did his *Common Sense* of January 1776 persuade many thousands of Americans that they should seek independence, but his *Crisis* essays, beginning in December 1776, also persuaded many that they could defend their independence against a massive British Army at the very low point of the war. Finally, the British utterly failed to shape American public opinion and hardly even tried to do so. British officers either overestimated Loyalist strength or mistrusted the Loyalist leaders who wanted to work with them. Either way, they did not harness Loyalist opinion effectively.

American public opinion, favoring first intellectual and economic resistance to Britain, then armed resistance, and finally independence, but always with doubts, gradually grew more confident over time. By the arrival of Britain's Carlisle Peace Commission in 1778, any rejection of independence was unthinkable. Thereafter, American public opinion, although with many hesitating steps, became more surely focused on its own major national institution, Congress, and upon the major national question that faced it—not independence, but the character of a new nation that was already independent yet still unsure of the degree of power and unity it wished to exercise both within America and with other nations.

CHARLES ROSENBERG

See also

Associated Loyalists; Border Warfare; Boston, Massachusetts; Boston Port Act; Boston Tea Party; Boycotts; Coercive Acts; Congress, First Continental; Congress, Second Continental and Confederation; Declaration of Independence; Georgia; Hancock, John; Loyalists; Paine, Thomas; Propaganda; Regulator Movement; Religion

References

East, Robert A., and Jacob Judd, eds. *The Loyalist Americans: A Focus on Greater New York*. Tarrytown, NY: Sleepy Hollow, 1975.

Jensen, Merrill. *The American Revolution within America*. New York: New York University Press, 1974.

Lynn, Kenneth S. *A Divided People*. Westport, CT: Greenwood, 1977.

Martin, Thomas S. *Minds and Hearts: The American Revolution as a Philosophical Crisis*. Lanham, MD: University Press of America, 1984.

Pearson, Michael. *Those Damned Rebels: The American Revolution as Seen through British Eyes*. New York: Putnam, 1972.

Smith, Paul H. "The American Loyalists: Notes on their Organization and Numerical Strength." *William and Mary Quarterly*, 3rd ser., 25(2) (1968): 259–277.

Trevelyan, George Otto. *The American Revolution*. New York: David McKay, 1964.

The unpopularity of the American Revolutionary War, deliberately launched by Britain in an effort to regain control of the thirteen American colonies, was evident in numerous places: the serious doubts of several high military officers, regular denunciations in the press, many critical municipal resolutions, the hostility of most major merchants, and the outright mockery of the opposition in Parliament. The *London Magazine* observed in 1768 that "nine persons in ten, even in this country, are friends to the Americans and thoroughly convinced they have right on their side." Six years later, however, when British colonial rule was moving toward a crisis, contrary opinions became more common, such as that appearing in the *Morning Chronicle:* "The sword alone can decide this dispute . . . to prevent the ruin of the British Empire, which will inevitably take place if we are defeated." From the beginning of the colonial troubles until the end of the war, British attitudes toward the conflict were sharply divided, often along lines of political affiliation, social class, occupation, and even religion.

British parliamentary politics were divided roughly between Tories and Whigs, ancestors of the nineteenth-century Conservative and Liberal Parties. Tories favored a powerful monarchy and the preservation of class privileges, and they naturally sided with King George III, who could generally command a majority in Parliament, in part by relying on massive patronage and, occasionally, direct bribery. This left the Whigs through most of the late eighteenth century as the opposition. And the Church of England in the late eighteenth century was almost unanimously identified with the Tory landowning aristocracy. Only two of its bishops expressed any support for the American colonists.

British Whigs, like their American counterparts, believed that there was a fundamental law that limited the actions of the highest authorities—Parliament as well as the king. British sympathizers of the American colonists were even known as "the patriots of the nation." A writer to the *London Magazine* signed himself "A devoted friend of the constitution as it was settled at the revolution," meaning the Glorious Revolution of 1688 that overthrew King James II. To preserve liberty, he wrote, the legislative body "should not depart out of the instrument, the frame that the people when they last settled the legislative ordained." "An Old Correspondent" declared that legislative authority must remain within lawful bounds, "which if they exceed, their authority ceases, whatever power from their guns may remain." Most English nonconformists also favored the colonial cause, a sympathy strengthened by large numbers of nonconformist sectarians in many of the American colonies.

Tories were, above all, more approving of passive obedience to authority, resolving all colonial claims to liberty with the statement of the prime minister, Lord Frederick North: "the whole reasoning on this question may be fairly deduced from one single postulate, viz., that the Inhabitants of the British Colonies are Subjects of the British State." The writer "A.B." called this "the favourite Doctrine of all Tyrants, namely, that the supreme Power of a Nation has Authority to pass what Laws they please, and that the People are

The interior of a blacksmith's shop with Lord Mansfield forging the links to a chain; Lord North standing to the left holding a lorgnette and, in his right hand, a paper titled "An act for prohibiting all trade"; Lord Sandwich holding a hammer in one hand and an anchor in the other; Lord Bute working the bellows; and other men in the background. Looking through a window is George III. (Library of Congress)

guilty of Arrogance, Presumption, and I know not what, if they pretend to interfere with them in any Degree."

British newspapers in the late eighteenth century had not begun to publish editorials, but they did print lengthy and colorful letters from readers, many of whom used pen names such as "Philo-Britanniae" (lover of Britain), "Philocolonas" (lover of the colonies), "Pompilius," "Candidus," "Rationalis," "Bristoliensis" (man of Bristol), or even the name of the philosophic Roman emperor, Marcus Aurelius. Letters from America, under names such as "A Virginian" and "Mercator" (a merchant, from Boston) were also published in English newspapers.

Merchants in Britain's seaports overwhelmingly took the side of the colonies in the disputes that culminated in the Declaration of Independence. The Sugar Act of 1764 and the Stamp Act of 1765 threatened to drain the colonies of hard money and generally interrupt trade, to the detriment of many British merchants. The Townshend Acts in 1767 incited nonimportation agreements in most colonies, agreements that soon distressed British commerce. The *London Chronicle* reported on 1 September 1764 that the principal merchants of Bristol "intend to support with all their interest the independent free trade of the North American colonies."

In supporting the Americans' objections to British policy, British merchants and manufacturers were not only voicing their principles but also trying to protect their prosperity. Americans were increasingly producing their own cloth and talking about developing their own manufactures. Little hard currency was available in the colonies to pay for imports, and Britain's new controls on the sugar trade with the West Indies and other new taxes were taking what little currency remained out of circulation. Colonists turning to nonimportation as a form of protest naturally promoted local manufacturing as a substitute. In 1766 the *St. James's Chronicle* reported that exports to America were "near 600,000 pounds less this past summer than has been known for 30 years past."

Edmund Burke, a Whig leader in the House of Commons in 1774, urged that the careful regulation of trade policy, rather than the imposition of deeply resented taxes, was the key to restoring peace in the colonies. When the Boston Port Act suspended trade with that city in 1774, petitions poured into Parliament from merchants in London and other cities who saw their profits dropping. When word of the battles at Lexington and Concord reached London in 1775, members of the Constitutional Society called for donations for the relief of "our beloved American fellow subjects." And when heralds subsequently read a proclamation at the Royal Exchange

Building in London declaring that anyone aiding the rebels would be prosecuted as a traitor, the crowd present openly hissed in response.

Merchants who did want the government to enforce obedience on the colonies often feared to say so openly because colonial traders had threatened to default on their debts to British houses of commerce if Britain used force in the colonies. A petition from the industrial city of Birmingham did advocate that coercive measures against Boston be strictly enforced. Friends of the Americans, however, replied that Birmingham's arms makers simply wanted a war so as to make money by selling weapons to both sides and charged that munitions were already being sold to the colonial militia through Holland and Germany.

Another body of opinion bitterly criticized the growth of manufactures in the colonies, which the writers "Old England" and "No Bostonian" viewed as contrary to the entire purpose of having colonies. According to mercantilism, the dominant economic theory in eighteenth-century Britain, colonies were expected to strengthen and serve the empire by supplying commodities that the mother country could not produce and by serving as markets for British manufacturers, not by becoming economic powers themselves.

But the cry "no taxation without representation" from the colonies had its counterpart in Whig demands for electoral reform in England. The list of boroughs from which representatives to Parliament were elected had not been changed since medieval times, so some large cities had no representatives, while long-depopulated rural villages sent one or two members, chosen by the lord who held title to the land. Some boroughs were even publicly advertised for sale to the highest bidder. These "rotten boroughs" led "A Plain Dealer" to assert that "the Americans, by showing us what they would, teach us what we ought to do."

Tories replied to these demands by asserting the doctrine of virtual representation. Every member of Parliament, they argued, represented the entire nation, not merely the borough that elected him. A few large cities might not elect any members, but the people who lived there were represented in Parliament by other members of their own class elected elsewhere in the kingdom. One "Britophilus" asserted that the American colonies likewise had virtual representation in Parliament. But the American pamphleteer James Otis Jr., who rejected this argument for the colonies, also asserted in his *Considerations on Behalf of the Colonists* that all major English cities should indeed have their own representatives, to which many English Whigs firmly agreed.

One recurrent British argument against the Stamp Act, and against coercive measures generally, was that the colonies were becoming so strong and their population so large that coercion would soon be impossible. Defenders of the act insisted that repealing it would harm the dignity and authority of the government and compared the Americans to ungrateful spoiled children turning upon Mother England. The Reverend James Scott, chaplain to First Lord of the Admiralty Lord Sandwich, writing in opposition to the repeal of the Stamp Act, was unable to keep his identity hidden behind the pen name "Anti-Sejanus." He described the protests in America as "such an undutiful return to the mother country, for that paternal care and tenderness" supposedly extended to cultivate colonial settlement, and emphasized that the American tax burden was very light compared to that borne by English taxpayers.

One writer stated that British America's population was one-fifth of all the king's subjects, yet they paid only one-twentieth of all taxes to the royal government. Another estimated that American taxes paid to the British government each year averaged 8 pence per person, while in England the average tax burden came to 12 shillings (144 pence) a year. One commonly held view prior to the Stamp Act was that Britain's huge debt from the Seven Years' War (known in America as the French and Indian War) was incurred solely in defense of the colonies and colonial interests. If "our timid and ill-judging Ministers intend to give way to the tumultuous Americans," Scott wrote, "can it be supposed that the Colonists will ever submit to bear any share in those grievous burdens and taxes, with which we are loaded?"

By 1774–1775, however, considerable opinion in Britain openly favored an amicable separation from the colonies. Dean Tucker, a churchman who published pamphlets on economics with views similar to those of Adam Smith, proposed to separate the colonies from Britain but guarantee their freedom and independence against any invader. He asserted that trade, the real source of prosperity on both sides of the Atlantic, could only improve. The *Monthly Review* partially agreed, since many in England had come to believe that "we can neither *govern* the Americans, nor be *governed by them*; . . . we can neither *unite* with them, nor ought to think of *subduing* them; . . . nothing remains but to part with them on as friendly terms as we can." Even the anti-American "Philo-Britanniae" proposed to cut all ties with America "as an unhappy Parent would with a disobedient Child, who had well nigh ruined him."

"Rationalis," writing to the *London Chronicle,* frankly advocated restraint to advance a policy of divide and rule toward the colonies. Given the colonies' strength from their growing population, he argued, the only sound way to retain control by the mother country "would be found in their disunion, from rival interest and their discordant religious principles, . . . but what would never probably be effected among themselves is likely to be accomplished by an ill-judged measure of the mother country's to involve them in a common calamity of oppression."

When in early 1774 the British government decided on harsh measures in response to the Boston Tea Party, public opinion was deeply divided. The *Middlesex Journal* demanded punishment for Boston, saying that any other approach would be "an infamous instance of servile pusillanimity," while another writer referred to the atmosphere in Boston as seditious, turbulent, and insolent. A writer in the *London Packet,* however, remarked that the "miserable Cabinet Junto in whom *only* the King thinks proper to confide, are as cordially despised in America as they are detested in England."

General Jeffrey Amherst, experienced in leading British and colonial forces in North America during the French and Indian War, emphatically refused an offer to take command of British forces suppressing the rebellion and substantially agreed with Adjutant General Harvey, Britain's most senior

America's population was one-fifth of all the king's subjects, yet they paid only one-twentieth of all taxes.

staff officer, that trying to conquer the American colonies using land forces "is as wild an idea as ever contraverted common sense." Many officers declined to serve in America, and when Lord Effingham resigned his military commission, he was publicly thanked by the citizens of London, Southwark, Dublin, and Newcastle. One reason that George III's government hired Hessian mercenaries to reassert royal authority is that army enlistment rates in Britain dropped in anticipation of a war in America.

In mid-1774, with the news of widespread resistance from Boston and other colonies giving political ammunition to the Whig opposition, the king dissolved Parliament. The subsequent election of many Tory members in the fall satisfied George III that he had the support to carry out military measures to regain control of the colonies. To achieve this electoral victory, he paid at least £70,000 in bribes from the Secret Service Fund, which had been established to pay spies. The means he employed suggests that British public opinion may have been poorly reflected in the composition of his new Parliament. Even without the bribes, however, the rotten boroughs and the property requirements to qualify as a voter guaranteed that Parliament would not accurately express the whole nation's views. But while the Whig opposition remained loud and mocking throughout the war, the king had voting majorities for his policy until early 1782. He also had popular support among the upper classes. Whig Parliament member Charles James Fox was thrown out of a London dinner party in December 1777 after offering a toast to George Washington.

When open warfare began after Lexington and Concord, one correspondent after another wrote that the majority of the people "are very friendly to the Americans, and view them as an injured people," or that "the greatest part of the nation are ardent in wishing success to the Americans, and in deprecating the arms employed by their Sovereign." The Whigs stressed the importance of defending England against a possible invasion from the Bourbon monarchy of France and repeatedly called for the armies in North America to be brought home where they were truly needed. A petition was addressed to the king from "Lord Mayor, Aldermen and Commons of the City of London" asking that the coercive treatment of the Americans be suspended. (The lord mayor was John Wilkes, fervently favorable to the rebellious Americans and survivor of a twenty-two-month prison sentence for sedition.)

But in regard to the entire colonial crisis and especially the War for American Independence itself, it is virtually impossible to measure the actual numbers in the British population who adhered to each side of the conflict. Britain's Tories argued that the public press was no accurate gauge and insisted that "one disaffected person makes more clamour than fifty loyal subjects." Public opinion hardly divided 50 to 1 in either direction, but Britain, deeply divided over war with America in 1774, remained deeply divided at the war's end in 1783.

CHARLES ROSENBERG

See also

Amherst, Jeffrey; Boston Port Act; Boycotts; Burke, Edmund; Coercive Acts; Fox, Charles James; France; Montagu, John, 4th Earl of Sandwich; Religion;

Smith, Adam; Stamp Act; Sugar Act; Tories; Townshend Acts; Trade; Whigs; Wilkes, John

References

Bailyn, Bernard. *The Ideological Origins of the American Revolution.* 1967. Reprint, Cambridge: Harvard University Press, 1992.

Gould, Eliga H. *The Persistence of Empire: British Political Culture in the Age of the American Revolution.* Chapel Hill: University of North Carolina Press, 2000.

Hinkhouse, Fred Junkin. *The Preliminaries of the American Revolution as Seen in the English Press.* New York: Octagon, 1969.

Pearson, Michael. *Those Damned Rebels: The American Revolution as Seen through British Eyes.* New York: Putnam, 1972.

Trevelyan, George Otto. *The American Revolution.* New York: David McKay, 1964.

Pulaski, Casimir
(1748–1779)

Count Casimir Pulaski, a Polish Patriot and soldier, served the American Revolutionary cause as a volunteer but developed much ill will against himself by grumbling about the way he was being treated. He first saw service as a soldier outside Poland by joining the guard of Charles, Duke of Courland. Pulaski returned to Poland in 1767, and on 29 February 1768 he joined the Confederation of Barr, which his father and six associates had founded to resist Russian domination of their homeland. His father was arrested and killed, and Pulaski inherited the title of count. He was successful in partisan warfare for a time, and in 1769 he encouraged the Lithuanians to rebel. Although besieged in the monastery of Czenstochova for a time, he repelled the Russians and with assistance from others forced them to retreat across the Vistula River. Finally, his resistance was crushed, and Poland was partitioned in 1773. He was declared an outlaw, his estates were confiscated, and he fled to Turkey. From there he attempted unsuccessfully for two years to incite the Turks to attack Russia.

Penniless, Pulaski traveled to Paris in 1775 and for two years searched for employment suitable to a dispossessed revolutionary Polish count. French agents suggested that he might wish to aid the Americans in their rebellion against Britain. They put him in touch with Benjamin Franklin and Silas Deane, who were looking for European officers to join the hard-pressed Continental Army. After several conversations with these two men, Pulaski sailed for America in June 1777, carrying in his pocket a letter of introduction from Franklin to General George Washington. Pulaski arrived in Boston in July, and when he met Washington a month later the commander in chief quickly identified the young Pole as an officer who might take command of and regularize the Continental Army's four cavalry regiments. On 25 August, while waiting for Washington to act, Pulaski gave Congress a plan for the organization of a corps of volunteers. Two days later, Washington recommended to Congress that Pulaski be employed as a leader of Continental cavalry.

Before Congress acted on either of these ideas, a British army commanded by General William Howe marched toward Philadelphia in southeastern Pennsylvania. Pulaski joined Washington's army as a volunteer to oppose the enemy. In the Battle of Brandywine on 11 September, Pulaski commanded Washington's personal bodyguard, under orders to observe enemy movements. He warned Washington that Howe was attempting to surround the American army and allowed the commander in chief to take defensive measures. During the retreat that followed, Pulaski defended the army's rear. As a reward for his services, Washington recommended to Congress on 15 September that Pulaski be promoted to brigadier general. When Congress complied, Washington gave Pulaski command of the Continental cavalry and ordered him to scout British positions. Pulaski saved Washington from being surprised by the enemy at Warren's Tavern on 16 September and fought in the Battle of Germantown on 4 October. In the winter of 1777–1778, Pulaski served under Brigadier General Anthony Wayne. On 29 February 1778, he and Wayne successfully attacked a British detachment commanded by Lieutenant-Colonel Thomas Stirling at Cooper's Ferry, New Jersey. Although Wayne praised Pulaski's military abilities and bravery, the two men quarreled in March, and Pulaski resigned his commission in a huff.

Lingering at Valley Forge without a command, Pulaski petitioned Washington to allow him to organize a body of light infantry and lancers for independent service. Both Washington and Congress agreed, and so the famous Pulaski's Legion was born. By summer 1778, Pulaski had recruited 350 men, half cavalry and half infantry. On the

Casimir Pulaski, a Polish national in search of adventure, joined the Patriot cause in 1777 as a cavalry commander. He fought at Brandywine and raised an independent unit of dragoons, at the head of which he was mortally wounded during a charge at the siege of Savannah. (National Archives and Records Administration)

night of 15 October, at Little Egg Harbor, New Jersey, he was surprised in camp by the British and lost 40 dead before fighting them off. The following winter at Minisink, New York, he threatened to return to Europe because he felt neglected, but Washington talked him out of it. Pulaski was ordered southward to join Major General Benjamin Lincoln at Charleston in early February 1779. On 8 May, Pulaski attacked a British force under General Augustine Prevost that was threatening Charleston and was repulsed after a severe firefight. Five days later, Prevost withdrew toward Savannah, and Pulaski, although sick with a fever, was ordered by Lincoln to follow and harass the British army's flanks.

On 19 August, Pulaski wrote a letter to Congress complaining bitterly about the ill treatment he had received since arriving in America and again threatening to resign. Still, he expressed a hope that he would receive suitable attention in the future. In early September, still hounding Prevost's troops, he cooperated with General John McIntosh in surprising and capturing an enemy outpost. Pulaski also continued to skirmish with small British units. At Beaufort, he contacted French and American warships that were to cooperate with Lincoln in capturing Savannah. When Lincoln arrived from

Charleston and took command of operations, Pulaski served under him. On 9 October, during Franco-American operations against British defenses around Savannah, he bravely but rashly led a cavalry charge and was wounded by a grapeshot in his right thigh. Evacuated to the American brig *Wasp*, he died two days later and was probably buried at sea. Unpopular in late 1779 because of his grousing, Pulaski died a noble death, thus erasing the bad impression he had made. In 1855, Charlestonians completed the erection of a monument to his memory.

PAUL DAVID NELSON

See also
Brandywine, Battle of; Deane, Silas; Franklin, Benjamin; Germantown, Battle of; Lincoln, Benjamin; Philadelphia Campaign; Prevost, Augustine; Savannah, Georgia, Operations against; Valley Forge, Pennsylvania; Wayne, Anthony

References
Abodaher, David J. *Freedom Fighter: Casimir Pulaski.* New York: J. Messner, 1969.
Gordon, William W. "Count Casimir Pulaski." *Georgia Historical Quarterly* 13 (1929): 167–227.
Griffin, Martin I. J. "General Count Casimir Pulaski, 'The Father of American Cavalry.'" *American Catholic Historical Researches* 6 (1910): 1–128.
Manning, Clarence A. *Soldier of Liberty: Casimir Pulaski.* New York: Philosophical Library, 1945.
Thompson, C. H. *Historical Facts in the Lives of Count Pulaski and Baron de Lovzinski.* Plattsburg, MO: Leader Publishing Company, 1928.

Putnam, Israel
(1718–1790)

Israel Putnam, Continental soldier, has been celebrated in American history as the very model of a republican citizen, second only to George Washington in the pantheon of heroes. Putnam's fame derives not so much from his military abilities, which were not outstanding, as from his personal virtues of bravery and rough-hewn wisdom.

Growing up on a Massachusetts farm, Putnam was used to hard labor, and although he was only about five feet six inches tall at maturity, he was powerfully built. Long before the Revolution, many stories circulated among his neighbors about his various exploits of strength and bravery. His father bequeathed to him an estate worth £2,500, which he used to buy a rich farm near Pomfret, Connecticut, in 1740. He sired a large family and developed deep Christian beliefs. When the French and Indian War began in 1755, he joined the Connecticut militia as a volunteer but was quickly promoted to lieutenant. He took part in the unsuccessful expedition against Fort Crown Point in 1755, then joined Rogers's Rangers.

Commissioned a captain in the Rangers in the fall of 1755, Putnam did much scouting of the French and Indians around Fort Ticonderoga. He was promoted to major in 1758 and in the same year was captured by the Indians.

Tied to a tree to be burned, with wood heaped about his feet, he was rescued by a French officer who prevailed upon the Indians to release him into French captivity. In 1759 Putnam was exchanged and promoted to lieutenant-colonel, then led troops in Sir Jeffrey Amherst's operations northward by way of Albany. Serving again with Amherst in 1760, Putnam led a regiment on the successful march from Fort Oswego to Montreal. In 1762 he joined in a British expedition to capture Havana, led by Major-General George Keppel, Earl of Albemarle. Although Havana surrendered to Albemarle's force on 14 August, Putnam was not in the fight. The ship on which he sailed was caught in a hurricane off the Cuban coast, and he and his company, barely escaping death, were shipwrecked on the coast. He was finally rescued, but only after many of his men succumbed to disease and starvation.

By the end of the French and Indian War, Putnam was widely known in America for his near-death martial exploits, bravery, and skill as a frontier fighter. In 1763–1765, during Pontiac's Rebellion, he joined in the Anglo-American struggle against Indians on the frontier, commencing the war as a major. He was promoted to lieutenant-colonel in May 1764 and commanded five companies of Connecticut militia during Colonel John Bradstreet's march to Detroit. For a few years afterward, he settled peacefully into farming and running a tavern, The General Wolfe. In 1766 and 1767 Putnam served two terms in the Connecticut legislature and was elected a selectman. He was commissioned by General Phineas Lyman in 1772–1773 to take part in an expedition that sailed through the West Indies, the Gulf of Mexico, and up the Mississippi River as far as Natchez, seeking land to exploit. He kept a journal during these adventures, parts of which were published in 1931.

As troubles between Britain and America grew in the 1770s, Putnam joined the Sons of Liberty and took part in every subsequent manifestation of colonial resistance. In August 1774, after the port of Boston was closed by the Coercive Acts, he drove a herd of 125 sheep into the city to feed hungry citizens. That October he was commissioned lieutenant colonel of the 11th Regiment of Connecticut militia. For years it was said that when news reached him that war had broken out on 19 April 1775 at Lexington and Concord, he was plowing in a field. Supposedly, like the famous Roman Lucius Quinctius Cincinnatus, he unhitched one of the horses, notified his militiamen to follow him, and rode 100 miles in eighteen hours to Cambridge, Massachusetts. This story is probably untrue, but he did quickly march with his regiment to Boston. Promoted to colonel of the 3rd Connecticut Regiment on 1 May and to brigadier general of Connecticut militia a month later, he helped plan for and execute the Battle of Bunker Hill on 17 June. Two

Israel Putnam led the Connecticut militia at the Battle of Bunker Hill, at which action he is said to have instructed his men with the famous words, "Don't fire until you see the whites of their eyes"—a phrase not, however, original to him. Later he served as a brigadier general in the battles at Long Island and Princeton, but he was removed from field duty by George Washington owing to his poor performance. (Library of Congress)

days later he was commissioned major general in the Continental Army and commanded the American center at the siege of Boston in the winter of 1775–1776.

For a short time in the spring of 1776, Putnam was in overall command of American troops at New York. When General George Washington assumed command on 13 April, Putnam was made second in command. Up to this point in the war, he had performed well militarily, handling relatively small groups of men in a type of fighting reminiscent of his earlier experiences on the frontier. But in the Battle of Long Island, on 27 August, he found himself completely out of his depth, commanding the American left wing that he had taken over from General John Sullivan three days before. Badly outmaneuvered by General William Howe, Putnam's defensive line was overwhelmed, and the entire Continental Army collapsed. Many Americans, Washington included, believed that Putnam was responsible for this debacle. On 15 September, during the American retreat after the British landings at Kips Bay on Manhattan, Putnam successfully removed all stores and troops from New York City when it was in danger of being cut off.

In December 1776 Washington gave Putnam command of Philadelphia and in January 1777 ordered him to Princeton, New Jersey. The commander in chief was greatly annoyed when Putnam decided on his own judgment to delay obeying the order. Apparently on this occasion, as on others, Putnam misunderstood Washington's intentions and never exercised any deliberate design of insubordination against the commander in chief. Although Washington had decided by this time that Putnam was not a reliable officer, he ordered him in May to take command of the Highland forts on the Hudson River above New York. On the evening of 3 October, General Sir Henry Clinton began operations against the forts as a diversion to assist General John Burgoyne, who was in trouble at Saratoga. Two days later Clinton landed troops at Verplanck's Point and overwhelmed an American outpost. Putnam, compelled to retreat, drew reinforcements from the garrisons of Forts Clinton and Montgomery. On 6 October both forts fell to General Clinton, and the following day Fort Constitution, opposite West Point, also capitulated.

Furious at these reverses, Washington instituted court-martial proceedings against Putnam later in October, charging him with negligence and disobedience of orders. The court exonerated Putnam, but Washington had no desire to allow him to retain any field command and was anxious to shuffle him aside. Fortunately for the Americans, Clinton abandoned the Highland forts in late October and returned to New York. On 16 March 1778, Putnam requested leave to go home to Connecticut on recruiting service, and Washington quickly complied, replacing him in the Highlands with General Alexander McDougall. In May 1779 Putnam implored Washington to be allowed to rejoin the main army, and the commander in chief reluctantly gave him responsibility for the troops at White Plains, New York. Washington was relieved when Putnam's military service was brought to an abrupt end in December by a paralytic stroke. Putnam went home to Pomfret and spent the rest of his life running a tavern and telling stories. Despite his reverses during the Revolutionary War, during his lifetime Putnam retained his reputation for bravery in action and continued to be highly respected after his death.

PAUL DAVID NELSON

See also

Boston, Siege of; Bunker Hill, Battle of; Burgoyne, John; Clinton, Henry; Coercive Acts; Fort Clinton, New York; Fort Montgomery, New York, Assault on; Hudson River and the Hudson Highlands; Kips Bay, New York, Action at; Lexington and Concord; Long Island, Battle of; McDougall, Alexander; Saratoga Campaign; Sullivan, John; West Point, New York

References

Bates, Albert, ed. *The Two Putnams, Israel and Rufus, in the Havana Expedition, 1762, and the Mississippi River Exploration, 1772–1773.* Hartford: Connecticut Historical Society, 1931.

Hill, George. *General Israel Putnam (Old Put): A Biography.* Boston: E. O. Libby, 1858.

Humphreys, David. *An Essay on the Life of the Honorable Major-General Israel Putnam.* Brattleboro, VT: William Fessenden, 1812.

Livingston, William Farrand. "The Homes and Haunts of Israel Putnam." *New England Magazine* 17 (1897): 193–212.

———. *Israel Putnam: Pioneer, Ranger, and Major-General, 1718–1790.* New York: Putnam, 1905.

Luther, F. S. "General Israel Putnam." *Worcester Historical Society Proceedings* 20 (1904): 204–214.

Niven, John. *Connecticut Hero: Israel Putnam.* Hartford: American Revolution Bicentennial Commission of Connecticut, 1977.

Putnam, Eben. *A History of the Putnam Family in England and America,* Vol. 1. Salem, MA: Salem Press, 1891.

Tarbox, Increase N. *Life of Israel Putnam ("Old Put"), Major-General in the Continental Army.* Boston: Lockwood, Brooks, 1876.

Putnam, Rufus
(1738–1824)

Born 9 April 1738 in Sutton, Massachusetts, Rufus Putnam was the son of Elisha and Susan Fuller Putnam and was a cousin of Israel Putnam. Rufus Putnam lived with his grandfather and a brother-in-law after the death of his father in 1746, before apprenticing himself as a millwright to Daniel Matthews. When the French and Indian War broke out, Putnam joined a company of rangers based at Fort Edward and served successfully as a scout and later as a military engineer at Greenbush, where he learned the rudiments of building military fortifications. In 1761 he returned to Sutton, where he married first Elizabeth Ayers, who died in childbirth with their first child the following year, and then in 1765 Persis Rice, with whom he had eight children.

A successful farmer, Putnam branched out into planning and constructing mills, then taught himself surveying, a skill that qualified him to accompany a party of veterans to British West Florida in 1773 to choose land grants as a bonus for their service in the French and Indian War. Although the settlement plans were abandoned, Putnam, who had laid out nineteen town sites for the party, increasingly felt drawn to engineering and surveying. In 1775 he received a commission in the Continental Army as a lieutenant colonel on the basis of his technical skills, and he planned the rebuilding and reinforcement of breastworks and fortifications at Boston and New York City. However, he was also a skillful military commander, leading a regiment at the Battle of Saratoga. In the last years of the Revolution, he was responsible for fortifying West Point, a crucial fortress on the Hudson River, and Newport, Rhode Island. Putnam was rewarded with the rank of colonel.

An early member of the Society of the Cincinnati as well as an enthusiastic Freemason, Putnam parlayed his network of friends and colleagues into a 1786 surveying job for the Commonwealth of Massachusetts, during which he negotiated a land cessation with the Penobscot tribe and mapped the acquired territory. In 1792, he was promoted to brigadier general and sent to negotiate a similar treaty with the Wabash tribe. During this period, Putnam was also a founding director and major investor in the Ohio Company and in April 1788 helped to choose and lay out the company's first settlement at Marietta, Ohio (named for Marie Antoinette, in recognition of France's aid in the Revolution).

Putnam and his family moved to Marietta, where he worked to found schools, served as a trustee for the newly established Ohio University in Athens, and was named a district judge. Particularly fascinated with the local Native American mounds, he worked hard to preserve them from destruction by settlers. Putnam lost his position as surveyor general of the United States in 1803, a position given by George Washington in 1796, because of complaints made to Thomas Jefferson about Putnam's mathematical and technical skills. When Ohio became a state, it named Putnam surveyor general, and despite criticism of his self-taught methods, he established the system of contracting out surveying work used by the federal and state governments until 1910. Putnam died in Marietta on 4 May 1824.

MARGARET SANKEY

See also
Boston, Siege of; Saratoga Campaign; West Point, New York

References
Putnam, George Haven. *Israel Putnam, Major-General in the Continental Army, Rufus Putnam, Brigadier-General in the Continental Army, and Their Service in the French and Indian War, and in the American Revolution.* London: n.p., 1923.
Putnam, Rufus. *The Memoirs of Rufus Putnam.* Boston: Houghton Mifflin, 1903.
Thompson, Eben Francis. *A Brief Chronicle of Rufus Putnam and His Rutland Home.* Worcester, MA: Commonwealth Press, 1930.

Q

The British Parliament passed two acts that mandated and regulated the quartering of British troops among civilian populations in America during the growing imperial crisis. The first of these, enacted shortly after the Stamp Act, was the more visible and important, especially as it led to a brief curtailment of the powers of the recalcitrant New York Assembly. The second Quartering Act, as the last of the four Coercive Acts of 1774, was overshadowed by its three companions: the Boston Port Act, the Massachusetts Government Act, and the Administration of Justice Act (called by many colonists the Murder Act). The colonists, however, did consider the new Quartering Act to be an important grievance until independence.

The first Quartering Act, enacted on 15 May 1765, required local civil authorities to provide barracks and supplies for the British troops stationed in their communities or provinces in North America and directed the quartering of troops in taverns, inns, alehouses, and, if necessary, even uninhabited houses and barns where barracks were not available. Although the act was not a tax, it compelled local assemblymen to provide supplies for the quartered troops without reimbursement by the Crown, which would in turn have raised local taxes. For this reason, the New York Assembly would not provide to General Thomas Gage, the commander in chief of British forces in North America, and his troops stationed in New York City the provisions called for in the act. Gage pressed the legislators to comply, but in December 1766 they again refused to supply his troops.

As tensions mounted in New York City, soldiers and citizens displayed a growing frustration over the issue. The controversy over the Quartering Act continued, finally prompting the British government to seek legislation from Parliament to discipline the defiant Assembly. In July 1767, King George III signed the New York Suspending Act, which empowered the government to direct New York's governor to withhold his approval of any action by the legislature until that body provided the funds needed to sustain the troops. Wills Hill, the Earl of Hillsborough, who became Britain's first secretary of state for the colonies in 1768, soon exercised this new power. New York's legislators continued their defiance until December 1769 but finally appropriated the

The S P E E C H of the Right Honourable the Earl of C H A T-H A M, in the Houſe of LORDS, upon reading the Amend-ments in the QUEBEC BILL, on Friday, the 17th June, 1774. Together with his Lordſhip's S P E E C H, on the Third Reading, in the Houſe of Lords, of the Bill for PROVIDING WITH QUARTERS, the Officers and Troops in AMERICA.

MOST ILLUSTRIOUS LORDS;

THE unfavourable ſtate of health, under which I have long laboured, could not prevent me from laying before your Lordſhips my thoughts on the Bill now before you; and on the American affairs in general.

If we take a tranſient view of thoſe motives which induced the anceſtors of our fellow-ſubjects, in America, to leave their native country to encounter the innumerable difficulties of the unexplored regions of the weſtern world, our aſtoniſhment at the preſent conduct of their deſcendants will naturally ſubſide. There was no corner of the world into which men of their free and enterprizing turn would not fly, with alacrity, rather than ſubmit to the ſlaviſh and

"they have avoided ſome ſubjects of diſ-"pute, and have laid a foundation for re-"moving ſome cauſes of former alterca-"tion."

This, my Lords, was the temper of the Americans; and would have continued ſo, had it not been interrupted by your fruitleſs endeavours to tax them without their conſent; but the moment they perceived your intention was renewed to tax them, through the ſides of the Eaſt India Company, their reſentment got the aſcendant of their duty, and hurried them into actions contrary to all laws of policy, civilization, and humanity, which, in their cooler hours, they would have thought on with horror; for I ſeriouſly believe, the deſtroying of the Tea was much more the effect of deſpair, than that of deſign.

"into the Britiſh conſtitution as a funda-"mental law, and ever held ſacred and ir-"revocable by the ſubjects within the "realm; and that what a man has honeſtly "acquired, is abſolutely his own; which "he may freely give, but which cannot be "taken from him without his conſent."

This, my Lords, though no new doctrine, has been always my received and unalterable opinion; and I will carry it to my grave, *that this country had no right, under Heaven, to tax America*. It is contrary to all the principles of juſtice and civil policy, which neither the exigencies of the ſtate, or even the acquieſcence in the taxes, could juſtify upon any occaſion whatſoever. Such proceedings will never meet with their wiſhed for ſucceſs; and inſtead of adding to their miſeries, as the Bill now before you

William Pitt the Elder's speech in the House of Lords supporting the Quartering Act printed on a 1774 American broadside. (Library of Congress)

sum of £2,000 to supply the British regulars. But New York's civilians continued to clash with British soldiers. For the second time, British troops cut down a liberty pole. The colonists responded by preventing British troops from posting broadsides and then finally staging a full-scale riot on the city's Golden Hill in January 1770.

After the Golden Hill riot and then the Boston Massacre in March 1770, most British troops were kept in barracks that were fairly well removed from civilians, and friction between the two groups subsided in the so-called quiet period of 1770–1773. But in 1774, the deepening imperial crisis led the British government to give its officers in America new flexibility to quarter troops among civilians if they concluded that such quarters would give them a tighter control of colonial populations, especially in Massachusetts. In the wake of the Boston Tea Party, Parliament passed three acts to reassert British control of that rebellious province: the Boston Port Act (March 1774), the Massachusetts Government Act (May 1774), and the Administration of Justice Act (May 1774). To enforce these acts, the government appointed Gage the new governor of Massachusetts.

The Quartering Act of 2 June 1774 was intended to strengthen Gage's hand, although it applied to all of North America, not just to Massachusetts. This statute, unlike the 1765 act, authorized the housing of British troops in taverns and empty buildings, rather than barracks, whenever their commanders judged this helpful to their mission of suppressing popular resistance to British authority. Furthermore, for the first time Parliament legalized the use of occupied dwellings for British soldiers. The new Quartering Act officially expired on 24 March 1776, which happened to coincide exactly with the British Army's departure from Massachusetts. But by that date, full-scale war had broken out in North America, and the British Army operated thereafter under wartime rules, with no effective limits on the quartering of its troops, for the duration of the Revolutionary War.

CHRISTOPHER N. FRITSCH

See also
Boston Massacre; British Army; Coercive Acts; Gage, Thomas; Massachusetts; New York, Province and State; New York City

References
Alden, John Richard. *General Gage in America: Being Principally a History of His Role in the American Revolution*. Baton Rouge: Louisiana State University Press, 1948.

Ammerman, David. *In the Common Cause: American Response to the Coercive Acts of 1774*. New York: Norton, 1975.

Countryman, Edward. *A People in Revolution: The American Revolution and Political Society in New York, 1760–1790*. Baltimore, MD: Johns Hopkins University Press, 1981.

Shy, John. *Toward Lexington: The Role of the British Army in the Coming of the American Revolution*. Princeton, NJ: Princeton University Press, 1965.

Varga, Nicholas. "The New York Restraining Act: Its Passage and Some Effects, 1766–1768." *New York History* 37 (1956): 233–258.

Quebec, Siege of
(November 1775–May 1776)

The siege of Quebec City, in the province of Quebec, marked the successful defense of the last British stronghold in Canada by Major-General Guy Carleton against rebel forces led by Major General Richard Montgomery and Colonel Benedict Arnold.

Quebec had been founded in 1608, on the site of an Indian village named Stadacona. It was no stranger to conflict, having been besieged by the British successfully in 1629 and 1759 and unsuccessfully in 1690 and 1711 during the interminable colonial wars between France and Great Britain. By 1775, it had more than 1,500 houses and more than 5,000 inhabitants, the majority of them French-speaking but with a powerful merchant class of English-speaking British and American immigrants. The loyalty to the Crown of this group, which had arrived since 1763, was questionable, while that of the former French subjects was ambivalent at best. The city was divided into an upper and lower town, separated by a stockade that had two gates. One, for carriages, ran up a winding road, and the other, for pedestrians, led to a steep stairway cut into the rock. There were several churches but only two taverns, one in the upper town and one in the lower. The city was the seat of government in Canada and the home of Carleton, the governor of the province. At the outbreak of hostilities, Carleton had moved to

Benedict Arnold's attack on Quebec in the winter of 1775. (North Wind Picture Archives)

Montreal to be closer to the anticipated scene of operations on the Richelieu River and had left his lieutenant governor, Hector Cramahé, in charge of the city and of preparing its defenses.

Not surprisingly, the city figured large in the plans of Congress. Soon after the capture of Fort Ticonderoga in May 1775, Jonathan Brewer of Massachusetts submitted a plan for an attack on Quebec by 500 men through upper Massachusetts (present-day Maine) along a route long known to Indians, French missionaries, and, since 1761, the British Army (which had rejected it as a feasible route for moving large bodies of men). Though rejected initially, the plan was resurrected in July as part of a two-pronged invasion, designed to make Carleton disperse his numerically inferior forces across a wide area, preventing them from supporting each other. The western column, 3,000 men under Philip Schuyler (referred to as the Separate or Northern Army), would head north up Lake Champlain and the Richelieu River to St. John's, then on to Montreal, and finally east along the St. Lawrence. The eastern column, 1,050 volunteers led by Benedict Arnold, would head up the Kennebec River, over Height of Land and then down the Chaudière River to the St. Lawrence. The final target for both forces was Quebec City, possession of which would virtually guarantee victory in the struggle for Canada.

The Separate Army left Crown Point on 30 August and entered Canada via Île-aux-Noix at the head of Lake Champlain. With Montgomery taking over from Schuyler, who was ill, by mid-November the army had captured the British forts at St. John's and Chambly and also the city of Montreal. However, the two months taken to capture St. John's had left Montgomery precious little time to reach and capture Quebec before the onset of winter and the expiration of his soldiers' enlistments. Resting briefly to accumulate supplies and winter clothing, he set off for Quebec late in November.

Arnold's command had a rather less straightforward journey. Leaving Cambridge on 11 September, he and his troops sailed from Newburyport to the mouth of the Kennebec River. For the next seven weeks they trekked through the Maine wilderness, losing most of their supplies and equipment and suffering from hunger, thirst, and disease that forced a third of the troops to turn back. On the evening of 3 November, Arnold's column—now down to just 675 men—reached Sartigan, where he recruited 50 Abenaki warriors. He also learned of the capture of St. John's and immediately sent an officer to find boats and some riflemen to reconnoiter the St. Lawrence. As dawn broke on 8 November, the riflemen saw Quebec and the two warships in the middle of the river guarding it.

Unaware of the proximity of the enemy, Cramahé was trying to keep order inside Quebec. The city gates were shut at 6:00 every night, militia patrolled the streets, and American sympathizers were kept under surveillance. As reports came in of armed men seen at Point Levis, Cramahé had all canoes and boats removed from the south bank of the river and Île d'Orléans. On 3 November, the frigate *Lizard* arrived with money, uniforms, and 100 volunteers from Newfoundland, raising the morale of the citizens. Nine days later, Allan MacLean, Carleton's military deputy, returned from Sorel and—to the relief of the civilian Cramahé—took charge of the garrison of 1,126 men.

Despite Cramahé's efforts, Arnold found forty canoes, and on the night of 13 November his leading unit crossed the St. Lawrence and landed a mile above Wolfe's Cove. Although this group was spotted by a British patrol, by dawn the next day more than 500 men were across the river, but the ladders and 100 men were still stuck on the south bank. Moving onto the Plains of Abraham, Arnold called a council of war to discuss whether they should attack Quebec that night. Daniel Morgan, whose company of riflemen had led the invasion into Canada, was in favor but was outvoted; in fact, one of the city gates was unlocked and only lightly guarded. Morgan relieved his frustration by occupying the suburb of St. Foye, seizing large quantities of cattle and potatoes and looting houses.

That evening, one of Morgan's sentries was captured by a British patrol. Arnold quickly saw how to use the aggressive mind-set of the enemy to his advantage and tried to provoke an attack by forming his men in front of the city walls. Some shots were exchanged without loss to either side, but MacLean had several houses near Fort St.-Jean burned to deny cover to Morgan's riflemen. Arnold then sent a summons offering to spare private property if the city surrendered, but on 16 November a council of war voted unanimously to hold out. Two days later Arnold discovered that MacLean planned a sortie, but when an inventory showed that more than one hundred muskets were broken beyond repair and that there were fewer than five rounds each for the rest, even the belligerent Morgan agreed that they should retreat to Pointe aux Trembles, 20 miles west, and await Montgomery.

Once there, Arnold's men found plenty of food and winter clothing, but problems were emerging over his leadership style, and subordinates increasingly challenged his orders or refused to obey them at all (several later asked to be removed from his command). On 2 December, Montgomery landed at Pointe aux Trembles with around 1,000 men, and the combined force immediately left for Quebec. Montgomery set up headquarters in St. Foye, with his own men camped on the Plains of Abraham and Arnold's occupying St. Roche and the meadows by the St. Charles River. Montgomery had Arnold's Indians shoot messages to the merchants over the city walls and sent a summons to Carleton.

Carleton read it, had it burnt, and jailed the old woman who had carried it into the city. He then divided the garrison among his subordinates: MacLean took the regular and provincial troops (the 7th Foot, Marines, and Royal Highland Emigrants); the 150 sailors went to the naval officer, John Hamilton; Henry Caldwell took control of the British (English-speaking) militia; and Noël Voyer took control of their Canadian (French-speaking) counterpart. Meanwhile, Carleton's engineer, James Thompson, had block-houses, gun platforms, and barricades built to cover the main streets of the lower town.

Montgomery began bombarding the city with five mortars in St. Roche, but two days of shelling produced few casualties (thereby boosting civilian morale). More damaging were the riflemen picking off defenders on the city walls, though the danger was far from one-sided, with cannon fire making life equally dangerous for the Americans (one shell killed Montgomery's horse and destroyed his sleigh during an officers' conference). Montgomery responded by having a second battery built 700 yards from Fort St.-Jean, behind some houses. Temperatures had fallen to the point where digging was impossible, and the gunners built the breastworks from ice. This battery's location prevented the British from observing the effect of their return fire, so Carleton ordered the artillery to demolish the houses; however, his gunners accidentally set them on fire, and the blaze almost reached the city. With the houses gone, the battery was exposed and had to be abandoned on 17 December, after two guns were destroyed and ten gunners were killed or wounded. The next morning, Montgomery sent Arnold to the walls with another summons, this time offering Carleton and Cramahé safe passage to England. Arnold was forced to wait outside the gates until one of Carleton's staff leaned over the wall and said that the governor would neither read the letter nor negotiate with rebels.

With shortages of food and firewood and with enlistments due to expire, Montgomery was urged to storm the city without further delay. He informed General George Washington that he would attack during the first heavy snowstorm, concentrating his forces while the garrison watched their entire perimeter. On Christmas Day, Montgomery announced his scheme to the army and was cheered enthusiastically, but secretly many were pessimistic. Two days later, a snowstorm blew up that lasted into the night, and the troops made ready. Four companies of Arnold's men and the four New York regiments would assault the Cap Diamond bastion, while the rest broke into the lower town along the causeway beneath it. Just after midnight the weather cleared, and the attack was postponed—fortunately for the rebels, as a deserter had warned Carleton. At this time, total British strength stood at approximately 1,500, of whom 440 were regular or provincial troops and 860 were militia. The Americans mustered approximately 1,700 men.

Montgomery changed his plan but now found that smallpox had infected his troops. He set up a separate hospital, 3 miles to the rear, that was soon full, and his men defied orders not to inoculate themselves. On the afternoon of 30 December another storm developed, and at about 4:00 A.M. the next day Montgomery led 300 New Yorkers down to the river, planning to pass along the base of Cap Diamond and enter the lower town from the south. At the same time, Arnold took the main force of 600 men in from the north, via St. Roche and a long, winding road called the Sault au Matelot. Once in the lower town, Montgomery and Arnold would rendezvous and head into the upper town, hoping that the merchants would panic and force Carleton to surrender. (Carleton had anticipated such a plan and had issued

American troops, many of whom became lost in the streets of Quebec during the failed assault on the city in December 1775, were either killed or captured by the British and Canadian defenders. (Library of Congress)

orders to burn the warehouses and wharves if it happened.) Feints by James Livingston's Canadians against Fort St.-Jean and by John Brown against the Cap Diamond bastion would distract the garrison.

Montgomery led his men down to Wolfe's Cove and along a causeway just 24 feet wide, with a 300-foot precipice on the landward side and a steep drop down to the St. Lawrence on the other. As they neared Prés de Ville, they heard the bell of Notre Dame des Victoires above the blizzard—sentries had spotted lanterns in the swirling snow, and the city was being roused. Below Cap Diamond, a line of picket posts running from the river's edge to the cliff blocked their path. Montgomery slipped through a gap cut by his men and moved on to the next line, where he used a saw to cut through two posts next to the cliff. Leading a dozen officers and men through the second obstacle, he held a brief conference before ordering the group to head for a two-story blockhouse. Inside were four cannon, manned by fifty sailors and militiamen. Observing human shapes advancing through the snow, they opened fire at a range of 50 yards, killing Montgomery and most of the men with him. Command passed to Montgomery's deputy quartermaster, Donald Campbell, who, after consulting with the surviving officers, ordered a retreat. Unknown to Campbell, the occupants of the blockhouse were in such a state of panic that they could only be kept at their posts at bayonet point.

Arnold's column was led by 30 riflemen and a 6-pounder on a sled, then the remaining riflemen, two detachments of musket men, and about 150

Indians and Canadians, with more troops expected to join them from the north bank of the St. Charles. The column left St. Roche but was spotted near the Porte Palais and struck by musket fire and grenades, during which the gun became stuck in a drift and was abandoned. As the troops passed through the dockyard, they encountered the first barrier across the Sault au Matelot, defended by 30 militiamen and three cannon. With no artillery, Arnold could only launch a frontal attack but almost immediately was wounded in the leg and carried to the rear. Morgan took command, ran to the barrier, and sprang up the first ladder. Fire from the defenders' muskets scorched his face, and he fell off but climbed back up again, accompanied by two riflemen. More followed, and the post was captured in minutes, at the cost of 1 man dead and 6 men wounded. Morgan then sprinted to the next barricade, found the gate unguarded and unlocked, and looked inside. He returned to collect support, but his colleagues refused to move until the main body arrived; the delay—about thirty minutes—proved fatal.

Caldwell, in command at Cap Diamond, had realized that Brown's attack was a feint. As Caldwell went to report to Carleton, he learned of Arnold's attack on the Sault au Matelot and set off at once with some British militia, 30 Royal Highland Emigrants, and 50 sailors. At the second barricade, he found 200 French militia under Voyer and a company of the 7th Foot. Sending the militia and Emigrants into the surrounding houses, he formed up the 7th Foot in a double line behind the twelve-foot-high barricade and had cannon mounted on a platform immediately behind them pointing straight down the road.

Reinforced by some Pennsylvanians and the two detachments of musket men, Morgan went back to the second barricade. As he arrived, some sailors blocked his way, and their officer called on him to surrender. Morgan shot him dead, and the sailors retreated through the gate. Morgan and his men surged forward, shouting "Quebec is ours!" However, they were beaten back by a hail of musketry from the upper windows of the houses, and there was bayonet fighting in some of the buildings. The Americans might still have escaped had not several officers been hit simultaneously, at which Morgan ordered his men into unoccupied houses, where they were effectively trapped.

Carleton, now aware of events in the Sault au Matelot, ordered 500 Royal Highland Emigrants and sailors to sally out of the Porte Palais and retake the first barricade. By chance, they blundered straight into the American detachment from north of the St. Charles, which had become lost in St. Roche. With their powder damp from the snow, the entire detachment had to surrender. The commander of the British force then approached the first barricade alone and tried to bluff Morgan into surrendering, but he was captured at once. However, his men soon sealed off the barricade, and by 10:00 A.M. the Americans had run out of ammunition and were forced to surrender. The last to do so was Morgan himself, insisting on handing his sword to a priest rather than to a British officer.

Carleton then sent a small force to capture the battery in St. Roche and bring the guns back into the city, but that was as far as he went in exploiting his victory—much to the frustration of several subordinates (especially Caldwell, who believed that one big effort would have finished the enemy). Back on the Plains of Abraham, the wounded Arnold also believed that Carleton would follow up his success and issued muskets to the patients in the hospital while sending frantic messages for help to David Wooster at Montreal. In addition to Montgomery and 9 of the 12 men with him, Arnold had lost at least 30 dead and 382 captured, including 1 lieutenant colonel, 2 majors, 8 captains, 15 lieutenants, 1 adjutant, 4 volunteers, 1 quartermaster, and 350 enlisted men. Another 44 officers and men had been wounded and were prisoners. The spring thaw would reveal 30 more dead, and there were reports that others had fallen through the ice while fleeing across the St. Charles. Carleton's losses were 6 dead and 1 wounded.

Montgomery's body was found the next day, and on 2 January 1776 Carleton allowed the personal belongings of the prisoners to be brought into the city. With 100 enlistments expiring on 31 December, Arnold now had barely 600 fit men and could do no more than stop food and firewood from entering the city. He also had buildings close to the city and even some of the ships moored in the river burned, though this had little impact. Wooster, who also had only 600 men left, had refused to leave Montreal, fearing an uprising in his absence. He had sent word to Schuyler, at Albany, but the latter was also short of men, and his few remaining troops were needed to defend the Mohawk Valley against raids by Loyalists and Indians. Congress still refused to authorize long-term enlistments (or even to offer bounties for reenlistment) and asked New Hampshire, Massachusetts, and Connecticut to raise another regiment each to serve in Canada. However, even these prolific colonies were struggling to find recruits. Informed of the situation in Canada, Washington contemplated resignation.

The winter of 1775–1776 was one of the worst in living memory. Eventually, reinforcements came in from New Jersey and Pennsylvania, but even they were in a poor state physically and militarily after their long journey, and they arrived to find that many of Arnold's troops had smallpox. Equally worrying was the lack of hard cash: in March, Arnold announced that civilians accepting paper money would receive full payment in gold within four months. It was a lie, but it kept his men supplied for a few more months. Even so, looting at bayonet point became rife and led even pro-American Canadians to reconsider their loyalties. On 23 March, 300 militiamen marched against Arnold's outpost at Point Lévis but were ambushed by a mixed force of New Yorkers and rebel Canadians.

Total American strength by the end of March stood at approximately 2,900, of whom 800 were unfit due to smallpox (either sick or inoculated) and 426 were prisoners in Quebec. At about this time, Wooster replaced Arnold, who went back to take control of Montreal. By now, the Americans were reduced to indiscriminate shelling of the upper and lower towns. A battery at Point Lévis opened fire on 2 April, throwing red-hot shot into the town and at ships in the St. Lawrence. The following day another battery appeared opposite the Porte St. Louis, and several days later a third appeared on the north side of the St. Charles. However, lack of trained gunners stopped them from competing with the 150 guns mounted on the walls of Quebec or with Carleton's industry and manpower. When a foraging party found scaling ladders hidden in front of the St. Louis bastion, Carleton ordered the snow cleared from the ditch, barricaded the lower town with blocks of ice from the river, built two blockhouses outside the walls, and cut a trench in the river ice under Cap Diamond to prevent the picket barriers from being outflanked. In reality, though, there was more threat from the prisoners inside Quebec; both the officers (in the seminary) and the enlisted men (in the Récollet Monastery, and later the Dauphine Bastion) attempted mass escapes, but each attempt was thwarted. Some did find a way out: 94 men were recruited into MacLean's regiment from among the British-born prisoners, but within days 14 had deserted, and Carleton had the rest disarmed.

On 1 May, as the spring thaw began, John Thomas of Massachusetts replaced Wooster and brought 1,200 more men. Two days later, the river was open, and a fireship was sent against the vessels moored at the Queen's Wharf under cover of darkness. The operation, which failed, proved to be the last aggressive act of the American forces against Quebec. Concerned at the condition of his men, Thomas was already considering a withdrawal to Jacques Cartier and Deschambault when the British frigate *Surprise* and the sloops *Isis* and *Martin* unloaded 200 soldiers and marines. Carleton ordered an immediate sortie, attacking the American camp with 900 men and turning their withdrawal into a rout. By 7 May, Thomas was in Deschambault and under heavy bombardment from British ships. With many troops sick and Carleton now able to land troops in his rear, Thomas fell back to Sorel. Once again, Carleton did little to follow up his success, preferring to keep the smallpox-ridden enemy at a healthy distance; initiating a charm offensive by behaving humanely to his prisoners (the officers taken at Quebec were paroled, each receiving gold and a new shirt as he went home); and sending out militia to collect starving American stragglers and nonwalking wounded. With the arrival of a new army, commanded by John Burgoyne, at the beginning of June, the threat to Quebec was finally removed.

BRENDAN D. MORRISSEY

See also
Arnold, Benedict; Canada, Operations in; Carleton, Guy; Chambly, Quebec, Action at; Montgomery, Richard; Montreal, Operations against; Morgan, Daniel; Schuyler, Philip; St. John's, Actions against

References
Hatch, Robert. *Thrust for Canada: The American Attempt on Quebec, 1775–1776*. Boston: Houghton Mifflin, 1979.

Lanctot, Gustave. *Canada and the American Revolution, 1774–1783*. London: Harrap, 1967.

Morrissey, Brendan. *Quebec 1775: The American Invasion of Canada*. Oxford, UK: Osprey, 2004.

Stanley, George. *Canada Invaded, 1775–1776*. Toronto: Canadian War Museum, 1973.

In May and June 1774, Parliament and King George III devised and approved the Quebec Act, thereby reorganizing a government for Quebec, which Britain had seized from France at the end of the Seven Years' War.

The Quebec Act was an attempt to deal with problems that had arisen for Britain as it assimilated an old and large French colony into the British Empire. Under the first British governor, James Murray, and his successor, Guy Carleton, a number of major questions arose, such as whether the province should have a legislative assembly. Most of the old French inhabitants did not want one, and as Roman Catholics they would in any case be excluded from membership, under prevailing British law, because of the Test Acts. But newly arrived English settlers wanted an assembly. Also at issue was whether the Roman Catholic religion should be allowed to continue (and under what restrictions or regulations) and whether French or English law should be used in the province's courts. Carleton, who became governor in 1766, generally supported the French citizens in these matters and conducted surveys of the populace for the home government in preparation for making the changes that he felt were necessary. He firmly believed that the old French citizens should be allowed to keep their religion, and he forcefully asserted that no assembly was needed or desired by the majority of the inhabitants. As for the law, he advised that the French inhabitants be allowed to retain French legal codes. In fact, on 1 February 1770, he and his council enacted legal reforms that allowed French law to be used for the court of Common Pleas, without waiting for approval from Britain.

In August 1770, Carleton returned to London in order to expedite the process of legislative reform. He continued to argue for French usages, but by 1773 he was disgusted at the slowness with which Parliament dealt with the creation of a new government for Quebec. Progress looked even more doubtful in early 1774, as Parliament passed the Coercive (Intolerable) Acts in response to the destruction of tea at Boston in December 1773. Finally, however, the Lord North ministry was stung into action by the fear that Quebec's French-speaking citizens might join the growing rebellion in the neighboring British colonies to the south. On 17 May, North introduced the Quebec bill into the House of Lords, and a few days later it came down to the House of Commons. In a deposition to the Commons in early June, Carleton reiterated most of his earlier views in favor of the French-speaking Canadians but conceded that the use of English criminal law should be incorporated into the new judicial system. Despite some opposition, the Quebec bill passed both houses of Parliament with ease and was ratified on 22 June 1774 by George III.

The provisions of the Quebec Act generally pleased Carleton, for they strongly reflected his advice. The governor and his council were given full power to legislate, because Parliament believed it was inexpedient to erect an elective assembly. Full freedom of religion was allowed for Roman Catholics, and the Church was permitted to continue to collect tithes. The Test Acts

A cartoon attacking the Quebec Act of 1774, showing Lord Bute and a member of Parliament threatening colonial America, with the French Catholic city of Quebec high in the background and, below, the British Protestant town of Boston in flames and a blindfolded figure of Britannia about to stumble into a pit. (Library of Congress)

were rescinded for Quebec, and an oath of allegiance was substituted to allow Roman Catholics to hold civil offices. French civil law was retained, but the criminal law was to be English. The boundaries of Quebec were vastly extended, to the Ohio and Mississippi Rivers to the south and west and as far as the Hudson's Bay Company territory to the north. This last measure was approved because the government had found no other alternative for governing old French settlers who lived on the frontier and for the effective administration of the Native American tribes. The Quebec Act was essentially a statesmanlike measure, designed to deal with a number of separate problems.

In August 1774 Carleton returned to Quebec, and on 20 September he reported to London that the French-speaking citizens were delighted with the new law. He probably exaggerated, for the strongest support was limited to Quebec's clergy and its quasi-feudal seigneurs, with the majority of the inhabitants assuming a more wait-and-see attitude. The English settlers in the western parts of Canada, however, despised the new legislation. On 18 November, Carleton reported to London that they were seething with outrage, even though they had submitted to the new arrangements. He believed that they were emulating the reactions of the southern colonists, where the measure was violently resented because of its recognition of the Roman Catholic religion and the act's engrossing of territories long claimed by several colonies based on boundary clauses in their original charters.

To most British North Americans, the Quebec Act was seen as nothing less than a restoration of the old French empire destroyed in 1763 and the cutting off of their destiny in the West. The Roman Catholic provisions were particularly resented in New England, where anti-Catholic feeling was virulent. The lack of an assembly for Canada was universally seen in the thirteen colonies south of Canada as a direct assault upon representative government. Therefore, the lower colonists considered the Quebec Act as simply another Coercive Act, as further proof of British tyranny, and it thus became yet another cause of the American Revolution. In time, however, the Quebec Act became as important to French Canadians as the Magna Carta was for the English because it established the basis of their religious, legal, and cultural rights as a distinct people.

PAUL DAVID NELSON

See also
British Parliament; Canada; Carleton, Guy; Coercive Acts; George III, King of England; North, Lord Frederick

References
Cavendish, Henry. *Debates in the House of Commons in the Year 1774 on the Bill for Making More Effectual Provision for the Government of the Province of Quebec.* London: J. Wright, 1839.

Christie, Ian R. *Crisis of Empire: Great Britain and the American Colonies, 1754–1783.* New York: Norton, 1966.

Coupland, Sir Reginald. *The Quebec Act: A Study in Statesmanship.* Reprint. Oxford: Oxford University Press, 1968.

Nelson, Paul David. *General Sir Guy Carleton, Lord Dorchester: Soldier-Statesman of Early British Canada.* Madison, NJ: Fairleigh Dickinson University Press, 2000.

Quinby Bridge, South Carolina, Action at
(17 July 1781)

At Quinby Bridge, north of Charleston, South Carolina, a Patriot militia force failed to halt the withdrawal of a British garrison from Moncks Corner to Charleston. The frontal-assault tactics of Patriot commander Thomas Sumter did result, however, in Francis Marion, known as the "Swamp Fox," and Lieutenant Colonel Henry Lee refusing to cooperate with a commander whom they viewed as reckless with the lives of his men.

A series of small Patriot victories in South Carolina continued to drive British troops back from their country garrisons to their main base of operations in Charleston. The British evacuated their garrison at Moncks Corner in July 1781. As the troops marched southward to Charleston, Patriot forces pursued them. The British commander, Lieutenant-Colonel John Coates, ordered his men, numbering between 650 and 750 regulars and Loyalist militia, to burn their supplies at Biggin Church and slip away at night to avoid the Patriot troops in the area. The Patriots, led by Marion, Sumter, and Lee, spotted the flames and initiated a chase to catch the British force.

Coates split his unit and sent the majority toward Quinby Bridge but directed approximately 150 dragoons to a ferry point. The Patriots divided their force as well and continued to chase both groups of British soldiers. The British dragoons safely crossed the river ahead of a pursuit force led by Lee and tied the single boat at the far shore, thereby frustrating a Patriot attempt to cross. The other British soldiers reached Quinby Bridge, where they loosened the boards in anticipation of removing them after all of their troops crossed. They also erected a hasty defensive position at the crossing. But Lee's cavalry quickly rejoined the main Patriot force and caught up to the British rear guard. Most of the inexperienced British recruits threw down their weapons and fled at the sight of the American cavalry, but a sufficient number of them resisted stoutly enough to delay Lee. A small number of his cavalry continued after Coates, while Lee remained with the main body to gather prisoners.

Lee's advance force emerged out of the darkness suddenly and crossed the still-intact bridge before the British troops could gather their weapons and form a defensive line, but Lee's horses kicked off many of the loosened boards in the process. A second force leaped across the gaps, thereby causing more damage. The third force could not cross the bridge and join the others, who were now fighting the British troops on the far side of the river. With Lee overseeing the gathering of prisoners from the British rear guard, the American cavalry lacked the leadership capable of organizing the two separated groups of men at the bridge. Many British recruits fled the scene, but others offered such stout resistance that vicious hand-to-hand fighting broke out at the site before Lee finally arrived. It was too late, however, to organize the cavalry for a rescue of those stranded on the far side of the river. The Americans finally broke contact with the British and fled upstream to a ford to try to join the other Americans later.

The British force withdrew to a plantation situated on a hill overlooking the bridge. The next day, Sumter and Marion joined Lee, and the overall command passed to Sumter, who ignored prudent advice to await an artillery piece and ordered an assault on the British forces in the plantation buildings. The assault proved ineffective and resulted in numerous casualties. The Patriot leaders immediately began arguing about the day's events and criticized Sumter for his rash frontal assault. Lee and Marion then refused to allow Sumter to command their troops and departed from the area. Without the assistance of the other two leaders, Sumter was also forced to withdraw. Coates then moved his force to the safety of Charleston. The Patriot forces lost approximately 60 total casualties, while the British casualties numbered 6 dead and 38 wounded.

TERRY M. MAYS

See also
Lee, Henry; Marion, Francis; Sumter, Thomas

Reference
Bass, Robert. *Swamp Fox: The Life and Campaigns of General Francis Marion.* 1959. Reprint, Orangeburg, SC: Sandlapper, 1989.

Josiah Quincy Jr., often called "the Patriot" to distinguish him from his father and his son, who both shared the name, was an eloquent orator and publicist for the Patriot cause. His premature death, in the same month as the battles at Lexington and Concord, ended the career of one of the Revolution's most dedicated young leaders.

The Quincy family of Boston and Braintree (later Quincy), Massachusetts, was one of the most prominent in its province, with a rich legacy of Harvard-educated merchants, landowners, and magistrates. Young Quincy was the son of Colonel Josiah Quincy, a prosperous merchant, and Hannah Sturgis. His older brother Samuel (1735–1789) was a prominent barrister whose allegiance to the Loyalist cause led him to break with his Patriot father and depart the colonies for England in May 1775, immediately after young Josiah's death.

Quincy graduated from Harvard College in 1763. Three years later, he was awarded a master's degree from Harvard and was selected to deliver the first English oration given at a commencement. Speaking in the euphoric aftermath of the repeal of the hated Stamp Act, Quincy chose the topic of patriotism for his address, drawing upon the rhetoric of William Shakespeare and the political ideas of John Locke. In these same years, under the guidance of his older brother, Quincy pursued a career in law, procuring an apprenticeship with Oxenbridge Thacher, one of Boston's leading attorneys. When Thacher died in 1765, Quincy inherited his lucrative practice. Quincy also established himself as Massachusetts's first court reporter, recording cases tried in the Superior Court of Judicature from 1761 through 1772. With his professional career well established, he married Abigail Phillips, the daughter of Boston merchant William Phillips, in October 1769. The marriage produced two children, and the couple's son, Josiah Quincy (1772–1864), later called "the President," served as a member of Congress, mayor of Boston, and president of Harvard University.

Although he was an ardent Patriot, Quincy was opposed to mob protest and violence. At the same time, however, he was an avid foe of Massachusetts's leading royal officeholder, Thomas Hutchinson, toward whom Quincy expressed both personal and political animosity. During the late 1760s, he wrote numerous anonymous newspaper essays opposing British policy toward the colonies. His reputation as an attorney and as a Patriot led to his being tapped by Thomas Cushing, Samuel Adams, John Hancock, and his father-in-law William Phillips to assist John Adams in defending Captain Thomas Preston and eight British solders accused of murder arising from the Boston Massacre of March 1770. Many Patriot leaders believed that

Portrait of Josiah Quincy Jr., Patriot orator and publicist (1744–1775). (Library of Congress)

the British soldiers must receive the best available defense in order to establish that the rule of law and not vigilante justice governed Boston. The eloquent Quincy maintained that if a crime was committed, it was manslaughter rather than murder. He argued that all true friends of liberty and the rights of citizens would vote to acquit the soldiers. The arguments of Quincy and Adams were persuasive. The jury totally acquitted Preston and six of the soldiers and convicted the other two soldiers of manslaughter.

Following the publicity of the Boston Massacre trials, Quincy grew increasingly vocal in his denunciation of British policy, penning numerous essays for the Patriot cause. In 1772 he was elected to Boston's radical new Committee of Correspondence. Along with James Otis Jr. and Samuel Adams, Quincy was charged with preparing a pamphlet to protest the Crown's control of the province's judiciary. Before he could complete this task, he suffered from a severe bout of tuberculosis. His physicians suggested that he travel to South Carolina for his health. While in South Carolina and during his overland return to Massachusetts, he used his political skills to develop channels of communication between Patriots in Boston and those in the Carolinas, the Chesapeake region, and Pennsylvania.

After his return to Massachusetts in May 1773, Quincy maintained an active role as a Whig publicist. Perhaps his most significant piece was *Observations on the Act of Parliament Commonly Called the Boston Port-Bill, with Thoughts on Civil Society and Standing Armies* (1774). In criticizing Parliament's response to the Boston Tea Party, he condemned the punishment of an entire community for the actions of a few private individuals. He also attacked the standing armies established by Britain as "armed monsters" who threatened liberty. He asserted that if defending one's country amounted to treason and rebellion, then "like my fathers [his Puritan and politically dissenting seventeenth-century ancestors], I will glory in the name of rebel and traitor."

Although he continued to suffer from tuberculosis, Quincy undertook a journey to London in September 1774 hoping to provide his Boston colleagues with political intelligence regarding British plans for the colonies and perhaps to find a way to accommodate the growing rift between Britain and its colonies. While in London, he used his contacts to arrange meetings with powerful English politicians such as Lords North, Dartmouth, and Shelburne. Quincy believed that the results of his investigations were too sensitive to entrust to written correspondence. Accordingly, on 10 March 1775, he set sail for Boston, intending to convey his findings personally to American leaders. Some six weeks later, on 26 April 1775, just as his ship reached the harbor in Gloucester, Massachusetts, he died from his recurring tuberculosis. His political intelligence for the Boston Patriots died with him, although the battles at Lexington and Concord just one week earlier must have rendered much of his information obsolete.

RON BRILEY

See also
Boston Massacre; Massachusetts

References

Brown, Richard D. "Quincy, Josiah." Pp. 36–37 in *American National Biography*, Vol. 18. New York: Oxford University Press, 1999.

Quincy, Josiah. *Memoir of the Life of Josiah Quincy, Jun. of Mass: By His Son, Josiah Quincy*. Boston: Cummings, Hillier, 1825.

Quincy Family Papers, 1639–1930. Unpublished. Boston: Massachusetts Historical Society, 36 linear feet.

Shaw, Peter. *American Patriots and the Ritual of Revolution*. Cambridge: Harvard University Press, 1981.

R

Nathaniel Ramsay is best known for his heroic resistance to the British at the Battle of Monmouth, a resistance that bought General George Washington time to reverse General Charles Lee's retreat and regain control of the field of battle.

Ramsay was born to Irish immigrants in Lancaster County, Pennsylvania, on 1 May 1741. He was the older brother of historian David Ramsay. Nathaniel, who generally spelled his surname "Ramsey" but was usually named "Ramsay" in contemporary records, graduated from the College of New Jersey (now Princeton) and settled in Maryland to practice law. He signed the Declaration of Freemen at the Maryland Convention in 1775 and later served as a delegate to the Continental Congress.

On 14 January 1776, Ramsay was selected as captain of Colonel William Smallwood's Maryland Regiment. When this became the 3rd Maryland Regiment of the Continental Army on 10 July, Ramsay was commissioned as lieutenant colonel. Barely a month later, on 27 August, his regiment distinguished itself against Hessian troops during the Battle of Long Island.

Ramsay and his unit gained fame for halting the American retreat at Monmouth on 28 June 1778, giving Washington time to rally his army. Washington personally credited Ramsay's 3rd Maryland and Colonel Walter Stewart's 13th Pennsylvania Regiments with keeping the enemy from gaining the ground that other American units abandoned. The British forced the two rebel regiments back, but slowly enough on that sweltering afternoon to give Washington an estimated half hour to regroup his forces.

Ramsay was the last American commander to retreat at Monmouth. After his horse was shot from beneath him, he fought on foot with several soldiers of the British 16th Dragoons, dueling man-to-man with his sword. He was wounded and taken prisoner, but the British commander, General Sir Henry Clinton, was so impressed by Ramsay's bravery that he ordered the injured captive released on parole. Ramsay was returned to the Continental Army on 29 June or soon thereafter and was taken to Princeton to recuperate.

The 3rd Maryland Regiment went on to take part in the battles at Camden, South Carolina, and at Yorktown, but the British did not officially

Ramsay, Nathaniel
(1741–1817)

exchange Ramsay until 14 December 1780, and he retired from the army on 1 January 1781. Along with his brother David, he served in Congress from 1785 through 1787. From 1790 to 1798, he was U.S. marshal for Maryland, and he served as naval officer at the port of Baltimore from 1794 until his death on 23 October 1817.

KELLY HENSLEY

See also
Maryland; Monmouth, Battle of; Smallwood, William; Stewart, Walter

References
Boatner, Mark. *Encyclopedia of the American Revolution.* Mechanicsburg, PA: Stackpole, 1994.

Montross, Lynn. *The Reluctant Rebels: The Story of the Continental Congress, 1774–1789.* New York: Harper, 1950.

Smith, Samuel Stelle. *The Battle of Monmouth.* Monmouth Beach, NJ: Philip Freneau, 1964.

Stryker, William S. *The Battle of Monmouth.* 1927. Reprint, Port Washington, NY: Kennikat, 1970.

Ramseur's Mill, North Carolina, Action at
(20 June 1780)

On 20 June 1780, North Carolina militia forces under Colonel Francis Locke attacked and defeated a party of North Carolina Loyalists commanded by Colonel John Moore at Ramseur's Mill in Lincoln County, North Carolina. After Charleston surrendered on 12 May 1780 to General Charles Cornwallis, the British proceeded to occupy the interior parts of South Carolina. They established strong posts at Camden, Cheraw, Georgetown, Rocky Mount, and Ninety-Six in preparation for an advance into North Carolina. The North Carolina Loyalists enthusiastically welcomed this news, sending Cornwallis reports of their strength and urging him to march northward. But Cornwallis, preferring to stay put during the heat of the summer, instructed the Loyalists to remain quiescent until later in the year.

However, there were a number of Loyalists in North Carolina who refused to delay. One of these was Moore, who lived near Ramseur's Mill. In early June he returned from service under Cornwallis, wearing a battered Provincial uniform and a sword. He announced himself a lieutenant colonel in John Hamilton's North Carolina Loyalist regiment and called for the Loyalists to rally to the king's standard at Ramseur's Mill on 13 June. Within a week he had collected 1,300 men, three-fourths of them armed. Meanwhile, Patriots from North Carolina prepared to resist Cornwallis's coming invasion. General Griffith Rutherford called on the state's militia to rally at a plantation near Charlotte, and 800 responded. Locke gathered 400 men at Mountain Creek, not far from Ramseur's Mill. A third group collected under the command of Major Joseph McDowell. When Rutherford learned of Moore's Loyalist army at Ramseur's Mill, he realized that it was too dangerous to be ignored, but he did not wish to leave Charlotte undefended. He therefore ordered Locke, who was closest to Moore's camp, to attack the Loyalists there.

On 19 June, Locke and his militia marched out to surprise the Loyalists at Ramseur's Mill. Leading the expedition were three small groups of mounted men and the rest of Locke's force; an unorganized body of undisciplined, amateur soldiers followed in double file. Moore's troops, equally undisciplined and amateur, were encamped along the crest of a ridge, about 300 yards from the mill. They appeared to be in a fairly secure defensive position, and they also outnumbered their attackers by more than three to one. The ridge in front of their position was free of undergrowth and offered them an open field of fire. In front of their position, at a distance of 600 yards, Moore had posted a picket guard of a dozen men. When Locke's horsemen approached quietly through the woods on 20 June, the pickets fired an irregular volley and fled to the camp, throwing it into a panic. The horsemen thundered after them up the hill, far ahead of their own infantry, causing the unarmed Loyalists to flee. But the rest of Moore's men, seeing that the attackers were few in number, rallied, opened fire, and drove the horsemen back down the hill. Then the Loyalists attacked, pursuing the retreating Patriots.

Just then, the rest of Locke's men arrived. They quickly formed a line at the foot of the slope, commenced firing, and drove the Loyalists back up the slope and over the brow of the ridge. The Loyalists rallied and came forward again, but by then Locke's men had surrounded the ridge, with small parties gaining the Loyalists' right and left flanks. Moore's men then retreated once more, this time to the top of the hill. In none of these movements did either Moore or Locke exercise any control, and the battle was becoming chaotic. It was only by haphazard movement that the Patriots had flanked Moore's position, but they had gained the rear of the Loyalists and closed with them in hand-to-hand combat. Neither side had bayonets, so they used clubbed muskets, rocks, and fists to batter each other. Although for identification the Loyalists wore green sprigs in their hats and the Patriots wore pieces of white paper, these were lost in the melee, and it became difficult to discern friend from foe. Quite likely, friend assaulted friend on both sides in the frenzy of hatred let loose by civil war.

For a time, the contest was equal as a Loyalist captain named Warlick rallied his men over and over again. Then a Patriot, William Shays, shot and killed Warlick, causing the Loyalists to break and flee down the far side of the hill and across a creek. There they halted, while Locke attempted to form his men along the hilltop in anticipation of another Tory assault. He could collect only 150 of his original 400 men, so he sent an urgent message to Rutherford, who was marching to his assistance, asking him to hasten forward. But Moore's men were in no mood for further combat. They sent a flag to Locke, asking for a truce to bury their dead and collect their wounded, but before Locke could reply they departed the field by ones and twos. Locke's men were in such disarray that he could not pursue the Loyalists, so Moore finally led 30 men to Camden, where he joined Lieutenant-Colonel Francis Rawdon. Despite the comic opera aspects of the affair, both sides suffered about 70 killed and 100 wounded. The North Carolina Loyalists, however, suffered more grievously. Demoralized that the Patriots seemed to be winning the war, they never again rallied to support the British in the numbers that might have made a strategic difference.

PAUL DAVID NELSON

See also
Charleston, South Carolina, Expedition against (1780); Cornwallis, Charles; Loyalist Units; Militia, Patriot and Loyalist; Rawdon, Francis

References
DeMond, Robert O. *The Loyalists in North Carolina during the Revolution*. Durham, NC: Duke University Press, 1940.

Morrill, Dan L. *Southern Campaigns of the American Revolution*. Baltimore, MD: Nautical and Aviation Publishing Company of America, 1993.

Rankin, Hugh. *North Carolina in the American Revolution*. Raleigh, NC: Division of Archives and History, 1959.

Ward, Christopher. *War of the Revolution*. 2 vols. New York: Macmillan, 1952.

Randolph, Edmund Jennings
(1753–1813)

Edmund Jennings Randolph was a leading Virginia politician during and after the Revolutionary War, served as the nation's first attorney general in the cabinet of President George Washington, and succeeded Thomas Jefferson as secretary of state, an office that Randolph was forced to resign in a dispute with Washington over America's relations with the French Republic.

Randolph was born into one of Virginia's most powerful and respected families. On the eve of the Revolutionary War, his father, John Randolph, who was the king's attorney in the province, decided to remain loyal to Great Britain. The young Randolph, however, supported the Revolution, and when the war commenced he refused to follow his father into exile in Great Britain. He went instead to live with his uncle Peyton Randolph, who was both the Speaker of Virginia's House of Burgesses and president of the Continental Congress. The younger Randolph also joined the Continental Army in 1775, and Washington, acting upon the joint recommendation of Jefferson, Patrick Henry, and Richard Henry Lee, appointed Randolph an aide-de-camp. He did not remain in the army for long, however, but returned to Virginia following the sudden death of Peyton Randolph in October 1775.

In 1776, Randolph was chosen as a member of the Virginia Convention, where he helped draft the first Virginia Constitution. He was also appointed to oversee the muster of the Williamsburg militia, a position he resigned because of his responsibilities at the convention and in a new political office. In November 1776, he was elected attorney general of the Commonwealth of Virginia, a post he held until 1786. While serving in that office, he was elected mayor of Williamsburg, and in 1779 he was elected to the Continental Congress. In Congress, he was noted for his efforts to enact a tariff to provide funds for the national government. He was particularly effective in ensuring that Virginia complied with congressional requests for monies to support the Continental Army. In the last two years of the war, he also attempted, unsuccessfully, to pass legislation to prevent the reestablishment of trade between the United States and Great Britain.

After the Revolutionary War, Randolph defeated Richard Henry Lee in Virginia's 1786 gubernatorial election. The following year, Randolph was elected to represent his state at the national Constitutional Convention. There he presented the Virginia Plan for constitutional reform, which favored the more populous states. As the convention proceeded with its work, however, he became increasingly critical of its decisions, and he finally joined Virginia's George Mason and Massachusetts's Elbridge Gerry in refusing to sign the finished document.

When Washington formed his cabinet in 1789, he chose Randolph as the nation's first attorney general. In 1794, Randolph succeeded Jefferson as secretary of state but did not hold this post for long. Randolph disagreed with Washington over the Jay Treaty with Great Britain, unsuccessfully urging the president not to sign it. And in 1795, the British minister to the United States charged that Randolph had revealed secrets to the French envoy. After heatedly denying the charge to Washington, Randolph resigned his post. He later served as Aaron Burr's chief counsel during Burr's treason trial in 1807. After several years of financial difficulties and poor health, Randolph died in 1813.

Tom Lansford

Virginia Governor Edmund Randolph initially refused to sign the U.S. Constitution, fearing that it gave the executive too much power. However, he pressed for ratification when he realized that Virginia needed the stability and resources that accompanied membership in the newly forming nation. (Library of Congress)

See also

Congress, Second Continental and Confederation; Constitution, United States; Henry, Patrick; Jay, John; Jefferson, Thomas; Lee, Richard Henry; Randolph, Peyton; Virginia; Washington, George

References

Daniels, Jonathan. *The Randolphs of Virginia.* Garden City, NJ: Doubleday, 1972.
Reardon, John J. *Edmund Randolph: A Biography.* New York: Macmillan, 1975.

One of the most respected leaders in colonial Virginia, Peyton Randolph became an early defender of American political rights in the years leading up to the Revolution and was the first president of the Continental Congress.

Randolph was a member of one of the most prominent families in the Tidewater. His father, John Randolph, had studied law at the Inns of Court

Randolph, Peyton
(1721–1775)

Peyton Randolph, a Virginian, served as president of the First Continental Congress. He served in various assemblies before the war but died a month after hostilities began. (National Archives and Records Administration)

in London and later served as the representative from the College of William and Mary in the Virginia House of Burgesses. When on a mission to England on behalf of the college, he was knighted on the recommendation of Prime Minister Robert Walpole. Sir John Randolph, the only Virginian ever so honored in the colonial period, returned home to Williamsburg and continued his political career. He eventually became the Speaker of the House of Burgesses and the treasurer of Virginia. He died soon after leaving his library and substantial holdings to Peyton, his eldest son, along with other property to his wife, daughter, and another son named John.

Following in his father's footsteps, Randolph studied law at the Middle Temple in London before returning home to Virginia to begin his own political career. He married Elizabeth Harrison, the oldest daughter of another prominent Virginia family, and won election to the House of Burgesses as the representative from Williamsburg. He quickly won the respect of all who knew him in the Virginia capital. He was calm and pleasant, and he listened attentively to the concerns of his fellow legislators. He was also far better educated than most of the other lawyers in the region. He soon came to the attention of Lieutenant Governor William Gooch, who named Randolph attorney general for the colony in 1748. For most of the next twenty years, he served Virginia by providing legal advice to the governor and his council on all matters related to English and colonial law. Randolph won the respect of his fellow Virginians and even many Englishmen for the role he played in the Pistole Fee Dispute in 1752. Robert Dinwiddie, the new lieutenant governor had decided to affix the seal of the colony to every land patent and charge a fee of one pistole in the process. The representatives in the House of Burgesses protested that they had the exclusive right to lay taxes on the colony and that Dinwiddie had overstepped his powers. They sent Randolph to England to appeal their case directly to the Privy Council.

Although seemingly a minor issue, the Pistole Fee Dispute laid out the essential debate that would continue between Great Britain and its colonies in the coming years. While Virginians believed that only the House of Burgesses had the right to tax the colony, representatives for the Crown argued before the Privy Council that the "little assembly" in Williamsburg had no real power. The king owned all the land in America, and therefore the lieutenant governor, his rightful representative, could dispose of it as he pleased. Randolph returned to Virginia with a compromise. The lieutenant governor could place the seal on all pending land patents. In the future, he could also place it on any land patent of one hundred acres or more east of the Alleghenies. Patents for land west of the mountains would not require a seal.

Randolph arrived back in Virginia just as the French and Indian War broke out. He resumed his post as attorney general and worked to arm the militia on the western frontier. After the war ended, he found himself at the center of the growing conflict between Britain and the colonies. As a member of the House of Burgesses, he participated in the many debates over the best way to respond to higher taxes and tighter imperial controls. During the Stamp Act crisis of 1765, he worked to craft a clear statement of colonial rights without using the extreme language proposed by his fellow representative Patrick Henry.

In 1766, John Robinson, the longtime Speaker of the House and treasurer of Virginia, died suddenly. Robinson had loaned currency to friends instead of removing it from circulation and had thus left the colony with a £100,000 debt. Randolph was elected Speaker of the House and set to work restoring the tarnished image of his office. He made the position of treasurer an independent post and recommended that the Speaker be paid a salary. He also increased the size of standing committees in order to give younger burgesses a voice in colonial affairs. But his efforts to reform Virginia politics were soon overshadowed by the colonial reaction to the Townshend duties. Randolph oversaw the passage of the Virginia Resolves, which declared the right of the House of Burgesses to tax the colony, the right of colonists to petition the Crown directly for redress, and the right of colonists accused of crimes to be tried in the colonies.

Conflict between Great Britain and the colonies grew more violent after the passage of the Tea Act. When the port of Boston was closed, Randolph called for a day of prayer and fasting in Virginia so that the colony could show its support for Massachusetts. The royal governor, Lord Dunmore, promptly dissolved the House of Burgesses. Randolph joined his fellow burgesses at the Raleigh Tavern, where they formed the Virginia Association. The group elected Randolph as its moderator, urged a boycott of British goods, and recommended that a congress be called to plan the response of the colonies to the Intolerable Acts.

Randolph was chosen as a delegate to the First Continental Congress along with leaders such as Henry, George Washington, Richard Henry Lee, and Benjamin Harrison. Randolph was elected president of the Congress in September 1774 and was again elected president by the Second Continental Congress in May 1775. Between congressional sessions, he regularly returned to Virginia, where he served as Speaker of the House when it was in session and as president of the Virginia Association. Despite his failing health, he returned to the third session of Congress, more convinced than ever that the colonies were moving toward independence. On 22 October 1775, however, Randolph died of a stroke before he could affect the movement of Congress in this direction.

MARY STOCKWELL

See also

Congress, First Continental; Congress, Second Continental and Confederation; Randolph, Edward Jennings; Virginia

Reference

Reardon, John J. *Peyton Randolph, 1721–1775: One Who Presided*. Durham, NC: Carolina Academic Press, 1975.

Rankin, William
(?–?)

The Loyalist William Rankin played an unusual role in the American Revolutionary War. Nearly all of the many thousands of Loyalists in arms or in leadership positions and many of the many thousands more who were common civilians were known to the Patriot leadership and to the general population as Loyalists and never pretended to be Patriots. Rankin, however, played a double game for nearly five years, holding both civil and military Patriot posts in York County, Pennsylvania, while developing increasingly ambitious plans to aid the British cause.

The dates and locations of Rankin's birth and death are unknown, but in 1775 he was a landholder, local justice, member of the Revolutionary committee of correspondence, and militia colonel in York County. As Congress moved toward independence, however, Rankin quietly agreed to aid local Loyalists while retaining his civil and military offices. Beginning in 1776, he secretly helped Loyalists whom he was supposed to arrest to evade capture, and for the next two years he secretly organized Loyalists in York and Lancaster Counties in Pennsylvania and in adjacent northern Maryland.

By 1778 Rankin was in contact with Britain's army commander, Sir Henry Clinton, through the Germantown Loyalist Christopher Sowers and Clinton's aide, Major John André, and soon claimed that 6,000 Pennsylvania and Maryland Loyalists "would answer his call for an uprising." As the time for such a venture was not yet ripe, Rankin tried but failed in 1779 to have a secret Loyalist placed in command of the Pennsylvania militia forces that would accompany General John Sullivan's invasion of the Iroquois country. He also informed Clinton that if the frontier Loyalist leader John Butler would move south to attack Carlisle, Pennsylvania, Rankin would provide him with local support. Following Major André's arrest and execution in the fall of 1780, Rankin contacted British General John Simcoe with a proposal to lead an uprising of local Loyalists in the Chesapeake Bay area.

In March 1781, Rankin was discovered and arrested by the Patriots, but he soon escaped to New York City. He briefly visited Lord Charles Cornwallis's army in Virginia with plans to aid the general's ongoing invasion of that state, but Cornwallis ignored him. In 1783, Rankin left New York with the British Army. He later submitted a petition from Nova Scotia to Britain's claims commission seeking £313 for his losses.

KATIE SIMONTON AND RICHARD ALAN RYERSON

See also

André, John; Butler, John; Clinton, Henry; Cornwallis, Charles; Loyalists; Simcoe, John Graves; Sowers, Christopher, III

Reference

Van Doran, Carl. *Secret History of the American Revolution: An Account of the Conspiracies of Benedict Arnold and Numerous Others from the Secret Service Papers of the British Headquarters in North America.* New York: Viking, 1941.

Rathbun, John Peck
(1746–1782)

One of the most enterprising and successful captains in the Continental Navy, John Peck Rathbun is best known for his victorious one-vessel assault on New Providence (Nassau) in the Bahamas in 1778. He was also primarily responsible for the capture of eight British merchant vessels off Newfoundland in 1779, which proved to be the Continental Navy's most profitable seizure of prizes during the Revolutionary War.

Rathbun's service in the Continental Navy began in 1775 when he left his Rhode Island home to become lieutenant on the sloop *Providence*. In February 1776, he took part in the capture of New Providence under the direction of Esek Hopkins. That October, Rathbun served under John Paul Jones when Jones escaped two British frigates and wrought considerable damage upon British shipping at Canso, Nova Scotia. Rathbun became first lieutenant under Jones on the *Alfred* and returned to the coast of Nova Scotia to stalk British vessels.

In April 1777, Rathbun assumed command of the *Providence* and soon after captured one of four British vessels that he met off Sandy Hook. Later that year, he took a British privateer and put into Charleston, where he made plans to again strike British-held New Providence. In early January 1778, he escaped three British armed vessels while en route to Abaco in the Bahamas to make final preparations for the assault. On the evening of 27 January, his attack party of twenty-six men landed at New Providence and took the fort without firing a shot. Rathbun's twelve-gun sloop held New Providence for three days. His daring operation resulted in the release of thirty American prisoners and two ships, the destruction of four British vessels, and the taking of a sixteen-gun ship and a brig. He also seized 1,600 pounds of gunpowder and a large supply of muskets.

Rathbun's success continued with five more prizes in early 1779. In May he accepted command of the frigate *Queen of France* (28 guns). Two months later, he played the lead role in deceiving and capturing eight vessels of a Jamaica convoy under British escort off the Grand Banks of Newfoundland. The ships and their cargoes were valued at more than $1 million.

In May 1780, Rathbun was stationed at Charleston when the British seized the port. Captured and imprisoned for more than a year, he was released on parole in August 1781. Soon after his release, he took command of the *Wexford* (20 guns), a Massachusetts privateer. Within a month, he was again apprehended. He was sent to Mill Prison in Plymouth, England, where he died the next year.

MICHAEL F. DOVE

See also

Bahamas; Charleston, South Carolina, Expedition against (1780); Continental Navy; Naval Operations, American vs. British

Reference

Miller, Nathan. *Sea of Glory: A Naval History of the American Revolution.* 1974. Reprint, Charleston, SC: Nautical and Aviation Publishing Company, 2000.

Rawdon, Francis
(1754–1826)

Francis Rawdon, later Rawdon-Hastings, 1st Marquis of Hastings and 2nd Earl of Moira, was a distinguished British soldier in the Revolutionary War, serving longer than most of his colleagues and still in his twenties when he departed America in 1781. He was the son of Baron John Rawdon, later 1st Earl of Moira, and Lady Elizabeth Hastings, eldest daughter of Thophilus, 9th Earl of Huntingdon. Known by the courtesy title of Lord Rawdon from 1761 to 1783, he was raised to the peerage as Baron Rawdon by the king. He was educated at Harrow and University College, Oxford, and at the latter institution befriended another student, Banastre Tarleton, with whom he would be closely associated in the American Revolutionary War. Rawdon was thin and gangly in youth, and later in life he was described as being the ugliest man in Britain. His portraits belie this description. He was tall and athletic, with a stately air and impressive manner. A young lady of his acquaintance remarked of him, "I well remember what we thought of the haughty look of Lord Rawdon." On 7 August 1771 he was gazetted an ensign in the 15th Foot. He matriculated at University College, Oxford, on 23 October 1771 and remained there for two years. Promoted to lieutenant in the 5th Foot on 20 October 1773, he embarked with his regiment at Monkstown, near Cork, Ireland, for America on 7 May 1774.

Rawdon landed at Boston in July, just as tensions between the colonists and Britain were reaching the boiling point, and joined the military forces of General Thomas Gage, the British commander in chief. He was posted to the grenadier company of the 5th Foot, commanded by Captain George Harris, to replace a subaltern who had been wounded at Lexington, Massachusetts, on 19 April. On 17 June, at the Battle of Bunker Hill, Rawdon and the grenadiers were in the thick of the fighting. Although he came through unscathed, a bullet passed through his cap. After Harris was wounded, Rawdon took command of the grenadiers and distinguished himself. General John Burgoyne observed that Rawdon had that day made his military reputation for life because of his gallantry under fire. On 12 July Rawdon was promoted to captain in the 63rd Foot, and in the fall he joined other officers in an amateur theatrical group that staged plays in Faneuil Hall. On 15 January 1776 he was appointed aide-de-camp to General Sir Henry Clinton, who was organizing an expedition against the southern colonies. Rawdon was with Clinton in May during abortive operations on the Cape Fear River in North Carolina and a month later in similarly futile attempts against Charleston, South Carolina.

In July 1776 Rawdon sailed with Clinton to New York, arriving there in early August just as General William Howe, the new British commander in chief, was commencing the campaign of 1776. Rawdon was present with Clinton at the Battle of Long Island on 27 August, the landing at Kips Bay on Manhattan on 15 September, the Battle of White Plains on 28 October, and the capture of Forts Washington and Lee on 16 and 20 November, respectively. In all these operations Rawdon was often so busy that he went for ten days at a time without removing his clothes. He accompanied General Charles Cornwallis during the army's march through New Jersey to the Delaware River in December 1776. Directly afterward, Rawdon went home to Britain with Clinton for the winter, returning to New York in the spring of 1777 and remaining there with Clinton when Howe took the main army southward in the summer to attack Philadelphia. Rawdon took part in Clinton's capture of Forts Clinton, Montgomery, Independence, and Constitution in the Hudson Highlands in October and later that month was chosen by Clinton to carry the good news to Howe in Philadelphia.

Portrait of Francis Rawdon (1754–1826), British military officer and politician. (Library of Congress)

Returning to New York, Rawdon spent the winter of 1777–1778 living a relaxed life of parties and fine dining. On 1 May 1778 he sailed with Clinton to Philadelphia, where Clinton assumed command of British forces in America. Clinton and Rawdon began organizing a provincial corps, the Volunteers of Ireland, on 25 May, to be composed of Irish deserters from the Continental Army. When it was completed, partly with financial assistance from Rawdon, he was appointed its commander with the provincial rank of colonel. This corps would later distinguish itself in battles in the South. He was also promoted to permanent lieutenant-colonel and appointed adjutant-general on 15 June. In the Battle of Monmouth on 28 June, fought during Clinton's march from Philadelphia to New York, Rawdon formed the British line of battle for the commander in chief and otherwise assisted in the action. In July, after reaching New York City, Rawdon volunteered for service on board the fleet under Admiral Lord Richard Howe that was defending New York from a threatened attack by French warships. A month later Rawdon accompanied Clinton and General Charles Grey on a relief expedition to save the British garrison on Rhode Island. Sent ahead on a reconnoitering expedition on 30 August, Rawdon reported back the following day that the Americans had abandoned attempts to take the garrison.

Over the next few months Rawdon and Clinton began to develop a coolness toward each other, and by August 1779 Clinton was publicly scolding his young protégé for perceived lapses in military protocol. On 3 September 1779 Rawdon resigned as adjutant-general, declaring that he could no longer work closely with a superior who had lost confidence in him. When Clinton sailed with an army of 7,600 men on 26 December to commence military operations against Charleston, Rawdon remained in New York. By March, however, Clinton ordered reinforcements from New York, and on 18 April Rawdon arrived with 2,500 men. He was given command of forces on the left bank of the Cooper River, where on 24 April he captured defensive works on Haddrell's Point. After Charleston surrendered on 12 May, Clinton dispatched three columns to occupy Camden and Ninety-Six in upper South Carolina and Augusta in Georgia. Rawdon was given command of the garrison at Camden, which consisted of 2,500 men, and was later promoted to brigadier-general by Clinton (although his commission did not arrive until he had departed America for Britain in August 1781). Clinton having departed for New York on 5 June, Cornwallis was left in overall command of forces in the South, with headquarters at Charleston.

At Camden, Rawdon had to contend with partisan warfare conducted by General Thomas Sumter and with the approach from North Carolina of an American army led by Major General Horatio Gates. In early August, Rawdon advanced northward to cover the retirement of his outlying detachments, then fell back to Camden. On 14 August Cornwallis assumed command and marched north to fight Gates's army. In the Battle of Camden on 16 August, Rawdon led the British left and fought well against Gates's Continental regulars. After the rout of the Americans, Cornwallis marched northward to Charlotte but fell back after Major Patrick Ferguson was defeated at Kings Mountain on 7 October. During the withdrawal to Winnsboro, South Carolina, Cornwallis fell sick, and Rawdon assumed command of the army. Ordered back to Camden for the winter of 1780–1781, he assumed overall command in South Carolina when Cornwallis advanced northward in January 1781 to confront General Nathanael Greene and finally abandoned the Carolinas entirely.

Over the next two months, Rawdon was gradually isolated at Camden as Greene, assisted by Sumter, Henry Lee, and Francis Marion, seized posts along the Santee River that protected Rawdon's supply lines to Charleston. In April, Greene advanced on Rawdon's position at Camden with his main army of 1,500 men, and Rawdon could muster only 900 troops to counter the threat. On 25 April, at Hobkirk's Hill, just north of Camden, Rawdon attacked and defeated Greene's forces in a brilliantly conducted battle. Nevertheless, Rawdon was compelled to abandon Camden on 10 May, falling back to Moncks Corner, 30 miles from Charleston on 24 May. In rapid succession, his posts at Orangeburg, McCord's Ferry, Friday's Ferry, Nelson's Ferry, Georgetown, and Augusta were either abandoned or captured as he contracted his defensive lines to protect Charleston and Savannah. On 22 May, Greene besieged Ninety-Six, but a force of 550 New York Loyalists refused to surrender the post. Rawdon, reinforced by three British regiments from Ireland on 3 June, marched with 1,800 men to the relief of the post.

Reaching Ninety-Six on 21 June, Rawdon discovered that Greene had retreated northward the day before. Rawdon abandoned Ninety-Six on 3 July and eleven days later concentrated his forces at Orangeburg. There, on 20 July, his health broken by the rigors of field duty, he handed over his command to Colonel Alexander Stewart, marched with 500 men to Charleston, and on 21 August 1781 departed for home. The vessel he traveled on was captured by a French privateer, which sailed to Virginia and then to Brest. In December, Rawdon was exchanged and returned to Britain. In February 1782 the Duke of Richmond laid charges against Rawdon in the House of Lords, claiming that Rawdon had behaved with excessive cruelty in executing an American prisoner, Colonel Isaac Hayne, without trial. Rawdon defeated the charges and exacted a public apology from Richmond. On 21 March 1782 Rawdon was appointed lieutenant-colonel of the 105th Foot, and on 20 November another promotion made him colonel and an aide-de-camp to the king.

While still in America, Rawdon had entered British politics during the parliamentary recess of 1780–1781, being elected to the Irish House of Commons. After his return from the war he became a member of the British House of Lords. He had an active political career for almost three decades and gained a reputation for serving the interests of the Prince of Wales. In June 1793 Rawdon succeeded his father as Earl of Moira and on 12 October was promoted to major-general. He served with the Duke of York in June and July 1794, fighting French revolutionary forces in Flanders. On 1 January 1798 Rawdon was promoted to lieutenant-general and on 25 September 1803 to general. He was given the colonelcy of the 27th Foot on 23 May 1804 and made constable of the Tower of London on 1 March 1806. In the so-called Ministry of All the Talents formed under Lord George Grenville in February 1806, Rawdon was master-general of the ordnance. He married Flora, Countess of Loudoun, in 1804, and they had six children. He was invested with the Order of the Garter on 12 June 1812.

Owing to his financial extravagance, Rawdon (now 2nd Earl of Moira) had to seek employment as governor-general of Bengal in 1812 and a year later sailed to Calcutta. While in India, he led a number of campaigns and expanded British territory. In February 1817, in recognition of his services in operations against Nepal, he was created Marquis of Hastings and given a unanimous vote of thanks by Parliament. The following year he was endowed with other honors. Appointed governor of Malta in 1824, he held that office until he died in 1826.

PAUL DAVID NELSON

See also

Augusta, Georgia, Operations at; Bunker Hill, Battle of; Burgoyne, John; Camden Campaign; Charleston, South Carolina, Expedition against (1776); Clinton, Henry; Cornwallis, Charles; Ferguson, Patrick; Fort Clinton, New York; Fort Lee, New Jersey; Fort Montgomery, New York, Assault on; Fort Ninety-Six, South Carolina, Sieges of; Fort Washington, New York, Fall of; Gage, Thomas; Gates, Horatio; Greene, Nathanael; Grey, Charles; Hayne, Isaac; Hobkirk's Hill, Battle of; Howe, Richard; Hudson River and the Hudson Highlands; Kings Mountain, Battle of; Lexington and Concord; Long Island, Battle of; Monmouth, Battle of; New Jersey, Operations in; New York, Operations in; Rhode Island, Battle of; Southern Campaigns; Stewart, Alexander; Sumter, Thomas; White Plains, Battle of

References

Bass, Robert D. *The Green Dragon: The Lives of Banastre Tarleton and Mary Robinson.* 1957. Reprint, Orangeburg, SC: Sandlapper, 2003.

Conrad, Dennis, et al., eds. *The Papers of General Nathanael Greene.* 13 vols. Chapel Hill: University of North Carolina Press, 1976–2005.

McCrady, Edward. *The History of South Carolina in the Revolution, 1775–1780.* 1901. Reprint, New York: Russell and Russell, 1969.

Pancake, John S. *This Destructive War: The British Campaign for the Carolinas, 1780–1782.* University, AL: University of Alabama Press, 1985.

Tarleton, Banastre. *History of the Campaigns of 1780 and 1781, in the Southern Provinces of North America.* 1787. Reprint, New York: New York Times, 1968.

Ward, Christopher. *War of the Revolution.* 2 vols. New York: Macmillan, 1952.

Wickwire, Franklin, and Mary Wickwire. *Cornwallis: The American Adventure.* Boston: Houghton Mifflin, 1970.

Read, George

See Declaration of Independence Signers

Reed, Joseph
(1741–1785)

Joseph Reed was one of the most important leaders in Pennsylvania throughout the Revolution as well as a key member of the command staff of the Continental Army in the early years of the war. He began his Revolutionary career in a characteristically ambivalent fashion. Between 1773 and 1775, he urged reconciliation between Britain and America in correspondence with William Legge, Lord Dartmouth, while at the same time rising to the leadership of Philadelphia's resistance movement. Soon thereafter Reed became General George Washington's first secretary and later served as adjutant general of the Continental Army, before assuming the role of chief executive of Pennsylvania. Even after independence, Reed appears to have had some hopes for reconciling America and Britain, but he supported the Revolution faithfully until his early death.

Reed was born in Trenton, New Jersey, on 27 August 1741, and spent many of his early years in Philadelphia before returning to New Jersey, where he graduated from the College of New Jersey (Princeton) in 1757. He studied law in England from 1763 to 1765, where he became informally engaged to Esther De Berdt, daughter of Dennis De Berdt, the colonial agent for the Massachusetts legislature. Reed returned to New Jersey to become deputy secretary of the province and clerk of the council. In 1770, he took a second trip to London, married De Berdt, and returned to Philadelphia to practice law.

In December 1773, through the good offices of his brother-in-law, Dennis De Berdt Jr., Reed began corresponding with Dartmouth, Britain's secretary of state for America. Just as he began this correspondence, however, Reed, as a highly successful lawyer and a leader of Philadelphia's increasingly powerful Presbyterians, entered public life as a member of the committee chosen to coordinate the opposition to the shipment of East India Company tea. He served on every resistance committee thereafter, and until his health began to fail in 1784, he always held either an important civil office in Pennsylvania or a key position in the Continental Army.

The resistance movement in Philadelphia had been led from its beginning in 1765 by Charles Thomson, who worked closely with John Dickinson, Pennsylvania's leading Whig spokesman. But in September 1774, Thomson became secretary of the Continental Congress, and in October Dickinson entered the Pennsylvania Assembly and then entered Congress. This left Reed as the leader of Philadelphia's resistance movement, a position confirmed by his election as chairman of the Committee of Observation, Inspection, and Correspondence chosen in November 1774. He retained his leadership role until June 1775, when he startled Philadelphians by accepting an appointment from Washington as secretary to the new commander in chief and then proceeded to Boston. Thereafter, Reed's four-month absence, followed by his attempts to moderate the policies of Philadelphia's most radical leaders upon his return to Philadelphia, began to reduce his influence.

Joseph Reed, a Revolutionary leader in Philadelphia before independence, served as secretary to General George Washington and then as president of the Executive Council of Pennsylvania. (Bettman/Corbis)

Reed soon resigned his position as secretary to Washington and was back in Philadelphia by October 1775, where he was elected to the Pennsylvania Assembly. And in February 1776 he was elected chairman of Philadelphia's last Committee of Observation, Inspection, and Correspondence. Over the next four months, he strongly supported independence but also tried to moderate the growing hostility toward the Assembly. In mid-June 1776, he abandoned his attempts to bring Pennsylvania's partisans together and joined the Continental Army. He was soon appointed adjutant general and played a key role in assisting Washington from the disastrous New York Campaign through the triumphs at Trenton and Princeton, then the difficult Philadelphia Campaign, and finally at Monmouth. Reed also became a close friend of General Nathanael Greene, and the two men later maintained an important correspondence during Greene's southern campaign. Also during the war, Reed's wife organized the women of Philadelphia to perform relief work for the soldiers until her death in 1780.

While Reed was still in the army, he was offered and declined the position of chief justice of Pennsylvania. He sat briefly in Congress in the fall of 1777, when he signed the Articles of Confederation. In the summer of 1778, Governor George Johnstone, the feckless member of Britain's Carlisle Peace Commission, offered Reed a bribe to use his influence to persuade Congress and Washington to abandon independence and negotiate peace and reconciliation with Britain. Despite his personal moderation and his strong desire for conciliation from the time of his correspondence with Dartmouth, Reed rejected the bribe and promptly reported it to Congress. This incident finally sealed the fate of the ineffective Carlisle Peace Commission and resulted in a nasty pamphlet war between Johnstone and Reed.

In 1778, Reed left the army and reentered public life in Pennsylvania. His first role was as a prosecutor of several persons charged with collaborating with the British during General William Howe's recent occupation of Philadelphia. In November 1778, Reed became president of Pennsylvania's Executive Council, the nominal equivalent of governor but with less power than most governors in Pennsylvania's legislative-centered, unicameral government. His three years in this role were perhaps the most important, and most difficult, of his career. He clashed with the state's moderate Republicans, whom he saw as so partisan that they would not concentrate on defeating Britain, and criticized them for welcoming open collaborators into their ranks. And he clashed with the radical Constitutionalists, whose aggressive support of mob action to intimidate merchants and bring down food prices made orderly government difficult. At one point, he had to call out the militia to disperse a crowd that had forced several Republicans to seek refuge in the house of the Republican leader James Wilson (the Fort Wilson Incident). And, inevitably, Reed experienced friction with General Benedict Arnold, whom Washington had unwisely appointed to supervise the securing and distributing of supplies for the recovering city after the British departure.

Reed's last years were difficult. He failed to secure election to the Pennsylvania Assembly and then to the post of chief justice. He was accused by John Cadwalader of considering abandoning the Revolution in 1776, a charge that most contemporaries, and later historians, found unpersuasive. Reed was successful in arguing Pennsylvania's case against Connecticut for ownership of the Wyoming Valley. By 1784, however, he was quite ill, and he died on 5 March 1785.

Reed was an unusually conciliatory person to play a prominent role in leading a revolution. At virtually every stage of his career, he showed a rare combination of a strong commitment to the Patriot cause and a keen desire to see contending parties, from Britain versus America in the mid-1770s to Pennsylvania's Republicans versus its Constitutionalists during the war years, conciliate their differences. His sudden, unpredictable career changes in 1775 and 1776 perhaps suggest a certain indecisiveness in his character. But his great dedication to each of the roles he filled, especially as Washington's adjutant general from 1776 to 1778 and as president of Pennsylvania's Executive Council from 1778 to 1781, makes him one of the most important Patriot leaders of the Revolution.

RICHARD ALAN RYERSON

See also
Cadwalader, John; Carlisle Peace Commission; Continental Army; Correspondence, Committees of; Dickinson, John; Pennsylvania; Philadelphia; Thomson, Charles; Washington, George

References

Brunhouse, Robert L. *The Counter-Revolution in Pennsylvania, 1776–1790*. Harrisburg: Pennsylvania Historical and Museum Commission, 1942.

Roche, John F. *Joseph Reed: A Moderate in the American Revolution*. New York: Columbia University Press, 1957.

Rosswurm, Steven. *Arms, Country, and Class: The Philadelphia Militia and the "Lower Sort" during the American Revolution*. New Brunswick, NJ: Rutgers University Press, 1987.

Rowe, G. S. "Joseph Reed." Pp. 270–272 in *American National Biography*, Vol. 18. New York: Oxford University Press, 1999.

Ryerson, Richard Alan. *The Revolution Is Now Begun: The Radical Committee of Philadelphia, 1765–1776*. Philadelphia: University of Pennsylvania Press, 1978.

Religion

Horace Walpole believed that he knew what caused the American Revolution: "Cousin America has run off with a Presbyterian parson, and that's an end of it." Although few Britons or Americans have believed that it was as simple as that, historians have always assumed that religion and religious concerns were among the most fundamental causes of the American Revolution. A more helpful way to look at the relationship, however, might be to think about the ways in which religion helped *shape* the colonists' experience of independence and revolution and at the ways in which that experience, in turn, radically transformed American religious culture.

Virtually all historians would agree that for most Americans in 1776, religion remained the primary means for ordering and understanding the world and their place in it. It is not surprising, then, that religion shaped in fundamental ways the colonists' responses to the imperial crisis, the war that followed it, and the revolutionary developments that then flowed from both.

American religious culture in 1776 had been shaped itself not only by the immediate experience of the Great Awakening and the colonial wars with France, both extending through the 1740s and 1750s, but also by two centuries of struggle in the mother country over the shape and nature of Christianity in England. Through the Reformation, the English Civil War, and the Glorious Revolution, the British and, then, their American colonies developed a religious tradition that was characterized by a firm sense of being the chosen people of God, a toleration of dissent and a concern for liberty of conscience within Protestantism, an often virulent anti-Catholicism, and the conviction that political and religious tyranny were inseparable. The controversy over the appointment of an Anglican bishop for the colonies just before the Revolution brought into play most of those dynamics.

Ironically, the effort to consolidate and centralize church authority and discipline in the late colonial period had been least successful in the Church of England, which was established in all of the colonies south of Pennsylvania. Most of the Anglican laity in the colonies and much of the colonial clergy welcomed the lack of episcopal oversight, while the hierarchy in England

The Great Awakening, which swept through much of colonial America from the 1730s to the 1750s, aroused intense religious fervor and sometimes inspired believers to march in singing processions. (North Wind Picture Archives)

and some Anglican colonists understood the all-too-obvious advantages for the Church in the appointment of a bishop resident in the colonies. Such an appointment was never seriously considered by the Church, but during the twenty years or so before 1776 rumors persisted about the imminent arrival of a spiritual lord for the colonies. Those rumors easily fed into a parallel controversy over allegations that some royal officials and their colonial allies were scheming to create a colonial aristocracy. When the Reverend East Apthorp began to build a rather elaborate residence in Cambridge, Massachusetts, colonists immediately believed that it was actually intended to house the new lord spiritual, an Anglican bishop. There would follow, then, the suppression of all religious dissent, the union of spiritual and political tyranny, and, for all the colonists knew, the final introduction, somehow, of papacy itself. And worst of all, they noted, this fundamental threat to their dearest liberties came not from Catholic France, as it had in the French and Indian War, but from that late defender of Protestantism, England.

When the debates over the imperial crisis itself began in 1764 and 1765, the colonial clergy immediately assumed in it the leadership role that one would expect of the colonies' only real profession. Ordained men of God remained the most respected leaders in society and, with access to both pulpit and print, were its most effective opinion makers. This they had most recently demonstrated in the war with France. Moreover, they were heir to the English tradition of clerical involvement in political controversy, and throughout the colonial period they had roused the faithful in holy war, not only with papist France but also with Indians in the wilderness and with the Devil and his covened minions closer to home. The clergy now turned the themes and tropes from those battles against the mother country: constant vigilance against tyranny in all its forms, selfless exertion in a sacred cause, and a humbled, repentant posture before the great God upon whom all depended. They preached sermons supporting the boycotts against British goods and the nurturing of American manufactures. They enthusiastically officiated at the public days of prayer, fasting, and humiliation that the emerging Patriot legislatures regularly recommended as the crisis with England intensified. And they were especially vocal in condemning the Boston Massacre in 1770 and were quick to urge united efforts to relieve the blockade of the beleaguered city after the Boston Tea Party in 1773.

Clerical involvement in the imperial crisis became especially pronounced with the passing by Britain in 1774 of the Quebec Act. The act was a politic and even humane attempt by the British to arrange for the effective government of the Catholic province that had just been added to the Protestant British Empire. In order to enfranchise these new British subjects, the legislation waived the Test Acts for Catholics in Canada and preserved the rights of the Catholic Church to collect the tithe in the province. And it ominously, at least from the perspective of the Protestant colonists to the south, extended the boundaries of Catholic Quebec both south and west, to the confluence of the Ohio and the Mississippi Rivers. The clergy now pressed even harder the assertion, first made in the Bishop Controversy, that there had developed recently a lamentable but alarming affinity between Britain and the papists, who were now positioned to threaten the Protestant colonies not only from the North but also in the West.

Not all the clergy supported the Patriot cause after fighting broke out, independence was declared, and Britain moved to subdue the rebellion. But the majority who did contributed significantly to defending the colonists' actions and to ensuring public support for the war. The most important of those contributions was undoubtedly the clergy's role in elaborating the republican political theory that became the ideological foundation of the American Revolution. Republics were assumed in eighteenth-century political theory to be especially vulnerable governments because they depended upon selfless, virtuous, and disinterested citizens who could be trusted with the responsibility for electing their own rulers. More than any other part of the colonial leadership, the Patriot clergy persuaded the American rebels that they were capable of that demanding task. They argued that in the heat of the controversy with Britain and the armed conflict that followed it, the colonists were abandoning selfishness and contention and were uniting in defense of their liberties. Indeed, the more extravagant of the clergy suggested that the crisis was transforming the essential character of the colonists. They insisted that there was a natural affinity between pure Christianity and republicanism and that transformed Christian Americans, products of both the recent Great Awakening and the current crisis, were, in fact, republicans by nature.

The complex response of the several religious denominations to the imperial crisis and the question of independence reveals the many ways in which the choice between Patriotism and Loyalism was shaped by ethnicity and widely varying specific historical traditions as well as by denominational affiliation. The question of independence posed the most immediate and dramatic challenge, of course, to the Church of England. The Anglican clergy had sworn an oath of loyalty to the monarch, the titular head of the Church, upon being ordained, and the Book of Common Prayer contained prayers for the sovereign. A little more than half of the Anglican clergy remained loyal. Some, such as Charles Inglis of New York and Samuel Seabury of Connecticut, became pamphleteers for the Tory cause. Others simply rode out the crisis as best they could, while many joined the thousands of Anglican Loyalists who opted simply to return to England. But a very large minority of the Anglican clergy and a majority of the Anglican laity in several colonies supported the Patriot cause with varying degrees of enthusiasm. In some colonies, such as Connecticut, virtually all of the Anglicans were assumed to be Loyalists, while in parts of Virginia, Anglican lay support for the Patriot cause was overwhelming. Finally, more than half of the signers of the Declaration of Independence were members of the Church of England who now became spiritual as well as political rebels.

The other established denomination in colonial America, New England's Congregational descendants of the seventeenth-century Puritans, was itself the product of rebellion against an English king. The Congregational clergy of New England were the earliest and most fervent supporters of the Patriot cause. Men such as Jonathan Mayhew reminded their countrymen of the duty to hold to account an unjust ruler and drew upon the experience of the seventeenth-century English Civil War against Stuart absolutism to urge rebellion against the dynasty's Hanoverian successor. There were, of course, Congregational clerics and laity who were Loyalists. But the Congregationalists, firmly established in all of the New England colonies except Rhode Island, had found ways in the late colonial period to accommodate dissent, and during the Revolutionary War and its aftermath, both in Massachusetts and Connecticut, they were able to protect their privileged legal position.

Despite Walpole's conviction that "Cousin America" had eloped with "a Presbyterian parson," the Presbyterians were, in fact, somewhat divided on the question of independence, especially early on in the imperial crisis. The Presbyterians were the most widely and evenly distributed of the colonial denominations, and the English Presbyterians of New England were firm in their support of independence. But the far more numerous, and more recently arrived, Scots-Irish Presbyterians who dominated the backcountry from Pennsylvania to Georgia were often alienated by the failure of the eastern elites who led the war against Britain to attend to the frontier's political, economic, and, especially, military needs in the late colonial period. The great majority of Presbyterians, however, finally did support the war, under the leadership of Patriot ministers such as Princeton President John Witherspoon and North Carolina's David Caldwell. Scots-Irish Presbyterians were especially numerous in the Continental Army and the state militias, leading King George III finally to call the rebellion simply "the Presbyterian war."

As Puritanism had been born in the seventeenth-century rebellion against the Stuarts, so American Methodism was born of the rebellion against their Hanoverian successors. A product of the pietistic revival led by John Wesley within the Church of England in the mid-eighteenth century, Methodism had barely established itself mostly in the middle and upper southern colonies by the time of the imperial crisis. Its adherents met in lay-controlled societies that were served occasionally by the ministers sent by Wesley from England. When independence came, all of those ministers returned to England except Francis Asbury. Wesley, who still maintained a troubled and tenuous position in the Church of England, staunchly opposed independence. Asbury spent the war years holding the small Methodist connection together, supporting the American cause and doing all he could to distinguish Methodism from the embattled Church of England.

Portrait of Samuel Seabury (1729–1796), the first American Episcopal bishop. (Library of Congress)

The Baptists had led the fight against both the Congregational and Anglican establishments in the late colonial period. During the Revolution the Baptists continued that struggle, led in New England by Isaac Backus and in Virginia by John Leland. The Baptist leaders and their followers overwhelmingly supported the Patriot cause, which they persistently compared to their own struggle with the Congregational and Anglican establishments. In 1773 Backus explicitly compared the tea tax to the tax dissenters in Massachusetts who were forced to pay to support religion and declared that they both violated the Patriots' call for no taxation without representation. The Baptists proved to be vexing allies at times for Patriot leaders, especially in Massachusetts, but allies they surely were.

The American Baptists, most of whom were of English origin, had much in common with the great array of Pietist and Anabaptist sects that were concentrated in the middle colonies, especially their mutual insistence on the baptism of adult believers. But unlike the English Baptists, these continental Pietists and Anabaptists—Mennonites and Amish, Moravians, Schwenkfelders, German Baptists, and, most important, Quakers—were pacifists. Their refusal to pay war-related taxes and serve in local militias kept them in constant conflict with Patriot authorities throughout the war. They were whipped, fined, and sometimes imprisoned, and in some colonies, especially Pennsylvania, they were disenfranchised well into the early republic.

Woodcut of colonial parishioners during a worship service. Note the spinning wheel in the foreground. (North Wind Picture Archives)

Unlike most of these small continental sects, the predominantly English Quakers were a numerous and powerful force in a few colonies, especially North Carolina and, of course, Pennsylvania. There the Society of Friends had been intimately involved in colonial politics. But disputes with the Scots-Irish Presbyterians over defense of the frontier and contentions with several factions over the end of proprietary rule in Pennsylvania had forced a growing number of Quakers to withdraw from politics in the years immediately preceding the imperial crisis. Most Friends probably opposed British efforts to establish firmer control over the colonies. But most also rejected independence because they believed that not even unjust rulers should be deposed through violence. The Quakers were among the most extreme of those who refused to support the war effort; some would not even use Continental currency. Removed from political life, some Quakers began, even as the military struggle progressed, to support efforts to reform American society and were among the first to apply the egalitarian force of the Revolution's rhetoric to the institution of human bondage that made a mockery of it.

The Pietistic and Anabaptist sects were part of a larger community of continental Protestant groups in late colonial America. Lutherans, mostly German, and Reformed Dutch and German communities were a growing presence, especially in the middle colonies. The Lutherans had remained rather separate from colonial society and were somewhat apolitical in the Revolution, although some, mindful of the German origins of the House of Hanover, opted to leave the rebellious colonies and cast their lot with coreligionists in loyal Canada. The Lutherans' most important clerical leader, Henry Muhlenberg, was sympathetic to that position but decided to remain and to lead the German Lutherans into a closer identification with the Patriot cause and the republican society it created. The German Calvinists in Pennsylvania had received very little aid from the Reformed Churches in Europe and had established ties instead with the Dutch Reformed community in New York and New Jersey. Majorities in both Calvinist groups immediately and enthusiastically supported the Patriot cause, although many Dutch Calvinists became Loyalists.

Two groups—Roman Catholics and Jews—stood apart altogether from the Protestantism that so thoroughly dominated and defined the British North American colonies on the eve of independence. Both groups used the crisis with Britain to certify their basic allegiance to America. This was easier for the Jews than it was for the Catholics. Although tiny colonial Catholic communities, numerous only in the middle colonies (including Maryland), had coexisted quietly with Protestants for decades, the war with France and, then, the Quebec Act had reignited anti-Catholic fears and prejudice that were never far below the surface among the British. The all-important American alliance with the French Catholic king in 1778 instantly complicated matters even further. There were, of course, Catholic Loyalists, but most Catholics favored the Revolution, and many served with distinction in the Patriot army and state militias, especially in Pennsylvania. The Catholics who were Irish (not nearly so many in the eighteenth century as there would be later) were only too willing to fight the British again. And in Charles Carroll of Carrollton and his cousin, the Jesuit priest John Carroll, American Catholics found distinguished spokesmen, lay and spiritual, for their community. At the end of the war, George Washington pointedly thanked Catholics for their support in the conflict with England.

There were 2,000–3,000 Jews in the English colonies in 1776, the largest concentrations being in the ports of Charleston, Philadelphia, New York City, and Newport. The Puritans had long identified with the original "chosen people" of God, and the Hebrew scriptures figured prominently in the Patriot critique of English absolutism. The inscription on the Liberty Bell came from Leviticus: "Proclaim Liberty to all the land and unto all the inhabitants thereof." There were a few Jewish Loyalists, especially among the wealthier merchants of occupied New York City. But most Jewish colonists seemed to sense that the liberal bias of representative government and the egalitarian thrust of the Revolution's rhetoric simply offered them a more attractive future than traditional European religious arrangements. Jewish merchants supported the boycotts of the 1760s and 1770s, and whereas Jews had not participated in military operations in Europe, in Revolutionary America they did. More than 100 Jews served, many of them becoming officers. Several Jewish financiers, the most important of them being the Philadelphia broker Haym Salomon, assisted in arranging for the colonial and international loans that made the war effort possible. As he had done with America's Catholics, Washington at the end of the war made a special point of writing to "the children of Abraham" (at Newport's congregation, Jeshuat Israel) to thank them for their support of the Patriot cause and declare his belief in the value of broad religious toleration.

Just as they had helped persuade the colonists into rebellion and into the experiment with republican government, the clergy also led in explaining the amazing outcome of the war with Britain. Their sermons on the colonial victory were replete with references to David and Goliath, and in the course of the imperial crisis and the war they discovered repeated instances of the Providential direction of events toward American independence. Most important of all, the clergy insisted that the colonial victory demonstrated that the Americans were indisputably capable of sustaining the republican governments they were in the process of creating.

The frames for those governments were laid out in the constitutions that the several states wrote between 1776 and 1781. And it was in those years that the colonists first grappled with the implications of independence and the Revolution's rhetoric for the relationship between church and state in the new republic. The most significant of the state debates occurred, predictably, in Virginia, where the Declaration of Independence made inevitable a significant change in the privileged status of the Anglican Church, which was now the church of the enemy. In 1776 dissenters were exempted from paying taxes to support the Church, and in 1779 Virginia ended the Anglicans' established status. Many Presbyterian ministers and some Baptists and leaders of other evangelical groups favored replacing the Anglican establishment with a General Assessment on the whole population to support not one denomination but Christianity in general. Thomas Jefferson, James Madison, and probably the majority of Virginia's evangelical laity supported instead a radical departure in which all connections between church and state would be severed. After an intense debate, the legislature in 1786 finally adopted Jefferson's Statute of Religious Freedom, which for the first time stated that there should be no connection whatsoever between the citizen's civil personality and his religious beliefs.

The establishment of a single denomination survived the Revolution and its aftermath only in the heavily Congregational states of Connecticut and Massachusetts. However, in their constitutions and in their legislatures, several states demonstrated in the decade or so after independence the abiding attraction of the idea of a general establishment of Christianity. South Carolina briefly established the Christian Church, while Maryland and Massachusetts required that certain officeholders be of the Christian religion. Other states—Georgia, New Hampshire, New Jersey, and North Carolina— had more specifically Christian requirements. Delaware required that all believe in the Trinity, while even Pennsylvania, which had never had any form of religious establishment, still required that officeholders believe in a future system of rewards and punishments. Several states disenfranchised Catholics, even as Father Carroll attempted to defuse Protestant suspicions about his coreligionists by opposing all forms of a general establishment and supporting the complete separation of church and state. And by 1789, all of the states except New York and Virginia had passed legislation that in some way restricted the civil liberties of Jews.

When the Constitutional Convention met in 1787, all assumed that no single denomination could force acquiescence in its own national establishment, but there was pressure to at least acknowledge the Christian nature of the new nation. The delegates, however, mindful of the explosive nature of any question relating to religion and influenced also by the liberal sentiments just embodied in Jefferson's Virginia Statute, decided to omit any reference to religion or even to God in the nation's basic frame. The single exception was a negative one: Clause Three of Article Six specifically prohibited any religious test for public office in the new republic. Four years later, in the Bill of Rights, the national Congress was enjoined from passing any act that either created a national establishment of religion or interfered with the citizen's right to exercise his religious freedom.

In the years immediately following the Revolutionary War, the process of denominational consolidation that had characterized the late colonial period began anew, intensified now by the need for religious groups with British or European connections to establish American identities and denominational structures. The first to do so was, understandably, the American branch of the Church of England. By 1784 the English Church, and Parliament, had agreed upon the rubrics whereby men who did not live in England could be elevated to the episcopacy, and in 1789 the American Anglican Church was incorporated as the Protestant Episcopal Church. Also in 1784, Asbury led the American Wesleyans in establishing, with Wesley's reluctant blessing, the Methodist Episcopal Church. Wesley's death in 1791 finally settled the issue of the independence of the American church.

Denominations without strong ties to England also sought a stronger American identity. America's Lutherans had never been burdened with ties to a European church and thus had little trouble in simply continuing to function as an independent community. The Dutch Calvinists declared their independence from Amsterdam in 1784 and established the Reformed Protestant Dutch Church. Their German Calvinist brethren, in turn, severed their ties with the American Dutch church and established their own German Reformed Church in 1791. A year earlier, in 1790, Father Carroll persuaded Rome to establish an American Catholic Church that would be free of the Vatican's Congregation for Propaganda, answer only to the pope, and, in effect, elect its own leaders. For his efforts, in 1790 Carroll was named the first Catholic bishop in the United States. And in 1789 the one American denomination that had succeeded in creating a genuine hierarchical structure during the colonial period turned that structure into a national hierarchy. The Presbyterians created a General Assembly and adopted a uniform book of discipline and worship that made the Presbyterians at once the most unified and purposive denominational community in the nation.

As this process of consolidation proceeded, however, the Revolution generated powerful forces that in the nineteenth century would challenge the basic institutions of American religion and society. The institution of human bondage made a mockery of the ideological foundation of the American Revolution. While the War for Independence was still in progress, the dissonance between the language of liberty and the institution of slavery led many Christians, white and black, to organize to end the international slave trade and slavery itself. And in the 1780s, blacks, both slave and free, in the North and in the South, began to organize black churches that were free, in varying degrees, from white control. When a group of free black Methodists in Philadelphia in 1787 were pulled from their knees while praying in a church gallery closed to them, Richard Allen led them out of the church and established the first of a series of free black churches that in 1816 were organized as the African Methodist Episcopal Church. And in the last two decades of the eighteenth century, American Quakers slowly but successfully completed the work begun in the colonial period by John Woolman and Anthony Benezet to purge the Friendly churches of slaveholders. The Revolution did not rid the republic of slavery, of course. But for parts of American religion, at least, it defined the institution as a problem, one that had to be resolved if the ideals of the Revolution were to be realized.

Like African Americans, white women too would have to wait for the redemption of the Great Declaration's pledge of equality in America. The Great Awakening of the 1740s and 1750s had honored the affective, emotive dimensions of evangelical religious response and, in the doing, had elevated women and female religious experience. In the heat of that revival, several denominations, Quakers and Methodists in particular, had allowed women to exhort and even to preach. And men as well as women were urged toward a conversion experience and Christian life that was grounded in affective and emotional response, introspection, submission, and confession and was conceived of and described in terms distinctly feminine.

All of that changed in the late eighteenth century. The Revolution itself sharply distinguished between the male world of politics and power and the female world of home and church and began the process of separation that would in the nineteenth century differentiate the spheres appropriate to men and to women. The opportunities for women to exhort and to preach were diminished by the Revolution. But the Revolution did produce two dramatic female examples of the potential power of its basic message of equality when applied to religion. Within a few miles of each other in western New England and upstate New York after 1776 emerged two remarkable women who in one way or another claimed to be the female incarnation of the spirit of Christ. Mother Ann Lee, the founder of the American Shakers, and Jemima Wilkinson, the "Public Universal Friend," were different in many ways. But they both inspired men as well as women to forsake all and follow them, Wilkinson by denying her femaleness and Lee by emphasizing it.

Wilkinson and Lee were part of the remarkable ferment of radical religious sects that swept through rural New England and New York during and after the American Revolution. Few in number, these radical sectarians are nonetheless very important for understanding the religious impact of the American Revolution. Most were products of the New Light Separatist movement in New England that began during the Great Awakening. Freewill Baptists, Universalists, Come-Outers, Irelandites, New Israelites, Merry Demons—they all accepted enthusiastically the Awakening's injunction to look to one's own salvation and to reject all who would impede that task. And they had drunk deeply of the Revolution's transforming rhetoric of individual freedom and responsibility. They were seekers impatient of all authority and believed that the instructed conscience of any Christian could discern religious truth and divine will as well as the most educated religious professional. They were radically antinomian and held all things accountable to their individual judgment. This was a culture that sought knowledge in the occult as easily as in sacred texts and soon would produce in a young man named Joseph Smith one who would both dabble in the occult and produce his own sacred text. The radically democratized religious world of the early nineteenth century that produced Smith and his new dispensation was the most important result, in religion, of the American Revolution.

HOWARD MILLER

See also

Backus, Isaac; Carroll, Charles; Constitution, United States; Constitutions, State; Jefferson, Thomas; Lee, Mother Ann; Loyalists; Quebec Act; Witherspoon, John

References

Andrews, Dee. *The Methodists and Revolutionary America: The Shaping of an Evangelical Culture*. Princeton, NJ: Princeton University Press, 2000.

Bonomi, Patricia. *Under the Cope of Heaven: Religion, Society and Politics in Colonial America*. New York: Oxford University Press, 1986.

Butler, Jon. "A Revolutionary Millennium?" Pp. 194–224 in *Awash in a Sea of Faith: Christianizing the American People*. Cambridge: Harvard University Press, 1990.

Endy, Melvin B., Jr. "Just War, Holy War, and the Millennialism in Revolutionary America." *William and Mary Quarterly*, 3rd ser., 42 (January 1985): 3–25.

Hatch, Nathan O. *The Sacred Cause of Liberty: Republican Thought and the Millennium in Revolutionary New England*. New Haven, CT: Yale University Press, 1977.

Hoffman, Ronald, and Peter J. Albert, eds. *Religion in a Revolutionary Age*. Charlottesville: University of Virginia Press, 1994.

Hutson, James H., ed. *Religion and the New Republic: Faith in the Founding of America*. Lanham, MD: Rowman and Littlefield, 2000.

Juster, Susan. *Disorderly Women: Sexual Politics and Evangelicalism in Revolutionary New England*. Ithaca, NY: Cornell University Press, 1994.

Keller, Rosemary Skinner. "Women, Civil Religion and the American Revolution." Pp. 368–380 in *Women and Religion in America*, Vol. 2, *The Colonial and Revolutionary Periods*. Edited by Rosemary Ruether and Rosemary Skinner Keller. San Francisco: Harper and Row, 1983.

McLoughlin, William G. *Isaac Backus and the American Pietistic Tradition*. Boston: Little, Brown, 1967.

———, ed. *Isaac Backus on Church, State and Calvinism: Pamphlets, 1754–1789*. Cambridge: Harvard University Press, 1968.

———. *New England Dissent, 1630–1833: The Baptists and the Separation of Church and State*. 2 vols. Cambridge: Harvard University Press, 1971.

———. "The Role of Religion in the Revolution: Liberty of Conscience and Cultural Cohesion in the Revolution." Pp. 197–225 in *Essays on the American Revolution*. Edited by Stephen G. Kurtz and James H. Hutson. Chapel Hill: University of North Carolina Press, 1973.

Miller, William Lee. *The First Liberty: America's Foundation in Religious Freedom*. Expanded and updated ed. Washington, DC: Georgetown University Press, 2003.

Murrin, John M. "No Awakening, No Revolution? More Counterfactual Speculations." *Reviews in American History* (1983): 161–171.

Noll, Mark A. "The American Revolution and Protestant Evangelicalism." *Journal of Interdisciplinary History* (1993): 615–638.

Sassi, Jonathan D. *A Republic of Righteousness: The Public Christianity of the Post-Revolutionary New England Clergy*. New York: Oxford University Press, 2001.

Stout, Harry S. "Religion, Communications, and the Ideological Origins of the American Revolution." *William and Mary Quarterly*, 3rd ser., 34 (October 1977): 519–541.

Wood, Gordon S. "Religion and the American Revolution." Pp. 173–205 in *New Directions in American Religious History*. Edited by Harry S. Stout and D. G. Hart. New York: Oxford University Press, 1977.

Revere, Paul
(1734–1818)

Paul Revere was a highly regarded Boston silversmith who became a leader in the town's resistance to British rule. Baptized on 22 December 1734, he was one of eleven children born to Paul Revere and Deborah Hitchborn. His father, a French Huguenot originally named Apollos Rivoire, had emigrated from the Channel Island of Guernsey to Boston in 1715 at the age of thirteen. Following an apprenticeship to a Boston silversmith, the elder Revere Anglicized his birth name. After attending Boston's North Writing School and becoming an apprentice to his father, young Revere took over the family business after his father's death in 1754.

Because of his skill and his father's clientele, Revere rapidly developed a thriving business as a silversmith and goldsmith. From repairing damaged silver pieces to making simple picture frames, spoons, buttons, and candlesticks to creating expensive tea services, in less than a decade he was drawing customers from Boston's commercial elite as well as the artisan class. His exceptional status as a respected artisan is confirmed in John Singleton Copley's superb 1768 portrait of the craftsman, with his tools in front of him and holding a fine example of his work. By the early 1760s, Revere had also mastered copperplate engraving and had begun to supply illustrations for Boston printers. He even dabbled in dentistry, wiring false teeth. One reason for his ever more diverse and growing business interests was the need to provide for a rapidly expanding family. In 1757 he married Sarah Orne, with whom he had eight children. When she died, he married Rachel Walker, and she also had eight children.

Though a busy entrepreneur and family man, Revere led an active social and political life. He faithfully attended the Second Church, joined the Freemasons, frequented several taverns in Boston's North End where he lived and worked, joined the militia as an artillery officer, and became a member of several political clubs, including the North End Caucus. When the imperial crisis began with Britain, Revere emerged as a leading Patriot.

In 1765, Revere joined the Sons of Liberty, a group that organized many of the demonstrations against British authorities. In 1768, he engraved a silver punch bowl to commemorate the refusal of Massachusetts's legislators to rescind a letter that they had dispatched to other colonies, urging them to resist the Townshend duties on imports recently imposed by Parliament. Among the many engraved drawings and cartoons Revere produced, and by far the most famous, was his depiction of the Boston Massacre (1770), which inaccurately shows British soldiers firing into an orderly crowd of innocent citizens. Because of its wide circulation, the engraving contributed significantly to the image of a British government that too easily resorted to the use of arbitrary power. In December 1773, he helped plan and may have participated in the Boston Tea Party. After the incident, he made the first of more than a dozen rides as a courier carrying news of Boston's resistance to the British, traveling as far south as Philadelphia.

The best known of these missions took place on the night and early morning of 18–19 April 1775. When Boston Patriots learned that the British commander in chief in North America, General Thomas Gage, was planning to order several hundred soldiers to seize resistance leaders Samuel Adams and John Hancock, who had fled from Boston to nearby Lexington, and destroy the munitions of the provincial militia stored in Concord, they dispatched Revere and William Dawes to warn Adams, Hancock, and the countryside. The two riders, joined by Samuel Prescott in Lexington, succeeded in their mission. Adams and Hancock escaped, and the warned militiamen drove the British regulars back to Boston.

Once the war began, Revere lobbied for a field commission. He was a veteran of the French and Indian War, having served as a junior officer of artillery in a failed 1756 campaign to take Crown Point on Lake Champlain from the French. In the first year of the Revolutionary War, however, he was busy making engraved copper plates to print currency for the province and helping design a much-needed gunpowder mill. He did receive a commission as a lieutenant colonel of artillery in 1776 but saw little action in the conflict. He commanded *Castle William* in Boston Harbor for a time, and in 1779 he led Massachusetts troops aboard Captain Dudley Saltonstall's disastrous naval expedition against a British force at Penobscot Bay. Accused of cowardice and insubordination, Revere resigned from the service, although a court-martial three years later cleared him of the charges.

At the war's conclusion, Revere returned to his silver shop and opened a hardware store. In 1788 he built an iron foundry, where he cast church bells and cannon, and twelve years later he built a copper rolling mill. He supplied the copper to resheath the hull of USS *Constitution*, boilers for Robert Fulton's steamboats, and the dome of the Massachusetts statehouse. Revere remained active in politics, rallying Boston artisans to support the ratification of the 1787 U.S. Constitution. Although he served as Suffolk County coroner and as president of Boston's board of health, he held no major political office. Contending that he had never truly been a supporter of democracy, he became a strong supporter of the Federalist Party in the 1790s. He died on 10 May 1818. Although he was a man of many accomplishments, he is most widely known through the words of Henry Wadsworth Longfellow, who immortalized Revere's midnight warning to Lexington in the 1861 poem, "Paul Revere's Ride."

LARRY GRAGG

Portrait of Paul Revere (1735–1818), American Patriot by John Singleton Copley. (Freelance Photography Guild/Corbis)

See also

Boston Massacre; Boston Tea Party; Copley, John Singleton; Lexington and Concord; Minutemen; Penobscot Expedition; Saltonstall, Dudley; Sons of Liberty; Townshend Acts

References

Fischer, David Hackett. *Paul Revere's Ride.* New York: Oxford University Press, 1994.
Forbes, Esther. *Paul Revere and the World He Lived In.* Boston: Little, Brown, 1942.

Triber, Jayne E. *A True Republican: The Life of Paul Revere*. Amherst: University of Massachusetts Press, 1998.

Zannieri, Nina, and Patrick Leehey. *Paul Revere: Artisan, Businessman, and Patriot: The Man behind the Myth*. Boston: Paul Revere Memorial Association, 1988.

Rhode Island

Although only one major battle, the Battle of Rhode Island (28–29 August 1778), which ended the Continental Army's attempt to drive the British from Newport, was fought on Rhode Island's soil, the American Revolutionary War left its political, social, and military mark on the state. Its soldiers and sailors served in widely scattered areas in several states and on several coasts throughout the war, and the British blockaded Rhode Island's ports and occupied Newport for more than three years. Estimates indicate that the Revolution cost Rhode Island $1 million, with heavy damages from battle casualties, the decline in trade, and the flight of Loyalists from the state. Following the war, Rhode Island, heavily influenced by Quaker antislavery sentiment, which supported the Antifederalist opposition to a new Constitution that countenanced slavery, was the last of the original thirteen states to join the new federal union.

The Revolution did not change Rhode Island's governmental structure, but it did bring about legal and political changes, producing legislation that affected Catholics and African slaves. The Revolution prompted the decline of Newport in favor of Providence as the center of the state's population and commerce. Partially because of the three-year British occupation, Newport's growth was arrested, while Providence flourished. Newport's almost total commitment to marine commerce had created a society of people who were highly dependent on each other; merchant and dockworker, sailmaker and ropewalk owner united to achieve their common goal of the success of each voyage. Dependency also extended to social networks through which the wealthy took responsibility for other community members. In 1764 Britain began to resolutely enforce new import duties and commercial regulations, and the interests of Newport and the British government suddenly clashed after several decades during which the successful evasion of British customs duties by Newport residents had maintained peace in the colony. The long British occupation of Newport encouraged the Loyalism that had existed among its townspeople before the war. By 1782, the population of Newport had dwindled from 9,209 to 5,532. Providence, more sheltered from the Royal Navy at the head of Narragansett Bay and a center of Revolutionary activity, remained stable during the Revolution.

Perhaps the largest irony of the American Revolution for Rhode Island lies in the fact that this first colony to declare its independence from Britain, in May 1776, became the last state to ratify the U.S. Constitution, in May 1790, when the new federal government had been in operation for more than a year. Rhode Island's distinctive history, both before and during the Revolutionary War, provides some keys to understanding this seeming contradiction.

Angry Rhode Islanders burn the British revenue cutter *Gaspée* in 1772. (North Wind Picture Archives)

Nonconformist, committed to religious toleration, and emphatically hostile to the Puritan leaders in Boston, Roger Williams established the first permanent settlement in Rhode Island at Providence Plantation in 1636, the year that Harvard College was established in Massachusetts. Williams believed that local Indians owned the land on which they lived, and he set the important precedent of purchasing it from them. Other settlers who thought like Williams on matters of church and state flocked to the new settlement, and soon communities were established in Portsmouth (1638), Newport (1639), and Warwick (1642). In March 1644, England granted Williams a parliamentary patent that united the four towns into a single colony, and other settlements soon joined them.

In 1663, King Charles II granted Dr. John Clarke the Royal Charter to Rhode Island, guaranteeing complete religious liberty and establishing a self-governing colony with nearly total autonomy. The charter also strengthened Rhode Island's territorial claims and officially established its name: Rhode Island and Providence Plantations. This was the most liberal charter that England issued during the colonial era, and many persecuted religious groups, including Baptists, Quakers, Jews, and French Huguenots, settled in Rhode Island to enjoy its religious freedom and easy government.

By the end of the seventeenth century, Newport was a prosperous port and Rhode Island's dominant community. There were nine incorporated towns, and the population had increased to more than 6,000 people. By the eve of the Revolution in 1774, Rhode Island had 59,707 people who lived in twenty-nine towns. Utilizing the labor of black and Indian slaves, Rhode Island farmers produced livestock, dairy products, and crops of apples, onions, and flax. Its residents harvested lumber and barrel staves from its forests, and whaling and fishing provided wealth from the sea.

One of the less savory aspects of Rhode Island's commerce involved the molasses, rum, and slaves of the triangular trade. The colony built a brisk commerce with nearly every quarter of the Atlantic community, including England, the Portuguese Islands, Africa, South America, the West Indies, and several other British mainland colonies. The most lucrative and infamous part of this commerce was the slave trade, in which Rhode Island's merchants surpassed their counterparts in every other mainland colony. The Rhode Island traffic formed one part of the triangular route that brought molasses from the West Indies to Rhode Island, where it was distilled into rum. The rum was bartered along the African coast for slaves, who were carried in slave ships to the West Indies and the southern colonies, performed domestic service in the mansions of the merchants, or labored as workers on the plantation-size farms of southern Rhode Island.

Britain's passage of the Sugar Act in 1764, levying new duties on the sugar and molasses imports that were so essential to Providence distilleries and to the triangular trade in rum and slaves, generated a tide of local protest that swept Rhode Islanders into the Revolution in the 1770s. As a succession of arbitrary British laws such as the Stamp Act, the Townshend duties, the Tea Act, and finally the Coercive Acts moved the colony toward separation from Britain, the town of Providence became a leader of the resistance movement, its citizens agitating for total autonomy, including the exclusive power to tax themselves.

The Rhode Island General Assembly opened the year 1776 by reclaiming a right it had abandoned more than seventy years earlier and voted to commission privateers to seize British ships engaged in operations against the united colonies and to appoint a court with a jury to hear claims for prizes. Then, on 4 May 1776, the General Assembly voted to repudiate its allegiance to King George III, the first state to take this measure. From this point on, citizens of Rhode Island were not to invoke the name or authority of the king, since their colony had severed its slender ties with Britain. In the Continental Congress in July, Rhode Island solidly backed the resolution to declare independence from Britain.

These actions highlighted two important Rhode Island traditions. Declaring independence from Britain voiced the old spirit of independence in Rhode Island and the willingness to follow the path of conviction that had brought pioneers such as Williams and Anne Hutchinson to found the colony. Rhode Islanders had been opposing the Royal Navy and its encroachments on local trade for some time, and led by Stephen Hopkins, Rhode Island had early on called for the union of the rebellious colonies.

As America's Continental Army attempted unsuccessfully to expel the British from Newport, Rhode Island shippers rushed into privateering. The closing of Narragansett Bay by Britain's navy hampered this activity, but both Rhode Island's maritime investors and its mariners operated from bases at New Bedford or Boston, often merging their ventures with local interests. Toward the end of the war, privateering returned to Providence and Newport on a small scale but did not reach the volume seen earlier in neighboring states. But the seafaring communities of Rhode Island had to keep commercially active to escape poverty, and many people took great risks and lost both their lives and their fortunes defending their "sacred honor" as members of an independent state.

Rhode Island's commerce, like its privateering, enjoyed an early burst of activity following independence but then had to redirect its activity into other channels because of the British blockade and occupation of Newport. Ships could escape Narragansett Bay by stealth and expert seamanship, but the risks were great, and maritime traffic shifted to safer ports in Massachusetts. Even in these difficult circumstances, however, Rhode Island merchants sought new commercial connections in France, Spain, the Netherlands, and the Caribbean, where huge central marketing cities beckoned. Despite the new markets, however, Rhode Island merchants hastened to resume trade with British ports at the end of the Revolution. During the war, they also turned to new kinds of business, including the filling of supply contracts for the armed forces. Wartime scarcities also generated increased profits in manufacturing items such as cannon.

To finance its participation in the Revolutionary War, Rhode Island turned to paper currency and for some time put its faith in the Continental dollar. The state firmly controlled its Revolutionary War financial obligations in the early years, taxing its citizens more than most states and forcing them to subscribe to federal loans when Congress began borrowing. This Revolutionary zeal cooled when in 1780 the United States repudiated most of its Continental currency and switched to a system of requisitions on the states to supply men, arms, provisions, uniforms, and other items needed to fight the war.

The Revolutionary War kept quenching the initial ardor of Rhode Islanders for a union of the states. The failure to develop an equitable fiscal policy that would distribute costs reasonably was just one obstacle. The Continental Congress consistently relegated recapturing Newport to low priority and never made serious efforts to protect the New England coast from raids by the British navy. When the United States launched its navy, its officials condemned the predatory approach to fighting at sea that Rhode Island skippers thought natural and logical, and the same officials abandoned all efforts to maintain the naval strength that Rhode Islanders thought essential.

Rhode Island rushed to ratify the Articles of Confederation in 1778 but afterward grew so distrustful of the Continental Congress that the legislature allowed the voters to choose their representatives to Congress at the annual general election. Generations of Rhode Islanders had taught themselves how to use their colonial government to watch out for local interests and head off the centralization of authority in London. Naturally, they resisted centralization in Philadelphia and sought to use their state power even more extensively than they had employed their influence as a colony. The height of that influence came in 1782 and again in 1786, when the state refused to approve Congress's plan to acquire an independent source of income through an impost on imports, an arrangement to which every other state initially agreed. This refusal contributed to the effort to reform the Articles of Confederation and ultimately led to the U.S. Constitution.

The Revolutionary War and its spirit of freedom also influenced Rhode Island's attitude toward slavery and was the impetus for the General Assembly to pass the Gradual Emancipation Act in 1784 and to ban the slave trade in October 1787. And in 1783, the Rhode Island General Assembly removed the arbitrarily civil disabilities against Roman Catholics that dated from 1719 by giving Catholics "all the rights and privileges of the Protestant citizens of this state." The manumission law of 1784 was the most significant of several laws regarding African slaves. Following a Lockean preface, the measure granted freedom to all children born to slave mothers after 1 March 1784. Although encouraging, this law did not abolish slavery because it failed to require the emancipation of the state's existing slaves. But the manumission measure did inspire Rhode Island reformers, especially Quakers, to work for the banning of the slave trade. After much agitation, the General Assembly passed a law in October 1787 that prohibited any Rhode Island citizen from engaging in the slave trade. The legislature termed the trade inconsistent with "that more enlightened and civilized state of freedom which has of late prevailed."

Between September 1787 and January 1790, however, Rhode Island was finally forced to confront the issue of national identity it had largely ignored, or stoutly resisted, throughout the 1780s. The General Assembly rejected at least eleven attempts by the representatives from the mercantile ports to convene a state convention to ratify the U.S. Constitution. Instead, the Assembly, dominated by rural members, defied the ratifying instructions inserted in the Constitution by the Founding Fathers by conducting a popular referendum on the Constitution. That election, which was boycotted by many supporters of a stronger union, rejected the Constitution by a vote of 2,708 to 237. A primary reason for the rejection was the fear of most Rhode Island citizens that any central government, whether it was located in London, New York, or Philadelphia, would encroach on local authority. This ideology, local economic concerns, and a centuries-old independent spirit explain the wariness of Rhode Island toward the Constitution.

Finally, in January 1790, more than eight months after George Washington's inauguration as the first president of the United States and with the federal government making claims that it would, in all its commercial relations, treat Rhode Island as a foreign nation, the state's dominant Country Party called the required Constitutional Conventional. After two separate sessions, one in South Kingstown from 1 to 6 March and the second in Newport from 24 to 29 May, approval was finally obtained. The ratification tally—34 in favor and 32 opposed—was the narrowest of any state, and the ratification vote was favorable only because four Antifederalists either deliberately absented themselves or abstained from voting.

Despite its deep reservations about central government, however, Revolutionary-era Rhode Island entered the Early National Period of American history with the will and ability to grow and expand with the new nation.

KATHY WARNES

See also

Articles of Confederation; Coercive Acts; Constitution, United States, Ratification of; Newport, Rhode Island, Naval Operations against; Privateering; Rhode Island, Battle of; Stamp Act; Sugar Act; Sullivan, John; Tea Act; Townshend Acts

References

Alderman, Clifford Lindsey. *The Rhode Island Colony.* London: Crowell-Collier, 1969.

Crane, Elaine Forman. *A Dependent People: Newport, Rhode Island, in the Revolutionary Era.* 1985. Reprint, New York: Fordham University Press, 1992.

James, Sydney V. *Colonial Rhode Island: A History.* New York: Scribner, 1975.

James, Sydney V., Shelia L. Skemp, and Bruce C. Daniels, eds. *The Colonial Metamorphoses in Rhode Island.* Hanover, NH: University Press of New England, 2000.

"The Revolutionary Era, 1763–1790." *State of Rhode Island General Assembly History Pages.* http://www.rilin.state.ri.us/studteaguide/RhodeIslandHistory/chapt3.html.

Rhode Island, Battle of
(29 July–31 August 1778)

From 29 July to 31 August 1778, American and French forces campaigned to regain control of Newport, on the south end of Aquidneck (or Rhode) Island, that had been lost to General Sir Henry Clinton and a British army of 6,000 men in December 1776. As a result of the Franco-American treaty of alliance, signed on 6 February 1778, an American land force commanded by Major General John Sullivan coordinated its assaults against Newport with operations conducted by a French fleet commanded by Admiral Jean-Baptiste d'Estaing. The failure of the operation soured relations between America and France at the very beginning of the alliance and led to considerable name-calling and second-guessing on both sides. Ultimately, cooler heads from among both sides prevailed. Differences were reconciled, rhetoric was toned down, and the relationship was not crippled. Finally, everyone admitted—at least for public consumption—that the allies' lack of success was due more to failures in communication between commanders, bad weather, geographical difficulties, intervention of a British fleet, and plain bad luck than to stupidity or turpitude on the part of either Sullivan or d'Estaing.

In the early summer of 1778, Sullivan commanded 1,000 Continental regulars at Providence, Rhode Island, and British General Robert Pigot held

American troops advancing on the British at Newport on 25 August 1778. The 1st Rhode Island Regiment, a unit of African American soldiers, held off attacks by the British in the Battle of Rhode Island, thereby allowing American troops to escape a trap. (Library of Congress)

Newport with a reinforced garrison of 6,700 troops. D'Estaing, arriving with a French fleet off the mouth of New York Harbor on 11 July, discovered that his ships were too large to safely cross the bar at Sandy Hook. Therefore, he could not attack the British fleet of Admiral Richard Howe at anchor in the harbor. General George Washington, in consultation with Congress, proposed to d'Estaing that he take his fleet to Rhode Island. There he would coordinate his operations with an American army commanded by Sullivan for an attack against Pigot at Newport. D'Estaing agreed and on 22 July sailed eastward toward Rhode Island. Sensing a great opportunity, Washington called upon the New England states to mobilize 5,000 militiamen and dispatched the veteran Continental brigades of Generals James Varnum and John Glover to reinforce Sullivan. He also sent Generals Nathanael Greene, a Rhode Islander, and the Marquis de Lafayette to assist Sullivan. It was ten days after d'Estaing arrived before the militia was fully mobilized, but finally 6,000 men, commanded by John Hancock, marched to Sullivan's assistance. The American army at full strength numbered 10,000 troops, and d'Estaing also had 4,000 French men on transports in his impressive fleet.

On 29 July d'Estaing reached Rhode Island and established contact with Sullivan. The tone of d'Estaing's correspondence with the American general was excessively complimentary, but from the very beginning frictions began to emerge. The admiral was anxious to begin operations immediately, but Sullivan still had not collected the New England militia. Moreover, Sullivan adopted a tone of correspondence with d'Estaing that the admiral thought was too blunt and too suggestive of orders to an inferior officer. D'Estaing was totally unimpressed with the American army, referring to the two veteran Continental brigades as militia, and he was disappointed that his fleet was not supplied with water and provisions as he had expected. Nevertheless, when Sullivan met d'Estaing on his flagship on 30 July, the Frenchman agreed to follow Sullivan's plan of operations. The French fleet would sail up the Middle Passage on 8 August, bombarding the British in Newport on the way, and a day later Sullivan would shift his troops from Tiverton on the mainland to the northeastern end of Aquidneck Island. Early on 10 August, acting in unison with the Americans, d'Estaing would land French troops on the west side of the island, and the allies would carry out a general assault against Pigot's lines around Newport.

On 5 August, preparatory to these maneuvers, d'Estaing sent Admiral Pierre de Suffren on a preliminary mission against British ships in Rhode Island Harbor. With two frigates, Suffren sailed up the Seakonnet, or East, Passage, while two ships of the line supported him in the Middle Passage. The British were thrown into a panic. They abandoned Conanicut Island, and their warships fled in total disarray. The frigate *Cerberus* (32 guns), in Narragansett Bay, tried to reach Newport but ran aground, was set afire by its own captain, and exploded. Also grounded and destroyed were the frigates *Juno*, *Orpheus*, and *Lark* (all 32 guns); the *Kingfisher* (16 guns); and the galley *Pigot*. The *Flora* (32 guns), the *Falcon* (18 guns), and several transports were scuttled to block Newport Harbor against French warships. On 8 August, according to plan, d'Estaing sailed up the Middle Passage, bombarding Newport as he passed, and anchored off Conanicut Island. While waiting for the scheduled attack on 10 August, he allowed sailors suffering from scurvy to land on the island to restore their health. Sullivan meanwhile collected his army at Tiverton and prepared to cross over to Aquidneck Island at the appointed time. He dispatched Lafayette with 1,000 troops to join the French allies in preparing for the assault.

Learning that Pigot had abandoned his works on the northern end of Aquidneck Island and withdrawn to fortifications around Newport, Sullivan crossed over to occupy these lines on 9 August, a day earlier than the plans called for. D'Estaing apparently was offended by this violation of military etiquette: the Americans landing ahead of the French and without prior consultation. Nevertheless, the admiral realized that Sullivan's movement made tactical sense and began landing troops in accordance with the original plan. In any case, the point quickly became moot, for on that same day, 9 August, at about noon the British fleet under Howe arrived off Rhode Island from New York. Despite Sullivan's entreaties that d'Estaing leave the French troops under his command, the admiral reembarked his men and sailed out on 10 August to engage Howe's fleet. After two days of maneuvering, both fleets were battered by a great gale. The crippled British vessels eventually returned to New York, and d'Estaing's fleet ultimately reached Rhode Island on 20 August.

On 11 August, Sullivan decided to advance against Pigot's lines around Newport, even though he did not have support from the French. Delayed by

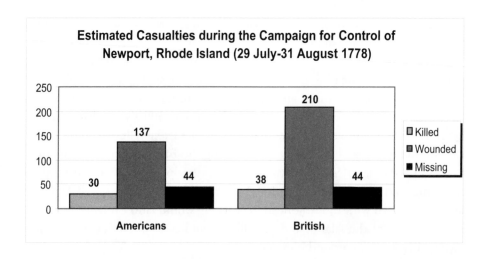

Estimated Casualties during the Campaign for Control of Newport, Rhode Island (29 July–31 August 1778)

the storm, he pushed southward on 15 August and started regular approaches on the eastern end of his lines. Four days later he began firing artillery at the British lines, with his opponents reciprocating without much effect. When d'Estaing reappeared on 20 August, Sullivan pleaded with him to disembark French troops to assist the American army. Sullivan and his general officers, Lafayette excepted, even wrote a letter to d'Estaing suggesting that French honor was in the balance. No amount of entreaty sufficed, and on 22 August d'Estaing proceeded to Boston to repair his battered fleet. Suddenly the American army was in serious trouble. That same day, Greene declared that neither the evacuation nor the continued occupation of Aquidneck Island seemed to be a viable option. The situation quickly got worse over the next few days, for d'Estaing's departure led to wholesale desertions by the New England militia. On 26 August, Lafayette rode to Boston and unsuccessfully pleaded with d'Estaing to return to Rhode Island. Although Sullivan at first blustered that the Americans could go it alone and that Pigot would never attempt any offensive action, he began withdrawing the remainder of his army, about 7,000 men, on the evening of 28 August.

Contrary to Sullivan's optimistic assertions, Pigot quickly pursued the American army, and Sullivan ordered light infantry covering forces under Colonels Henry Beekman Livingston and John Laurens to slow their adversary's progress. By 3:00 A.M. on 29 August, the Americans were busy fortifying the south face of Butt's Hill, on the northwest end of Aquidneck Island near Bristol Ferry. By 9:00 the light infantry forces were driven into these defensive works by the Hessian jaegers of General Baron von Lossberg. Greene was in command of the American left flank, and Sullivan personally commanded the center and right. Greene advocated an attack on Lossberg's jaegers but was overruled. Instead, Sullivan waited for an attack by Pigot's right wing, which was commanded by General Francis Smith. This assault was repulsed by General John Glover's brigade, which drove the British back to Quaker Hill in confusion.

Meanwhile, the American right came under artillery fire from British warships in the Middle Channel, and Lossberg, commanding the British left, charged forward and captured a number of outer works. Bringing guns forward, the Hessians commenced firing into the American lines, which were reinforced by Sullivan and remained steadfast in the face of their opponent's pounding. Three times Lossberg sent his jaegers charging against the American positions, and three times they were repulsed with great loss. A newly raised regiment of black troops, the Black Rhode Islanders, commanded by Major Samuel Ward, fought valiantly in the repulse of the Hessian regulars. Greene then counterattacked, pushing Lossberg back in considerable disarray. Sullivan wanted very much to continue the advance and drive the opposition off Turkey and Quaker Hills, but realizing that his men were exhausted and hungry after thirty-six hours of constant action, he called off the pursuit. By 3:00 P.M. the battle settled into an artillery duel, with Pigot bringing up additional guns from Newport and Sullivan preparing for further Anglo-Hessian attacks that did not materialize.

During the following day, 30 August, the rival armies maintained their positions, eyeing each other warily. The Americans were proud of the way they had conducted themselves the previous day, for they had performed with spirit and discipline under difficult circumstances. They had lost 30 killed, 137 wounded, and 44 missing, while the British had suffered 38 killed, 210 wounded, and 44 missing. But the Americans had failed in their mission of capturing Newport, and on the night of 30–31 August they were faced with the difficult and dangerous maneuver of evacuating Aquidneck Island. Glover conducted the operation, using Salem boatmen under his supervision. Sullivan then dismissed the few remaining militiamen under his command and marched back to Providence with 1,200 Continental regulars. His escape was as timely as it was fortunate, for on 1 September Clinton arrived by sea at Newport with 5,000 fresh troops.

American recriminations against the French, particularly d'Estaing, however, continued, for some time, and the admiral expressed anger and resentment at what he called ill-conceived complaints. Washington finally intervened, writing to Sullivan, Greene, William Heath, and other prominent Patriot leaders to recommend that they cultivate "harmony and good agreement" between Americans and Frenchmen. Congress did its part, resolving that d'Estaing had "behaved as a brave and wise officer" and had done all "which the circumstances and nature of the service would admit of." D'Estaing chose to be appeased by these slightly ambiguous words, and harmony between the allies was gradually restored.

PAUL DAVID NELSON

See also

Estaing, Jean-Baptiste, Comte d'; Glover, John; Greene, Nathanael; Lafayette, Marquis de; Newport, Rhode Island, Naval Operations against; Suffren, Pierre-André de; Sullivan, John

References

Billias, George A. *General John Glover and His Marblehead Mariners*. New York: Holt, 1960.

Deardon, Paul F. *The Rhode Island Campaign of 1778: Inauspicious Dawn of Alliance*. Providence: Rhode Island Bicentennial Foundation, 1980.

Gruber, Ira D. *The Howe Brothers and the American Revolution*. New York: Norton, 1972.

Miller, Nathan. *Sea of Glory: The Continental Navy Fights for Independence, 1775–1783*. New York: David McKay, 1974.

Simister, Florence Parker. *The Fire's Center: Rhode Island in the Revolutionary Era, 1763–1790*. Providence: Rhode Island Bicentennial Foundation, 1979.

Stinchcombe, William C. *The American Revolution and the French Alliance*. Syracuse, NY: Syracuse University Press, 1969.

Ward, Christopher. *War of the Revolution*. 2 vols. New York: Macmillan, 1952.

Whittemore, Charles P. *A General of the Revolution: John Sullivan of New Hampshire*. New York: Columbia University Press, 1961.

Riedesel, Friedrich Adolph, Baron von

(1738–1800)

Friedrich von Riedesel was credited with introducing the Christmas tree to North America.

A Brunswick general, Baron Friedrich Adolph von Riedesel commanded German troops in Canada and upper New York in 1776 and 1777, playing a prominent role in the Saratoga Campaign and later commanding the Convention Army. His full correct name and title are General F. A. Riedesel, Freiherr zu Eisenbach.

Riedesel was born on 3 June 1738 in Lauterbach, the third of seven children of Johann Wilhelm Riedesel by his first wife, Sophie Hedwig von Borke (daughter of a general in the Prussian army). The Riedesel family belonged to the lesser nobility of Hesse and, since 1680, had held the title "Freiherr (Baron) zu Eisenbach." However, the family was not wealthy, and Friedrich's father worked as a government official to supplement the income from his estates. The Riedesels were devout Lutherans, and Friedrich was destined to become a minister until, at age fifteen, his father sent him to Marburg to study law, in preparation for a diplomatic career. Young Riedesel apparently preferred watching the city's garrison at drill and was befriended by an officer who tricked him into believing that his father had consented to his entering the army. In fact, his father was so angry at the news that he cut off all financial support.

As a seventeen-year-old officer cadet, Riedesel was sent to London when his regiment was hired by the British government, but in 1757 he returned to Europe and served in the army commanded by Duke Ferdinand of Brunswick. Though nominally still an officer in the forces of the Landgrave of Hesse, Riedesel became an aide to Ferdinand and eventually transferred into Brunswick service to improve his career prospects. Over the next four years, Riedesel served with sufficient distinction (particularly at the Battle of Minden) to gain the notice of both the duke and Frederick the Great, and by the age of twenty-three Riedesel was a colonel commanding two regiments.

In 1760, while posted to Minden, he had met Charlotte von Massow (called Frederika in modern works), the fifteen-year-old daughter of a Prussian military official, and had proposed but was recalled to duty before they could marry. In August 1762, he was wounded and returned to Minden to convalesce, with Massow nursing him. Despite his father's objections (the

Massows were apparently even poorer than the Riedesels), the couple was married at Paderborn in December 1762 and spent the next thirteen years living in Wolffenbüttel, producing four children (the first two died before one year of age). During this period, Riedesel was appointed adjutant general to the Duke of Brunswick, and in January 1776 he was promoted to major general and given command of the corps that the duke had contracted to send to America.

With 4,300 men, Riedesel left Brunswick in February, arriving in Portsmouth in March. He then spent six weeks crossing the Atlantic, arriving at Quebec City on 1 June. At this point, Massow, who was pregnant, was still in Wolffenbüttel but determined to join him. Just two months after giving birth to their fifth child, she arrived in England. She spoke no English, had no money, and did not qualify for any official assistance. Fortunately, a former colleague of Riedesel looked after her, and she was eventually presented to the king and queen. After eleven months in Britain, she sailed for Canada with three children (all under five years of age), their nurse, two maids, and a coachman and was reunited with Riedesel at Chambly.

Baron Friedrich von Riedesel, the commander of German forces in the Saratoga Campaign. (National Archives and Records Administration)

Riedesel's corps had played only a minor role in the campaign of 1776, but it was chosen to take part in the ill-fated expedition under General John Burgoyne that left Canada in June 1777. Despite difficulties with logistics and the terrain, Burgoyne's overconfidence led him to exclude Riedesel from his initial councils of war and ignore the Brunswicker's objections to the foraging expedition to Bennington. Disregarding these snubs, Riedesel was a good subordinate and performed well, rescuing Simon Fraser's outnumbered Advance Corps at Hubbardton and Hamilton's brigade at Freeman's Farm. Throughout the campaign, Riedesel was cool and decisive under fire and sufficiently sensitive to aver to the greater experience of American conditions of nominal subordinates, such as Fraser.

After the surrender at Saratoga, Burgoyne's army was taken to Boston. At first, the Riedesels lived in the attic of a farmhouse but were then moved to Cambridge, where Riedesel celebrated his fortieth birthday. Later that year, he led the Convention Army on its long march into Virginia (dining with the Marquis de Lafayette en route), but the following summer found him suffering from heat stroke and depression. He was returned to New York City toward the end of 1779 (though not officially exchanged until October 1780) and lived with the British commander in chief, Sir Henry Clinton (who spoke good German, having also served as aide to the Duke of Brunswick during the Seven Years' War). Another daughter, Amerika, was born in 1780.

Surviving a bout of typhus, Riedesel was promoted to lieutenant general in 1781 and took charge of the troops around New York City and Long Island, settling his family in Brooklyn. However, they were forced to move back to Sorel, where Riedesel reorganized the German forces in Canada, and there they spent the last two years of the war (during which time he was credited with introducing the Christmas tree to North America). A seventh child, Canada, was born in November 1782 but died a few months later and was buried at Sorel. Soon after, Riedesel learned that his father had also died, and with the war now virtually over, the Riedesels and the remaining Brunswick troops left Canada in August 1783. After a brief stop in London, they arrived in Brunswick in October.

Riedesel could now spend more time in Lauterbach, and between 1785 and 1788 he and his wife had two more children. In 1788, the Duke of Brunswick loaned troops to Austria to quell a revolt in the Low Countries, and Riedesel spent the next three years on campaign, with his family living in Maastricht. (During this conflict, one of his subordinates was his younger brother Johann; their only previous common service was in the Seven Years' War, when they had been on opposite sides.) In 1792, the Netherlands was invaded by the armies of the French Republic, and Riedesel took part in the campaign to expel them. After a brief period in retirement at Lauterbach, he was recalled to service as commandant of the city of Brunswick, a post he held for six years. In increasingly poor health, Riedesel died in his sleep on 6 January 1800. His reputation was such that despite the difficulties of cross-border travel caused by the French Revolution, several rulers allowed his wife to take his body across their territory without tolls so that he could be buried at Lauterbach. Massow left Brunswick for her native Berlin in 1801 and died there on 29 March 1808.

It is unfortunate that the most frequently seen artistic image of Riedesel shows him in his fifties rather than in his prime—strongly built, vigorous, and hardy—as he was in America. As well as being courageous, sound in judgment, and tactful, he was always attentive to the comfort and well-being of his men and was a popular commander with all ranks. It was entirely fitting that he returned to Brunswick a hero. Of his nine children, four daughters and one son—Georg—outlived him, though the latter produced no male children.

Riedesel's wife—born Frederika Charlotte Louise von Massow (1746–1808) but known in the Riedesel family as Charlotte and nicknamed "Fritschen"—produced a journal describing their experiences in America that was published in the year that her husband died. She appears to have been a resilient woman, capable of pitching in when needed—for example, supervising the care of the wounded prior to the surrender at Saratoga and rescuing the Brunswick regimental colors—but maintaining an obvious distance from the wives of the ordinary soldiers.

German authorities with access to the family archives are clear that the Hessian Riedesels, despite belonging to a noble family dating back to the twelfth century, did not use "von" until very recently (and then only as a shorter alternative to "Riedesel Freiherr zu Eisenbach"). In fact, the first such usage may have been in the memoirs of the general and his wife, as the original publishers were based in Berlin and incorporated the standard Prussian noble predicate, used to indicate the geographical location of a family's estate (equivalent to "de" in France, or "of" in Britain). However, Riedesel was a family name, not a place name—meaning either "donkey rider" or a table on which reeds are cut, according to the method of translation—and had Riedesel followed the Prussian practice, he would have been Friedrich Adolph von Eisenbach.

BRENDAN D. MORRISSEY

See also

Bennington, Battle of; Burgoyne, John; Canada, Operations in; Convention Army; Fraser, Simon; German Mercenaries; Hubbardton, Battle of; Saratoga Campaign

References

Brown, Marvin, trans. *Baroness von Riedesel and the American Revolution: Journal and Correspondence of a Tour of Duty, 1776–1783.* Chapel Hill: University of North Carolina, 1965.
Stone, William, trans. *Memoirs, Letters and Journals of Major General Riedesel.* New York: New York Times and Arno, 1969.
Tharp, Louise. *The Baroness and the General.* Boston: Little, Brown, 1962.

Rifle

Despite having much greater accuracy than muskets, rifles were generally not used as military weapons in the eighteenth century. A rifle, by definition, has grooves cut down the length of the barrel, a technique known as "rifling." These grooves grip the ball tightly so that when the weapon is fired the ball leaves the barrel with a spin. The projectile thus travels with greater range and accuracy than when fired from a smoothbore musket.

The rifle was perfected in Germany by gunsmiths and hunters, where it was known as a Jäger rifle (*Jäger* is German for "hunter"). These were heavy, short-barreled, large-caliber weapons. German settlers in Pennsylvania later began to lengthen the barrel and reduce the caliber. The Pennsylvania rifle simply adapted the Old World weapon to the conditions of the New World. From Pennsylvania, gunsmiths and traders brought the weapon to the frontiers of New York, the Old Northwest, and the Southeast.

Whereas a soldier armed with a musket might hit an individual target at perhaps 80 or 100 yards at best, a rifleman could hit a target 200–300 yards away. The rifle was a hunting weapon specifically designed to be loaded and fired slowly. Its handler had to load it carefully before taking aim at his target. Most rifles required about a full minute to load as opposed to perhaps half that time for a musket. Thus, in combat, riflemen generally fired at will rather than in volleys. With each man loading at his own pace, riflemen produced a steady rolling fire.

The process of loading followed a prescribed sequence. First, powder was measured from a horn into a measuring horn or flask. This charge was then poured down the barrel. Next, a greased patch, usually a scrap of paper or cloth, was put over the muzzle with a ball. Rifles often had a patch box built into the stock for storing greased patches. The marksman then rammed

> Most rifles required about a full minute to load.

American rifleman (*left*) and a soldier with the Pennsylvania Continental line. (Library of Congress)

this down the barrel. The tight-fitting ball was more difficult to ram down the barrel of a rifle than that of a smoothbore musket. Often the ramrod was wooden, and care had to be taken not to break it by loading the ball too quickly. Last, the soldier primed the pan from his horn.

In addition to the slowness of loading, the rifle suffered the additional disadvantage of not accommodating a bayonet. On the other hand, most had sights at the muzzle for aiming, and in any event a rifleman never wished to be close enough to the enemy to require the use of a bayonet. By definition, his advantage lay in his ability to strike a target from a considerable distance. Other features mitigated against the use of rifles in hand-to-hand combat: they were light and delicate, their parts were small and fragile, and their stocks were thin. In short, they could not be wielded as clubs or tolerate rough handling.

Unlike muskets, which were mass-produced, rifles were individually crafted by gunsmiths. Rifle ammunition and parts, moreover, were not interchangeable, as was the case with a military musket. Supplying an army of riflemen, each of whom fired a different-sized ball and required different spare parts, would have been unfeasible in the eighteenth century, and hence the continued reliance of all armies of the day on the far less accurate but cheaper musket for the ordinary infantryman.

For civilians, the rifle served as a tool used by families for their personal protection and as a means of putting food on their tables. Passed down through generations, these weapons became important family heirlooms and were often ornately carved and decorated. Rifles were generally found in the hands of militia from frontier areas, such as the Carolina backcountry or western Pennsylvania. In more settled regions, such as New England or coastal Virginia, there was less game and little threat of Indian attack. Militia units from these areas generally carried smoothbore fowlers, trade muskets, or captured military muskets.

Riflemen generally served in units of their own during the Revolution. They were most effective as skirmishers and sharpshooters but always relied on musket-armed troops to support them. At the start of hostilities, the Continental Congress authorized Virginia, Maryland, and Pennsylvania to provide rifle companies to the Continental Army outside Boston. Later in the war, Generals Daniel Morgan and Nathanael Greene demonstrated the effective use of riflemen in the battles at Cowpens (17 January 1781) and Guilford Courthouse (15 March 1781). Instructing their riflemen to fire only a few shots and aim for officers, they were able to disrupt advancing British forces. The riflemen were then to fall back and leave the main battle to musket-wielding Continental forces.

Military rifles used during the Revolution included the German Jäger rifle and the Ferguson Rifle. Patrick Ferguson, a major in the British Army, developed a breech-loading rifle that did not require a ramrod. A trigger guard unscrewed to reveal a hole on top of the barrel breech. Ball and powder were inserted, and the trigger guard was rotated to close it. Only 200 Ferguson Rifles were made, and the rifle saw limited use at Brandywine. Ferguson's death at the Battle of Kings Mountain (7 October 1780) ended efforts to promote this unique and highly effective weapon.

The American Long Rifle was a deadly accurate weapon, but its practical use in the field was limited. The notion of American riflemen winning the Revolution is a myth: in reality, Washington's musket-armed infantry had to master linear tactics and meet similarly armed British regulars in the open field.

ROBERT M. DUNKERLY

See also

Cowpens, Battle of; Ferguson, Patrick; German Mercenaries; Greene, Nathanael; Guilford Courthouse, Battle of; Kings Mountain, Battle of; Morgan, Daniel; Musket

References

Blackmore, Howard L. *British Military Firearms, 1650–1850*. London: Greenhill, 1994.

Hughes, Maj.-Gen. B. P. *Firepower: Weapons Effectiveness on the Battlefield, 1630–1850*. London: Arms and Armour, 1974.

LaCrosse, Richard, Jr. *The Frontier Rifleman*. Union City, TN: Pioneer, 1997.

Neumann, George. *Battle Weapons of the American Revolution*. Texarkana, TX: Scurlock, 1998.

Westwood, David. *The Military Rifle*. Santa Barbara, CA: ABC-CLIO, 2004.

Wright, John. *Some Notes on the Continental Army*. New York: Temple Hill, 1975.

Rivington, James
(1724–1802)

James Rivington published *Rivington's New-York Gazette or the Connecticut, Hudson's River, New-Jersey, and Quebec Weekly Advertiser* (later, *Rivington's Royal Gazette*), the most important Loyalist newspaper in America during the Revolution and the first daily newspaper in America.

Rivington was born into a printing family in London but fled to America after pursuing a youth of gambling, expensive tastes, and illegal printing that caused him to file for bankruptcy in 1760. Promoting himself as the only London bookseller in the colonies, he opened bookstores in Philadelphia, New York, and Boston. By 1766 he confined his book selling to New York, but the following year he settled in Annapolis, where he undertook a land scheme known as the Maryland Lottery. When this plan failed, Rivington returned to New York, where his finances and his fortunes improved upon his marriage in 1769 to a wealthy widow, Elizabeth Van Horne, with whom he would have three children.

In 1773 Rivington established his newspaper, which quickly became renowned for its coverage of European news and its transcripts of parliamentary debates. Within two years *Rivington's New-York Gazette* boasted 3,600 subscribers. Isaiah Thomas, publisher of the *Massachusetts Spy*, praised his fellow printer and remarked that no colonial paper was better printed or contained more foreign intelligence than *Rivington's Gazette*. Rivington espoused a nonpartisan press representing all sides in political debates. But his presentation of multiple political perspectives soon earned him criticism from his readers. Angry Patriots hanged the printer in effigy in April 1775. His own Tory-leaning sentiments quickly earned the disdain of many New Yorkers after the battles at Lexington and Concord, and in May he barely escaped an attack on his press by the Connecticut Sons of Liberty, who forced him to sign a loyalty oath to the Patriot cause. In November 1775 a mob headed by the New York City radical Isaac Sears attacked his printing office, confiscated his type, and destroyed his presses. Rivington and his family fled to London.

In September 1777, Rivington returned to New York with an appointment as the king's printer in the British-occupied city and resumed publishing his newspaper, this time under the masthead *Rivington's New York Loyal Gazette*. He changed the name to the *Royal Gazette* in December and forthrightly adopted the British cause. Offended Patriots dubbed his publication "The Lying Gazette." As the tide of the war turned in favor of the Americans, Rivington's partisan voice in print grew weaker. Some sources indicate that he spied for General George Washington by providing the comte de Grasse, via Allan MacLean, with the communication code of the British fleet in time for the siege of Yorktown. Because of Rivington's contribution to America's victory, the story goes, he was spared punishment for his support of the British for several years.

Rivington remained in New York when the British departed the city in 1783. He kept publishing but changed the name of his paper again, this time to *Rivington's New-York Gazette and Universal Advertiser*. His newly titled publication, however, was unable to win public support, and he printed his final issue at the end of 1783. Retiring from printing, he turned to book selling but wound up in debtors' prison from 1797 to 1801 and died impoverished in New York on 4 July 1802.

While Rivington's career seems both checkered and tragic, he did contribute to the American printing tradition by advocating freedom of the press in the early years of America's conflict with Britain, especially in the early 1770s. As printer of the *Royal Gazette*, he also established a publishing schedule with other New York printers from May 1778 to July 1783 that essentially created the first daily newspaper in America.

MARTHA J. KING

See also

New York, Province and State; Washington, George

References

Cray, Catherine Snell. "The Tory and the Spy: The Double Life of James Rivington." *William and Mary Quarterly* 16 (1959): 61–72.

Humphrey, Carol Sue. "James Rivington." Pp. 575–576 in *American National Biography*, Vol. 18. New York. Oxford University Press, 1999.

Robinson, Beverly
(1721–1792)

Beverly Robinson was a New York Loyalist who is best known for his role in the conspiracy of General Benedict Arnold to deliver the fort at West Point to the British Army in 1780.

Beverly (originally Beverley) Robinson was born into a prominent Virginia family. His father, the Honorable John Robinson, president of Virginia's Council, served briefly as acting governor upon the retirement of Governor William Gooch. Young Robinson traveled to New York in 1746 to raise and lead a military company against French Canada during King George's War and stayed to marry Susanna Phillipse, daughter of Frederick Phillipse, owner of the vast Phillipse manor on the Hudson River. This marriage soon involved Robinson in bitter conflicts with tenants who were challenging the great Hudson Valley patroons. When the Revolutionary War began, Robinson was living at Beverly, a home that he built just a few miles south of West Point, and enjoying the large income from the Phillipse estate that had been left to his wife.

Although he was a friend of George Washington and was critical of British imperial trade and taxation policies, Robinson wished to take no part in the colonies' armed conflict with the mother country and opposed American independence. In February 1777, when he was pressured to declare his allegiance to the independent State of New York, he fled from his home in the Hudson Valley to the safety of British-occupied New York City. Now pressured by his friends, he entered the military service of the Crown and served as colonel of the Loyal American Regiment and commanded a corps called the Guides and Pioneers. In October 1777, Robinson fought well during Sir Henry Clinton's capture of Fort Montgomery on the Hudson River, below West Point. Four of Robinson's sons also served with the British forces. The State of New York retaliated by confiscating all of his family's land in the Hudson Valley and legally banishing both him and his wife.

Robinson's most important contribution to the British military effort came in espionage and intelligence. The British consulted him on the possible defection of Patriot leaders of Vermont to the Crown, and he wrote a letter to Ethan Allen that expressed support for a separate Vermont. Robinson was also involved in a clandestine attempt to bring American General Israel Putnam, who was stationed in Robinson's confiscated home, over to the British side.

In the conspiracy of Arnold in 1780, Robinson played his most important role in espionage, and it was supposed that he was among the first persons privy to the traitorous general's purpose. There is evidence that Arnold addressed a letter to him on the subject of going over to the British side before soliciting the command of West Point from Washington. Robinson also accompanied Major

John André to Dobb's Ferry to meet Arnold, but an accident prevented an interview, and both men returned to New York. Arnold then sent a letter to Robinson, who was on board the British warship *Vulture*, anchored on the Hudson River just south of West Point. Shortly thereafter, André, whom Arnold had finally met clandestinely, was captured behind American lines and sent as a prisoner to Robinson's own house, which had been confiscated by the State of New York and which Arnold had occupied as his headquarters. After André's trial and conviction for spying, Clinton sent commissioners to the American camp in the hope of proving the major's innocence and attached Robinson to the commission as a character witness for André because Robinson had been Washington's friend. But both the commission and a letter from Robinson to Washington proved futile, and André was hanged.

Fleeing to England in 1782, Robinson was compensated for his wartime services under an act of Parliament. He was awarded £23,287, and his wife was awarded £800. Robinson spent the rest of his life in England. He lived in retirement at Thornbury, near Bath, until his death in 1792. Beverly, Robinson's home on the Hudson River below West Point, is still standing.

LINDA MILLER

See also

Allen, Ethan; André, John; Arnold, Benedict; Clinton, Henry; Fort Montgomery, New York, Assault on; Loyalists; Putnam, Israel; Washington, George; West Point, New York

References

Countryman, Edward. *A People in Revolution: The American Revolution and Political Society in New York, 1760–1790*. Baltimore, MD: Johns Hopkins University Press, 1981.

Kim, Sung Bok. *Landlord and Tenant in Colonial New York: Manorial Society, 1664–1775*. Chapel Hill: University of North Carolina Press, 1978.

Van Doren, Carl. *Secret History of the American Revolution: An Account of the Conspiracies of Benedict Arnold and Numerous Others from the Secret Service Papers of the British Headquarters in North America*. New York: Viking, 1941.

Ward, Harry. "Robinson, Beverly." Pp. 639–640 in *American National Biography*, Vol. 18. Edited by John Garraty. New York: Oxford University Press, 1999.

Rochambeau, Comte de

See Vimeur, Jean-Baptiste, Comte de Rochambeau

Rodney, Caesar
(1728–1784)

Heir to a wealthy Delaware family and an early advocate of resistance to British policy, Caesar Rodney was a signer of the Declaration of Independence who is best known for riding from his home in Delaware to Congress to cast a decisive vote in favor of independence.

Rodney had been active in public life for several years before the beginning of the American Revolution. At the time of the French and Indian (Seven Years') War, he worked to form a militia company. In the mid-1760s, he participated in Delaware's opposition to the Stamp Act. He also helped with the preparation of a letter sent to King George III protesting the Townshend Acts of 1767–1768. As tensions between Britain and the colonies reached a crisis in the mid-1770s, Rodney was elected to represent Delaware in the First Continental Congress. He quickly became known as one of Congress's most radical members, and in the Second Continental Congress he supported separation from Britain at all costs.

Rodney was frequently absent from Congress throughout 1775 in order to rally support for independence among the citizens of Delaware. When the time came for the thirteen colonial delegations at Philadelphia to vote on the issue, he was in Dover, and Delaware's other two representatives, the radical Thomas McKean and the conservative George Read, were deadlocked. During the night of 1–2 July 1776, Rodney achieved his moment of historical fame for his dash to Philadelphia to break the tie in favor of independence.

Portrait of Caesar Rodney, delegate from Delaware to both the First and Second Continental Congresses and a signer of the Declaration of Independence. Rodney is best known for riding to Congress while gravely ill to break a tie vote in his delegation to approve the Declaration of Independence. (Library of Congress)

In response to his aggressive support for separation, Delaware's moderates and Loyalist sympathizers joined forces to oust Rodney from Congress. Rather than seek political retribution against his opponents, he immediately returned to his home state and joined a militia unit similar to the one he had led at the time of the French and Indian War. He was soon appointed general of Delaware's militia. In recognition of his service in defense of the state and as a sign of the rapidly decreasing influence of the state's Loyalist faction, Delaware voters elected him president (governor) of the state, a position he held until 1781, when ill health forced his retirement.

WILLIAM E. DOODY

See also

Congress, First Continental; Congress, Second Continental and Confederation; Declaration of Independence; Declaration of Independence Signers; Delaware; McKean, Thomas; Stamp Act; Townshend Acts

References

Frank, William P., and Harold B. Hancock. "Caesar Rodney's Two Hundred and Fiftieth Anniversary: An Evaluation." *Delaware History* 18(2) 1978: 63–74.
Ryden, George, ed. *Letters to and from Caesar Rodney, 1756–1784.* 1933. Reprint, Philadelphia: University of Pennsylvania Press, 1970.

Rodney, George
(1719–1792)

One of the boldest and most innovative British admirals of the eighteenth century, George Brydges Rodney won naval victories in the West Indies at the end of the American Revolution that were instrumental in preserving British dominance in the area, creating a stronger position for British negotiators at the peace conference, and altering traditional naval tactics.

During a naval career that began at age fourteen, Rodney cut a dashing figure. Remarkably successful in command by reason of his boldness and his keen eye for strategy and tactics, rewarded with a baronetcy and a seat in Parliament, he was handsome, clever, irascible, indiscreet, unscrupulous, and irresistibly drawn to women and gaming tables. Though he made a fortune in prize money (in part, it was alleged, by cheating fellow officers), he lost it and more gambling and piled up at least £30,000 in election expenses. Appointed a rear-admiral in 1771 with an annual salary of £232 but denied the far more lucrative governorship of Jamaica, he conceived a lively hatred for the Earl of Sandwich, the first lord of the Admiralty. Unable to cope with his creditors and fearful of debtors' prison, Rodney fled to Paris early in 1775, just prior to the outbreak of the American Revolution. Early in 1778 he was promoted to admiral of the White and found his residence in Paris threatened by the impending war between France and Britain. Securing a loan from the Marèchal de Biron, Rodney returned to Britain, laid his hands on his back pay, and cleared his debts. He now desired a sea command, but the ill-feeling between himself and Sandwich was an obstacle. Only when other senior officers began refusing commands to protest Sandwich's management of the Admiralty did Rodney get his chance, accepting on 1 October 1779 command of the Leeward Islands station, important because of the extensive French and British economic interests in the Caribbean.

On 24 December 1779, Rodney left Britain with 22 ships of the line, 8 frigates, 66 supply ships, and about 300 transports bound for the relief of Gibraltar. He was fortunate enough to capture a Spanish convoy of 16 ships off Cape Finisterre on 8 January 1780. A week later he engaged a squadron of 9 Spanish ships off Cape St. Vincent in a night action known as the Moonlight Battle, destroying 1 ship and capturing 6 others with their commander, Admiral Don Juan de Langara. The acclaim that Rodney won from this battle was richly deserved, for he had pioneered a new tactic of naval warfare, beating upwind from the lee position to block from port and trapping an enemy whose possession of the weather gauge should have enabled him to control the battle. The recent sheathing of British warships with copper to retard bottom fouling and provide greater speed and mobility was crucial in this maneuver. With the captured vessels en route to Britain to be sold for prize money, Rodney hoped to alleviate his financial problems. Sandwich was forced to praise him publicly, and Rodney paused briefly in Gibraltar to enjoy the accolades due his success and then sailed for the West Indies, arriving in St. Lucia on 22 March.

The following month Luc-Urbain du Bouexic de Guichen arrived to command French naval forces in the area, and when he put to sea with this fleet, Rodney was not far behind. On 15 April, Rodney unveiled his plan of attack, notifying his captains that he intended to disregard the Admiralty's standing orders to engage the enemy ship-by-ship along the whole length of the enemy line, opting instead to concentrate his entire force on one part of the enemy line to win a crushing victory. The following day, he sighted Guichen to the lee of the island of Martinique. Rodney had the weather gauge and, operating to windward of the French, could control the encounter. On the morning of 17 April, with the French fleet heading south and the British about 12 miles away heading north on a parallel course, Rodney signaled his intent to attack the enemy's rear. He did not, however, refer specifically to the plans he had unveiled two days previously, and by the time the French and British were sailing parallel in the same direction, a variety of other signals had been exchanged within the British fleet.

Thus, just before noon when Rodney gave the order to attack, the commanders at the head of his line, Captain Robert Carkett and Rear-Admiral Hyde Parker, attacked the head of the French line, and other captains arranged their ships accordingly along the whole of the French line. Instead of the decisive victory that Rodney had envisioned, he found himself fighting a brisk battle that badly damaged several ships on both sides without any conclusive result. Furious, he accused Carkett and Parker of insubordination, but the fault was clearly Rodney's for not issuing clear and specific orders in a timely fashion. Despite the disappointing outcome of the engagement, Rodney later claimed that

Admiral George Rodney, commander in chief of the Lee-ward Islands station. Prior to taking up his post, he defeated the Spanish off Cape St. Vincent in January 1780 before bringing badly needed supplies to the besieged British garrison at Gibraltar. He fought the French twice off Dominica as well as at the Saintes. (Library of Congress)

his greatest feat was matching wits with the wily Guichen and forcing him into battle on disadvantageous terms. For his part, Guichen resolved never again to yield the weather gauge to Rodney if he could help it. The following month, both fleets maneuvered off Martinique for several days, with Guichen holding the weather gauge and declining battle.

During the summer Guichen sailed for France, and Rodney, fearing that he might be reinforcing Admiral Charles Ternay at Newport, Rhode Island, sailed up the East Coast to New York. Though his presence there was resented by Vice-Admiral Marriot Arbuthnot, with whom he quarreled about prize money, it was instrumental in forestalling George Washington's plan for a Franco-American assault on the city by sea and land. Rodney returned to the West Indies at the beginning of December. Reinforced by Sir Samuel Hood, he soon learned that the Netherlands and Britain had commenced hostilities. In February 1781 Rodney mounted an attack on the Dutch islands of St. Eustatius and St. Martin, whose neutral trade, so vital to the American colonies, was now fair game. Genuinely irate at the British merchants there who had sustained this trade in defiance of their nation's interests, he was intent upon punishing them. At the same time, his greed was excited at the prospect of his share in the millions of pounds of seized merchandise. Immediately selling off a part of it, he shipped the rest to England. Preoccupied with the governance of St. Eustatius and plagued by gout and kidney stones, Rodney failed to press on to seize the other Dutch possessions at Curaçao and Surinam. Moreover, he failed to support Hood in the blockade of Martinique that was lost to a French fleet under François de Grasse that brushed Hood aside.

In May, Rodney arrived at Tobago too late to prevent its capture by de Grasse and, despite holding the weather gauge, declined to attack de Grasse's fleet. In July, de Grasse left for North American waters with twenty-five ships, and Rodney, assuming that he would leave some ships in the Caribbean and send off others to escort a convoy to France, sent a message to New York underestimating the size of the French fleet and supplying faulty intelligence that contributed to the decisive Franco-American victory at Yorktown. Rodney had to cede his command to Hood and return to Britain both to recuperate and to defend in Parliament his conduct at St. Eustatius as well as his conduct of naval operations. The news that Rodney had been promoted to vice-admiral was more than offset by news of the capture by the French of more than half of his convoy of seized merchandise. Moreover, the subsequent recapture of St. Eustatius meant the loss of his profits from the sale of merchandise there. The British merchants of St. Eustatius then sued Rodney for wrongful seizure of their assets, and he was plagued for some time afterward by the bother and expense of legal actions.

Somewhat refreshed by his furlough, Rodney returned to the West Indies in February 1782, meeting Hood at Barbados and taking command of their combined fleet of 37 ships of the line. De Grasse was at Martinique. Fresh from the capture of the island of St. Kitts, he loaded 6,500 troops onto his 36 warships and sailed with 260 supply ships to rendezvous with a Spanish force of 14 ships and 8,000 troops and seize Jamaica. Based at St. Lucia, Rodney waited for the French to move. On 9 April, leading a fleet of 36 ships of the line on his flagship *Formidable* (90 guns), he sighted de Grasse's fleet between Dominica and the Iles des Saintes and skirmished inconclusively. De Grasse tried to escape through the Saintes passage but could not. On the morning of 12 April the evenly matched lines of battle passed at close quarters, the British heading north, the French sailing south. Though the French held the weather gauge, Rodney's fleet crowded them from the lee, and the French had trouble trying to turn onto the same tack as the British. When a shift in the wind created two large gaps in the French line, Sir Charles Douglas pointed out the opportunity to Rodney, who at first balked, then went below after giving Douglas permission to break the line of battle. The *Formidable* quickly sailed through one gap, firing at the French vessels on both sides, while Sir Edmund Affleck on the *Bedford* led the rear division through the other gap (anticipating Horatio Nelson's tactics in 1805 at the Battle of Trafalgar). His line ruptured, his ships raked stem to stern with fire by British vessels firing broadsides simultaneously from port and starboard while breaching the French line, de Grasse tried to withdraw and regroup, but all order was lost, his rear was destroyed, and 5 ships of the line were captured.

The last of them, de Grasse's flagship *Ville de Paris*, surrendered only after having been fired upon by 7 British ships in succession. At dark Rodney called off the chase, infuriating Hood.

Controversy raged afterward, with Rodney claiming that in the darkness his ships might have been at a disadvantage and that some French ships might have seized the opportunity to attack islands in the British rear. This is patently absurd. It is more likely, as Hood contended, that Rodney's lust for prize money made him fear that he would lose his prizes in the confusion of a night pursuit, and probably Rodney's poor physical condition and fatigue after a lengthy battle played an important role as well. At any event, his victory saved Jamaica, decisively established British command of the area, and dealt a severe blow to French naval confidence and prestige. While this came too late to affect the outcome of the American Revolution, it certainly strengthened the hand of the British government in negotiating a peace treaty, quite possibly forestalling British cession of Canada to the Americans with consequences incalculable for North American and world history. Rodney was entitled to his famous boast, "In the little year I have taken two Spanish, one French and one Dutch admiral." Though he was rewarded with a peerage and a pension of £2,000, he spent his last years short of money and harassed by the St. Eustatius lawsuits.

JOSEPH M. MCCARTHY

See also
Cape St. Vincent, Battle of; Dominica, Second Battle of; Grasse, François-Joseph-Paul, Comte de; Guichen, Luc-Urbain du Bouexic, Comte de; Hood, Samuel; Martinique, Battle of; Saintes, Battle of the; West Indies; Yorktown, Virginia, Siege of

References
Breen, Kenneth. "George Bridges, Lord Rodney." Pp. 225–246 in *Precursors of Nelson: British Admirals of the Eighteenth Century*, ed. Peter Le Fevre and Richard Harding. London: Chatham, 2000.
Hart, Francis R. *Admirals of the Caribbean*. Boston: Houghton Mifflin, 1935.
Hurst, Ronald. *The Golden Rock: An Episode of the American War of Independence, 1775–1783*. Annapolis, MD: Naval Institute Press, 1996.
Macintyre, Donald G. *Admiral Rodney*. New York: Norton, 1963.
Mahan, Alfred Thayer. *Types of Naval Officers Drawn from the History of the British Navy*. Freeport, NY: Books for Libraries, 1969.
Rodney, George. *The Rodney Papers: Selections from the Correspondence of Admiral Lord Rodney*. Burlington, VT: Ashgate, 2005–.
Spinney, David. *Rodney*. London: Allen and Unwin, 1969.

Rodrigue, Hortalez et Cie

Due to the number of its ships, Rodrigue, Hortalez et Cie was probably the first French firm to provide aid to the United States, but its role was very controversial, and the American government took fifty years to

Pierre-Augustin Caron de Beaumarchais founded Rodrigue, Hortalez et Cie, which supplied the Patriots with war munitions. (Library of Congress)

reimburse its chairman and principal shareholder, Pierre-Augustin Caron de Beaumarchais.

Beginning in the fall of 1775, the Continental Congress entered into secret negotiations with the French government for the purpose of purchasing arms. The rebels were a very attractive market for French arms dealers because the British government had forbidden the manufacture of gunpowder and weapons in its colonies. Officially, King Louis XVI expressed no desire to help the Americans, and the Continental Congress, for its part, did not want the French to know how much the Americans were short of everything.

Congress assigned the job of procuring arms to Arthur Lee. At the beginning of 1775, Lee and Beaumarchais met in London after the latter sent a memorandum to the king (also read by the foreign minister, Charles Gravier, the comte de Vergennes) concerning the possibility of supporting the colonists. Toward the end of the year, Lee reestablished contact with Beaumarchais and with various other French businessmen, especially in Nantes. As a result, in June 1776, 15,000 firearms from the Royal Arsenals were exported from Nantes. Other shipments were sent in September under the cover of the slave trade. The banker Schweighauser, in concert with the firm of Dobrée in Nantes, advanced large sums to Thomas Morris, the rebels' business representative.

Another business in Nantes, Perret, Dacosta et Cie, constructed and armed ten ships in the period 1776–1778. However, this private help was not provided free of charge, and the rebels were desperately short of funds, as revealed by the correspondence in May 1776 between Benjamin Franklin and the members of the commission that had been charged with the purchase of war matériel. Beaumarchais' intervention through the cover of Rodrigue, Hortalez et Cie was, therefore, particularly important to the independence of the American colonies.

Following his discussions with Lee, Beaumarchais, in February 1776, sent Louis XVI a new and private memorandum encouraging the provision of arms to the rebels. As a result, the king authorized Vergennes to offer a loan of 1 million livres to the Americans. This constituted the equivalent of a new ship of the line of 110 guns, completely equipped for a six months' cruise and with 950 men on board. Vergennes set the following condition: the transaction was to be managed so as to appear to the British government—and even to the American public—as a private enterprise with no connection to the French government.

To achieve this, Vergennes suggested that a business enterprise be created to camouflage the shipment of firearms and war matériel to the rebels. Beaumarchais' entanglements with the courts provided a perfect cover with which to disguise his commercial dealings from British spies, and his association with the financier Pâris-Duverney gave him a solid commercial cover.

On 10 June 1776, Vergennes duly made the sum available to Beaumarchais, who founded the firm of Rodrigue, Hortalez et Cie. A second 1 million livres was provided by the Spanish government. He was instructed to establish a large commercial firm with which, at his own risk, he was to furnish to the Americans arms and other materials necessary to conduct a war. French arsenals would deliver the armaments and munitions, but Beaumarchais would be responsible for paying for them. He was not to demand payment from the Americans since they were unable to make them, but, in return, he could demand goods in kind from their future production. And so began the ambiguous role of Rodrigue, Hortalez et Cie that, to the American government, was a cover for the French government. As far as Vergennes was concerned, if the first 2 million livres were spent for the rebels, this was to be considered a private arrangement, and the aid would have to be repaid by the Americans. But first, of course, it was necessary to furnish them with the sort of assistance that had become indispensable to them.

In June 1776, the British had 32,000 troops in North America to oppose 18,000 men under General George Washington. At this time Congress sent Silas Deane, who arrived in Paris at the beginning of July, to secure whatever aid he could acquire. Deane wanted to negotiate through Dr. Jacques Dubourg and the financier Le Ray de Chaumont, but on 13 July Vergennes insisted that they conduct business through Beaumarchais, who was the sole coordinator of all details concerning exports and imports between the United States and France, whether they were munitions or ordinary goods. Beaumarchais was to manage all deadlines, determine all prices, reach agreements, and establish all financial commitments and the rate of repayment.

On 19 July, Beaumarchais met with Deane. They agreed that in addition to certain shipments of arms funded by the 2 million livres supplied by the kings of France and Spain, Deane would make purchases on credit in the name of the Continental Congress, with payment to be made in exchange for colonial goods. On 6 September, Beaumarchais rented a large building, the old residence of the Dutch ambassador, at 47 rue du Vieille du Temple, as the location for Rodrigue, Hortalez et Cie.

Deane could not give a fixed time for repayment, but Beaumarchais was prepared to be flexible. In August, Deane bought 30,000 uniforms, 4,000 tents, 200 pieces of artillery, and 30,000 muskets. The muskets were of French army regulation. They included a bayonet and were manufactured by the royal factory in Saint Etienne. Although Beaumarchais had not yet officially established the firm of Rodrigue, Hortalez et Cie, Deane had already ordered directly from Beaumarchais 6 million livres' worth of purchases without having provided any down payment and had stated that Congress would be considerably late in paying. Nonetheless, Beaumarchais was able to have 8 ships loaded by December 1776, and he left for Le Havre to supervise their departure. But David Murray, Lord Stormont, the British ambassador to France, who probably had been warned by Edward Bancroft, a double agent, forced the French government to order the unloading of the ships. It was while supervising the loading of the ship *Amphitrite* at Le Havre that Beaumarchais learned of Franklin's arrival at Quiberon on 4 December

1776. Together with the *Amphitrite*'s cargo, many French volunteers sailed to aid the rebels, long before the Marquis de Lafayette did so. The engineers and the artillerymen on board the ships owned by Rodrigue, Hortalez et Cie brought the Americans valuable technical help. More ships embarked for America in 1777.

Rodrigue, Hortalez et Cie was a limited partnership in which the two principal partners were, unofficially, the French and Spanish governments but included the most prominent French shipowners: de Monthieu et Carrier (Nantes), Vincent et Gradis (Bordeaux), and such noblemen as the Marquis de Saint-Aignan and the Marquis de l'Aubépine, among others. Beaumarchais committed his entire fortune to this venture. Though this was already considerable, he also persuaded his suppliers to invest in it. Beaumarchais' two closest contributors were the treasurer Cantini, who was followed by Gudin de la Ferlière and Thévenaud de Francy, who was initially his secretary and then his personal representative in the French ports and ultimately in America.

By the end of 1776, Rodrigue, Hortalez et Cie had chartered ten ships. Since Nantes and Le Havre were under particularly close scrutiny by British spies, Beaumarchais used other ports and varied certain sailings. As a result, Pierre Landais, in charge of the *Flamand*, left from Marseilles and arrived without incident at Portsmouth in 1777. Taking advantage of his enhanced reputation, the result of his success in providing shipments to the rebels and of his trips to many French ports, Beaumarchais established contact with traders and shipfitters there. On 6 June 1777, Franklin and Deane ordered, through Monthieu of Nantes, 10,000 uniforms, 8,000 firearms, and other equipment valued at 917,820 livres. This consignment was loaded aboard Beaumarchais' ships, but since Monthieu was one of Beaumarchais' partners, it is difficult to know if this transaction was solely or only partially the concern of Rodrigue, Hortalez et Cie.

At that time, it was essential for Deane to receive deliveries, for spending had by September 1777 greatly exceeded available funds, without the prospect of receiving any payment from his government. Nevertheless, Beaumarchais and his partners, in full expectation of ultimately getting paid, continued to send ships to America. From 1778 to 1783, therefore, Rodrigue, Hortalez et Cie fitted out and sent fifteen additional ships to the rebels.

There is a great disparity in losses before and after June 1778, by which time Rodrigue, Hortalez et Cie was in business. From 1775 to June 1778, shipowners reported 132 ships, worth 15.6 million livres, captured by the British in the North Atlantic. Not all of them were carrying supplies for the rebels. A large number of ships were carrying the usual goods—cloth of all kinds, tools, grain, and many other articles—looking to profit from the high prices paid along the American coast due to the state of war. Rodrigue, Hortalez et Cie lost 4 ships in 1778. Two vessels were captured off Virginia in 1779, and another sank in the Chesapeake toward the latter part of that year during the expedition to Savannah. Three were captured in 1782 at a time when French convoys were suffering virtually no losses. Conversely, on 30 June 1780, 2 ships, which were escorting a convoy of 35 vessels from Yorktown, captured 2 British ships, the *Marlborough* and the *Nelly*, with the help of 2 other ships from Bordeaux. These prizes were sold in Bordeaux for 430,000 livres, of which Rodrigue, Hortalez et Cie received 319,000 livres.

In eighteenth-century France, the term "shipfitter" did not mean the owner but rather the party responsible for outfitting a ship. Each ship, and in particular ships for the colonial trade, had at least a dozen owners, sometimes as many as one hundred. The shipfitter rarely owned more than 20 percent of the cargo; the rest was the property of other shipfitters and traders. It was in this way that Beaumarchais bought and shipped various goods destined for the rebel forces as well as some consignments, including French cloth and wine, for American businessmen. There was also rum and sugar from the Antilles for the king or for private French consumers.

Like most French shippers, Rodrigue, Hortalez et Cie chartered its ships to transport products sent by the king to the colonies and to the United States. The king reserved for himself about 80 percent of the ships' holds, leaving the rest for the shippers. On arrival at the Antilles or the United States, a captain was free to acquire cargo for the return trip. The king paid a premium price for that cargo, and a large number of shippers became rich.

Controversy surrounding American debt. The problem of the repayment of the debt due to Rodrigue, Hortalez et Cie by the United States is very complex. It is at once a financial, legal, and political issue: financial because Congress did not have any money, legal because the French government's exact role in Beaumarchais' enterprise was poorly defined, and political because the relationship between Lee and Deane accounts for most of the cause of the Americans' refusal to repay the debt.

While Vergennes wanted everything to be handled through Beaumarchais, Lee preferred to manage affairs through Chaumont. During his stay in Paris in December 1776, Lee consented to the financial agreements reached between Franklin and Chaumont without worrying if the latter, who was giving Franklin free lodging in his Passy residence, was actually motivated by profit alone. Lee never accepted the agreements reached between Deane and Beaumarchais regarding Vergennes and Rodrigue, Hortalez et Cie. Instead, Lee chose to believe that the kings of France and Spain were the principals in this enterprise, although they had provided only 3 million livres.

When Beaumarchais sold part of the *Amphitrite*'s cargo to the rebels, to be repaid to the accounts of his shareholders and not to the kings of France and Spain, Lee suspected that Beaumarchais was profiting heavily. Lee accused Beaumarchais and Franklin of collusion and dissuaded Congress from paying Beaumarchais. In March 1778, Beaumarchais had only received 300,000 livres in the form of rice and tobacco for resale to help recover the initial investment.

Deane and Lee had been consistently at odds about the purchase of arms in France. When Deane returned to America, Congress demanded an explanation about the material bought in France and found itself divided into two factions, one supporting Deane, the other supporting Lee. Nothing could be proven against Deane, Franklin, and Beaumarchais. Finally, on 15 January 1779, John Jay, president of Congress, acknowledged the latter's debt to Rodrigue, Hortalez et Cie and wrote to Beaumarchais expressing Congress's immense appreciation for all he had done for the United States. A few months later, Beaumarchais received statements acknowledging a debt of 2.544 million livres, payable in three years, even though Congress actually owed Beaumarchais 5 million livres.

In 1781, Deane estimated the debt to be 3.6 million livres. In 1784, Thomas Barclay, the new American consul to France, lowered that claim. On 12 January 1786, Beaumarchais wrote to Charles Alexandre de Calonne, the finance minister, stating that the U.S. Congress owed him 9 million livres. In 1787, Lee estimated that, on the contrary, it was Beaumarchais who owed 1.8 million livres, but in 1793 Alexander Hamilton raised that debt to 2.28 million. This discrepancy can be explained by the disagreement between the French government and Congress. In 1783, the young United States owed 9 million livres to the French government, but Congress estimated that 1 million should have been subtracted as, they claimed, Beaumarchais had concealed that million. Until an explanation for this was forthcoming, Congress refused all payments to Rodrigue, Hortalez et Cie.

There were two conflicting ideas. According to Beaumarchais, the French government had only given him 1 million livres in 1776 to support the American cause. He had to be accountable only to Louis XVI and Vergennes about the use of that million. The same applied to the other 2 million that had been loaned to him for the exclusive use of arms procurement. The American government, therefore, was expected to pay him for all the goods that he had furnished. Because of the Americans' failure to repay the debt, Beaumarchais had to borrow money and thus had become personally indebted to the suppliers who had provided various goods to the United States.

On the other hand, in the postwar period Congress had to rebuild the country, and tax revenue was poor. With a dispute over Rodrigue, Hortalez et Cie's claims, it was considered better to forgo payment for as long as possible. On 10 April 1795, Beaumarchais, in exile in Hamburg and out of funds, requested that Congress pay him while, at the same time, he abandoned his claim to the contested million livres. He wrote to Congress explaining his bitter disappointment at having served America with zeal yet with nothing offered in return. Being close to death, he asked that the debt be paid to his daughter. In view of the troubles in France and the large number of financiers and businessmen who were condemned to die during the Terror, Beaumarchais had hoped that he would not have to reimburse some of his old partners. In the end Beaumarchais, who had helped the Americans so much, died a pauper.

Congress would probably never have paid Beaumarchais' heirs had it not decided, in 1835, to demand from France, Spain, Portugal, and the Kingdom of Naples restitution for the losses incurred by the American merchant marine during the Revolutionary War. To settle affairs with France, President Andrew Jackson demanded 25 million francs (France's post-Revolutionary currency) in gold. Louis Philippe's government called in all unpaid American debts, including those to Beaumarchais. Ignoring the issue of interest for late payment, the United States arbitrarily set that debt at 800,000 francs in gold. Beaumarchais' heirs lost a substantial amount of money—when the total debt owed Beaumarchais between 1776 and 1783 is considered—but they resigned themselves to it, and the matter was finally closed.

PATRICK VILLIERS

See also
Beaumarchais, Pierre-Augustin Caron de; Deane, Silas; France; Franklin, Benjamin; Gravier, Charles, Comte de Vergennes; Lee, Arthur; Louis XVI, King of France

References
Clark, Ronald W. *Benjamin Franklin: A Biography.* New York: Random House, 1983.
Hale, Edward. *Franklin in France.* 2 vols. Boston: Roberts Brothers, 1888.
Kite, Elizabeth S. *Beaumarchais and the War of American Independence.* Boston: R. G. Badger, 1918.
Lafon, R. *Beaumarchais le brillant armateur.* Paris: Société d'Editions Géographiques, Maritimes et Coloniales, 1928.
Lever, Maurice. *Pierre-Augustin Caron de Beaumarchais.* Paris: Fayard, 1999.
Loménie, L. *Beaumarchais et son temps.* Geneva: Slatkine Reprints, 1970.
Marsan J. *Beaumarchais et les affaires d'Amérique: Lettres inédites.* Paris: n.p., 1919.
Morton, Brian N., and Donald C. Spinelli. *Beaumarchais and the American Revolution.* Lanham, MD: Lexington Books, 2003.
Robinson, Philip, ed. *Beaumarchais: Homme de lettres, homme de société.* New York: P. Lang, 2000.
Shewmake, Antoinette, ed. *For the Good of Mankind: Pierre-Augustin Caron de Beaumarchais's Political Correspondence Relative to the American Revolution.* Lanham, MD: University Press of America, 1987.
Sillié, Ch. J. *Beaumarchais and the Lost Million: A Chapter of the Secret History of the American Revolution.* Philadelphia: n.p., 1886.
Villiers, Patrick. *Le commerce colonial atlantique et la guerre d'indépendance des États-Unis d'Amérique, 1778–1783.* New York: Arno, 1977.

Rogers, Robert
(1731–1795)

The American frontier soldier Robert Rogers became a local hero in New England while still in his twenties for battling Indians allied with the French during the French and Indian (Seven Years') War. During the American Revolutionary War, however, he lost his reputation with many of those same New Englanders as well as with other Americans when he was suspected of being a British spy and then became a Loyalist officer.

Rogers was born in Methuen, Massachusetts, the son of Scots-Irish immigrants. Brought up in Dunbarton, New Hampshire, he became an accomplished Indian trader and scout. During the French and Indian War, he served as a captain in the New Hampshire Regiment and was authorized to raise an independent ranger company in 1756. This command, eventually raised to battalion strength, became famous as Rogers's Rangers, a unit skilled in irregular guerrilla warfare. Rogers led this force in the destruction of French-allied Indians at Crown Point in 1759, in the Quebec Campaign under General James Wolfe later that year, and at Montreal in 1760. Sir Jeffrey Amherst gave

Robert Rogers organized Rogers's Rangers, one of the most successful military units on the New England and New York frontiers during the French and Indian War. Rogers's Loyalist unit, the Queen's Rangers, was less successful in the Revolutionary War. (Library of Congress)

Rogers a regular commission as captain in 1761 and dispatched him to Detroit to take possession of the far western French outposts. In the West, he commanded an independent ranger company during the Cherokee War and fought during Pontiac's Rebellion in 1763.

An individual of intemperate, avaricious, and quite possibly dishonest character, Rogers fled to London to escape his creditors in 1764. In a city interested in all things American, he attempted to capitalize on his fame by writing his memoirs and a play, *Ponteach; or the Savages of America* (1766). Failing to convince King George III to finance an expedition to discover the Northwest Passage, Rogers returned to America to the command of Fort Michilimackinac on the upper Great Lakes. His continued irregular behavior, however, led to his removal from command in 1768 and a spell in debtors' prison after his return to London.

Determined to develop his western land grants, Rogers returned to America in 1775, but as a regular British officer, albeit on half pay, he was suspected of being a British spy and was twice imprisoned. Escaping from captivity in Philadelphia, he made his way through British lines and was authorized by General William Howe to raise a Loyalist command, the Queen's Rangers, in August 1776. During October and November 1776, the Queen's Rangers became one of the most feared Loyalist forces on Long Island Sound. When the Loyalist forces were reorganized in November 1776, however, Rogers's leadership was questioned by the new British inspector general, Alexander Innes, and he was relieved from command. While Rogers now began to sink into obscurity, the Queen's Rangers became one of the most distinguished of all Loyalist military units, and the unit was later brought into the regular establishment of the British Army as the 1st American Regiment.

Following his evacuation from New York City with other Loyalists in 1782, Rogers spent another spell in debtors' prison in London. He died in obscurity, a poor half-pay officer, in May 1795. His career was later resurrected by Francis Parkman, and he became something of a romantic figure due to Kenneth Roberts's novel, *Northwest Passage* (1936), which was later made into a popular movie with Spencer Tracey playing a more sober Rogers.

RORY T. CORNISH

See also
Associated Loyalists

References
Cuneo, John R. "The Early Days of the Queen's Rangers, August 1776–February 1777." *Military Affairs* 22(2) (1958): 65–74.
———. *Robert Rogers of the Rangers*. New York: Oxford University Press, 1959.

Betsy Ross is a favorite legendary figure of the American Revolution, popularly credited with sewing, and in part designing, the first American flag. And this legend, like most, appears to be a blending of colorful myth and hard facts.

Ross was born Elizabeth Griscom in Philadelphia on 1 January 1752. She was the seventh daughter of the seventeen children of Samuel Griscom, a carpenter who helped to build the tower of Independence Hall, and Rebecca James. Betsy was raised in the Quaker religion. She attended her mother's school for Quaker children and later the Friends Public School. She also served as an apprentice to John Webster, an upholsterer, where she met a fellow apprentice and her future husband, John Ross. On 4 November 1773, she married Ross at Huggs Tavern in Gloucester, New Jersey. Because he was not a Quaker, the new Mrs. Ross was expelled from her Quaker meeting. The Rosses rented a house on Arch Street in Philadelphia, where they opened an upholstery business. On 21 January 1776, John died from wounds he received from an explosion of gunpowder that he was guarding for the Revolutionary resistance at a Delaware River dock. Ross continued to operate the family business on her own. In addition to upholstery work, she also made flags as part of her business.

The story of Ross's role in creating the first American flag was first told by her grandson, William Canby, to a meeting of the Pennsylvania Historical Society in 1870. Canby recounted a visit by General George Washington and Continental Congress members Robert Morris and George Ross in the spring of 1776 to Betsy Ross's shop. Washington showed Ross a drawing of the flag he proposed, and she made suggestions to change the stars to five-pointed ones and to place the stars in a circle instead of in a row as he had drawn. Washington and the committee members agreed, and Ross was given the job of making the first flag of the United States of America. Later that spring, she delivered several flags for use on the ships of the Continental Navy on the Delaware River.

There is, however, little contemporary evidence to support the story of this meeting or of Ross's role in designing America's first flag. Washington was with the Continental Army in New York in June 1776, and Congress did not authorize the familiar design for America's first national battle flag until 14 June 1777, when it passed the Flag Resolution. This act determined that the naval flag of the United States should have thirteen alternating red and white stripes, with thirteen white stars on a blue field.

Yet Ross evidently did make battle flags during the Revolutionary War. She is first recorded in this role in May 1777, when she made ship colors for the Pennsylvania State Navy, and she may have made early national flags as

According to a late nineteenth-century claim by her family, Betsy Ross, a Philadelphia Quaker seamstress, sewed and helped design the first flag of the United States and showed it to George Washington. Ross did indeed do seamstress work for Congress and may have made flags, but there is no evidence that she worked on the first flag, designed any flag, or ever met General Washington. (Library of Congress)

well. Perhaps the earliest national flag used in a land battle, at Bennington in August 1777, was of a different pattern from the naval flag, and it took some time for Congress's general design to prevail.

As she continued her upholstery business and made occasional flags, Ross got on with her personal life as well. On 15 June 1777, she married a seaman, Joseph Ashburn, at Gloria Dei Church in Philadelphia and had two daughters, Zillah and Elizabeth. Ashburn was captured by the British while serving as first mate on the brigantine *Patty*. He died on 3 March 1782 at the Old Mill prison in Plymouth, England. Ross learned of her husband's death from John Claypoole, a fellow prisoner and longtime friend of the Ashburns. She married Claypoole on 8 May 1783. Ross later moved her business to another location on Second Street. She and Claypoole had five daughters together, Clarissa Sidney, Susannah, Rachel, Jane, and Harriet. Claypoole died on 3 August 1817 after a long illness. Ross gave up her business in 1827, turning it over to her daughter Clarissa Sidney Wilson, who operated it until she moved to Fort Madison, Iowa, in 1856. Ross went first to live with her daughter Susannah Satterthwaite in nearby Abington, Pennsylvania, and later returned to Philadelphia and lived in the home of her son-in-law, Caleb Candy, where she died on 30 January 1836 at age eighty-four.

ARTHUR HOLST

See also
Congress, Second Continental and Confederation; Continental Navy; Flags and Standards

References
Norton, Mary Beth. *Liberty's Daughters: The Revolutionary Experience of American Women, 1750–1800*. Boston: Little, Brown, 1980.

Weigley, Russell F., ed. *Philadelphia: A 300-Year History*. New York: Norton, 1982.

Wulf, Karin A. "Ross, Betsy." Pp. in 900–901, *American National Biography*, Vol. 18. New York: Oxford University Press, 1999.

Ross, George

See Declaration of Independence Signers

Royal Navy

The Royal Navy during the War of American Independence did not enjoy the reputation that it would attain a generation later under Lord Horatio, Viscount Nelson. In the 1770s it was comparatively weaker than its French counterpart and, owing to the priorities of British squadrons having to operate along the lengthy coast of North America and in the English Channel, stronger French fleets were able to cross the Atlantic to the West Indies than

The Second Battle of Dominica, 12 April 1782, where the French, under Admiral François de Grasse, failed to make best use of their superior numbers to crush the British under Admiral Lord George Rodney, whose rear division never reached the action because of becalmed conditions. (Naval Historical Center)

in any other war in the eighteenth century. The unusual result was that most of the Anglo-French naval encounters were fought in the Caribbean, whereas in all the other conflicts of that century the great majority of battles were fought in European waters. A number of significant actions also took place in the Indian Ocean.

Ship construction and design. Ships were constructed of wood, with the most preferred type being oak, which was both durable and resilient. Teak, grown in India, also proved to be an excellent material. Fir was sometimes used for hulls, although it was best for deck planks. Elm was also sometimes used for hulls. Very large quantities of wood were required for even the smaller-sized vessels, not to mention ships of the line, with the largest ships requiring more than 5,000 cartloads of timber, each of fifty cubic feet (the equivalent of approximately one full-grown oak). There was never enough timber, with shortages of oak being particularly acute. Pine was also important, as it served well for the masts. The Royal Navy suffered from shortages of timber from the very beginning of the conflict, since many of its needs were met from the forests of Maine, which were of course in rebel hands, while the pine forests of Norway and other Baltic nations would, by 1780, be controlled by countries that had formed the League of Armed Neutrality against Britain.

Forward deck of an eighteenth-century British ship of the line. Although the Royal Navy fought a number of ship-to-ship actions against the Continental Navy, it was principally engaged with the French in the West Indies. (Jim Harter, ed., *Nautical Illustrations*, 2003)

Shipbuilders understood the practical limits that could be placed on the length of a vessel and the need for sufficient strength to protect a vessel from enemy fire. Consideration was also made for a ship's ability to carry itself and its cargo—in good as well as bad weather—and this together with its stability at sea all dictated the number of decks that a ship could contain. Everything was a compromise. The heavier the ship, the slower it moved. The longer the ship, the faster it sailed but the more space it required to turn. A smaller ship, equipped with plenty of sails, would have an advantage in speed over a larger vessel, but in adverse weather conditions the larger vessel could sustain the strain of the wind longer and was slowed down less by the effect of the waves. Thus, ship types were specialized, with larger vessels boasting strength, size, and the ability to mount more guns and small vessels displaying superiority in weatherliness and speed.

Although no perfect system of standardization of ship types existed, such types can be broken down into categories and readily distinguished. Middle-sized ships, that is, frigates, constituted a compromise. The larger ships of war were three-masted vessels with square sails on all three masts, known as square-rigged, though most ships also carried a number of sails fore and aft as well. Although there existed a bewildering number of ship types, warships of this era were divided into two main groups, with all vessels carrying at least twenty guns and having a specific rating.

There were six rates, each defined by the number of guns carried. A first-rate ship carried one hundred guns or more, while a ship of the second rate mounted ninety to ninety-eight guns and normally served as an admiral's flagship. There were very few of these in commission, but they were particularly powerful and deployed their guns on three decks. The most common vessels used in-line of battle warfare belonged to the third rate, which had between sixty-four and eighty-four guns, with almost all ships of this rate having guns on two decks. First-, second-, and third-rate vessels were called line of battle ships or ships of the line and were those that stood end-to-end in battle delivering their broadsides to the enemy in the principal formation employed in combat. Ships whose complement of guns fell below sixty-four did not normally take a place in the line of battle, since their armaments were considered too light and their hulls insufficiently strong to bear up against fire delivered by larger vessels.

Two-deckers, which were seldom seen in the line, were mostly used as escorts for larger warships or for troop transports and merchant vessels. Such ships were sometimes classed as fourth rates of fifty to sixty guns or fifth rates of thirty to forty-four guns. Frigates, which generally fell into the category of fifth rates, were used extensively at this time. They contained a single gun deck and carried between twenty-eight and forty guns. They were built for speed, though powerful enough to defend themselves even against ships of the line for a short period. The larger types were fifth rates and the smaller ones sixth rates, with twenty to twenty-eight guns. Sixth rates were usually known as post ships. Below these were the unrated sloops, which carried between eight and twenty guns. Unrated vessels also included a variety of other types including brigs, schooners, bomb ships, fire-ships, and transports.

Weaponry. The principal weapons aboard ships of this period were smoothbore cannons mounted on carriages. Naval ordnance amounted to little more than iron tubes, closed at one end, down which were loaded various forms of ammunition. Guns were classified according to the weight of the shot they fired—for example, 32-pounder, 24-pounder, etc. Guns were placed in rows along each deck and were shifted into position by a system of ropes and pulleys together with handspikes that enabled the crew to man-handle the weapons into position, particularly after discharge. The gun carriage sat on wheels, also known as trucks, enabling the crew to run the gun back inboard for loading. The barrel first had to be cleaned of any burning fragments left by the previous powder carriage. A bag containing gunpowder packed in the form of a cartridge was then pushed down the barrel from the muzzle, followed by a felt wad. The shot was then pushed after it, followed by another wad meant to hold the shot in place. After ramming all these materials home, a member of the gun crew used a spike to pierce the cartridge bag by inserting it into the touch hole near the breech of the gun. A small amount of fine-grain gunpowder was inserted into the touch hole. The men then ran the gun out through the port, the position adjusted for proper elevation and aim. Then, when a slow match was applied, the flame was transmitted down to the cartridge, and ignition was achieved. The weapon discharged and violently recoiled, but the force was partly controlled by the weight of the gun itself and the rope breechings, which stopped the gun from rolling back farther than was necessary to reload it.

The heaviest piece of ordnance, a 32-pounder, required a crew of fifteen men to operate, though it could be fired by fewer men once losses were incurred. A gun crew underwent constant and repetitive training in order to perfect the routine of loading and firing its weapon as rapidly and as accurately as possible—no mean feat when conducted under battle conditions complete with thick, swirling smoke; cramped conditions; deafening noise; and the cries of the wounded. A crew could certainly be trained to execute its functions quickly; having the gunners fire their weapon accurately took rather more time to perfect.

A skilled gun crew, firing with the right type of ammunition and in good weather conditions, could hit a target more than a mile away, but effective range of typical gunners was closer to a quarter of a mile. Ideally, ships would be within pistol shot, where hitting the target was more or less guaranteed. In such a case, rate of fire took precedence over accuracy, and a good crew could fire an average of once every ninety seconds. A great psychological effect could be achieved by firing a broadside simultaneously, but inevitably, different standards of gunnery between different gun crews, together with

A skilled gun crew could hit a target more than a mile away.

the effect of casualties, made this very difficult after a few discharges. Simultaneous firing, moreover, took a toll on the ship itself. More commonly, crews fired in quick succession down the deck, creating a kind of ripple of fire. Depending on the purpose to be achieved, crews fired at the enemy above the bulwarks to slow down the ship's speed by damaging masts and rigging or at the hull to create holes beneath the water line and disable the opponents' guns, and kill their crews.

Several forms of projectiles were available to gunners. For short ranges, grapeshot, consisting of a bundle of musket shot secured together in canvas, could be fired to create the effect of a shotgun when it left the barrel. Similarly, canister or case shot consisted of a tin containing small shot that burst after emerging from the muzzle. Where the objective was to disable an enemy vessel's masts and rigging, a host of shot types were available, including bar shot and chain shot. Bar shot consisted of two halves of an iron ball attached to a bar, making the shape of a dumbbell. When fired, this projectile did great damage to ropes and spars. Chain shot consisted of two balls connected by several inches of chain. These cut and tangled ropes.

Such projectiles were very effective against the motive power of the ship and against men, but they were very inaccurate and traveled only a short distance. At greater distances, crews used round shot—what is often referred to now as a cannonball. This was spherical, iron, and solid and was meant to smash the enemy's hull. The heaviest type, of thirty-two pounds, had a velocity of 1,600 feet per second on leaving the muzzle and could crash through 2.5 feet of oak planking. Where round shot hit thinner planking, the resulting shower of splinters could disable and kill men, not to mention dismount a gun or destroy its carriage. Any man unfortunate enough to find himself in its path was either badly maimed or killed. Limbs were commonly lost through such fire.

Even more effective at close range were double-shotted guns—those loaded with two shots. Normally, opponents fought in parallel lines, thus exposing only their strongest sides. Great damage could, however, be achieved if a captain could maneuver his ship so as to cross the bow or stern of his opponent, thus enabling him to rake the target with most of his broadside guns while himself suffering comparatively little from the few guns that the enemy had mounted on his bow and stern. These were the most vulnerable parts of the ship, and shot fired along the whole length of the decks often dismounted guns.

The accepted, conventional method of fighting was in line of battle, that is, with both squadrons or fleets deployed in more or less parallel lines (whether on the same or opposite courses) so that their broadsides could be brought to bear against the enemy. Ships were said to be in line ahead, that is, one behind the other in single file. Once the lines passed one another they maneuvered in an oval or elliptical formation and returned to engage their opponent once again. Such methods rarely led to decisive victories, since the quality of the various fleets was not as distinguishable as it would become a generation later. Moreover, the idea of breaking the line (deliberately driving through the line and forcing the opponent to fight individual ship-to-ship actions when one possessed an advantage in numbers, seamanship, and morale) did not come into practice until the Battle of the Saintes in 1782 and was not fully appreciated until the Napoleonic Wars.

Whether fleet or single-ship actions, most encounters were fought at close range, so close in fact that small arms were regularly employed, together with edged weapons carried by boarding parties. The most common form of firearm at sea, as on land, was the musket, though the blunderbuss could still be seen during this period, and the Americans sometimes used rifles. Sea service muskets were like the land version, though slightly shorter. Blunderbusses, with a bell-shaped mouth and firing irregular-sized objects such as bits of iron, were used with deadly effect at close range, particularly against boarders. Muskets were discharged from across rival decks, particularly by marines, but could be wielded by boarding parties. Once discharged in hand-to-hand fighting, however, there was no time to reload, so the weapon was usually reversed to make use of its butt end as a club.

If rival crews actually confronted one another face-to-face in a boarding action, then recourse was most often made to boarding pikes, pistols, tomahawks or boarding axes, and knives or daggers. Boarding pikes were about six feet long, made of ash, and tipped with a triangular steel blade that narrowed to a point. It was most effective in defending against boarders attempting to mount the side of an enemy vessel. Boarding pikes came in long and short versions, depending on the area on the ship where they were to be used. There was little room on the cramped decks of a ship to employ long weapons, and these were therefore designed for such conditions. The cutlass was short, heavy, and bereft of unnecessary ornamentation with a strong hand guard on the hilt both to protect the hand and to use as a knuckle duster in the event that lack of space prevented its user from swinging the blade. Officers' swords were similar, very unlike the straight dress swords seen in portraits, which were only used for ceremonial purposes on land. Midshipmen, who were generally only in their teens, often employed a simple dirk—much like a dagger—or a very short sword. Pistols were very similar to the patterns used ashore, but plainer and sturdier, and were sometimes modified with a belt hook to enable a soldier to carry more than one slung across his front and to prevent him from dropping it in combat. Hand grenades were also used, particularly by sailors positioned in the fighting tops (platforms mounted on the masts about halfway up). Grenades were of simple design, consisting of hollow spheres filled with gunpowder and lit with a slow match.

During the American Revolutionary War, the Royal Navy introduced a new type of gun, the carronade, that served it very well, particularly at the Battle of the Saintes in 1782. The carronade was shorter than a standard great gun, as cannon were officially designated, and fired a 68-pound shot for larger ships and smaller weights for smaller vessels. Employing a small charge and a short barrel, the benefit of the carronade derived from the smashing power produced by the weight of its shot rather than from the velocity at which it traveled.

Copper sheathing was another innovation by the Royal Navy during the war. The longer a ship had been in commission, especially if it served in

Ship Designations during the American Revolution

Common Name	Rating	Number of Guns
Ship of the Line	First	100+
	Second	90–98
	Third	64–84
Frigate	Fourth	50–60
	Fifth	30–44
	Sixth	20–28

tropical waters such as the West Indies, the more it was likely to have small sea creatures and vegetation attached to its bottom. As this marine growth grew, the ship slowed in its progress through the water owing to the resistance caused by friction. The underside of a ship could also be attacked by a small burrowing creature known as the teredo worm, which would bore its way into the ship from beneath, gradually eating away the timber and thus weakening the ship's structure.

A method had to be found to protect ships from such pests, thereby increasing a ship's longevity and preventing the decrease in its speed. Coppering a ship's bottom would also decrease the time that a vessel had to be laid up in dock in order to scrape and burn off the growth clinging to the underside. The principle of protecting a ship in this way had been understood since the sixteenth century, but the lead sheathing used at that time proved unsatisfactory on many grounds. In 1776 copper sheathing was used on four ships and the following year on a dozen more. By 1778, practically the whole of the Royal Navy's ships were copper-bottomed. Although this innovation was expensive, it was effective against marine growth and boring animals, for copper in contact with water soon forms a layer of oxide that is poisonous to most marine animals and is too slick to allow adhesion for plants. Hardly any enemy vessels were coppered at this time, giving the Royal Navy the advantage of superior speed.

Higher direction and support. The Royal Navy was backed by a complex organization, made necessary by the fact that warships were the most complicated man-made objects then in existence, whose construction and maintenance required a complex system of officials, dockyards, and skilled workers to manage, direct, and support. The navy employed more men than any other occupation or institution and was naturally the most expensive to maintain. The Royal Navy was managed by the Admiralty in London and maintained at various dockyards, the six major ones being Portsmouth, Plymouth, and Chatham, all on the south coast of England; Deptford and Woolwich on the Thames River; and Sheerness in Scotland. Such yards constructed ships and refitted them, though with its worldwide responsibilities the navy also had to rely on overseas dockyards that maintained and refitted local squadrons. Gibraltar in the Mediterranean, Antigua and Jamaica in the West Indies, Halifax on the Canadian coast, and Bombay in India were the principal overseas ports of the Royal Navy. Ships requiring repairs or resupply could usually depend on such yards to stock their needs. Captured ports, such as New York, were used during the war, and improvised dockyards could be established, such as on Lake Champlain, using available manpower in the form of shipwrights and carpenters from the nearest squadron or fleet.

Recruitment. Manning the Royal Navy was a perennial problem, as there was never enough available manpower to satisfy the navy's needs. Conscription largely brought in men already connected with the sea, but landsmen were sometimes drafted as well. Many others were obtained by the more ruthless method of the press gang, by which seamen—being already acquainted with life aboard ship—were in effect seized from merchant ships or abducted from the streets of port towns and compelled to serve aboard a vessel of the

Warships were the most complicated man-made objects then in existence.

Royal Navy. Men already serving the navy or in possession of a certificate of exemption could avoid being pressed, but this unjust method of manning the fleet was a legal, if unofficial, means at the government's disposal. Pressed men, like convicts, were held aboard ships until the end of the war.

About half the sailors in the Royal Navy were pressed, the remainder being volunteers (who themselves may have been pressed to the extent that once caught they may have been offered to "volunteer" and receive higher pay rather than protest at the injustice of their predicament). Those who genuinely volunteered often did so with dreams of glory and adventure, but for the most part their motivation lay in acquiring prize money—a specified payment made to every officer and seaman as a reward for the capture of an enemy vessel in reasonable enough condition for the navy to commission it for its own use. Men sometimes volunteered under the influence of drink, only afterward realizing that they had become virtual prisoners in the hands of their captain.

The strength of the Royal Navy at the beginning of the war was about 16,000 men, of whom a quarter were marines, men specially trained to serve aboard ships on sentry duty, to maintain discipline, and to provide musket fire in battle and landing parties in amphibious operations. Their chief function was to prevent mutiny aboard ship. The navy expanded rapidly during the Revolutionary War, but while Parliament voted for a strength of 90,000 men in 1781, of whom 20,000 were to be marines, these figures were never reached.

Officers and men. Noncommissioned officers (NCOs) were in charge of the guns and the men performing their respective tasks in the rigging. The more senior of the NCOs were the warrant officers. The boatswain held responsibility for the seamen, the carpenter was responsible for the ship's structure, and the purser managed the system of pay and the provision of food and clothing aboard ship. The navigation of the ship fell largely to the master. Officers held commissions from the king authorizing them to hold a position of command, either lieutenant, captain, or admiral. Prior to becoming an officer, a boy between thirteen and eighteen years old would serve for a number of years as a sort of apprentice or cadet, known as a midshipman, though older men could remain midshipmen if they failed their lieutenant's examination or were unable to secure promotion through patronage.

The system of patronage was extremely important at the time, not only within the armed forces but also in politics. Receiving a post or promotion in the navy usually came as the result of distinguished service or, more frequently, through the assistance of a friend or family member with influence within the service. A patron might wish to support a young man's professional aspirations, have a family or political connection with him, or need to return a political or financial favor performed by the aspirant's family.

Having passed his lieutenant's examination as a midshipman, a man had to rely on patronage to rise to a captaincy or had to depend on the fate of circumstances. Battle might disable or kill off those of higher rank, thereby opening up positions. Distinguished conduct in combat might also secure the rank of captain, giving the independent command of a ship to an ambitious lieutenant. Beyond captain came the rank of admiral, divided into rear admiral, vice-admiral, and admiral, the last rank itself divided into three parts to distinguish them according to seniority. After a lieutenant became a captain, promotion was achieved by seniority, and though this was more or less a simple waiting game, patronage could still make the difference between a desirable or an undesirable posting, whether that be the quality of the squadron or fleet he commanded or the station (theater of operations) to which he was assigned. During peacetime a ship was usually paid off, which meant that its crew was released from service and the captain placed on half pay, unless he could find another ship onto which he could immediately transfer.

GREGORY FREMONT-BARNES

See also
Continental Navy; French Navy; Saintes, Battle of the

References
Clowes, William Laird. *The Royal Navy: A History from the Earliest Times to 1900.* 7 vols. London: Chatham, 1996.

Gardiner, Robert, ed. *Navies and the American Revolution, 1775–1783.* London: Chatham, 1996.

James, William. *The British Navy in Adversity: A Study of the War of American Independence.* 1926. Reprint, New York: Russell and Russell, 1970.

Preston, Antony, David Lyon, and John H. Batchelor. *Navies of the American Revolution.* Englewood Cliffs, NJ: Prentice-Hall, 1975.

Syrett, David. *The Royal Navy in American Waters, 1775–1783.* Brookfield, VT: Gower, 1989.

———. *The Royal Navy in European Waters during the American Revolutionary War.* Columbia: University of South Carolina Press, 1998.

Tunstall, Brian. *Naval Warfare in the Age of Sail: The Evolution of Fighting Tactics, 1650–1815.* Edited by Nicholas Tracy. Annapolis, MD: Naval Institute Press, 1990.

Rush, Benjamin
(1746–1813)

The passionate, idealistic, and contentious Dr. Benjamin Rush was perhaps the most prominent medical, educational, and social reformer in Revolutionary America as well as one of its more important political figures.

Rush was born on 4 January 1746 in Byberry, near Philadelphia. After the death of his Anglican father, he was raised in the Presbyterian faith of his mother. The young Rush was exposed to perhaps the three most dynamic spokesmen for the evangelical wing of the colonial Presbyterian Church, first as a member of Gilbert Tennent's Second Presbyterian Church in Philadelphia; then as a pupil in his maternal uncle, Samuel Finley's, Presbyterian West Nottingham Academy in Maryland (1754–1759); and finally as a student at the Presbyterian College of New Jersey (Princeton) under its minister-president, Samuel Davies (1759–1760). Rush heard the three evangelicals, at the height of the French and Indian (Seven Years') War, call for all true Christians to selflessly exert themselves to defeat the enemies of God and thereby prepare the way in America for the Second Coming. By the time Rush, barely sixteen, graduated from Princeton in 1760, he was firmly grounded in Christian utopian millennialism and was committed to engaged public service in the name of Jesus Christ.

As he graduated, however, Rush concluded that he had not experienced the intense conversion required of ministers, and after briefly considering the law, he began in 1761 to study medicine with Philadelphia's John Redman. Near the end of that apprenticeship, in 1765, Rush enthusiastically supported Philadelphia's rather raucous response to the Stamp Act: the hanging of an official in effigy and the adoption and enforcement of a nonimportation agreement.

Soon thereafter, Rush sailed to Britain to study medicine with the celebrated William Cullen at the University of Edinburgh. There the young evangelical Christian encountered the Scottish Enlightenment, with its emphasis on religious skepticism, scientific empiricism, and political liberalism. Rush embraced Cullen's rejection of Hermann Boerhaave's assertion that all diseases originated in the body's fluids and accepted his teacher's alternative explanation, that disease originated in the body's solid organs and muscles as they responded, through the nervous system, to the energy of the brain. Disease occurred when the brain malfunctioned and caused the body to become either too lax or too tense. Drugs and diet treated the former condition; bleeding and purging treated the latter. Rush also studied chemistry with Joseph Black, whose studies on fixed air helped lead to the discovery of oxygen. Yet it is clear that Rush never fully comprehended the empirical basis of Enlightenment science, probably because, like Jonathan Edwards, his essential sense of the world, even the material world, was, basically, theological.

Benjamin Rush served as a delegate from Pennsylvania in the Second Continental Congress and signed the Declaration of Independence. He was also briefly surgeon general of the Continental Army but had to resign in 1778 because of his association with George Washington's critics in the so-called Conway Cabal. Rush was an early opponent of slavery and a strong supporter of the U.S. Constitution. (National Archives and Records Administration)

Outside the classroom, Rush encountered in Edinburgh, and then in London, a world that influenced fundamentally his role in the American Revolution. A fellow student introduced him to the literature of seventeenth-century English republicanism, especially the writings of Algernon Sidney and John Hampden, with their critique of monarchy and their assertion that legitimate government must be based on the consent of the governed and must pursue only the good of the people. Rush joined the Revolution Club in Edinburgh and, later in London, attended The Club of the Honest Whigs, where he met John Wilkes, Joseph Priestley, Richard Price, James Brugh, and, most important, the great Whig historian Catherine Macaulay. When to these broadening experiences was added, in 1769, a brief tour of France, where he met several of the leading philosophes and was repulsed by a brief sight of King Louis XV and his mistress, Madame Du Barry, at Versailles, Rush had become a confirmed republican.

Rush's role in the American Revolution was also shaped by his encounter in Scotland with the writings of John Locke and David Hartley. Rush seems to have instinctively accepted Locke's denial of innate ideas and his parallel assertion that man can know only through the evidence of his senses. On the basis of that sensationalism, the Enlightenment erected a doctrine of environmentalism that became the foundation of Rush's response to the American Revolution and the society it created. Equally important to that response, however, was the physiological psychology of Hartley's associationalism. Hartley, influenced by Newton's "Opticks" (1704), suggested that sensory stimuli operated by producing vibrations through the nervous system, causing the brain to build up clusters or sequences of impressions from repeated experiences. Lockean sensationalism and Hartley's associationalism became the basis for Rush's assertion, in America, that by changing man's environment and, thereby, the impressions received from it, man, and by extension society, could scientifically, mechanically, be improved, even perfected.

Returning to Philadelphia in 1769, Rush set up a medical practice and in 1770 began to lecture on chemistry at the College of Philadelphia. Writing under the pseudonym "Hampden" and then under his own name, he was an early critic of parliamentary threats to colonial liberties as well as an early critic of slavery. He was disappointed by what he took to be the lukewarm response of Philadelphia's merchants to the Coercive (Intolerable) Acts passed by Parliament in early 1774, and he was a well-informed, close observer of the deliberations of the First Continental Congress in the fall of that year. In the winter of 1774–1775 he published two articles on the manufacture of saltpeter, essential to making gunpowder, and briefly headed the local United Company for Promoting American Manufactures. He favored independence after Lexington and Concord and promoted George Washington as commander in chief of the Continental Army by having reprinted a 1755 sermon by Samuel Davies in which the Presbyterian divine predicted that the Virginian would one day serve his country well.

In the summer of 1775 Pennsylvania's Committee of Safety authorized Rush and others to supervise the construction of a factory for making saltpeter and a small fleet of galleys, or gunboats, to protect the city. In September he was named physician surgeon to that fleet. Earlier that year he had met, in a local bookstore, the recent immigrant Thomas Paine. After Lexington and Concord, Rush encouraged Paine to write a pamphlet urging immediate independence. When Paine presented the pamphlet, then titled *Plain Truth*, to him, Rush suggested he call it instead *Common Sense*, and then, having determined the pamphlet's name, arranged for its publication in January 1776.

In this first month of the year of independence, Rush also married Julia Stockton, the sixteen-year-old daughter of New Jersey's affluent political leader Richard Stockton. A month later Rush was elected to the Philadelphia Committee of Inspection and Observation. For the next few months he maneuvered to force the Pennsylvania delegation to Congress to vote for independence. In June 1776 he was elected to the provincial congress that drew up rules for a subsequent convention to write a constitution for what was hoped would soon be an independent Pennsylvania. Before that convention met, the Continental Congress adopted the Declaration of Independence, with Pennsylvania's marginal and last-minute approval. When Pennsylvania's convention did meet on 15 July, it elected Rush to the Continental Congress, and in early August he proudly signed the Declaration of Independence.

In Congress, Rush served on committees dealing with medical issues, intelligence, and prisoners of war. And as the year ended, he served, as a civilian and without pay, in the mobile hospital that traveled with Washington's forces as they crossed the Delaware into New Jersey on their way to the battles at Trenton and Princeton. Rush began, almost immediately, to criticize the apparently wretched conditions in the medical department, especially after he observed on several occasions what he described as the well-ordered hospitals in the British Army.

As Rush served with the Continental Army, he also became vocal in his criticisms of the new Pennsylvania Constitution of 1776, which the state convention had written and adopted after his departure to the Continental Congress. He objected to the document's provision for a single, unrestrained legislative house; to its provision for annual elections and a review of the government every seven years by a Council of Censors; and to the lack of an independent judiciary or any provision for amending the basic frame of government. For Rush, the Pennsylvania Constitution of 1776 was a textbook for mob rule. Largely because of his intense and continued opposition to the document, he lost his position in Congress in February 1777.

Several months later, Rush was appointed surgeon general for the all-important Middle Department of the army, the department over which Washington had direct command. Rush served under Dr. William Shippen Jr., the new director general of the army's medical services. Charged with organizing medical services for the department, Rush grew increasingly critical of Shippen's leadership, which, in Rush's view, was responsible for the service's inability to control a horrific epidemic in the army camp at Valley Forge in the winter of 1777–1778. He also accused the wealthy Shippen of illegally selling some of the service's precious wine stock, at a profit to himself. Rush finally put his accusations in a letter to Washington, who referred them to Congress without immediately responding to Rush himself.

His failure to secure Washington's endorsement of his charges, which the volatile Rush took as a deliberate slight, solidified his growing reservations about the commander in chief's military abilities. Rush knew that Washington and Shippen were friends and did not think much of Washington's choice of friends. Rush believed that the indecisive general was all too prone to be manipulated by unscrupulous subordinates, friends, and hangers-on and saw no place in a republic for what he called the "idolization" of the Virginian. Rush unwisely put these reservations into an unsigned letter to Patrick Henry on 12 January 1778, coincidentally the same date on which Washington got around to answering Rush's earlier letter to him. Henry showed the letter to Washington, who recognized Rush's handwriting and became furious.

In the meantime, a congressional committee headed by Princeton's president, John Witherspoon, had to choose between Shippen and his subordinate, both distinguished and proud graduates of Nassau Hall. Witherspoon reluctantly told Rush, who had helped Princeton's board of trustees recruit Witherspoon while Rush was a student at Edinburgh, that he had to resign. This Rush did on 31 January 1778. Unfortunately for Rush, his feud with Shippen came before Washington just as the general began to hear about the Conway Cabal. Rush's impolitic letter to Henry quoted some of General Thomas Conway's more incendiary criticisms of Washington, but nothing beyond that fact appears to link Rush directly to any machinations to replace the commander in chief. Rush's reputation was nonetheless irreparably damaged. For decades he was believed by many to have been involved with the alleged plot, especially after his letter to Henry became public knowledge.

After resigning from his service with the army, Rush concentrated on his medical practice and resumed teaching chemistry at the reorganized College of Philadelphia, which had become the University of Pennsylvania. He led the effort to control the yellow fever epidemic that decimated Philadelphia in 1793 but surely did more harm than good with the purging and bloodletting regimen that he had learned from Cullen in Edinburgh. But most of Rush's effort after the war went into creating a physical and social environment in the city, state, and nation that would produce citizens capable of sustaining the republican governments that the Americans were creating.

On the basis of Locke's sensationalism and Hartley's associationalism, Rush was convinced that by changing social, educational, political, and legal institutions within the proper physical environment, man could change himself through the mechanical effects of the environmental changes upon his mind. Rush said on numerous occasions that it was possible in the volatile, malleable world created by the Revolution to produce "republican machines," that the mind of man could be perfected by the combined effects of education, freedom, and the Christian gospel upon it. To that end, he helped organize societies to reform American society and became the foremost advocate for the early reform movement in the new republic. He worked to abolish slavery and capital punishment. He promoted temperance and what he considered appropriate forms of punishment as well as the humane care of the insane. Because he considered Christianity and republicanism to be virtually synonymous, he helped organize the first Bible and Sunday School societies in Philadelphia. He believed that education was the key to all republican institutions and advocated improved educational opportunities for women; helped establish Dickinson College in Carlisle, Pennsylvania, in 1783; and campaigned for a national university to educate the future leaders of the new republic.

Rush continued to serve the nation even as he strove to reform it. He was a member of Pennsylvania's ratifying convention in 1787, where he assisted James Wilson in making sure that the state supported the U.S. Constitution. From 1797 until his death, Rush served as the director of the national mint. And in 1811 he rendered one of his most important services to the republic he helped create. It was he who persuaded Thomas Jefferson and John Adams to renew their friendship, which produced, between 1812 and the virtually simultaneous deaths of the two founders on 4 July 1826, the correspondence that is now one of the monuments of American literature. Rush died on 19 April 1813, the thirty-eighth anniversary of Lexington and Concord.

HOWARD MILLER

See also

Adams, John; Congress, Second Continental and Confederation; Continental Army; Conway, Thomas; Conway Cabal; Jefferson, Thomas; Paine, Thomas; Pennsylvania; Philadelphia; Shippen, William; Washington, George; Wilson, James

References

Brodsky, Alyn. *Benjamin Rush: Patriot and Physician.* New York: Truman Talley, 2004.

Butterfield, Lyman H., ed. *Letters of Benjamin Rush.* 2 vols. Princeton, NJ: Princeton University Press, 1951.

D'Elia, Donald J. *Benjamin Rush: Philosopher of the American Revolution.* Philadelphia: American Philosophical Society, 1974.

Good, Harry Gehman. *Benjamin Rush and His Services to American Education.* Berne, IN: Witness Press, 1918.

Goodman, Nathan G. *Benjamin Rush: Physician and Citizen, 1746–1813.* Philadelphia: University of Pennsylvania Press, 1934.

Hawke, David F. *Benjamin Rush: Revolutionary Gadfly.* Indianapolis: Bobbs-Merrill, 1971.

Russia

See Catherine II, Empress of Russia

Rutherford, Griffith
(1721?–1805)

The North Carolina militia officer and political leader Griffith Rutherford led troops in several important campaigns against the British and their Loyalist and Indian supporters through nearly the entire Revolutionary War.

Rutherford was born in Ireland about 1721. He immigrated to America in 1739 and settled in North Carolina in the 1750s. By 1769 he was a member of the provincial assembly, where he served several terms in addition to holding local offices and a commission as a militia captain. Rutherford's strong stance in favor of American rights during the growing dispute with Great Britain soon brought him to the forefront of North Carolina's Revolutionary movement. He was a member of the Rowan County Committee of Safety and won election to the provincial congress that took effective control of North Carolina's government in 1775. He was an early advocate of American independence.

The provincial congress appointed Rutherford brigadier general of militia in the Salisbury District in April 1776, but he had already led his troops to South Carolina in late 1775 to assist the rebels of that state in suppressing Loyalist unrest in the backcountry.

When the Cherokees attacked the southern frontier in the summer of 1776, Rutherford assembled a force of more than 2,000 militia and marched against the Cherokee towns. His troops destroyed several Cherokee settlements along with the Indians' crops and food stores, which forced the tribal leaders to sue for peace. Rutherford then focused his attention on keeping North Carolina's numerous Loyalists in check. He also brought his troops to assist in the defense of South Carolina in 1779.

After the British captured Charleston in May 1780 and began to occupy South Carolina, Rutherford gathered 1,100 militia to assist the Continental Army's relief force under General Horatio Gates. Rutherford occupied Charlotte, North Carolina, from whence he could monitor British operations in South Carolina and resist the expected British advance northward. Meanwhile, some 1,000 North Carolina Loyalists assembled at Ramseur's Mill, intending to join the British Army. On learning of this threat, Rutherford ordered a subordinate to prepare to attack the Loyalists after Rutherford joined the much smaller American unit with reinforcements, but the militia attacked and defeated the Loyalists on 20 June 1780, before Rutherford arrived. Rutherford then dispersed another group of Loyalists who were gathering at the Yadkin River.

At the approach of Gates's army, Rutherford united his militia with the Continentals and marched into South Carolina. At the disastrous Battle of Camden on 16 August, Rutherford was wounded and captured, while most of his militiamen fled the battlefield. He remained a prisoner until his exchange in the summer of 1781. He then assembled a militia force to operate against the British garrison at Wilmington, but the British evacuated the town in November, prior to Rutherford's arrival. He then assumed command of the American forces there.

Rutherford returned to North Carolina politics after the war and was elected state senator from Rowan County in 1786. Shortly afterward he moved to Tennessee, where he was appointed to the territorial council and in 1794 became its president. He died in August 1805.

JIM PIECUCH

See also

Camden Campaign; Cherokees, Operations against; Ramseur's Mill, North Carolina, Action at

References

Ashe, Samuel, Stephen B. Weeks, and Charles L. Van Noppen, eds. *Biographical History of North Carolina from Colonial Times to the Present*. Vol. 5. Greensboro, NC: Charles L. Van Noppen, 1906.

Long, Minnie Rutherford Harsh. *General Griffith Rutherford and Allied Families: Harsh, Cathey, Locke, Holeman, Johnson [and] Chambers*, Milwaukee: Wisconsin Cuneo Press, 1942.

A member of the First and Second Continental Congresses and a signer of the Declaration of Independence, Edward Rutledge was a prominent South Carolina officeholder for nearly his entire adult life and became a leader of his state's Federalist Party in his last decade.

Born on 23 November 1749, the son of Dr. John Rutledge and Sarah Hext, Rutledge was a member of South Carolina's plantation elite. He studied classics with David Smith and law under his elder brother John before entering the Middle Temple in London in 1769 and joining the English bar in 1772. Rutledge returned to Charleston in 1773, married Henrietta Middleton, and then, as a member of the powerful family network of Draytons, Middletons, Pinckneys, and Rutledges, practiced as a popular lawyer. He made his name as a lawyer by successfully defending Thomas Powell against prosecution for printing the proceedings of the South Carolina Council, on the grounds that they were not entitled to legislative privilege.

As a delegate to the First Continental Congress, Rutledge advocated the boycott of imports and exports to bring America's grievances to Britain's attention, but in the Second Continental Congress he resisted independence until late in the congressional debates, when he changed his mind and worked to convince the South Carolina delegation of the need to break with Britain. Although he eventually signed the Declaration of Independence, joined Benjamin Franklin and John Adams in Congress's delegation that met with Lord Richard Howe in late July 1776 and defended Congress's decision to leave the empire, and served on Congress's Board of War, Rutledge had grave misgivings about the weak executive government of the Confederation and the participation of African Americans from several states in the Continental Army.

In 1777 Rutledge left Congress, and on his return to Charleston he served in the new South Carolina legislature, where he advocated harsh measures against the state's Loyalists. He also defended his state in an artillery unit. In the 1780 siege of Charleston, he was captured while serving as a messenger and was held at St. Augustine for more than a year before he was exchanged. Immediately resuming his leading role in South Carolina politics, he negotiated the British withdrawal from Charleston in 1782.

After the war, Rutledge served continuously in the South Carolina House of Representatives from 1782 to 1795 and then in the Senate from 1795 to 1799 until his election as governor. He strongly supported the ratification of the U.S. Constitution and the addition of the Bill of Rights, and as a Federalist he advocated internal improvements, such as canals; helped found the South Carolina Society for Promoting and Improving Agriculture; and backed the Bank of the United States and a strong national

Edward Rutledge was a very active member of the South Carolina legislature, leading the fight for the prosecution of British Loyalists in his home state. (Library of Congress)

defense. But he also found common ground with anti-British Republicans in opposing the Jay Treaty and favoring improved relations with revolutionary France. He declined a Supreme Court nomination in 1794 as well as other federal posts in order to serve his state and handle family property, but he was a recognized leader of the emerging southern Federalists who supported national unity and honor but demanded economic and political concessions to their region on slavery and trade. He served as governor of South Carolina from 1799 until his sudden death from a stroke on 23 January 1800.

MARGARET SANKEY

See also
Congress, First Continental; Congress, Second Continental and Confederation; Rutledge, John; South Carolina

References
Edgar, Walter B., and N. Louise Bailey, eds. *Biographical Directory of the South Carolina House of Representatives*, Vol. 2, *1692–1775*. Columbia: University of South Carolina Press, 1977.

Haw, James. *John and Edward Rutledge of South Carolina.* Athens: University of Georgia Press, 1997.

Hilborn, Nat, and Sam Hilborn. *Battleground of Freedom: South Carolina in the Revolution.* Columbia: Sandlapper, 1970.

Salley, Alexander Samuel. *Delegates to the Continental Congress from South Carolina.* Columbia, SC: State Company, 1927.

Starr, Rebecca. "Edward Rutledge." P. 775 in *The Blackwell Encyclopedia of the American Revolution.* Edited by Jack P. Greene and J. R. Pole. Oxford, UK: Blackwell, 1991.

Rutledge, John
(1739–1800)

John Rutledge, a highly conservative member of South Carolina's elite, became the new state's Revolutionary governor in 1776. He only slowly became committed to the cause of independence and did his best to contain the more egalitarian tendencies of the Revolution. Yet his dedication to the Patriot cause kept it alive in South Carolina during the darkest days of the Revolutionary War.

Rutledge was born into the family of a prosperous Charleston doctor and attorney in 1739. In 1757, Rutledge began preparation for the legal profession when he sailed to England to study at the Inns at Court. Returning to Charleston in 1760, he began his legal career, taught law to his younger brother, Edward, and pursued the traditional Carolinian interest in acquiring land. By 1775, Rutledge would own close to 30,000 acres.

Rutledge's political career began in 1761 with his election to South Carolina's Commons House of Assembly. In 1762, he would emerge as a spokesman for the rights of the Commons House against Thomas Boone, the royal governor, in the Gadsden Election Controversy. In 1765, Rutledge helped represent South Carolina at the Stamp Act Congress where, at age twenty-six, he was the youngest delegate. Rejoicing at the repeal of the Stamp Act in 1766, he always saw this as a victory for the traditional rights of Englishmen rather than as the beginning of any kind of Revolutionary movement. Similar feelings about English rights caused him to represent fellow conservative Henry Laurens in 1768 when one of Laurens's merchant ships was seized by the zealous new collector of customs and to support the nonimportation movement after 1767.

Yet despite his conservatism, Rutledge's prominence as a leading citizen of Charleston led to his service on a series of resistance committees in the early 1770s. In 1774 he was chosen to represent South Carolina at the First Continental Congress, where he became a favorite of the moderate faction that remained hopeful of reconciliation with Britain. Rutledge took the lead in supporting Joseph Galloway's proposal to create, in effect, an American parliament that would approve legislation related to the American colonies, but Congress rejected this proposal.

In 1775, at the Second Continental Congress, Rutledge again called for firm resistance to what he perceived as the overreaching of the British ministry while he continued to hold out hope for reconciliation. The radicalism of some of his fellow South Carolinians horrified Rutledge who, in early 1776, said that he would be "willing to ride post, by day and night to Philadelphia, in order to assist in reuniting Great Britain and America."

Due in part to his moderation, a new South Carolina Assembly House elected Rutledge governor in March 1776. He entered the task even as South Carolina's Patriot leaders worried over an imminent attack from the British by sea and an uprising of Indians and Loyalists on the frontier. An energetic executive, Rutledge helped prepare the state to deal with both threats, aided by the fact that the new conservative South Carolina constitution gave the governor broad powers.

Rutledge resigned his position as governor in 1778 in opposition to South Carolina's new constitution of that year, which limited executive power in favor of popular democracy. He did, however, continue to serve in South Carolina's General Assembly and in 1779 was reelected governor under the constitution that he so much feared. Rutledge's reputation for energetic leadership made him a natural choice, given that the British had once again begun to concentrate their military efforts in the South. Throughout 1779, Rutledge conscripted militiamen in hopes of driving the British from Georgia before they could concentrate against Charleston and urged the South Carolina legislature to raise taxes in order to pay for military supplies.

Ultimately, Rutledge's preparations did not prevent the British Army and Royal Navy from beginning the siege of Charleston in February 1780.

Planter-aristocrat John Rutledge represented South Carolina in the First Continental Congress and became the state's governor in 1779. He left Charleston before the British captured the city the following year but later returned as state representative to Congress between 1782 and 1783. (Collection of the Supreme Court of the United States)

By March the harbor of the port city was completely sealed off. Rutledge fled the city on 13 April, one day before British dragoons cut off Charleston's communications completely. Rutledge became South Carolina's governor in exile, eventually fleeing to North Carolina in order to escape the reach of Britain's cavalry commander Banastre Tarleton.

From wherever he was located, Rutledge worked consistently for the liberation of Charleston, and after General Charles Cornwallis's surrender at Yorktown in October 1781, Rutledge urged George Washington to make the recapture of the city his primary goal. As the war drew to a close in 1782, Rutledge joined the South Carolina legislature that had begun to meet regularly in Jacksonboro. The government returned to Charleston after the British abandoned the city in December 1782, but Rutledge stepped down from the governorship, although he continued to hold a seat in the South Carolina legislature throughout the following decade.

Rutledge remained staunchly conservative in the tumultuous era after the American Revolution. In state politics, he opposed moving the state capital to the interior, a move meant to conciliate the rapidly developing backcountry. Rutledge represented South Carolina at the Constitutional Convention in 1787 where, like many of South Carolina's low-country elite, he held strongly Federalist views. He played a key role in articulating the position of southern slaveholders toward the new central government, insisting that the new federal constitution protect both slavery and southern commercial interests as the price of their joining the union. In 1789, he was appointed an associate justice of the new U.S. Supreme Court but resigned his seat in 1791 to become chief justice of South Carolina.

In the 1790s, however, Rutledge faced a deluge of personal tragedies. The deaths of his mother and then of his wife in 1792 combined with illness and overwhelming personal debts drove Rutledge into a deep depression. Thereafter, he acquired a reputation for eccentricity but continued to hold public office as chief justice. In July 1795, President Washington nominated Rutledge to head the U.S. Supreme Court, but the Senate rejected him, in part because of rumors about his increasingly erratic personal behavior but also because he had made many enemies among the Federalists for his outspoken opposition to the Jay Treaty. Rutledge lived much of the remainder of his life as a recluse and died in July 1800.

W. Scott Poole

See also

Charleston, South Carolina, Expedition against (1776); Charleston, South Carolina, Expedition against (1780); Constitution, United States; Laurens, Henry; Rutledge, Edward; South Carolina

References

Edgar, Walter B., and N. Louise Bailey, eds. *Biographical Directory of the South Carolina House of Representatives*, Vol. 2, *1692–1775*. Columbia: University of South Carolina Press, 1977.

Haw, James. *John and Edward Rutledge of South Carolina*. Athens: University of Georgia Press, 1997.

Starr, Rebecca. "John Rutledge." Pp. 775–776 in *The Blackwell Encyclopedia of the American Revolution*. Edited by Jack P. Greene and J. R. Pole. Oxford, UK: Blackwell, 1991.

Weir, Robert M. *Colonial South Carolina: A History*. Columbia: University of South Carolina Press, 1997.

Index

Index